Encyclopedia Sherlockiana

My name is Sherlock Holmes. It is my business to know what other people don't know.

("The Blue Carbuncle")

Encyclopedia Sherlockiana

AN A-TO-Z GUIDE TO THE
WORLD OF THE GREAT DETECTIVE

Matthew E. Bunson

MACMILLAN · USA

This book is dedicated to Sir Arthur Conan Doyle (1859–1930)

MACMILLAN
A Prentice Hall Macmillan Company
15 Columbus Circle
New York, NY 10023

Library of Congress Cataloging-in-Publication Data

Bunson, Matthew.
    Encyclopedia Sherlockiana : an A-to-Z guide to the world of the
great detective / Matthew E. Bunson.
      p.   cm.
    Includes bibliographical references and index.
    ISBN 0-671-79826-X : $25.00
     1. Doyle, Arthur Conan, Sir, 1859–1930—Characters—Sherlock
Holmes—Encyclopedias.   2. Detective and mystery stories, English—
Encyclopedias.   3. Holmes, Sherlock (Fictitious character)—
Encyclopedias.   I. Title.
PR4623.A3B86   1994
823'.8—dc20   94-10714
                                                     CIP

Designed by Irving Perkins Associates, Inc.
Manufactured in the United States of America
10 9 8 7 6 5 4 3 2 1
First Edition

Contents

Foreword

"Never has so much been written by so many for so few," Christopher Morley, a distinguished American author and cofounder of The Baker Street Irregulars organization, once wrote. This was an accurate statement when he made it many years ago, but now there is so much being published about Sherlock Holmes and his milieu that one can fill an entire room with a Holmesian library. I know, I have done it.

One wonders why this incredible, enthusiastic, and effusive interest in a man who flourished a century ago, a man who lived in a time different and now mostly outdated, a man who, some dare to say, was but a fictional character created by Sir Arthur Conan Doyle, has all come about. Yet today, the accounts in the sixty published cases of Holmes are read by millions and countless parodies, pastiches, and look-alike tales are published annually. The Canon is rewritten for children, adapted to radio and television and for the legitimate theatre. These sixty tales have been translated into some sixty-five languages, into braille, Esperanto, two forms of shorthand, and even one tale into pig Latin. And there are listed more than three hundred Sherlockian societies which flourish in many countries.

Certainly this is a literary phenomenon without comparison. Sherlock Holmes is an exemplar for reasoning, action, and success and is thought of as a living person, one far greater than mere literary creation: a hero who lives! Holmes, the character, is a thinking man of action; one who serves his fellow men in his own unique, forceful, and useful manner. He represents truth, justice, law, order, and country. One other attractive virtue is that he is almost always successful. Sherlock Holmes is, as he once said of Watson, ". . . a fixed point in a changing world." There can be no question but that these sixty stories will be read again and again and again by many for many years to come.

It is my desire that the information supplied in this volume will help introduce and enhance any reader's interest in these sixty absorbing stories concerning a true hero—Mr. Sherlock Holmes of Baker Street. It is a well-planned and much needed book.

I continue, after a lifetime of reading the Doylean Holmesian Canon, to urge others to share the experience. Then to go a step further and to read the many parodies, biographies (not only of Holmes but of Watson and Moriarty), poems, and historical research about the Great Detective and his time. And, of course, to read about the true creator Sir Arthur Conan Doyle and to explore his other fiction and historical writings.

I close with another quotation from the writings of Christopher Morley, who wrote of the Holmesian Canon, "The saga of Holmes and Watson endures as a unique portrait of a friendship and of a civilization."

—John Bennett Shaw, B.S.I.
Santa Fe, New Mexico

Introduction

The *Encyclopedia Sherlockiana* is intended to provide both the general reader and the devoted Sherlockian or Holmesian with an easy to use, comprehensive, A-to-Z guide to the world of Sherlock Holmes. Included in this book are entries covering virtually every aspect of the Canon, with a broad, additional focus on the incarnations of the detective in film, radio, stage, pastiche, parody, and other non-Canonical writings. Sherlockians will naturally be familiar with the material presented throughout this volume, but hopefully they will find it a readable consultative source, good for browsing, fact checking, and simply enjoying a subject that can preoccupy the interest and the imagination of a lifetime and still call one back as Holmes might have called upon Watson with a terse telegram—"Come at once if convenient, if inconvenient, come all the same."

For those many readers, however, who have come to this book with little familiarity with Sherlock Holmes or the fascinating offshoots of the "Sacred Writings," there are certain steps that can be taken to make one's initiation into Sherlockiana a painless one. This encyclopedia has been written and organized with the general reader in mind and with maximizing its reader friendliness. One does not have to be an expert on all of the stories to enjoy it; indeed, this book could be of interest to those persons who have only read a few of the stories or who are only familiar with the Basil Rathbone-Nigel Bruce films or the non-Canonical works of fiction, such as those by Nicholas Meyer or John Gardner. For the first-time Sherlock Holmes fan, it might be useful to familiarize oneself with the Canon (see p. xv), reading the entries pertaining to the original stories and then moving on to the longer topics such as Sherlock Holmes, John H. Watson, and Professor Moriarty to examine the more detailed or obscure points of interest. Furthermore, throughout the book there are extensive lists, tables, maps, and illustrations of pertinent subjects such as the actors who have played Holmes, Watson, and Lestrade, Holmes's American Connection, Butlers of the Canon, and even the participants in the Wessex Cup. Finally, there is also a complete index with a listing of all possible names, places, events, and titles to which entries may make reference. If, therefore, a reader does not find a specific name in the A to Z portion (e.g. Van Deker, Morgan, or *De Jure inter Gentes*), please consult the index for the pages where information on them is to be found. This author, of course, cannot recommend strongly enough the importance of actually reading all of the stories of the Canon, but if one is uncertain where to start or if one is limited by time, then the entries in this book on each of the cases may help clarify a few of the points worth considering when determining which stories should be read first. The reader may even want to start with the ten stories chosen by Sir Arthur Conan Doyle as the best or the ones picked by the public in the competition held by the *Strand* (p. xviii). Each of the stories has something to offer, and collectively, they represent one of the greatest bodies of work in the history of detective literature.

Holmes once declared that "There is nothing new under the sun. It has all been done before." Many Sherlockians may have thought of this maxim upon seeing this book, remembering fondly the brilliant work of the same name by Jack Tracy that was published in 1978. Unlike that excellent tome, however, this encyclopedia is concerned not only with the Canon, but with the hundreds of related issues and topics that have been part of the evolution of Sherlockiana in the years following the cessation of Dr. Watson's published accounts. Tracy also placed his encyclopedia in the era of Sherlock Holmes, a setting quite impossible and undesirable when one covers the Great Detective fighting Count Dracula, appearing in Science Fiction, solving crimes in film, and battling evil in late 20th century San Francisco.

This book has taken years to create and there are many individuals to whom I owe a debt of gratitude for their kind assistance. Among them are Peter

Blau; Ronald De Waal; Frank Langella; Cinema Collector's; Jerry Ohlinger's; June Wyndham Davies of Granada Television; WGBH Boston; and the staff of the Sahara West Library. In addition I would like to give special thanks to two important individuals: John Bennett Shaw, B.S.I., for his advice, patience, wisdom, and boundless generosity, and Deirdre Mullane, my editor, for her enthusiasm, vision, and friendship. I would also like to acknowledge the many thousands of devoted Sherlockians and Holmesians over the years and across the globe. Their labors, writings, researches, and love of the Master made this book possible. I hope that in some small way this book will encourage others to continue the work of these remarkable men and women.

A Chronology of Sherlockiana

(1852–1987)

The following is a chronology of Sherlockiana from the estimated date of birth of Dr. John Watson to the 100th anniversary of the publication of A *Study in Scarlet* in 1887. Dates given here include the major events in the lives of the Great Detective, Dr. Watson, and Sir Arthur Conan Doyle. Dates are also provided for the cases recounted in the Canon. The principal source for these is W. S. Baring-Gould, the brilliant and respected Holmesian who painstakingly researched the probably chronology of the detective's career and life. As many of the cases written by Watson were deliberately structured to disguise or hide the date of their occurrence there has long been discussion as to their proper dating. Baring-Gould's dates are used here to provide some approximate source of reference for readers. Opinions naturally vary about some of them.

1852	August 7	Birth of John H. Watson (Estimated).
1854	January 6	Birth of Sherlock Holmes (Estimated).
1858	September 7	Birth of Irene Adler in Trenton, New Jersey.
1859	May 22	Birth of Arthur Conan Doyle in Edinburgh, Scotland.
1861	May 4	Birth of Mary Morstan (future Mrs. Watson).
1872	Summer	Possible period of schooling for Sherlock Holmes by Professor James Moriarty.
1872	September	Possible entry of John Watson into the University of London Medical School.
	October	Possible entry of Holmes into a university (perhaps Christ Church College at Oxford, although Cambridge is also mentioned).
1874	August-September	The case of "The 'Gloria Scott' " solved while still attending university; first case of Holmes's career.
1877 (or 1878)		Holmes moves to London to embark upon a career as a consulting detective; he takes rooms in Montague Street, near the British Museum, and begins learning what he will need to succeed. Early cases will include the Tarleton Murders, Vamberry, the Wine Merchant, the Singular Affair of the Aluminum Crutch, and Ricoletti of the Club Foot and His Abominable Wife.
1878	June	Watson takes the degree of doctor of medicine at the University of London; he soon moves to Netley where he goes through the course prescribed for surgeons in the army.
	November	Watson is attached to the Fifth Northumberland Fusiliers; outbreak of the Second Afghan War.
1879	October 2	"The Musgrave Ritual"
	November 23	Possible departure of Holmes to America in the guise of an actor.
1880	Spring	Watson is attached to Berkshires (66th Foot).
	July 27	Battle of Maiwand; Watson is seriously wounded and saved by the heroism of Murray.
	August 5	Holmes sets sail from America for home.

November Watson returns to England aboard the *Orontes*.

1881 January Watson begins search for new lodgings, meeting Stamford, an old friend at the Criterion Bar. Stamford takes Watson to meet Sherlock Holmes. The next day Holmes and Watson visit 221B Baker Street.

March A Study in Scarlet; the first case investigated by Holmes and Watson together.

1882 June Arthur Conan Doyle opens a medical practice at 1 Bush Villa, Elm Grove, Southsea.

1883 April "The Adventure of the Speckled Band"

1885 August 6 Arthur Conan Doyle marries Louise Hawkins, who died in 1906.

1886 August Watson possibly journeys to America, meeting Constance Adams (see "Angels of Darkness").

1886 October "The Resident Patient"

"The Adventure of the Noble Bachelor"

"The Adventure of the Second Stain"

November Watson perhaps marries Constance Adams, opening a practice in Kensington.

1887 April "The Reigate Squires"

May "A Scandal in Bohemia"

June "The Man with the Twisted Lip"

September "The Five Orange Pips"

October "A Case of Identity"

"The Adventure of the Red-Headed League"

November "The Adventure of the Dying Detective"

A Study in Scarlet first published, in *Beeton's Christmas Annual*.

December Death of Mrs. Watson.

December 27 "The Adventure of the Blue Carbuncle"

1888 January *The Valley of Fear*

April "The Yellow Face"

September "The Greek Interpreter"

The Sign of Four

The Hound of the Baskervilles

1889 April "The Adventure of the Copper Beeches"

May Marriage of Watson and Mary Morstan; purchase by Watson of a practice in the Paddington district from Old Farquhar.

June "The Boscombe Valley Mystery"

"The Stockbroker's Clerk"

July "The Naval Treaty"

August-September "The Cardboard Box"

September "The Adventure of the Engineer's Thumb"

"The Crooked Man"

1890 March "Wisteria Lodge"

October *The Sign of Four* first published, in *Lippincott's Monthly Magazine*.

September "Silver Blaze"

December "The Adventure of the Beryl Coronet"

Service to the royal family of Scandinavia.

1891 December-March Service in a "matter of supreme importance" to the French government.

January-April Holmes wages war against the criminal empire of Professor Moriarty, the Napoleon of Crime.

April 24-May 4 "The Final Problem"; Holmes is hunted across Continent by Moriarty and is apparently killed at the Reichenbach Falls in Switzerland.

May 4 Holmes embarks on the Great Hiatus (it will last until April 5, 1894).

July The first "Adventures of Sherlock Holmes" short story by Dr. Watson appears in the *Strand Magazine*, under the title "A Scandal in Bohemia."

1891–1892 Death of Mary Watson sometime in late 1891 or early 1892.

1892 October *The Adventures of Sherlock Holmes*, first collection of Holmes stories in book form, is published, with a foreword by Dr. Joseph Bell.

1893 November "Under the Clock," the earliest stage work on the detective, is presented in London.

December "The Final Problem" is published in the *Strand* causing massive public protest.

1894 April 5 *The Return of Sherlock Holmes* and "The Adventure of the Empty House"; capture of the last known lieutenant of Professor Moriarty.

May Watson sells his Paddington practice and returns to Baker Street.

November "The Adventure of the Golden Pince-Nez"

Second book collection of Holmes stories is published as *The Memoirs of Sherlock Holmes*.

1895 April "The Adventure of the Three Students"

"The Adventure of the Solitary Cyclist"

July "The Adventure of Black Peter"

August "The Adventure of the Norwood Builder"

November "The Adventure of the Bruce-Partington Plans"

1896 Known to many Sherlockians as "the missing year," a period of little documented activity.

October "The Adventure of the Veiled Lodger"

November "The Adventure of the Sussex Vampire"

December "The Adventure of the Missing Three-Quarter"

1897 January "The Adventure of the Abbey Grange"

March "The Adventure of the Devil's Foot"

1898 July "The Adventure of the Retired Colourman"

August "The Adventure of the Dancing Men"

1899 January "The Adventure of Charles Augustus Milverton"

November 6 *Sherlock Holmes* starring William Gillette opens in New York.

1900 June "The Adventure of the Six Napoleons"

October "The Problem of Thor Bridge"

1900–1903 Doyle volunteers his medical services to British forces in South Africa during the Boer War.

1901 May "The Adventure of the Priory School"

August *The Hound of the Baskervilles* published in the *Strand*; hopes that Holmes has returned to life in print are dashed however as the work is a "reminiscence."

May "The Adventure of Shoscombe Old Place"

June "The Adventure of the Three Garridebs"

July "The Disappearance of Lady Frances Carfax"

Watson takes up residence at Queen Anne Street

August 9   Arthur Conan Doyle is knighted at Buckingham Palace for his many achievements on behalf of England.

September   "The Adventure of the Illustrious Client"

"The Adventure of the Red Circle"

October   The third marriage of Dr. Watson.

1903   January   "The Adventure of the Blanched Soldier"

May   "The Adventure of the Three Gables"

Summer   "The Adventure of the Mazarin Stone"

September   "The Adventure of the Creeping Man"

October 8   The death of Irene Adler in New Jersey.

The retirement of Sherlock Holmes to the Sussex Downs and his villa on the coast at Fulworth.

Doyle is made a Knight of Grace of the Order of St. John of Jerusalem.

Around this time, the film *Sherlock Holmes Baffled* is made by American Mutoscope.

1904   Christmas   A card game entitled Sherlock Holmes is published by Parker Bros.

1905   Additional stories published in the collection, *The Return of Sherlock Holmes*.

1907   August   "The Adventure of the Lion's Mane"

Doyle marries Jean Leckie, with whom he has three children.

1910   June 4   The play *The Speckled Band* premieres at the Adelphi Theatre in London.

1912   July   "Studies in the Literature of Sherlock Holmes" is published in the Oxford undergraduate journal, *The Blue Book*, the first writing of Sherlockiana by Ronald Knox.

1912–1913   Holmes is asked by the British government to assist it in counterintelligence activities against the Germans. He agrees and becomes the Irish-American agent Altamont, penetrating the spy ring headed by Von Bork.

1914   August   "His Last Bow"

1914–1918   Watson rejoins the army and serves as physician.

1916   William Gillette stars as Holmes in the film *Sherlock Holmes*.

1917   The collection *His Last Bow* is published.

1920   Holmes active in Constantinople (theory proposed by Vincent Starrett in *221B: Studies in Sherlock Holmes*).

1921   The play *The Crown Diamond*, by Sir Arthur Conan Doyle, opens for a brief theatrical life in England.

1923   Colorful cards created by Alexander Bogulavsky, featuring Holmes and characters from the Canon, are offered by Turf cigarettes.

1924   *Memories and Adventures*, the autobiography of Sir Arthur Conan Doyle, is published.

1927   March   "A Sherlock Holmes Competition" is held by the *Strand*.

March 5 "Shoscombe Old Place," the final account of the Canon, is published in *Liberty Magazine* in the United States (published in the *Strand* in April).

The collection *The Casebook of Sherlock Holmes* is published.

1929 July 24 The possible date of Dr. Watson's death.

1930 July 7 Sir Arthur Conan Doyle dies at Crowborough.

The Complete Sherlock Holmes, including all sixty adventures, with an introduction by Christopher Morley, is published by Doubleday.

1933 *The Private Life of Sherlock Holmes* by Vincent Starrett is published.

1934 The organization *The Baker Street Irregulars* (BSI) is founded by Christopher Morley in New York; the first Holmesian society in America.

1935 The first meeting of the Sherlock Holmes Society of London is held in June.

First Scion Society is founded (in New York).

1939 *The Hound of the Baskervilles* is released by 20th Century-Fox; it is the first film featuring Basil Rathbone and Nigel Bruce as Holmes and Watson.

1944 *The Misadventures of Sherlock Holmes*, edited by Ellery Queen, is published; it is subsequently suppressed.

1946
November 19 The possible date of Mycroft Holmes's death.

The Baker Street Journal begins publication.

1948 An obituary of Sherlock Holmes, written by E. V. Knox, is published by the *Strand*.

1950 The *Strand Magazine* goes out of business.

1951 The Festival of Britain is held; a reconstruction of Baker Street is offered. It is later moved to the public house, the "Sherlock Holmes."

The Sherlock Holmes Society of London is founded.

1954 *The Exploits of Sherlock Holmes*, a collection of pastiches by Adrian Conan Doyle and John Dickson Carr, is published.

1957 January 6 The possible date of Sherlock Holmes's death.

1967 *The Annotated Sherlock Holmes*, edited by W. S. Baring-Gould, is published.

1968 The Sherlock Holmes Society of London tours the Reichenbach Falls in Switzerland; the event receives worldwide publicity.

Women Sherlockians form The Adventuresses of Sherlock Holmes (ASH).

1974 The novel *The Seven-Per-Cent Solution* by Nicholas Meyer is published; it is later made into a successful film.

The novel *The Return of Moriarty* by John Gardner is published.

1978 January 6 The play *The Crucifer of Blood* by Paul Giovanni premieres in Buffalo, New York.

1987 100th anniversary of the publication of *A Study in Scarlet*.

1992   January   Women are invited to attend the Annual Dinner of the BSI.

For the complete list of Sherlock Holmes adventures see THE CANON, which follows.

For the many stage, radio, and film treatments of the detective, see HOLMES ON SCREEN AND TELEVISION under HOLMES, SHERLOCK; see also STAGE; see also the Appendix.

The Canon

Also called the Sacred Writings, the published cases of Sherlock Holmes are comprised of sixty works: four novels and fifty-six short stories. Before the title, an * denotes a story told by a third person narrator and a † denotes a story told by Holmes himself. After the title, the accepted abbreviation of the work is given, as recognized by scholars (e.g. *The Sign of Four*—SIGN). With the exception of the four noted, all of the adventures are recounted by Watson.

A STUDY IN SCARLET (STUD)—November, 1887, *Beeton's Christmas Annual*; first published separately as a novel in 1888.

THE SIGN OF FOUR (SIGN)—February, 1890, *Lippincott's*; published separately as a novel in 1892. Also called *The Sign of the Four* in the United States.

"A SCANDAL IN BOHEMIA" (SCAN)—July, 1891, *Strand*; collected in *The Adventures of Sherlock Holmes*.

"THE RED-HEADED LEAGUE" (REDH)—August, 1891, *Strand*; collected in *The Adventures of Sherlock Holmes*.

"A CASE OF IDENTITY" (IDEN)—September, 1891, *Strand*; collected in *The Adventures of Sherlock Holmes*.

"THE BOSCOMBE VALLEY MYSTERY" (BOSC)—October, 1891, *Strand*; collected in *The Adventures of Sherlock Holmes*.

"THE FIVE ORANGE PIPS" (FIVE)—November, 1891, *Strand*; collected in *The Adventures of Sherlock Holmes*.

"THE MAN WITH THE TWISTED LIP" (TWIS)—December, 1891, *Strand*; collected in *The Adventures of Sherlock Holmes*.

"THE ADVENTURE OF THE BLUE CARBUNCLE" (BLUE)—January, 1892, *Strand*; collected in *The Adventures of Sherlock Holmes*.

"THE ADVENTURE OF THE SPECKLED BAND" (SPEC)—February, 1892, *Strand*; collected in *The Adventures of Sherlock Holmes*.

"THE ADVENTURE OF THE ENGINEER'S THUMB" (ENGR)—March, 1892, *Strand*; collected in *The Adventures of Sherlock Holmes*.

"THE ADVENTURE OF THE NOBLE BACHELOR" (NOBL)—April, 1892, *Strand*; collected in *The Adventures of Sherlock Holmes*.

"THE ADVENTURE OF THE BERYL CORONET" (BERY)—May, 1892, *Strand*; collected in *The Adventures of Sherlock Holmes*.

"THE ADVENTURE OF THE COPPER BEECHES" (COPP)—June, 1892, *Strand*; collected in *The Adventures of Sherlock Holmes*.

"SILVER BLAZE" (SILV)—December, 1892, *Strand*; collected in *The Memoirs of Sherlock Holmes*.

"THE CARDBOARD BOX" (CARD)—January, 1893, *Strand*; collected in some editions of *The Memoirs of Sherlock Holmes* (1894) and in *His Last Bow* (1917).

"THE YELLOW FACE" (YELL)—February, 1893, *Harper's*; collected in *The Memoirs of Sherlock Holmes*.

"THE STOCKBROKER'S CLERK" (STOC)—March, 1893, *Harper's*; collected in *The Memoirs of Sherlock Holmes*.

"THE 'GLORIA SCOTT' " (GLOR)—April, 1893, *Strand*; collected in *The Memoirs of Sherlock Holmes*.

"THE MUSGRAVE RITUAL" (MUSG)—May, 1893, *Harper's*; collected in *The Memoirs of Sherlock Holmes*.

"THE REIGATE SQUIRES" (REIG)—June, 1893, *Harper's*; collected in *The Memoirs of Sherlock Holmes*. Also called "The Reigate Puzzle" in the United States.

"THE CROOKED MAN" (CROO)—July, 1893, *Strand*; collected in *The Memoirs of Sherlock Holmes*.

"THE RESIDENT PATIENT" (RESI)—August, 1893, *Strand*; collected in *The Memoirs of Sherlock Holmes*.

"THE GREEK INTERPRETER" (GREE)—September, 1893, *Strand*; collected in *The Memoirs of Sherlock Holmes*.

"THE NAVAL TREATY" (NAVA)—October and November, 1893, *Harper's*; collected in *The Memoirs of Sherlock Holmes*.

"THE FINAL PROBLEM" (FINA)—December, 1893, *Strand*; collected in *The Memoirs of Sherlock Holmes*.

THE HOUND OF THE BASKERVILLES (HOUN)—August, 1901–April 1902, *Strand*; published separately in novel form.

"THE ADVENTURE OF THE EMPTY HOUSE" (EMPT)—September 26, 1903, *Collier's*; October, 1903, *Strand*; collected in *The Return of Sherlock Holmes*.

"THE ADVENTURE OF THE NORWOOD BUILDER" (NORW)—October 31, 1903, *Collier's*; November, 1903, *Strand*; collected in *The Return of Sherlock Holmes*.

"THE ADVENTURE OF THE DANCING MEN" (DANC)—December, 1903, *Collier's*; collected in *The Return of Sherlock Holmes*.

"THE ADVENTURE OF THE SOLITARY CYCLIST" (SOLI)—December 26, 1903, *Collier's*; January, 1904, *Strand*; collected in *The Return of Sherlock Holmes*.

"THE ADVENTURE OF THE PRIORY SCHOOL" (PRIO)—January 30, 1904, *Collier's*; February, 1904, *Strand*; collected in *The Return of Sherlock Holmes*.

"THE ADVENTURE OF BLACK PETER" (BLAC)—February 27, 1904, *Collier's*; March, 1904, *Strand*; collected in *The Return of Sherlock Holmes*.

"THE ADVENTURE OF CHARLES AUGUSTUS MILVERTON" (CHAS)—March 26, 1904, *Collier's*; April, 1904, *Strand*; collected in *The Return of Sherlock Holmes*.

"THE ADVENTURE OF THE SIX NAPOLEONS" (SIXN)—April 30, 1904, *Collier's*; May, 1904, *Strand*; collected in *The Return of Sherlock Holmes*.

"THE ADVENTURE OF THE THREE STUDENTS" (3STU)—June, 1904, *Strand*; September, 1904, *Collier's*; collected in *The Return of Sherlock Holmes*.

"THE ADVENTURE OF THE GOLDEN PINCE-NEZ" (GOLD)—July, 1904, *Strand*; collected in *The Return of Sherlock Holmes*.

"THE ADVENTURE OF THE MISSING THREE-QUARTER" (MISS)—August, 1904, *Strand*; collected in *The Return of Sherlock Holmes*.

"THE ADVENTURE OF THE ABBEY GRANGE" (ABBE)—September, 1904, *Strand*; collected in *The Memoirs of Sherlock Holmes*.

"THE ADVENTURE OF THE SECOND STAIN" (SECO)—December, 1904, *Strand*; January, 1905, *Collier's*; collected in *The Memoirs of Sherlock Holmes*.

"WISTERIA LODGE" ("A Reminiscence of Mr. Sherlock Holmes") (WIST)—August 15, 1908, *Collier's*; September and October, 1908, *Strand*; collected in *His Last Bow*.

"THE ADVENTURE OF THE BRUCE-PARTINGTON PLANS" (BRUC)—December, 1908, *Strand*; collected in *His Last Bow*.

"THE ADVENTURE OF THE DEVIL'S FOOT" (DEVI)—December, 1910, *Strand*; collected in *His Last Bow*.

"THE ADVENTURE OF THE RED CIRCLE" (REDC)—March and April, 1911, *Strand*; collected in *His Last Bow*.

"THE DISAPPEARANCE OF LADY FRANCES CARFAX" (LADY)—December, 1911, *Strand*; collected in *His Last Bow*.

"THE ADVENTURE OF THE DYING DETECTIVE" (DYIN)—November 22, 1913, *Collier's*; December, 1913, *Strand*; collected in *His Last Bow*.

THE VALLEY OF FEAR (VALL)—September, 1914–May, 1915, *Strand*; published separately as a novel.

*"His Last Bow" (LAST)—September, 1917, *Strand*; collected in *His Last Bow*.

*"The Adventure of the Mazarin Stone" (MAZA)—October, 1921, *Strand*; collected in *The Case Book of Sherlock Holmes*.

"The Problem of Thor Bridge" (THOR)—February and March, 1922, *Strand*; collected in *The Case Book of Sherlock Holmes*.

"The Adventure of the Creeping Man" (CREE)—March, 1923, *Strand*; collected in *The Case Book of Sherlock Holmes*.

"The Adventure of the Sussex Vampire" (SUSS)—January, 1924, *Hearst's International*; collected in *The Case Book of Sherlock Holmes*.

"The Adventure of the Three Garridebs" (3GAR)—October 25, 1924, *Collier's*; January, 1925, *Strand*; collected in *The Case Book of Sherlock Holmes*.

"The Adventure of the Illustrious Client" (ILLU)—November 8, 1924, *Collier's*; May, 1925, *Strand*; collected in *The Case Book of Sherlock Holmes*.

"The Adventure of the Three Gables" (3GAB)—September 18, 1926, *Liberty*; October, 1926, *Strand*; collected in *The Case Book of Sherlock Holmes*.

†"The Adventure of the Blanched Soldier" (BLAN)—October 16, 1926, *Liberty*; November, 1926, *Strand*; collected in *The Case Book of Sherlock Holmes*.

†"The Adventure of the Lion's Mane" (LION)—November 27, 1926, *Liberty*; December, 1926, *Strand*; collected in *The Case Book of Sherlock Holmes*.

"The Adventure of the Retired Colourman" (RETI)—December 18, 1926, *Liberty*; January, 1927, *Strand*; collected in *The Case Book of Sherlock Holmes*.

"The Adventure of the Veiled Lodger" (VEIL)—January 22, 1927, *Liberty*; February, 1927, *Strand*; collected in *The Case Book of Sherlock Holmes*.

"The Adventure of Shoscombe Old Place" (SHOS)—March 5, 1927, *Liberty*; April, 1927, *Strand*; collected in *The Case Book of Sherlock Holmes*.

Collections
The Adventures of Sherlock Holmes (1892)
The Memoirs of Sherlock Holmes (1894)
The Return of Sherlock Holmes (1905)
His Last Bow (1917)
The Casebook of Sherlock Holmes (1927)

The Best of Sherlock Holmes

In March 1927, the *Strand Magazine* attempted to answer the oft asked question: "Which Sherlock Holmes stories are the best?" At the request of the magazine, Conan Doyle chose twelve stories from the growing Canon (only forty-four had been published at the time) that he would rank as superior. This list was then given to the editor in a sealed envelope. A contest was held to identify the most stories named by Conan Doyle—the first prize being 100 pounds and an autographed copy of his autobiography, *Memories and Adventures*.

In January 1927 the *Strand* inaugurated the competition with an article "Mr. Sherlock Holmes to His Friends." All entries had to be filled out by placing corresponding numbers on a coupon and returned to the magazine by March 26, 1927. The winner was R.T. Norman, who successfully named ten of twelve cases chosen by Conan Doyle. The results were published in the June 1927 issue. In his piece, "How I Made My List," Conan Doyle explained his choices, declaring, for example, "There is the grim snake story, 'The Speckled Band.' That I am sure will be on every list. Next to that in popular favour and in my own esteem I would place 'The Red-Headed League' and 'The Dancing Men,' on account in each case of the originality of the plot."

Conan Doyle's list included the following:

1. "The Speckled Band"
2. "The Red-Headed League"
3. "The Dancing Men"
4. "The Final Problem"
5. "A Scandal in Bohemia"
6. "The Empty House"
7. "The Five Orange Pips"
8. "The Second Stain"
9. "The Devil's Foot"
10. "The Priory School"
11. "The Musgrave Ritual"
12. "The Reigate Squires"

In 1959, the *Baker Street Journal* polled its readers and came up with the following list of favorites:

1. "The Speckled Band"
2. "The Red-Headed League"
3. "The Blue Carbuncle"
4. "Silver Blaze"
5. "A Scandal in Bohemia"
6. "The Musgrave Ritual"
7. "The Bruce-Partington Plans"
8. "The Six Napoleons"
9. "The Dancing Men"
10. "The Empty House"

Abbreviations of the Canon

ABBREVIATIONS:*

ABBE	The Abbey Grange	NAVA	The Naval Treaty
BERY	The Beryl Coronet	NOBL	The Noble Bachelor
BLAC	Black Peter	NORW	The Norwood Builder
BLAN	The Blanched Soldier	PREF	Preface to "His Last Bow"
BLUE	The Blue Carbuncle	PRIO	The Priory School
BOSC	The Boscombe Valley Mystery	REDC	The Red Circle
BRUC	The Bruce-Partington Plans	REDH	The Red-Headed League
CARD	The Cardboard Box	REIG	The Reigate Squires
CHAS	Charles Augustus Milverton	RESI	The Resident Patient
COPP	The Copper Beeches	RETI	The Retired Colourman
CREE	The Creeping Man	SCAN	A Scandal in Bohemia
CROO	The Crooked Man	SECO	The Second Stain
DANC	The Dancing Men	SHOS	Shoscombe Old Place
DEVI	The Devil's Foot	SIGN	The Sign of Four
DYIN	The Dying Detective	SILV	Silver Blaze
EMPT	The Empty House	SIXN	The Six Napoleons
ENGR	The Engineer's Thumb	SOLI	The Solitary Cyclist
FINA	The Final Problem	SPEC	The Speckled Band
FIVE	The Five Orange Pips	STOC	The Stock-broker's Clerk
GLOR	The "Gloria Scott"	STUD	A Study in Scarlet
GOLD	The Golden Pince-Nez	SUSS	The Sussex Vampire
GREE	The Greek Interpreter	THOR	The Problem of Thor Bridge
HOUN	The Hound of the Baskervilles	3GAB	The Three Gables
IDEN	A Case of Identity	3GAR	The Three Garridebs
ILLU	The Illustrious Client	3STU	The Three Students
LADY	The Disappearance of Lady Frances Carfax	TWIS	The Man With the Twisted Lip
LAST	His Last Bow	VALL	The Valley of Fear
LION	The Lion's Mane	VEIL	The Veiled Lodger
MAZA	The Mazarin Stone	WIST	Wisteria Lodge
MISS	The Missing Three-Quarter	YELL	The Yellow Face
MUSG	The Musgrave Ritual		

* These abbreviations are taken from the accepted form established by Professor Jay Finley Christ of the *Baker Street Irregulars*.

Unchronicled Cases of the Canon

Throughout his long career as a consulting detective, Sherlock Holmes investigated or advised upon a staggering number of cases. In April, 1891 he commented to Watson that he had been engaged on over a thousand cases ("The Final Problem"). Given his remarkable success following his return to practice from the Great Hiatus (1891–1894), particularly his brilliant year of 1895, it can be calculated that the detective investigated over two thousand cases, if not more. As the Canon only presents sixty cases, there is a vast amount of material that has never been published, remaining unknown and hidden in Holmes's and Watson's archives, save for a few tantalizing titles or references. The following is a list of unchronicled or unpublished cases to which reference is made in the Canon.

Abergavenny Murders (PRIO)
Abernetty Family (SIXN)
Abrahams in danger (HOUN)
Addleton tragedy (GOLD)
Agar, Dr. Moore, a dramatic meeting (DEVI)
Alicia (THOR)
Aluminum crutch (MUSG)
Amateur Mendicant Society (MUSG)
Ancient British Barrow (GOLD)
Arnsworth Castle business (SCAN)
Atkinson Brothers of Trincomalee (SCAN)

Backwater, service to Lord (NOBL)
Bishopgate Jewel Case (SIGN)
Blackmail of a "revered name in England" (HOUN)
Black Pearl of the Borgias (SIXN)
Bogus Laundry Affair (CARD)
Brooks and Woodhouse (BRUC)

Camberwell Poisoning (FIVE)
Carruthers, Colonel (WIST)
Clay, John (REDH)
Coiner run to ground (SHOS)
Conk-Singleton Forgery (SIXN)
Coptic Patriarchs (RETI)
Crosby the banker (GOLD)

Darlington Substitution Scandal (SCAN)
Dowson, Baron (MAZA)
Dundas Separation Case (IDEN)

Etherege's husband (IDEN)

Farintosh, Mrs. (SPEC)
Fashionably dressed young girl (STUD)
Ferrers Documents (PRIO)
Forgery case (STUD)
Forrester, Mrs. Cecil (SIGN)
French Republic, service to (FINA)
Friesland (NORW)

Grafenstein, Count von und zu (LAST)
Grice-Paterson (FIVE)
Grosvenor Square furniture van (NOBL)

Harden, J. Vincent (SOLI)
Hobbs, Fairdale (REDC)
Holland's royal family (SCAN)
Hopkins, Inspector Stanley (ABBE, 7 cases, 4 untold)
Huret, the Boulevard Assassin (GOLD)

Jewish peddler (STUD)

Lynch, Victor (SUSS)

Maberley, Mortimer (3GAB)
MacDonald, Alec (VALL)
Manor House Case (GREE)
Margate woman (SECO)
Maseilles (IDEN)
Matilda Briggs (SUSS)
Matthews (EMPT)
Maupertuis, Baron (REIG)
Merridew (EMPT)
Montpensier, Madame (HOUN)

ABBAS PARVA. A small village in Berkshire in "The Veiled Lodger." Its name was derived from the Latin *abbas* (meaning abbot), and *parvus* (meaning small), parva in this case referring to little. Abbas Parva was the site chosen by the Ronder circus to camp the night that Ronder, the owner, was killed and Eugenia Ronder, his wife, was mauled by the lion King Sahara.

ABBEY GRANGE. The residence and estate of Sir Eustace and Lady Mary Brackenstall, situated at Marsham in Kent, in "The Adventure of the Abbey Grange." Watson described it: "The avenue ran through a noble park, between lines of ancient elms, that ended in a low, widespread house, pillared in the front after the fashion of Palladio."

"ABBEY GRANGE, THE ADVENTURE OF THE" (ABBE). Published: *Strand*, September 1904, *Collier's* December 1904; collected in *The Return of Sherlock Holmes* (1905). Case date: January 1897. Major players: Holmes, Watson, Mary Brackenstall, Capt. Jack Croker, Theresa, Sir Eustace Brackenstall, Inspector Stanley Hopkins. A perplexing case for Holmes who, at one point, tells Watson, "We have not yet met our Waterloo, Watson, but this is our Marengo, for it begins in defeat and ends in victory." The detective is summoned to the Abbey Grange, near Chislehurst where Sir Eustace Brackenstall has been murdered brutally, apparently by burglars. Based on the testimony of Lady Brackenstall and her maid Theresa, the murderers are seemingly the Randall Gang, a local band of thieves. The case proves much more complex, and in the end, Holmes demonstrates not only his skills as a detective but his sense of justice, allowing the real murderer to escape arrest after conducting his own "trial" of the crime with

Watson as his jury. "The Abbey Grange" contains the now famous Holmesian quote: "Come, Watson, come! The game is afoot!"

ABBEY SCHOOL. A name used by Holmes almost certainly to refer to the Priory School during his writing of "The Blanched Soldier." According to the detective, Holmes was just finishing the case when James Dodd involved him in the new investigation. Holmes spoke of it, saying it was "the case which my friend Watson has described as that of the Abbey School, in which the Duke of Greyminster was so deeply involved."

ABDULLAH KHAN. One of the Four in *The Sign of Four*.

ABERDEEN. This coastal city in Scotland was said by Holmes to be notable because a case similar to that of St. Simon in "The Noble Bachelor" took place there. Inspector Alec MacDonald of Scotland Yard came from Aberdeen in *The Valley of Fear*.

ABERDEEN SHIPPING CO. In full, Aberdeen Steam Navigation Company, a shipping firm located in the City, on Fresno Street, off of Upper Swandam Lane in "The Man With the Twisted Lip." Mrs. Neville St. Clair received a telegram that "a small parcel of considerable value which she had been expecting was waiting for her at the Aberdeen Shipping Company." Her journey to these offices precipitated the disappearance of her husband.

ABERGAVENNY. A murder that possibly took place in the town of Abergavenny in Wales ("The

1

Priory School"). The so-called Abergavenny Murder was coming to trial at the same time that Holmes had been retained in the case of the Ferrers Documents. The detective was thus doubtful that he and Watson would be able to involve themselves in the investigation brought to them by Dr. Thorneycroft Huxtable. As Holmes declared, "Only a very important issue could call me from London at present." The abduction of the son of the duke of Holdernesse was important enough.

ABERNETTY FAMILY. An investigation considered by Holmes to be one of his "classic cases." The "dreadful business" mentioned in "The Six Napoleons" was brought to his attention "by the depth which the parsley had sunk into the butter upon a hot day."

ABRAHAMS. A case that was ongoing at the start of Holmes's investigation into the disappearance of Lady Frances Carfax in "The Disappearance of Lady Frances Carfax." The detective felt that he could not leave London while "old Abrahams is in such mortal terror of his life." Watson was therefore sent to Lausanne to begin the search for the missing woman.

ACHMET. A merchant, the servant of a rajah in northern India and the bearer of the Agra Treasure in *The Sign of Four*. He was described as "a little, fat, round fellow, with a great yellow turban, and a bundle in his hand, done up in a shawl." Achmet was murdered in 1857 by the men of the Four for the treasure he carried.

ACID. Holmes was very familiar with these chemical compounds through his extensive study of chemistry. The chemical table used by Holmes was acid stained ("The Empty House," "The Mazarin Stone"), and his fingers were frequently discolored from contact with various acids (*A Study in Scarlet*). The odor of acids was no doubt often present at 221B. Watson, for example, deduced Holmes's labors in chemistry by the smell that greeted his arrival at 221B during one of their cases ("A Case of Identity"): "A formidable array of bottles and test-tubes, with the pungent smell of hydrochloric acid, told me that he had spent his day in the chemical work which was so dear to him."

Acids figured in a number of Holmes's cases. John Clay could be recognized by the white splash

of acid upon his forehead in "The Red-Headed League." Eugenia Ronder in "The Veiled Lodger" sent Holmes a bottle of prussic acid as a symbol of her acceptance of his advice concerning her own life—"Your life is not your own ... Keep your hands off it." Bottles of acid were found in Bartholomew Sholto's laboratory in *The Sign of Four*, and Kitty Winter chose vitriol (sulphuric acid) as her weapon of revenge against the odious Baron Adalbert Gruner in "The Illustrious Client." Other cases in which acid appeared were: "The Cardboard Box," "The Engineer's Thumb," and "The Blue Carbuncle." (See also CHEMISTRY.)

ACTON. A wealthy, elderly gentleman whose house was burgled in "The Reigate Squires." Colonel Hayter said of him: "Old Acton, who is one of our country magnates, had his house broken into last Monday. No great damage was done, but the fellows are still at large."

ADAIR, HILDA. Daughter of the earl of Maynooth and Lady Maynooth, and sister of Ronald Adair in "The Empty House." With her mother, she discovered her brother's body.

ADAIR, HON. RONALD. The son of the earl of Maynooth and Lady Maynooth who was murdered in the spring of 1894 "under the most unusual and inexplicable circumstances" in "The Empty House." Adair was described as an easygoing aristocrat who had no enemies and no particular vices save that he "was fond of cards, playing continually, but never for such stakes as would hurt him." His card playing was the cause of his death as he caught a fellow club member cheating and was murdered by that dangerous person to prevent the cheat's embarrassment. The inquest, however, could uncover no motive for his brutal killing, his head "horribly mutilated by an expanded revolver bullet." The solution of his murder was tied to the triumphant return of Holmes in 1894.

ADDLETON TRAGEDY. A case dated to 1894 ("The Golden Pince-Nez"). An account of the case was offered in "The Adventure of Foulkes Rath" in the collection *The Exploits of Sherlock Holmes* (1954).

ADELAIDE-SOUTHAMPTON LINE. The largest of the two shipping companies that connected Australia with Britain in "The Abbey

Grange." Its London offices were located "at the end of Pall Mall." Jack Croker served aboard the company's liner *Rock of Gibraltar*, and later became captain of the new ship *Bass Rock*.

ADLER, IRENE. Called "*the* woman," an American born opera singer and adventuress (1858–c.1890) who earned Holmes's lasting respect for providing a capable and wily opponent in the affair chronicled in "A Scandal in Bohemia." The king of Bohemia had approached Holmes to engage his services in recovering a compromising photograph that he had given Adler during their relationship in Warsaw. The consultation had come about after the ruler's agents had failed to recover the picture through burglary and assault. Holmes looked her up in his index to the Commonplace Books: "Hum! Born in New Jersey in 1858. Contralto—hum! La Scala, hum! Prima donna Imperial Opera of Warsaw—yes! Retired from operatic stage-ha! Living in London—quite so!" At the conclusion of the case, Watson wrote: "He used to make merry over the cleverness of women, but I have not heard him do it of late. And when he refers to her photograph, it is always under the honourable title of *the* woman." He also wrote: "to Sherlock Holmes she is always *the* woman. I have seldom heard him mention her under any other name. In his eyes, she eclipses and predominates the whole of her sex. It was not that he felt any emotion akin to love for Irene Adler. All emotions, and that one particularly, were abhorrent to his cold, precise but admirably balanced mind."

Much has been made of Holmes's relationship with Irene Adler, particularly by those writers who chose to ignore Watson's assurances of Holmes's logic, focusing instead on possible romantic associations with her. W. S. Baring-Gould, in his *Sherlock Holmes of Baker Street*, proposed that Holmes and Adler had a son together, an idea that received development in the television film "Sherlock Holmes in New York" (1976) and in the literature surrounding the famous detective Nero Wolfe, who was thought to be the son of Holmes and Adler. It is generally acknowledged by scholars that Adler was based (or disguised) on the adventuress Lola Montez. At the time of the Bohemian affair, Adler resided at Briony Lodge, Serpentine Avenue, St. John's Wood. Adler has also been the title character in a series of very successful romance-mystery novels by Carole Nelson Douglas, focusing on her years after the Bohemian affair at a time when the

Irene Adler, "The Woman"; by an unknown French artist, dated to around 1920.

world believed her to be dead. The entries in the series thus far have been *Good Night, Mr. Holmes* (1989), *Good Morning, Irene* (1990), and *Irene At Large* (1992). (See also NORTON, GODFREY.)

"ADVENTURE OF." See under the actual title, e.g. "SECOND STAIN, THE ADVENTURE OF."

ADVENTURES OF SHERLOCK HOLMES, THE. Published in 1892, this volume was the first collection of the detective's cases that had originally appeared in the *Strand Magazine*. The compiled stories were: "A Scandal in Bohemia," "The Red-Headed League," "A Case of Identity," "The Boscombe Valley Mystery," "The Five Orange Pips," "The Man With the Twisted Lip," "The Adventure of the Blue Carbuncle," "The Adventure of the Speckled Band," "The Adventure of the Engineer's Thumb," "The Adventure of the Noble Bachelor," "The Adventure of the Beryl Coronet," and "The Adventure of the Copper Beeches." The British edition included all 104 illustrations drawn by Sidney Paget for the *Strand* and included a dedication by Conan Doyle to "My old teacher, Joseph Bell, M.D." Bell, considered the inspiration or model for Holmes, wrote a review of the collection for the magazine *Bookman*, noting that Conan Doyle "knows how delicious brevity is, how everything tends to be too long, and he has given us stories that we can read at a sitting between dinner and coffee, and we have not a chance to forget the beginning before we reach the end." The American edition contained only sixteen of the Paget drawings. Immensely successful, the collection eclipsed another non-Sherlock work by Doyle published the same month, the Napoleonic era novel, *The Great Shadow*.

ADVENTURES OF SHERLOCK HOLMES, THE. [Films]

Of the many film and television treatments of the great detective, three appeared under this title.

ADVENTURES OF SHERLOCK HOLMES, THE.

U.S. 1905. Dir: J. Stuart Blackton. Cast: Maurice Costello (Holmes). (Vitagraph) Known also in the United States as *Held for a Ransom* and in England as *Sherlock Holmes*, or *Held for Ransom*, this is one of the earliest Holmes films, and the first with a Holmes (Costello) who was clearly identified as such. Eight minutes long, it has the detective rescuing a woman from the clutches of kidnappers. It may have originally been the first of a planned series of films, but the next Vitagraph release in the same vein, *Caught*, based loosely on "The Adventure of the Red-Headed League," did not include Holmes at all.

ADVENTURES OF SHERLOCK HOLMES, THE.

U.S. 1939. Dir: Albert Werker. Cast: Basil Rathbone (Holmes), Nigel Bruce (Watson), George Zucco (Moriarty), Ida Lupino (Ann Brandon), Mary Gordon (Mrs. Hudson). The second

and one of the best of the beloved Rathbone-Bruce film cycle, released by 20th Century-Fox (the subsequent movies were made by Universal Pictures). The follow up to the immensely successful *Hound of the Baskervilles* (1939), this was supposedly "based on the play *Sherlock Holmes* by William Gillette with the permission of the executors of the late Sir Arthur Conan Doyle," although the story bore little resemblance to the original source material, offering up instead a very convoluted plot to steal the crown jewels and bring discredit and humiliation to the Great Detective. Holmes solved the well-known case of the Hound in the previous film, so the producers decided that they needed something equally titanic. They thus chose the Napoleon of Crime, PROFESSOR MORIARTY, and the film featured a bitter, inventive, and often exciting struggle between the two great minds. BASIL RATHBONE and George Zucco were both superb as Holmes and Moriarty, playing their deadly game with gusto. NIGEL BRUCE, bumbling about as Watson, was not equal to his steady performance in *Hound*, starting on the road to buffoonery that handicapped his Watson in later productions.

"ADVENTURES OF SHERLOCK HOLMES, THE" [Television]

England. Dates: 1984–1985, with ongoing series. Cast: Jeremy Brett (Holmes), David Burke (Watson), and Rosalie Williams (Mrs. Hudson). This first series of the excellent and enormously popular adaptation from Granada Television, produced by Michael Cox and developed by John Hawkesworth, is still continuing both in production and popularity, due in large measure to the brilliant performances of Brett as Holmes, the ingenious interpretations of the cases, and the high quality of the productions. The series (with seven stories in the first season and six more in the second), began with "A SCANDAL IN BOHEMIA" and ended with Holmes's dramatic and heart-wrenching "death" at the REICHENBACH FALLS in the midst of a struggle with Professor Moriarty (played by Eric Porter). Some cases were changed to ease their adaptation or to increase their suspense, but the genuine atmosphere of the Canon was retained throughout, including a particularly authentic looking Baker Street. Changes in story lines include the robbery in "The Adventure of the Red-Headed League" masterminded by Professor Moriarty, adding to frustrations with Holmes that finally erupt in "The Final Problem,"

A poster from *The Adventures of Sherlock Holmes* (1939), with Basil Rathbone and Nigel Bruce.

the last episode of the second season, and the last appearance of David Burke as Watson (he would be replaced in subsequent episodes by Edward Hardwicke). Among the notable performances in the first seasons were Gayle Hunnicutt as Irene Adler, Jeremy Kemp as Grimesby Roylott, Joss Acklund as Jephro Rucastle, and Rosalyn Landor as Helen Stoner. Charles Gray (Mycroft Holmes) and Colin Jeavons (Inspector Lestrade) began playing recurring characters.

"ADVENTURES OF SHERLOCK HOLMES, THE." [Radio] Several important radio programs under this title were presented over the air in the United States and England:

1) U.S. 1930–1931, 1931–1932, 1932–1933, 1934–1935. Cast: William Gillette, Richard Gordon, Louis Hector (Holmes), and Leigh Lovell

(Watson). The first American radio program featuring the duo, the "Adventures" was written by Edith Meiser who adapted the Canon and then created original stories. Famed actor WILLIAM GILLETTE played Holmes only in the first broadcast before handing the microphone to Richard Gordon who completed the first three seasons; Louis Hector completed the fourth season, while Leigh Lovell played Watson throughout. The first season's stories were all derived from the Canon, but thereafter they were a combination of the Canon and original case ideas from Meiser who went on to write for the Basil Rathbone and Nigel Bruce radio series. Among Meiser's original cases were "The Voodoo Curse," "The Jewish Breastplate," and "The Syrian Mummy."

2) U.S. 1939–1940. Cast: Basil Rathbone (Holmes) and Nigel Bruce (Watson). The first radio program featuring the beloved Rathbone and

Bruce, these adaptations of the Canon were written by Edith Meiser and aired in twenty-four broadcasts. The pair went to star in the "Sherlock Holmes" radio series throughout the decade.

3) England 1954. Cast: John Gielgud (Holmes) and Ralph Richardson (Watson). A series of twelve spirited adaptations written by John Keir Cross that began with "Dr. Watson Meets Sherlock Holmes," a combination of A Study in Scarlet and "The Adventure of Charles Augustus Milverton." Orson Welles, who adapted the William Gillette play Sherlock Holmes for radio in "The Mercury Theatre on the Air" in 1938, guest starred as Professor Moriarty in the episode "The Final Problem." The series debuted in America in February, 1955. (See also under RADIO.)

ADVENTURES OF SHERLOCK HOLMES'S SMARTER BROTHER, THE.   U.S. 1975.

Dir: Gene Wilder. Cast: Gene Wilder (Sigerson), Marty Feldman (Sacker), Douglas Wilmer (Holmes), Thorley Walters (Watson), and Leo McKern (Moriarty). (20th Century-Fox) This largely slapstick comedy attempts to spoof the Sherlock Holmes story in the tradition of Mel Brooks's Young Frankenstein or Blazing Saddles. Unfortunately, it is only intermittently funny, despite the spirited efforts of most of the cast. Smarter Brother presents the exploits of Sherlock's younger brother Sigerson, a detective perpetually in the shadow of his more famous sibling. Finally receiving a case of his own, Sigerson soon finds himself embroiled in a struggle with the nefarious Professor Moriarty for some important documents. Sigerson is aided by a policeman, Ormond Sacker, who takes part in most of the adventures in the film.

AFGHANISTAN.   This East Asian country was the site of several major wars during the reign of Queen Victoria. Afghanistan will always be remembered by Holmesians because of the first words ever spoken by Holmes to Watson: "How are you? You have been in Afghanistan, I perceive." Watson travelled to Afghanistan in 1878 via India to join his regiment, the Fifth Northumberland Fusiliers, to which he was attached as assistant surgeon. Arriving in India, he discovered that the regiment had gone on to Afghanistan as the Second Afghan War had erupted. Watson went to Candahar and subsequently fought at Maiwand where he was wounded by the now famous "Jezail bullet." Con-

tracting enteric fever (typhoid), he was sent home, although it took many years for him to recover fully from his terrible ordeal ("The Noble Bachelor," The Sign of Four), writing in A Study in Scarlet that he had had enough noise and excitement in Afghanistan to last for the remainder of his natural existence.

While in the country, Watson became physician to Colonel Hayter, whom he would meet some years later on a case in "The Reigate Squires." Afghanistan provided the doctor with reminiscences that he told to Mary Morstan in The Sign of Four and Percy Phelps in "The Naval Treaty" who had little interest in Afghanistan, India, or social questions. Camp life made Watson more lax in his personal habits than might be proper for a medical man ("The Musgrave Ritual"), but it also had the favorable effect of making him flexible to sudden changes in routine. When summoned by Holmes to aid in the investigation of the murder of Charles McCarthy in "The Boscombe Valley Mystery," and with only half an hour to reach Paddington Station, Watson sprung into action: "My experience in camp life in Afghanistan had at least the effect of making me a prompt and ready traveller. My wants were few and simple, so that in less than the time stated I was in a cab with my valise, rattling away to Paddington Station." Other cases in which Afghanistan figured include: "The Empty House"—Colonel Sebastian Moran served there, fighting at Charasiab, Sherpur, and Kabul; and "The Crooked Man"—Henry Wood spent years there wandering among the Afghans after his escape.

AFRICA.   The continent is mentioned in several cases. Dr. Leon Sterndale, the famous explorer, had spent many years in central Africa and was allowed to return there to complete his work after the dreadful affair involving the radix pedis diaboli in "The Devil's Foot." Ralph Smith travelled to South Africa in 1870, dying there after acquiring his fortune. His choice of Violet Smith, daughter of his brother James, as his heir precipitated the conspiracy by Bob Carruthers and Jack Woodley recorded in "The Solitary Cyclist."

AGAR, DR. MOORE.   A Harley Street physician who, in March of 1897, ordered Holmes to take a much needed vacation in "The Devil's Foot." When "Holmes' iron constitution showed some symptoms of giving way in the face of con-

stant hard work of a most exacting kind, aggravated, perhaps, by occasional indiscretions of his own," the doctor "gave positive injunctions that the famous private agent would lay aside all cases and surrender himself to complete rest if he wished to avert an absolute breakdown." Holmes agreed to a rest in Cornwall, but was soon embroiled in another case. Agar's introduction to Holmes was "dramatic," and Watson wrote that he hoped one day to recount it. What the introduction was remains unknown, but a possible first meeting was offered by Nicholas Meyer in his pastiche *The West End Horror* (1976). In it, Agar meets Holmes under the most terrible of circumstances, playing a small, but decisive role in the solution of the case.

AGATHA. The housemaid of the blackmailer Charles Augustus Milverton who fell in love with and became engaged to Escott, a plumber with a rising business in "Charles Augustus Milverton." Escott, of course, was Holmes. Trusting completely in her love, Agatha provided him with information about her master and his estate, Appledore Towers. To allow Escott to visit her at night, she locked up the dog that routinely wandered the garden, thereby also allowing Holmes access to Milverton's study.

AGENCY. The name given by Holmes to members of his own "small, but very efficient organization" in "The Disappearance of Lady Frances Carfax" who assist him in his investigations. It has generally been assumed that Holmes was aided throughout his career by Watson and the Baker Street Irregulars, but this was largely in the early years. For the most part, the detective worked alone, receiving assistance from the Irregulars (in *The Sign of Four*, "The Crooked Man," and *A Study in Scarlet*), or from young individuals such as Simpson ("The Crooked Man"), Cartwright (*Hound of the Baskervilles*), or Wiggins (*A Study in Scarlet, The Sign of Four*), the head of the Irregulars. In "A Scandal in Bohemia," Holmes hired a gang of street toughs and others to help gain entry to Briony Lodge, home of Irene Adler. He also procured the assistance of several agencies in *The Sign of Four* to help him search for the steam launch *Aurora*.

Later in his career, Holmes seems to have had in place a large, professional organization. In a number of cases he was aided by various individuals: Langdale Pike in "The Three Gables," Mercer in "The Creeping Man," and Johnson in "The Illus-

trious Client," as well as the unknown agent who wired Josiah Amberley from Little Purlington in "The Retired Colourman." He was assisted as well by various "agents" in his efforts to recover the "Mazarin Stone." The firm's motto was Compound of the Busy Bee and Excelsior. We Can But Try.

AGONY COLUMN. The name used for personal advertisements that appeared in the various newspapers read by Holmes. The detective held a rather strong opinion of the columns. "What a chorus of groans, cries, and bleatings! What a rag-bag of singular happenings! But surely the most valuable hunting-ground that ever was given to a student of the unusual." He thus faithfully maintained a "great book in which day by day, he filed the agony columns of the various London journals" ("The Red Circle"). Holmes also remarked that he read nothing in the press save the agony column and the criminal news ("The Noble Bachelor"). Clipping the column in "The Copper Beeches," and "The Engineer's Thumb," he also often enjoyed reading the cryptic messages encoded there as in *The Valley of Fear*.

Holmes employed the agony column in several cases: to find the *Aurora* in *The Sign of Four*; to find a certain cabdriver in "The Naval Treaty"; to locate Henry Baker in "The Blue Carbuncle"; and to find the owner of the ring found on Brixton Road in *A Study in Scarlet*. Other advertisements noted were for Lady Frances Carfax in "The Disappearance of Lady Frances Carfax" and Paul and Sophy Kratides in "The Greek Interpreter"; the latter advertisement was placed by Mycroft Holmes.

AGRA TREASURE. This magnificent collection of jewels that had belonged to an Indian *rajah* became the motivation for murder and revenge in *The Sign of Four*. The Agra Treasure was originally stolen by the Four after they murdered the merchant Achmet who was carrying it for his master, the *rajah*. Named for the city in North India that is the home of the Taj Mahal, it was later taken by Major Sholto and finally came to Jonathan Small. Unable to bear anyone else enjoying the gems other than himself, Small cast the treasure into the Thames when his capture by Holmes became inevitable. Later describing the treasure, Small said that "the light of the lantern gleamed upon a collection of gems such as I have read of and thought about when I was a little lad in Pershore. It was blinding to look upon them." Watson greeted the loss of the treasure with an exclamation of relief as it meant that Mary Morstan, who had stood to inherit the fortune, was once more within his reach. He told Mary that "this treasure, these riches, sealed my lips. Now that they are gone I can tell you how I love you. That is why I said, 'Thank God'." Mary agreed, and the doctor added in his account, "Whoever had lost a treasure, I knew that night that I had found one."

AINSTREE, DR.   "The greatest living authority upon tropical diseases." He was living in London at the time of Holmes's apparent illness in "The Dying Detective," and Watson wished to consult him on behalf of his deathly sick friend. For his own important reasons, Holmes would not allow the doctor near him.

AIR GUN.   This dangerous rifle was first wielded to deadly effect in "The Empty House" and was intended for use on several occasions to assassinate Holmes. As designed, the air gun utilized condensed air to propel a ball or projectile, perhaps a soft-nosed revolver bullet, with the velocity of a high-powered rifle, thereby confusing police and forensic experts who would be at a loss to explain how a revolver bullet could do such terrible damage to a person's head. Holmes first encountered air guns in 1891 during his prolonged campaign against the vast criminal organization of Professor Moriarty. Entering Watson's consulting room, he closed the shutters to avoid having his head blown off, expressing to the doctor his fear of air guns. The same concern returned in 1894 when Holmes once more entered into practice. He was targeted for death by the last lieutenant of Moriarty. This dangerous criminal planned to use an air gun built by the blind German Von Herder. The weapon was eventually put on display in the Scotland Yard Museum. Another air gun was constructed some years later by the gunsmith Straubenzee for Count Sylvius in "The Mazarin Stone." This one, however, was never fired at Holmes. An interesting cinematic version of the air gun was presented in the 1946 film *Terror By Night*, with Basil Rathbone and Nigel Bruce. Here the weapon was not a rifle but a cleverly constructed pistol, carried by Colonel Moran.

AKBAR DOST.   One of the Four in *The Sign of Four*.

ALDERSHOT.   A town in Hampshire that possessed the largest military camp in England. Among the troops stationed there was the First Battalion of the Royal Mallows Regiment. Its commanding officer, Colonel James Barclay, was found dead in his home. The case was investigated and solved by Holmes in "The Crooked Man."

ALDGATE STATION.   The eastern-most metropolitan station in the underground and suburban railway system of nineteenth-century London. The body of Arthur Cadogan West was found near it in "The Bruce-Partington Plans."

ALDRIDGE.   A man who aids Holmes and Inspector Lestrade in the Bogus Laundry affair. He looked something like Jim Browner in "The Cardboard Box," "a big, powerful chap, clean-shaven, and very swarthy."

ALEXANDRIA.   This Egyptian city was the source of cigarettes for Professor Coram who ordered 1,000 at a time from Ionides, of Alexandria. A chain smoker, Coram needed a fresh supply every fortnight. Holmes apparently enjoyed the taste of Alexandrian cigarettes himself, smoking them profusely during an interview with the professor. (The ashes he used to solve the case in "The Golden Pince-Nez.") Nathan Garrideb stated a preference for the coins of ancient Syracuse over those of Alexandria in "The Three Garridebs."

ALEXIS.   A Russian Nihilist and a member of a group known as The Brotherhood or The Order in "The Golden Pince-Nez." Alexis was arrested for the murder of a police officer by the Russian police and sentenced to labor in a Siberian salt mine on the testimony of Professor Coram. Anna, Coram's wife, was in love with Alexis, declaring that he "was noble, unselfish, loving, all that my husband was not." Although Alexis was innocent and wrote strenuously against the crime, Coram hid the letters to Anna that would have secured his freedom and testified against him out of jealous hatred. The recovery of the letters became Anna's quest.

ALGAR.   A friend of Holmes's who was on the Liverpool police force. Holmes wired Algar for information that helped solve the case of "The Cardboard Box."

ALICE.   The maid and close confidante of Hatty Doran in "The Noble Bachelor." Lord St. Simon described Alice as an American who came from California with her mistress. He felt that the maid was allowed to take great liberties, adding: "Still, of course, in America they look upon these things in a different way."

ALICIA. The disappearance of this cutter ranked among Holmes's unsolved cases. The vessel "sailed one spring morning into a small patch of mist from where she never emerged, nor was anything further ever heard of herself and her crew" ("The Problem of Thor Bridge"). Philip Jose Farmer, writing as Harry Manders, proposed a wild explanation for the disappearance of the *Alicia* in his short pastiche "The Problem of the Sore Bridge—Among Others."

ALISON'S. Also Alson's Rooms, an establishment (perhaps a public house) at which boxing or prizefighting was held (*The Sign of Four*). Holmes fought three rounds with McMurdo the night of the latter's benefit in either 1883 or 1884.

ALLARDYCE. A London butcher shop where Holmes spent an energetic morning stabbing a harpoon at a pig that was hung from the ceiling by a hook in "Black Peter." He satisfied himself that by no exertion of his strength could he transfix the pig with a single blow. This activity had a direct bearing on solving the murder of Captain Peter Carey.

ALLAN BROTHERS. The principal land agents in the village of Esher, Surrey in "Wisteria Lodge." Aloysius Garcia rented Wisteria Lodge from them.

ALLEN, MRS. The housekeeper at Birlstone Manor in *The Valley of Fear*. She was a "buxom and cheerful person" who was also a little hard of hearing. Following the discovery of a body in the study, Mrs. Allen took Mrs. Douglas to her bedroom and stayed with her throughout most of the night.

ALPHA INN. A small public house near the British Museum, in Bloomsbury, on the corner of one of the streets that connect with Holborn. A goose club was organized here, to which Henry Baker belonged and from which he obtained a Christmas goose in "The Blue Carbuncle." (See also WINDIGATE.)

ALTAMONT. This highly successful disguise and alias was adopted by Holmes to penetrate a German spy ring just before the start of World War I in "His Last Bow." As Altamont, Holmes assumed the persona of an Irish-American agent who came to work for the German master spy Von Bork. He was described by Von Bork as "a wonderful worker. If I pay him well, at least he delivers the goods, to use his own phrase. Besides he is not a traitor. I assure you that our most Pan-Germanic Junker is a sucking dove in his feelings towards England as compared with a real bitter Irish-American." Altamont had a nice taste for wine, particularly Von Bork's Tokay, and spoke with an accent so severe that the German often had trouble understanding him, declaring to a colleague that, "He seems to have declared war on the King's English as well as on the English king." So convincing was Holmes's performance that the spymaster was completely surprised when Holmes sprung his trap.

Holmes as Altamont closes the trap on Von Bork, the German spymaster, in "His Last Bow"; by A. Gilbert.

ALUMINUM CRUTCH.   An untold investigation conducted by Holmes and mentioned in "The Musgrave Ritual." The case of the Aluminum Crutch dates to the period before Holmes met Watson.

AMATEUR MENDICANT SOCIETY.   An organization that was investigated by Holmes in 1887, and thus also ranked among the detective's unchronicled cases. The society "held a luxurious club in the lower vault of a furniture warehouse" ("The Five Orange Pips").

AMATI.   The famed Italian manufacturer of violins. In *A Study in Scarlet*, Holmes spoke to Watson about "Cremona fiddles, and the differences between a Stradivarius and an Amati."

AMBERLEY, JOSIAH.   The junior partner of Brickfall & Amberley manufacturers of art materials hired Holmes to locate his missing wife in "The Retired Colourman." Amberley wished the detective to find his wife, whom he said had run off with her lover, a neighbor named Ray Ernest. Holmes remarked of him: "He made his little pile, retired from business at the age of sixty-one, bought a house at Lewisham, and settled down to rest after a life of ceaseless grind . . . Early in 1897 he married a woman twenty years younger than himself—a good-looking woman, too, if the photograph does not flatter. A competence, a wife, leisure—it seemed a straight road which lay before him. And yet within two years he is, as you have seen, as broken and miserable a creature as crawls beneath the sun."

AMERICAN ENCYCLOPEDIA.   A reference work used periodically by Holmes. In "The Five Orange Pips," Holmes consulted it to find information on the Ku Klux Klan.

AMES.   The butler of Birlstone Manor in *The Valley of Fear.*

ANATOMY.   Watson included this area of study in his listing of "Sherlock Holmes—his limits" in *A Study in Scarlet*. Watson wrote of Holmes's knowledge as "Accurate, but unsystematic." He looked back humorously upon it some years later in "The Five Orange Pips." Holmes's familiarity with the subject allowed him to identify the bone shown to him and Watson by John Mason as a femur in

"Shoscombe Old Place" and to note the similarity between the ear of Susan Cushing and another that had been mailed in "The Cardboard Box."

ANCIENT BRITISH BARROW.   An unchronicled investigation undertaken by Holmes in 1894 in "The Golden Pince-Nez." The case involved "the Addleton tragedy and the singular contents of the ancient British barrow."

ANDAMAN ISLANDS.   These islands, situated in the Bay of Bengal in the Indian Ocean, entered into the story of the Four in *The Sign of Four*. Jonathan Small was sent there for incarceration, an act that involved Major Sholto and Captain Morstan in the affair of the Agra Treasure. Small first met the dangerous Andaman islander Tonga during his imprisonment. So memorable was Tonga, that Watson wrote he would always associate "the dreary marshes of the Thames and the long, sullen reaches of the river" with the "pursuit of the Andaman islanders" ("The Gold Pince-Nez"). Most of the information cited by Holmes concerning the islands from his gazetteer was inaccurate.

ANDERSON.   A companion of James Dodd and Geoffrey Emsworth in "The Blanched Soldier" who, in 1900, during the Boer War, was killed at the "morning fight at Buffelspruit, outside Pretoria, on the Eastern railway line." Emsworth, Anderson, and Simpson (another soldier, nicknamed Baldy), had become separated from their associates— Emsworth was wounded and the other two killed. Anderson is also the name of the constable of Fulworth who investigated the death of Fitzroy MacPherson in "The Lion's Mane." Out of his depth, he soon called upon the retired Holmes to assist him, for which the detective credited him with "good sense."

ANDERSON MURDERS.   Killings that occurred in North Carolina, said by Holmes to be very similar to the case he investigated in *The Hound of the Baskervilles.*

ANDOVER.   A town in Hampshire where a case occurred in 1877 that was analogous to the one Holmes investigated concerning Mary Sutherland in "A Case of Identity."

"ANGELS OF DARKNESS."   One of the two unpublished works by Sir Arthur Conan Doyle

The American Connection

Sherlock Holmes was always delighted to meet Americans and knew a great deal about the United States, possessing both friends in the country and considerable familiarity with American slang or colloquialisms (such as "a herd of buffaloes."). While it is known that Holmes was in America in the years just prior to the start of World War I impersonating the Irish-American Altamont while penetrating the German spy ring of Von Bork ("His Last Bow"), it is a matter of some speculation that he may have spent time in the United States prior to his meeting Watson. This idea was developed by such writers as W. S. Baring-Gould in his biography of Holmes, Michael Hardwick in *Sherlock Holmes, My Life and Crimes*, and H. Paul Jeffers in *The Adventure of the Stalwart Companions*, among others.

Throughout his career, the detective was engaged in a number of known cases involving Americans or America. Among these are:

"The Dancing Men"
"The Five Orange Pips"
His Last Bow
The Hound of the Baskervilles (a Canadian)
"The Noble Bachelor"
"The Problem of Thor Bridge"

"The Red Circle"
A Study in Scarlet
"The Three Garridebs"
The Valley of Fear
"The Yellow Face"

(See under individual entries related to these cases, e.g. Hope, Jefferson; or Slaney, Abe; see also Adler, Irene; Buffalo (1); Buffalo (2); Canada; Chicago; Escott; Florida; Georgia; New York; Pennsylvania; San Francisco; also *Sherlock Holmes in New York*; *Sherlock Holmes in Washington*; *The Scarlet Claw*; and *Enter the Lion*.)

(along with "The Stonor Case") that have not been released or seen by the public at the insistence of the Doyle Estate. "Angels of Darkness" was apparently a three-act play, written in 1890, with Dr. Watson as its principal character. It was based on the flashbacks featured in *A Study in Scarlet*, but was set in San Francisco. It is believed that the doctor becomes romantically involved in the drama.

ANGLO-INDIAN CLUB. A club that Colonel Moran was a member of in "The Empty House."

ANISEED. Highly aromatic, the seed of the anise plant found in the Mediterranean was sprayed by Holmes onto the hind wheel of Leslie Armstrong's brougham, thereby allowing the track dog Pompey to follow it in "The Missing Three-Quarter."

ANSTRUTHER, DR. This physician maintained Watson's medical practice when he was away, presumably with Holmes, on some case of deadly importance. In the case of the murder of Charles McCarthy in "The Boscombe Valley Mystery," Watson was uncertain if he had the time to join Holmes because of his heavy caseload. Mrs. Watson then suggested that the doctor consult Anstruther, as he might be willing to take over his practice for a few days. Watson also made reference to "an accommodating neighbour" ("The Final Problem" and "The Stockbroker's Clerk"), once calling him Jackson ("The Crooked Man"). Watson presumably knew several physicians who were available to cover for him, friends who were aware of the special nature of Watson's relationship with Holmes. (See also Practices under WATSON, DR. JOHN.)

ANTHONY.   The old manservant to the Stapletons at Merripit House in Devonshire in *The Hound of the Baskervilles*, Anthony probably had served the Stapletons for some years before they arrived in Devonshire, perhaps as far back as Stapleton's schoolmaster days. Following the affair of the Hound, Anthony disappeared. Holmes doubted that Anthony was the servant's real name, suggesting the name was Antonio, implying a Spanish or South American origin.

ANTHROPOID, SERUM OF.   This mysterious potion is taken by Professor Presbury in "The Creeping Man," in the hopes that it would make him younger. The serum was provided to him by Lowenstein of Prague. His "wondrous strength-giving serum" was "tabooed by the profession because he refused to reveal its source." Despite the dangers, Presbury took the serum anyway, with terrible consequences.

ANTHROPOLOGICAL JOURNAL.   In full, *Journal of the Anthropological Institution of Great Britain and Ireland*, a journal of the society established in 1871. Holmes contributed two short monographs on ears to the journal, making him eminently qualified to examine the ears that were delivered by mail to Sarah Cushing in "The Cardboard Box." The titles of the articles remain unknown, but the Holmesian H.W. Bell, in his work *Sherlock Holmes and Dr. Watson*, has dated the case to 1885, meaning that the two articles appeared in the journal in 1884.

APPLEDORE TOWERS.   The residence of Charles Augustus Milverton, situated in Hampstead. Holmes was familiar with the layout of Appledore Towers through his courtship of Milverton's maid Agatha while he was disguised as the plumber Escott in "Charles Augustus Milverton."

ARCADIA MIXTURE.   Watson's favorite tobacco mixture. The doctor continued to smoke it even after his marriage, the fact deduced by Holmes when he noted the ash of the mixture upon Watson's coat at the start of "The Crooked Man."

ARMITAGE, PERCY.   The second son of Armitage, of Crane Water, near Reading in "The Speckled Band." Percy was engaged to Helen Stoner, stepdaughter of Dr. Grimesby Roylott of Stoke Moran, and presumably married her following her stepfather's gruesome death.

ARMSTRONG, DR. LESLIE.   The formidable friend of Godfrey Staunton, one of the heads of the medical school of Cambridge and a thinker of European reputation in more than one branch of science, appeared in "The Missing Three-Quarter." Armstrong impressed Holmes greatly, the latter stating that he had never "seen a man who, if he turned his talents that way, was more calculated to fill the gap left by the illustrious Moriarty." The physician waged an often brilliant battle of wits with the detective, foiling Holmes's search for the missing Staunton, in the assumption that Holmes was in the employ of Lord Mount-James. As Armstrong's purpose was entirely noble, he "wrung Holmes by the hand" upon learning that the sleuth was equally concerned for Staunton's well-being. Watson considered him "a man of deep character, a man with an alert mind, grim, ascetic, self-contained, formidable."

ARNSWORTH CASTLE.   In full, the Arnsworth Castle business, an unchronicled case investigated by Holmes before 1888. In the solution, Holmes used a false alarm of fire: "When a woman thinks that her house is on fire, her instinct is at once to rush to the thing that she values most. It is a perfectly overpowering impulse, and I have more than once taken advantage of it. In the case of the Darlington Substitution Scandal it was of use to me, and also in the Arnsworth Castle business" ("A Scandal in Bohemia"). A pastiche of the case, "The Adventure of the Red Widow," was included in the collection *The Exploits of Sherlock Holmes* by Adrian Conan Doyle. For another case involving the use of a false fire alarm, see "NORWOOD BUILDER, THE ADVENTURE OF THE."

ARSENE LUPIN CONTRA SHERLOCK HOLMES.   Germany 1910–1911. Cast: Viggo Larsen (Holmes), Paul Otto (Arsene Lupin). A series of five one- and two-reel German-language films, featuring the great detective and the well-known French thief, based on *Arsene Lupin Contra Sherlock Holmes* (1903) by Maurice Leblanc, and directed by Viggo Larsen. Vitascope Pictures in Germany, the production company, was able to use the loose copyright law concerning films and film adaptations to change Leblanc's original character

Herlock to the proper Sherlock. The five segments were similar to the Holmes-Raffles films that VIGGO LARSEN had made during his stay at Nordisk in Denmark. Lupin proves quite a match for the detective, donning apparently foolproof disguises and leading Holmes on a number of merry chases. Holmes finally catches up with the thief in episode five. The segments were 1) *Der Alte Sekretar* (*The Old Secretaire*); 2) *Der Blaue Diamant* (*The Blue Diamond*); 3) *Die Falschen Rembrandts* (*The Fake Rembrandts*); 4) *Die Flucht* (*The Escape*); 5) *Arsene Lupin Ende* (*The End of Arsene Lupin*). (See also LUPIN, ARSENE.)

ART. Holmes was surprisingly well versed in the arts. Watson wrote that Holmes had only the "crudest of ideas" concerning art, but the detective protested, suggesting that they spend some time in a gallery in Bond Street in *The Hound of the Baskervilles*. Holmes was the descendent of the French artist Horace Vernet—the artist's sister was his grandmother—telling Watson that "art in the blood is liable to take the strangest forms." ("The Greek Interpreter"). Holmes also gave the artistic name to *A Study in Scarlet*.

As for the role of art in other adventures, Baron Gruner was a noted collector of art in "The Illustrious Client," while Thaddeus Sholto declared himself to be knowledgeable on the subject in *The Sign of Four*. Laura Lyons's husband was an artist in *The Hound of the Baskervilles*. The St. Pancras case was said to involve a picture-frame maker ("Shoscombe Old Place"). The duke of Balmoral was also forced to sell his family's art collection in order to support the family in "The Noble Bachelor."

ASSAULT AND BATTERY. This crime occurred numerous times in the Canon, both upon clients of Holmes's and the detective himself. By definition, assault implies the attempt to inflict injury, while battery is the actual committing of the attack. Among the notable episodes of assault and battery upon clients are Violet Smith's abduction by Jack Woodley and Reverend Williamson in "The Solitary Cyclist"; and Victor Hatherley's attack by Lysander Stark in "The Engineer's Thumb." Other episodes involving nonclients include: the assault on Henry Baker by street toughs in "The Blue Carbuncle"; the murderous rages of Dr. Grimesby Roylott, especially toward the local blacksmith in "The Speckled Band"; and the actions of the Spencer John Gang in "The Three

Gables." Professor Moriarty practiced assault and battery, one of his many crimes.

There were several attacks upon Holmes himself. The most severe of them was launched by the hired thugs of Baron Gruner in Regent Street, an assault that earned newspaper headlines in "The Illustrious Client." The detective was also set upon by the Cunninghams in "The Reigate Squires"; by Jack Woodley in "The Solitary Cyclist"—where Holmes demonstrated his boxing prowess; by Joseph Harrison in "The Naval Treaty"; and by Jefferson Hope in *A Study in Scarlet*, although Hope was wrestling also with Watson, Gregson, and Lestrade.

ASTRONOMY. While Holmes may have initially known little about this subject, his knowledge of the science increased throughout the Canon. Watson expressed total disbelief in *A Study in Scarlet* that Holmes was so ignorant on a wide variety of subjects, adding: "My surprise reached a climax, however, when I found incidentally that he was ignorant of the Copernican Theory and of the composition of the Solar System. That any civilized human being in the nineteenth century should not be aware that the earth travelled round the sun appeared to be to me such an extraordinary fact that I could hardly realise it." As the years went by, however, the doctor's assessment had to be revised as Holmes displayed more than a casual astronomical familiarity, despite the detective's own admission of ignorance in *A Study in Scarlet*. Holmes discussed the Personal Equation in "The Musgrave Ritual" and the obliquity of the Eliptic in "The Greek Interpreter," and compared Mycroft's visit to Baker Street with a planet leaving its orbit ("The Bruce-Partington Plans"). See also DYNAMICS OF THE ASTEROID.

ATKINSON. An unchronicled investigation by Holmes, dated to around 1888 in "A Scandal in Bohemia." Watson reported that because of his marriage, he and Holmes had drifted away from each other, but from time to time he heard some vague account of the detective's doings, including "his clearing up the singular tragedy of the Atkinson brothers at Trincomalee."

ATWILL, LIONEL. A well-known performer (1885–1946) of the 1930s and 1940s, Atwill appeared in such memorable films as *The Vampire Bat* (1933), *Son of Frankenstein* (1939), and *Mark of the Vampire* (1935), frequently playing mad scientists

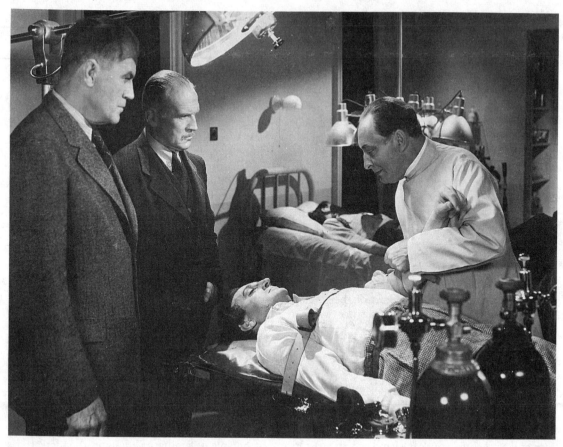

Lionel Atwill (r.) seen here as Professor Moriarty, prepares to drain Holmes of his blood in *Sherlock Holmes and the Secret Weapon* (1942).

or dutiful police inspectors. Atwill worked in two Holmes pictures, *The Hound of the Baskervilles* (1939) and *Sherlock Holmes and the Secret Weapon* (1942), opposite Basil Rathbone and Nigel Bruce. In the former he played Dr. Mortimer while in the latter he had the coveted role of Professor Moriarty. As the evil professor, Atwill had the fun of strapping Holmes to an operating table and slowly draining him of every last drop of blood. Holmes, of course, had the last laugh.

"AUGUST, 1914." The code used by the German spymaster Von Bork for his double combination safe in "His Last Bow." The lock required a letter (or word) / number combination, thus August, 1914. The code was appropriate given the events of the summer and the work of the spy.

AUSTRALIA. This former British colonial possession was mentioned in several cases, normally as the backdrop of a person's dark past, or the place of origin for characters. The most dramatic sojourn in Australia was by John Turner, a onetime prospector who became the bushranger Black Jack of Ballarat and who was later blackmailed by Charles McCarthy, a robbery victim he once spared in "The Boscombe Valley Mystery." Another case involved the Norfolk squire Trevor Senior who was once transported aboard the prison barque *Gloria Scott* for embezzlement. He managed to survive the ship's destruction, reaching Australia not as a prisoner but a free man. Over the next years he made his fortune in the goldfields ("The 'Gloria Scott' "). Lady Mary Brackenstall in "The Abbey Grange" and Holy Peters in "The Disappearance of Lady

Frances Carfax" came from Australia and the earl of Maynooth served as governor of one of the colonies in Australia in 1894 in "The Empty House." Watson also visited Australia many years before meeting Holmes, as is clear from his references to it in *The Sign of Four*.

AUSTRIA.   This kingdom was known in full as Austria-Hungary (or the Austro-Hungarian Empire) during Holmes's day. The odious Baron Gruner was an Austrian in "The Illustrious Client," Lowenstein wrote a letter to Professor Presbury that bore an Austrian stamp in "The Creeping Man," and Holmes consulted his index to the Commonplace Books for information on "Vampirism in Hungary." The country figured much more prominently in Nicholas Meyer's novel *The Seven-Per-Cent Solution* (1974), which featured Holmes and Watson travelling to Vienna and there meeting Dr. Sigmund Freud.

AVELING.   The mathematics master at the Priory School in "The Priory School." He proved useful to Holmes in the investigation by confirming that Heidegger, the missing German master, used Palmer tires on his bicycle.

B DIVISION.   One of the twenty-two administrative divisions of the Metropolitan Police of London. Its jurisdiction extended over Kensington south and a portion of Westminster. At the time of "The Blue Carbuncle" (dated variously to 1887, 1889, or 1890), Inspector Bradstreet was assigned to B Division. (See also SCOTLAND YARD.)

BACKWATER, LORD.   The owner of Capleton (or Mapleton) Stables, Dartmoor, whose horse, Desborough, lost to Silver Blaze in the Wessex Cup in "Silver Blaze." Backwater, who had no doubt heard of Holmes's brilliance (perhaps in the Silver Blaze affair), also attended the wedding of Lord Robert St. Simon, recommending to the nobleman that he consult with Holmes in solving the disappearance of his new bride, the former Hatty Doran, in "The Noble Bachelor." The Sherlockian scholar W. S. Baring-Gould proposed that Holmes had done some service for Lord Backwater between March 1881 and October 1886. Lord St. Simon was to honeymoon at Backwater's estate near Petersfield.

BADEN.   This city and health spa in Switzerland was part of the Grand Duchy of Baden in Holmes's time. Watson was able to trace Lady Frances Carfax to the Englischer Hof in Baden in "The Disappearance of Lady Frances Carfax." There she made the acquaintance of Dr. and Mrs. Shlessinger, subsequently leaving with them.

BAGATELLE CARD CLUB.   A London club to which Ronald Adair and Colonel Sebastian Moran belonged in "The Empty House." On the night that he was killed, Adair had played a rubber of whist with Moran at the club.

BAIN, SANDY.   A jockey in the service of Sir Robert Norberton in "Shoscombe Old Place," at Shoscombe Stables, in Berkshire. Sir Robert strangely ordered Bain to give Lady Beatrice Falder's favorite spaniel to Josiah Barnes, keeper of the Green Dragon Inn.

BAKER, HENRY.   A member of the goose club at the Alpha Inn in "The Blue Carbuncle," he lost both his hat and his goose during an attack by a group of roughs. When both the hat and goose were brought to Holmes by the commissionaire Peterson, Holmes kept the hat and gave the goose to Peterson, whose wife discovered the Blue Carbuncle in its crop. Based upon his observations of the hat, Holmes stated that Baker was: "a man who leads a sedentary life, goes out little, is out of training entirely, is middle-aged, has grizzled hair which he has had cut within the last few days, and which he anoints with lime-cream. These are the more patent facts which are to be deduced from his hat. Also, by the way, that it is extremely improbable that he has gas laid on in his house." The detective, of course, was proven completely correct, including his statement that Baker's wife, for whom the goose was intended as a peace offering, had ceased to love her husband.

BAKER STREET.   This London street, situated in the West End, became immortalized as the address of Sherlock Holmes from around 1881 until 1903 and his retirement to the Sussex Downs. Baker Street is known throughout the world. Down its straight way ran, rode, and walked clients, police, criminals, and suspects, each proceeding to 221B and the suite of rooms occupied for so long and with such distinction by the Master Detective.

Contrary to its depiction in film (the various Baker Streets of the Rathbone-Bruce cycle for example), the street is straight, its rigidness confirmed by Watson's account in "The Empty House" when he reported the attempted assassination of Holmes from Camden House, situated directly across from 221 Baker Street.

Much to the disappointment no doubt of many devotees of the Canon who make pilgrimages to London, there is no actual 221B Baker Street, let alone a 221. In Holmes's time, Baker Street was short, stretching barely over a quarter of a mile. Numbered addresses ran from south to north, with Nos. 1–42 on the east side of the street, and Nos. 44–85 on the west going south. Thus, there could not have been a 221. In 1930, however, the entire length of the street was renamed Baker Street, requiring a renumbering. A Georgian house, No. 41 Upper Baker Street, was redesignated 221 Baker Street. That same year, however, it was demolished to make room for Abbey House. Abbey House eventually occupied 215–229 Baker Street, also serving as the Abbey National Building Society.

During the period known as the Great Hiatus (1891–1894), Mrs. Hudson, Holmes's long-suffering landlady, maintained his rooms exactly as he left them, thanks to the financial intervention

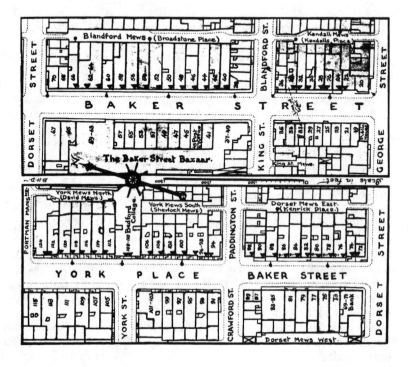

Baker Street in 1894, site of one of the world's most famous addresses.

Holmes and Watson at Baker Street; by Howard Elcock.

of his brother Mycroft Holmes. One of the most famous addresses in all literature and film, 221B became as synonymous with the Great Detective as his cap and deerstalker, his pipe, and the redoubtable Dr. Watson who lived with Holmes for many years and later returned to 221B from time to time between his frequent marriages. While the number used for the residence, 221B, was clearly a camouflage to hide the "real" address, it is generally accepted that B (also spelled b) signified the French "bis," designating Holmes's address as a subsidiary to the general household of Baker Street.

The earliest description of the suite of rooms at Baker Street was provided by Watson in A Study in Scarlet: "They consisted of a couple of comfortable bedrooms and a single large airy sitting-room, cheerfully furnished, and illuminated by two broad windows. So desirable in every way were the apartments, and so moderate did the terms seem when divided between us, that the bargain was concluded upon the spot, and we at once entered into possession." The remaining fifty-nine works of the Canon contain interesting and vital clues as to the layout and general appearance of the rooms that were for so long the *sanctum sanctorum* of Sherlockiana.

Contrary to some film versions of Baker Street,

Holmes's rooms were on the second floor (or, in correct English terms, on the first floor). Mrs. Hudson obviously retained for herself the entire ground floor, although it has been theorized that the detective may have rented the cellar to use as an additional storage area or, more likely, as a secret laboratory where he could perform his largest experiments (see also LUMBER ROOM). While Watson lived there, his bedroom was upstairs from Holmes's dwelling place. Its location can be confirmed by references (as in "Thor Bridge" and "The Beryl Coronet") to Watson coming *down* to breakfast.

There is a tendency to imagine the "humble lodgings" as static, frozen in time around 1895. As with any long-term residence, changes, even subtly introduced, would, inevitably, have manifested themselves in the surroundings, for example, as Watson moved out, moved back in, and then out again as various Mrs. Watsons attached themselves to his life. Such departures and returns would have altered to some degree the layout of the Baker Street interior; at the very least, Watson's prized portrait of Henry Ward Beecher would have travelled with him. Furniture would have worn out, curtains would have been replaced, and new technologies—such as the telephone—would have crept their way into the domestic scene.

A number of attempts have been made to recreate the Baker Street lodgings with as much authenticity as possible. In 1951, Michael Wright undertook an ambitious reconstruction of 221B for a Sherlock Holmes Exhibition that was part of the Festival of Britain. The exhibit was eventually moved to the upstairs of the public house the "Sherlock Holmes" in the Northumberland Hotel (where Sir Henry Baskerville stayed in *The Hound of the Baskervilles*). Other memorable reconstructions were supervised by Adrian Conan Doyle at the Château de Lucens in Switzerland that have regrettably not survived; and by John Bennett Shaw, a scale model that has recently been donated to the University of Minnesota.

Baker Street on film has not always been to the particular tastes of Holmesians. Early film Baker Streets were remarkably simple and surprisingly sparse, especially given the multitude of details to which the stories allude. The suite of rooms in John Barrymore's 1922 *Sherlock Holmes* was an excellent exception, even if shades of the Gillette play (cushions before the fire for example) found their way into the production. Certainly the most shocking

A notable 221B Baker Street, from *The Adventures of Sherlock Holmes* (1939).

of the early 221Bs was that featured in *The Speckled Band* (1931) with Raymond Massey. This residence was nothing like the small home of Mrs. Hudson. The detective had not a simple set of rooms but a large office, with stenographers, secretaries, and a host of modern appliances! Other notable cinematic 221Bs were in the Basil Rathbone–Nigel Bruce series (1939–1946), *The Hound of the Baskervilles* (1959), *A Study in Terror* (1965), *The Private Life of Sherlock Holmes* (1970), *Murder by Decree* (1979), and the particularly good Baker Street of the Granada Television series with Jeremy Brett.

Each year, thousands of letters addressed to Holmes or to Watson arrive at 221B Baker Street. Many are tongue in cheek or simply contain salutations to the Great Detective; some, however, are serious inquiries for Holmes's advice or help in solving some personal mystery or crisis. The Abbey

National Building Society dutifully answers each piece of mail, the replies written by The Secretary to Sherlock Holmes. Near the main entrance to Abbey House is a plaque commemorating 221B Baker Street and the detective, including the quote from *A Study in Scarlet*: "We met next day and inspected the rooms at 221 B Baker Street . . . and at once entered into possession."

The noted Sherlockian W. S. Baring-Gould wrote in "The Problem of Number 221" (*Baker Street Journal*) that "The evidence of The Empty House, The Hound of the Baskervilles, The Red-Headed League, The Blue Carbuncle, and The Beryl Coronet would seem to indicate that '221' Baker Street was a house on the west side (or left side going north) of Baker Street, *below* Dorset Street, and most probably *between* Blandford and Dorset Streets." A. L. Shearn proposed that

Holmes, in his usually brilliant manner, would have anticipated the inevitable renumbering of Baker Street and so resided in the building that was to become 221. This has been disputed by many scholars in favor of other addresses they deem more likely: Baring-Gould favored a house somewhere between 19 and 35 Baker Street; Bernard Davies chose 31 Baker Street (the onetime 72 Baker Street); and Vincent Starrett, author of *The Private Life of Sherlock Holmes*, liked 66 Baker Street for what he described as its "occult sense of rightness." Starrett, however, concurred with the labors and researches of Dr. Gray Chandler Briggs of St. Louis, who deduced the residence of 221 not by searching for it but by locating Camden House, which was supposed to be across from Mrs. Hudson's house. Briggs followed the route taken by Holmes when he led Watson circuitously to the Empty House. Having found it, he decided that the house opposite was Holmes's famed dwelling place—11 Baker Street—making Camden House No. 118. As for Sir Arthur Conan Doyle, the story was told by the writer Sebastian Lamb that one day while walking with Conan Doyle, Sir Arthur pointed to No. 61 Baker Street and said that that was where Sherlock Holmes lived. Ironically, his statement has not been accepted by Sherlockians who point out that No. 61 is not facing directly opposite from any house that could be termed a likely candidate for Camden House. To complicate matters even further, Russell McLaughlin and Robert G. Harris, in "What Price Baker Street" (*Baker Street Journal*, 1952) argued that Mrs. Hudson's residence was not even located on Baker Street. The Baker Street location was simply an "accommodation" address; the rooms Holmes lived in were located someplace nearby, at Gloucester Place.

BAKER STREET. U.S. 1964–1965. Dir: Harold Prince. Cast: Fritz Weaver (Holmes), Peter Sallis (Dr. Watson), Martin Gabel (Professor Moriarty), and Inga Swenson (Irene Adler). In full, *Baker Street: A Musical Adventure of Sherlock Holmes*, a major musical production with music and lyrics by Marian Grudeff and Raymond Jessel that opened in New York at the Broadway Theatre in February 1965, subsequently running for nine months. This lively work was based loosely on "A Scandal in Bohemia," "The Empty House," and "The Final Problem," weaving together the characters of Irene Adler, Moriarty, and Holmes and Watson. The plot centered on the professor's scheme to

Fritz Weaver (with Inga Swenson) sings and smokes in the musical "Baker Street" (1965).

steal the Crown Jewels *à la* the Basil Rathbone film *The Adventures of Sherlock Holmes* (1939). Among the notable musical numbers was "Leave It to Us, Guv," performed by Wiggins and the Baker Street Irregulars. The show was never moved to London, nor was a film version ever developed.

BAKER STREET IRREGULARS (1). This group of street urchins was recruited by Holmes to perform various missions, generally to search London following clues and to go places where the detective himself could not. Watson first encountered the Irregulars in *A Study in Scarlet*, describing them as "six dirty little scoundrels [who] stood in line like so many disreputable statuettes." Their chief was the energetic and inventive Wiggins. Holmes said to Watson about them: "There's more work to be got out of one of those little beggars than out of a dozen of the force . . . The mere sight of an official looking person seals men's lips. These youngsters, however, go everywhere and hear everything. They are as sharp as needles, too; all they want is organization." In return for their labors, the detective paid them a shilling a day with a guinea bonus to the one who found the object of their search; they were also paid for expenses (*The Sign of Four*). Holmes used the Irregulars to hunt down the cab driven by Jefferson Hope in *A Study in Scarlet*; to find the ship *Aurora* in *The Sign of Four*; and to watch over Henry Wood at Aldershot in "The Crooked Man."

The Irregulars have figured in a number of interesting films and productions. In the musical *Baker Street* (1965), they sang and danced the song "Leave It to Us, Guv," while in the film *Without a Clue* (1990), they took fiendish delight in tormenting the incompetent Holmes played by Michael Caine. (See also BAKER STREET IRREGULARS, THE CASE OF THE; EXIT, SHERLOCK HOLMES; GLENDOWER CONSPIRACY, THE; and QUALLSFORD INHERITANCE, THE.)

BAKER STREET IRREGULARS (2).

The oldest and most prestigious of the societies devoted to the study and appreciation of Sherlock Holmes, the BSI was founded in 1934 by a group of remarkable Sherlockians, inspired by one of the greatest of all Sherlockians, Christopher Morley, as a means of sharing their fascination with all things related to the great detective. Morley, who had already organized several clubs and was a member of the famed Algonquin Round Table, conceived of the Baker Street Irregulars, naming them after Holmes's rather unorthodox band of street urchin assistants. He used as a required test for admission a crossword puzzle created by his brother Frank which he included in the May 19, 1934 issue of *The Saturday Review of Literature* in his column "The Bowling Green." Morley declared that those persons successfully completing the puzzle would be granted admission to the first dinner of the society.

That now famous dinner was held at the Christ Cella Restaurant in New York. Early members included Rex Stout, Frederic Dorr Steele, and the noted Sherlockian John Bennett Shaw. It would later include Franklin Delano Roosevelt and Harry Truman. "The Buy-Laws of the Baker Street Irregulars," written by Elmer Davis, were also published in "The Bowling Green" and are still read at the Annual Dinner.

The founder of the Baker Street Irregulars were obliged to complete this puzzle to gain membership. Created by Frank V. Morely, it appeared in *The Saturday Review of Literature* in May 1934.

CROSSWORD 221 B (*Baker Street Irregular*)   *Mycroft Holmes*

ACROSS

1. A treatise on this, written at the age of twenty-one, had a European vogue and earned its author a professorship. (2 words, 8, 7)
8. It was of course to see these that Holmes enquired the way from Saxe-Coburg Square to the Strand (2 words, 10, 5)
11. How the pips were set (2)
13. Not an Eley's No. 2 (which is an excellent argument with a gentleman who can twist steel pokers into knots) but the weapon in the tragedy of Birlstone (3)
14. What was done on the opposite wall in bullet-pocks by the patriotic Holmes (2)
15. What Watson recognized when he put his hand on Bartholomew Sholto's leg (5)
18. Where Watson met young Stamford, who introduced him to Sherlock Holmes (3)
20. A kind of pet, over which Dr. Grimesby Roylott hurled the local blacksmith (4)
21. Holmes should have said this before being so sure of catching the murderers of John Openshaw (2)
22. The kind of Pedro whence came the tiger (3)
23. Though he knew the methods, Watson sometimes found it difficult to do this (3)
25. Patron saint of old Mr. Farquhar's affliction and perhaps of Abe Slaney's men (5)
27. Perhaps a measure of Holmes's chemicals (2)
28. In short, Watson (2)
29. 𝕏𝕏 (2)
30. Curious that he did nothing in the nightime (1)
31. This would obviously not describe the empty house opposite 221b Baker Street (2)
34. It seems likely that Watson's elder brother suffered from this disease (2)
35. Though you might have taken this at Lodge 29, Chicago, nevertheless, you had to pass a test as well at Lodge 341, Vermissa (4)
37. The *Star* of Savannah (4)
40. Mrs. Barclay's reproach (in The Crooked Man, of course) suggests the parable of this (2)
41. Scrawled in blood-red letters across the bare plaster at No. 3, Lauriston Gardens (5)
43. Holmes found this, because he was looking for it in the mud (5)
44. Suggests Jonathan Small's leg (4)
45. The brother who left Watson no choice but to relate The Final

DOWN

Problem (2 words, 5, 8)

1. A country district in the west of England where "Cooee" was a common signal (2 words, 8, 6)
2. Charles Augustus Milverton dealt with no niggard hand; therefore this would not describe him (4)
3. The kind of practice indulged by Mr. Williamson, the solitary cyclist's unfrocked clergyman—"there was a man of that name in orders, whose career has been a singularly dark one." (3)
4. There is comparatively as much sense in Hafiz. Indeed, it's a case of identity. (3 words, 2, 2, 6)
5. Caused the rift in the beryl coronet (3)
6. Many of Holmes's opponents had cause to (3)
7. Begins: 'Whose was it?' 'His who is gone.' 'Who shall have it?' 'He who will come.' (2 words, 3)
9. of four (4)
10. The number of Napoleons plus the number of Randall gang (4)
12. One of the five sent 'S.H. for J.O.' (3)
16. To save the dying detective trouble, Mr. Culverton Smith was kind enough to give the signal by turning this up (3)
17. The blundering constable who failed to gain his sergeant's stripes in the Lauriston Gardens Mystery (5)
19. There was a giant one of Sumatra; yet it was unwritten (3)
23. How Watson felt after the Final Problem (3)
24. He was epollicate (8)
26. Initials of the second most dangerous man in London (2)
32. Though Miss Mary Sutherland's boots were not unlike, they were really odd ones; the one having this slightly decorated, and the other plain (3)
33. You may forgive the plural form of these tobaccos, since Holmes smoked so much of them (3)
36. Behind this Black Jack of Ballaret waited and smoked an Indian cigar, of the variety which are rolled in Rotterdam (4)
38 and 39. The best I can make of these is the Latin for the sufferers of the epidemic which pleased Holmes so extremely that he said 'A long shot, Watson, a very long shot,' and pinched the Doctor's arm (4)
42. One of the two in the cardboard box (2)
44. Initials of the street in which Mycroft lodged (2)

The Annual Dinner, the BSI grand event for the year, is held on the Friday closest to the generally accepted date of the birth of Sherlock Holmes, January 6, 1854. Should that day fall too close to New Year's Day, the dinner is moved to the next week. It has long been a custom to follow the repast with readings of monographs and poetry and with the granting of awards and investitures (or memberships).

By the end of the first year, the BSI had come to inspire other individuals to form their own societies. These came to be called Scion Societies because they took as their model the BSI and were loosely affiliated with it. The first was the "Five Orange Pips of Westchester County" in New York, begun in 1935 by Richard Clarke. Later Scion Societies included "The Hounds of the Baskerville" in Chicago in 1943, "The Sons of the Copper Beeches" of Philadelphia in 1947, "The Giant Rats of Sumatra" and "The Brothers Three of Moriarty," among literally hundreds of others. New Scion Societies are added every year to the lengthy list kept by the BSI.

The society also began publishing in 1946 *The Baker Street Journal,* a quarterly publication that remains the foremost source of exacting Sherlockian scholarship in the United States. It is enthusiastically recommended for anyone with an interest in the investigating detective. (See also Appendix on Sherlock Holmes Societies.)

BUY-LAWS OF THE BAKER STREET IRREGULARS

ARTICLE I
The name of this society shall be the Baker Street Irregulars.

ARTICLE II
Its purpose shall be the study of the Sacred Writings.

ARTICLE III
All persons shall be eligible for membership who pass an examination in the Sacred Writings set by officers of the society, and who are considered otherwise suitable.

ARTICLE IV
The officers shall be a Gasogene, a Tantalus, and a Commissionaire.

The duties of the Gasogene shall be those commonly performed by a President.

The duties of the Tantalus shall be those commonly performed by a Secretary.

The duties of the Commissionaire shall be to telephone down for ice, White Rock, and whatever else may be required and available; to conduct all negotiations with waiters; and to assess the members pro rata for the cost of same.

BUY LAWS
(1) An annual meeting shall be held on January 6th, at which toasts shall be drunk which were published in the *Saturday Review* of January 27th, 1934; after which the members shall drink at will.

(2) The current round shall be bought by any member who fails to identify, by title of story and context, any quotation from the Sacred Writings submitted by any other member.

Qualification A.—If two or more members fail so to identify, a round shall be bought by each of those so failing.

Qualification B.—If the submitter of the quotation, upon challenge, fails to identify it correctly, he shall buy the round.

(3) Special meetings may be called at any time or any place by any one of three members, two of whom shall constitute a quorum.

Qualification A.—If said two are of the opposite sexes, they shall use care in selecting the place of meeting, to avoid misinterpretation (or interpretation, either, for that matter).

Qualification B.—If such two persons of opposite sexes be clients of the Personal Column of the *Saturday Review,* the foregoing does not apply; such persons being presumed to let their consciences be their guides.

(4) All other business shall be left for the monthly meeting.

(5) There shall be no monthly meeting.

Elmer Davis
"The Bowling Green," February 17, 1934

BAKER STREET IRREGULARS, THE CASE OF THE.

A 1978 novel by Robert Newman, intended for children. A young Cornish lad, Andrew Craigie, comes to London in the company of his guardian Herbert Dennison. Soon, however, Dennison disappears and Andrew is nearly abducted, finding sanctuary with some of the Baker Street Irregulars, including a young girl nicknamed Screamer. Andrew naturally comes to know Holmes, serving as his assistant while the detective is in disguise. Holmes not only finds Dennison, but finds for Andrew what he had always wanted, his mother. The novel is notable for providing insight into the life of the Irregulars.

BALDWIN, TED. One of the bosses of the Scowrers in Vermissa Valley in *The Valley of Fear*. He competed with John McMurdo (Birdy Edwards) for the attentions of Ettie Shafter before being imprisoned through Birdy's efforts for involvement in the numerous illegal activities of the Vermissa Lodge. He later travelled to England under the alias Hargrove (or Hargrave) to murder McMurdo, but was killed before carrying out his mission. Baldwin was described as "a handsome, dashing young man of about the same age and build as McMurdo himself."

BALDWIN CLUB. One of the clubs of which young Ronald Adair was a member in "The Empty House."

BALLARAT. A city in Australia, noted in Holmes's day for its rich goldfields. Watson had visited there during his time in Australia and compared the holes that had been dug in the grounds around Pondicherry Lodge in the search for the Agra Treasure to the side of a hill, near Ballarat, where prospectors had been at work (*The Sign of Four*). The name **Ballarat Gang** was given to a gang of robbers (bushrangers) in Australia who were active during the 1860s. John Turner was a member of the gang, earning the nickname "Black Jack of Ballarat" ("The Boscombe Valley Mystery").

BALMORAL, DUKE OF. A nobleman of the St. Simon family, onetime secretary for foreign affairs, inheritor of Plantagenet blood by direct descent, Tudor on the distaff side, and father of Lord Robert Walsingham de Vere St. Simon. His son consulted Holmes about the disappearance of his wife, Hatty Doran, in "The Noble Bachelor." The duke was himself mentioned in several cases. In "The Noble Bachelor," it was said to be an open secret that the duke had been forced "within the last few years," to sell his artworks. He apparently did not attend St. Simon's wedding, although his wife, the duchess, his daughter Lady Clara St. Simon, and his third son, Lord Eustace St. Simon, were on hand. His horse Iris competed in the Wessex Cup, but came in a disappointing third behind Silver Blaze and Desborough ("Silver Blaze"). He was also a card player, playing with Godfrey Milner and losing as much as 420 pounds in one night to Ronald Adair and Colonel Sebastian Moran a few weeks before Adair's brutal murder in "The Empty House."

BANKS. Financial institutions figure in a number of cases recorded in the Canon. Holmes maintained an account at the Capital and Counties Bank, Oxford Street branch ("The Priory School"). Watson kept a tin dispatch box in the vaults of Cox & Co. crammed full of papers "nearly all of which are records of cases to illustrate the curious problems which Mr. Sherlock Holmes had at various times to examine" ("Thor Bridge"). The good doctor once had a depleted bank account that delayed his holiday ("The Cardboard Box"), the cause for his financial straits said by some scholars to be related possibly to his gambling or drinking. Such personal weaknesses would explain the reference made in "The Dancing Men" to his cheque-book being locked in Holmes's desk, with the detective possessing the key. Professor Moriarty was said by Holmes to have cheques drawn on six different banks, and it was suspected that the Napoleon of Crime had as many as twenty accounts (*The Valley of Fear*).

BANNISTER. The servant to Hilton Soames of the College of St. Luke's, Bannister had served for over ten years by the time of the affair recounted in "The Three Students," and was assumed to be above reproach. Bannister, however, was once the butler to Sir Jabez Gilchrist and his loyalty to the memory of his former employer was such that he went to great lengths to assist Sir Jabez's son. According to Watson, Bannister was "a little, white-faced, clean-shaven, grizzly-haired fellow of fifty."

BARCLAY, COLONEL JAMES. Commanding officer of the Royal Mallows Regiment (or the

Royal Munsters in some editions) at Aldershot in "The Crooked Man." Barclay was found dead and his wife unconscious in the locked morning room of his villa, Lachine, during the summer of 1888 or 1889. He was considered a gallant veteran who began his career as full private, was raised to commissioned rank for bravery during the Sepoy Rebellion, or Mutiny, and eventually came to command the very regiment in which he had once carried a musket. As Holmes reported to Watson, based upon the facts given to him by Major Murphy of the regiment, "Barclay's devotion to his wife was greater than his wife's to Barclay. He was acutely uneasy if he were absent from her for a day." He was also prone to terrible depressions and disliked being left alone. His peculiarities had their origin years before in India during the mutiny. Competing with a rival soldier, Henry Wood, for the affections of Nancy Devoy, Barclay betrayed Wood to the Sepoys. Marrying Nancy, he went on to a successful career while Wood began decades of misery.

BARCLAY, NANCY. The wife of Colonel James Barclay in "The Crooked Man" was very popular with the ladies of the Royal Mallows Regiment at Aldershot and was said to have been a woman of great beauty in her youth, and "even now, when she has been married for upward of thirty years, she is still of a striking and queenly appearance." When a young girl in India, Nancy Devoy, the daughter of a regimental colour-sergeant, was the object of attentions from both James Barclay and Henry Wood. Barclay won her hand through terrible means, and her meeting with Wood some thirty years later set off the events recorded in "The Crooked Man."

BARDLE. An inspector in the Sussex constabulary who investigated the strange death of Fitzroy McPherson in "The Lion's Mane." Said by Holmes to be "a steady, solid, bovine man with thoughtful eyes," Bardle displayed good sense in acknowledging the detective's "immense experience," consulting him on the case, particularly concerning the arrest of Ian Murdoch for the "crime."

BARITSU. Also *bartitsu*, a type of martial art that Holmes described as a "Japanese system of wrestling, which has more than once been very useful to me." It was of particular assistance on May 4, 1891, during his vicious hand-to-hand struggle with Professor Moriarty on the edge of the Reichenbach Falls in "The Final Problem." Using *baritsu*, the detective "slipped through his grip, and he with a horrible scream kicked madly for a few seconds, and clawed the air with both his hands. But for all his efforts he could not get his balance, and over he went." It is interesting to speculate on the reaction of Mrs. Hudson, or even Dr. Watson, on walking in on Holmes while he was practicing his *baritsu* to maintain his proficiency, although Mrs. Hudson would have found *baritsu* exercises preferable to the target practice the detective undertook in his rooms ("The Musgrave Ritual"). It is also intriguing to ponder where Holmes first learned and later mastered the art.

BARKER. A private detective with a practice in London, Barker was said by Holmes to be his "hated rival upon the Surrey shore." Barker was seen in the street in front of Amberley's house during the investigation of "The Retired Colourman." Watson said that "he was a tall, dark, heavily-moustached, rather military-looking man." He had been hired by the family of Dr. Ray Ernest after Ernest's disappearance with Amberley's wife.

BARKER, CECIL. A close friend and long-time business partner of John Douglas with whom he mined for gold in California (*The Valley of Fear*). A resident of Hales Lodge, Hampstead, he was suspected for a time of murdering Douglas, whose body was discovered at Birlstone Manor.

BARNICOT, DR. A respected London practitioner and owner of two plaster busts of Napoleon in "The Six Napoleons." One statue remained in the principal consulting room of his residence at Kensington Road, the second at his surgery and dispensary at Lower Brixton Road. Both were stolen and smashed by an apparently deranged culprit.

BAR OF GOLD, THE. A riverside opium den situated in Upper Swandam Lane in "The Man With the Twisted Lip." Watson wrote that it was "between a slop-shop and a gin-shop, approached by a steep flight of steps leading down to a black gap like the mouth of a cave." The doctor went there to find the opium addict Isa Whitney, a friend, but he also discovered Sherlock Holmes there. The detective, in disguise as a wretched addict, had taken up post in the hopes of learning the whereabouts of the missing Neville St. Clair who had disappeared from the Bar of Gold. Holmes mentioned that he used the den previously for his own purposes, "And the rascally lascar who runs it has sworn to have vengeance upon me. There is a trap-door at the back of that building, near the corner of Paul's Wharf, which could tell some strange tales of what has passed through it upon the moonless night."

BARRETT. This London police constable was passing along Godolphin Street when he noticed that the door to No. 16 was ajar in "The Second Stain." Knocking but receiving no answer, he entered to find the body of Eduardo Lucas "stabbed to the heart" with an Indian dagger.

BARRYMORE, ELIZA. A servant at Baskerville Hall, Eliza was the wife of the butler John Barrymore in *The Hound of the Baskervilles*. The escaped convict Selden was her brother. Watson wrote of her: "She was a large, impassive, heavy-featured woman with a stern set expression of mouth. But her telltale eyes were red and glanced at me from between swollen lids. It was she, then, who wept in the night . . ."

BARRYMORE, JOHN. The butler of Baskerville Hall in *The Hound of the Baskervilles* whose family had served at the hall for several generations. Upon the arrival of Sir Henry Baskerville as master of the hall, Barrymore announced that he and his wife Eliza would be leaving the family's service. Sir Charles Baskerville's generosity gave them the opportunity to establish themselves in business. While still at the hall, Barrymore engaged in very peculiar behavior, particularly signalling to the moor with a light in the dead of night. Barrymore "was a remarkable-looking man, tall, handsome, with a square black beard and pale, distinguished features."

BARTON. An inspector from Scotland Yard who took charge of the investigation into the disappearance of Neville St. Clair in "The Man With the Twisted Lip." He made a careful search of the premises in which the beggar Hugh Boone was found, but he could find nothing related to Neville St. Clair, although he subsequently arrested Boone. By the time Holmes arrived at Bow Street to interview the beggar, Inspector Bradstreet was on duty.

BARTON, DR. HILL. An alias used by Watson to gain entry to the residence of Baron Gruner while Holmes was searching the baron's study in "The Illustrious Client." Watson pretended to be an expert in Chinese wares who was willing to sell to Gruner a unique set of Ming china. Sensing that Dr. Barton may have been an emissary of Holmes, the baron trapped the disguised Watson by asking him questions to test his knowledge. Barton supposedly resided in Half Moon Street.

BASIL, CAPTAIN. Holmes used this alias during his investigation into the murder of Peter Carey in "Black Peter." Watson realized that the detective was using one of his many disguises and names when "several rough-looking men called . . . and inquired for Captain Basil." Holmes had drawn them to Baker Street under the pretext of looking for harpooners to serve under a Captain Basil in an arctic expedition. One of the men who appeared was a murderer.

BASKERVILLE FAMILY. The Baskerville family in Devonshire on Dartmoor that resided at Baskerville Hall was apparently cursed in *The Hound of the Baskervilles*. Hugo Baskerville, living around the time of the Great Rebellion (c. 1647), was the foundation for the legend of the curse as he was supposedly killed in an attack by an agent of the devil in the shape of an enormous hound. His descendant, another Hugo Baskerville, wrote down the legend of the Hound as a warning and lesson to his two sons, Rodger and John, in 1742. It was his wish that nothing be told of the matter to their sister Elizabeth. Other members of the line were Rear Admiral Baskerville (c.1782), who served under Rodney in the West Indies; Sir William Baskerville, who had served under William Pitt as chairman of committees of the House of Commons; and Rodger Baskerville, who was considered the black sheep of the family—he went to Central or South America and had a son there, Rodger, before dying of yellow fever in 1876.

Sir Charles Baskerville was successful in restoring the fortunes of the Baskervilles by making his vast wealth through South African speculation. Returning to England, he occupied the family estate in Devonshire; his habitation of the hall, however, was brief for he died under mysterious circumstances a short time later. While his death was officially attributed to heart failure, the seemingly supernatural events surrounding it, and the imminent arrival of

Sir Henry Baskerville as his heir, prompted Dr. Mortimer to consult Holmes.

Sir Henry Baskerville inherited not only the large Baskerville estate and fortune, but the dread curse of the Hound of the Baskervilles as well. Young Sir Henry was a Canadian farmer who came into the Baskerville title suddenly and unexpectedly. Arriving in England he was immediately involved in peculiar and mysterious events, having two different boots stolen, being followed by a bearded man, and receiving a threatening letter. Fortunately for him a friend of his late uncle Charles had consulted Holmes before his arrival and the detective was thereafter involved in the unraveling of the mystery surrounding the terrible hound. Sir Henry "was a small, alert, dark-eyed man about thirty years of age, very sturdily built, with thick black eyebrows and a strong, pugnacious face." (See THE HOUND OF THE BASKERVILLES.)

BASKERVILLE HALL. The ancestral home of the Baskervilles, situated in Dartmoor near the hamlet of Grimpen and the terrible Grimpen Mire in *The Hound of the Baskervilles*. Many of the events described in the account took place at the hall. Upon seeing it, Sir Henry Baskerville commented, "My word, it isn't a very cheerful place." Watson described the hall in great detail: "The whole front was draped in ivy, with a patch clipped bare here and there where a window or a coat-of-arms broke through the dark veil. From this central block rose the twin towers, ancient, crenellated, and pierced with many loopholes. To right and left of the turrets were more modern wings of black granite."

BATES, MARLOW. The manager of J. Neil Gibson's estate in Hampshire in "Thor Bridge." "He was a thin, nervous wisp of a man with frightened eyes and a twitching, hesitating manner." Bates arrived at Baker Street shortly before his employer to warn Holmes that Gibson was "a villain . . . A hard man, Mr. Holmes, hard to all about him . . . But his wife was his chief victim. He was brutal to her—yes, sir brutal!" Gibson's wife had been found shot to death on Thor Bridge.

BAXTER, EDITH. A maid to John Straker at King's Pyland Stables, in Dartmoor in "Silver Blaze," Edith brought a supper of curried mutton to the stable boy Ned Hunter. The food was laced with opium, rendering the lad unconscious and allowing the removal of the horse Silver Blaze from the stable. Edith was completely ignorant of the presence of the opium.

BAYARD. A horse owned by Colonel Ross that was supposed to run in the Wessex Cup with Silver Blaze in "Silver Blaze." Following the disappearance of Silver Blaze, Colonel Ross scratched Bayard from the race.

BAYNES, INSPECTOR. A member of the Surrey costabulary and one of the most competent policemen whom Holmes would meet, encountering him in "Wisteria Lodge." Baynes "was a stout, puffy, red man, whose face was only redeemed from grossness by two extraordinary bright eyes, almost hidden behind the heavy creases of cheek and brow." Baynes conducted his own investigation into the brutal death of Aloysius Garcia of Wisteria Lodge and the "grotesque" experience of John Scott Eccles, largely free of the advice and wisdom of Holmes. The detective was ultimately quite impressed with Baynes, as the inspector proved as successful as Holmes himself. Holmes complimented him, "You will rise high in your profession. You have instinct and intuition."

BEAUCHAMP ARRIANCE. A small wood situated near Poldhu Bay in Cornwall in "The Devil's Foot." Dr. Leon Sterndale lived in Beauchamp Arriance during his stays in England between his expeditions to Africa.

BECHER, DR. The owner of a house at Eyford to which Victor Hatherley travelled to repair a hydraulic press in "The Engineer's Thumb." His accomplice was Colonel Lysander Stark, and he himself was introduced to Hatherley as "Ferguson." Becher was said to be "an Englishman, and there isn't a man in the parish who has a better lined waistcoat."

BEDDINGTON BROTHERS. The two clever thieves attempted the ingenious robbery of Mawson & Williams', a famous London stockbroking firm, of 10,000 pounds in bonds in "The Stockbroker's Clerk." One brother, posing as both Arthur and Harry Pinner, of the Franco-Midland Hardware Company, Ltd., kept the clerk Hall Pycroft occupied in Birmingham while the other brother impersonated Pycroft at Mawson & Williams'. The impersonator failed in the robbery, killed the watchman, and was captured. The other brother, learning of the failure, tried to commit suicide. It was revealed that one of the Beddingtons was a famous forger and cracksman who, with his brother, had just completed a five-year term in prison.

BEECHER, HENRY WARD. Watson owned an unframed picture of Beecher (1813–1887), the American preacher during the era of the Civil War, which stood upon the top of the doctor's books at 221B Baker Street ("The Cardboard Box"). In the pastiche novel *The Private Life of Dr. Watson*, Michael Hardwicke wrote that Watson had met Beecher while a young man in America.

BEE CULTURE, PRACTICAL HANDBOOK OF. In full, *Practical Handbook of Bee Culture, with Some Observations upon the Segregation of the Queen*, a monograph written by Holmes sometime before 1914, the product of his extensive researches into the honeybee during his retirement on the Sussex Downs ("The Second Stain"). Holmes told Watson: "Alone I did it. Behold the fruit of pensive nights and laborious days, when I watched the little working gangs as once I watched the criminal world of London." Considered by the detective to be the *magnum opus* of his latter years, the fruit of his leisured ease, the book was small and blue, with golden letters printed on the cover. It is now virtually unobtainable despite the best efforts of Sherlockians throughout the world to locate a copy. One person who definitely held the book was the German spymaster Von Bork ("His Last Bow"). Around November of 1887, Holmes had used beeswax to form a crust on his lips to increase the appearance that he was about to expire in "The Dying Detective," and it has been theorized that Holmes may have used his vast knowledge to extend his life through a concoction made of royal jelly. It was this expertise that allowed Holmes to live until 1957, according to the Sherlockian W. S. Baring-Gould. David Dvorkin theorized a similar practice in his 1983 novel *Time for Sherlock Holmes*.

BEESWING. A filmy crust that forms in some wines, such as port, that is an indicator of age. In "The Abbey Grange," Holmes discovered beeswing in a glass of wine while investigating the death of Sir Eustace Brackenstall. The observation was pivotal to the solution of the case.

BELLADONNA. A type of poisonous plant found in England. Holmes was said by Watson to have a "variable" knowledge of botany, but was "well up in belladonna, opium, and poisons generally" (*A Study in Scarlet*). In a demonstration of the detective's experience with the poison, in "The Dying Detective," Holmes put belladonna in his eyes to dilate the pupils and create a glistening appearance to make himself appear severely ill.

BELLAMY FAMILY. A family that lived in Fulworth, Sussex in "The Lion's Mane." **Tom** Bellamy, father of **William** and **Maud**, was a one-time fisherman who came to own "all the boats and bathing-cots at Fulworth." William became a business partner of his father. Holmes found him to be "a powerful young man, with a heavy, sullen face." His sister Maud was the fiancée of the murdered Fitzroy McPherson. Holmes was impressed by her "composed concentration" upon hearing the details of McPherson's terrible death, adding that it showed "she possessed strong character as well as great beauty." Her appearance was such that even Holmes was moved to declare "that no young man would cross her path unscathed."

BELL, DR. JOSEPH. This gifted medical practitioner served as one of the leading models for Sherlock Holmes. Arthur Conan Doyle had known Bell during Doyle's years at Edinburgh University. Bell had been a lecturer and surgeon who also possessed an amazingly acute power of deductive reasoning. Doyle wrote that Bell would sit in the waiting room, his "face like a Red Indian," diagnosing his visitors as they came in: "You are a soldier, and a non-commissioned officer at that. You have served in Bermuda. Now how do I know that, gentlemen? Because he came into the room without even taking his hat off, as he would go into an orderly room. He was a soldier. A slight authoritative air, combined with his age, shows that he was a non-commissioned officer. A rash on his forehead tells me he was in Bermuda and subject to a certain rash known only there." Bell's abilities were so amazing to his students that Conan Doyle looked no further for possible models for a great detective. Years later, in 1882, Conan Doyle dedicated *The Adventures of Sherlock Holmes*, the first collection of Holmes cases in book form, to "My old teacher, Joseph Bell, M.D." Bell, in turn, reviewed the collection for the magazine *Bookman*.

BELLINGER, LORD. The two-time premier of England engaged Holmes's services in recovering the important letter that had been stolen from the dispatch box of the Rt. Hon. Trelawney Hope in "The Second Stain." Bellinger at first refused to provide the detective with any information concerning the contents of the letter, but his brusque dismissal by Holmes coupled with the desperation of his situation compelled the premier to be completely honest. He was described by Watson as being "austere, high-nosed, eagle-eyed, and dominant." At one point, "The Premier sprang to his feet with that quick, fierce gleam of his deep-set eyes before which a Cabinet has cowered." Holmes was not intimidated.

BENDER. A member of the ill-fated Ferrier wagon train in *A Study in Scarlet*, Bender was the first member of the party to die on the Great Alkali Plain after they became lost. Of the expedition, only John and Lucy Ferrier came out alive.

BENNETT, TREVOR ("JACK"). The professional assistant to Professor Presbury and fiancé of the professor's daughter Edith appears in "The Creeping Man." "He was a tall, handsome youth about thirty, well dressed and elegant, but with something in his bearing which suggested the shyness of the student rather than the self-possession of the man of the world." Bennett went to Holmes in the hopes that the detective might be able to discover the cause of Professor Presbury's very strange behavior.

BENTINCK STREET. A street in the West End, between Marylebone Lane and Welbeck Street, where Holmes was nearly run down by a van at the corner of Bentinck and Welbeck in "The Final Problem." The attack was the first made upon his life by the agents of Professor Moriarty.

BEPPO. An Italian sculptor who became involved with the Black Pearl of the Borgias in "The Six Napoleons." Beppo was "a well known ne'er-do-well among the Italian colony. He had once been a skillful sculptor and had earned an honest living, but he had taken to evil courses, and had twice already been in gaol." He had worked in the Gelder & Co. sculptor works and later at Morse Hudson's shop. In the former he hid the pearl and used the latter to aid his efforts at recovering it. During his relentless campaign to acquire and destroy the Devine busts of Napoleon, he encountered the Mafia assassin Pietro Venucci, killing him

on the doorstep of Horace Harker. Holmes's success in tracking and capturing Beppo at Chiswick impressed Inspector Lestrade greatly.

BERKSHIRE. Victor Hatherley was hired by Colonel Lysander Stark to repair a hydraulic press in Eyford, Berkshire, a county to the west of London, in "The Engineer's Thumb." Berkshire was also the setting of Shoscombe Old Place ("Shoscombe Old Place"), Abbas Parva ("The Veiled Lodger"), and Crane Water ("The Speckled Band"). The Roylotts of Stoke Moran, once one of the richest families in England, owned an estate on the western border of Surrey that "extended over the border into Berkshire in the north, and Hampshire in the west."

BERKSHIRES. Also the Royal Berkshire Regiment, or, more properly, the Princess Charlotte of Wales's Royal Berkshire Regiment, this British infantry regiment comprised the onetime forty-ninth and sixty-sixth Foot. Dr. Watson, originally attached to the Fifth Northumberland Fusiliers as an assistant surgeon in India, was later removed and attached to the Berkshires. He served with the regiment at the Battle of Maiwand (1881), where the Berkshires suffered horrendous losses, and Watson was severely wounded (*A Study in Scarlet*).

BERNSTONE, MRS. The housekeeper to Bartholomew Sholto at Pondicherry Lodge, Upper Norwood in *The Sign of Four*, Mrs. Bernstone was arrested by Inspector Athelney Jones along with Thaddeus Sholto, the Indian butler Lal Rao, a porter, and the gatekeeper McMurdo for the possible murder of her employer.

BERTILLON, ALPHONSE. This French criminologist (1853–1914) developed the Bertillon system, called the Bertillonage, for the swift identification of criminals. The system used various measurements of the body with extensive files of descriptions and photos. While superceded from around 1900 by fingerprinting, Bertillon won Holmes's admiration ("The Naval Treaty") and his jealousy (*The Hound of the Baskervilles*), due to the French savant's wide reputation.

"BERYL CORONET, THE ADVENTURE OF THE" (BERY). Published: *Strand*, May 1892; collected in *The Adventures of Sherlock Holmes*

(1892). Case Date: December 1881 to 1890. Major players: Holmes, Watson, Alexander Holder, Arthur Holder, Sir George Burnwell, Mary Holder, Lucy Parr. Alexander Holder, of the banking firm Holder & Stevenson, enlists the aid of the detective in recovering the Beryl Coronet. The priceless jewelry, given to Holder as collateral for a short-term loan of 50,000 pounds to a person whose name is "a household word all over the earth," was stolen from Holder's home. His son Alexander was found apparently tearing apart the coronet for his own obviously nefarious plans. The jewelry was recovered, but three of the jewels were missing. Holmes's investigation completely exonerated the son and the detective made a declaration to Alexander Holder that has been the source of much speculation by Sherlockians: "You owe a very humble apology to that noble lad, your son, who has carried himself in this matter as I should be proud to see my own son do, should I ever chance to have one."

Holmes draws a gun on Sir Alec Cunningham in "The Beryl Coronet"; by Sidney Paget.

BIBLE. Holmes confessed to Watson that his biblical knowledge was "a trifle rusty," but he was nevertheless able to point the doctor to the story "in the first or second of Samuel" that was germane to the case the detective had just solved in "The Crooked Man." In attempting to decipher the message sent to him by his informant in the lair of Professor Moriarty in *The Valley of Fear*, Holmes thought the code might refer to the Bible, though he could "not name any book less likely to be at the elbow of one of Moriarty's associates."

BILLIARDS. Watson was fond of the game and played billiards with his friend Thurston at a club shortly before the commencement of Holmes's investigation into the Dancing Men. The detective deduced that Watson played billiards as he had chalk between his left finger and thumb when he returned from the club the previous night; Watson routinely placed chalk there to steady the cue, and he never played billiards except with Thurston.

BILLY. A youth named Billy serves as a page at Baker Street in the 1880s in *The Valley of Fear*. Another page at Baker Street, also named Billy, appears around the turn of the century. More is known about this young man because of his direct involvement in "The Mazarin Stone." The youth was a "very wise and tactful page, who had helped a little to fill up the gaps of loneliness and isolation which surrounded the saturnine figure of the great detective," and during the case Holmes pondered "That boy is a problem, Watson. How far am I justified in allowing him to be in danger?" At the start of "Thor Bridge," Billy announced Marlow Bates and probably did the same for J. Neil Gibson. The date of his employment probably began after 1894, as he declared that certain events, recounted in "The Empty House," dated to 1894, were before his time. See also BRECKINRIDGE.

BINOMIAL THEOREM. This theorem, first devised by Sir Isaac Newton, asserts that for any real numbers a and b, and for any positive integer n, $(a+b)$ to the nth power can be expanded into terms involving the power of a and b. At the age of twenty-one, Professor Moriarty authored a treatise upon the Binomial Theorem, which had a European vogue, and on the basis of it he won a mathematical chair at one of England's small universities ("The Final Problem"). The question remains as to what Moriarty may have contributed to the subject. As Poul Anderson presents in his "A Treatise on the Binomial Theorem" (1955) for the *Baker Street Journal*, the theorem states:

$$(a + b)^n = a^n + na^{n-1}b + \frac{n(n-1)}{1.2} a^{n-2b^2} + \ldots$$

$$+ \ldots \frac{n(n-1)\ldots(n-r+1)}{r!} a^{n-r}b^r \ldots + \ldots b^n$$

Anderson argues that it must have been original and obviously important enough to be known throughout Europe. He proposes "that Moriarty was working on the basic idea of number itself, and that he developed a general binomial theorem applicable to other algebras than the one we know. If he could do this at the three-cornered age of 21, it is obvious that in his case, as in the Master's, genius flowered early."

BIRDS.   Birds figure directly in several cases. Canaries played an important role in the unchronicled business involving Wilson, "the notorious canary trainer," whose arrest removed "a plague spot" from London's East End ("Black Peter"). (This case was presented as "The Adventure of the Deptford Horror" in the collection *The Exploits of Sherlock Holmes* by Adrian Conan Doyle.) Another unchronicled case in Watson's notes was that of "the politician, the lighthouse and the trained cormorant" ("The Veiled Lodger"). Holmes and Watson walked through Surrey "rejoicing in the music of the birds" ("The Solitary Cyclist"), and Holmes suggested giving a few hours "to the birds and the flowers" ("Black Peter"). During his disguised encounter with Watson in "The Empty House," the detective was peddling a book, *British Birds*, among others. Mrs. Watson was said by her husband to attract folk in grief "like birds to a lighthouse" ("The Man With the Twisted Lip").

BIRLSTONE MANOR HOUSE.   The residence of John Douglas was situated one-half mile from Birlstone village in *The Valley of Fear*. "The Manor House, with its many gables and its small, diamond-paned windows, was still much as the builder had left it in the early seventeenth century." The manor was fashioned after Groombridge Place, between Sussex and Kent, near the village of Groomsbridge. Its true identification was made by Sir Arthur Conan Doyle himself, who stayed there several times.

BIRMINGHAM.   Holmes and Watson journeyed to this large Midlands city to investigate Hall Pycroft's odd story in "The Stockbroker's Clerk." Howard Garrideb supposedly had offices in Birmingham in the suburb of Aston ("The Three Garridebs"); Steve Dixie, a prizefighter hired by the voluptuary Isadora Klein, claimed that he was in training in Birmingham at the time of young Perkins's death ("The Three Gables"); and the daughter of Trevor Senior died in Birmingham of diptheria ("The 'Gloria Scott' ").

BISHOPGATE JEWEL CASE.   This unchronicled investigation is described by Holmes as "a piece of very simple reasoning" in *The Sign of Four*. The detective apparently had instructed the police on the details of the affair. One officer, Athelney Jones, told Holmes: "I'll never forget how you lectured us all on causes and inferences and effects in the Bishopgate jewel case. It's true you set us on the right track; but you'll own now that it was more by good luck than good guidance."

"BLACK BARONET, THE ADVENTURE OF THE."

A pastiche written by Adrian Conan Doyle and John Dickson Carr and first published in *Collier's* magazine (131, No. 21) on May 23, 1953, with illustrations by Robert Fawcett. The story was later collected in *The Exploits of Sherlock Holmes* (1954). The case involves Holmes's investigation into the gruesome stabbing death of Colonel Jocelyn Dalcy at Lavington Court in Kent, while staying as the guest of Sir Reginald Lavington. An excellent rendering of the Watsonian style, the case is notable for offering an account of the unfortunate Madame Montpensier mentioned in *The Hound of the Baskervilles* and for having been produced on American television on May 26, 1953, starring Basil Rathbone as Holmes and Martyn Green as Watson.

BLACK FORMOSA CORRUPTION.   A dreadful-sounding disease described in "The Dying Detective," of which Watson confessed he had never heard.

BLACKHEATH.   This residential district of Lewisham just below Greenwich and north of Lee, near the famous Blackheath Common, figures in several cases. Watson ("The Sussex Vampire") and Godfrey Staunton ("The Missing Three-Quarter") both played for the Blackheath Football Club. The "unhappy" John Hector McFarlane lived with his parents at Torrington Lodge, Blackheath ("The Norwood Builder").

BLACKMAIL.   Holmes considered this crime to be particularly odious. The detective was thus very animated when telling Watson of the "King of Blackmailers," Charles Augustus Milverton. Holmes also declared Moriarty to be at the head of a criminal chain that ended with the pickpocket and the blackmailer (*The Valley of Fear*). Blackmail or extortion is attempted in several of Holmes's cases.

"BLACK PETER, THE ADVENTURE OF" (BLAC).   Published: *Collier's*, February 1904, *Strand*, March 1904; collected in *The Return of Sherlock Holmes* (1905). Case date: July, 1895. Major players: Holmes, Watson, Inspector Hopkins, John Hopley Neligan, Captain Peter Carey, Patrick Cairns. This case took place in 1895 when, Watson writes, "I have never known my friend to be in better form, both mental and physical." That year brought to the detective such investigations as the death of Cardinal Tosca, the arrest of Wilson, "the notorious canary trainer," and "the very obscure circumstances which surrounded the death of Captain Peter Carey," known as Black Peter, who was found impaled on a wall by a harpoon in a cabin in the garden of his retirement home in Woodman's Lee. Inspector Hopkins arrests the young, skinny John Neligan for the crime, but Holmes has serious doubts. The solution to the crime is made by Holmes with the help of a "Captain Basil," organizer of an arctic expedition. Inspector Hopkins plays an interesting role in the affair, demonstrating that while he has studied Holmes's methods, his application of them has not been mastered.

"BLANCHED SOLDIER, THE ADVENTURE OF THE" (BLAN).   Published: *Liberty*, October 1926, *Strand*, November 1926; collected in *The Case Book of Sherlock Holmes* (1927). Case date: January, 1903. Major players: Holmes, James Dodd, Godfrey Emsworth, Colonel Emsworth. This is one of two chronicles written by Holmes himself, the result of his constant criticism of Watson's accounts of his cases. " 'Try it yourself, Holmes!' he has retorted, and I am compelled to admit that, having taken my pen in my hand, I do

begin to realize that the matter must be presented in such a way as may interest the reader." While the Holmesian composition does not rival the good doctor's (and the detective leaves the audience as much in the dark as is his custom with Watson), the story does provide some insight into Holmes's methods. James Dodd, the "Blanched Soldier," engages Holmes's services to find the whereabouts of a friend and comrade, Godfrey Emsworth, with whom Dodd had served in the Boer War.

BLESSINGTON.   According to Holmes, Blessington, whose real name was Sutton, was the worst of the Worthingdon Bank Gang in "The Resident Patient." Having turned on his criminal partners and thus avoided punishment for the robbery and murder of a bank caretaker, Sutton changes his name and spends the rest of his life in mortal terror for his life from his betrayed fellows. As Blessington, he established Dr. Percy Trevelyan in his Brook Street practice, receiving for payment rooms in the residence, the physician's medical attentions, and three-quarters of the practice's earnings. His shield, however, could not save him, and the vengeance of the gang inevitably caught up with him.

BLOODSTAINS.   This evidence of a crime was often vitally important to its solution. The crucial nature of bloodstains to the detection of crime was important to Holmes early on in his career, hence his jubilation at discovering a reagent that was precipitated by hemoglobin and by nothing else, a test for blood that was thus infallible and much superior to the test used at the time, the old Guaiacum Test. In *A Study in Scarlet*, blood is spattered on the floor near the body of Enoch Drebber (although not his as he was unmarked) and on the wall was written in blood the word RACHE. The blood at Deep Dene House seems to prove conclusively the guilt of John Hector McFarlane in "The Norwood Builder." The most intriguing bloodstains are on the carpet where the stabbed body of Eduardo Lucas is found in "The Second Stain." Strangely, the stain on the carpet did not correspond to the impression left on the floor beneath.

BLOUNT.   A student at Harold Stackhurst's coaching establishment, the Gables, in "The Lion's Mane." It is Blount who discovers the carcass of the Airedale belonging to Fitzroy McPherson. The terrier has died "on the very edge of the pool where its master's body had also been found."

"BLUE CARBUNCLE, THE ADVENTURE OF THE" (BLUE).

Published: *Strand*, January 1892; collected in *The Adventures of Sherlock Holmes* (1892). Case date: December 1887, 1889, or 1890. Major players: Holmes, Watson, James Ryder, Henry Baker, Peterson, Mrs. Oakshott, Mr. Windigate, John Horner. The plot of this tale centers on the pursuit of a Christmas goose in the crop of which is hidden the Blue Carbuncle, a gem stolen from the countess of Morcar's hotel room at the Hotel Cosmopolitan. The reward for its return is 1,000 pounds which, according to Holmes, is not a twentieth of its market value, adding that there were "sentimental considerations in the background which would induce the Countess to part with half her fortune if she could but recover the gem." The stone had a violent history, including two murders, a vitriol throwing, a suicide, and several robberies. Holmes is first introduced to the case by Peterson after the commissionaire had found the goose and a hat in the street—the owner had dropped them both in a scuffle in the Tottenham Court Road. Holmes performs a brilliant bit of deduction on the hat, his analysis of the owner proven totally correct when the owner, Henry Baker, is located. The detective's investigation leads him to the Alpha Inn and then to the windswept, chilly Covent Garden and the stall of the fowl dealer Mr. Breckinridge. In the end, the detective proves generous indeed in allowing the culprit to escape, declaring to Watson, "I am not retained by the police to supply their deficiencies." "The Blue Carbuncle" was ranked third on the list of favorite stories of the readers of the *Baker Street Journal* in 1959.

BOB.

The brother of Lucy Ferrier in *A Study in Scarlet*. He died in 1847 when the Ferrier wagon party became lost on the Great Alkali Plain.

BOER WAR.

See EMSWORTH, GEOFFREY and "BLANCHED SOLDIER, THE"; see also under the profile of Sir Arthur Conan Doyle in the Appendices.

BOGUS LAUNDRY AFFAIR.

An unchronicled case solved by Holmes and Inspector Lestrade ("The Cardboard Box"). Help was provided to them by a man named Aldridge who was big, clean-shaven, swarthy, and powerful.

Holmes captures the real thief of "The Blue Carbuncle"; by Sidney Paget.

BOHEMIA.

The most notable case involving Bohemia, a region of northwestern Austria and a onetime principality, is the Irene Adler affair, recorded as "A Scandal in Bohemia," in which Holmes is engaged by the king of Bohemia to recover a compromising photograph. The note the detective receives anonymously from the monarch bears the watermark of the *Egria Papier Gesellschaft*. Egria was a town near Carlsbad in Bohemia. Dorak, the London agent for the infamous Lowenstein, was a Bohemian ("The Creeping Man").

BOHEMIA, KING OF.

In full, Wilhelm Gottsreich Sigismond von Ormstein (born 1858) grand duke of Cassel-Felstein, and hereditary king of Bohemia, one of several monarchs to enlist the services of the detective. In this case, chronicled as "A Scandal in Bohemia," the king is anxious that Holmes recover from Irene Adler certain compromising letters and a photograph. The adventuress Adler had threatened to send the photographs to the family of the king's bride-to-be, Clotilde Lothman von Saxe-Meningen, second daughter of the king of Scandinavia. Even though Holmes fails in recovering the photograph, the king was satisfied with the turn of events, giving the detective a valuable snuff-box as a token of gratitude, and also allowing him to keep a photograph of Adler that she had left for the king.

BOHEMIAN. This term, used to describe someone who leads an unconventional life and who has little regard for the constraints and demands of society, may very well apply to Holmes. While Watson claimed that he possessed a natural bohemianism of disposition ("The Musgrave Ritual"), he was perfectly normal compared to the socially eccentric and maladjusted Holmes. The detective was a true bohemian who "loathed every form of society with his whole Bohemian soul" ("A Scandal in Bohemia"). He could, certainly, be an entertaining and energetic dinner companion as Athelney Jones discovers during the case of Jonathan Small (*The Sign of Four*). Holmes that evening served oysters (a favorite) and a brace of grouse, with an excellent white wine, and spoke about miracle plays, medieval pottery, Stradivarius violins, the Buddhism of Ceylon, and the warships of the future. His skills as an actor would allow him to be charming, but beneath the air of congeniality lurks the bohemian who describes social invitations as "those unwelcome summonses which call upon a man either to be bored or to lie." ("The Noble Bachelor.")

"BOOK OF LIFE, THE". This article was written by Holmes sometime around March 1881 for an English magazine, but published anonymously. Reading the piece on the morning of March 4, 1881 during breakfast, Watson described the title as "somewhat ambitious." Unaware of the authorship, he declared it to be "ineffable twaddle," adding that he had "never read such rubbish in my life," and that it was "evidently the theory of some armchair lounger who evolves all these neat little paradoxes in the seclusion of his own study." The occasion of the remark allowed Holmes to claim authorship of the article and to explain to Watson much of what the consulting detective did for a living. "The Book of Life" was an explanation of the science of deduction and analysis, presenting the idea that through it, one could "infer the existence of the Atlantic through a single drop of water."

BOONE, HUGH. A crippled professional beggar arrested for the murder of Neville St. Clair in

"The Man With the Twisted Lip." He resided part of the time in the upper room of the Bar of Gold, a dangerous opium den where St. Clair was last seen. He spent his days in a small angle in the wall on the left-hand side, some little distance down Threadneedle Street. There, sitting cross-legged, the pitiful creature made money by selling wax vestas (a kind of match), drawing attention to himself by his appearance and his remarkable wit, for he was "ever ready with a reply to any piece of chaff which may be thrown at him by the passers-by."

BOOTS. Patent leather boots were worn by Sir Henry Baskerville in *The Hound of the Baskervilles*. Upon arriving in England, he purchased a pair of brown boots, among many other items, paying six dollars for them. One of the boots was stolen before he had a chance to wear them. The missing boot suddenly reappeared, but an older, much more worn one disappeared. The thefts were of interest to Holmes. Enoch Drebber in *A Study in Scarlet* and Lord Robert St. Simon in "The Noble Bachelor" wore patent leather boots. Watson owned a pair of patent leather slippers ("The Stockbroker's Clerk").

"BOSCOMBE VALLEY MYSTERY, THE" (BOSC). Published: *Strand*, October 1891; collected in *The Adventures of Sherlock Holmes* (1892). Case date: June 1889. Major players: Holmes, Watson, Inspector Lestrade, James McCarthy, Charles McCarthy, Alice Turner, John Turner. Another of Holmes's investigations in which the detective allows a murderer to avoid the gallows, in this case he grants only a brief reprieve as death soon comes to the guilty party anyway. Charles McCarthy is found murdered in a wood next to Boscombe Pool, near his home on one of the farms owned by John Turner in Boscombe Valley, a country district near Ross, in Herefordshire. Turner also owned the vast Boscombe Valley Estate, residing at Boscombe Hall.

McCarthy's son, James, is arrested as the obvious suspect in his father's murder—he has quarrelled with his father moments before the elder McCarthy's death, and was very reluctant to discuss the details of his disagreement. Inspector Lestrade, who has been retained by young McCarthy's supporters, summons Holmes. The detective quickly decides the man's innocence. After an analysis of the area of the crime, Holmes is able to describe the mur-

Holmes at his best in "The Boscombe Valley Mystery"; by Sidney Paget.

derer as "a tall man, left-handed, limps with the right leg, wears thick-soled shooting-boots and a grey cloak, smokes Indian cigars, uses a cigarette holder, and carries a blunt penknife in his pocket." In an interestingly philosophical reflection at the end of the case, Holmes tells Watson: "God help us! Why does fate play such tricks with poor helpless worms? I never hear of such a case as this that I do not think of Baxter's words, and say, 'There, but for the grace of God, goes Sherlock Holmes.' "

BOSWELL, JAMES.   Scottish lawyer and author (1740–1795) and the close friend and biographer of Dr. Samuel Johnson. His *Life of Samuel Johnson* is often considered the greatest biography in the English language. Holmes remarked to Watson at the outset of his investigation into the Irene Adler affair ("A Scandal in Bohemia"), "I am lost without my Boswell."

BOTANY.   Holmes's knowledge in this field of study was rated by Watson as "variable. Well up in belladonna, opium, and poisons generally. Knows nothing of practical gardening" (*A Study in Scarlet*). During his investigation into the strange events at Wisteria Lodge, Holmes observed Aloysius Garcia's neighbors while appearing to study elementary books on botany ("Wisteria Lodge").

BOW STREET.   A street in Westminster where London's main police court was situated. Holmes and Watson solved the affair of "The Man With the Twisted Lip" there during an examination of the crippled beggar Hugh Boone.

BOW WINDOW.   It is now generally accepted that there was a bow window, a type of window that projects from a wall, or windows at 221B Baker Street, as was examined by the esteemed members of the Baker Street Irregulars Julian Wolff in his article "I Have My Eye on a Suite in Baker Street" (1946), for the *Baker Street Journal*. A bow window was mentioned specifically twice, in "The Beryl Coronet" and "The Mazarin Stone." Other references were made as well. In *The Sign of Four*, Watson "sat in the window" pondering his first meeting with Mary Morstan; the doctor and Percy Phelps watched Holmes return to Baker Street from the window in "The Naval Treaty"; and from "the recess of the window," Holmes observed Dr. Mortimer in *The Hound of the Baskervilles*.

BOXING.   Holmes was surprisingly proficient in this often brutal sport. Watson wrote that his friend was capable of great muscular effort "and he was undoubtedly one of the finest boxers of his weight that I have ever seen" ("The Yellow Face"). Holmes boxed while at college, telling Watson

Holmes displays his pugilistic skills in "The Solitary Cyclist" against Jack Woodley; by Sidney Paget.

"Bar fencing and boxing I had few athletic tastes" ("The 'Gloria Scott' "). Clearly, he retained much of his skill and interest in the sport for he attended boxing matches and took part in at least one benefit, against McMurdo at Alison's Rooms (*The Sign of Four*). Pugilistic talent also came in handy when fighting "Roaring" Jack Woodley ("The Solitary Cyclist"), Joseph Harrison ("The Naval Treaty"), and the agent of Professor Moriarty who attacked him in the street ("The Final Problem"). Other boxers in the Canon were McMurdo, Sam Merton ("The Mazarin Stone"), Williams (*The Sign of Four*), and Steve Dixie ("The Three Gables").

BOX-ROOM. A storage room for keeping trunks and boxes. Holmes wrote that his own mind was "like a crowded box-room with packets of all sorts stowed away therein—so many I may well have but a vague perception of what was there." ("The Lion's Mane.") (See also LUMBER ROOM.)

BRACKENSTALL, SIR EUSTACE. An English baronet and one of the wealthiest men in the country who, in 1897, was brutally murdered in "The Abbey Grange." According to Stanley Hopkins, Brackenstall "was a good-hearted man when he was sober, but a perfect fiend when he was drunk, or rather when he was half drunk, for he seldom really went the whole way." His drunken rages included beating his wife, Lady Mary, throwing a decanter at her maid Theresa Wright and drenching Lady Mary's dog in petroleum and setting it on fire.

BRACKENSTALL, LADY MARY. The young, beautiful, and long-suffering wife of Sir Eustace Brackenstall in "The Abbey Grange." Originally from Adelaide, Australia, Miss Mary Fraser sailed to England on the *Rock of Gibraltar*, where she met the first officer, Jack Croker, who fell in love with her. Arriving in England, however, she wed Sir Eustace, won over by his title, money, and "London ways." After a short time, she was utterly miserable—her husband was a drunkard who beat her, burned her dog, and threw a decanter at her maid Theresa. Though she did not murder her husband herself, she and Theresa went far to shield the real killer. Holmes, who solved the case, refrained from exposing the murderer to the police. Instead, Watson, acting as an English jury, found the murderer not guilty in a very informal trial.

BRACKWELL, LADY EVA. A client of Holmes in "Charles Augustus Milverton." Lady Eva was "the most beautiful debutante of last season," whose plans to marry the earl of Dovercourt were being threatened by the odious Charles Augustus Milverton. The "king of blackmailers" had acquired several imprudent letters written by the lady to a young country squire and promised to send them to the earl should a certain sum, 7,000 pounds, not be paid. Engaged initially to negotiate with Milverton, Holmes undertook a large operation against the criminal on Lady Eva's behalf.

BRADLEY'S. A London tobacconist that supplied Watson. Holmes asked the good doctor on his way out to have Bradley's send up a pound of its strongest shag tobacco to aid him in pondering the death of Sir Charles Baskerville in *The Hound of the Baskervilles*. By the time Watson returned several hours later, the doctor thought a fire had broken out in 221B, but his fears were put to rest when he smelled the acrid fumes of strong coarse tobacco. Later, upon the moor, Holmes remarked, "when I see the stub of a cigarette marked Bradley, Oxford Street, I know that my friend Watson is in the neighborhood."

BRADSHAW'S RAILWAY GUIDE. One of several railway guides available to the traveller of the English rail system during Holmes's time. Published monthly, *Bradshaw's* was the most comprehensive of the publications available to the detective when planning his numerous rail journeys. In "The Copper Beeches," Holmes was considering meeting Miss Violet Hunter at the Black Swan Hotel in Winchester and asked Watson to look up trains in his *Bradshaw*. In *The Valley of Fear*, Holmes did not accept Watson's suggestion that the coded message from his informant in Moriarty's lair had as its key *Bradshaw's*, and, of course, Holmes was correct.

BRADSTREET, INSPECTOR. A member of Scotland Yard who joined the force probably in 1862, Bradstreet took part in the investigation of at least three of Holmes's cases. During the affair of "The Man With the Twisted Lip," Bradstreet was on duty at the Bow Street police-court when Holmes and Watson arrived to interview the cripple Hugh Boone. Around June 1889, as a member of B Division, he gave evidence concerning the arrest of John Horner, taken into custody for possibly stealing Countess Morcar's gem in "The Blue Carbuncle." Finally, in 1889, he journeyed with Holmes to Eyford along with Victor Hatherley and a plainclothesman to investigate the strange and savage severing of Hatherley's finger in the "Engineer's Thumb." At the time, Bradstreet was most likely assigned to the central headquarters of Scotland Yard.

BREAKFAST. See Food under HOLMES, SHERLOCK.

BRECKINRIDGE. The dealer in geese at Covent Garden Market who sold fowl to Mr. Windigate of the Alpha Inn in "The Blue Carbuncle." The geese were then distributed to the members of the Christmas goose club, including Henry Baker, who was given a very special goose. Billy, or Bill, a small boy who assisted Breckinridge, may have been his son. (See also *PINK 'UN*.)

BRETT, JEREMY. English actor (b. 1942), best known for his highly successful portrayal of Holmes in the ongoing Granada Television adaptations of the Canon. Brett earned early notoriety for his performance in the film *My Fair Lady* opposite Rex Harrison and Audrey Hepburn. An accomplished stage actor, Brett starred as Watson in *Crucifer of Blood* with Charlton Heston as Holmes in a 1981 staging of the Paul Giovanni play at the Ahmanson Theatre in Los Angeles. The Eton graduate first played Holmes in the series *The Adventures of Sherlock Holmes* in 1984. His Watson was David Burke for the first two seasons. In 1986, Burke left and was replaced by Edward Hardwicke, son of Sir Cedric Hardwicke. As a young man growing up in Los Angeles, Edward knew Basil Rathbone through his father. Hardwicke has remained a steady and capable Watson for all of the subsequent seasons, appearing with Brett in *The Return of Sherlock Holmes*, *The Casebook of Sherlock Holmes*, and the two films *The Sign of Four* and *The Hound of the Baskervilles*. Brett's performance as Holmes is generally ranked as the finest of all time, better even than that of Basil Rathbone. Of the detective, the actor said in an interview: "Sherlock Holmes is a free spirit, you cannot pin him down—he is probably the most complicated character I've played in my life."

BREWER, SAM. A Curzon Street moneylender and chief creditor of Sir Robert Norberton in "Shoscombe Old Place." Norberton nearly came to Holmes's attention once when he horsewhipped Brewer almost to death upon Newmarket Heath. The assumption that Brewer would not extend his credit forced Sir Robert to drastic measures.

BRITISH MEDICAL JOURNAL. Watson was reading the journal published by the British Medical Association one morning in June (1888 or 1889) after breakfast at the commencement of the case involving "The Stock-Broker's Clerk." In his investigation of "The Blanched Soldier," Holmes desired to know what Godfrey Emsworth's caretaker was reading, especially if it was the *Lancet* or the *British Medical Journal*.

BRITISH MUSEUM. The renowned London museum was one of the sources of information used by Holmes to aid in the solution of several cases. Trevor Hall, in his collection *Sherlock Holmes: Ten Literary Studies*, postulated that Holmes made up for any deficiencies in learning and erudition by

Jeremy Brett is one of the most popular of recent incarnations of the Great Detective in the MYSTERY! series on public television. (Photo courtesy of MYSTERY!/WGBH Boston.)

utilizing the available sources of the time, especially the British Museum. It was thus perhaps not a mere coincidence that upon arriving in London, the young detective took rooms at Montague Street, "just round the corner from the British Museum" ("The Musgrave Ritual"). Taking advantage of the museum's resources, during *The Hound of the Baskervilles*, Holmes looked up the reputation of Jack Stapleton, an expert on bugs, and during "Wisteria Lodge," he studied Eckermann's *Voodooism and the Negroid Religion*, among other works to understand some of the peculiar clues found in the kitchen of Wisteria Lodge.

BRIXTON ROAD.   In their effort to save the eponymous in "The Disappearance of Lady Frances Carfax," Holmes and Watson drove frantically down the Brixton Road, in the southern London suburbs. In *A Study in Scarlet*, Enoch Drebber was found murdered at Lauriston Gardens, just off the Brixton Road, and Maggie Oakshott, the egg and poultry raiser in "The Blue Carbuncle," lived on the street. The Brixton district also figured in several cases. The Tangeys in "The Naval Treaty," who worked at the Foreign Office, lived at No. 16 Ivy Lane, Brixton, while Stanley Hopkins resided in Brixton. The branch surgery of Dr. Barnicot was in the lower Brixton Road in "The Six Napoleons." The murder of Enoch Drebber was also called the Brixton Mystery by the newspapers.

BROMLEY BROWN, LIEUTENANT.   One of the officers in command of the native garrison at the Blair Island penal colony in the Andaman Islands in *The Sign of Four*.

BROOK, CLIVE.   The English born actor (d. 1974) portrayed Holmes three times in film: *The Return of Sherlock Holmes* (1929), *Murder Will Out* (1930; part of *Paramount On Parade*), and *Sherlock Holmes* (1932). Brook is generally given the distinction of being the first talking Holmes, although the film *The Return of Sherlock Holmes* was available in both a sound and a silent version as not every theatre had yet installed sound equipment. Critics were hard on Brook's portrayal of the Great Detective, calling it "heart-breaking" and crying that "Sherlock Holmes was left out and Sherlock Brook put in." (*Film Weekly*, 1930). (See also OWEN, REGINALD.)

The classic silhouette: Clive Brook in *Sherlock Holmes* (1932).

BROOKS.   A criminal whose plans were obviously foiled by Holmes, for the detective ranked him among the fifty men who had good reason for taking Holmes's life. ("The Bruce-Partington Plans.")

BROWN, JOSIAH.   The owner of one of the six busts of Napoleon that were being stolen and smashed in "The Six Napoleons," Brown lived at Laburnum Lodge, Laburnum Vale, Chiswick. Holmes was convinced that Brown's bust would the next victim.

BROWN, SAM.   The Scotland Yard inspector participated in the pursuit of Jonathan Small with Holmes, Watson, and fellow officer Athelney Jones in *The Sign of Four*. He was on board the police launch that went after the *Aurora*, and later accompanied Watson to Mrs. Cecil Forrester's with the box thought to contain the Agra Treasure.

BROWN, SILAS.   The manager at Capleton Stables in Dartmoor, and the trainer of Desborough, Brown was the second favorite for the Wessex Cup in "Silver Blaze." Brown was involved in the disappearance of Silver Blaze until his role was privately exposed by Holmes. After meeting Brown, the detective declared: "A more perfect compound of the bully, coward and sneak than Master Silas Brown I have seldom met with."

BROWNER, JAMES. The steam packet steward married Mary Cushing in Liverpool in "The Cardboard Box." Originally a steward on a South American line, he moved to the Liverpool, Dublin, and London Steam Packet Company vessel *May Day.* A jealous husband, he was convinced that his wife had taken a lover, Alec Fairbairn. His violent response and vindictive declaration of his act that was sent by accident to Mary's elder sister Susan instead of Sarah (whom Browner hated), involved both the police and Holmes and was one of the most unique and gruesome cases of the Canon.

BRUCE, NIGEL. The English actor (1895– 1953) played Dr. Watson in fifteen films and more than two hundred times on radio, usually opposite Basil Rathbone as Sherlock Holmes. As with his friend Rathbone, Bruce, more than any other actor, became synonymous with John H. Watson, imprinting the image of the screen doctor with his own unique interpretation. Bruce was born in Ensenada, Mexico, the son of a Scottish baronet and wife who were travelling through Mexico at the time of his birth. Educated in England, he served in World War I and was wounded in the leg. His injury left him wheelchair bound for three years. Bruce's acting career began in 1920, when he made his stage debut in *The Creaking Chair.* He eventually moved into silent pictures, and then into sound films, appearing in such memorable works as *Treasure Island* (1934), *The Scarlet Pimpernel* (1935), *The Charge of the Light Brigade* (1936), and *Suez* (1938). In 1939 he began his long Watsonian association in *The Hound of the Baskervilles* for 20th Century-Fox, giving what critics consider his best of all outings as the doctor. He was still excellent in *The Adventures of Sherlock Holmes* (1939), but from then on his Watson was increasingly buffoonish, described by many writers as epitomizing "*Boobus Britannicus.*" Bumbling, unobservant, silly, at times even petulant and utterly mystified by the deductions of his close friend, throughout the long-running Universal series of films Bruce's Watson seemed incapable of writing the exciting accounts

of Sherlock Holmes's adventures and would certainly never have been trusted by Holmes to carry out any but the most innocuous tasks. Nevertheless, Bruce was immensely popular as Watson, his fame increasing with the radio adventures with his friend Rathbone from 1939 to 1946 and with Tom Conway from 1946 to 1947. Bruce's last broadcast with Rathbone was "The Singular Affair of the Baconian Cipher," which aired on May 27, 1946.

Bruce failed to comprehend Rathbone's departure from the role of Holmes, feeling that Rathbone was throwing away a virtual career as the Great Detective. It was Rathbone's hope, however, that Bruce would play Watson once more in the stage play *Sherlock Holmes* written by Rathbone's wife Ouida, but Bruce was too ill. He died on October 8, 1953, just a few weeks before the play's opening. Rathbone wrote of Bruce in his autobiography *In and Out of Character*: "There is no question in my mind that Nigel Bruce was the ideal Watson, not only of his time but possibly of and for all time."

"BRUCE-PARTINGTON PLANS, THE ADVENTURE OF THE" (BRUC). Published: *Strand,* December 1908, *Collier's,* December 1908; collected in *His Last Bow* (1917). Case date: November 1895. Major players: Holmes, Watson, Mycroft Holmes, Arthur Cadogan West, Sir James Walter, Colonel Valentine Walter, Sidney Johnson, Miss Westbury, Hugo Oberstein. This tale involved an interesting reworking of the themes encountered by Holmes and Watson in "The Second Stain." At the behest of his brother Mycroft, the Great Detective launches into an investigation of the theft of the Bruce-Partington Submarine Plans from the Woolwich Arsenal. One of the most jealously guarded of all government secrets, the vessel is said to be so powerful that "naval warfare becomes impossible within the radius" of its operation. A major crisis erupts when some of the plans are stolen; then seven of the ten missing plans turn up in the pockets of the murdered Arthur Cadogan West, a junior clerk at Woolwich whose body is found just outside Aldgate Station.

The case allows Holmes to perform some truly brilliant deductions and analyses, particularly in locating the actual site of the murder of Cadogan West and in trapping the foreign spy who masterminded the theft. For his achievement, Holmes is offered, but refuses, his name on the queen's honors list. Watson writes, however: "Some weeks

Radio: Basil Rathbone and Nigel Bruce perform one of their "adventures" on radio. Their radio programs ran from 1939 to 1961.

afterwards I learned incidentally that my friend spent a day at Windsor, whence he returned with a remarkably fine emerald tie-pin. When I asked him if he had bought it, he answered that it was a present from a certain gracious lady in whose interest he had once been fortunate enough to carry out a small commission." A variation on the submarine theme is seen in the film *The Private Life of Sherlock Holmes* (1970), in which Mycroft (Christopher Lee) oversees the secret construction of a sub on Loch Ness.

BRUCE-PINKERTON PRIZE. The prominent medical prize won by Dr. Percy Trevelyan while at King's College Hospital, for his monograph upon obscure nervous diseases. In "The Resident Patient," Watson expressed familiarity with the work.

BRUISES. This aspect of forensic pathology was of considerable interest to Holmes. In *A Study*

in *Scarlet*, it was said that he was known at St. Bartholomew's Hospital for beating the corpses in the dissecting rooms with a stick to determine how long after death bruises could be produced.

BRUNTON, RICHARD. Of the butler of Hurlstone, the Musgrave family estate in Sussex in "The Musgrave Ritual," Reginald Musgrave said: "He was a young schoolmaster out of place when he was first taken up by my father, but he was a man of great energy and character, and he soon became quite invaluable in the household ... With his personal advantages and his extraordinary gifts— for he can speak several languages and play nearly every musical instrument—it is wonderful that he should have been satisfied so long in such a position, but I suppose that he was comfortable and lacked energy to make any change. The butler of Hurlstone is always a thing that is remembered by all who visit us." He had two weaknesses, however, one was an eye for the ladies, and the second was a curious obsession with the family history of the Musgraves. The latter earned him a dismissal and the former his death.

BUDAPEST.   Also Buda-Pesth, the capital of Hungary. In a Budapest laboratory was to be found the only specimen of the so-called Devil's Foot, the *Radix pedis diaboli*, other than that owned by Leon Sterndale ("The Devil's Foot"). Months after the conclusion of the affair of "The Greek Interpreter," a curious newspaper report reached Holmes and Watson from Budapest, relating that two Englishmen, who had been travelling with a woman, had been stabbed to death, and the Hungarian police were of the opinion that they had quarreled and killed each other. Holmes believed the victims to be the same villains in the case he had investigated in England—Harold Latimer and Wilson Kemp—their deaths caused, he surmised, by the vengeful Sophy Kratides, whose fate remained unknown.

BUDDHA.   Holmes knew a great deal about the Buddhism of Ceylon, as he displayed one evening at dinner with Watson and Inspector Athelney Jones in *The Sign of Four*. The Agra Treasure chest had a hasp (a metal fastener) in the image of a sitting Buddha, and the detective sat upon the floor like some strange Buddha as he consulted his numerous commonplace books for information on Eugenia Ronder in "The Veiled Lodger."

BUFFALO.   The detective uses the expression "a herd of buffaloes" twice in the Canon—first in *A Study in Scarlet* and then again in "The Boscombe Valley Mystery." This phrase, in conjunction with other clues, has led many scholars to theorize that Holmes had some association with America prior to his meeting Watson.

BUFFALO, NEW YORK.   Holmes journeyed there disguised as the Irish-American Altamont, joining a secret Irish society as part of his effort to penetrate the spy ring of Von Bork just before the start of World War I in "His Last Bow."

BULLDOG.   Holmes once compared Inspector Lestrade to a bulldog in tenacity, adding that it had brought him to the top of Scotland Yard ("The Cardboard Box"). Watson claimed in *A Study in Scarlet* that one of his shortcomings was that he kept a bull-pup, but if he meant a dog, it was never mentioned again. He may have been referring to a

tendency toward sudden anger, as mentioned in Michael Hardwick's *The Private Life of Dr. Watson*. In *A Study in Scarlet*, on the body of Enoch Drebber was found a gold pin in the shape of a bulldog's head, with rubies for its eyes.

BURGLARY.   Holmes was remarkably skilled in burglarious enterprises, remarking to Watson in "The Retired Colourman," "Burglary has always been an alternative profession had I cared to adopt it, and I have little doubt that I should have come to the front." This crime is distinguished from robbery by the fact that it is done at night and involves breaking and entering. Holmes used his skills at burgling to enter the homes of Hugo Oberstein ("The Bruce-Partington Plans"), Baron Adalbert Gruner ("The Illustrious Client"), Josiah Amberley ("The Retired Colourman"), and Charles Augustus Milverton ("Charles Augustus Milverton"). In the cases of Gruner and Amberley, the detective was discovered, by the baron and the detective Barker respectively. Holmes admitted that his methods were sometimes irregular but they were effective. Lestrade exclaimed once: "We can't do these things in the force, Mr. Holmes ... No wonder you get results that are beyond us. But some of these days you'll go too far, and you'll find yourself and your friend in trouble" ("The Bruce-Partington Plans").

BURNET, MISS.   The Englishwoman who served as the governess to the children of Mr. Henderson of High Gable, in Surrey in "Wisteria Lodge." Her real name was Signora Victor Durando and her husband, the minister of San Pedro in London, had been murdered on orders from Don Murillo, dictator of San Pedro. The Signora thus became a member of the conspiracy to murder the ex-dictator.

BURNWELL, SIR GEORGE.   A friend and gambling partner of Arthur Holder, Burnwell is the secret courter of Arthur's cousin Mary in "The Beryl Coronet." Alexander Holder, Arthur's father, found him to be "a man of the world to his fingertips, one who has been everywhere, seen everything, a brilliant talker, and a man of great personal beauty," but also someone to be deeply distrusted. Holmes had an even lower opinion of him: "He is one of the most dangerous men in England—a ruined gambler, an absolutely desperate villain; a man without heart or conscience."

The abduction of Miss Burnet in "Wisteria Lodge"; by Sidney Paget

BUTLERS OF THE CANON.   As Holmes frequently dealt with England's upper classes, it was inevitable that he should encounter a number of menservants. While most of the butlers of the Canon were rather unremarkable, there were several who were quite memorable, such as John Barrymore, Bannister, and Jose. The most impressive was, of course, Brunton, of whom Reginald Musgrave declared: "The butler of Hurlstone is always a thing that is remembered by all who visit us."

NAME	PLACE OF SERVICE	CASE
Ames	Birlstone Manor House	*The Valley of Fear*
Anthony	Merripit House	*The Hound of the Baskervilles*
Bannister	St. Luke's College (to Hilton Soames); earlier to Sir Jabez Gilchrist	"The Three Students"
Barrymore, John	Baskerville Hall	*The Hound of the Baskervilles*
Brunton, Richard	Hurlstone	"The Musgrave Ritual"
Hudson	Donnithorpe Estate	"The 'Gloria Scott' "
Jacobs	Whitehall Terrace	"The Second Stain"
John	The home of Dr. Leslie Armstrong	"The Missing Three-Quarter"
Jose	Manservant of Don Murillo	"Wisteria Lodge"
Khitmutgar	The homes of Thaddeus and Bartholomew Sholto	*The Sign of Four*
Old Ralph	Tuxbury Old Hall	"The Blanched Soldier"
Staples	The home of Culverton Smith	"The Dying Detective"
Stephens	Shoscombe Old Place	"Shoscombe Old Place"
Unknown	India (Killed by Grimesby Roylett)	"The Speckled Band"

Note: There are several other unnamed butlers mentioned in "The Illustrious Client," "The Noble Bachelor," "The Priory School," "The Reigate Squires," and "Wisteria Lodge."

CADOGAN WEST, ARTHUR. A clerk at the Woolwich Arsenal, Cadogan becomes the leading suspect in the theft of "The Bruce-Partington Plans" when his body is found just outside Aldgate Station on the underground with some of the plans stuffed in his pockets. While events seem to point toward his guilt, both Holmes and his brother Mycroft are not satisfied with this apparently obvious fact. The detective attempts to discover why Cadogan West, while walking with his fiancée Violet Westbury, had darted off suddenly, leaving her alone in the fog—the last time she saw him alive. Westbury refused to believe that the hot-headed, impetuous Cadogan West could steal the plans: "Arthur was the most single-minded, chivalrous, patriotic man upon earth. He would have cut his right hand off before he would sell a State secret confided to his keeping."

CAIRNS, PATRICK. Holmes hunted this harpooner in the guise of Captain Basil in "Black Peter." Cairns had been a harpooner for twenty-six years and had sailed on the *Sea Unicorn*, out of Dundee. His "fierce, bull-dog face was framed in a tangle of hair and beard, and two bold dark eyes gleamed behind the cover of thick, tufted, overhung eyebrows."

CALHOUN, CAPTAIN JAMES. The mastermind of the Openshaw murders in "The Five Orange Pips," Calhoun was an American ship captain of the barque *Lone Star* out of Savannah, Georgia. He was also a member of the Ku Klux Klan, leading the conspiracy against three members of the Openshaw family. Calhoun and the *Lone Star* were both apparently lost at sea in 1887 in an Atlantic gale.

CAMBERWELL. A letter is mailed to Holmes from his informant in the criminal organization of Professor Moriarty from this London borough in *The Valley of Fear*. The detective sent money to his agent via an address in the Camberwell post office. Mrs. Cecil Forrester (*The Sign of Four*), Mary Sutherland ("A Case of Identity"), Miss Dobney ("The Disappearance of Lady Frances Carfax"), and the Charpentier boardinghouse (*A Study in Scarlet*), were all in Camberwell. (See next entry.)

CAMBERWELL POISONING CASE. An unchronicled investigation dated to 1887. "Holmes was able, by winding up the dead man's watch, to prove that it had been wound up two hours ago, and that therefore the deceased had gone to bed within that time—a deduction which was of the greatest importance in clearing up the case." ("The Five Orange Pips.") The case was developed in the short story "The Adventure of the Gold Hunter" in *The Exploits of Sherlock Holmes* by Adrian Conan Doyle and John Dickson Carr.

CAMBRIDGE UNIVERSITY. Holmes may have attended this prestigious English university; the other possibility is Oxford. Holmes himself never admitted which school he attended, merely making reference to his time at college in "The Musgrave Ritual" and "The 'Gloria Scott'." Watson only added to the mystery by disguising the universities he and Holmes visited in "The Three Students" and "The Creeping Man." Percy Phelps had a "triumphant" career at Cambridge ("The Naval Treaty"). Willoughby Smith also attended the school ("The Golden Pince-Nez.") (See also HOLMES, SHERLOCK.)

CAMDEN HOUSE. The residence opposite Holmes's quarters at 221B Baker Street, Camden House was empty in April 1894, with "bare planking" and wallpaper "hanging in ribbons." It thus served admirably the purposes of Moriarty's last known lieutenant in planning the assassination of Holmes in "The Empty House." The location of the residence has been the subject of considerable speculation among scholars. (See BAKER STREET for other details.)

CAMFORD UNIVERSITY. A university said by Holmes to be composed of "ancient colleges." It was here that the detective investigated the case of "The Creeping Man" involving Professor Presbury.

CAMPDEN HOUSE. A thoroughfare in Kensington where a plaster cast of Napoleon was found smashed in the garden of an empty house in "The Six Napoleons." The bust had belonged to Horace Harker.

CANADA. Henry Baskerville had worked on a farm in this onetime British colony (it was still in Holmes's time) prior to his inheriting the accursed estate of Sir Charles Baskerville in *The Hound of the Baskervilles.* Canada was also a subject Mycroft knew much about, as mentioned in "The Bruce-Partington Plans."

CANARY TRAINER, THE. The third pastiche novel by Nicholas Meyer (with *The Seven-Per-Cent Solution* and *The West End Horror*), published in 1993. Here Holmes recounts to Watson a previously unchronicled case into which the detective was drawn while on the Great Hiatus: he hunts down the Phantom of Opera. The plot is nicely interwoven with the events of the original Gaston Leroux novel, although there is a missing air of anticipation due to the proliferation of phantom versions in the last years. The climax is also unequal to the reputations of both characters. Once again, Meyer captures the atmosphere of the times, with Irene Adler thrown in to spice things up. Watson, however, is acutely missed, especially after the finely drawn characters of the previous novels.

CANDLE. Candles proved helpful to Holmes in solving the murder of Hilton Cubitt in "The Dancing Men." Holmes knew that the window in the room in which Cubitt was found murdered had been opened for only a brief period of time because the candle in the room was not guttered (melted wax had not dripped down the side opposite a breeze or draft). Knowing this, and later proving that the draft had blown gun powder fumes through the house, the detective deduced that a third party had been present, clearing Elsie Cubitt of suspicion.

CANE. Holmes used a cane in several cases. He carried a cane in "Thor Bridge" and struck it upon the stone side of the bridge to determine how hard a blow would have to be in order to cause the marks left upon the bridge during the murder of Mrs. Gibson. A cane was of vital service during his investigation at Stoke Moran in "The Speckled Band," as Holmes used it to repel the advancing swamp adder. A sword cane also figured in the film *Murder By Decree* (1979).

CANTLEMERE, LORD. This high government official was involved in the efforts to recover the Mazarin Stone and opposed Holmes's involvement in the affair. Unable to resist the temptation, Holmes had fun at Cantlemere's expense by "finding" the stone on the lord's person.

CAPITAL AND COUNTIES BANK. This banking firm served as the financial agent of the detective; he banked at the Oxford branch as revealed in "The Priory School." Other patrons of the bank were Arthur Cadogan West ("The Bruce-Partington Plans") and Neville St. Clair ("The Man With the Twisted Lip").

"CARDBOARD BOX, THE" (CARD). Published: *Strand*, January 1893, *Harper's*, January 14, 1893; collected in *The Memoirs of Sherlock Holmes* (1894) and *His Last Bow* (1917). Major players: Holmes, Watson, Susan Cushing, Mary Cushing, Inspector Lestrade, Sarah Cushing, James Browner. Case date: August, late 1880s. This case of adultery, revenge, and murder caused quite a stir at the time of its publication because of its discussion of extramarital activities. Holmes is summoned to Croydon on a blazing August day where Inspector Lestrade shows him some kind of a gruesome practical joke—Susan Cushing has received a box filled with coarse salt and two severed human ears. Holmes, of course, is an expert on ears (he wrote two monographs upon the subject) and decides that there is much more here than a peculiar sense of fun. The solution centers on the three

Cushing sisters and the man who had married one of them, to the jealous rage of another. When faced with the issue of adultery, Holmes typically becomes morbid, glumly telling Watson: "What object is served by this circle of misery and violence and fear? It must tend to some end, or else our universe is ruled by chance, which is unthinkable."

Because of the public unease, the account was omitted from some editions of *The Memoirs of Sherlock Holmes* in 1894 and was later added to *His Last Bow*, by which time adultery had become less shocking. Because of the removal of the story from some editions, the popular mind-reading incident that began "The Cardboard Box" was added to the opening of "The Resident Patient." In some collections of the entire Canon, the episode appears in both accounts.

CARERE, MADEMOISELLE. The stepdaughter of the unfortunate Madame Montpensier (*The Hound of the Baskervilles*). Her apparent murder hung over Madame Montpensier, but she was found alive six months later and married in New York.

CAREY, PETER. Nicknamed Black Peter, the captain of sealing and whaling vessels resided at Woodman's Lee, in Sussex, and was found impaled on a door by a harpoon in "Black Peter." Born in 1845 he had been a "daring and successful" captain, commanding in 1883 the steam sealer *Sea*

Holmes, Watson, and Lestrade inspect some ears—on which Holmes is an expert—in "The Cardboard Box"; by Sidney Paget.

Unicorn before retiring the following year. Stanley Hopkins, told Holmes and Watson: "In ordinary life he was a strict Puritan—a silent, gloomy fellow . . . The man was an intermittent drunkard, and when he had the fit on him he was a perfect fiend . . . he was loathed and avoided by everyone of his neighbors."

CARFAX, LADY FRANCES. The sole survivor of the direct family of the late earl of Rufton disappeared quite suddenly and was the focus of Holmes and Watson's frantic searches in "The Disappearance of Lady Frances Carfax." Holmes said of her, "The estates [of the family] went, as you may remember, in the male line. She was left with limited means, but with some very remarkable old Spanish jewellery of silver and curiously cut diamonds to which she was fondly attached—too attached, for she refused to leave them with her banker and always carried them about with her. A rather pathetic figure, the Lady Frances, a beautiful woman, still in fresh middle age, and yet, by a strange chance, the last derelict of what only twenty years ago was a goodly fleet."

CARINA. A singer at the Albert Hall whom Holmes went to hear with Watson, interrupting his investigation into the Amberley affair ("The Retired Colourman") and escaping "this weary workaday world by the side door of music."

CARLO. Dogs of this name appear in two Holmes stories. Jephro Rucastle threatened Violet Hunter with a mastiff guard dog in "The Copper Beeches," and only Toller the groom could handle it. Carlo was killed by Watson when it was mauling its master. A spaniel owned by Robert Ferguson in "The Sussex Vampire" is also named Carlo. It had considerable difficulty walking as its hind legs moved erratically and its tail was always on the ground. The problem was diagnosed as spinal meningitis, but Holmes's discovery of the real cause contributed to the solution of the case.

CARLTON CLUB. One of the members of this prominent Conservative club, located in London in Pall Mall, Sir James Damery, sent a note to Holmes from the club requesting an appointment in "The Illustrious Client." The Diogenes Club, Mycroft Holmes's own club, was "some little distance from the Carlton" in Pall Mall ("The Greek Interpreter").

CARLYLE, THOMAS. In *A Study in Scarlet*, Watson quoted the well-known Scottish historian and essayist (1795–1881) to Holmes and was surprised when the young detective "inquired in the naivest way who he might be and what he had done." This contributed to Watson's assessment that Holmes's "ignorance was as remarkable as his knowledge." A short time later, however, Holmes paraphrased Carlyle: "They say that genius is an infinite capacity for taking pains." (See also RICHTER, JOHANN.)

CARRUTHERS, BOB. The employer of Violet Smith who gave to the poor young woman the good-paying position as music teacher to his daughter in "The Solitary Cyclist." Carruthers made the invitation out of ulterior motives, however, and was partner of the rogue and bully, Jack Woodley. Their original plan to steal the inheritance that was unknown to Smith was upset by Carruthers's falling unexpectedly in love with her. His subsequent actions caused Smith to consult Holmes. Carruthers "was a dark, sallow, clean shaven, silent person; but he had polite manners and a pleasant smile." He resided at Chiltern Grange.

CARRUTHERS, COLONEL. An otherwise unknown criminal whom Holmes and Watson locked up just before undertaking the case at "Wisteria Lodge."

CARTWRIGHT. This fourteen-year-old lad "with a bright, keen face" was of assistance to Holmes in *The Hound of the Baskervilles*. A district messenger-boy, Cartwright had originally aided the detective when Holmes saved the good name, and possibly the life, of Wilson, the manager of the district messenger station. Cartwright searched for the newspaper from which had been clipped the letter of warning to Sir Henry Baskerville in London, and later journeyed to Dartmoor. Disguised as a country youth, he kept Holmes supplied with food while the detective was encamped upon the moor. (See also WORTHINGDON BANK GANG.)

CASEBOOK. Holmes recorded details about his many cases in this small book. Also referred to as his "indexed list of cases," the casebook was consulted on a number of occasions: in *The Hound of the Baskervilles*, "The Speckled Band," and "The Sussex Vampire." (See also COMMONPLACE BOOK and NOTEBOOK.)

CASE BOOK OF SHERLOCK HOLMES, THE. The fifth and final published collection of cases, released in 1927, three years before the passing of Sir Arthur Conan Doyle. It brought to a close the initial publishing history of the Canon and was comprised of the last twelve Holmes cases written by Dr. Watson. In order of their appearance in *Strand Magazine*, they were:

"The Adventure of the Mazarin Stone"
"The Problem of Thor Bridge"
"The Adventure of the Creeping Man"
"The Adventure of the Sussex Vampire"
"The Adventure of the Three Garridebs"
"The Adventure of the Illustrious Client"
"The Adventure of the Three Gables"
"The Adventure of the Blanched Soldier"
"The Adventure of the Lion's Mane"
"The Adventure of the Retired Colourman"
"The Adventure of the Veiled Lodger"
"The Adventure of Shoscombe Old Place"

In his introduction to the volume, Conan Doyle wrote: "Had Holmes never existed I could not have done more, though he may perhaps have stood a little in the way of my more serious literary work. And so, reader, farewell to Sherlock Holmes! I thank you for your past constancy and can but hope that some return has been made in the shape of that distraction from the worries of life and stimulating change of thought which can only be found in the fairy kingdom of romance."

"CASEBOOK OF SHERLOCK HOLMES, THE." This third series of television adventures featuring Jeremy Brett (Holmes) and Edward Hardwicke (Watson) was first broadcast in England during the 1991–1992 season. Produced by Granada Television, the adaptations included "The Disappearance of Lady Frances Carfax," "The Problem of Thor Bridge," "The Boscombe Valley Mystery," "The Illustrious Client," "The Master Blackmailer" (based on "Charles Augustus Milverton"), and "The Last Vampire" (based on "The Sussex Vampire"). Sherlockians have taken note of the fact the choices for the "Casebook" are not properly Canonical, as "Lady Frances" was published as part of *His Last Bow* and "The Boscombe Valley" was published in *The Adventures of Sherlock Holmes*. Certain liberties have always been taken with the stories, but "Lady Frances Carfax" and especially "The Last Vampire," as presented by Granada, were severely reworked, much to the disappointment of devotées of the Canon.

"CASE OF IDENTITY, A" (IDEN). Published: *Strand*, September 1891; collected in *The Adventures of Sherlock Holmes* (1892). Case date: 1890. Major players: Holmes, Watson, Mary Sutherland, Hosmer Angel, Mr. Windibank. An investigation by Holmes that Watson noted was free of legal crime. Holmes's assistance is enlisted by Miss Mary Sutherland to find her fiancé, Hosmer Angel, who had vanished from the cab carrying him to their wedding. The case leads Holmes to learn of the very strange relationship between Sutherland and Angel: she had no idea where he lived and knew little of him save that he courted her very aggressively. Of the actual mind behind the affair, Holmes declared: "That fellow will rise from crime to crime until he does something very bad, and ends on a gallows. The case has, in some respects, been not entirely devoid of interest."

CASE OF THE REVOLUTIONIST'S DAUGHTER: SHERLOCK HOLMES MEETS KARL MARX, THE. A 1983 pastiche by Lewis S. Feuer that depicts the title encounter while burying the reader into a detailed account of the lives of the early Communist philosophers and their theories. Much like Randall Collins in his *The Case of the Philosopher's Ring*, Feuer devotes the bulk of his story to extensive discussions on Marx and Engels. Holmes is consulted by Engels in 1881 concerning the intense personal troubles of Karl Marx and his family. The detective is thus drawn into the peculiar world of the socialists in what Watson describes as "the most political case in which Holmes was ever involved." The reader may have an almost impossible time keeping up with dialogue laced with deep theory and philosophical analysis.

"CASES OF SHERLOCK HOLMES, THE." England 1968. Dir: Henri Safran, et al. Cast: Peter Cushing (Holmes), Nigel Stock (Watson), and Grace Arnold (Mrs. Hudson). This BBC television series, which was aired in 1968, once again offered Cushing the chance to return to Baker Street. Although increasingly old, he was quite active in the role, aided by Stock, one of the best of all Watsons. The adaptations included:

"The Second Stain," "A Study in Scarlet" (rarely filmed in modern productions), "The Hound of the Baskervilles" (of course), "Thor Bridge," "Black Peter," and "The Blue Carbuncle." Filmed in black and white, the series was not the equal to its immediate predecessor, "Sherlock Holmes," with Douglas Wilmer and Nigel Stock.

CASTALOTTE, TITO. The senior partner of the firm Castalotte & Zamba, New York's foremost fruit importers in "The Red Circle," was saved from a gang of ruffians in the Bowery by Gennaro Lucca. As a reward, he made Lucca a department head and came to treat him as the son he never had. Gennaro and his wife Emilia thus loved Castalotte as they would a father, and Gennaro was horrified when he received orders from the terror organization, the Red Circle, to blow up Castalotte and his house with dynamite because Tito had refused to bend to the will of the society. Gennaro's unwillingness to undertake the murder caused the events described in "The Red Circle."

CATARACT KNIFE. A delicate knife used for the surgical removal of the lens of the eye for cataracts. One such knife was inexplicably found in the dead hand of John Straker in "Silver Blaze."

CAVENDISH. Tobacco that has been sweetened with molasses (or syrup) and pressed into cakes can be smoked or chewed. Half an ounce of cavendish was found in the pocket of the dead John Straker in "Silver Blaze."

CAVENDISH CLUB. One of the London clubs, located in Regent Street, to which Ronald Adair belonged in "The Empty House."

CEDARS, THE. In "The Man With the Twisted Lip," Holmes and Watson stayed at the Cedars, the villa of Neville St. Clair and family near Lee, in Kent. During the investigation into the disappearance of Neville, Holmes solves the case with a bath sponge borrowed from a Cedars bathroom.

CHALDEAN LANGUAGE. The language of the ancient civilization of the Chaldeans, also called Aramaic, that was one of the tongues of the ancient Semitic people. In studying the ancient Cornish language during his enforced rest in Cornwall in "The Devil's Foot," Holmes concluded the

Cornish branch of the great Celtic speech had its roots in the Chaldean language.

CHARING CROSS.   This district in the London borough of the City of Westminster plays a role in numerous adventures. The bank of Cox & Co. was located in Charing Cross ("Thor Bridge"). Related sites were:

1. Charing Cross Hospital. From 1882–1884, James Mortimer served there as house surgeon, receiving a commemorative walking stick with "To James Mortimer, M.R.C.S., from his friends of the C.C.H." engraved upon it. He left the stick by accident at 221B and it became the object of observation by Holmes and Watson in *The Hound of the Baskervilles*. Following the vicious, murderous attack upon Holmes by the ruffians hired by Baron Gruner, the detective was taken to C.C.H. and later moved to Baker Street in "The Illustrious Client."

2. Charing Cross Post Office. John Scott Eccles sent a telegram to Holmes from the post office situated at the intersection of the Strand and Charing Cross concerning his "most incredible and grotesque experience" at Wisteria Lodge in "Wisteria Lodge." The letter of warning to Sir Henry Baskerville in *The Hound of the Baskerville* bore a Charing Cross postmark. (See also Hotel.)

3. Charing Cross Station. Holmes mentioned that a criminal named Matthews, one of the rogues in the fine M section of the detective's index of biographies, knocked out his left canine in the waiting room at Charing Cross Station ("The Empty House"). Madame Fournay, wife of the international agent Eduardo Lucas, "attracted much attention at Charing Cross Station . . . by the wildness of her appearance and the violence of her gestures" ("The Second Stain"). Irene Adler left London with her husband from the station in "A Scandal in Bohemia."

CHARLES I.   In "The Musgrave Ritual," it was said that Charles, king of England from 1625 to 1649, entrusted the safekeeping of his crown to the Musgrave family so that it could be passed along to his son Charles II. The crown subsequently disappeared. In the Musgrave Ritual, Charles was referred to in the line "his who is gone." The king also supposedly hid at Birlstone Manor for a few days during the Civil War (*The Valley of Fear*). His

son, **Charles II**, was king of England from 1660 to 1685. The Musgrave Ritual referred to him in the line "his who will come" ("The Musgrave Ritual"). Sir Ralph Musgrave was "a prominent Cavalier, and the right-hand man of Charles II in his wanderings."

"CHARLES AUGUSTUS MILVERTON, THE ADVENTURE OF" (CHAS).   Published: *Collier's*, March 1904, *Strand*, April 1904; collected in *The Return of Sherlock Holmes* (1905). Case date: Various, 1882–1899. Major players: Holmes, Watson, Milverton, Lestrade. A case that pitches Holmes against the King of All Blackmailers, Milverton. The detective has been hired by Lady Eva Brackenwell to recover some letters being used by Milverton to blackmail her. When reason fails with the villain, Holmes resolves to burgle Milverton's residence, Appledore Towers. Toward this end, he assumes the guise of Escott, a plumber with a rising business, wooing and becoming engaged to Milverton's housemaid. Watson is horrified, but the information and assistance Holmes receives from the maid Agatha allows him and Watson to enter Appledore Towers with greater ease. There follow the tragic and bloody events in which Milverton's cruel profession finally catches up with him. Because of the circumstances of the case and the very prominent name associated with it, Watson wrote of his deliberate efforts to conceal names and dates, hence the difficulty encountered in determining the date.

CHARLINGTON HALL.   A large house in Surrey, situated between Chiltern Grange and the village of Farnham in "The Solitary Cyclist," the hall was tenanted by the defrocked clergyman Williamson, who lived alone with a small staff of servants. "The house was invisible from the road, but the surroundings all spoke of gloom and decay."

CHARPENTIER FAMILY.   The family owns the Charpentier's Boarding Establishment in Torquay Terrace, Camberwell in *A Study in Scarlet*. The proprietress was Madame Charpentier. Her daughter, Alice, described by Inspector Gregson as "an uncommonly fine girl," received the very improper advances of Enoch Drebber while Drebber and Stangerson were staying at the boardinghouse. Drebber's conduct caused Alice's brother Arthur, a sub-lieutenant in the Royal Navy, to give him a

Charles Augustus Milverton, the "King of Blackmailers," in "Charles Augustus Milverton"; by Sidney Paget.

thrashing. As Drebber was killed that night, Inspector Gregson arrested Arthur for Drebber's murder.

CHARTER. Early English Charters, written grants, dating from around 1066 to 1500, that conferred certain rights or privileges upon a person, the people, or a body, were the subject of laborious researches by Holmes in 1895. Watson wrote that Holmes's studies were so striking that they might be the subject of a future narrative. At the time of his efforts, Holmes visited one of the great university towns where the detective became involved in the affair of "The Three Students." (See also FERRERS DOCUMENTS.)

CHARWOMAN. Mrs. Tangey, in "The Naval Treaty," worked at the Foreign Office where her husband served as commissionaire. She was suspected for a time of stealing the Naval Treaty. There was also a charwoman employed in the home of the Amberleys in "The Retired Colourman." Holmes also encountered a clever villain disguised as a charwoman in the film *Dressed to Kill* (1946).

CHEESEMAN'S. The home of Robert Ferguson and family near Lamberley, Sussex, Holmes and Watson investigate the possible predations of a vampire in "The Sussex Vampire." Watson wrote: "It was a large, straggling building, very old in the centre, very new at the wings with towering Tudor chimneys and a lichen-spotted, high-pitched roof of Horsham slabs. The doorsteps were worn into curves, and the ancient tiles which lined the porch were marked with the rebus of a cheese and a man after the original builder."

CHEMISTRY. Watson wrote in *A Study in Scarlet* that Holmes possessed a "profound" knowledge of chemistry, and that he was "uncomfortable" without his chemicals ("The Three Students"). The doctor was often complaining about Holmes's experiments, noting in "The Musgrave Ritual,"

Holmes pursuing his chemistry experiments, a favorite activity, in "The Naval Treaty"; by Sidney Paget.

Peter Cushing as Holmes at work at the detective's famed chemistry table; from *The Hound of the Baskervilles* (1959). Note the proper clay pipe.

that their "chambers were always full of chemicals and criminal relics . . ." The detective conducted his experiments in a corner of Baker Street, on an "acid-stained, deal-topped table" ("The Mazarin Stone" and "The Empty House"). Prior to their sharing lodgings at 221B, Holmes did some of his experimentation at St. Bartholomew's Hospital. It was there that he created an infallible test for bloodstains and where he first met Dr. Watson. Cases where he performed experiments included: *A Study in Scarlet*, "The Dancing Men," "The Copper Beeches," "A Case of Identity," "The Naval Treaty," *The Sign of Four*, and in the original edition of "The Resident Patient."

CHEQUERS.   Holmes and Watson stay at this inn or hotel in Lamberley, Sussex during their investigation into the activities of a suspected vampire in "The Sussex Vampire." They also stay at the Chequers, an inn at Camford, during the investigation of "The Creeping Man." The detective was familiar with the hotel, commenting that "the port used to be above mediocrity and the linen was above reproach."

CHESS.   Josiah Amberley excelled at this board game in "The Retired Colourman"; Holmes notes to Watson that it was one mark of a scheming mind. Of interest to chess players is Raymond Smullyan's book *Chess Mysteries of Sherlock Holmes* (1979). Surprisingly, Holmes is never mentioned in the Canon playing chess. The cause could be attributed to the difficult time he probably had finding a partner equal to his skill.

CHESTERFIELD.   A town in Derbyshire where the father of Neville St. Clair served as a schoolmaster ("The Man With the Twisted Lip"). Reuben Hays was arrested here ("The Priory School").

CHESTERTON.   A village situated to the north of Cambridge. In "The Missing Three-Quarter," Holmes searched for the missing Godfrey Staunton, the player for the Cambridge University rugby team, at Chesterton, but with no success.

CHICAGO.   This large Midwest city is the home of a dangerous gang to which Abe Slaney, "the most dangerous crook in Chicago," belonged in "The Dancing Men." Holmes claimed to have knowledge about Chicago gangsters, but he relied upon a friend in the New York Police Bureau for information about Slaney. The admission could be taken as an indication that Holmes had greater experience with America than he was willing or disposed to discuss. Chicago was featured in several cases: in *The Valley of Fear*, Birdy Edwards journeyed to Vermissa Valley from Chicago, returned and was married there, but was ultimately forced to leave the city; Killer Evans, in "The Three Garridebs," was a native of Chicago, the city supposedly where Alexander Hamilton Garrideb made a portion of his vast wealth; finally, in "His Last Bow," Holmes, in the disguise of the Irish-American Altamont, began his penetration of Von Bork's spy ring in Chicago.

CHINA.   Jabez Wilson visited this Asian country, a journey deduced by Holmes in "The Red-Headed League" by the coin upon his watch chain and the tattoo above his wrist. In "The Blue Carbuncle," the Blue Carbuncle was said to have been found in the banks of a river in southern China. In "The Dying Detective," the terrible disease that had apparently mortally inflicted Holmes was said by him to have been contracted while he was working among some Chinese sailors down on the docks of London. In "The Illustrious Client," Chinese pottery was a specialty of Baron Gruner, so much so that he authored a book on the subject. Finally, the *Gloria Scott* had been built originally for the coastal tea trade.

CHLOROFORM.   A colorless liquid that can be used for anaesthetic purposes. Lady Frances Carfax was rendered unconscious with chloroform in "The Disappearance of Lady Frances Carfax," as were

Mary Maberley in "The Three Gables," and Von Bork in "His Last Bow."

CHOPIN, FREDERIC. In *A Study in Scarlet*, Holmes looked forward to spending an afternoon at Halle's where Norman-Neruda was playing. "Her attack and her bowing are splendid. What's that little thing of Chopin's she plays so magnificently: Tra-la-la-lira-lira-lay."

CHRISTMAS. This case recounted in "The Blue Carbuncle" takes place on the second day after Christmas. Holmes allowed the thief of the prized jewel, the Blue Carbuncle, to retain his liberty, justifying his leniency by telling Watson that he was not retained by the police to supply their deficiencies and that it was the season of forgiveness, not the only time that Holmes stayed the hand of justice for unique circumstances (see "The Abbey Grange" and "The Devil's Foot" for example). Christmas has been used in several non-Canonical stories, including "A Christmas Episode" by Charles Fisher, "Death in the Christmas Hour" by James Powell, and "A Sherlock Holmes Christmas Story" by John Hogan. In the latter, Professor Moriarty sends Holmes a gift—the giant rat of Sumatra!

CHURCH STREET. A street in Kensington where Holmes, in the guise of an old bibliophile, claimed to own a bookshop in "The Empty House." (See also GELDER & CO.)

CIGAR. Holmes made a special study of cigar ashes, authoring the monograph "Upon the Distinction Between the Ashes of the Various Tobaccos" (*The Sign of Four*). The detective kept his own cigars in a coal-scuttle ("The Musgrave Ritual"). Cigar ash or butts figured in a number of cases: Blessington smoked Havanas, but the cigar ends found in his fireplace were imported from Dutch East India ("The Resident Patient"); the murderer of Charles McCarthy smoked Indian cigars, cut with a blunt penknife and smoked through a cigar holder ("Boscombe Valley Mystery"); and Dr. Grimesby Roylott smoked Indian cigars ("The Speckled Band"). In an excellent demonstration of deductive ability, Dr. Mortimer in *The Hound of the Baskervilles* told Holmes that he knew how long Sir Charles Baskerville had stood at the Yew Alley gate by the ash that had fallen from his cigar, causing

Holmes to exclaim "Excellent! This is a colleague, Watson, after our own heart." (See also TOBACCO.)

CIGARETTE. Cigarettes were also included in Holmes's monograph "Upon the Distinctions Between the Ashes of the Various Tobaccos" (*The Sign of Four*; also "The Boscombe Valley Mystery"). Watson smoked cigarettes that were made by Bradley (*The Hound of the Baskervilles*), while Dr. Mortimer made his own. The most interesting case involving cigarettes was "The Golden Pince-Nez" featuring the chain smoker Professor Coram, who devoured cigarettes from Ionides of Alexandria at the rate of 1,000 per fortnight. Holmes apparently loved them as well, smoking several of them in one sitting and then using the fallen ash to solve the case. (See also TOBACCO.)

CITY AND SUBURBAN BANK. A London banking firm featured in "The Red-Headed League." Its Coburg branch office, located around the corner from the pawnshop of Jabez Wilson, onetime member of the Red-Headed League, was the target of a gang of clever burglars. Their attempt to rob it was foiled by Holmes.

CLARET. A name used in England for various red wines from France. James Windibank in "A Case of Identity" travelled for the claret importer Westhouse & Marbank. Following the arrest of the culprit in the case of "The Dying Detective," Holmes refreshed himself with a glass of claret, and Holmes and Watson shared a bottle during the case of "The Cardboard Box."

CLAY, JOHN. A murderer, thief, smasher, and forger who was a mastermind behind the attempt to rob the City and Suburban Bank in "The Red-Headed League." Holmes considered Clay to be the fourth smartest man in London and the third most daring. Peter Jones of Scotland Yard said of him: "I would rather have my bracelets on him than on any criminal in London. He's a remarkable man, is young John Clay. His grandfather was a Royal Duke, and he himself has been to Eton and Oxford. His brain is as cunning as his fingers, and though we meet signs of him at every turn, we never know where to find the man himself. He'll crack a crib in Scotland one week, and be raising money to build an orphanage in Cornwall the next." In appearance, he was small, stoutly built, very quick in his

Holmes puts the hands of justice on John Clay in "The Red-Headed League"; by Sidney Paget.

ways, had a splash of acid on his forehead, and had ears pierced for earrings. (See also SPAULDING, VINCENT.)

CLAYTON, JOHN. A London cabdriver who operated cab No. 2704, out of Shipley's Yard, near Waterloo Station in *The Hound of the Baskervilles*. He picked up a fare in Trafalgar Square and was paid two guineas to do exactly what the passenger wanted all day and to ask no questions. The fare was observing Sir Henry Baskerville, with very sinister intentions. Clayton was ultimately told that his ride was named Sherlock Holmes, an alias that struck the real Holmes as very humorous. Clayton lived at 3 Turpey Street, Borough.

CLEESE, JOHN. English actor, writer, and comedian, onetime member of the group Monty Python. Cleese horrified many of the faithful of Sherlockiana with his two slapstick satires on Holmes, "Elementary, My Dear Watson" (1973) and "The Strange Case of the End of Civilization As We Know It" (1977), both for British

television. The first, shown in January 1973, had Cleese as Holmes and William Rushton as Dr. Watson attempting to solve the strange case involving Fu Manchu, five dead solicitors, and the panel of the television show *Call My Bluff*. The second, assailed harshly by Sherlockian critics, again featured Cleese as a detective, with Arthur Lowe, debuting on British television in September 1977. Here, the descendants of Holmes and Watson are featured, attempting to save the earth from destruction at the hands of the grandson of Professor Moriarty.

CLEFT TOR. A Dartmoor tor from which the butler John Barrymore received signals at Baskerville Hall in the dark of the night in *The Hound of the Baskervilles*.

CLEVELAND. The Ohio city where Enoch Drebber and Joseph Stangerson lived until Jefferson Hope caught up with them in *A Study in Scarlet*. In the pocket of the dead Drebber were found cards with his name and Cleveland address.

CLUBS. See table below.

MAJOR CLUBS OF THE CANON

CLUB	NOTABLE MEMBERS	CASES
Anglo-Indian	Colonel Sebastian Moran	EMPT
Bagatelle	Colonel Sebastian Moran Ronald Adair, Mr. Murray, Sir John Hardy, Godfrey Milner, and Lord Balmoral	EMPT
Baldwin	Ronald Adair	EMPT
Carlton	Sir James Damery	ILLU
Cavendish	Ronald Adair	EMPT
Diogenes	Mycroft Holmes	GREE and BRUC
Tankerville	Colonel Sebastian Moran and Major Prendergast	EMPT and FIVE

COAL AND IRON POLICE. A special police force that was raised by the railway and colliery owners of Vermissa Valley to support the police who were working with great difficulty against the terrorist organization of the Scowrers in *The Valley of Fear*.

COAL TAR. A foul-smelling, viscous black fluid obtained by the distillation of tar, and used in dyes, medicines, and for waterproofing. During the Great Hiatus, Holmes spent some months researching coal tar derivatives ("The Empty House"). During his investigation into the case of "The Blanched Soldier," the detective noted that the butler of Tuxbury Old Hall had the "tarry odour" of disinfectant on his gloves. Bartholomew Sholto's laboratory and the garret above it at Pondicherry Lodge had a "tarlike odour" upon which Watson remarked in *The Sign of Four*.

COBB, JOHN. The groom employed by Charles McCarthy at the Hatherley Farm in "The Boscombe Valley Mystery."

COCAINE. Holmes was long under the influence of the highly addictive stimulant from which Dr. Watson was apparently successful in freeing him. The earliest indications that Holmes might have been using some kind of drug were given in the first work of the Canon, *A Study in Scarlet*, when Watson, who was still coming to know the detective, wrote: ". . . for days on end he would lie upon the sofa in the sitting-room, hardly uttering a word or moving a muscle from morning to night. On these occasions I have noticed such a dreamy, vacant expression in his eyes, that I might have suspected him of being addicted to the use of some narcotic, had not the temperament and cleanliness of his whole life forbidden such a notion." Watson's fears are confirmed in *The Sign of Four*, as Holmes's addiction serves as the opening and closing segments to the novel, with the detective declaring at the end, "For me . . . there still remains the cocaine-bottle."

Watson called Holmes a "self-poisoner" ("The Five Orange Pips") and impressed upon him the dangers of taking cocaine ("The Twisted Lip"). While Holmes admitted that the effects of the drug were physically bad (*The Sign of Four*), he took the so-called seven-per-cent solution as a means of relieving the ennui that so easily afflicted his great brain. The mantelpiece in his bedroom had a litter of syringes scattered over it ("The Dying Detective"). The syringe and drug dosage being used were carried in a "neat morocco case." Watson wrote that Holmes would remain "in our lodgings in Baker Street, buried among his old books, and alternating week to week between cocaine and ambition, the drowsiness of the drug, and the fierce energy of his own keen nature" ("A Scandal in Bohemia").

After Holmes's return from the Great Hiatus in April 1894, Watson was able to write: "For years I had gradually weaned him from that drug mania which had threatened once to check his remarkable career. Now I knew that under ordinary conditions he no longer craved for this artificial stimulus, but I was well aware that the fiend was not dead but sleeping, and I have known that the sleep was a light one and the waking near when in periods of idleness I have seen the drawn look upon Holmes' ascetic face, and the brooding of his deep-set and inscrutable eyes" ("The Missing Three-Quarter"). That Holmes was not necessarily free of the drug was clear from references made in "The Devil's Foot" and "The Creeping Man," although Watson's concerns, at least as expressed in his writings, were substantially reduced.

Holmes's addiction was not a particularly enviable one and naturally received little attention in early films featuring the detective. It was thus shocking to hear Holmes (as played by Basil Rathbone) exclaim to the doctor at the end of *The Hound of the Baskervilles* (1939), "Oh, Watson, the needle!" By far, the most serious examination of the addiction was by Nicholas Meyer in his novel *The Seven-Per-Cent Solution*, and its film version.

COLONNA, PRINCE OF. The owner of the ill-fated Black Pearl of the Borgias in "The Six Napoleons." It was stolen by the maid of the princess of Colonna from the prince's bedroom at the Dacre Hotel.

COMMISSIONAIRES. Members of the Corps of Commissionaires comprised of retired soldiers who worked as messengers and guides. Two notable commissionaires were Tangey in "The Naval Treaty," who was at the Foreign Office, and Peterson in "The Six Napoleons," who found Henry Baker's hat and goose; in the goose was a very remarkable gem. Other commissionaires appear in "The Mazarin Stone" and *A Study in Scarlet*.

COMMONPLACE BOOKS. Holmes kept a mammoth collection of books containing his accumulation of knowledge on a nearly endless number of subjects. So vast was this compilation that the detective created an index for it, although references to the index throughout the Canon often mean the commonplace books themselves. Additionally, in "The Empty House" and "A Scandal in Bohemia," Watson writes of an "index of biographies." It is unclear whether he refers to a separate compilation or to the index itself. Such commonplace books were labor intensive and required extensive updating; hence Watson's observation in "The Five Orange Pips" that "Sherlock Holmes sat moodily at one side of the fireplace cross-indexing his records of crime," and in "The Bruce-Partington Plans" that he had spent time "cross-indexing his huge book of references." Other mentionings were in "The Red Circle" and in "The Musgrave Ritual" concerning his indexing. Holmes consulted his records for a number of cases: *B* for the Baskerville case; *V* for vampires; *S* for Godfrey Staunton; *H* for the duke of Holdernesse, in the "encyclopedia of reference," and *M*, a collection that was "a fine one" for his index of biographies, for Colonel Sebastian Moran. Holmes also looked up the biography of Irene Adler (an entry sandwiched between headings on a Hebrew rabbi and a staff commander who had authored a monograph on deep sea fishes) in "A Scandal in Bohemia." Watson wrote in "The Creeping Man" that Holmes looked upon him as an institution "like the violin, the shag tobacco, the old black pipe, the index books, and others less excusable."

"CONAN DOYLE." A made-for-British-television film (1972), part of the "Edwardians" series, it was shown in America in 1974 as part of the series "Masterpiece Theatre" on Public Television. Cast: Nigel Davenport (Conan Doyle), Alison Leggett (Ma'am), and Sam Dastor (George Edalji). The film focuses not on Sherlock Holmes, but on Sir Arthur Conan Doyle, specifically his efforts to free the young Eurasian Georg Edalji from the charges of maiming animals, for which he was falsely imprisoned in 1907.

CONDUIT STREET. A street in Westminster where the dangerous Colonel Sebastian Moran keeps a residence ("The Empty House").

CONFEDERATE STATES OF AMERICA. The Confederacy, the eleven states in America that seceded from the Union in 1861, figure in two Holmes adventures. The Ku Klux Klan, according to Holmes's *American Encyclopedia*, was created by former Confederate soldiers ("The Five Orange Pips"). In the pastiche novel, *Enter the Lion, A Posthumous Memoir of Mycroft Holmes* (1979), the Confederacy figured prominently.

CONK-SINGLETON FORGERY. Holmes initiated this case following the successful conclusion of "The Six Napoleons." W. S. Baring-Gould, the noted Sherlockian, put the date of the case at early June 1900. It may be argued, however, that Holmes and Watson had been working on the matter prior to the affair of the Six Napoleons as Holmes was able to instruct the good doctor immediately after the recovery of the Black Pearl of the Borgias to get out the papers of the Conk-Singleton forgery case. The writer John Dickson Carr offered his interpretation with the short play, "The Adventure of the Conk-Singleton Papers," first staged in 1948, at the Mystery Writers of America's Annual Edgar Allan Poe Awards Dinner.

CONTINENTAL GAZETTEER. A reference book used by Holmes in "A Scandal in Bohemia" to look up information about Egria, a town in Bohemia.

"COOEE." A call originally used by the Australian aborigines and adopted by some colonists for use as a signal in the bush, it was heard in "The Boscombe Valley Mystery" between James McCarthy and his father, Charles McCarthy.

COOK. A London constable of H Division. While on duty near Waterloo Bridge in "The Five Orange Pips," he found the body of John Openshaw.

COOK'S TOURIST OFFICE (or Thomas Cook). A travel bureau that had booked the journey of Lady Frances Carfax from Lausanne to Basel through its local Lausanne office in "The Disappearance of Lady Frances Carfax." Watson interviewed the manager of the Lausanne branch and learned of the Lady's movements from that city.

COOMBE TRACEY. A town on Dartmoor in Devonshire in *The Hound of the Baskervilles*. During

Holmes and Watson face the rage of Jephro Rucastle in "The Copper Beeches"; by Sidney Paget.

his time on the moor, Holmes received his supplies from there, and Inspector Lestrade's train stopped at Coombe Tracey. Laura Lyon, daughter of Frankland, lived there.

COPERNICAN THEORY.   See ASTRONOMY.

"COPPER BEECHES, THE ADVENTURE OF THE" (COPP).   Published: *Strand*, June 1892; collected in *The Adventures of Sherlock Holmes* (1892). Case date: Various. Major players: Holmes, Watson, Violet Hunter, Jephro Rucastle, Alice Rucastle, Mrs. Rucastle, Mr. Fowler. The case begins with Holmes lamenting that his practice "seems to be degenerating into an agency for recovering lost lead pencils and giving advice to young ladies from boarding schools." It would apparently have reached bottom with a letter from Violet Hunter asking for his advice on whether to accept an offered position as governess. This rather demeaning request introduces Holmes and Watson to

the affair involving Jephro Rucastle, owner of the Copper Beeches, near Winchester, and his weird family. As part of her employment, Miss Hunter must cut her lustrous hair, wear any dress chosen by Rucastle, and listen each day to a set of uproariously funny stories. Holmes, with the help of Watson and Hunter, uncovers the dark secret of the Copper Beeches. Violet Hunter described it as "a large square block of a house, whitewashed, but all stained and streaked with damp and bad weather . . . A clump of copper beeches immediately in front of the hall door has given its name to the place."

COPTIC MONASTERIES.   The *magnum opus* of Professor Coram in "The Golden Pince-Nez" was an analysis of the documents found in the Coptic monasteries of Egypt and Syria. Coram believed that it would "cut deep at the very foundations of revealed religion." The case of the **Coptic Patriarchs** was an unchronicled matter investigated by Holmes and dated to around 1898. At the time the detective began his work on the affair of "The Retired Colourman," Holmes was "preoccupied with this case of the two Coptic Patriarchs." The matter came to a head on the day that Holmes first involved Watson in the Josiah Amberley investigation.

CORAM, PROFESSOR.   An invalid who resided at Yoxley Old Place in Kent in "The Golden Pince-Nez," and a scholar (whose *magnum opus* was an analysis of documents found in the Coptic monasteries of Syria and Egypt). Coram was actually named Sergius and had been a member of the Russian Nihilists (or The Brotherhood), a revolutionist group, together with his wife **Anna**. He betrayed The Brotherhood and allowed her to go to a czarist prison in Siberia. She hunted him down in England and attempted to retrieve documents from his home at Yoxley Old Place in Kent that would prove the innocence of her friend, Alexis, an honorable man wrongly imprisoned through Sergius's testimony. This dark past ultimately caught up with him. Coram spent half his time in bed "and the other half hobbling round the house with a stick or being pushed about the grounds by the gardener in a Bath chair." He was also a chain smoker, consuming 1,000 Alexandrian cigarettes per fortnight. Holmes performed some brilliant deductions and analysis on Anna's gold glasses (pince-nez).

CORNELIUS, MR.   An alias used by Jonas Oldacre to swindle his creditors in "The Norwood Builder." Prior to his apparent death, Oldacre transferred money in large amounts to Mr. Cornelius.

CORNWALL.   Holmes, under medical orders, vacationed in the southwestern region of England with Watson in 1897, becoming embroiled in the horrifying affair of "The Devil's Foot." The failure of the West Country bank of Dawson & Neligan caused the ruin of half the families of Cornwall, impacting upon the case of "Black Peter." John Clay, the industrious criminal in "The Red-Headed League," was said by Inspector Peter Jones of Scotland Yard to crack a crib in Scotland one week and raise money to build an orphanage in Cornwall the next.

CORPORATION STREET.   A street in Birmingham where, at 126B, were situated the temporary offices of the Franco-Midland Hardware Company in "The Stockbroker's Clerk."

CORRESPONDENCE.   Watson wrote that Holmes's unanswered correspondence was customarily "transfixed by a jack-knife into the very centre of his wooden mantelpiece" ("The Musgrave Ritual"). Holmes himself was of the opinion that his "correspondence has certainly the charm of variety . . . and the humbler are usually the more interesting" ("The Noble Bachelor"), but he was understandably careful about opening packages, telling Watson: "My correspondence, however, is, as you know, a varied one, and I am somewhat upon my guard against any packages which reach me" ("The Dying Detective").

COUNTERFEITING.   Holmes encountered this criminal activity several times in the Canon. The most ambitious counterfeiters were the gang of Lysander Stark in "The Engineer's Thumb," said to be coiners on a large scale. In "The Three Garridebs," Killer Evans had been imprisoned for shooting the counterfeiter Rodger Prescott, and worked to acquire Prescott's printing outfit by posing as a Garrideb. Holmes was once able to trace a coiner by the copper and zinc filings in the seam of his trouser cuff in "Shoscombe Old Place." Other cases with mention of counterfeiting include "The Red-Headed League," *The Valley of Fear*, and "The Crooked Man."

COVENT GARDEN.   Also Covent Garden Theatre or Royal Italian Opera House, a theatre in Westminster where Holmes attended musical events. At the conclusion of "The Red Circle," Holmes took Watson there to hear Wagner Night. Covent Garden Market was situated nearby. Here, on a snowy, cold night in 1900, Holmes visited the poultry dealer Breckinridge at Covent Garden Market in the hopes of learning the source of the geese sold to the Alpha Inn in "The Six Napoleons."

COVENTRY.   A city in Warwickshire where Cyril Morton, fiance of Violet Smith, was employed by the Midland Electric Company at the time of "The Solitary Cyclist." John Openshaw, in "The Five Orange Pips," owned a small factory in Coventry.

COVENTRY, SERGEANT.   A constable in Hampshire who was assigned to the investigation into the apparent murder of Maria Gibson, wife of the wealthy J. Neil Gibson, who was found shot on Thor Bridge in "Thor Bridge."

COWPER.   A Mormon living in Salt Lake City in *A Study in Scarlet*, to whom Jefferson Hope had rendered services at different times. He informed Hope that Lucy Ferrier had been forced to marry Enoch Drebber.

COX & CO.   Watson kept a tin dispatch box with his name JOHN H. WATSON, M.D., Late Indian Army, painted on the lid, at this London banking firm in Charing Cross. "It is crammed with papers, nearly all of which are records of cases to illustrate the curious problems which Mr. Sherlock Holmes had at various times to examine" ("Thor Bridge"). Watson mentioned his box also in "The Creeping Man" and "The Veiled Lodger." Cox & Co. was featured in the interesting opening of the film *The Private Life of Sherlock Holmes* (1970) and served as the "source" for the cases presented in *The Exploits of Sherlock Holmes* by Adrian Conan Doyle and John Dickson Carr.

COXON & WOODHOUSE.   The stockbroking firm, of Draper's Gardens, for whom Hall Pycroft had worked as a clerk in "The Stockbroker's Clerk." He was let go after Coxon & Woodhouse "were let in early in the spring through the Venezuelan loan, as no doubt you remember, and came a nasty cropper. I have been with them five years, and old Coxon gave me a ripping good testimonial when the smash came, but of course we clerks were all turned adrift, the twenty-seven of us."

CREAM-LAID PAPER.   A type of writing paper noted for its heaviness, cream color, and ribbed texture. The note received by Aloysius Garcia in "Wisteria Lodge" was on cream-laid paper, as was the note to Mycroft Holmes from J. Davenport in "The Greek Interpreter," although it was on royal cream paper, which meant that the sheet was 19-by-24 inches.

CREDIT LYONNAIS.   Marie Devine cashed a check from the missing Lady Frances Carfax at the Montpelier branch of the famous French bank in "The Disappearance of Lady Frances Carfax." Holmes suspected that Professor Moriarty used the Credit Lyonnais to hold the bulk of his fortune in *The Valley of Fear*, and Count Sylvius denied that he had forged a check on the Credit Lyonnais in "The Mazarin Stone."

"CREEPING MAN, THE ADVENTURE OF THE" (CREE).   Published: *Strand*, March 1923, *Hearst's International*, March 1923; collected in *The Case Book of Sherlock Holmes* (1927). Case date: September 1903. Major players: Holmes, Watson, Professor Presbury, Trevor Bennett, Alice Morphy, Edith Presbury, Dorak, Mercer, and Roy. The case was identified by Watson as one of the last undertaken by Holmes before his retirement in 1903 to the Sussex Downs. One of the most bizarre and poorly written entries in the Canon, the investigation brought Holmes and Watson to the university town of Camford. There, Professor Presbury, eminent physiologist of Camford University, has been behaving very strangely, including pursuing

Professor Presbury behaves rather strangely in "The Creeping Man"; by Howard Elcock.

the young Alice Morphy with relentless ardor. Of particular note is the strained give and take between Holmes and Watson. "The relations between us in those latter days were peculiar. He was a man of habits, and I had become one of them. As an institution, I was like the violin, the shag tobacco, the old black pipe, the index books, and others perhaps less excusable." Watson had been summoned by Holmes with the note, "Come at once if convenient—if inconvenient come all the same. S.H."

CREMONA VIOLINS.   Violins from the city of Cremona, noted for its Stradivarius and Amati fiddles. At the outset of the investigation into the murder of Enoch Drebber in *A Study in Scarlet*, Holmes "was in the best of spirits, and prattled away about Cremona fiddles, and the difference between a Stradivarius and an Amati."

CREOSOTE.   An oily liquid obtained by distilling wood tar and used as a wood preservative and disinfectant. In *The Sign of Four*, with the help of the dog Toby, Holmes and Watson tracked Jonathan Small and Tonga after Tonga stepped in creosote. Toby was able to pick up the scent.

CRIMEAN WAR.   The conflict in which England, France, and Turkey fought Russia from 1853 to 1856. The Hon. Philip Green's father commanded the Sea of Azov fleet during the war ("The Disappearance of Lady Frances Carfax"), and Colonel Emsworth earned the Victoria Cross there ("The Blanched Soldier"). The barque *Gloria Scott* was used to transport convicts to Australia because the usual convict vessels were being used to transport troops to Crimea.

CRITERION BAR.   This restaurant, bar, and theatre in Regent Circus, Piccadilly will forever be remembered as the place where, in *A Study in Scarlet*, Watson, newly returned from the Second Afghan War, met young Stamford, his former dresser at Barts. As Watson was looking for lodgings cheaper than the ones he had in the Strand, Stamford suggested that they go and speak with someone he knew who was desirous of sharing a nice suite of rooms. Stamford introduced Watson to Sherlock Holmes. (See also HOLBORN.)

CROCKFORD'S CLERICAL DIRECTORY. An annual directory that provided a listing of the

clergy belonging to the Church of England. In "The Retired Colourman," Holmes consulted *Crockford's* concerning Vicar J. C. Elman.

CROKER, JACK.   Croker was captain of the vessel *Bass Rock* and onetime first officer on the *Rock of Gibraltar* where he met and fell in love with Mary Fraser in "The Abbey Grange." She returned his love with friendship, and he accepted with honorable equanimity her marriage to Sir Eustace Brackenstall. Upon learning of her miserable life from Mary's maid, Croker visited her at the Abbey Grange. Holmes tested Croker's honor and was impressed that he rang true every time. Watson wrote that Croker "was a very tall young man, golden-moustached, blue-eyed, with a skin which had been burned by tropical suns, and a springy step, which showed that the huge frame was as active as it was strong." Some editions spell his name Crocker.

"CROOKED MAN, THE" (CROO).   Published: *Strand*, July 1893, *Harper's*, July 1893; collected in *The Memoirs of Sherlock Holmes* (1894). Case date: 1888 or 1889. Major players: Holmes, Watson, Nancy Barclay, Colonel James Barclay, Henry Wood, and Teddy. Holmes fetches Watson from his wife and Paddington practice and journeys to Aldershot where Colonel James Barclay, commanding officer of the Royal Munsters, has been found dead in his residence with his wife in an apparent coma beside him. Holmes's investigation of the murder scene determines that there was another person in the room, and a small creature that expressed a culinary interest in a caged canary. Pivotal to the solution to the case is Holmes's interview with Barclay's neighbor, Miss Morrison. Holmes soon finds the "Crooked Man" and hears his tale of love, betrayal, and revenge.

CROSBY.   A banker who met a "terrible death" in 1894 and was associated by Watson with "the repulsive story of the red leech." ("The Golden Pince-Nez.")

CROWDER, WILLIAM.   A gamekeeper in the service of John Turner at his estate in "The Boscombe Valley Mystery." He witnessed Charles McCarthy walk toward Boscombe Pool, followed by his son. McCarthy was later found dead, and his son was arrested for the murder.

CROWN DIAMOND.   Known in full as *The Crown Diamond, An Evening with Sherlock Holmes*, a play written by Sir Arthur Conan Doyle and first performed in Bristol on May 2, 1921, starring Dennis Neilson-Terry (Holmes) and R. V. Taylour (Watson). A one-act play, *The Crown Diamond* has been subject to considerable debate over the years as to its year of creation and the purpose of Conan Doyle in taking to his pen. Sir Arthur's son, Adrian, was of the view that it was written early in this century, after the debut and success of the play *Sherlock Holmes* by William Gillette. Given the presence in the play of Colonel Sebastian Moran, the wax bust, and an air-gun, it was perhaps written before "The Empty House" (1903) but was not published at the time because Conan Doyle desired to use many of its elements in his story marking the return of Sherlock Holmes. Many years would pass before *The Crown Diamond* would see life on the stage. After its debut, it ran for a week in London and then again in London for another week in August. In all, there were a mere twenty-eight performances before the play disappeared and was forgotten. In October, 1921, the ghost of *The Crown Diamond* surfaced in the body of "The Mazarin Stone" in the *Strand Magazine*. The original play was essentially the same, only Moran was replaced by Count Negretto Sylvius, the colonel having already appeared in "The Empty House." The transformation of the play to a short story was a poor one, with the result that Conan Doyle produced an uneven and implausible theatrical work and a major disappointment for the Canon. The connection of *The Crown Diamond* with "The Mazarin Stone" was first uncovered in 1949 by the respected Holmesian Anthony Boucher.

CRUCIFER OF BLOOD.   A very successful stage play written by Paul Giovanni that premiered at the Studio Arena Theatre in Buffalo in January 1978. It soon moved to Broadway, opening at the Helen Hayes Theater in September 1978, starring Paxton Whitehead (Holmes), Timothy Landfield (Watson), Dwight Schultz (Major Alistair Ross), Nicolas Surovy (Captain Neville St. Claire), and Glenn Close (Irene St. Claire). *Crucifer of Blood* was essentially a version of *The Sign of Four*, relying on both the Canon and William Gillette's play *Sherlock Holmes* for inspiration. The plot roughly follows *The Sign of Four*, although Giovanni changed the character, shifted part of the action to a limehouse opium den, and rendered both Holmes and Watson as more realistic figures, although there is a cruel streak to much of the presentation as the detective at times seems both harsh and arbitrary. The play's dark nature, however, made it ideally suited for riveting melodrama and it eventually moved to London. Brilliant actor Keith Michell played Holmes there, while in Los Angeles, at the Ahmanson Theater, Charlton Heston took on the role, opposite Jeremy Brett (Watson) who was to go on to become the great Holmes in the recent British television productions by Granada Television. Heston also starred in a television version of the play for the American cable channel TNT in 1991. The adaptation was remarkable for its sets.

CRYPTOGRAPHY.   The study of codes or secret writings, of which Holmes was a genuine expert, authoring the "trifling" monograph *Secret Writings: Analysis of 160 Separate Ciphers*. His knowledge was both demonstrated and tested in "The Dancing Men" in which he justified his claim that he was "fairly familiar with all forms of secret writings." The writing encountered in this case was the so-called Dancing Men cipher, a type of substitution cipher in which stick figures represented letters of the alphabet.

Abe Slaney, who was familiar with it, described the cipher: "There were seven of us in a gang in Chicago, and Elsie's father was the boss of the Joint. He was a clever man, was old Patrick. It was he who invented that writing, which would pass as a child's scrawl unless you just happened to have the key to it." The Dancing Men code, broken by Holmes, was used to lure the murderer of Hilton Cubitt to his capture. The cipher also reappeared in the film *Sherlock Holmes and the Secret Weapon* (1942), starring Basil Rathbone and Nigel Bruce.

There were several other cryptographic puzzles

The enigmatic Dancing Men code, deciphered by Holmes.

solved by Holmes. In "The 'Gloria Scott'," he was faced with uncovering why a peculiar message caused the death of Trevor Senior: "The supply of game for London is going steadily up. Head keeper Hudson, we believe, has been now told to receive all orders for fly-paper and for preservation of your hen pheasant's life." A little more challenging was the code sent from Porlock, Holmes's agent in the lair of Professor Moriarty in *The Valley of Fear*. It read:

> 534 C2 13 127 36 31 4 17 21 41
> DOUGLAS 109 293 5 37 BIRLSTONE
> 26 BIRLSTONE 9 47 171

Solving the message depended upon finding the correct book from which the code source was used. Holmes and Watson eventually chose *Whitaker's Almanack*. The detective also intercepted and translated the alarming message to the mysterious lodger of the Warrens in "The Red Circle": *"ATTENTA! PERICOLO!"*—"Beware! Danger!" Holmes also enjoyed reading the crude ciphers found in the agony columns of newspapers (*The Valley of Fear*.) In the 1946 film *Dressed to Kill*, Holmes (Rathbone) had to solve an intriguing code based on the notes of music played by several music boxes.

CUBITT, HILTON. A Norfolk squire who lived at Ridling Thorpe Manor and who involved Holmes in the affair of "The Dancing Men." Cubitt was "a tall, ruddy, clean shaven gentleman, whose clear eyes and florid cheeks told of a life led far from the fogs of Baker Street." While not a rich man, his family had been at Ridling Thorpe for five centuries. He journeyed to London for the Jubilee (1887 or 1897) and there met Elsie Patrick, falling in love and marrying her despite her admission of previously "disagreeable associations." Their union was happy until June the following year when a letter arrived from America for Elsie. From that time, his wife had been behaving very strangely. Cubitt turned to Holmes for advice, but was murdered within a day of the consultation.

CUBITT, ELSIE. The former Elsie Patrick of Chicago, wife of Hilton Cubitt whom she married in "The Dancing Men" shortly after the Jubilee in 1887 or 1897. She gave Hilton every opportunity to withdraw from the marriage, citing her past "disagreeable associations," but he loved her enough to

agree to her request never to discuss her previous life in America. Their marriage was happy until she received a letter from America and later began finding the curious stick figures, the Dancing Men, around the outside of the house. A short time later, her husband was killed and she, in grief, tried to kill herself. (See CRYPTOGRAPHY.)

CULLIN, ARTHUR. Also spelled Cullen, an American actor who twice played Dr. Watson, in *The Valley of Fear* (1914) with H. A. Saintbury as Holmes, and *The Sign of Four* (1923), with Eille Norwood as Holmes. He replaced Hubert Willis as Watson in *The Sign of Four* because he looked much younger and would be more believable while romancing Mary Morstan (Isobel Elsom, wife of director Murice Elvey). Cullin also had a part in the 1923 film *Fires of Fate*, based on the novel by Sir Arthur Conan Doyle.

CUMMINGS, JOYCE. A barrister hired to defend Grace Dunbar, governess of the children of J. Neil Gibson in "Thor Bridge." She had been arrested for the apparent murder of Gibson's wife Maria on Thor Bridge.

CUNNINGHAM. A squire in Surrey, one of "The Reigate Squires" whose coachman, William Kirwin, was killed in the "robbery" of Cunningham's house. **Alec Cunningham**, his son, was closely involved in father's affairs and nearly succeeded in murdering Holmes. The elder Cunningham was an "elderly man, with a strong, deep-lined, heavy-eyed face," while Alec was a "dashing young fellow, whose bright, smiling expression and showy dress were in strange contrast with the business which had brought us there."

CUSACK, CATHERINE. The maid to the Countess Morcar at the time the Blue Carbuncle was stolen from the countess's dressing room at the Hotel Cosmopolitan in "The Blue Carbuncle."

CUSHING, PETER. The London born actor (b. 1913) best known for his long career in horror movies, particularly for Hammer Films of England, who produced such hits as *Curse of Frankenstein* (1957) and *Horror of Dracula* (1958). Cushing has also played Holmes on screen and television. Despite his short stature, shorter at least than the very tall Holmes, Cushing proved himself a very able Sherlock throughout the years, basing his

Peter Cushing, one of the finest of all screen Sherlocks, from *The Hound of the Baskervilles.* (1959)

a television series (1968) with Nigel Stock and in the British television film "Masks of Death" (1984) with John Mills.

CUSHING, SARAH.   The younger sister of Susan Cushing in "The Cardboard Box." After the marriage of her other sister Mary, she went to live with Mary and her husband, James Browner, in Liverpool. This arrangement proved disastrous and Sarah departed and moved in with Susan for a time before settling in New Street, Wallington. Immediately after Susan received the cardboard box containing two severed human ears, Sarah took to her bed with a brain fever.

CUSHING, SUSAN.   A maiden living in Cross Street, Croydon, the eldest of the three sisters who figured in "The Cardboard Box." Susan received in the mail a cardboard box containing two severed human ears, an event so uncommon and grotesque that Lestrade called in Sherlock Holmes. The *Daily Chronicle* wrote: "There is no indication as to the sender, and the matter is the more mysterious as Miss Cushing, who is a maiden lady of fifty, has led a most retired life, and has so few acquaintances or correspondents that it is a rare event for her to receive anything in the post."

CYANEA CAPILLATA.   A type of common jellyfish found in the Atlantic, known by the name "Lion's Mane" because of its shape and color. A *Cyanea capillata* figured in the story "The Lion's Mane." Holmes consulted the work *Out of Doors* by J. G. Wood for information on the creature.

appearance as closely as possible on the original Paget drawings in the *Strand.* His Holmes was always slightly manic, bubbling with suppressed energy just waiting to be released like a pent-up geyser. This interpretation played out well opposite Andre Morell in his first Holmesian outing, *The Hound of the Baskervilles* (1959). He later starred in

D'ALBERT, COUNTESS. A noblewoman whose name was used by the assassin of Charles Augustus Milverton to gain an appointment with the blackmailer in "Charles Augustus Milverton." The killer posed as a servant of the Countess D'Albert who was willing to sell compromising letters about her mistress.

DAMERY, SIR JAMES. The representative of "The Illustrious Client" who enlisted the aid of the great detective over the affair of Baron Adalbert Gruner. Colonel Sir James Damery was well known for his meticulous care in dress and his "bluff, honest personality." Holmes said of him, "He has rather a reputation for arranging delicate matters which are to be kept out of the papers." He was instrumental in negotiating the solution to the Hammerford Will case with Sir George Lewis. In this case, he was anxious that the impending marriage of Baron Gruner to Violet De Merville be terminated. Damery was a member of the Carlton Club and could be reached in emergencies at the number XX.31.

"DANCING MEN, THE ADVENTURE OF THE" (DANC). Published: *Collier's, Strand,* December 1903; collected in *The Return of Sherlock Holmes* (1905). Case date: 1898. Major players: Holmes, Watson, Hilton Cubitt, Elsie Cubitt, Abe Slaney. The case poses Holmes with a challenging code, the Dancing Men cipher. It is brought to him by Hilton Cubitt of Ridling Thorpe Manor in Norfolk. His American wife, Elsie, has been made extremely agitated by the sudden appearance of the Dancing Men, scrawled on various locations and also placed on paper. Heightening the sense of mystery is the fact that she refuses ever to speak about her American past, a history of which she is

obviously ashamed. The matter for Holmes soon escalates from an intriguing puzzle to a murder investigation as Hilton is shot dead and his wife, the obvious suspect, has turned the gun on herself. Sir Arthur Conan Doyle thought very highly of this case, ranking it number three on his list of favorite cases. The readers of the *Baker Street Journal* in 1959 ranked it number nine on their list. The cipher was, according to Conan Doyle, based on a child's scribble, although the influence of Edgar Allan Poe's story "The Gold Bug" is apparent. See also CRYPTOGRAPHY.

DANIELL, HENRY. Gifted British actor best known in Sherlockian film circles for his performance as Professor Moriarty in *The Woman in Green* (1945). Daniell first appeared in a Holmes film in the Universal release *Sherlock Holmes and the Voice of Terror* (1942), playing a small role as Sir Alfred Lloyd. He played another minor character, William Easter, in *Sherlock Holmes in Washington* (1943). Finally, in 1945, he was given the coveted role of Professor Moriarty in *The Woman in Green*, opposite Basil Rathbone and Nigel Bruce as Holmes and Watson, and Hillary Brook as the title character. Daniell's work as the professor earned him a justifiable place as one of the great all-time professors. Rathbone considered him the best of all Moriartys, saying in his autobiography that there were other Moriartys, "but none so delectably dangerous."

DANITE BAND. (Also, Danites, The Sons of Dan, and The Avenging Angels) A secret society that was first organized among the Mormons in 1838 by Dr. Samson Avard. The Danite Band was intended to root out enemies of Mormonism and to punish those Mormons who swayed from doctrine, although it was quickly suppressed by Joseph Smith and never operated in Utah. The society was featured in *A Study in Scarlet* where it was said: "To this day, in the lonely reaches of the West, the name of the Danite Band, or the Avenging Angels, is a sinister and ill-omened one."

DARBYSHIRE, WILLIAM.   A name used by John Straker, the trainer at the stables of Colonel Ross in "Silver Blaze." As Darbyshire (some editions spell it Derbyshire), he kept a mistress and acquired enormous debts. (See also LESURIER, MADAME.)

DARLINGTON SUBSTITUTION SCANDAL.   One of Holmes's unchronicled cases, perhaps in the town of Darlington, in the county of Durham. The case was solved by Holmes using a false alarm of fire ("A Scandal in Bohemia").

DARTMOOR.   A region of high moorland in southwestern Devon. The affairs of "Silver Blaze" and *The Hound of the Baskervilles* took place there.

DARWIN, CHARLES.   Holmes referred to the famous English naturalist (1809–1882) in remembering an afternoon spent listening to the music of Norman-Neruda at Halle's in *A Study in Scarlet*: "Do you remember [Watson] what Darwin says about music? He claims that the power of producing and appreciating it existed among the human race long before the power of speech was arrived at. Perhaps that is why we are so subtly influenced by it. There are vague memories in our souls of those misty centuries when the world was in its childhood." The *Daily Telegraph* mentioned Darwin in its editorial on the murder of Enoch Drebber in *A Study in Scarlet*.

DATING OF DOCUMENTS.   Also *On the Dating of Documents*, a monograph written by Holmes sometime before the case recounted in *The Hound of the Baskervilles* (possible dates for the book given by experts include before 1886 or before 1889). The work apparently had a wide distribution, at least in the scientific community, as the detective asked Dr. Mortimer if he had read it. Holmes's knowledge on the subject allowed him to date the old manuscript that Mortimer brought to him to 1730. The actual date was 1742. As with other writings by Holmes, this monograph has proven extremely difficult to find.

DAUBENSEE.   A small lake near the summit of the Gemmi Pass in Switzerland. In "The Final Problem," as Watson and Holmes passed along the shore of Daubensee, "A large rock which had been dislodged from the ridge upon our right clattered down and roared into the lake behind us." This was an apparent attempt on their lives by the forces of Professor Moriarty.

DAVENPORT, J.   An acquaintance of Sophy Kratides in "The Greek Interpreter," who responded to Mycroft Holmes's advertisements in the *Daily News* concerning Paul and Sophy Kratides. (See also CREAM-LAID PAPER.)

DAWSON.   The manager of Abel White's indigo plantation in India in *The Sign of Four*. He and his wife were killed at the start of the Sepoy Rebellion (or Indian mutiny) in 1857. Dawson was also the name of a groom in the service of Lord Backwater at Capleton Stables, in Dartmoor in "Silver Blaze."

DECAMERON.   In *A Study in Scarlet*, a pocket edition of the book, a collection of ribald tales authored by the fourteenth-century Italian novelist Giovanni Boccaccio, with the name Joseph Stangerson on the flyleaf, was found in the pocket of the murdered Enoch J. Drebber.

DE CROY, PHILIPPE.   A seventeenth-century printer who published the work *De Jure inter Gentes* (*On the Law of Nations*). While waiting for the murderer of Enoch Drebber in *A Study in Scarlet*, Holmes read the "queer old book." He had purchased it at a stall the day before. The detective professed to knowing nothing about Philippe de Croy. Its previous owner was Guliolmi Whyte (or William White).

DEEP DENE HOUSE.   The residence of Jonas Oldacre, situated, according to the *Daily Telegraph*, "at the Sydenham end of the road of that name" in "The Norwood Builder." Holmes told Watson that it was "a big modern villa of staring brick, standing back in its own grounds, with a laurel-clumped lawn in front of it."

DEERSTALKER AND CAPE.   More properly, a close-fitting ear-flapped travelling cap and "long-grey travelling cloak" (or Inverness), two of the

Deerstalker, cape, and pipe: John Neville wears the world-famous garb of Holmes, from *A Study in Terror* (1965).

most familiar items in the required habilement of the Sherlock Holmes of the imagination. The majority of readers and fans of the detective would immediately identify him by his cap and cape, so much so that no caricature, no reference would be complete without some mention or depiction of the deerstalker and cape. In the Canon, it was customary for Holmes to adopt this attire only for cases that took him to the country. Watson, however, did not specifically write about a deerstalker, describing instead "his long gray travelling-cloak and close-fitting cloth cap" in "The Boscombe Valley Mystery." Credit for the deerstalker-Holmes association goes to the artist Sidney Paget who, for his illustrations of the story, drew the detective in a deerstalker. It was used again in the drawings for subsequent stories such as "Silver Blaze," "The Priory School," and "The Final Problem." Frederic Dorr Steele, the illustrator of cases appearing in the American magazine *Collier's*, adopted the clothing, although he seemed to prefer the cap alone, drawing the detective wearing it with some tasteful and well-fitting suits. The deerstalker and cape worked well in film, setting Holmes instantly apart from those around him and making his arrival on the scene—with pipe between his lips and Watson dutifully following behind—all the more dramatic.

DE MERVILLE, GENERAL. The famous soldier "of Khyber fame" and father of Violet De Merville in "The Illustrious Client" who resided at 104 Berkeley Square. He strongly opposed her intended marriage to Baron Gruner, but he could not sway his daughter in any way. As a result, the general was a broken man. Colonel Sir James Damery added: "The strong soldier has been utterly demoralized by this incident. He has lost the nerve which never failed him on the battlefield and has become a weak, doddering old man, utterly incapable of contending with a brilliant forceful rascal like this Austrian."

DE MERVILLE, VIOLET. The daughter of General De Merville who became engaged to Baron Gruner despite the strenuous objections of her father in "The Illustrious Client." She was completely under the control of the awful Austrian baron, accepting his explanations of his dark, murderous past. So devout was her fidelity that she resisted both the words of Holmes (who had been brought into the case by Colonel Sir James Damery) and the spirited Kitty Winter (who had been ruined by the baron). She was finally convinced of his true nature by reading his "lust diary." Holmes described her as "beautiful, but with the ethereal other-worldly beauty of some fanatic whose thoughts are set on high. I have seen such faces in the pictures of the old masters in the Middle Ages."

DEMON DEVICE, THE. This 1979 pastiche novel by Robert Saffron was written supposedly by Sir Arthur Conan Doyle, as transmitted to Saffron from beyond the grave. The story centers on Doyle's efforts on behalf of the British government to locate and destroy some secret weapon being developed by the Germans. The tale is different from most in that Saffron is given the account by Conan Doyle from the nether world.

DENNIS, SALLY. The name used by the equally false Mrs. Sawyer in *A Study in Scarlet*. After Holmes had advertised the discovery of the ring in the road between the White Hart Tavern and Holland Grove, Mrs. Sawyer insisted that the ring belonged to her daughter Sally Dennis, who had wed Tom Dennis, supposedly a steward aboard a Union ship. Mrs. Sawyer was actually a cleverly disguised man and the Dennis family did not exist.

DE RESZKE, JEAN AND EDOUARD. Edouard was the more famous of the two well-known nineteenth-century opera singers, performing with the Metropolitan Opera in New York. At the conclusion of *The Hound of the Baskervilles*, Holmes asked Watson if he had heard of the De Reszkes, inviting him to hear them in *Les Huguenots*.

"Devil's Foot, The Adventure of the" (DEVI).

Published: *Strand*, December 1910, *Strand* (U.S.), February 1911; collected in *His Last Bow* (1917). Case date: March 1897. Major players: Holmes, Watson, Leon Sterndale, Mortimer Tregennis, Vicar Roundhay. One of the most horrifying of cases, "The Devil's Foot" was ranked ninth on Conan Doyle's list of favorite stories and was included in the collection *Sherlock Through Time and Space*. Known also as the Cornish Horror, this lurid affair takes place while Holmes is on enforced vacation. Watson writes that it was "in the spring of the year 1897 that Holmes' iron constitution showed some symptoms of giving way in the face of constant hard work of a most exacting kind, aggravated, perhaps, by occasional indiscretions of his own." Watson takes Holmes to a small

Holmes and Watson have barely escaped death by "The Devil's Foot," (*Radix pedis diaboli*); by Gilbert Haliday.

cottage near Poldhu Bay, on the Cornish coast. While there, they become involved in the terrible events surrounding the Tregennis family. In his effort to prove the method of murder, Holmes nearly kills himself and Watson, displaying afterward a rare outburst of friendship and emotion. As occurred in other cases, Holmes allows one of the murderers in the case to escape justice (see also "The Abbey Grange" and "The Blue Carbuncle" for other examples). In an interesting moment, the detective tells one of the suspects, " 'I followed you.' 'I saw no one.' 'That is what you may expect to see when I follow you.' "

Devine. This nineteenth-century French sculptor created the bust of Napoleon from which casts were made by the Stepney sculptor-works of Gelder & Co. Casts of the bust were being destroyed all over London in the case recounted in "The Six Napoleons."

Devine, Marie. The maid of Lady Frances Carfax in "The Disappearance of Lady Frances Carfax." Devine lived in Montpelier. Watson journeyed there to interview her about the disappearance of Lady Frances. Her address was 11 Rue de Trajan. She was engaged to one of the head waiters at the Hotel National at Lausanne.

Devon County Chronicle. A paper in the West Country in which appeared an account of the death of Sir Charles Baskerville in *The Hound of the Baskervilles*.

Devonshire. Dartmoor, situated in southern Devonshire, a county in southwest England, with agricultural land and cattle, was the site of the events recounted in *The Hound of the Baskervilles* and "Silver Blaze."

Diamond. The jewel was found in abundance in the Agra Treasure in *The Sign of Four*. There were 143 diamonds in the Agra Treasure, including the Great Mogul, said to have weighed 280 carats. The Mazarin Stone, which Holmes recovered in "The Mazarin Stone," was a great yellow diamond named after Cardinal Jules Mazarin (1602–1661). Lady Frances Carfax inherited "some very remarkable old Spanish jewellery" of silver and curiously cut diamonds to which she was fondly attached and for which she was abducted and nearly murdered in "The Disappearance of Lady Frances Carfax." Violet Smith was offered diamonds if she would marry Jack Woodley in "The Solitary Cyclist." The eponymous blackmailer in "Charles Augustus Milverton" lamented that a woman should have her marriage destroyed because she would not turn her diamonds to paste.

DIOGENES CLUB.   A London club situated in Pall Mall to which Mycroft Holmes belonged and of which he was a founding member. Watson was given considerable detail about this very unusual club by Holmes on the way to meet Mycroft in "The Greek Interpreter." "There are many men in London, you know, who, some from shyness, some from misanthropy, have no wish for the company of their fellows. Yet they are not averse to comfortable chairs and the latest periodicals. It is for the convenience of these that the Diogenes Club was started, and it now contains the most unsociable and unclubable men in town. No member is permitted to take the least notice of any other one. Save in the Stranger's Room, no talking is, under any circumstances, allowed, and three offences, if brought to the notice of the committee, render the talker liable to expulsion. My brother was one of the founders, and I have myself found it a very soothing atmosphere." The club also figured in "The Bruce-Partington Plans." The Diogenes Club has long been a source for speculation and study by Sherlockians and has been considered a possible cover for espionage or secret activities by the British government. This theory was presented in *The Private Life of Sherlock Holmes* (1970) with Robert Stephens (Holmes) and Christopher Lee (Mycroft). The club, according to Holmes, was obviously involved in secret work from the Himalayas to Loch Ness. The Diogenes also appeared in *The Seven-Per-Cent Solution*, the novel by Nicholas Meyer and its film adaptation.

"DISAPPEARANCE OF LADY FRANCES CARFAX, THE" (LADY).   Published: *Strand*, December 1911; collected in *His Last Bow* (1917). Case date: Various (1894–1903). Major players: Holmes, Watson, Lady Frances Carfax, Philip Green, Dr. Shlessinger, Mrs. Shlessinger. A case that nearly ends in disaster for Holmes and death for Lady Frances, the woman for whom he is searching desperately, "The Disappearance" features Watson in a very prominent role. He is sent to

Switzerland by Holmes in search of the missing Carfax as the detective is too busy to go himself. This naturally leads to events similar to those in *The Hound of the Baskervilles* in which Holmes secretly shadows the good doctor, saves him from an embarrassing confrontation with a rough Englishman, and then declares to him, "I cannot at the moment recall any possible blunder which you have omitted." Holmes is definitely challenged by the disappearance, realizing the solution barely in time. Notable from the affair was the appearance of the con man, thief, and would-be murderer Holy Peters, with his odious accomplice Annie Fraser.

DISTRICT MESSENGER SERVICE CO.
This messenger service, operating in London, was used by Holmes throughout his career, calling it by the various names of "express office" (*The Hound*

Holmes rushes to Watson's aide in "The Disappearance of Lady Frances Carfax"; by Alec Ball.

Disguises of Sherlock Holmes

Holmes possessed a genuine talent for disappearing into various disguises while engaged on cases. His disguises permitted him to pursue criminals and also to search for information that was beyond the reach of any policemen or investigators. It is believed that he used five safehouses around London where he most likely kept various changes of clothing and character to be used in emergencies or when circumstances warranted.

"It was not merely that Holmes changed his costume. His expression, his manner, his very soul seemed to vary with every fresh part that he assumed. The stage lost a fine actor, even as science lost an acute reasoner, when he became a specialist in crime."

—Dr. Watson
"A Scandal in Bohemia."

Disguise	Case	Disguise	Case
Common loafer	"The Beryl Coronet"	Old woman	"The Mazarin Stone"
Captain Basil	"Black Peter"	Drunken-looking groom	"A Scandal in Bohemia"
Escott, a plumber	"Charles Augustus Milverton"	Nonconformist clergyman	"A Scandal in Bohemia"
Elderly, deformed bookseller	"The Empty House"	Sailor	*The Sign of Four*
Italian priest	"The Final Problem"	Asthmatic old master mariner	*The Sign of Four*
French *ouvrier*	"The Disappearance of Lady Carfax"	Opium smoker	"The Man With the Twisted Lip"
Altamont, an Irish-American spy	"His Last Bow"		
Old sporting man	"The Mazarin Stone"		

(See also BROOK, CLIVE; LONDON; NORWOOD, EILLE; and SAWYER, MRS.)

of the *Baskervilles*) and "express messenger" ("The Six Napoleons"). Holmes had a generally high opinion of the service, declaring during the affair of "The Six Napoleons" that nothing less than attempted murder would hold the London messenger-boy from keeping on his way. Holmes employed the young messenger Cartwright during his investigation into *The Hound* and had saved Cartwright's employer Mr. Wilson, manager of the district office.

DIXIE, STEVE.   A black prizefighter, called Black Steve by Holmes in "The Three Gables," Dixie was hired by the adventuress Isadora Klein to intimidate Holmes. The detective was unimpressed, turning the tables quickly after Dixie burst threateningly into 221B. The figure of Dixie has been criticized by some readers as poorly drawn and highly jingoistic, proof that Holmes could not have participated in the case, or that Watson could not have written it.

DIXON, JEREMY.   A resident of Trinity College, Cambridge University and owner of the formidable tracker dog Pompey in "The Missing Three-Quarter." Holmes used Pompey in his efforts to locate the missing Godfrey Staunton.

DIXON, MRS.   The housekeeper in the employ of Bob Carruthers at Chiltern Grange in "The Solitary Cyclist."

Sherlock Holmes (played here by Jeremy Brett) assumes the disguise of a plumber in a recent production of "The Master Blackmailer." (Photo courtesy of MYSTERY!/WGBH Boston.)

DOBNEY, SUSAN.   The old governess of Lady Frances Carfax, long retired and living in Camberwell, who involved Holmes in the search for her onetime charge in "The Disappearance of Lady Frances Carfax." Carfax was in the habit of writing Miss Dobney every second week and nearly five weeks had passed when she finally consulted Holmes about not hearing from her. The Hon. Philip Green knew her, calling her "Old Susan Dobney with the mad cap!"

DOCTOR JEKYL AND MR. HOLMES. Novel by Loren D. Estleman, the author of the pastiche *Sherlock Holmes vs. Dracula, or the Adventure of the Sanguinary Count* (1978). According to this tale, Holmes not only manages to solve the famous affair of Dr. Jekyl and Mr. Hyde, but actually brings it to an end by shooting Jekyl dead. The detective then assists Robert Louis Stevenson in the writing of his story, only Holmes receives no credit—supposedly at his own insistence.

"DOCTOR WATSON AND THE DARK-WATER HALL MYSTERY."   A 1974 BBC Television film, starring Edward Fox as Watson, written by Kingsley Amis and directed by James Cellan Jones. Distinguished by a spirited performance by Fox, this mystery focuses only on Watson, while Holmes is away on a rest cure. In his absence, the physician journeys to a manor house in the Cotswolds to conduct his own investigation into a murder. The most notable characterization in the production is its presentation of Watson as the womanizer he claimed to be in *The Sign of Four*. Watson here wastes little time, bedding a maid in the house on the first night of his visit.

DODD, JAMES.   The title character in "The Blanched Soldier," Dodd asks for Holmes's help in finding his "closest pal," Godfrey Emsworth. Dodd had recently returned from South Africa where he had served in the Boer War in the Imperial Yeomanry, Middlesex Corps, and was, at the time he consulted Holmes, working as a stockbroker in

Throgmorton Street. Emsworth was Dodd's closest friend in South Africa, so Dodd was surprised when he did not hear from Emsworth for six months, and was rebuffed brusquely when he visited Tuxbury Old Park and searched the estate for him.

DOG-CART. A type of cart, so named for the box beneath the rear seat once used to carry dogs. Holmes was often able to deduce that a person had travelled by dog-cart by the splashes of mud that could be seen on their clothing, usually on one side where they had been sitting. Dog-carts were used by Helen Stoner ("The Speckled Band"), White Mason (*The Valley of Fear*), and Inspector Martin ("The Dancing Men"). A dog-cart was owned by Jephro Rucastle ("The Copper Beeches"), Bob Carruthers ("The Solitary Cyclist"), Neville St. Clair ("The Man With the Twisted Lip"), Reuben Hays ("The Priory School"), the Trevors ("The 'Gloria Scott'"), Vicar Roundhay ("The Devil's Foot"), and Dr. Mortimer (*The Hound of the Baskervilles*).

DOGS OF THE CANON. A number of memorable dogs appear in the Canon serving both as weapons of justice and of crime. The most notable canine in all of Watson's writings was the Hound of the Baskervilles, supposedly a hound from hell that cursed the Baskerville family of Dartmoor. Other dogs were:

DOG (BREED)	CASE
Carlo (Mastiff)	"The Copper Beeches"
Carlo (Spaniel)	"The Sussex Vampire"
Chester Wilcox's Dogs (Bloodhound)	*The Valley of Fear*
Fitzroy McPherson's Dog (Airedale)	"The Lion's Mane"
Mrs. Hudson's Dog (Terrier)	*A Study in Scarlet*
Pompey (Part Foxhound, part Beagle)	"The Missing Third-Quarter"
Roy (Wolfhound)	"The Creeping Man"
Toby (Part Spaniel, part Lurcher)	*The Sign of Four*
Watson's Dog (Bull-pup)	*A Study in Scarlet*

DOLORES. The maid and longtime companion of Mrs. Ferguson in "The Sussex Vampire," Dolores was more like "a friend rather than a servant," having been with Mrs. Ferguson from before her marriage to Robert Ferguson.

DOLSKY. A victim of poison in Odessa. In *A Study in Scarlet*, Holmes pointed to the cases of Dolsky in Odessa and Leturier in Montpellier for examples of the "forcible administration of poison."

DONNITHORPE. In "The 'Gloria Scott'," Trevor Senior owned an estate here, a hamlet to the north of Langmere, in Norfolk, and it was the site of Holmes's first case.

DORAK. The London agent for Lowenstein of Prague who represented him to two clients in England in "The Creeping Man." A. Dorak maintained a general store in London.

DORAN, ALOYSIUS. A San Francisco millionaire, father of HATTY DORAN in "The Noble Bachelor," Doran had made his fortune as a prospector in the Rockies. His daughter married Lord St. Simon, and the party at the wedding was to return to the furnished house at Lancaster Gate that had been taken by Doran. Lord St. Simon said that Doran was "the richest man on the Pacific slope," adding, "He had nothing a few years ago. Then he struck gold, invested it, and came up by leaps and bounds."

DORAN, HATTY. The only daughter of Aloysius Doran, Esq., the millionaire of San Francisco in "The Noble Bachelor." Hatty wed Lord St. Simon, bringing with her a dowry said to be considerably over six figures, with expectations for the future. At her wedding breakfast, she disappeared mysteriously, much to the surprise of her husband. He thus consulted Holmes in the hopes that the detective might find her. Lord St. Simon said of her: "my wife was twenty before her father became a rich man. During that time she ran free in a mining camp and wandered through woods or mountains, so that her education has come from Nature rather than the schoolmaster. She is what we call in England a tomboy, with a strong nature, wild and free, unfettered by any sort of traditions. She is impetuous—volcanic, I was about to say. She is swift in making up her mind and fearless in carrying out her resolutions."

DORKING, COLONEL. One of the many victims of the eponymous blackmailer in "Charles Augustus Milverton." Dorking was to wed the Honourable Miss Miles, but the marriage was called off two days before it was to take place because of Milverton's evil intervention: "It was almost incredible, but the absurd sum of twelve hundred pounds would have settled the whole question."

"DO WE PROGRESS."   An article authored by Dr. Mortimer for the *Journal of Psychology* in *The Hound of the Baskervilles*.

DOWNING.   A member of the Surrey constabulary who was injured while capturing the mulatto in "Wisteria Lodge." Downing was badly bitten around the thumb in the struggle.

DOWSON, BARON.   A criminal who had been brought to justice by Holmes. In "The Mazarin Stone," the detective informed Count Negretto Sylvius that "old Baron Dowson said the night before he was hanged that in my case the law had gained what the stage had lost."

DRACULA.   Bram Stoker's famous and influential vampire first appeared in the 1897 novel *Dracula*. In the Canon, the closest that Holmes ever came to encountering the count was in "The Sussex Vampire," but he never had the opportunity to match wits with the King Vampire. It was, of course, inevitable that writers should bring the two titans together. Fred Saberhagen was the first, with his novel *The Holmes-Dracula File* (1975) in which it was proposed that Dracula was the detective's uncle, an idea no doubt abhorrent to devotees. A more conventional confrontation was offered by Loren D. Estleman in his *Sherlock Holmes vs. Dracula, or the Case of the Sanguinary Count* (1978), written as one of Watson's unpublished accounts. Other meetings of the two were staged in the novel *The Probability Pad* by T. A. Waters and *A Night in the Lonesome October* by Roger Zelazny (1993). In the 1970s, it was hoped that Hammer Films was in production with a Holmes-Dracula film, but the work proved only a rumor. It has also been proposed that Professor Moriarty may have been Dracula.

DRAGHOUND.   A dog that has been trained to follow an artificial scent. Holmes used draghounds several times. Pompey, "the pride of the local draghounds," helped track the missing Godfrey Staunton in "The Missing Three-Quarter," and Toby followed Jonathan Small and Tonga, although the creosote used for the scent did lead him astray in *The Sign of Four*. Toby reappeared in the pastiche novel, *The Seven-Per-Cent Solution* by Nicholas Meyer, pursuing Professor Moriarty all the way to Vienna.

DREBBER, ENOCH J.   The son of one of the four principal elders of the Mormon Church at Salt Lake City, Utah in *A Study in Scarlet*. He was "a bull-necked youth with coarse, bloated features" and was given control of his father's mills. Meeting Lucy Ferrier, Drebber competed with Joseph Stangerson for her attentions. He eventually forced her to marry him despite his having played a leading part in the persecution and murder of her father. Lucy soon died, and Drebber, with Joseph Stangerson as his secretary, fled from Utah before the wrath of Jefferson Hope, who loved Lucy utterly and who swore vengeance upon them. His flight eventually took him to England. There, in London, his body was found in the house at 3 Lauriston Gardens, the word RACHE scrawled in blood upon the wall. In the years since his time in Utah, Drebber's moral character had not improved, as Mme. Charpentier, the owner of a boardinghouse in which he stayed, would attest to: "He was coarse in his habits and brutish in his ways."

DRESSED TO KILL.   U.S. 1946. Dir: Roy William Neill. Cast: Basil Rathbone (Holmes), Nigel Bruce (Watson), Patricia Morison (Hilda Courtney), Mary Gordon (Mrs. Hudson), and Carl Harbord (Inspector Hopkins). Known in England as *Sherlock Holmes and the Secret Code*, this was the fourteenth and final film to star Rathbone and Bruce, and one that made a conscious effort to identify with the Canon. Thus, Watson is seen early on reading an issue of *Strand Magazine* containing "A Scandal in Bohemia," described by Holmes as one of the good doctor's "slightly lurid stories." Holmes is also very Holmesian, performing some excellent deductions and laboring relentlessly to crack a musical code. The puzzle is presented in three music boxes made by an imprisoned thief who is trying to communicate the whereabouts of stolen plates used in the engraving of five pound notes. The counterfeiters, searching and murdering for the boxes, are led by the fiendishly clever Hilda Courtney. She proves a talented opponent for Holmes, one of several deadly females he encountered at Universal (in *Sherlock Holmes and the Spider Woman*, 1944; *The Pearl of Death*,

1944; and *The Woman in Green*, 1945). Courtney uses a smoke bomb (as in "A Scandal in Bohemia") to fool Watson into revealing the location of one of the music boxes, wears the disguise of a charwoman to fool Holmes, and lures the detective into a trap by leaving behind a cigarette butt, knowing Holmes's familiarity with tobacco will lead him right to her and his death by gas in a garage. Holmes escapes, naturally, and at the end he gives credit to Watson for solving the case—the doctor had provided the vital clue—and the faithful Watson assures everyone that "I don't think I could have done it entirely without Mr. Holmes's help, you know." This was a charming farewell for the two actors who remain the most popular duo of all time.

DRESSING GOWN.   Holmes enjoyed wearing a lounging robe while at 221B, whether performing chemical researches, sitting pondering a case while enshrouded in pipe smoke, or looking up a criminal in his index of biographies. Based on references made in the Canon, it has been estimated by scholars that Holmes owned at least three dressing gowns: a purple one ("The Blue Carbuncle"), a blue one ("The Man With the Twisted Lip"), and a mouse-colored one that was mentioned twice ("The Bruce-Partington Plans" and "The Empty House"). The mouse-colored garment was draped around the wax figure of Holmes used as a decoy for the assassin in "The Empty House" and was put on shortly after the detective returned to his lodgings following the arrest of the deadly sniper. Some scholars have used the changing color of the gown to point to the possible effects of the alcoholic tendencies of Dr. Watson in his accountings. Other references to the dressing gown were made in "The Beryl Coronet," "The Cardboard Box," "The Engineer's Thumb," "The Final Problem," *The Hound of the Baskervilles*, "The Disappearance of Lady Frances Carfax," "The Mazarin Stone," "The Resident Patient," and *The Valley of Fear*. The solution to the case of "The Reigate Squires" was found by Holmes in the dressing gown of Alec Cunningham.

DUBUQUE, MONSIEUR.   A member of the Paris police who, with the criminal specialist Fritz Von Waldbaum, conducted an interview with Holmes concerning the true facts in the case of "The Second Stain." Watson retained an almost verbatim report of the meeting ("The Naval Treaty"). In some editions, his name appears as Dubugue.

DUNBAR, GRACE.   The governess to the children of J. Neil Gibson in "Thor Bridge," Dunbar was the immediate suspect when Mrs. Maria Gibson was found murdered upon the Thor Bridge. The governess was arrested for the killing, especially after the apparent murder weapon was found on the floor of Dunbar's wardrobe. Gibson attempted to hire Holmes to clear her, but refused to divulge certain details of his relationship with her. The Gold King loved Dunbar and attempted to win her affections only to have her reject his advances. The governess, however, had a strong influence over Gibson, guiding him to make good use of his vast wealth, remaining in his service to continue this noble aim. Holmes clears her of all charges, telling Watson "we have helped a remarkable woman . . ."

DUNDAS SEPARATION.   An unchronicled case in which Holmes was engaged to clear up some small points in connection with it, as mentioned in "A Case of Identity." "The husband was a teetotaler, there was no other woman, and the conduct complained of was that he had drifted into the habit of winding up every meal by taking out his false teeth and hurling them at his wife . . ." The case was brought up by Holmes during his discussion with Watson as to whether commonplace occurrences held any interest for the reasoner. Watson brought forward an article entitled, "A Husband's Cruelty to his Wife," saying: "There is half a column of print, but I know without reading it that it is all perfectly familiar to me. There is, of course, the other woman, the drink, the push, the blow, the sympathetic sister or landlady. The crudest of writers could invent nothing more crude." Holmes then gave him the details, adding that such actions were not "likely to occur to the imagination of the average story-teller."

DURANDO, VICTOR.   The minister of San Pedro in London mentioned in "Wisteria Lodge." He had met and married his wife there. In a premonition of his fate, he refused to take her with him when he was recalled on some pretext to San Pedro by Don Murillo, the country's dictator. Durando was subsequently shot, his estates confiscated, and his wife "left with a pittance and a broken heart." (See next entry.)

"DYING DETECTIVE, THE ADVENTURE OF THE" (DYIN).   Published: *Collier's*, November 1913; collected in *His Last Bow* (1917).

"The Dying Detective"—Holmes in the grips of an incurable Asian malady; by Walter Paget.

Case date: 1887 or 1890. Major players: Holmes, Watson, Culverton Smith, Victor Savage, Inspector Morton. This account by Watson begins with a nicely written passage complimenting Mrs. Hudson, the "long-suffering" landlady of Sherlock Holmes. It is she who informs Watson that the detective is dying, summoning him to Baker Street to attend his friend in what seem to be his last hours. Holmes apparently has contracted some horrible disease from the East while "working among Chinese sailors down in the docks." Watson wishes to consult Dr. Ainstree to assist his dreadful-looking friend, but Holmes will allow him to bring only one man, Culverton Smith, a planter from Sumatra and an expert on tropical afflictions. At one point, the delirious detective blurts out: "I cannot think why the whole bed of the ocean is not one solid mass of oysters, so prolific they seem. Ah, I am wandering! Strange how the brain controls the brain! What was I saying, Watson?"

DYNAMICS OF THE ASTEROID, THE. This celebrated book written by Professor Moriarty was noted by Holmes to ascend "to such rarefied heights of pure mathematics that it is said that there was no man in the scientific press capable of critiquing it." (*The Valley of Fear*.) There are, unfortunately, no copies available today to collectors. (See also BINOMIAL THEOREM.)

EARS. This subject of human anatomy was the focus of special study by Holmes. It was particularly helpful in the case recounted in "The Cardboard Box," in which severed human ears arrive in a box delivered to Susan Cushing. He told Watson: "As a medical man, you are aware, Watson, that there is no part of the body which varies so much as the human ear. Each ear is as a rule quite distinctive and differs from all other ones. In last year's *Anthropological Journal* you will find two short monographs from my pen upon the subject." Regrettably, those works have never been located by scholars.

EAST END. The East End, a working class and immigrant section of London, noted for its deplorable conditions, dense population, and heavy crime, encompassed the London docks and was the site of several days' investigation by Holmes during the "Black Peter" case. In the East End, Holmes was able to procure the arrest of Wilson, the notorious canary trainer, thereby removing a plague spot from the area. Holmes also claimed to have contracted an Asiatic disease while working among Chinese sailors in the East End in "The Dying Detective." (See also JACK THE RIPPER.)

ECLAIR SERIES. The name given to the series of silent Holmes films made from 1912 to 1913 by the Franco-British Film Company/Eclair (Fenning), under the copyright of *Société Français des Filmes et Cinématographes Eclair*. The films in the series were: *The Speckled Band* (1912), *Silver Blaze* (1912), *The Beryl Coronet* (1912), *The Musgrave Ritual* (1913), *The Reigate Squires* (1912), *The Stolen Papers* (1912), *A Mystery of Boscombe Vale* (1912), and *The Copper Beeches* (1912). The films starred George Trevilles (Holmes) and Mr. Moyse (Watson), although Moyse may not have starred in the first episode.

EDALJI, GEORGE. A real-life individual (d. 1953) whose cause was undertaken by Sir Arthur Conan Doyle, Edalji was a junior barrister and a Eurasian (Parsee). He had been arrested and convicted of maiming animals, and Conan Doyle, convinced of his innocence, became involved in the latter part of 1906. He was allowed by Scotland Yard to examine the evidence of the case and subsequently wrote a series of articles for the *Daily Telegraph* in the early part of 1907. Conan Doyle's campaign finally succeeded and Edalji was released from prison, but the Parsee was never officially cleared. A character based on Edalji appeared in the Nicholas Meyer novel *The West End Horror*. Also, the 1972 British television production of "Conan Doyle" (with Nigel Davenport) featured the Edalji case.

EDMUNDS. A member of the Berkshire constabulary who investigated the Abbas Parva tragedy in "The Veiled Lodger." Baffled by one or two points regarding the case, Edmunds "dropped in and smoked a pipe or two" with Holmes while discussing the tragedy. Holmes considered him "a smart lad," but some time after his investigation, Edmunds was sent to Allahabad.

EDWARDS, BIRDY. A member of the Pinkerton Detective Agency, Edwards was responsible for the destruction and suppression of the Scowrers (the Ancient Order of Freemen) of Vermissa Valley in *The Valley of Fear*. Originally from Ireland, Edwards posed as one John ("Jack") McMurdo, a supposed member of the Freemen of Chicago who fled to Vermissa Valley after murdering a man. Accepted as genuine by most of the Scowrers, especially the so-called bodymaster of the lodge 341, John McGinty, McMurdo became a trusted member. After his labors in the valley, Edwards married Ettie Shafter, fleeing to Chicago to escape the vengeance of the Freemen. He later went to California where he was highly successful prospecting for gold. There he was known as John Douglas. Ettie died and Douglas, still pursued by the Scowrers, went to London. Here he was involved in the tragedy of Birlstone Manor and was apparently murdered.

EGRIA. A town in Bohemia, not far from Carlsbad, with numerous glass factories and paper mills. In "A Scandal in Bohemia," Holmes looked up Egria in his *Continental Gazetteer* after noting the letters *Eg P Gt* woven into the paper used by the anonymous visitor to Baker Street. They stood for *Egria Papier Gesellschaft* and told Holmes that the paper, and hence the client, were from Bohemia. The towns **Eglonitz** and **Eglow** were also mentioned.

EGYPT. The North African country was, in Holmes's time, under the overall control of England but under the nominal authority of Turkey. In "The Golden Pince-Nez," Professor Coram claimed that his analysis of documents found in the Coptic monasteries of Egypt and Syria would cut deep at the very foundations of revealed religion. He also ordered 1,000 cigarettes every fortnight from the Alexandrian tobacconist Ionides. In "His Last Bow," Holmes found a pigeon hole marked "Egypt" in the safe of the German master spy Von Bork. Holmes also asked Mrs. Maberley if she would like a trip to Cairo in "The Three Gables." The detective's first experience with Egypt supposedly came in his youth for, according to the film *Young Sherlock Holmes*, he uncovered in London a cult of Egyptian human sacrificers.

"ELEMENTARY, MY DEAR WATSON." Arguably Sherlock Holmes's most famous maxim, as associated with him as his deerstalker and cape and his pipe. Unfortunately, this celebrated phrase was never actually uttered by the detective anywhere in the Canon. It is a combination of two Holmesian lines that were used by William Gillette in his play *Sherlock Holmes*. In "The Cardboard

Box," Holmes performs the feat of reading Watson's mind, saying afterward that "it was very superficial, my dear Watson, I assure you." Meanwhile, at the start of "The Crooked Man," Holmes responds to Watson's surprise at one of his deductions by saying that it was "elementary." The best-known user of the maxim was, of course, Basil Rathbone, considered by many to be the quintessential Holmes.

ELEY BROS.   An English ammunition manufacturer whose cartridges were used by Watson for his revolver. In preparing to do battle with Dr. Grimesby Roylott in "The Speckled Band," Holmes asked Watson to slip a revolver into his pocket. "An Eley's No. 2 is an excellent argument with a gentleman who can twist steel pokers into knots."

ELISE.   A woman in the house of Colonel Lysander Stark in "The Engineer's Thumb." She tried to warn Victor Hatherley to flee the house and was later instrumental in helping him to escape.

ELMAN, J. C.   The vicar of Mossmoor-cum-Little Purlington, of Little Purlington, Essex in "The Retired Colourman." Described as "a big, solemn, rather pompous clergyman," he supposedly sent a telegram to Josiah Amberley. "Come at once without fail. Can give information as to your recent loss—Elman. The Vicarage." When Amberley and Dr. Watson journeyed to Little Purlington, Elman denied ever sending a message. Holmes looked up Elman in his *Crockford's Clerical Dictionary*.

ELRIGE.   A farmer in Norfolk in "The Dancing Men," he owned Elrige's Farm where Abe Slaney stayed during his efforts to communicate with Elsie Patrick.

EMERALD.   There were ninety-seven emeralds in the Agra Treasure in *The Sign of Four*. For his brilliant work in the affair of "The Bruce-Partington Plans," Holmes was given an emerald tiepin by Queen Victoria, and for his services to the king of Bohemia in the Irene Adler affair in "A Scandal in Bohemia," he was offered by the ruler an emerald snake ring. The detective declined his gift and asked for something far more valuable, a photograph of Adler.

"EMPTY HOUSE, THE ADVENTURE OF THE" (EMPT).   Published: *Collier's*, September 1903, *Strand*, October 1903; collected in The

Return of Sherlock Holmes (1905). Major players: Holmes, Watson, Ronald Adair, Inspector Lestrade, Colonel Sebastian Moran, Mrs. Hudson. Case date: April 1894. This story brought the triumphant return of Sherlock Holmes both to life and practice, marking the final resurrection of the detective after his posthumous appearance in the novel *The Hound of the Baskervilles* in 1901. The same gloom that surrounded the narrative of "The Final Problem" seems to enshroud the opening of "The Empty House": Holmes is still dead some three years after his terrible struggle with Professor Moriarty at the Reichenbach Falls; Watson's beloved Mary has died, forcing the doctor to move out of his Paddington practice to Kensington; and all London is abuzz with talk of the bizarre murder of the Hon. Ronald Adair, inexplicably shot with a revolver at close range while in a locked room on the second floor. Watson's efforts to apply his late friend's methods prove fruitless. In the midst of the darkness, Holmes returns suddenly and Watson writes, "I rose to my feet, stared at him for some seconds in utter amazement, and then it appears that I must have fainted for the first and the last time in my life." Holmes is truly back, giving Watson an account of his years of wandering after Reichenbach (see GREAT HIATUS). They then set out together to capture the murderer of Adair, laying an ingenious trap with a wax bust of Holmes. The killer is none other than one of the dead Professor Moriarty's most dangerous lieutenants who is anxious to take revenge upon Holmes for the destruction of his master and his vast criminal organization.

EMSWORTH, COLONEL.   A retired army officer, winner of the Victoria Cross, and father of Godfrey Emsworth in "The Blanched Soldier," Colonel Emsworth lived with his wife at Tuxbury Old Park in Berfordshire. Despite his advancing years, he still had tremendous strength and purpose of will, using it to intimidate other people. He tried to keep the condition of his son secret, working against the curiosity of James Dodd. Dodd described him as "a huge, bow-backed man with a smoky skin and a straggling gray beard, seated behind his littered desk. A red-veined nose jutted out like a vulture's beak, and two fierce gray eyes glared at me from under tufted brows. I could understand now why Godfrey seldom spoke of his father." Mrs. Emsworth, the colonel's long-suffering wife, was "a gentle little white mouse of a woman."

EMSWORTH, GODFREY. Onetime English soldier in the Boer War, the only son of Colonel Emsworth and his wife of Tuxbury Old Park in Berfordshire in "The Blanched Soldier." As the son of a holder of the Victoria Cross, Godfrey was said to have "the fighting blood in him" and had volunteered for service in the war. The finest lad in the regiment, he was soon the closest friend of James Dodd, himself an "upstanding Briton." The two were mates for a year until Godfrey was wounded by a bullet from an elephant gun in action near Diamond Hill, outside Pretoria. Dodd lost touch with him and his efforts to learn the condition of his friend went unanswered. He did learn that Emsworth had been shipped home via Southampton. Dodd's efforts to learn the true condition of his friend were defeated by the obstinacy of Colonel Emsworth. Holmes discovered the truth about Godfrey, and brought with him to Tuxbury Old Place a medical specialist best equipped to deal with Godfrey's ailment.

ENCYCLOPEDIA BRITANNICA. The encyclopedia was to be copied by Jabez Wilson as his duty as a member of "The Red-Headed League." According to Wilson, he had copied Abbots, Archery, Armour, Architecture, and Attica, and hoped with diligence that he might get on to the B's before long. His work was cut short, however, by the dissolution of the league.

"ENGINEER'S THUMB, THE ADVENTURE OF THE" (ENGR). Published: *Strand*, March 1892; collected in *The Adventures of Sherlock Holmes* (1892). Case date: Summer 1892. Major players: Holmes, Watson, Victor Hatherley, Colonel Lysander Stark, Mr. Ferguson, Elise, Inspector Bradstreet. This was one of the only two cases placed before Sherlock Holmes by Dr. Watson, the other being Colonel Warburton's madness. Victor Hatherley is brought to Watson from Paddington Station, with his thumb hacked off, and Watson takes him to meet Holmes. The young engineer had been hired by Colonel Lysander Stark to fix a fuller's earth press at a house in Reading, Berkshire. Arriving at the estate, Hatherley underwent the wild adventures that ultimately cost him his appendage. Holmes told Hatherley about his thumb, "Indirectly it may be of value, you know; you have only to put it into words to gain the reputation of being excellent company for the remainder of your existence."

ENGLISH CHANNEL. From Holmes's villa in Sussex could be seen the English Channel in "The Lion's Mane," as he stated, "My villa is situated upon the southern slope of the downs, commanding a great view of the Channel." In "His Last Bow" one of the pigeon holes in the safe of the German spymaster Von Bork, under the specific name "The Channel," was also dedicated to information about this important waterway.

ENGLISCHER HOF. The hotel in the village of Meiringen, Switzerland, run by Peter Steiler the elder in "The Final Problem." Holmes and Watson stayed there on the night of May 3, 1894, the night before Holmes's fateful encounter with Professor Moriarty at the Reichenbach Falls. According to Michael Hardwick in his work *Sherlock Holmes, My Life and Crimes*, the Englischer Hof was the site of very different events than recorded by Watson. Lady Frances Carfax stayed for a fortnight in another hotel by the same name in Baden in "The Disappearance of Lady Frances Carfax." It was here that she made the acquaintance of Dr. and Mrs. Shlessinger, in whose company she left the hotel.

ENTER THE LION. In full, *Enter the Lion, A Posthumous Memoir of Mycroft Holmes*, a 1979 novel by Michael P. Hodel and Sean M. Wright, supposedly drawn from Mycroft Holmes's own account. A lively and well-written work, it focuses on the heretofore largely ignored subject of Mycroft, the brilliant and rotund elder brother of the Great Detective. In the story, he and Sherlock become embroiled in a plot by old members of the Southern Confederacy to resurrect their fortunes.

ERNEST, RAY. A London physician and friend and chess-playing neighbor of Mr. and Mrs. Josiah Amberley in "The Retired Colourman," Ernest was accused by Amberley of being the lover of his wife and of running away with the lady and his fortune. Unable to locate the missing doctor, Ernest's family engaged the detective Barker to find him, while Holmes was hired by Amberley.

ESCOTT. A disguise adopted by Holmes to gain entry into the household of the blackmailer Charles Augustus Milverton in "Charles Augustus Milverton." As Escott, Holmes donned a goatee, and pretended to be a swaggering plumber with a rising business. Escott wooed and won the heart of Milverton's maid Agatha, using her as his prime

Holmes disguised as Escott, a plumber with a rising business in "Charles Augustus Milverton"; by Sidney Paget.

source of information about the odious blackmailer. In the Granada Television adaptation of the story, extensive time was given to use of the alias by Holmes (played by Jeremy Brett), with special attention paid to the winning of Agatha's love and its effect upon the detective. The name Escott may have been used by Holmes during his time in America as a young actor, prior to his embarking upon his career as a detective; this idea is proposed by H. Paul Jeffers in the novel *The Adventure of the Stalwart Companions* (1978), in which Holmes meets Theodore Roosevelt.

ETHEREGE. A man who had disappeared and who was found by Holmes easily, even though the police and everyone else had given him up for dead ("A Case of Identity"). Mrs. Etherege was so impressed that she advised Mary Sutherland to consult Holmes about the disappearance of her fiance, Hosmer Angel.

ETON COLLEGE. Colonel Sebastian Moran was educated at Eton ("The Empty House"), and

John Clay, a "murderer, thief, smasher, and forger," had attended Eton as well ("The Red-Headed League"). The college is Britain's most famous public school, in Buckinghamshire, established in 1440 by King Henry VI.

EVANS. The real name of the country squire Beddoes in "The 'Gloria Scott'." Evans had been convicted of committing forgery and, in 1855, was sentenced to transportation to Australia on the *Gloria Scott*. He joined in the convict mutiny on board and survived the ship's destruction. Reaching Australia, he prospered with Trevor Senior in the goldfields, changed his name to Beddoes, and returned to England. His many quiet years came to an end with the arrival of the seaman Hudson. Evans's message to Trevor in code caused the latter's death by apoplexy. A member of the Vermissa police in Vermissa Valley in *The Valley of Fear* is also named Evans. He was shot and killed when he ventured to arrest one of the Scowrers.

EVANS, "KILLER." This American career criminal, whose real name was James Winter, also went by the alias Morecroft in "The Three Garridebs." His Scotland Yard dossier was quite detailed. "Aged forty-four. Native of Chicago. Known to have shot three men in the States. Escaped from penitentiary through political influence. Came to London in 1893. Shot a man over cards in a nightclub in the Waterloo Road in January, 1895. Man died, but he was shown to have been the aggressor in the row. Dead man was identified as Rodger Prescott, famous as forger and coiner in Chicago. Killer Evans released in 1901. Has been under police supervision since, but so far as known has led an honest life." Evans returned to crime in the affair of the Garridebs, but was apprehended by Holmes and Watson. He came close to being killed by Holmes after wounding Watson.

EXIT, SHERLOCK HOLMES. This 1977 novel by Robert Lee, known in full as *Exit, Sherlock Holmes, The Great Detective's Final Days*, begins as a straightforward version of a Sherlock Holmes adventure as recorded by John Watson and ends as a science fiction tale. Holmes is featured in the book in only a limited way as the focus of the story is devoted to the private and very competent investigation of Watson in attempting to find the missing Holmes. The story begins in 1903 with Watson summoned to 221B to learn that Moriarty was not killed in 1891. Holmes, determined to rid the world finally of the professor's evil, undertakes his mission by "retiring" to the Sussex Downs to raise bees. Watson soon begins to unravel the complicated life of the detective and learns the shocking truth about him.

EXPLOITS OF SHERLOCK HOLMES, THE.

This collection of original short stories, actually brilliant pastiches of the cases of the Canon, was written by Adrian Conan Doyle and John Dickson Carr. Originally published individually, the adventures were collected and appeared in book form in 1954. Eleven of the twelve stories were first published in *Collier's Magazine*, the one exception being "The Adventure of the Seven Clocks," by Conan Doyle and Carr, which appeared in *Life Magazine* in December, 1952. Conan Doyle and Carr began the new cases together, authoring, aside from the "Seven Clocks": "The Adventure of the Gold Hunter," "The Adventure of the Wax Gamblers," "The Adventure of Highgate Miracle,"

"The Adventure of the Black Baronet," and "The Adventure of the Sealed Room." Carr fell ill, however, and Conan Doyle completed the last six adventures: "The Adventure of Foulkes Rath," "The Adventure of the Abbas Ruby," "The Adventure of the Dark Angels," "The Adventure of the Two Women," "The Adventure of the Deptford Horror," and "The Adventure of the Red Widow."

EXTORTION.

Both the Red Circle ("The Red Circle") and the Scowrers (*The Valley of Fear*) procured money through extortion, an often violent and brutal crime in which money, information, or goods are obtained from another through intimidation, coercion, and/or force. (See also BLACKMAIL.)

EYFORD.

Dr. Becher and his house guest Colonel Lysander Stark, in "The Engineer's Thumb," lived in Eyford, a village in Berkshire, near Reading and the border of Oxfordshire. It was there that the engineer Victor Hatherley was asked to come to repair a hydraulic press.

FABER, JOHANN.

A type of pencil manufactured in Nuremberg. A Johann Faber was used to copy a passage of Thucydides in "The Three Students," a fact deduced by Holmes because all that remained of the pencil were the letters *N N*. Critics have pointed to the obvious inconsistency in this as the letters *N N* could not be the only ones left on the stub given the name Johann Faber since sharpening the pencil from either end would have left other letters.

FAIRBANK.

The residence of Alexander Holder in the London district of Streatham, from

which was stolen the Beryl Coronet in "The Beryl Coronet." Watson wrote that "Fairbank was a good-sized square house of white stone, standing back a little from the road. A double carriage sweep, snow-clad lawn, stretched down in front to two large iron gates which closed the entrance."

FAIRBORN, ALEC.

The lover of Mary Browner in "The Cardboard Box." According to James Browner: "He was a man with winning ways, and he made friends wherever he went. He was a dashing, swaggering chap, smart and curled, who had seen half the world and could talk of what he had seen." Warned off by Mary's husband James, Fairborn persisted in his relationship with a terrible result.

FALDER, LADY BEATRICE.   The sister of Sir Robert Norberton and title holder of her late husband's estate "Shoscombe Old Place," Lady Beatrice took a special interest in Sir Robert's stables and had a love for the famous Shoscombe spaniels. Upon her death, the Shoscombe estate reverted to her husband's brother, a fact that was to prove of supreme importance in explaining the strange behavior of Sir Robert just prior to the running of the Derby. The apparently cruel behavior of Sir Robert toward his sister prompted John Mason, head trainer at the stables, to consult with Holmes. Other members of the Falder line included Sir James Falder, Lady Beatrice's late husband; Hugo and Odo, who lived during the Norman era; and Sir William and Sir Denis of the eighteenth century, who were buried in the crypt of the ruined chapel on the grounds of Shoscombe Park. (See also SHOSCOMBE OLD PLACE, SHOSCOMBE PARK, and NORBERTON, SIR ROBERT.)

FARINTOSH, MRS.   An early client of Holmes's, before Watson's time, who consulted the detective concerning an opal tiara. She recommended him to Helen Stoner and thereby made possible Holmes's involvement in the affair of "The Speckled Band."

FARMER, PHILIP JOSÉ.   The prolific American writer (b. 1935) was the author of several important Holmesian literary efforts. *The Adventure of the Peerless Peer* (1974) featured Holmes and Watson meeting Lord Greystoke, known as Tarzan of the Apes, while the duo is on a secret mission in 1916 to Cairo in pursuit of the German master spy Von Bork (made famous in "His Last Bow"). "The Problem of Sore Bridge—Among Others" (1975) presents Raffles, the notorious cracksman, solving the three unchronicled cases mentioned in "The Problem of Thor Bridge": the disappearance of the cutter *Alicia*, the disappearance of James Phillimore, and the bizarre affair of Isadora Persano. Farmer also created *The Other Log of Phileas Fogg* (1973), in which the identity of Captain Nemo is revealed (hint: he is a certain mathematics professor); and "A Scarletin Study," by Jonathan Swift Somers III, with the superintelligent Ralph Von Wau Wau, a German shepherd with an artificially

high intelligence; and "The Adventure of the Three Madmen" (1948), in which Holmes and Watson meet Mowgli, the creation of Rudyard Kipling.

FARNHAM.   A small town in Surrey, near Chiltern Grange, the home of Bob Carruthers in "The Solitary Cyclist." Holmes described the area as a "beautiful neighbourhood, and full of the most interesting associations." It was near here that Holmes and Watson captured Archie Stamford, the forger.

FARQUHAR, MR.   An old general medical practitioner from whom Watson purchased his practice in Paddington, as reported in "The Stockbroker's Clerk." Farquhar "had at one time an excellent general practice, but his age, and an affliction of the nature of St. Vitus' dance from which he suffered, had very much thinned it."

"FATHER'S TALE, A."   A short story by Sterling Lanier that was first published in *The Magazine of Fantasy and Science-Fiction* in 1974. This is another entry in the speculation by writers about the giant rat of Sumatra, originally associated with the vessel *Matilda Briggs*, one of Holmes's unchronicled cases, a story for which the world, until this point anyway, has not been prepared.

FENCING.   Watson considered Holmes to be an excellent swordsman (*A Study in Scarlet*, "The Five Orange Pips"), largely the result of his participating in the sport during his brief university career ("The 'Gloria Scott' "). The detective's talents in fencing were, unfortunately, never displayed in the Canon, mainly because of the cerebral nature of the chronicles. In film, however, where the detective has been forced to take part in adventures more suited to a superhero, his skill with the sword has proven a useful and exciting plot device. A stunning duel between Holmes and the evil Baron Leinsdorf in the novel and film version of *The Seven-Per-Cent Solution* was conducted on a moving train, the contest won by the sleuth because the nobleman had no backhand. Two other notable duels were in *Young Sherlock Holmes* (1985) and the comedy *Without a Clue* (1988).

FERGUSON.   The secretary to J. Neil Gibson, the Gold King in "Thor Bridge," is named Ferguson, as is a retired sea captain and onetime owner of the Three Gables before its purchase by the

Maberleys. Holmes theorized that Ferguson may have buried a treasure in the Three Gables. See also BECHER, DR.

FERGUSON, ROBERT.   A London tea-broker and senior partner of Ferguson & Muirhead who consulted Holmes when it appeared that Mrs. Ferguson was practicing vampirism on their baby son in "The Sussex Vampire." Watson had once known Big Bob Ferguson as the finest three-quarter that the team from Richmond had ever had. His strength was such that he was able to throw Watson over the ropes and into the crowd when Richmond played the team from Blackheath. By the time Ferguson met the doctor again, however, his "great frame had fallen in, his hair was scanty, and his shoulders were bowed." By Ferguson's own admission, he had been especially aged by his wife's more than unusual behavior. His son **Jack** ("Jacky") Ferguson was a fifteen year old who had been deformed in a fall during childhood. The offspring of Ferguson's first marriage (which ended in the death of the wife), Jack hated his new stepmother, a Peruvian lady, and his new baby brother. He was "a remarkable lad, pale-eyed and fair-haired, with excitable blue eyes." Although "circumscribed in action," he was said to have a "very developed mind."

FERN.   In examining the apparent scene of struggle between Holmes and Professor Moriarty at the Reichenbach Falls in "The Final Problem," Watson noted the torn up ferns at the rim of the falls leading to the inescapable conclusion that both the detective and the archvillain had plummeted to their deaths. Ferns were also mentioned in *The Hound of the Baskervilles*, "Silver Blaze," and "Thor Bridge."

FERRERS DOCUMENTS.   A case investigated by Holmes early in the century. He was engaged upon it at the time of his being consulted about the disappearance of Lord Saltire, son of the duke of Holdernesse in "The Priory School." The Ferrers Documents have been the source of considerable speculation by scholars. Michael Harrison, for example, in his *The World of Sherlock Holmes*, did extensive research into the subject and discovered what he believed to be the true nature of the case. Holmes conducted a thorough investigation that lasted some eight years, from April 1895 to October 1903. The documents sought to establish the complete genealogy of the Washington family

so that the British government could present them to America as a gift upon the 100th anniversary of Washington's death in 1899. The work also involved the detective looking into early English charters. (For details, the reader is encouraged to consult Harrison's excellent book.) Another possible version of the case was offered in the collection *The Exploits of Sherlock Holmes* (1954) in the short story "The Adventure of the Dark Angels" by Adrian Conan Doyle.

FERRIER, DR.   A physician who lived in Woking, near the home of Percy Phelps in "The Naval Treaty." When Phelps was brought home as "practically a raving maniac" following the theft of the Naval Treaty, Ferrier took care of him.

FERRIER, JOHN.   A frontiersman and farmer who, with his daughter Lucy, was rescued from certain death in the Great Alkali Plain by a group of migrating Mormons in *A Study in Scarlet*. Ferrier subsequently joined the Mormon Church, but his refusal to submit utterly to doctrine led to his murder in 1860 by the Danite Band. "His face lean and haggard, and the brown parchment-like skin was drawn tightly over the projecting bones; his long, brown hair and beard were all flecked and dashed with white; his eyes were sunken in his head, and burned with an unnatural lustre; while his hand which grasped a rifle was hardly more fleshy than that of a skeleton." The adopted daughter of John Ferrier, **Lucy Ferrier** was only a child when saved and grew up into the Flower of Utah. She loved JEFFERSON HOPE, but also received the unwanted advances of Enoch Drebber and Joseph Stangerson. Following the murder of her father by the Danites, she was forcibly wed to Drebber, becoming his eighth wife. Within a month of her marriage, she was dead. Jefferson Hope never forgave Drebber or Stangerson for her demise, pursuing them both across the world to inflict vengeance.

FETLOCK JONES.   A Sherlockian parody created in 1902 by Mark Twain. Jones appeared in *Harper's Monthly Magazine* in the story "A Double-Barreled Detective Story," and was later included in the collection that was suppressed by the Doyle estate, *The Misadventures of Sherlock Holmes* (1944). Twain created Fetlock Jones as a result of his desire to satirize the detective fiction of the time in general and Sherlock Holmes in particular. Twain particularly found frustrating Conan Doyle's willingness to kill off the detective in one story only to raise him from the dead in another.

"FIELD BAZAAR, THE." A charming Holmes parody written by Sir Arthur Conan Doyle for the undergraduate magazine of his alma mater, Edinburgh University, published in the *Student* in November, 1896. Significantly, it was penned at the time when Holmes was believed dead at the bottom of Reichenbach Falls in Switzerland, while Conan Doyle steadfastly refused to bring him back to life. "The Field Bazaar" thus represents Conan Doyle's first movement toward relenting to public pressure to revive the detective, a move that would culminate in the publication of *The Hound of the Baskervilles* in serialized form starting in 1901. Affectionately written, the brief work presents Holmes correctly (of course) deducing that Watson has been invited to help raise money for the university's cricket team.

FIFTH NORTHUMBERLAND FUSILIERS. A British army regiment first raised in 1674. As reported in *A Study in Scarlet*, Watson joined the Fifth Fusiliers in Afghanistan as assistant surgeon. He was removed from the regiment and attached to the Berkshires with whom he saw action at the bloody Battle of Maiwand (1880).

Holmes and Watson observe Professor Moriarty's special train in "The Final Problem"; by Sidney Paget.

"FINAL PROBLEM, THE" (FINA). Published: *Strand*, December 1893, *McClure's*, December 1893; collected in *The Memoirs of Sherlock Holmes* (1894). Major players: Holmes, Watson, Professor Moriarty, Peter Steiler. Case date: April 1891. Certainly the most traumatic of all cases recorded by Watson, one that caused massive public uproar. Watson begins his narrative ominously, "It is with a heavy heart that I take up my pen to write these the last words in which I shall ever record the singular gifts by which my friend Mr. Sherlock Holmes was distinguished." Indeed, the doctor had intended to make "The Naval Treaty" his final entry, but "the recent letters in which Colonel James Moriarty defends the memory of his brother" have forced him "to lay the facts before the public exactly as they occurred." As was no doubt guessed by the readers of the *Strand*, "The Final Problem" details the climactic struggle between Sherlock Holmes and the wicked Professor Moriarty. When Watson first meets Holmes in the story, the detective is obviously afraid of something—"air-guns." His concern stems from the fact that he has been working over the previous months to destroy the professor's vast criminal organization, this despite Moriarty's warning of the

Professor Moiarty pays a call on the Great Detective in "The Final Problem"; by Sidney Paget.

Holmes at the Reichenback Falls in "The Final Problem"; by Harry C. Edwards.

most dire consequences should Holmes's campaign continue. The detective completes his offensive, but even he recognizes the need to flee before the archvillain's wrath. He and Watson travel to the Continent with Moriarty hot on their trail as he has eluded capture by the police. The inevitable confrontation takes place in Switzerland at the Reichenbach Falls. Watson sadly writes: "An examination by experts leaves little doubt that a personal contest between the two men ended, as it could hardly fail to end in such a situation, in their reeling over, locked in each other's arms. Any attempt at recovering the bodies was absolutely hopeless, and there, deep down in that dreadful cauldron of swirling water and seething foam, will lie for all time the most dangerous criminal and the

foremost champion of the law of their generation." The public was horrified at Holmes's demise, wearing black armbands and writing abusive and demanding letters to Conan Doyle in protest. Holmes would not return in print until 1901 with the "posthumous" *The Hound of the Baskervilles* and would not return to life until 1903 in "The Adventure of the Empty House."

THE FINAL LETTER OF SHERLOCK HOLMES

The following note was discovered by Dr. Watson at the edge of the Reichenbach Falls in Switzerland in April, 1891 at the conclusion of the case recounted in "The Final Problem." According to tradition, the "original autograph manuscript of Sherlock Holmes' letter to Dr. Watson, regarding his last meeting with Professor Moriarty," was auctioned on December 8, 1915 in Philadelphia. It subsequently disappeared.

My dear Watson, I write these few lines through the courtesy of Mr. Moriarty, who awaits my convenience for the final discussion of those questions which lie between us. He has been giving me a sketch of the methods by which he avoided the English police and kept himself informed of our movements. They certainly confirm the very high opinion which I had formed of his abilities. I am pleased to think that I shall be able to free society from any further effects of his presence, though I fear that it is at a cost which will give pain to my friends, and especially, my dear Watson, to you. I have already explained to you, however, that my career had in any case reached its crisis, and that no possible conclusion to it could be more congenial to me than this. Indeed, if I may make a full confession to you, I was quite convinced that the letter from Meiringen was a hoax, and I allowed you to depart on that errand under the persuasion that some development of this sort would follow. Tell Inspector Patterson that the papers which he needs to convict the gang are in pigeon-hole M., done up in a blue envelope and inscribed 'Moriarty.' I made every disposition of my property before leaving England, and handed it to my brother Mycroft. Pray give my greetings to Mrs. Hudson, and believe me to be, my dear fellow,

Very sincerely yours,
Sherlock Holmes

FINGERPRINT.   The mark left by the fingertip provides a nearly infallible means of identification. Holmes noted that a letter from Neville St. Clair to his wife had been posted by a man with a dirty thumb in "The Man With the Twisted Lip"; he finds two thumb marks on "The Cardboard Box" mailed to Susan Cushing; and dismissed the thumb mark on the envelope of the letter sent to Mary Morstan as probably that of the postman in *The Sign of Four*. A thumb mark made in blood that was found at Deep Dene House seemed to provide final, absolutely damning proof that Jonas Oldacre had been murdered by the unfortunate John Hector McFarlane, but Holmes found it to be crucial to proving his innocence in "The Norwood Builder." Interestingly, the "advances" made in fingerprint analysis by Holmes were a model for Scotland Yard, which began using the fingerprint for identification starting in 1901. (See also BERTILLON, ALPHONSE.)

FIRST BENGALORE PIONEERS.   A regiment in the Indian army, mentioned in "The Empty House." Colonel Sebastian Moran was forced to retire from the regiment for various reasons. In some editions, it is spelled 1st Bangalore Pioneers.

FISHER, PENROSE.   One of the best medical practitioners in London. In "The Dying Detective," Watson proposed bringing Dr. Penrose to Holmes, but the detective refused.

FISHERMAN.   A disguise adopted by Holmes to visit Shoscombe Old Place.

"FIVE ORANGE PIPS, THE" (FIVE). Published: *Strand*, November 1891; collected in *The Adventures of Sherlock Holmes* (1892). Case date: September 1887, possibly 1888 or 1889. Major players: Holmes, Watson, John Openshaw, Elias Openshaw, and Joseph Openshaw. One of the few failures of the detective, this case pits Holmes against the Ku Klux Klan (KKK). John Openshaw, nephew of Colonel Elias Openshaw, had inherited his family's fortune and its curse upon the untimely demises of his father and uncle. Their deaths were preceded by envelopes containing Five Orange Pips—the seeds symbolizing their impending doom. Young John Openshaw also received one, learning of his family's associations with the KKK in the United States. He took his story to Holmes, who inexplicably allowed his client to journey back

to Sussex. John, of course, never reached his destination. The detective swore revenge upon the murderers and set himself to the task. Despite Holmes's failings, or possibly because of them, Sir Arthur Conan Doyle liked the case, ranking it seventh on his list of favorites.

FLAUBERT, GUSTAVE.   French novelist (1821–1880) whose well-known quotation from a letter to George Sand, *"L'homme n'est rien, l'oeuvre—tout"* ("The man is nothing, work everything") was used by Holmes, although quoted incorrectly (*"L'homme c'est rien—l'oeuvre c'est tout"*) in "The Red-Headed League."

FLEET STREET.   A thoroughfare in central London known for its newspaper and publishing offices. At the start of the "Resident Patient," Holmes and Watson took a leisurely stroll, watching the ever changing kaleidoscope of life as it ebbed and flowed through Fleet Street and the Strand. Upon returning to Baker Street, however, they found a brougham waiting at their door. The client was Dr. Percy Trevelyan. The offices of the "Red-Headed League" were found at 7 Pope's Court, Fleet Street.

FLEMING, IAN.   Australian born actor who portrayed Dr. Watson opposite Arthur Wontner from 1931 to 1937. (He was not the same Ian Fleming who authored the James Bond novels.) Fleming's Watson was traditionally competent, but distinguished himself by his eye for the ladies (particularly in *The Sleeping Cardinal*, 1931) and the use of his pipe. Wontner played the good doctor in: *The Sleeping Cardinal*, *The Missing Rembrandt* (1932), *The Triumph of Sherlock Holmes* (1935), and *Silver Blaze* (1937). Curiously, he was replaced in *The Sign of Four* (1932) by Ian Hunter because it was felt by the producers that a younger, more active Watson was needed to make the romance of Mary Morstan more believable.

FLORIDA.   Elias Openshaw became a planter in Florida and reportedly did very well in "The Five Orange Pips." According to Holmes's *American Encyclopedia*, the Ku Klux Klan was very active in Florida.

FOLKESTONE COURT.   The site of a burglary in May 1889, one of four considerable thefts during the last three years in the West Country, in *The*

Holmes and Watson stroll through Fleet Street and the Strand in "The Resident Patient"; by Sidney Paget.

Hound of the Baskervilles. The Folkestone Court burglary was notable because of the cold-blooded pistolling of the page who had surprised the masked and solitary burglar. Holmes believed that he knew who was the mastermind behind the robberies.

FOLLIOT, SIR GEORGE.   The owner of Oxshott Towers in Surrey. He was a neighbor of Aloysius Garcia of "Wisteria Lodge." In some editions, the name is spelled Ffolliot.

FOOLSCAP.   Writing-paper that received its name from the onetime watermark of a fool's head and cap with bells. It sometimes was thirty-four-by-thirty-four centimeters in size. Holmes referred to Watson's chronicling of his case as "laying out his foolscap" ("The Bruce-Partington Plans," "The Norwood Builder"), and the paper appeared in a number of cases: "The Cardboard Box," *The Hound of the Baskervilles*, "The Red Circle," "The Red-Headed League," "The Six Napoleons," "The Three Gables," and "The Three Garridebs."

FOOTSTEP.   Holmes felt the impression left by the foot was very important to the art of detection. In his opinion, no method was as important to the detective sciences as the tracing of the footstep, and no method so neglected (*A Study in Scarlet*). Holmes was the author of the monograph *The Tracing of Footsteps, with some Remarks upon the Uses of Plaster of Paris as a Preserver of Impresses*, dated to or before 1887 as he showed a copy of the work to Watson in *The Sign of Four*. It was also presumably translated into the French by François le Villard. A glimpse of his views on the subject was provided by his comment to Inspector Stanley Hopkins in "Black Peter": "As long as the criminal remains upon two legs so long must there be some indentation, some abrasion, some trifling displacement which can be detected by the scientific searcher."

FORBES.   A detective of Scotland Yard put in charge of the investigation to recover the Naval Treaty that had been stolen from Percy Phelps's office. Forbes, "a small foxy man with a sharp but by no means amiable expression," was at first against working with Holmes but his manner soon changed as he dealt with the detective.

FORDHAM.   An attorney in Horsham who drew up Elias Openshaw's will, leaving the estate, "all its advantages and all its disadvantages" to his brother, Joseph, in "The Five Orange Pips." Fordham is also the name of the attending physician of Trevor Senior in "The 'Gloria Scott'." Dr. Fordham was with Trevor when he died.

FORDINGBRIDGE.   A town in Hampshire where Beddoes, the old friend of Trevor Senior, had an estate in "The 'Gloria Scott'."

FOREIGN OFFICE.   A ministry in the British government headed by the secretary of state for foreign affairs with which Holmes had dealings throughout his long career, although probably only a few of his most important investigations for it were recounted by Watson. Holmes recovered the Naval Treaty that had been stolen from Percy Phelps's office in the Foreign Office (F.O.) under Lord Holdhurst, the foreign minister ("The Naval Treaty"). He was also helpful in finding the missing letter from a foreign potentate that had disappeared from the dispatch-box of the Rt. Hon. Trelawney Hope, the secretary for foreign affairs ("The Second Stain"). During the Great Hiatus (1891–1894), Holmes communicated to the F.O. the results of his visit to Khartoum ("The Empty House"). His greatest case undertaken at the behest of the F.O. was the infiltration and destruction of the spyring of Von Bork. The request was probably made by Sir Edmund Grey, foreign minister from 1905 to 1916 ("His Last Bow"). The duke of Balmoral was onetime secretary for foreign affairs ("The Noble Bachelor"); Sir Augustus Moran was once British minister to Persia ("The Empty House"); and Douglas Maberley was an attache to Rome ("The Three Gables").

FORGERY. Holmes investigated a number of forgery cases and forgers including the Conk-Singleton forgery ("The Six Napoleons"), Evans ("The 'Gloria Scott'"), Archie Stamford ("The Solitary Cyclist"), Victor Lynch ("The Sussex Vampire"), Arthur Staunton ("The Missing Three-Quarter"), and Count Sylvius, who denied forging a check on the Credit Lyonnais ("The Mazarin Stone"). John Clay ("The Red-Headed League") and Beddington ("The Stockbroker's Clerk") were both forgers, and Holmes suspected that the presence of Professor Moriarty could be felt in a number of forgery cases ("The Final Problem," *The Valley of Fear*). Lestrade also consulted Holmes on such a matter (*A Study in Scarlet*).

FORRESTER, MRS. CECIL. A lady to whom Holmes was once of help in solving some domestic trouble (*The Sign of Four*). She was later the employer of Mary Morstan as a governess and suggested to her that she consult Holmes about the strange matter confronting her. Throughout the case, Mrs. Cecil Forrester was very supportive of Mary.

FORRESTER, INSPECTOR. A member of the Surrey police in charge of the investigation into the burglary of Old Acton's home and the murder of William Kirwin in "The Reigate Squires." "A smart young fellow," he asked Holmes's assistance in solving the crimes.

FORTESCUE SCHOLARSHIP. The scholarship for which Gilchrist, McLaren, and Daulat Ras were competing and for which one of them was willing to cheat in "The Three Students." The first

examination for the scholarship was to translate half a chapter of Thucydides.

FOULMIRE. A farmhouse in Dartmoor, Devonshire, situated near Baskerville Hall in *The Hound of the Baskervilles*. It was the site of the death of Sir Charles Baskerville.

THE FOUR. The name used by the four members of the conspiracy to steal the Agra Treasure in *The Sign of Four*. The Four were Jonathan Small, Abdullah Khan, Dost Akbar, and Mahomet Singh. They murdered Achmet, the bearer of the treasure, stole the jewels, and hid them. Exposed, however, they were sent to prison from where Jonathan Small eventually escaped, promising to recover the treasure in their name. He succeeded, albeit briefly. On the bodies of Major Sholto and Bartholomew Sholto, two victims of the cursed treasure, were placed papers bearing the words The Sign of the Four, a declaration also found on the map of the Agra fort.

FOURNAYE, MADAME. The secret Parisian wife of Henri Fournaye (actually the international agent Eduardo Lucas), who was arrested by the Paris police for the London murder of her husband in "The Second Stain." Of Creole origin, she was of an extremely excitable nature and had suffered in the past from attacks of jealousy that had amounted to frenzy. The servants at her small villa on the Rue Austerlitz reported her to the police authorities as being insane and it was soon uncovered that she had been in London at the time of her husband's brutal murder and that she did indeed suffer from a mania of a dangerous and permanent form. She had presumably suffered an eruption of jealousy and killed him in her uncontrollable rage. The death of her husband had the most profound consequences in the resolution of the case of the missing letter from the dispatch box of Trelawney Hope for which Holmes was searching. Madame Fournaye had drawn much attention to herself at Charing Cross on Tuesday, the night of Lucas's death.

FOUR-WHEELER. Also known as a Clarence cab, a type of enclosed, four-wheeled cab. Four-wheelers were often used by the detective, appearing in several cases: "Black Peter," "The Blue Carbuncle," "The Greek Interpreter," "A Case of Identity," "The Naval Treaty," "The Norwood

Builder," "The Priory School," *The Sign of Four*, "The Six Napoleons," "The Stockbroker's Clerk," and *A Study in Scarlet*. In the 1979 film *Murder By Decree*, a four-wheeler assumed a diabolical nature as it was used by Jack the Ripper; while in *The Adventure of Sherlock Holmes' Smarter Brother* (1975), two four-wheelers were used to fight a bizarre duel between Sigerson Holmes and Moriarty's henchmen.

FRANCE.   Holmes was engaged on several important cases in France. In 1891 in "The Final Problem," the detective assisted the French in a "matter of supreme importance" and Watson received two notes from him from Narbonne and Nimes. It can only be theorized that he was somehow thwarting the plans of Professor Moriarty on the Continent, thereby hastening his climactic struggle with him. Three years later, Holmes received an autographed letter of thanks from the French president for tracking and arresting Huret, the so-called Boulevard Assassin ("The Golden Pince-Nez"). He also spent the final period of the Great Hiatus (1891–1894) in southern France ("The Empty House").

By his own admission, Holmes was of French descent through a grandmother who was the sister of the French artist Vernet ("The Greek Interpreter"). Holmes clearly knew French as he frequently used French words and phrases, and was able to observe that the note in "A Scandal in Bohemia" that was later learned to be from the king of Bohemia could not have been written by a Frenchman. His assorted monographs were also translated into French by Francois le Villard (*The Sign of Four*).

FRANCO MIDLAND HARDWARE COMPANY, LTD.   A company in "The Stockbroker's Clerk" that supposedly operated 134 branches in France, as well as one in Brussels and one in San Remo. It was also purported to be run by Harry Pinner, managing director and promoter, with his brother Arthur one of its financial agents. The stockbroker clerk Hall Pycroft soon learned the truth about the firm and its directors, thanks to Sherlock Holmes.

FRANKFURT.   Actually Frankfurt-am-Main, the site of the Von Bischoff case (*A Study in Scarlet*).

FRANKLAND.   "An elderly man, red-faced, white-haired, and choleric," who lived at Lofton Hall, Devonshire, and who was a neighbor of the Baskervilles in *The Hound of the Baskervilles*. An eccentric, he had a passion for British law, spending a fortune in litigation. "He fights for the mere pleasure of fighting and is equally ready to take up either side of a question, so that it is no wonder that he has found it a costly amusement." Frankland also maintained a close watch over the moor, using his high-powered telescope. Laura Lyons, of Coombe Tracy, was his daughter.

FRASER.   A tutor who met the bogus Mr. Vandeleur on board a ship sailing from Central America to England. Trusting Vandeleur, Fraser helped him to establish St. Oliver's School, a successful institution in East Yorkshire. He eventually died of consumption (*The Hound of the Baskervilles*). Fraser was also the name of the accomplice in assorted criminal deeds of Holy Peters in "The Disappearance of Lady Frances Carfax"—Annie Fraser was "a tall, pale woman, with ferret eyes." She played the part of his wife, Mrs. Shlessinger, in the attempted swindle of Lady Frances Carfax.

FRATTON.   A district in Portsmouth where Holmes, disguised as the Irish-American Altamont, apparently resided in "His Last Bow." He said that he had rooms "down Fratton way."

FREEBODY, MAJOR.   The commander of one of the forts upon Portsdown Hill who was visited by his old friend Joseph Openshaw on the day of the latter's death in "The Five Orange Pips."

FREEMASONRY.   The secret fraternal organization to which Jabez Wilson belonged. Holmes deduced his membership in the Freemasons by the arc-and-compass breast pin that Wilson wore ("The Red-Headed League"). Other members were the detective Barker ("The Retired Colourman"), Enoch Drebber (*A Study in Scarlet*), and John Hector McFarlane ("The Norwood Builder"). Holmes had a deadly encounter with the Masons in the dark 1979 film *Murder By Decree*, with Christopher Plummer.

FRESNO STREET.   A street in London where the offices of the Aberdeen Shipping Company were situated. Mrs. Neville St. Clair went to their offices to pick up a package, accidently causing the events recounted in "The Man With the Twisted Lip."

FREUD, SIGMUND. Austrian psychiatrist (1856–1934) and the developer of the theory of psychoanalysis. Dr. Freud met Holmes in the 1974 pastiche novel *The Seven-Per-Cent Solution* by Nicholas Meyer, helping the detective to overcome his addiction to cocaine. Michael Shepherd also proposed a meeting of the doctor and the detective in his scholarly work, *Sherlock Holmes and the Case of Dr. Freud.*

FROCK COAT. A man's body-coat, with knee-length skirts, usually double-breasted. Holmes apparently frequently wore a frock coat, at least once before the Great Hiatus (*The Hound of the Baskervilles*), and twice after ("The Empty House," "The Norwood Builder"). An excellent illustration of a frock coat was drawn by Sidney Paget, of Lysander Stark for the *Strand* publication of "The Engineer's Thumb," in March 1892.

FULWORTH. A small seaside village in Sussex, near the Fulworth Cove and a few miles from the retirement villa of Sherlock Holmes. Fulworth was situated in a semicircle around the bay ("The Lion's Mane").

FU MANCHU, DR. The fiendish Chinese villain created by the writer Sax Romer in the 1913 novel *Dr. Fu Manchu.* Fu Manchu spent most of his devilish career in constant struggle with Nayland Smith and the redoubtable Dr. Petrie, never, apparently, encountering Holmes, despite the close involvement of both in crime, albeit on either side of the law. According to Cay Van Ash, however, in his excellent novel *Ten Years Beyond Baker Street* (1984), the two did clash, in 1913, as Holmes aided Dr. Petrie in finding the abducted Nayland Smith. The film *Murder Will Out* (1930) also offered a confrontation between Holmes and Fu Manchu.

Another connection between the detective and the evil doctor was found in the various film versions made about him. A number of Holmesian film veterans took part in Fu Manchu productions—Christopher Lee, Thorley Walters, H. Marion Crawford, Douglas Wilmer, and Fred Paul.

GABLES, THE. A well-known coaching establishment (private tutor) that was run by Harold Stackhurst in "The Lion's Mane." The Gables was situated half a mile from Sherlock Holmes's retirement villa and was said to be quite a large place, containing some score of young fellows preparing for various professions.

"GAME IS AFOOT!, THE." This well-known maxim used by Sherlock Holmes was, unlike "Elementary, My Dear Watson!", actually voiced by the Great Detective in the Canon. The phrase had its origins in Shakespeare's *Henry V*, act III, scene I, "I see you stand like greyhounds upon the strip, Straining upon the start. The game's afoot: Follow your spirit; and upon this charge Cry 'God for Harry! England and St. George!'" It was first used in "The Adventure of the Abbey Grange" when Holmes told Watson: "Come, Watson, come!

the game is afoot. Not a word! Into your clothes and come!"

GARCIA, ALOYSIUS.

The occupant of Wisteria Lodge, near Esher, in Surrey in "Wisteria Lodge." He was the son of some high dignitary of San Pedro who had been mistreated by Don Murillo of San Pedro. Garcia himself was apparently connected to an embassy, spoke perfect English, and, according to John Scott Eccles, "was pleasing in his manner, and as good-looking a man as I ever saw in my life." Garcia invited Eccles to Wisteria Lodge as his guest, but during the night he and his entire staff disappeared. A short time later, Garcia was found dead.

GARRIDEB, ALEXANDER HAMILTON.

A fictitious landowner who supposedly left a peculiar will to the advantage only of other Garridebs ("The Three Garridebs"). Garrideb purportedly instructed that his vast fortune of fifteen million dollars could be dispersed only when three other Garridebs were found and stood "in a row." The prospect of inheriting millions was enthralling to the recluse Nathan Garrideb, but he was destined to receive only a crushing disappointment.

GARRIDEB, HOWARD.

A resident of Aston, near Birmingham, who was supposedly the constructor of agricultural machinery and who was apparently the third Garrideb who had to be found so that John and Nathan Garrideb could inherit, with him, the fifteen million dollar estate of Alexander Hamilton Garrideb ("The Three Garridebs"). His advertisement, found by John Garrideb, included the claim that he constructed binders, reapers, steam and hand plows, drills, harrows, farmer's carts, buckboards, and all other appliances, as well as artesian wells. Holmes noted that the advertisement was curious, adding that it was bad English but good American.

GARRIDEB, JOHN.

A supposed "counsellor at law" from Moorville, Kansas who was searching for two more Garridebs so that they could all inherit the fortune of Alexander Hamilton Garrideb ("The Three Garridebs"). John Garrideb was quite upset upon learning that Nathan Garrideb, whom he had found, had consulted Holmes and engaged his services to find the third Garrideb. Throughout his interview with the detective, John revealed that he had not just recently arrived

in England as he claimed, leading Holmes to ponder: "I think the fellow is really an American, but he has worn his accent smooth with years of London. What is his game, then, this preposterous search for Garridebs."

GARRIDEB, NATHAN.

A reclusive antiquarian, of Little Ryder Street, who was sought out by John Garrideb as one of the three Garridebs needed to inherit the vast estate of Alexander Hamilton Garrideb ("The Three Garridebs"). His room looked like a small museum and was crowded with specimens, geological and anatomical. He went out only very rarely, going down to Sotheby's or Christie's. So excited was he at the prospect of inheriting millions that he engaged Holmes to find the third Garrideb, a move that alarmed John Garrideb. Watson wrote that Nathan was "a very tall, loose-jointed, round-backed person, gaunt and bald, some sixty-odd years of age. He had a cadaverous face, with the dull dead skin of a man to whom exercise was unknown. Large round spectacles and a small projecting goat's beard combined with his stooping attitude to give an expression of peering curiosity. The general effect, however, was amiable, though eccentric."

GASOGENE.

A device for creating aerated water by combining alkali carbonate with acid, thereby producing soda or seltzer. In homes it was customarily used in drinks. There was a gasogene at Baker Street, mentioned twice ("The Mazarin Stone," "A Scandal in Bohemia"). The gasogene became a symbol of the meetings of the organization of the Baker Street Irregulars in New York.

GELDER & CO.

A sculptor-works located in Stepney in "The Six Napoleons." The Napoleonic busts by Devine that figured in the affair of the Six Napoleons were manufactured at Gelder & Co., and they supplied both Morse Hudson and Harding Brothers with their busts. The Italian Beppo was employed by them for a time.

GEMMI PASS.

A pass in southwestern Switzerland over which Holmes and Watson journeyed through Interlaken in "The Final Problem." While going along the banks of Daubensee, in the pass, Holmes and Watson were nearly struck by a rock that had been dislodged from a ridge on their right. This was an apparent attempt on their lives.

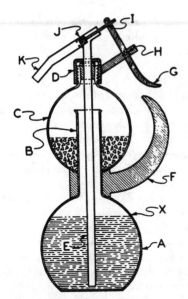

The gasogene at Baker Street, used to produce aerated water, evidenced Holmes's fascination with chemical processes; by Professor Jay Finley Christ, from *The Baker Street Journal*, January 1946.

GENEVA. A city in western Switzerland through which Holmes and Watson journeyed during their Continental sojourn in "The Final Problem." They proceeded to Geneva after learning in Strasbourg that Professor Moriarty had escaped the net of the London police.

GEOLOGY. A field of study in which Holmes was said by Watson to have knowledge that was "practical, but limited. Tells at a glance different soils from each other. After walks has shown me splashes on his trousers, and told me by their color and consistence in what part of London he had received them" (*A Study in Scarlet*). The doctor later looked back at his assessment with humor ("The Five Orange Pips"), and the detective never lost his skill at soil detection.

GEORGIA. The Ku Klux Klan was active in Georgia and had some of its branches there. The barque *Lone Star* was registered out of Savannah, Georgia in "The Five Orange Pips."

GERMANY. In both the Canon and in the films of Basil Rathbone for 20th Century-Fox Studios, the great detective was pitted against the evil empire. In print, Holmes's labors against the Germans centered on his efforts to unravel the spy ring of Von Bork by impersonating the Irish-American agent Altamont in "His Last Bow." His activities were undertaken at the personal request of the prime minister just before the start of World War I (1910–1914). Ironically, the detective had previously aided the king of Bohemia in "A Scandal in Bohemia" when Von Bork's cousin was the imperial envoy, and he saved Count Von und Zu Grafenstein from murder by the Nihilist Klopman. The count was Von Bork's mother's elder brother. Germans appearing in the Canon included the gun maker Von Herder ("The Empty House"), Lysander Stark ("The Engineer's Thumb"), the faithful Heidegger ("The Priory School"), Klein ("The Three Gables"), the manager of Gelder & Co. ("The Six Napoleons"), and the attendant of the Northumberland Hotel (*The Hound of the Baskervilles*).

Homes spoke some German as he was able to quote Goethe in the original German in *The Sign of Four*, and understood the meaning of the mysterious word *RACHE* in *A Study in Scarlet*. He considered the language to be the "most expressive" of all tongues in "His Last Bow," but described the German use of English to be "most uncourteous" to verbs in "A Scandal in Bohemia." The detective also preferred German music to French or Italian, finding it more to his taste. (See also WAGNER, RICHARD.)

In film, Holmes was the perfect choice to entertain American and English audiences with his efforts against the Nazis. Holmes fought the Gestapo or Nazi spies during World War II in such movies as *Sherlock Holmes and the Voice of Terror* (1942), *Sherlock Holmes and the Secret Weapon* (1942), and *Sherlock Holmes in Washington* (1943). While not considered the best of the Holmes films, these were helpful in improving morale in a world seemingly overrun by the Axis. (See also PRIVATE LIFE OF SHERLOCK HOLMES, THE.)

GIANT RAT OF SUMATRA. An unfortunately unchronicled case that involved the ship *Matilda Briggs*. Holmes said that the investigation was "a story for which the world is not yet prepared." Richard Boyer, in his pastiche *The Giant Rat of Sumatra*, offered a possible explanation of the case, while the rodent also appeared in the Christmas tale "A Sherlock Holmes Christmas Story" by John Hogan, in which Professor Moriarty sends the giant rat of Sumatra to Holmes as a gift.

The rodent also appeared in the short story "A Father's Tale" by Sterling Lanier.

GIANT RAT OF SUMATRA, THE.   A 1974 novel by Richard Boyer on the infamous rodent, associated with the ship *Matilda Briggs*. The story is told in the style of reminiscences by Dr. Watson, the publicity for the book declaring: "At last! The Sherlock Holmes adventure Conan Doyle could not bring himself to tell." The tale cleverly ties together several Holmesian points while resurrecting a very dangerous criminal of the Sacred Writings who was thought quite dead. Boyer captures the terror that a giant "rat" would generate, especially upon the Victorian psyche. The novel is considered a minor classic in pastiche literature.

GIBSON, J. NEIL.   American senator and the so-called Gold King in "Thor Bridge," who used his millions in gold to purchase an estate in Hampshire for his family. His wife, the hot-blooded former Maria Pinto, was found dead on Thor Bridge, and the governess of his children, Grace Dunbar, whom he loved, was apparently implicated in the murder. In an effort to clear Dunbar, Gibson engaged the services of Holmes. Bates, Gibson's manager, considered him an infernal villain. Watson was highly impressed with Gibson's appearance. "If I were a sculptor and desired to idealize the successful man of affairs, iron of nerve and leathery of conscience, I would choose Mr. Neil Gibson as my model. His tall, gaunt, craggy figure had a suggestion of hunger and rapacity. An Abraham Lincoln keyed to base uses instead of high ones would give some idea of the man. His face might have been chiseled in granite, hard-set, craggy, remorseless, with deep lines upon it, the scars of many a crisis."

GILA MONSTER.   A venomous lizard, *Helodermus suspectum*, found in the southwest of America and northern Mexico. Its bite, while painful and harmful, is not fatal to most humans. Holmes encountered a "venomous lizard or gila" in an unchronicled case, perhaps before 1896 or 1897, that was filed in his index of cases under V. In the novel *Ten Years Beyond Baker Street* (1984), by Cay Van Ash, the detective faces a gila monster in Wales, as part of his duel with Fu Manchu in 1913. It is therefore possible that the venomous lizard of the index was actually this one and Dr. Watson either unintentionally or purposely changed the date, especially given the fact that the story in which it was mentioned, "The Sussex Vampire," was published in 1924, years after Holmes's brief battle with Fu Manchu.

GILCHRIST.   A young scholar at the College of St. Luke's, a competitor for the Fortescue Scholarship, and one of the three suspects in the cheating scandal at the college that was investigated by Holmes in "The Three Students." Gilchrist, whose first name is never used by Watson in the account of the case, was a "fine scholar and athlete; plays in the Rugby team and the cricket team for the college, and got his Blue for the hurdles and the long jump. He is a fine manly fellow. His father was the notorious **Sir Jabez Gilchrist**, who ruined himself on the turf." By coincidence, Bannister, the butler at the college, had worked for many years for the Gilchrist family and knew young Gilchrist. Following the resolution of the affair, Gilchrist joined the Rhodesian police in South Africa, and Holmes trusted that he had a bright future.

GILLETTE, WILLIAM.   American actor, director, and playwright (1853–1937) who earned stage immortality for his innumerable performances as Sherlock Holmes. More than any single actor, Gillette helped to shape the public image of the Great Detective, bringing to life a character known previously only in literature. Gillette grew up in Connecticut, the son of a retired United States senator. He made his stage debut in 1875 in the play *Guilded Age* through the intervention of the author Mark Twain, who was also a friend of the family. Soon, however, the young performer was finding great success, starring in his own plays as early as 1881.

His first association with Holmes came about rather strangely. In an "interview" concocted by some newspaper reporter in the West, Sir Arthur Conan Doyle supposedly declared that his ideal choice to play the detective on stage was William Gillette. The actor was clearly intrigued and, as fortune would have it, he was the person considered to be the best suited to play Holmes by the Broadway producer Charles Frohman when that impresario began his work to bring Holmes to the stage. Frohman had received from Conan Doyle a five-act play on the detective, but the producer found it unworkable.

He received permission, however, to rework it, and Gillette made wholesale changes in the plot and characters, though he was careful to give

William Gillette, the greatest performer of Holmes on the stage. (Courtesy John Bennett Shaw.)

Conan Doyle billing as coauthor. Interestingly, Gillette had never read any Holmes stories prior to his involvement on the play. He did then read everything published to that point and did a surprisingly excellent job incorporating elements from various cases into the theatrical story. Aside from plotting taken from "A Scandal in Bohemia" and "The Final Problem," Gillette used such characteristic touches as Holmes noting that Watson's face on the right side is poorly shaved (from "The Boscombe Valley Mystery"), and the use of handcuffs (from A Study in Scarlet). He also coined the phrase "Oh, this is elementary, my dear Watson," that was to become so much a part of Basil Rathbone's interpretation.

Completing the play, called simply Sherlock Holmes, Gillette travelled to England in May 1899 to meet Conan Doyle. To Sir Arthur's delight, Gillette stepped off the train in Ulster cape and deerstalker cap, carrying a silver headed stick. Walking smartly up to him, Gillette took out an oversized magnifying lens, peered at him through it, and declared "Unquestionably an author." The two got on splendidly after that and the play Sherlock Holmes was a monumental success.

Gillette would ultimately play Holmes more than 1,300 times in the United States and in England. He was Sherlock Holmes for countless audiences, the image of the detective becoming his own through the artistic labors of Frederic Dorr Steele, who used his face and mannerisms as the model when illustrating newly published stories featuring the detective. Gillette had done more than merely bring Holmes to life—he made the part his own. A chain smoker, he was comfortable with a tobacco-loving sleuth, but he found that while cigars and cigarettes worked fine for the delivery of lines, the traditional straight pipe used by Holmes was very constricting to pronunciation. Thus, he adopted a curved pipe that he could clamp between his teeth and still be understood. This adjustment had the long-reaching effect of connecting the detective with a meerschaum pipe. About the only innovation that did not become a fixture of Holmesian attributes was Gillette's habit of reclining on cushions before a toasty fire.

As was true with Conan Doyle and later Basil Rathbone, Gillette eventually tired of the part, especially as audiences were mercilessly adamant that he play only the detective. Other productions he would stage would be booked only on agreement that Sherlock Holmes be included in the scheduled performances. Unlike Rathbone, Gillette stuck with Holmes and even used the character to poke fun at critics who attacked his acting style (he would stroll about puffing on his pipe, taking an excruciating amount of time to deliver a simple line). The revenge was a comedy spoof, The Painful Predicament of Sherlock Holmes, first staged by Gillette on March 24, 1905.

After retiring in 1910, Gillette would come back to the stage for so-called farewell tours. In 1916 he starred in a film version of the play, Sherlock Holmes. At the age of eighty-two, he was given the distinct honor of a final outing as Holmes, this time on radio. Broadcast on November 18, 1935, on WABC in New York, Gillette gave an hour-long performance, opposite Reginald Mason as Watson. Earlier that year, the recently formed organization of the Baker Street Irregulars made him guest of honor at their annual dinner. Conan Doyle praised Gillette with the words "You make the poor hero of the anemic printed page a very limp object as compared with the glamour of your own personality which you infuse into his stage presentment." [See also SHERLOCK HOLMES (play)].

GIPSIES.   Also Gypsies, the famed migratory people found in many parts of the world, particularly Europe. Gipsies lived in Dartmoor and thus figured in the two cases that were investigated there by Holmes and Watson: The Hound of the Baskervilles and "Silver Blaze." The Gipsy Murphy was a horse-dealer who heard the death cry of Sir Charles Baskerville, and gipsies were suspected in the disappearance of the horse Silver Blaze, particularly as traces of a gipsy camp had been found within a mile of the spot where John Straker's murder had taken place, a camp that was gone the following night. Dr. Grimesby Roylott reportedly had no friends save for a band of gipsies ("The Speckled Band"). He allowed them to encamp on the grounds of Stoke Moran and in return wandered away with them for weeks at a time. Gipsies were thus suspected in the death of Julia Stoner, especially as a result of her dying statement concerning a "speckled band." Gipsies also found the missing Lord Saltire's cricket-cap ("The Priory School"), and had supposedly pierced the ears of John Clay when he was a lad ("The Red-Headed League").

GLASSHOUSE STREET.   A Westminster thoroughfare by which the agents of Baron Gruner

A young Holmes working on his first case—"The 'Gloria Scott' "; by Sidney Paget.

who attacked and beat Holmes escaped in "The Illustrious Client."

GLENDOWER CONSPIRACY, THE. A
1990 pastiche by Lloyd Biggle, Jr., a published memoir from the Papers of Edward Porter Jones, Sherlock Holmes's reliable assistant. This time Holmes is involved in an affair in Wales, investigating the mysterious death of Eleanor Tromblay, wife of Emeric Tromblay, a wealthy mine owner. As is his custom, Holmes sends Porter Jones ahead of him, leaving the initial legwork to his reliable assistant. As usual, the case is not what it seems, expanding to assume national and even international dimensions. The work is steeped in Welsh history and nationalism, including lengthy accounts of Robert Owen and Owen Glendower. This well researched pastiche again largely omits Dr. Watson in the story as his presence in the case would obviate the need for Porter Jones. (See also QUALLSFORD INHERITANCE, THE.)

" 'GLORIA SCOTT', THE" (GLOR).
Published: *Strand*, April 1893, *Harper's*, April 1893; collected in *The Memoirs of Sherlock Holmes*

(1894). Major players: Holmes, Watson, Victor Trevor Jr., Victor Trevor Sr., Beddoes, Hudson. Case date: Possibly 1874. A very notable chronicle, delivered to Watson by Holmes, featuring the detective's first case. On a winter's evening, beside the fire, Holmes gives to Watson a full accounting of the affair, explaining how the following message "struck Justice of the Peace Trevor dead with horror when he read it:" "The supply of game for London is going steadily up [it ran]. Head-keeper Hudson, we believe, has been now told to receive all orders for fly-paper and for preservation of your hen-pheasant's life."

The future detective was introduced to the case by young Trevor, Holmes's only friend during the two years he was at college. "Trevor was the only man I knew, and that only through the accident of his bull terrier freezing on to my ankle one morning as I went down to chapel." Invited to the Trevor estate in Donnithorpe, Norfolk, Holmes meets Trevor Senior and performs an incisive analysis of the old justice of the peace. According to Trevor Senior, "the *Gloria Scott*, an English barque, had been in the Chinese tea-trade, but she was an old-fashioned, heavy-bowed, broad-beamed craft, and the new clippers had cut her out." In 1855, in the midst of the Crimean War, the vessel was pressed into service as a convict ship, transporting prisoners to Australia. Setting sail from Falmouth, it had a crew of twenty-six, with eighteen soldiers, a captain, three mates, a chaplain, a doctor, four warders, and thirty-eight convicts. It never reached Australia and was reported by the Admiralty as being lost at sea in that same year. The true events on board the doomed ship remained secret for many years until revealed by Trevor Senior to his grieved son. So impressed is the elder Trevor by Holmes's deductions that the justice urges Holmes toward a profession. "I don't know how you manage this, Mr. Holmes, but it seems to me that all the detectives of fact and fancy would be children in your hands. That's your line of life, sir, and you may take the word of a man who has seen something of the world."

GLOUCESTER ROAD.   A street in the Kensington area of West London, where Goldini's Restaurant and the Gloucester Road Station of the underground ("The Bruce-Partington Plans") could be found. Holmes initiated his investigation of Hugo Oberstein, of 13 Caulfield Gardens, at the Gloucester Road Station. There a rail worker kindly showed him that the back-stair windows of the Caulfield Gardens opened onto the line, an observation that had the most important relation to the solution of the case.

GODOLPHIN STREET.   A street in Westminster where, at No. 16, resided the international agent Eduardo Lucas in "The Second Stain." A newspaper article, detailing a MURDER IN WESTMINSTER, described the street as "one of the old-fashioned and included rows of eighteenth century houses which lie between the river [Thames] and the Abbey, almost in the shadow of the great Tower and the House of Parliament." It was an ideal location for a spy to take up residence.

GOETHE, JOHANN WOLFGANG VON.   A renowned German writer, scientist, and major figure of world literature (1794–1832). Holmes, betraying his knowledge of letters, quoted Goethe twice during the affair of *The Sign of Four*: "*Wir sind gewohnt, daß die Menschen verkohnen / Was sie nicht verstehen*" ("We are accustomed to seeing man despite what he does not understand"—*Faust*, 1790; the detective added that Goethe "is always pithy");

and "*Schade daß die Natur einen Mensch aus der schuf, / Dem zum würdigen Mann war und zum Schelmen der Stoff*" ("It is a shame that nature made only one person out of you, for there was material enough for a good man and a rogue"—*Xenian*, 1796). See also GERMANY.

"GOLDEN PINCE-NEZ, THE ADVENTURE OF THE" (GOLD).   Published: *Strand*, July 1904, *Collier's*, October 1904; collected in *The Return of Sherlock Holmes* (1905). Case date: November, 1894. Major players: Holmes, Watson, Professor Coram, Anna Coram, Mortimer, Mrs. Marker, and Susan Tarlton. A case investigated by Holmes at Yoxley Old Place in Kent that was part of the very active year 1894; a period that also included such cases as "the story of the red leech and the terrible death of Crosby, the banker . . . the Addleton tragedy . . . the famous Smith-Mortimer succession case . . . and the tracking of the Boulevard assassin, Huret, a feat that won Holmes the Legion of Honour and an autographed letter of thanks from the French president." The noted Holmesian Michael Hardwick writes: "It is hard to believe that 'none of them unites so many singular points of interest as the episode of Yoxley Old Place,' which Watson goes on to narrate instead." Holmes is summoned to Kent by young Inspector Hopkins to look into the murder of Willoughby Smith, secretary to the invalid Professor Coram. Holmes's chain-smoking Alexandrian cigarettes while throwing the ashes on the floor proves critical to the solution of the affair. The detective also performs a brilliant bit of deduction on a pair of spectacles.

GOLDINI'S RESTAURANT.   A "garish" Italian restaurant on the Gloucester Road, Kensington. Holmes dined there during the matter of "The Bruce-Partington Plans" and instructed Watson to meet him there and to bring with him "a jimmy, a dark lantern, a chisel, and a revolver." Upon Watson's arrival, the detective suggested a coffee and a curacao. "Try one of the proprietor's cigars. They are less poisonous than one would expect." Goldini's was also featured in the 1979 novel *Enter the Lion*, by Michael P. Hodel and Sean M. Wright.

GOOSE.   A fowl that figured prominently in the affair of "The Blue Carbuncle." The countess of Morcar's missing Blue Carbuncle, an extraordinary

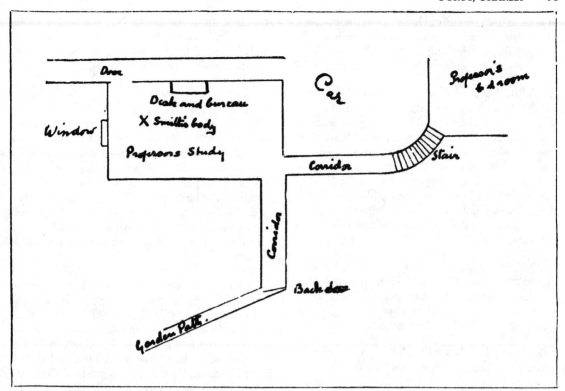

The unfortunate Willoughby is found murdered in "The Adventure of the Golden Pince-Nez."

piece of jewelry, was found in the crop of a Christmas goose belonging to Henry Baker. Holmes was able to determine his possible guilt by gauging his reaction to receiving a goose different from the one he purchased, and by offering him "the feather's, legs, crop, and so on" of his bird. Baker declined; "They might be useful to me as relics of my adventure," said he, "but beyond that I can hardly see what use the disjecta membra of my late acquaintance are going to be to me."

GORDON, SIR CHARLES. Famous British soldier (1833–1885) nicknamed Chinese Gordon. He earned great notoriety in the Chinese War of 1860, ended slavery in Egypt, and was killed at Khartoum by the troops of the Mahdi. Watson owned a newly framed picture of General Gordon ("The Cardboard Box"), and Holmes visited the site of his death, Khartoum, during the Great Hiatus ("The Empty House").

GORDON SQUARE. A square in London where Francis Hay Moulton took lodgings after arriving in England in "The Noble Bachelor."

GORGIANO, GIUSEPPE. A dreaded killer and assassin of the secret society of the Red Circle in "The Red Circle." Gorgiano was born in Posillipo, near Naples, becoming an agent of murder in southern Italy, where he was said to be "red to the elbow." Going to America, he served the Red Circle and was "at the bottom of fifty murders." He was known under several names, "Black Gorgiano," "Gorgiano of the Red Circle," and "Death." Emilia Lucca described him: "Not only was his body that of a giant but everything about him was grotesque, gigantic, and terrifying. His voice was like thunder in our little house. There was scarce room for the whirl of his great arms as he talked. His thoughts, his emotions, his passions, all were exaggerated and monstrous . . . He was a terrible and wonderful man." He pursued Gennaro and Emilia Lucca from New York to London.

GOROT, CHARLES. A fellow clerk, with Percy Phelps, in the Foreign Office who was briefly under suspicion in the theft of the secret "Naval Treaty." He was alone in Percy Phelps's office for a time the evening that the document disappeared and came from people of Huguenot extraction; but he was also English in sympathy and tradition. As Phelps added, "Nothing was found to implicate him in any way, and there the matter dropped."

GOVERNESS. Holmes was persuaded to become involved in several cases by governesses, including Violet Hunter in "The Copper Beeches," Violet Smith in "The Solitary Cyclist," Mary Morstan in *The Sign of Four*—Dr. Watson's future wife—and Miss Dabney, Lady Francis Carfax's old governess in "The Disappearance of Lady Frances Carfax." Grace Dunbar was governess to the children of J. Neil Gibson in "Thor Bridge," and Miss Burnet cared for the children of Mr. Henderson in "Wisteria Lodge."

GRAFENSTEIN, COUNT VON UND ZU. A German aristocrat whom Holmes saved from murder by the nihilist Klopman. Grafenstein was the elder brother of the mother of the German master spy Von Bork ("His Last Bow").

GRAHAM & MCFARLANE. A law firm located at 426 Gresham Buildings, E.C. in "The Norwood Builder." The unfortunate John Hector McFarlane was a junior partner.

GRAVESEND. A port city in Kent from which Jonathan Small and Tonga hoped to depart England on board the ship *Esmeralda* in *The Sign of Four*. Holmes wired Gravesend for information about the *Lone Star* in "The Five Orange Pips," and Mrs. St. Clair received a letter from her missing husband, posted at Gravesend in "The Man With the Twisted Lip."

GRAY, CHARLES. British actor best known for playing the archvillain Ernst Stavro Blofeld in the James Bond film *Diamonds Are Forever*. Gray is also one of the finest of all screen Mycroft Holmeses. He first portrayed Sherlock's brother in *The Seven-Per-Cent Solution* (1976), organizing Sherlock's fateful trip to Vienna with the help of Dr. Watson and Professor Moriarty. He reappeared as Mycroft twice in the Granada Television series on the Great Detective with Jeremy Brett as Sherlock. His first appearance came, obviously, in "The Greek Interpreter," followed later by "The Bruce-Partington Plans."

GREAT ALKALI PLAIN. An "arid and repulsive desert" found in central North America, stretching from the Sierra Nevadas to Nebraska, and the Yellowstone River to the Colorado. In *A Study in Scarlet*, John Ferrier and his daughter Lucy were rescued from the terrible place by a band of migrating Mormons.

"GREAT DETECTIVE, THE." England. 1953. Choreography: Margaret Dale. Music: Richard Arnell. Cast: Kenneth Macmillan (Great Detective, and Infamous Professor), Stanley Holden (His Friend the Doctor) and Walter Trevor (The Innocent Suspect). A Sherlock Holmes ballet, staged in London at the Sadler's Wells Ballet Theatre. Kenneth Macmillan enjoyed the distinction of playing both the detective and his enemy, the professor, as the two figures struggle for control of the city.

GREAT HIATUS. The period dating from May 1891 to April 1894 during which time it was generally believed that Sherlock Holmes was dead. The hiatus began with the detective's apparent demise at the hands of Professor Moriarty at the Reichenbach Falls in Switzerland and ended with Holmes's triumphant return to life in the case recounted as "The Empty House." Aside from the professor's wicked lieutenant who had witnessed Holmes's escape, the only other person who knew that he was alive was Mycroft Holmes. Where the Great Detective was during the hiatus was explained to Watson in "The Empty House": he journeyed to Tibet, Mecca, and Khartoum, before ending up in Montpelier, where he studied coal derivatives.

As there are a number of discrepancies in the account provided by Holmes to Watson concerning his alleged activities during this period, Sherlockians and Holmesians have long postulated theories as to what the Great Detective may truly have been up to during those long years from 1891–1894. The degree of scepticism among Sherlockians was brilliantly displayed by Edgar Smith in his article "Sherlock Holmes and the Great Hiatus" (1946) in *The Baker Street Journal*: "The doings at Reichenbach, we may all agree, are veiled in a mist of considerable doubt. But the Years of the Hiatus which lie beyond are enshrouded in a fog so thick that the streets of London itself have never known its like."

The errors or inconsistencies in the reported activities of Holmes have been examined thoroughly by scholars of the Sacred Writings and

THE STRAND MAGAZINE.

Vol. xxvi.   OCTOBER, 1903.   No. 154.

THE RETURN OF
SHERLOCK HOLMES.

By A. CONAN DOYLE.

I.—The Adventure of the Empty House.

IT was in the spring of the year 1894 that all London was interested, and the fashionable world dismayed, by the murder of the Honourable Ronald Adair under most unusual and inexplicable circumstances. The public has deeply in crime, and that after his disappearance I never failed to read with care the various problems which came before the public, and I even attempted more than once for my own private satisfaction to employ his methods in their solution, though with indifferent success. There was none, however,

Clues to Holmes's whereabouts during the Great Hiatus may be found in "The Empty Room," the first adventure published after his return.

many have reached the conclusion that something amiss is definitely afoot. For example, in "The Empty House," Watson spells lama with two l's, transforming the spiritual and temporal leader of Tibet into a docile pack animal of the Andes. Further, he misspells Montpellier, so that he has Holmes studying coal derivatives not in southern France but in one of several possible American cities, most notably the state capital of Vermont.

Among his superb writings on the Canon, W. S. Baring-Gould wrote the article "You May Have Read of the Remarkable Explorations of a Norwegian Named Sigerson . . ." in which he examined several schools of thought related to the Hiatus with very different positions *vis a vis* Holmes's journeys. One school, described by Baring-Gould as "an articulate group of Sherlockian commentators" holds steadfastly to the view that Holmes did all of the things mentioned in "The Empty House," crafting elaborate and ingenious reasons for the lapses of Watson. They were called by Baring-Gould the Apologists or Fundamentalists and they were opposed by the so-called Interpretive School. This group held that Watson and/or Holmes were not being entirely truthful. Their theories were finely tuned expositions such as that by Edgar Smith that Holmes was actually in America, assisting in the arrest of Lizzie Borden. It was during this time that he met and established his professional association with Wilson Hargreave of the New York Police Bureau mentioned in "The Dancing Men."

Baring-Gould identified a third group, the Sensationalist School. These radical theoreticians argued a number of such hypotheses: that both Holmes and Moriarty somehow survived their dramatic encounter at the Reichenbach Falls; that neither of them walked away from the Falls; or even more shocking, that Holmes was actually sent to a watery grave by the professor and the subsequent stories were all frauds.

Unfortunately, there will never be any definitive proof to confirm or deny the testimony of the Great Detective as recorded in "The Empty House." It will thus be the continuing task of Sherlockians to analyze, decipher, and debate the possible events of that day in May 1891 in Switzerland and the years that followed.

GREAT MOGUL, THE.   An Indian diamond said to weigh 280 carats and to be the second-largest diamond in existence. It was supposedly seen at the imperial Indian court in 1665, later reappearing in the Great Agra Treasure that was stolen by the Four in *The Sign of Four*.

GREAT MOUSE DETECTIVE, THE.   U.S. 1986. Cast: Voices of Vincent Price (Professor Ratigan), Barrie Ingham (Basil), Val Betlin (Dawson). This delightful animated Disney Films release features a brilliant but eccentric mouse, Basil of Baker Street, who resides in the same building as a certain other, albeit human, detective. The entire world of Mousedom parallels that of the humans who appear only briefly in the film, usually as shadows as the mice go about their business. The plot revolves around Basil's search for a little girl's father, a mouse toy maker who has been kidnapped by the evil Ratigan (wonderful voice by Price). He is aided by Dr. David Dawson, a slightly paunchy mouse who will remind afficianadoes of Thorley Walters. The dog Toby also appears. The animation is superb, assisted by the music of Henry Mancini. The film was based on *Basil of Baker Street*, a series of children's books by Eve Titus and Paul Geldone.

GREAT ORME STREET.   A street in central London, described as "a narrow thoroughfare at the north-east side of the British Museum." The Warrens owned "a high thin, yellow-brick edifice in Great Orme Street." Mrs. Warren consulted Holmes about the peculiar habits of one of her lodgers in "The Red Circle."

"GREEK INTERPRETER, THE" (GREE).
Published: *Strand*, September 1893, *Harper's*, September 1893; collected in *The Memoirs of Sherlock Holmes* (1894). Case date: Various, Baring-Gould date September 1888. Major players: Holmes, Watson, Mycroft Holmes, Mr. Melas, Paul Kratides, Sophy Kratides, Wilson Kemp, and Harold Latimer. An interesting case, made even more so by the presence of Mycroft Holmes, Sherlock's elder brother. Holmes suddenly informs Watson that he has a brother, a shadowy but apparently powerful servant in Whitehall and the founding member of the Diogenes Club. Mycroft introduces Holmes and Watson to a neighbor of his, Mr. Melas, a professional Greek

Mycroft Holmes pays a surprise visit to Baker Street in "The Greek Interpreter"; by Sidney Paget.

interpreter. Melas has recently been abducted and held hostage by Harold Latimer and Wilson Kemp, and has been forced to translate for his captors along with another of their victims, the unfortunate Paul Kratides. Eventually released, but with a promise of certain death should he ever talk of his experiences, Melas went immediately to Mycroft, who takes him to Holmes. The most lively portion of the account is the meeting with Mycroft at the Diogenes Club and the careful, delightful analysis he and Holmes make of an old soldier visible from a window in the club.

GREEN DRAGON.   An inn run by Josiah Barnes at Crendall, Berkshire in "Shoscombe Old Place." Holmes and Watson stayed there during their investigation into Shoscombe Old Place.

GREEN, HONORABLE PHILIP.   The son of Admiral Green (commander of the Azov fleet during the Crimean War) who loved Lady Frances Carfax in "The Disappearance of Lady Frances Carfax." He had been a wild youngster who found it better to go to South Africa. There he made a fortune, and some years later returned to England to seek out Lady Carfax, who had remained unmarried. He followed Lady Carfax across Europe and was seen near her just before she vanished, causing Dr. Watson to suspect him of having done away with her. Green subsequently aided Holmes and Watson in their investigation. Jules Vibart, the fiance of Lady Frances's maid Marie Devine, described Green as "*Un sauvage—un veritable sauvage!,*" while the landlord of the Englischer Hof in Baden said he was "a bulky, bearded, sunburned fellow, who looks as if he would be more at home in farmer's inn than a fashionable hotel. A hard, fierce man, I should think, and one I should be sorry to attend."

GREGORY, INSPECTOR.   A police inspector assigned to investigate the disappearance of the horse Silver Blaze and the murder of its trainer John Straker in "Silver Blaze." Holmes said that Gregory "is an extremely competent officer. Were he but gifted with imagination he might rise to great heights in his profession."

GREGSON, TOBIAS.   A Scotland Yard inspector who was involved in a number of Holmes's cases, often calling him in, unwillingly, when at an impasse or more often, utterly out of his depth. His known investigations involving Holmes were *A Study in Scarlet*, *The Sign of Four*, "The Greek Interpreter," "The Red Circle," and "Wisteria Lodge." Holmes had various opinions of him. In *A Study in Scarlet*, he told Watson: "Gregson is the smartest of the Scotland Yarders; he and Lestrade are the pick of a bad lot. They are both quick and energetic, but conventional—shockingly so. They have their knives into one another, too." He would later declare in "The Red Circle": "Our official detectives may blunder in the matter of intelligence, but never in that of courage"; and Watson wrote that Gregson was "an energetic, gallant, and, within his limitations, a capable officer" ("Wisteria Lodge"). Watson described him as "a tall, white-faced, flaxen-haired man, with a notebook in his hand" (*A Study in Scarlet*). Gregson was never as popular with filmmakers as was Lestrade.

GREUZE, JEAN BAPTISTE.   French artist (1725–1805), one of whose paintings was owned by Professor Moriarty. According to Holmes, in *The Valley of Fear*, a Greuze entitled *La Jeune Fille a l'Agneau* ("Young Girl with a Lamb") was sold in 1865 for 40,000 pounds at the Portalis sale (in some editions the amount is lowered to 4,000 pounds). The detective added: "Modern criticism has more than endorsed the high opinion formed of him by his contemporaries." The Greuze owned by Moriarty was hung in his study, depicting "a young woman with her head on her hands, peeking at you sideways." The painting figured in the John Gardner novels, *The Return of Moriarty* (1974) and *The Revenge of Moriarty* (1975).

GREYMINSTER, DUKE OF.   A client of Holmes's, mentioned in his account of "The Blanched Soldier." Holmes wrote of the duke of Greyminster's involvement in the case of the Abbey School. It is generally assumed that the detective was referring to the duke of Holdernesse and the affair of "The Priory School."

GRICE PATERSON.   An investigation conducted by Holmes in 1887. It involved "the singular adventures of Grice Patersons in the island of Uffa" ("The Five Orange Pips"), although it is unclear who or what the Grice Patersons were.

GRIGGS, JIMMY.   A clown in the Ronder Circus who did his best "to hold things together" as the circus declined due to Ronder's drinking in "The Veiled Lodger." Griggs saved Eugenia Ronder's life by driving off the lion Sahara King with a pole when it attacked her.

GRIMPEN.   A small village in Devonshire, on Dartmoor, near Baskerville Hall. It was the site of the events recounted in *The Hound of the Baskervilles* (see next entry).

GRIMPEN MIRE.   The terrible mire in Devonshire, in the parish of Grimpen where occurred the worst events recorded in *The Hound of the Baskervilles*. The Grimpen Mire dominated the countryside around Baskerville Hall and was, by legend, the home of the Hound of the Baskervilles. Watson wrote of it: "Ever since I have been here I have been conscious of shadows all around me. Life has become like that great Grimpen Mire, with little green patches everywhere into which one may sink and with no guide to point the track."

GRODNO.   A city in Russia, incorrectly said by Holmes to be in Little Russia. The detective spoke of an incident there in 1866 that was analogous to the case of *The Hound of the Baskervilles.*

GROSS & HANKEY'S.   Probably a jeweler's establishment located on Regent Street. In "A Scandal in Bohemia," Godfrey Norton, fiancé of Irene Adler, hurried there, in all likelihood to purchase a ring for their impending wedding.

GROSVENOR MANSIONS.   The residence of Lord Robert St. Simon in "The Noble Bachelor." It was on Victoria Street, Westminster. The letter from him to Holmes was dated from there.

GROSVENOR MIXTURE.   A type of tobacco mixture that was smoked by Grant Munro in "The Yellow Face."

GROSVENOR SQUARE.   A Mayfair square where Isadora Klein lived in "The Three Gables." Grosvenor Square was also the probable site of the "Little Problem of the Grosvenor Square Furniture Van," a case investigated by Holmes. At the time of his handling of the affair chronicled in "The Noble Bachelor," Holmes declared the case to be "quite cleared up now—though, indeed, it was obvious from the first."

GRUNER, BARON ADELBERT.   An Austrian aristocrat presented in "The Illustrious Client" who ranks with Dr. Grimesby Roylott as one of the most vile characters in the entire Canon. Known as the Austrian Murderer, Gruner had apparently managed to kill his wife in the Splugen Pass and escaped justice because of the untimely

Baron Adalbert Gruner in "The Illustrious Client"; by John Richard Flanagan.

demise of a witness. Having gone on a Mediterranean yachting voyage, he met the young, beautiful, and wealthy Violet de Merville, winning her love and devotion. Holmes was engaged by Sir James Damery, the discreet representative of the "Illustrious Client" to bring the planned union of de Merville and the baron to an end. The assignment proved very dangerous to Holmes as the baron had at his disposal a terrible arsenal of thugs and cutthroats.

HAFIZ. A Persian lyric poet of the fourteenth century. His collection of 700 poems, *The Divan*, was first published in English in 1891. Holmes quoted Hafiz at the end of "A Case of Identity." "There is danger for him who taketh the tiger cub, and danger also for whoso snatches a delusion from a woman," adding, "there is as much sense in Hafiz as in Horace, and as much knowledge of the world."

HAGUE, THE. Holmes pointed out that a parallel to the Mary Sutherland case ("A Case of Identity") occured in The Hague, the capital of the Netherlands, the previous year.

HAINES-JOHNSON. The name used by a disreputable auctioneer and appraiser in the pay of Isadora Klein in "The Three Gables." He attempted to purchase the Three Gables and all its furnishings at a good price from Mrs. Mary Maberley.

HALIFAX. The capital of Nova Scotia where Colonel Spence Munro accepted a post in "The Copper Beeches." Miss Violet Hunter, governess to Munro's children for five years, was thus forced to find another position.

HALLE, SIR CHARLES. British conductor and pianist (1819–1895), born in Westphalia, Germany. He married the well-known violinist Wilhelmine Norman-Neruda in 1888. During his investigation of the Drebber murder (*A Study in Scarlet*), Holmes took time to hear Norman-Neruda at Halle's.

HAMMERFORD WILL CASE. A delicate matter handled by Sir James Damery. He conducted the negotiations with Sir George Lewis over the Hammerford Will Case, one of many private affairs taken care of by Sir James ("The Illustrious Client").

HAMPSHIRE. A county in southern England where could be found the residence of J. Neil Gibson ("Thor Bridge"), Beddoes ("The 'Gloria Scott' "), and Jephro Rucastle ("The Copper Beeches"). At one time, the estate of the Roylotts of Stoke Moran extended over the Surrey border into Berkshire and Hampshire ("The Speckled Band"). While journeying through Hampshire to look into the Copper Beeches affair, Holmes spoke to Watson of the countryside. "You look at these scattered houses, and you are impressed by their beauty. I look at them and the only thought which comes to me is a feeling of their isolation and the immunity with which crime may be committed there ... look at these lonely houses, each in its own fields, filled for the most part with poor ignorant folk who know little of the law. Think of the hellish cruelty, the hidden wickednesses which may go on year in, year out, in such places, and none the wiser."

HAMPSTEAD. A largely residential area of London. Hall Pycroft ("The Stockbroker's Clerk"), Cecil James Barker (*The Valley of Fear*), and Charles Augustus Milverton ("Charles Augustus Milverton") lived in Hampstead. The large public area of Hampstead Heath was situated within Hampstead. Holmes and Watson ran two miles after burgling the home of Milverton, Appledore Towers, particularly after the climactic events there. Mr. Warren was set free by his captors here in "The Red Circle." Hampstead Heath was a scene of considerable activity in the 1987 novel, *The Revenge of the Hound*, by Michael Hardwick, in which the Hound of the Baskervilles had apparently returned and was apparently running loose on the heath.

"HANDS OF A MURDERER." A 1990 American television movie starring Edward Woodward and John Hillerman (Holmes and Watson), with Anthony Andrews (Professor Moriarty), and Kim Thomson (who also played the character Kitty Winter in "The Illustrious Client" on the BBC series with Jeremy Brett). Also titled "Sherlock Holmes and the Prince of Crime," this is a surprisingly disappointing production despite the best efforts of all concerned and lavish attention to detail. Andrews would have been an excellent Holmes and Woodward a superb Moriarty. The plot involves the professor's increasingly contrived efforts to best Sherlock, in the spirit of *The Adventures of Sherlock Holmes* (1939).

HANDWRITING. Handwriting analysis allowed Holmes to gain insight into numerous cases. In the affair of "The Reigate Squires," such analysis was of enormous help in solving the case, reflecting Holmes's view of handwriting in general. "In normal cases one can place a man in his true decade with tolerable confidence. I say normal cases because ill-health and physical weakness reproduce the signs of old age, even when the invalid is a youth." The detective analyzed the writing of Jonas Oldacre in "The Norwood Builder," Annie Harrison in "The Naval Treaty," and was able to recognize the writing of Porlock, his informant in the organization of Professor Moriarty in *The Valley of Fear*. Holmes could also date the Baskerville manuscript in *The Hound of the Baskervilles* to within ten years of its authorship. (See also TYPEWRITER.)

HARDEN, JOHN VINCENT. A well-known tobacco millionaire who in 1895 was subjected to a peculiar persecution. Holmes investigated the matter and found it to be "a very abstruse and complicated problem." His attentions were so focused upon the Harden case that he could not undertake personally the Violet Smith affair of "The Solitary Cyclist," sending Watson as his surrogate.

HARDING, LYN. Welsh-born actor (1867–1952) distinguished for having played two of the Canon's most wicked villains, Dr. Grimesby Roylott and Professor Moriarty. Harding was actually an accomplished performer before entering Sherlockian productions, having served, with fellow Holmesian alumnus H. A. Saintbury, in the acting company of Sir Herbert Tree. In 1910, he portrayed Grimesby Roylott (or Rylott as he is called in the play) on the stage, in Conan Doyle's play *The Speckled Band*, reprising the character in the 1921 film version with Saintbury. After taking on the role of Captain Hook in two stage versions of *Peter Pan* (1922, 1925), Harding was back as Rylott opposite Raymond Massey in *The Speckled Band* (1931). Four years later, he assumed the role of Professor Moriarty, facing Arthur Wontner in *The Triumph of Sherlock Holmes* (1935) and *Silver Blaze* (1937). Harding's wicked presence, piercing eyes, and menacing countenance, made him a natural Moriarty. (See also "SPECKLED BAND, THE.")

HARDING, MR. Founder and proprietor of Harding Brothers, an emporium in Kensington in "The Six Napoleons." Among his items for sale were plaster casts of Devine's head of Napoleon which were sold to Horace Harker, Mr. Sandeford, and Josiah Brown. Each bust was eventually destroyed.

HARDY. Foreman of the Sutherland plumbing firm, operating the business with the widow of Sutherland until her remarriage to James Windibank in "A Case of Identity." Hardy accompanied Mrs. Sutherland and her daughter, Mary, to the gasfitter's ball. There Mary met her future fiance, Hosmer Angel.

HARDY, SIR CHARLES. The author of a report that was in Trelawny Hope's dispatch box in "The Second Stain."

HARDY, SIR JOHN. A member of the Bagatelle Card Club who, on the afternoon of March 30, 1894, played whist with Ronald Adair and two other gentlemen—Adair was murdered that night in "The Empty House."

HARGREAVE, WILSON. A member of the New York Police Bureau and a friend of Holmes's. According to Holmes, Hergreave "more than once made use of my knowledge of London crime." The American policeman was willing to reciprocate, communicating to Holmes important information by cable to the detective that helped the solution of the affair of "The Dancing Men." How the two met is not stated in the Canon. H. Paul Jeffers, however, in his 1978 novel, *The Adventure of the Stalwart Companions*, postulated that they first worked together in New York in 1880, in the case that also brought together Holmes and Teddy Roosevelt.

HARGROVE.   An alias used by the murderer Ted Baldwin in *The Valley of Fear*. It has been spelled Hargrave in some editions.

HARKER, HORACE.   A reporter of the Central Press Syndicate who resided at No. 131 Pitt Street, Kensington in "The Six Napoleons." Early one morning he was stunned to find his plaster cast of Devine's head of Napoleon missing and a murder victim, later identified as Pietro Venucci, sprawled on his doorstep. Harker was so confused and bothered by the incident that he could not cover his own story. He went on to bemoan: "It's like my luck! You remember when the stand fell at Doncaster? Well, I was the only journalist in the stand, and my journal the only one that had no account of it, for I was too shaken to write it. And now I will be too late with a murder done on my own doorstep." Harker later unwittingly aided Holmes by placing a false statement in his published account.

HARLEY STREET.   A street in the West End, known for the many physicians and specialists who had offices there. Dr. Moore Agar lived on Harley Street ("The Devil's Foot"). Watson also wrote in *The Valley of Fear* that Holmes was regarded by White Mason as a Harley Street specialist was viewed by a village practitioner.

HARRINGBY, LORD.   A neighbor of Aloysius Garcia whose home, The Dingle, was near Wisteria Lodge and Oxshott, in Surrey in "Wisteria Lodge."

HARRIS.   The name used by Holmes when he posed as an accountant from Bermondsey in his interview with Harry Pinner, of the Franco-Midland Hardware Co., the employer of Hall Pycroft in "The Stockbroker's Clerk."

HARRISON, ANNIE.   The fiancée of Percy Phelps in "The Naval Treaty." Following the theft of the Naval Treaty from the Foreign Office and the subsequent collapse of Phelps from a brain fever, she nursed him back to health. Annie Harrison also helped Holmes to solve the case. Her brother was Joseph Harrison. Holmes said of her: "She is a good sort, or I am mistaken. She and her brother are the only children of an iron-master up Northumberland way."

HARRISON, JOSEPH.   The brother of Annie Harrison and the prospective brother-in-law of Percy Phelps in "The Naval Treaty." On the night that the treaty was stolen, he was in London and was to travel down to Woking by the eleven-o'clock train. Percy hoped to journey with him. Holmes summed up the deceptively dangerous man by saying, "I can only say for certain that Mr. Joseph Harrison is a gentleman to whose mercy I would be extremely unwilling to trust."

HARROW.   Also Harrow-on-the-Hill, a city in Middlesex. Honoria Westphail, aunt of Helen and Julia Stoner in "The Speckled Band," lived near Harrow. (See next entry.)

HARROW WEALD.   A district of Middlesex, north of Harrow, where Mary Maberley lived at "The Three Gables." Holmes was warned by the fighter Steve Dixie that it was not safe "out Harrow way."

HARVEY.   A stableboy at Shoscombe Park in "Shoscombe Old Place." He was in charge of the central heating furnace at Shoscombe Old Place, discovering one morning the upper condyle of a human femur while raking out the furnace's cinders.

HARWICH.   A port town in Essex where Holmes met Watson prior to their driving in the doctor's Ford automobile to the residence of the German spymaster Von Bork in "His Last Bow." Von Bork's house overlooked Harwich and the harbor, and one could see the lights of the city at night.

HATHERLEY, VICTOR.   A hydraulic engineer who had a dramatic introduction to Dr. Watson in "The Engineer's Thumb"—he was assisted to the doctor's office near Paddington Station by railway guard because he had lost his thumb. Hatherley informed Watson that he resided at 16A Victoria Street (3d floor) and had lost the appendage through a murderous attack. The physician took care of the thumb and introduced Hatherley to Holmes, one of only two cases that Watson personally brought to the detective's attention, the other being the unchronicled Colonel Warburton's madness. Hatherley had been hired by the mysterious Lysander Stark to repair a hydraulic press, a commission that led to his being set upon. Watson found Hatherley understandably not at his best. "He was quietly dressed in a suit of heather tweed, with a soft cloth cap which he had laid down upon my books. Round one of his hands he had a hand-kerchief wrapped, which was mottled all over with bloodstains. He was young, not more than five and twenty, I should say, with a strong, masculine face; but he was exceedingly pale and gave me the impression of someone who was suffering from strong agitation, which it took all his strength of mind to control."

HAVEN, THE.   The home of Josiah Amber-eley and his wife in Lewisham in "The Retired Colourman." Of it Watson said: "I have never seen a worse-kept place. The garden was all running to seed, giving me an impression of wild neglect in which the plants had been allowed to find the way of Nature rather than art . . . The house, too, was slatternly to the last degree, but the poor man seemed himself to be aware of it and to be trying to remedy it, for a great pot of green paint stood in the centre of the hall, and he was carrying a thick brush in his left hand. He had been working on the woodwork." Another home called The Haven was that of the Bellamy family, in Fulworth, Sussex in "The Lion's Mane."

HAYLING, JEREMIAH.   A young hydraulic engineer who disappeared approximately one year before Victor Hatherley was hired by the myste-rious Colonel Lysander Stark to repair a hy-draulic press in "The Engineer's Thumb." An advertisement that appeared in the papers at the time stated: "Lost on the 9th inst., Mr. Jeremiah Hayling, aged 26, a hydraulic engineer. Left his lodgings at ten o'clock at night, and has not been heard of since."

HAYS, REUBEN.   Also Reuben Hayes, the owner of the Fighting Cock Inn, in Hallamshire in "The Priory School." Hays had once been the head coachman at Holdernesse Hall, in the service of the duke of Holdernesse, but had been removed from his position by the duke "without a character on the word of a lying corn-chandler." An embit-tered, "squat, dark, elderly man," he was involved in the abduction of Lord Saltire. His wife, Mrs. Hays, was a kind woman who was under the control of her brutal husband.

HAYTER, COLONEL.   An owner of a house near Reigate in Surrey in "The Reigate Squires." He had served as an officer in India and had come under Watson's care in Afghanistan. Years later he invited Holmes and Watson for a rest at his home, the detective accepting the offer only after being assured that the establishment was a bachelor one and that he would be given complete freedom. The doctor added, "Hayter was a fine old soldier who had seen much of the world, and he soon found, as I had expected, that Holmes and he had much in common."

HEBRON, JOHN.   A lawyer in Atlanta with a good practice, the husband of Effie Hebron and father of Lucy Hebron in "The Yellow Face." He died in Atlanta of yellow fever.

HEBRON, LUCY.   The daughter of Effie and John Hebron in "The Yellow Face." Following the outbreak of yellow fever that killed her father, and left her weak, Lucy remained in America. Her mother claimed that she had died in Atlanta.

HEIDEGGER.   The German master at the Pri-ory School who disappeared on the same night that Lord Saltire, son of the duke of Holdernesse, was apparently abducted in "The Priory School." The instructor had come to the school with the best of references, "but he was a silent, morose man, not very popular with masters or boys." Sus-pected of complicity in the affair, Heidegger was later found murdered and was cleared of all sus-picion.

HEINRICH.   German imperial envoy and cousin to the German master spy Von Bork in "His Last Bow." Holmes told Von Bork that Heinrich was envoy during the time that he had brought about the "separation" between Irene Adler and the late king of Bohemia, an affair recounted in "A Scandal in Bohemia."

HENDERSON.   The name used by Don Murillo of San Pedro while living at High Gable, near Oxshott, in Surrey in "Wisteria Lodge."

HEREFORD ARMS.   A hotel in Ross where Holmes and Watson stayed while looking into the murder of Charles McCarthy in "The Boscombe Valley Mystery."

Holmes and Watson find the body of the German master Heidegger in "The Priory School"; by Sidney Paget.

HERLOCK HOLMES. A highly successful parody of the Great Detective that first appeared in a series of short stories in the *Greyfriar's Herald* (1915) under the name Peter Todd, the pseudonym of Charles Harold St. John Hamilton. The tales featured the detective and faithful friend and chronicler Jotson. *The Adventures of Herlock Holmes* ran for the entire life of the *Greyfriar's Herald* (eighteen issues), before appearing in other publications. In all, "Todd" wrote over a hundred stories, including such interesting adventures as "The Case of the Escaped Hun" (1917), "The Chopstick Venus" (1920), "The Purloined Pork" (1920), and "The Nabob's Elephant" (1925). According to Peter Haining, the noted anthologist, copies of the early editions of the *Greyfriar's Herald* are among the most sought after series in all of Sherlockiana.

HIGH GABLE. The residence near Oxshott, in Surrey, of Mr. Henderson in "Wisteria Lodge."

Holmes described it as "the famous old Jacobean grange of High Gable, one mile on the farther side of Oxshott, and less than half a mile from the scene of the tragedy [the murder of Aloysius Garcia]."

HIGH TOR. A farmhouse on Dartmoor, in Devonshire, near Baskerville Hall in *The Hound of the Baskervilles*. The strange death of Sir Charles Baskerville occured here.

HILL, INSPECTOR. A member of Scotland Yard in "The Six Napoleons" who made a specialty of Saffron Hill and the Italian Quarter. Hill recognized the dead man found on the doorstep of Horace Harker as Pietro Venucci, from Naples, one of the greatest cutthroats in London who had connections to the Mafia.

HIS LAST BOW. The fourth collection of Holmes's cases, published in 1917. The adventures written by Dr. Watson and included in the work were "The Adventure of Wisteria Lodge," "The Adventure of the Red Circle," "The Adventure of the Bruce-Partington Plans," "The Adventure of the Dying Detective," "The Disappearance of Lady Frances Carfax," and "The Adventure of the Devil's Foot." Two other cases were included that deserve special mention: "His Last Bow," with its "An Epilogue of Sherlock Holmes," was written in the third person and was clearly intended to be the last word on the subject of Sherlock Holmes; "The Adventure of the Cardboard Box," published originally in January 1893, has a confusing place in Holmes collections because of public objections to its content—namely adultery. It was included in some editions of the collection *The Memoirs of Sherlock Holmes* (1894), but was left out in others. By 1917, it was felt that such objections had ceased, or at least been mollified by time, and so "The Cardboard Box" was added to *His Last Bow*.

"His Last Bow" (Last).

Published: *Strand*, September 1917, *Collier's*, September 22, 1917; collected in *His Last Bow* (1917). Major players: Holmes, Watson, Martha, Von Bork, Von Herling. Case date: August 1914. Known also with the subtitles "An Epilogue of Sherlock Holmes" and "The War Service of Sherlock Holmes," a chronicle detailing Holmes's labors on behalf of England just before the start of World War I. Written in the third person, it was said to be the result of the question asked by a British general as to what Holmes might have done during the war. The Great Detective is lured from happy retirement on the Sussex Downs to serve England by penetrating a dangerous spy ring headed by one of the kaiser's greatest operatives, Von Bork. The master spy's house on the English coast has become the center of a vast web, penetrated ingeniously by Holmes under the guise of the Irish-American agent Altamont. The story itself details the final closing of the net around Von Bork, culminating with Holmes's well-known speech to Watson. "Good old Watson! You are the one fixed point in a changing age. There's an east wind coming all the same, such a wind as never blew on England yet. It will be cold and bitter, Watson, and a good many of us may wither before its blast. But it's God's own wind none the less, and a cleaner, better, stronger land will lie in the sunshine when the storm has cleared."

Hobbs, Fairdale.

A lodger in the Great Orme Street house of Mrs. Warren in "The Red Circle." In the year before Mrs. Warren brought her own case to Holmes, Fairdale Hobbs had engaged the detective in "a simple matter." When Holmes refused to aid Mrs. Warren, she successfully flattered him by saying that Hobbs would never cease talking about the case—"your kindness, sir, and the way in which you brought light into the darkness. I remembered his words when I was in doubt and darkness myself. I knew you could if only you would."

Hoby, Sir Edward.

A squire in Norfolk who worked with Trevor Senior to bring a poaching gang to justice in "The 'Gloria Scott'." He and Trevor were threatened by the gang with knives, and Hoby was actually attacked by them on one occasion. In some editions his name is spelled Holly.

Hoey, Dennis.

American actor who played the bumbling Inspector Lestrade in six of the Universal Holmes films starring Basil Rathbone (Holmes) and Nigel Bruce (Watson). Hoey appeared in *Sherlock Holmes and the Secret Weapon* (1942), *Sherlock Holmes Faces Death* (1943), *The Spider Woman* (1944), *The Pearl of Death* (1944), *The House of Fear* (1945), and *Terror By Night* (1946). His interpretation of Lestrade was not particularly faithful to the Canon, but it was certainly entertaining and contrasted well with Rathbone's brilliance as Holmes. Hoey's Lestrade also had excellent chemistry with Nigel Bruce, particularly when the pair was left alone to sort out a puzzle unaided by the luminescence of Holmes. In this Lestrade, Watson had a detective more hopeless at deductive reasoning than he.

"Hoffman Barcarolle."

A work by the French composer Jacques Offenbach for his opera *Les Contes d'Hoffman* (*The Tales of Hoffman*) which was first performed in 1881. (A barcarolle, or barcarole, is a composition intended to mimic the songs of a Venetian gondolier.) Holmes fooled Count Sylvius and Sam Merton into thinking that he was playing the "Hoffman Barcarolle" on the violin in "The Mazarin Stone." It was actually a recording.

Holborn, The.

A restaurant in High Holborn where Watson and Stamford had lunch after meeting at the Criterion Bar in *A Study in Scarlet*. While going there in a cab, the two discussed Watson's search for more economical lodgings, a conversation that led to the doctor's introduction to Sherlock Holmes. Young Parkins was killed outside the "Holborn Bar" in "The Three Gables," possibly another name for the Holborn. Holmes confronted Steve Dixie about the killing. The Holborn was also used in Nicholas Meyer's novel, *The West End Horror* (1975).

HOLDER, ALEXANDER. The highly respected senior partner of the private banking firm Holder & Stevenson, of Threadneedle Street, in London in "The Beryl Coronet." In return for a loan of 50,000 pounds to an exalted nobleman he was given the Beryl Coronet as collateral, one of the most precious possessions in the British Empire. When part of it was stolen the apparent thief turned out to be his unreliable, profligate, and plutocratic son **Arthur.** He immediately consulted Holmes, running to 221B from the direction of the Metropolitan Station. Watson wrote: "He was a man of about fifty, tall, portly, and imposing, with a massive, strongly marked face and a commanding figure. He was dressed in sombre but rich style, in black frockcoat, shining hat, neat brown gaiters, and well-cut pearly gray trousers. Yet his actions were in absurd contrast to the dignity of his dress and features, for he was running hard, with occasional little springs, such as a weary man gives who is little accustomed to set any tax upon his legs. As he ran he jerked his hands up and down, waggled his head, and writhed his face into the most extraordinary contortions." His son Arthur, viewed by his father as a wastrel always in need of money, was immediately suspected of trying to make off with the priceless Beryl Coronet, his guilt seemingly proven absolutely by the fact that he was found holding the damaged piece of jewelry, with three of its stones missing. Arrested by the police, Arthur remained curiously silent and was eventually cleared by Holmes. The detective told Alexander, "You owe a very humble apology to that noble lad, your son, who has carried himself in this matter as I should be proud to see my own son do, should I ever chance to have one." **Mary Holder,** the niece of Alexander Holder and cousin of Arthur Holder, lived with her uncle in Steatham after the death of her father. She was infatuated with Sir George Burnwell and disappeared after the attempted theft of the Beryl Coronet.

HOLDER, JOHN. A company sergeant in the Third Buffs who saved the life of Jonathan Small by rescuing him from the Ganges after an attack by a crocodile in *The Sign of Four.*

HOLDERNESSE, DUKE OF. A powerful, influential, and extremely wealthy nobleman whose son, Lord Saltire, disappeared from the Priory School run by Dr. Thorneycroft Huxtable in "The Priory School." Holmes read of the duke in his encyclopedia of reference, volume *H*: "Holdernesse, 6th Duke, K.G., P.C.—half the alphabet! 'Baron Beverley, Earl of Carlston'—dear me what a list! 'Lord Lieutenant of Hallamshire since 1900. Married Edith Appledore, daughter of Sir Charles Appledore, 1888. Heir and only child, Lord Saltire. Owns about two hundred and fifty thousand acres. Minerals in Lancashire and Wales. Address: Carlton House Terrace; Holdernesse Hall, Hallamshire; Carston Castle, Bangor, Wales. Lord of the Admiralty, 1872; Chief Secretary of State for—' well, well, this man is certainly one of the greatest subjects of the Crown!" The duke had offered a 5000 pound reward for information as to the whereabouts of his son, and an additional 1000 pounds for the identity of the kidnappers. In a rare instance of claiming a reward of large size for his services, Holmes accepted the check from the duke, pocketing it and declaring, "I am a poor man." Sherlockians point out, however, that Watson's subsequent testimony notwithstanding ("Black Peter"), there is no evidence that Holmes ever actually cashed the check. In writing his own account of "The Blanched Soldier," Holmes referred to "the case which my friend Watson has described as that of the Abbey Shool, in which the Duke of Greyminster was so deeply involved." It is generally assumed that Holmes here refers to the duke of Holdernesse, although it is unclear whether he is here using the nobleman's real name. The **duchess of Holdernesse**—the onetime Edith Appledore, daughter of Sir Charles Appledore—had married the duke of Holdernesse in 1888, a union that produced one son, Lord Saltire. At the time of the abduction of Lord Saltire, she had become estranged from the duke and was living in the south of France.

HOLDERNESSE HALL. The seat of the duke of Holdernesse, near Mackleton, in Hallamshire in "The Priory School." It had a famous avenue of yews and a magnificent Elizabethan doorway.

HOLDHURST, LORD.   British foreign minister, a powerful Conservative politician, future premiere, and the uncle of Percy Phelps by Phelps's mother in "The Naval Treaty." Through Holdhurst's influence, Phelps was given a good position in the Foreign Office, and it was his lordship's understandable view that the disappearance of the Naval Treaty would have "a very prejudicial effect upon his career." Watson wrote that Holdhurst "seemed to represent that not too common type, a nobleman who is in truth noble."

HOLGER-MADSEN, FORREST.   Danish-born actor and director who appeared in a number of the Nordisk series of silent films from 1908 to 1911. He first played the role of the clever and elusive thief Raffles in *Sherlock Holmes I* (1908) and *Sherlock Holmes II* (1908), opposite Viggo Larsen (Holmes) and possibly Alwin Neuss (Watson). He may have again performed as Raffles in *Sherlock Holmes I Gaskjeldfren* (*Sherlock Holmes and the Gas Cellar*, 1908), although there is some doubt as to whether he had the role of the thief. In *Den Graa Dame* (*The Grey Lady*, 1909), he was given a prominent but unknown part. Holger-Madsen next served as director for *La Femme* (*The Woman*, 1910) and possibly *Sherlock Holmes I Bondefangerklor* (*Sherlock Holmes in the Claws of the Confidence Men*, 1910), *Den Forklaedte Guvernante* (*The Bogus Governess*, 1911), and *Hotelmysterierne* (*The Hotel Mystery*, 1911); he had also directed and perhaps starred as Holmes in the little-known 1908 feature *The Adventure of Sherlock Holmes.*

HOLLAND, ROYAL FAMILY.   Holmes performed some service for this reigning family in *A Study in Scarlet*. The detective told Watson that "the matter in which I served them was of such delicacy that I cannot confide it even to you, who have been good enough to chronicle one or two of my little problems" ("A Case of Identity"). As a gesture of their gratitude, the royal family gave to Holmes "a remarkable brilliant which sparkled upon his finger."

HOLLIS.   A member of the spy ring of the German Von Bork in "His Last Bow." He was captured just before the start of World War I, most likely through the efforts of Holmes as Altamont. Von Bork was of the view that he was mad, while Altamont added, "Well, he went a bit woozy towards the end. It's enough to make a man bughouse when he has to play a part from morning to night with a hundred guys all ready to set the copper wise to him," an observation made from personal experience.

HOLMES, CREIGHTON.   A parody of Sherlock Holmes, written by Ned Hubbell and presented in a collection of cases, *The Adventures of Creighton Holmes* (1979). Creighton Holmes is the descendent of the Great Detective who, from childhood, desired to pursue the career of the family. His cases were recorded by his faithful assistant Mr. Harrington, and the adventures presented in the 1979 work were by Harrington's pen. Creighton's cases included "The Mysterious Death at Weatherby Manor," "The Case of the Scientific Recluse," "The Strange Death of Matthew Tidmore," "The Kohinoor Gem Shop Burglary," and "The Case of the Bewildering Alibi."

HOLMES, MYCROFT.   The elder brother of Sherlock Holmes who possessed greater powers of observation than his sibling, but who lacked both

The brilliant and enigmatic Mycroft Holmes in "The Greek Interpreter"; by Sidney Paget.

energy and ambition. Mycroft Holmes remains one of the most compelling figures in the Canon, even though he appeared in but two of Watson's chronicles: "The Greek Interpreter" and "The Bruce-Partington Plans" (references were made to him in "The Final Problem" and "The Empty House"). In the latter case, it was revealed to Watson that Mycroft alone knew that Holmes was still alive after the terrible events at the Reichenbach Falls in 1891. He maintained the Baker Street lodgings of his brother as they were before the Great Hiatus and provided his brother with any money that might be needed during Sherlock's grand journeys.

Watson wrote of his surprise in learning one day of Mycroft's existence in "The Greek Interpreter." Sherlock had never discussed his family and the doctor had come to believe the detective was an orphan. Mycroft was seven years older than his brother and possessed even greater deductive powers. Holmes declared: "If the art of the detective began and ended in reasoning from an armchair, my brother would be the greatest criminal agent that ever lived. But he has no ambition and no energy. He will not even go out of his way to verify his own solutions, and would rather be considered wrong than take the trouble to prove himself right. Again and again I have taken a problem to him and have received an explanation which has afterwards proved to be the correct one. And yet he was absolutely incapable of working out the practical points which must be gone into before a case could be laid before a judge or jury . . . Mycroft lodges in Pall Mall, and he walks round the corner into Whitehall every morning and back every evening. From year's end to year's end he takes no other exercise, and is seen nowhere else, except only in the Diogenes Club, which is just opposite his rooms." In "The Bruce-Partington Plans," Sherlock added that "Mycroft has his rails and he runs on them. His Pall Mall lodgings, the Diogenes Club, Whitehall—that is his cycle."

Meeting Mycroft at the Diogenes Club (a club of which Mycroft was a founding member), Watson wrote that he "was a much larger and stouter man than Sherlock. His body was absolutely corpulent, but his face, though massive, had preserved something of the sharpness of expression which was so remarkable in that of his brother. His eyes, which were of a peculiarly light, watery gray, seemed to always retain that far-away, introspective look which I had only observed in Sherlock's when he

was exerting his full powers." ("The Greek Interpreter.")

He visited Baker Street only twice—in "The Greek Interpreter" and during the state of the national crisis in "The Bruce-Partington Plans"; so remarkable was his second visit that Sherlock exclaimed "a planet might as well leave its orbit." In "The Greek Interpreter" Sherlock told Watson that Mycroft audited the books in some of the government departments. By the time of "The Bruce-Partington Plans," Sherlock was more forthcoming about Mycroft's position at Whitehall: "You are right in thinking that he is under the British government. You would also be right in a sense if you said that occasionally he *is* the British government . . . Well, his position is unique. He has made it for himself. There has never been anything like it before, nor will be again. He has the tidiest and most orderly brain, with the greatest capacity for storing facts, of any man living. The same great powers which I have turned to the detection of crime he has used for this particular business. The conclusions of every department are passed to him, and he is the central exchange, the clearing-house, which makes out the balance. All other men are specialists, but his specialism is omniscience . . . They began by using him as a shortcut, a convenience; now he has made himself an essential. In that great brain of his everything is pigeon-holed, and can be handed out in an instant. Again and again his word has decided the national policy."

Mycroft has certainly been of interest to writers and filmmakers over the years. Much as speculation has surrounded Professor Moriarty and his relationship with Holmes, so has there been fascination with the possible activities of Mycroft for his government. In the film *The Private Life of Sherlock Holmes* (1971), for example, Mycroft (played by Christopher Lee) is the master of important government secrets, using the Diogenes Club as a perfect cover for secret operations around the globe on behalf of the queen. Special mention must also be made of the actor Charles Gray, who played him three times, in *The Seven-Per-Cent Solution* (1976), and twice in the Jeremy Brett series on television, in the episodes "The Greek Interpreter" and "The Bruce-Partington Plans." Perhaps the most imaginative bit of speculation about Mycroft suggested that he might have been the father of the equally rotund detective Nero Wolfe.

HOLMES, SHERLOCK.

The world's first consulting detective.

"I am the last and highest court of appeal in detection."

—SHERLOCK HOLMES.

Early Years. It is unfortunate that so little is known with any high degree of certainty about the early life and family of Sherlock Holmes. Scholars have only a few references from which to work in piecing together some picture of his childhood. According to the detective, he was the descendent of country squires "who appear to have led much the same life as is natural to their class" ("The Greek Interpreter"). Additionally, one of his grandmothers was the sister of the French artist Vernet—"Art in the blood is liable to take the strangest forms." Two interpretations can be made of his declarations. The use of the phrase "appear to have led" points to the possibility that the child Holmes grew up in an environment removed from that of his parents. Where this might have been is difficult to say; perhaps a public school or perhaps even America. The other, arguably more likely place of Holmes's youth is with his family in the country. As such he would have come to know the area of his family's holdings quite well receiving a suitable education, possibly from a private tutor. Holmes most likely learned here to dread and dislike the country, largely because the crimes that he recognized would go unpunished; a view acquired from long experience in the countryside and, as has been postulated by many Sherlockians, from shocking personal tragedy.

Holmes was born sometime around 1854, the date calculated by two references to his age in the Canon. The first was in "The Boscombe Valley Mystery," when he said that he was "middle-aged" in 1889. The second came in "His Last Bow," and is much more specific. Holmes is here said to be sixty years old. As the case was written in 1914 simple arithmetic puts his birth date to 1854. His brother Mycroft, seven years his senior, would thus have been born in 1847.

Schooling would have been of a local variety to start with before the introduction of a tutor. Who the tutor might have been is one of the great questions surrounding Holmes's youth. If the instructor was James Moriarty, as is believed by such scholars

Three coats of arms devised by Holmes scholars. The one on the left, by Rolfe Boswell, bears the motto, "We can but try." The motto of the central figure, according to Belden Wigglesworth, is *Je pense, alors je suis* ("I think, therefore I am"), while the coat of arms on the right boasts the Latin motto *Justim et tenacem propositi* ("Just and firm of purpose").

as Trevor Hall, then the theories about the genesis of the Holmes-Moriarty conflict take on particular interest. As proposed by Hall in the essay "The Early Years of Sherlock Holmes" (in his *Sherlock Holmes Ten Literary Studies*), Moriarty was the tutor of both Sherlock and Mycroft. The professor was somehow involved with Sherlock's mother, the adulterous liaison ending in the death, by murder, of his mother by his father. This idea accounts for two major elements in Holmes's career—his relentless pursuit of criminals, especially Professor Moriarty, and his deep-seated mistrust of women (see p. 116).

Aside from assorted pastiche novels and "autobiographies" of the detective, the young years of Holmes have been examined in three notable productions. In Nicholas Meyer's novel and film version of *The Seven Per-Cent Solution* (1974), in which Holmes meets Sigmund Freud, Trevor Hall's theory was developed and expanded. Moriarty was not the wicked Napoleon of Crime but was merely a mathematics tutor who had been caught having an affair with Mrs. Holmes. She was killed by an enraged husband in front of young Holmes, a tragedy that left him emotionally scarred for life. *Young Sherlock*, an English television production, offered a glimpse into the teenage years of Holmes. In this show the precocious future detective already wears his traditional cap and cape; the pipe no doubt would be added a few years later. Drawing its probable inspiration from *Young Sherlock* was the 1985 film *Young Sherlock Holmes* presenting Holmes again as a teenager, this time in a London school. Here, too, are offered a clever Holmes-Moriarty genesis, his mistrust of women, and his habit of wearing the deerstalker and cape.

Education.   As noted, among the numerous questions surrounding the early life of Holmes is his preuniversity education. Gavin Brend, in his *My Dear Sherlock: A Study in Sherlock* wrote: "It is a great pity that we have no record of young Sherlock's schooldays. Was he an infant prodigy, or did his remarkable powers develop later in his life? Alas, there was no Watson present to tell us." W. S. Baring-Gould, in his *Sherlock Holmes of Baker Street*, theorized that Holmes was educated for a time at a boarding school in Lambeth. There he met and befriended the bird-stuffer Old Sherman. He was later tutored by Professor Moriarty.

Whether or not Baring-Gould was correct remains a matter of some debate. What is not questioned is that Holmes attended a university. This is known with certainty because of two cases—"The 'Gloria Scott'" and "The Musgrave Ritual." In "The 'Gloria Scott'" he told Watson of Victor Trevor, "the only friend I made during the two years I was at college." It was the advice of Trevor's father that Holmes should become a detective. "It seems to me that all the detectives of fact and fancy would be children in your hands. That's your line of life, sir, and you may take the word of a man who has seen something of the world.

"And that recommendation, with the exaggerated estimate of my ability with which he prefaced it, was, if you will believe me, Watson, the very first thing which ever made me feel that a profession might be made out of what had up to that time been the merest hobby."

Where Holmes spent his "two years" is unknown, although there are generally recognized only two possibilities—Oxford or Cambridge. Both would have been excellent places for his education even though Watson would, in *A Study in Scarlet*, express utter amazement that Holmes, or indeed anyone, could be so ignorant of astronomy or literature—deficiencies that would speak poorly of the teaching skills of Holmes's university.

The "hobby" of which Holmes spoke ultimately made him the figure of some notoriety at his college. In "The Musgrave Ritual," he tells Watson of Reginald Musgrave's arrival one day at his lodgings on Montague Street and their subsequent chat in which Musgrave declares: "I understand, Holmes, that you are turning to practical ends those powers with which you used to amaze us?" Thus, having become convinced of his abilities and opportunities, sometime in 1877 or 1878, he set out for London to establish himself as the world's first consulting detective.

Early Career.   Aside from those cases that were presumably solved while he was in school and thus pass into the period of his amateur years, Holmes's first actual case in which his services were engaged was the affair of the *Gloria Scott*. This was solved before he left to go to London. Once in London, he situated himself in Montague Street and began the long road to success. Among his early cases were several failures, possibly the ones referred to in "The Five Orange Pips" when Holmes declared "I have been beaten four times—three times by men, and once by a woman." Other memorable investi-

IN THIS NUMBER—"THE RETURN OF SHERLOCK HOLMES"
Beginning a New Series of Detective Stories by A. CONAN DOYLE

Collier's

Household Number for October

VOL XXXI NO 26   SEPTEMBER 26 1903   PRICE 10 CENTS

The cover of *Collier's Magazine*; this issue heralded the return of Sherlock Holmes.

gations were the Tarleton murders, the case of Vamberry, the wine merchant, the adventure of the old Russian woman, and the singular affair of the aluminum crutch, "as well as a full account of Ricoletti of the club-foot, and his abominable wife." For Holmes, the most remarkable and *recherche* of all the cases was the adventure of the Musgrave Ritual, dated by the detective as his third case.

Case by case, he grew in prominence both among the criminal classes and, begrudgingly, among the officers and men of Scotland Yard. By 1881 he was giving assistance to the Yard and was, apparently, called in by them on particularly troublesome matters. A fact of his increasing success was made clear by his desire to find new rooms. That he was still not completely independent financially can be seen by his need to have a fellow lodger. Equally, it can be wondered if Holmes desired a roommate to maintain some association with normalcy, especially given the bizarre parade of clients, informants, and policemen who were filling up his lodgings in Montague Street as they would 221B Baker Street.

As fortune would have it, Holmes knew young Stamford and through him met Dr. John Watson at St. Bartholomew. The two went on to inspect 221B and took possession of the suite of rooms available there. The two seemed well-suited together and, after Watson began recording the remarkable exploits of his friend, a new era dawned for the detective.

Watson would soon become involved in Holmes's affairs, starting with the investigation into the murder of Enoch Drebber. Holmes's skills and success were such that the good doctor could hardly resist the temptation of writing about them. He tells Holmes at the end of A *Study in Scarlet*: "Your merits should be publicly recognized. You should publish an account of the case. If you won't, I will for you."

Later Career.   By 1889, Holmes was able to say that he had investigated some five hundred cases "of capital importance" (*The Hound of the Baskervilles*). Only a few of these had been published by Watson. A mere two years later, in 1891, he claimed to have worked on a thousand cases ("The Final Problem"). The thirteen years of his labors brought Holmes from total obscurity as a sleuth to considerable renown as a detective on the European stage. Most importantly, he had conducted

several investigations on behalf of European monarchs, including the king of Bohemia in "A Scandal in Bohemia," the king of Scandinavia ("The Noble Bachelor" and "The Final Problem"), and the royal family of the Netherlands ("A Scandal in Bohemia" and "A Case of Identity").

Holmes told Watson in "The Final Problem": "Of late I have been tempted to look into the problems furnished by nature rather than those more superficial ones for which our artificial state of society is responsible. Your memoirs will draw to an end, Watson, upon the day that I crown my career by the capture or extinction of the most dangerous and capable criminal in Europe," a recognition that there was increasingly little left to accomplish save the removal of Professor Moriarty as a threat to the world. Through Holmes's efforts, the professor's vast criminal empire was destroyed and Moriarty was killed in Switzerland.

The demise of the professor gave Holmes the opportunity to relinquish his role as the Great Detective. This was accomplished by allowing Watson, and hence the rest of the world, to believe that he had joined Moriarty at the bottom of the Falls. Informing only his brother Mycroft (thereby maintaining his rooms at Baker Street and having access to money), Holmes embarked upon years of travel and exploration, the period known generally as the Great Hiatus. Few areas of Holmes's life have been subjected to as much speculation as these lost years from 1891–1894. Theories aside, there is Holmes's own account of his activities. He supposedly visited Tibet, Mecca, Khartoum, and Montpelier (where he spent some months studying coal-tar derivatives). (See also GREAT HIATUS for other details.)

There seems to be evidence that Holmes's desire to end his career in 1891 was a halfhearted one. He apparently had already planned to return to England (and practice) when his "movements were hastened by the news of this very remarkable Park Lane Mystery, which not only appealed to me by its own merits, but which seemed to offer some most peculiar personal opportunities." The Park Lane Mystery was, of course, the strange murder of Ronald Adair and the opportunities were to return immediately to work and to trap the last major lieutenant of Professor Moriarty.

So, in April, 1894, Holmes revealed himself to a flabbergasted Watson and proceeded to conduct the case of "The Empty House." Once established again at Baker Street, Holmes would work for many more years (1894–1903) handling hundreds of cases between 1894 and 1901 ("The Solitary Cyclist"). Of these, the most brilliant year was 1895, during which he excelled in the case of the Bruce-Partington Plans, for which he received a private audience with Queen Victoria at Windsor, and a beautiful tiepin from her. Also notable was his investigation around 1901 into the disappearance of Lord Saltire, son of the duke of Holdernesse, chronicled in "The Priory School." The case is made memorable because of the detective's acceptance of an enormous check from the duke. "Holmes folded up the check and placed it carefully in his notebook. 'I am a poor man,' said he, as he patted it affectionately, and thrust it into the depths of his inner pocket." This was an event so amazing to Watson that the doctor was still writing about it at the start of his next published case, "Black Peter." More in keeping with Holmes's austere nature was his declining, in June 1902, the offer of a knighthood ("The Three Garridebs").

Once again, however, Holmes was reaching the point where retirement was more and more desirable and the longings expressed years before in "The Final Problem" were now entirely valid. The major difference was that the detective was now approaching fifty and the relentless physical and mental exertions of his profession, combined with his many indiscretions (most notably his long cocaine habit) had probably caused severe strains on his health, making his retirement even more appealing.

Readers of the *Strand Magazine* in December, 1904 were shocked to discover Dr. Watson's statement that Holmes "has definitely retired from London and betaken himself to study and bee-farming on the Sussex Downs" ("The Second Stain"). The date of his retirement has been placed at 1903 (or less likely 1904). The two best portraits of his life on the Sussex Downs were provided in the preface to "His Last Bow" and, by Holmes himself in "The Lion's Mane." In the preface, Watson wrote: "The friends of Mr. Sherlock Holmes will be glad to learn that he is still alive and well, though somewhat crippled by occasional attacks of rheumatism. He has, for many years, lived in a small farm upon the downs five miles from Eastbourne, where his time is divided between philosophy and agriculture. During this period of rest he has refused the most princely offers to take up various cases, having determined that his retirement was a permanent

one." In "The Lion's Mane," the detective wrote: "My villa is situated upon the southern slope of the downs, commanding a great view of the Channel . . . My house is lonely. I, my old housekeeper, and my bees have the estate all to ourselves."

Such was the crisis facing England in the years before the start of the First World War that Holmes acquiesced to the request of the prime minister and came out of retirement. His task—to penetrate the spy ring of the German intelligence master Von Bork. Impersonating Altamont, an Irish-American enemy of the British Empire, Holmes slowly unraveled the entire spy web of the crafty German. The climax of his operation was presented in "His Last Bow."

While "His Last Bow" was the last case of Sherlock Holmes, it has been theorized by scholars that he was also involved in other affairs. Vincent Starrett in his *221B: Studies in Sherlock Holmes*, proposed that Holmes was in Constantinople during 1920 as the Turkish government believed him to be active in the city, at least according to the *Times*. Anthony Boucher and Manly Wade Wellman also thought that Holmes was still working for England during World War II.

Death.   Nowhere in the Canon is mention made of the final passing of Sherlock Holmes. Any date surrounding the death of the Great Detective must, therefore, be pure conjecture. W. S. Baring-Gould, in *Sherlock Holmes of Baker Street*, put the date at Sunday, January 6, 1957. As he is one of the great figures in Sherlockiana, some weight must be given to his estimate. Naturally such a date would have made Holmes 103, not an unusually long life span for someone of his physical strength and power, although a little surprising given his long-term smoking and cocaine habit.

There appeared in the *Strand Magazine* (December 1948) an obituary for Sherlock Holmes written by E. V. Knox. Coming a mere two years before the demise of the magazine itself, the obituary was more a product of postwar pessimism than a legitimate termination of public interest in the detective. His passing, if or when it ever occurred, could not have been marked better than by Dr. Watson, who wrote in 1891 when it was assumed that Holmes was dead at the Reichenbach Falls that Holmes was "the best and the wisest man whom I have known."

This is the last Will and Testament

of me *Sherlock Holmes*
of *221B. Baker Street in the parish of St. Marylebone*
in the County of *London* made this *Sixteenth*
day of *April, 1891* in the year of our Lord

I **hereby** revoke all former testamentary dispositions made by me and declare this to be my last Will.
I appoint *my brother*

Mycroft Holmes

to be my Executor   and direct that all my just Debts and Funeral and Testamentary Expenses shall
be paid as soon as conveniently may be after my decease.

I **give and bequeath** unto

my devoted friend and associate, Dr. John H. Watson, often tried, sometimes trying, but never found wanting in loyalty; my well-intentioned though unavailing mentor against the blandishments of vice; my indispensable foil and whetstone; the perfect sop to my wounded vanity and too tactful to whisper Norbury in my ear when necessary; the ideal listener and the audience par excellence for those little tricks which others more discerning might well have deemed meretricious; the faithful Boswell to whose literary efforts – despite my occasional unkindly gibes – I owe whatever little fame I have enjoyed: in short, to the one true friend I have ever had, the sum of £5,000; also the choice of any books in my personal library (with such reservations as are mentioned below); including my commonplace books and the complete file of my cases, published and unpublished, with the sole exception of the papers in pigeonhole M. contained in a blue envelope and marked Moriarty which the proper authorities will take over in the event my demise should make it impossible for me to hand them over in person.

—— *To George Lestrade, of Scotland Yard, my gilt-edged German dictionary, in the hope he will find it useful should he again see the handwriting of Miss Rachel on the wall.*

—— *To Tobias Gregson, ditto, my leatherbound Hafiz, the study of whose poetry may supply a dash of that imagination so necessary to the ideal reasoner.*

—— *To the authorities of Scotland Yard, one copy of each of my trifling monographs on crime detection, unless happily they shall feel they have outgrown the need for the elementary suggestions of an amateur detective.*

—— *To my good brother, Mycroft Holmes, the remainder and residue of my estate, which he will be agreeably surprised to find, even after the foregoing bequests, to be not inconsiderable; and which will enable him, I hope, to take a much needed holiday from governmental cares to surroundings more congenial than those of the Diogenes Club; in the expectation that he will remain celibate for the rest of his natural life — and unnatural too; for that matter.*

Sherlock Holmes

Signed by the Testator in the presence of us, present at the same time, who at his request, in his presence, and in the presence of each other, have subscribed our names as Witnesses.

1st WITNESS—Name *Thomas P. Stockton*
Address *Staple Inn Holborn*
Occupation *Solicitor*

2nd WITNESS—Name *Philip H Mace*
Address *Staple Inn Holborn*
Occupation *Solicitor*

N.B.—The person making the will should sign it at the end of the Will itself, that is, immediately at the end of the writing.

The last will and testament of Sherlock Holmes, discovered by Nathan L. Bengis, Keeper of the Crown of the Musgrave Ritualists of New York, appeared in *London Mystery Magazine* in June 1955. Other scholars, notably Jacques Barzun, have questioned its authenticity.

HOLMES AND:

Chemistry.   Among the many fields of study pursued by Holmes, the detective had a passion for chemistry that never subsided. He used his knowledge of chemistry to help solve cases, but he also performed experiments simply for the love of it. In *The Sign of Four*, Watson wrote: "He would hardly reply to my questions, and busied himself all the evening in an abstruse chemical analysis which involved much heating of retorts and distilling of vapours, ending at last in a smell which fairly drove me out of the apartment. Up to the small hours of the morning I could hear the clinking of his testtubes, which told me that he was still engaged in his malodorous experiment."

Holmes apparently was ready to devote more time to the subject in the years prior to his retirement in 1903. He told Watson in "The Final Problem" in 1891: "Of late I have been tempted to look into the problems furnished by nature rather than those more superficial ones for which our artificial state of society is responsible," having told him a short time before, "Between ourselves, the recent cases in which I have been of assistance to the royal family of Scandinavia, and to the French republic, have left me in such a position that I could continue to live in the quiet fashion which is most congenial to me, and to concentrate my attention upon my chemical researches."

Food.   Holmes was of a temperament that he would go days without eating, preferring to keep food away as he desired the excess energy not to go to waste. This habit, combined with his natural bohemianism and his ascetic lifestyle, have produced a general view that Holmes was indifferent to food and thought of it only as a means of stoking his intellectual energies when they needed reviving. Such a picture, while understandable, is not

This is the Last Will and Testament
of me [Sherlock Holmes]

I give and bequeath unto

my devoted friend and associate, Dr. John H.
Watson, often tried, sometimes trying, but never
found wanting in loyalty; my well-intentioned
though unavailing mentor against the blandishments of vice, my indispensable foil and whetstone; the perfect sop to my wounded vanity and
too tactful to whisper "Norbury" in my ear when
necessary; the ideal listener and the audience par
excellence for those little tricks which others
more discerning might well have deemed meretricious; the faithful Boswell to whose literary
efforts—despite my occasional unkindly gibes—I
owe whatever little fame I have enjoyed; in short,
to the one true friend I have ever had, the sum of
£5,000; also the choice of any books in my personal library (with such reservations as are mentioned below), including my commonplace books
and the complete file of my cases, published and
unpublished, with the sole exception of the papers
in pigeonhole "M," contained in a blue envelope
and marked "Moriarty" which the proper authorities will take over in the event my demise should
make it impossible for me to hand them over in
person.

—To George Lestrade, of Scotland Yard, my
gilt-edged German dictionary, in the hope he will
find it useful should he again see the handwriting
of Miss Rachel on the wall.

—To Tobias Gregson, ditto, my leatherbound
Hafiz, the study of whose poetry may supply a dash
of that imagination so necessary to the ideal reasoner.

—To the authorities of Scotland Yard, one copy
of each of my trifling monographs on crime detection, unless happily they shall feel they have outgrown the need for the elementary suggestions of
an amateur detective.

—To my good brother, Mycroft Holmes, the
remainder and residue of my estate, which he will
be agreeably surprised to find, ever after the foregoing bequests, to be not inconsiderable, and
which will enable him, I hope, to take a much
needed holiday from governmental cares to surroundings more congenial than those of the Diogenes Club; in the expectation that he will
remain celibate for the rest of his natural life—
and unnatural too, for that matter.

[SHERLOCK HOLMES]

accurate. Sherlock Holmes actually possessed a re-
fined taste in cuisine and a highly sensitive
palate—one certainly superior to Dr. Watson's.

Holmes clearly enjoyed breakfast and took delight in it when actually eating. In "The Naval
Treaty" he resolves the case over breakfast—
curried fowl, eggs, and ham—with the assertion
"Mrs. Hudson has risen to the occasion . . . Her
cuisine is a little limited, but she has as good an
idea about breakfast as a Scotchwoman." Other
breakfast references were found in "The Engineer's
Thumb," "The Norwood Builder," and "Thor
Bridge." It should be noted that Holmes enjoyed a
pipe before and after breakfast. The prebreakfast
pipe was composed of all the dottles and leftovers
from the day before. It was unclear as to what he
used for his after-breakfast pipe (see PIPE).

For larger meals, specifically dinner, there are
two major categories to be examined: meals and
food eaten at Baker Street and meals eaten out.
Superb dining at Baker Street would have been
difficult because of the inability of acquiring on a
consistent basis gourmet-quality food and because
of the "limited" cuisine of Mrs. Hudson. It is possible, however, that on rare occasions, Holmes undertook to prepare his own fabulous repast.
Fletcher Pratt, in his essay "The Gastronomic
Holmes" (1952), proposed that the detective enjoyed two gourmet meals: one in "The Sign of
Four" and the other in "The Noble Bachelor."
According to Pratt, Holmes himself prepared the
dishes. In *The Sign of Four*, he invited Athelney
Jones to dinner. "I have oysters and a brace of
grouse, with something a little choice in white
wines—Watson you have never yet recognized my
abilities as a housekeeper." In "The Noble Bachelor," Holmes had served "a couple of brace of cold
woodcock, a pheasant, a pate de foie gras pie with a
group of ancient and cobwebby bottles."

In dining out, Holmes probably enjoyed a wide
variety of restaurants, although only four were
mentioned: Marcini's (*Hound of the Baskervilles*),
Goldini's ("The Bruce-Partington Plans"), Simpson's ("The Dying Detective"), and the Cafe
Royal ("The Illustrious Client"). Presumably, he
enjoyed the best entrees that these restaurants had
to offer. Regrettably, his culinary choices remain
unknown. At Goldini's he was enjoying a curacao
and cigar when Watson joined him in preparation
for their nighttime assault on the residence of Hugo
Oberstein. Holmes dined out on one other
occasion—in *The Hound of the Baskervilles*, he ate

some bread while camped out in a hut on the moors, leaving untouched the canned tongue and canned peaches that had been brought to him by the young Cartwright. Other references to meals were found in "The Cardboard Box," "The Five Orange Pips," "The Mazarin Stone," "The Missing Three-Quarter," "The Noble Bachelor," "The Priory School," *The Sign of Four*, "Silver Blaze," "Thor Bridge," "The Three Students," *The Valley of Fear*, and "The Veiled Lodger." (See also OYSTERS.)

Honors. Throughout his long career, Holmes was to accomplish a great many feats for governments, nobles, and monarchs in Europe and possibly beyond. Watson wrote that Holmes was given a ring from the hand of the king of Bohemia in return for bringing about a satisfactory conclusion to the Irene Adler affair ("A Scandal in Bohemia"). The detective declined the gift, taking instead something far more valuable—a picture of Adler. Holmes did accept, some weeks later, "a snuff-box of gold, with a great amethyst in the centre of the lid" from the grateful ruler ("A Case of Identity"). He also received a ring from the ruling family of Holland for his services to them in a matter of great delicacy. ("A Case of Identity"). By 1891, he had aided also the Scandinavian royal house and had been to Odessa to investigate the Trepoff murder; it is unknown whether his investigation into the Trepoff murder brought him into contact with the czarist government. By the time of his retirement, his achievements would have included his coming to the aid of the French government and the sultanate of Turkey, two notable matters among what were probably numerous and often secret investigations. For the arrest of Huret, the Boulevard Assassin, the detective was rewarded with the Legion of Honour and autographed photograph of the French president.

Back home, Holmes was given a very generous check from the duke of Holdernesse for finding his son, Lord Saltire. For his brilliant work in recovering the Bruce-Partington Plans, he was given an audience at Windsor Castle with Queen Victoria and a tiepin that he wore quite conspicuously. He refused his name on the Honours List, however, and turned down a knighthood in 1902. It is unknown what great honors he was paid (or offered) for exterminating the spy ring of Von Bork before the start of World War I. Michael Harrison, the noted Sherlockian, has calculated that Holmes might have received the following medals: *Palmes*

Holmes in rapture listening to music in "The Red-Headed League"; by Sidney Paget.

Academique, Legion of Honour, St. Olaf, the Polar Star, and the Order of the Bath.

Music. According to Watson, Holmes "was an enthusiastic musician, being himself not only a very capable performer but a composer of no ordinary merit" ("The Red-Headed League"). The detective enjoyed music of all kinds, including opera, concert music, and even the obscure compositions (motets) of Orlandus Lassus. The special devotion of Holmes to music was clear from a number of episodes. The most important was his careful maintenance of his Stradivarius violin: it was kept in its case and stored in a corner of his sitting room at Baker Street. This treatment of a musical instrument is in sharp contrast to his many other possessions, even exceedingly delicate ones—needles and syringes on his mantelpiece, tobacco in the toe end of a Persian slipper, his unanswered correspondence transfixed by a jackknife into the middle of the mantelpiece, and chemical and criminal relics found in the butter-dish. His playing was so excellent that by the time of "The Mazarin Stone," listeners could not tell him apart from a record. At Watson's request, he would play some of Mendelssohn's lieder and would also create pieces extemporaneously.

In listening to music, Holmes found the German variety to be more to his tastes than Italian or French. He attended the opera, including a Wagner at Covent Garden in "The Red Circle." Concerts were far more common: Carina at the Albert Hall in "The Retired Colourman," the de Reszkes in "Les Huguenots" in *The Hound of the Baskervilles*, and Sarasate at St. James's Hall in "The Red-Headed League," among others. In listening to Sarasate, Holmes's mood was quite revealing. "All the afternoon he sat in the stalls wrapped in the most perfect happiness, gently waving his long, thin fingers, in time to the music, while his gently smiling face and his languid, dreamy eyes were as unlike those of Holmes, the sleuth-hound, Holmes the relentless, keen-witted, ready-handed criminal agent, as it was possible to conceive."

Women and Marriage. Throughout the Canon, the reader is provided with numerous examples of Holmes's dislike and distrust of women and the utter contempt in which he held marriage. The causes for this psychological disposition have long been discussed by Sherlockians and examined by writers, playwrights, and filmmakers. In *The Seven-Per-Cent Solution*, for example, by Nicholas Meyer, Holmes witnessed the brutal murder of his adulterous mother by his father and so came to the deep-seated conclusion that women were not to be trusted and that they would ultimately disappoint. Additionally, their motives and true intentions must be studied carefully for their real aim is not always apparent. Among the statements that exemplify Holmes's attitude were:

"Women are never to be entirely trusted—not the best of them." (*The Sign of Four*)
"How can you build on such a quicksand? Their most trivial action may mean volumes, or their most extraordinary conduct may depend upon a hairpin or a curling tongs." ("The Second Stain")
"He disliked and distrusted the sex, but he was always a chivalrous opponent." ("The Dying Detective")
"I am not a whole-souled admirer of womankind." (*The Valley of Fear*)
"He never spoke of the softer passions, save with a gibe and a sneer." ("A Scandal in Bohemia")
"Woman's heart and mind are insoluble puzzles to the male." ("The Illustrious Client")

At the same time, the detective was forced to admit an abiding respect and regard for *the* woman, Irene Adler. "In his eyes she eclipses and predominates the whole of her sex. It was not that he felt any emotion akin to love for Irene Adler. All emotions, and that one particularly, were abhorrent to his cold, precise, but admirably balanced mind." The opera singer and adventuress epitomized the statements by Holmes: "I have seen too much not to know that the impression of a woman may be more valuable than the conclusion of an analytical reasoner" ("The Man With the Twisted Lip"), and "I value a woman's instinct" ("The Lion's Mane").

In "The Devil's Foot," Holmes told Leon Sterndale "I have never loved." This is naturally an arguably broad declaration, but his dealings with clients and suspects would seem to support it. The lovely Violet Hunter in "The Copper Beeches" had no effect upon him. "As to Miss Hunter, my friend Holmes, rather to my disappointment, manifested no further interest in her when once she ceased to be the centre of one of his problems." It is indeed unfortunate that no details are available concerning his wooing of Agatha, the maid of Charles Augustus Milverton, "the King of All Blackmailers." His skill in winning the affections of Agatha were probably those mentioned by Watson in "The Golden Pince-Nez." "Holmes had, when he liked, a peculiarly ingratiating way with women, and that he very readily established terms of confidence with them." (See also ADLER, IRENE; and HUDSON, MRS.)

HOLMESIAN ATTRIBUTES.

Appearance. Throughout the long history of the development of Sherlock Holmes in literature, film, and stage, the original description of Holmes has largely been forgotten in favor of a Master Detective who is much handsomer than the sleuth who first appeared in *A Study in Scarlet*. Here, Watson wrote:

"His very person and appearance were such as to

strike the attention of the most casual observer. In height he was rather over six feet, and so excessively lean that he seemed to be considerably taller. His eyes were sharp and piercing, save during those intervals of torpor to which I have alluded; and his thin, hawk-like nose gave his whole expression an air of alertness and decision. His chin, too, had the prominence and squareness which mark the man of determination. His hands were invariably blotted with ink and stained with chemicals, yet he was possessed of extraordinary delicacy of touch . . ."

On several occasions his tallness was noted (in "The Boscombe Valley Mystery," *The Hound of the Baskervilles*, "His Last Bow," "The Mazarin Stone," "The Man With the Twisted Lip," and *The Valley of Fear*) as were his thinness and narrowness of his face. His apparent leanness, virtually to the point of emaciation, was actually deceptive, however, for Holmes kept himself in remarkably excellent conditioning and was "always in training." He refused to take exercise for its own sake ("The Yellow Face"), but probably kept in shape by boxing, running, fencing, and the use of such martial arts as *baritsu*. He declared in "The Beryl Coronet" that he was "exceptionally strong in the fingers," and it was said that he had a "grasp of iron" ("His Last Bow"), this last attribute noted at a time when the detective was sixty years old. In his prime, he was capable of exerting enormous strength, as was seen in "The Speckled Band" when he straightened out an iron poker that had been bent by Dr. Grimesby Roylott. Such strength and conditioning would have been essential given the incredible demands he placed upon himself—work and exertions for weeks straight, abstaining from food, and smoking excessively and taking cocaine throughout.

When not using a disguise to penetrate some home of a suspected criminal or to gain information in a dark and dangerous section of London's criminal underground, Holmes maintained a certain pride of appearance when away from 221B Baker Street. He had a "catlike love of personal cleanliness" (*The Hound of the Baskervilles*) and consequently was generally well dressed. In "The Musgrave Ritual" it was said that "he affected a certain quiet primness of dress." He customarily wore tweeds or a frock coat, although his dress while in the country was notable for the use of "a long gray travelling-cloak" ("The Boscombe Valley Mystery") and the close-fitting, ear-flapped, cloth travelling cap—both were to become essential elements in the image of Sherlock Holmes. In the city,

he would not have worn the deerstalker and cape. For a coat he would have donned an ulster on occasion. At home, his dress was a little more casual. Holmes virtually always wore a dressing gown while at 221B. It is estimated that he owned at least three dressing gowns: a purple one, a blue one, and a mouse-colored one. These he obviously took with him when travelling as evidenced by his wearing of the blue gown while staying at the Cedars during the search for Neville St. Clair in "The Man With the Twisted Lip."

Habits.   Despite Watson's assurances of his "natural Bohemianism," the good doctor was forced to admit that with him there was a limit compared to Sherlock Holmes. Holmes was, "in his personal habits one of the most untidy men that ever drove a fellow-lodger to distraction," adding that "when I find a man who keeps his cigars in a coal-scuttle, his tobacco in the toe end of a Persian slipper, and his unanswered correspondence transfixed by a jack-knife into the very centre of his wooden mantelpiece, then I begin to give myself virtuous airs" ("The Musgrave Ritual").

As is clear from Watson's observation, Holmes was extraordinarily bohemian, an extension in many ways of the unique and unusual lifestyle that he pursued as the world's first consulting detective. His tastes were remarkably "frugal" ("The Priory School"), "his diet was usually of the sparest, and his habits were simple to the verge of austerity. Save for the occasional use of cocaine, he had no vices, and he only turned to the drug as a protest against the monotony of existence when cases were scanty and the papers uninteresting." Aside from the drug, he had evident passions for only a few other amusements. Music was certainly one of them, as were oysters, and rare occasions of gourmet food. The pipe, cigar, and cigarette were all smoked, but these seemed to assist his brain in working on the solution to a case. The pipe was especially useful, and he smoked several types depending upon his mood and the circumstances. (See also PIPE.)

As a rule, he was a late riser, so his being dressed at quarter past seven came as a surprise to Watson at the start of "The Speckled Band." His hours naturally varied depending upon the demands of a case, "those not infrequent occasions when he was up all night" (*The Hound of the Baskervilles*). When not working on a case, he faced the terrible onset of ennui that would, for many years, compel him to turn to his seven-per-cent solution of cocaine. "Idleness exhausts me completely" (*The Sign of Four*), he would complain, moping listlessly around Baker Street. At the start of "The Three Garridebs," "Holmes had spent several days in bed, as was his habit from time to time," certainly an excellent way of restoring energy after a taxing investigation.

HOLMES AS A CONSULTING DETECTIVE.

By his own admission, Sherlock Holmes was the world's only unofficial (or consulting, or even private) detective: "I am the last and highest court of appeal in detection. When Gregson, or Lestrade, or Athelney Jones are out of their depth—which by the way, is their normal state the matter is laid before me. I examine the data, as an expert, and pronounce a specialist's opinion. I claim no credit in such cases. My name figures in no newspaper. The work itself, the pleasure of finding a field for my peculiar powers, is my highest reward" (*The Sign of Four*).

In developing his art, Holmes believed that "detection is, or ought to be, an exact science" (*The Sign of Four*), and "breadth of view is one of the essentials of our profession. The interplay of ideas and the oblique uses of knowledge are often of extraordinary interest" (*The Valley of Fear*). His skills in observation and protodeductive reasoning were, apparently, a combination of acquired ability (largely self-taught) and genetic inheritance—"Art in the blood is liable to take the strangest forms" ("The Greek Interpreter"). How early he began to manifest these abilities is unknown, but certainly by his university years he had already formed into a system "those habits of observation and inference . . . although I had not not yet appreciated the part which they were to play in my life."

The system that Holmes used and continued to develop throughout his long career became the marvel of Europe and placed him in the first place among the solvers of crime. His methods, he said, relied upon three qualities: observation, deduction, and knowledge. All three were ever on display in the cases recounted in the Canon and all three seemed flabbergastingly amazing to casual observers, until they were explained by the detective, at which time they became obvious and were dismissed with a chorus of "I thought at first that you had done something clever, but I see that there was

nothing in it, after all" ("The Red-Headed League").

Observation. Holmes told Watson on numerous occasions, "You know my methods." Among them, and crucial to the ultimate solution of any mystery, was observation. "It has long been a maxim of mine that the little things are infinitely the most important" ("A Case of Identity"); "You know my method. It is founded upon the observation of trifles" ("The Boscombe Valley Mystery"); and "I dare call nothing trivial when I reflect that some of my most classic cases have had the least promising commencement" ("The Six Napoleons").

He possessed, according to Watson, "extraordinary powers" of observation in "A Scandal in Bohemia" and had an "extraordinary gift for minutiae" in *The Sign of Four*. His obsession with paying attention to details ("there is nothing so important as trifles"—"The Man With the Twisted Lip") made him a formidable figure at the scene of a crime, and the bane of police officials who were often mystified by his peculiar habits. In *A Study in Scarlet*, for example:

"As he spoke, he whipped a tape measure and a large round magnifying glass from his pocket. With these two implements he trotted noiselessly about the room, sometimes stopping, occasionally kneeling, and once lying flat upon his face. So engrossed was he with his occupation that he appeared to have forgotten our presence, for he chattered away to himself under his breath the whole time, keeping up a running fire of exclamations, groans, whistles, and little cries suggestive of encouragement and of hope . . . For twenty minutes or more he continued his researches, measuring with the most exact care the distance between marks which were entirely invisible to me, and occasionally applying his tape to the walls in an equally incomprehensible manner. In one place he gathered up very carefully a little pile of gray dust from the floor and packed it away in an envelope. Finally he examined with his glass the word upon the wall [RACHE], going over every letter of it with the most minute exactness. This done, he appeared to be satisfied, for he replaced his tape and his glass in his pocket."

Having made his observations, Holmes had little patience for those individuals who did not see or refused to see the same clues and pieces of evidence as he. "You see, but you do not observe" he said in "A Scandal in Bohemia." The police were especially subject to his barbs, usually because they assiduously adhered to their theories, formulated immediately upon arrival at a crime scene or from one piece of evidence given excessive weight; despite Holmes's maxim in "A Study in Scarlet," "It is a capital mistake to theorize before you have all the evidence. It biases the judgment."

Deduction.   The second phase of Holmes's methods was the use of deduction, based upon observation, to reach conclusions, scientifically and logically, as to the important details of the case. "It is of the highest importance in the art of deduction to be able to recognize, out of a number of facts, which are incidental and which are vital" ("The Reigate Squires"). Once gathered together, all of the facts, clues, bits and pieces, and assorted data, would be placed before his mind and he would examine them. Holmes frequently would then sit and ponder all of the facts for hours as in *The Hound of the Baskervilles* when "he weighed every particle of evidence, constructed alternative theories, balanced one against the other, and made up his mind as to which points were essential and which immaterial." In "The Man With the Twisted Lip," the detective considered the case for an entire night, consuming a pile of shag. The result was his solution—the correct one.

Of paramount importance to deductive reasoning was the willingness of the observer to remain logical and wholly objective. Having "approached the case with an absolutely blank mind, which is always an advantage" ("The Cardboard Box"), he thought it "an error to argue in front of your data. You find yourself insensibly twisting them round to fit your theories" ("Wisteria Lodge"). "I make a point of never having any prejudices and of following docilely wherever fact may lead me" ("The Reigate Squires"), and "I never guess. It is a shocking habit—destructive to the logical faculty" (*The Sign of Four*).

Once formed, a hypothesis had to be tested, and Holmes generally was quite ruthless with others and especially himself. The weighing of this theory would take into account many factors, including the values of circumstantial evidence or first-hand evidence, and those of imagination and intuition. Of circumstantial evidence, Holmes observed that "it is a very tricky thing; it may seem to point very straight to one thing, but if you shift your own point of view a little, you may find it pointing in an equally uncompromising manner to something entirely different" ("The Boscombe Valley Mystery").

As for imagination and intuition, they were useful to go beyond the often overly constricting, inhibiting, or limiting nature of fact. "There is nothing more deceptive than an obvious fact." In "Silver Blaze," he commented to Watson as they traced the horse Silver Blaze: "See the value of imagination . . . We imagined what might have happened, acted upon the supposition, and find ourselves justified."

Collectively, however, all of these elements had to be tested. "One should always look for a possible alternative and provide against it. It is the first rule of criminal investigation" ("Black Peter"). Equally, "One forms provisional theories and waits for time to explode them" ("The Sussex Vampire"). In many cases, "when a fact appears to be opposed to a long train of deductions, it invariably proves to be capable of bearing some other interpretation" (*A Study in Scarlet*). Ultimately, the final maxim guiding his genius in deduction, and one of the most famous of all his ideas states simply: "When you have eliminated the impossible, whatever remains, however improbable, must be the truth" (*The Sign of Four*).

Knowledge.   When writing about "Sherlock Holmes—his limits" in *A Study in Scarlet*, Watson observed that his knowledge of sensational literature was "Immense. He appears to know every detail of every horror perpetrated in this century." While the doctor would later look back with humor on his early assessment, his listing for Holmes's familiarity with the history of crime would never change. It was, in fact, a demonstration of the great importance placed by the detective on knowledge. "All knowledge comes useful to the detective" (*The Valley of Fear*) he said, adding in the same case "the interplay of ideas and the oblique uses of knowledge are often of extraordinary interest."

In embarking upon his career as a consulting detective around 1878, Holmes apparently recognized his shortcomings or gaps of learning and so set out to arm himself with information. By the time of his meeting with John Watson in 1881, his knowledge of poisons, crime, criminals, and a host of related subjects had become enormous. Combined with his unusual powers of fact retention, he was probably the most well-informed individual of his time, even though his accumulation was weighted toward certain subjects or areas. Of his own knowledge, he wrote in "The Lion's Mane": "I hold a vast store of out-of-the-way knowledge without scientific system, but very available for the needs of my work. My mind is like a crowded box-room with packets of all sorts stowed away therein—so many that I may well have but a vague perception of what was there."

As for those areas where personal knowledge might be deficient, Holmes had his answer: "A man should keep his little brain-attic stocked with all the furniture that he is likely to use, and the rest he can put away in the lumber-room of his library, where he can get it if he wants it" ("The Five Orange Pips"). He thus used all of the resources that the great city of London had to offer, particularly the British Museum. At Baker Street, he would have also had his sources, including the *American Encyclopedia*, the trusty *Bradshaw's*, Watson's *Medical Directory*, vast collections of newspapers, and other handy reference volumes, not to mention the astonishing amounts of material in his commonplace books.

This accumulated knowledge would have provided the final element in the solution of a crime or mystery. From deductive hypothesis, the informed reasoner would tie up all of the details and create a complete, legally acceptable solution. "The ideal reasoner would, when he had once been shown a single fact in all its bearing, deduce from it not only all the chain of events which led up to it but also all the results which would follow from it." (See also COCAINE, DISGUISES.)

HOLMES, SHERRINGFORD.   An early name used by Sir Arthur Conan Doyle for the eventual Sherlock Holmes. Sherlockians would argue, however, that this was a name initially considered by Watson's literary agent, Conan Doyle, as a means of disguising the true identity of the detective.

HOLMESES OF BAKER STREET.   England. 1933. Writer: Basil Mitchell. Cast: Felix Aylmer (Holmes), Nigel Playfair (Watson), Rosemary Ames (Shirley Holmes), and Eva Moore (Mrs. Watson). A play that opened at the Lyric Theatre in February 1933 that provided the detective with a daughter, an idea that has been explored in such works as *Sherlock Holmes in New York* (1976) and in the rumored origins of the detective Nero Wolfe. Holmes's daughter, Shirley, has apparently inherited her father's brilliant detective abilities and plans on becoming the first woman detective at Scotland Yard. The play presents Holmes in retire-

ment on the Sussex Downs, but he journeys to London and becomes involved in an apparent case of theft. He is reunited with the Watsons. *The Holmeses of Baker Street* was not particularly successful in its London run, largely because of the liberties that had been taken with the recognized and accepted attributes of the detective. The play did move to Broadway, running at the Masque Theatre from 1936 to 1937. It starred Cyril Scott (Holmes), Conway Wingfield (Watson), and Helen Chandler (Shirley Holmes).

HOLY LAND.   Dr. Shlessinger was preparing a map of this region in "The Disappearance of Lady Frances Carfax." While supposedly recuperating in Baden at the Englischer Hof from an illness contracted in South America, Dr. Shlessinger spoke of "preparing a map of the Holy Land, with special reference to the kingdom of the Midianites, upon which he was writing a monograph."

HOLY WAR, THE.   One of the books carried by Holmes in the disguise of the old bibliophile and offered to Dr. Watson in "The Empty House."

HONES, JOHNNY.   One of the members of the Ferrier wagon train travelling over the Great Alkali Plain in *A Study in Scarlet*. He was not a survivor of the doomed expedition.

HOPE, JEFFERSON.   A pioneer in California who fell in love with Lucy Ferrier and was a favorite of John Ferrier, Lucy's adoptive father, in *A Study in Scarlet*. "He had been a pioneer in California, and could narrate many a strange tale of fortunes made and fortunes lost in those wild halcyon days. He had been a scout too, and a trapper, a silver explorer, and a ranchman. Wherever stirring adventures were to be had, Jefferson Hope had been there in search of them." His father had known John Ferrier. Lucy agreed to be his wife, their betrothal formalized when he left for his diggings in Nevada. John Ferrier was killed, however, by the Avenging Angels, and Lucy was forced to marry Enoch Drebber, dying a short time later. Hope swore revenge, pursuing Drebber and Joseph Stangerson across the world for twenty years. He finally caught up with them in London, by which time he was himself dying.

HOPKINS, EZEKIAH.   The supposed founder of the Red-Headed League. Hopkins was said to be from Lebanon, Pennsylvania and "had a great sym-

Holmes on Screen and Television

It is generally agreed that the first Sherlock Holmes film with a clearly identified person playing the detective was the 1905 short *The Adventures of Sherlock Holmes*, with Maurice Costello. Since that time, the sleuth has been portrayed by some of Hollywood's biggest names and by actors who have become synonymous with the eccentric resident of Baker Street. Each performer has brought something to the role, but, often to their surprise, Holmes has proven quite a challenge to bring to life.

ACTOR	FILM OR PROGRAM	ACTOR	FILM OR PROGRAM
Maurice Costello	*The Adventures of Sherlock Holmes* (1905)	Buster Keaton	*Sherlock Jr.* (1924)
		Kurt Brenkendorff	*Der Mord in Splendid Hotel* (1919)
Viggo Larsen	*Sherlock Holmes I* (1908)		
	Sherlock Holmes II (1908)	Georges Treville	*The Speckled Band* (1912)
	Sherlock Holmes III (1908)		*Silver Blaze* (1912)
	Sangerindens Diamanter (1908)		*The Beryl Coronet* (1912)
	Droske No. 519 (1909)		*The Musgrave Ritual* (1912)
	Den Graa Dame (1909)		*The Reygate Squires* (1912)
	Arsen Lupin contra Sherlock Holmes (1910–1911)		*The Stolen Papers* (1912)
			A Mystery of Boscombe Vale (1912)
Otto Lagoni	*Sherlock Holmes I Bondefangerklor* (1910)		*The Copper Beeches* (1912)
Forrest Holger-Madsen	*Forklaedte Barnepige* (1911)	Harry Benham	*Sherlock Holmes Solves the Sign of Four* (1913)
	Hotelmysterierne (1911)	James Bragington	*A Study in Scarlet* (1914)
	The Adventures of Sherlock Holmes (1908)	H. A. Saintbury	*The Valley of Fear* (1916)
Holger Rasmussen	*Mordet I Bakerstreet* (1911)	Francis Ford	*A Study in Scarlet* (1914)
Alwin Neuss	*Millionobligationen* (1911)	William Gillette	*Sherlock Holmes* (1916)
	Der Hund von Baskerville (1914–1920)	Eille Norwood	*The Adventures of Sherlock Holmes* (series—April 1921)
Eugen Burg	*Der Hund von Baskerville* (1914–1920)		*The Further Adventures of Sherlock Holmes* (series—March 1922)
Lu Jurgens	*Der Hund von Baskerville* (1914–1920)		
Hugo Flink	*Der Erdstrommotor* (1917)		*The Last Adventures of Sherlock Holmes* (series—March 1923)
	Die Kasette (1917)		
	Der Schlagenring (1917)		
	Der Indische Spinne (1917)	John Barrymore	*Sherlock Holmes* (1922)
Ferdinand Bonn	*Was Er Im Spiegel Sah* (1918)	Carlyle Blackwell	*Der Hund von Baskerville* (1929)
	Die Gifteplombe (1918)		
	Das Schicksal der Renate Yongk (1918)	Clive Brook	*The Return of Sherlock Holmes* (1929)
	Die Dose des Kardinals (1918)		*Paramount on Parade* (Murder Will Out; 1930)
Sam Robinson	*Black Sherlock Holmes* (1918)		
Burt Lytell	*Sherlock Brown* (1921)		*Sherlock Holmes* (1932)

ACTOR	FILM OR PROGRAM	ACTOR	FILM OR PROGRAM
Reginald Owen	*A Study in Scarlet* (1933)		"Sherlock Holmes, Incident at Victoria Falls" (TV—1991)
Raymond Massey	*The Speckled Band* (1931)		
Robert Rendel	*The Hound of the Baskervilles* (1931 or 1932)		"Sherlock Holmes and the Leading Lady" (TV—1992)
Arthur Wontner	*The Sleeping Cardinal* (1931)		
	The Missing Rembrandt (1932)	John Neville	*A Study in Terror* (1965)
	The Sign of Four (1932)	Robert Stephens	*The Private Life of Sherlock Holmes* (1970)
	The Triumph of Sherlock Holmes (1935)	Douglas Wilmer	*The Adventure of Sherlock Holmes' Smarter Brother* (1975)
	Silver Blaze (1937)		
Hans Albers	*Der Mann, Der Sherlock Holmes War* (1937)		"Sherlock Holmes" (TV—1964–1965)
Bruno Guttner	*Der Hund von Baskerville* (1937)	Louis Hector	"The Three Garridebs" (TV—1937)
Hermann Speelmans	*Sherlock Holmes, oder Graue Dame* (1937)	Alan Wheatley	"Sherlock Holmes" (TV—1951)
Basil Rathbone	*The Hound of the Baskervilles* (1939)	Ronald Howard	"The New Adventures of Sherlock Holmes" (TV—1953)
	The Adventures of Sherlock Holmes (1939)	Ray Alan	"High Jinks" (TV—1969)
	Sherlock Holmes and the Voice of Terror (1942)	George C. Scott	*They Might Be Giants* (1971)
	Sherlock Holmes and the Secret Weapon (1942)	Stewart Granger	"The Hound of the Baskervilles" (TV—1972)
	Sherlock Holmes in Washington (1943)	John Cleese	"Elementary, My Dear Watson" (TV—1973)
	Sherlock Holmes Faces Death (1943)		"The Strange Case of the End of Civilization as We Know It" (TV—1977)
	The Spider Woman (1944)		
	The Scarlet Claw (1944)	Leonard Nimoy	"The Interior Motive" (TV—1975)
	The Pearl of Death (1944)	Brent Spiner	"STAR TREK: The Next Generation": "Elementary, My Dear Data" and "Ship in a Bottle"
	The House of Fear (1945)		
	The Woman in Green (1945)		
	Pursuit to Algiers (1945)		
	Terror By Night (1946)	Larry Hagman	*The Return of the World's Greatest Detective* (1974)
	Dressed to Kill (1946)		
	Crazy House (1943)	Nicol Williamson	*The Seven-Per-Cent Solution* (1976)
	"The Adventure of the Black Baronet" (TV, 1953)	Roger Moore	*Sherlock Holmes in New York* (1976)
Peter Cushing	*The Hound of the Baskervilles* (1959)	Peter Cook	*The Hound of the Baskervilles* (1977)
	"Sherlock Holmes" (TV—1968)	Royal Dano	"My Dear Uncle Sherlock" (TV—1977)
	"The Masks of Death" (TV—1984)	Christopher Plummer	"Silver Blaze" (TV—1977)
Christopher Lee	*Sherlock Holmes und das Halsband des Todes* (1962)		*Murder By Decree* (1979)
		Frank Langella	"Sherlock Holmes" (TV—1980)

ACTOR	FILM OR PROGRAM
Geoffrey Whitehead	"Sherlock Holmes and Dr. Watson" (TV—1982)
Tom Baker	"The Hound of the Baskervilles" (TV—1982)
Guy Henry	"Young Sherlock" (TV—1982)
Ian Richardson	"The Sign of Four" (TV—1983)
	"The Hound of the Baskervilles" (TV—1983)
Jeremy Brett	"The Adventures of Sherlock Holmes" (TV—1984)
	"The Return of Sherlock Holmes" (TV—1986–88)
	"The Hound of the Baskervilles" (TV—1987)
	"The Sign of Four" (TV—1987)
	"The Casebook of Sherlock Holmes" (TV—1991)
Nicholas Rowe	*Young Sherlock Holmes* (1985)
Michael Pennington	"The Return of Sherlock Holmes" (TV—1987)
Charlton Heston	"The Crucifer of Blood" (TV—1991)
Edward Woodward	"Hands of a Murderer" (TV—1990)

pathy for all red-headed men; when he died, it was found that he had left his enormous fortune in the hands of trustees, with instructions to apply the interest to the providing of easy berths, to men whose hair is of that colour."

HOPKINS, STANLEY. A young police inspector from Scotland Yard in whom Holmes took an interest and in whose future he had high hopes. Hopkins worked with Holmes on at least three cases: the murders of Eustace Brackenstall in "The Abbey Grange," Peter Carey in "Black Peter," and Willoughby Smith in "The Golden Pince-Nez." He also referred Cyril Overton, captain of the Cambridge rugby team, to Holmes, as he considered the disappearance of Godfrey Staunton to be more a case for Holmes than the police. He was described by Watson as "an exceedingly alert man thirty years of age, dressed in a quiet tweed suit, but retaining the erect bearing of one who is accus-

tomed to official uniform." Hopkins held the detective in very high regard and "professed the admiration and respect of a pupil for the scientific methods of the famous amateur" ("Black Peter"). Holmes said to Watson, "Hopkins has called me in seven times, and on each occasion his summons has been entirely justified . . . I fancy that every one of his cases has found its way into your collection . . ." ("The Abbey Grange"). Holmes also considered him to be not an emotional man. He resided at 46 Lord Street, Brixton. (See also SCOTLAND YARD.)

HORNER, JOHN. A twenty-six-year-old plumber who was arrested for stealing the Blue Carbuncle that belonged to the countess of Morcar in "The Blue Carbuncle." Horner had a previous conviction for robbery and was thus the obvious suspect, but Holmes was able to clear his name and recover the missing gem.

HORSHAM. A town in Sussex where the Openshaws resided in "The Five Orange Pips." Horsham was just north of Lamberley, home of Robert Ferguson in "The Sussex Vampire."

HORSOM, DR. A physician who certified the demise of Rose Spender, the old woman whom Annie Fraser claimed to be her old nurse in "The Disappearance of Lady Frances Carfax." He was to be found at 13 Firbank Villas and stated that Spender died of senile decay.

HOTELS. Throughout the Canon a number of hotels are featured or mentioned as places visited by either the Great Detective or by clients and criminals. Holmes stayed at several hotels and inns in the accounts of his cases, usually with Watson. On notable exception was the **Hotel Dulong** in Lyons to which the doctor was summoned because Holmes had shattered his health in the pursuit of the swindler Baron Maupertuis and his colossal schemes in "The Reigate Squires." During the "Black Peter" affair, Inspector Stanley Hopkins arranged rooms for Holmes and Watson at the **Brambletye** in Forest Row, Sussex, while the detective looked into the murder of Peter Carey. Holmes and Watson stayed at the **Crown Inn** in the small village of Stoke Moran during the affair of "The Speckled Band." In the smoking room of the **Charing Cross Hotel** next to the Charing Cross Station,

Holmes laid a trap for the international agent behind the theft of "The Bruce-Partington Plans." Joseph Stangerson was found stabbed to death in his bed in **Halliday's Private Hotel** in London on Little George Street in *A Study in Scarlet*. Between the **Grand Hotel** in London and Charing Cross Station Watson encountered a "one-legged news-vendor" who displayed the evening papers, and there he saw the headline MURDEROUS ATTACK UPON SHERLOCK HOLMES in "The Illustrious Client."

Other hotels of the Canon include the following: **Bentley's Private Hotel,** in London, where the Cambridge rugby team arrived to stay two days before their important match with Oxford in "The Missing Three-Quarter"; **Claridge's Hotel,** a famous London hotel where the millionaire J. Neil Gibson stayed in "The Problem of Thor Bridge," and where Martha, Holmes's agent in the household of Von Bork, was to meet the detective the day after the capture of the German spymaster in "His Last Bow"; the **Dacre Hotel,** one of whose best rooms was occupied for a time by the Prince of Colonna from whom the Black Pearl of the Borgias was stolen in "The Six Napoleons"; the **Fighting Cock Inn,** a small establishment run by Reuben Hays on the Chesterfield High Road, in Hallamshire, figured in the abduction of Lord Saltire, son of the duke of Holdernesse in "The Priory School"; the **Hotel Cosmopolitan** in London where the countess Morcar was staying at the time the Blue Carbuncle was stolen in "The Blue Carbuncle"; the **Hotel Escurial** in Madrid, the site of the assassination of Don Murillo and his secretary, Signor Lopez, in "Wisteria Lodge"; the **Hotel National** in Lausanne where Lady Frances Carfax was staying just prior to her vanishing in "The Disappearance of Lady Frances Carfax"; the **Mexborough Private Hotel** in Craven Street, London, where the Stapletons stayed while Jack Stapelton pursued Henry Baskerville in *The Hound of the Baskervilles* (the note sent to Sir Henry Baskerville was prepared with paper and ink from the Mexborough); the **Westville Arms,** an inn in the village of Birlstone where Holmes, Watson, and Inspector MacDonald stayed during the investigation into the apparent murder of John Douglas in *The Valley of Fear*; and the **Northumberland,** a small London hotel where Henry Baskerville stayed after arriving in England from Canada in *The Hound of the Baskervilles*. It was here that he lost two boots, a new one and an old one—a peculiar series of events that Holmes found exceedingly interesting. The Northumberland is known today for the public house on its onetime ground floor, the "Sherlock Holmes." Located on Northumberland Street, the "Sherlock Holmes" is profusely decorated with Holmesian memorabilia. Also on permanent display is the well-known sitting room from Baker Street that was created in 1951 for the Festival of Britain.

HOUND OF THE BASKERVILLES, THE (HOUN).

Published: *Strand*, August 1901–April 1902; published in novel form by Newnes (London), 1902 and McClure, Phillips (New York), 1902. Major players: Holmes, Watson, Sir Henry Baskerville, Dr. Mortimer, Jack Stapleton, Beryl Stapleton. Case date: 1889. The most famous, most popular, and generally considered the best written of all the accounts by Dr. Watson. It is a tale with much to recommend it to Sherlockians and non-Sherlockians alike as it contains elements of the supernatural, the Gothic, the classic detective novel, and of course, Holmes and Watson at their very best. Fans of the good doctor are especially fond of this work as he figures prominently in the narrative.

Having become involved in the case brought to him by Dr. Mortimer, Holmes admits that he is too preoccupied with another matter to attend to young Sir Henry Baskerville himself. Watson, as always, is sent as his surrogate to Baskerville Hall on Dartmoor. When Holmes finally makes his dramatic appearance, the doctor is praised for his good work by the detective, a major departure from the verbal beatings he takes in "The Disappearance of Lady Frances Carfax" and "The Solitary Cyclist." Watson's diary, quoted extensively in the story, gives full rein to Watson's literary aspirations—the passages on Baskerville Hall and the Grimpen Mire make for riveting reading and enhance the suspenseful climax of the case as the reader has been carefully prepared throughout to expect something truly frightful. The case itself, involving the murder of Sir Charles Baskerville, the attempted murder of his heir Sir Henry, and the apparent return of the dreaded dog that curses the Baskervilles, is one of the darkest of the detective's career, made particularly so because of the skill and cunning of his vicious opponent.

The first publication of the early installments of the novel in the *Strand* caused a major eruption of

Watson meets the Man on the Moor, in *The Hound of the Baskervilles*; by Sidney Paget.

public enthusiasm as it seemed to mark the triumphant resurrection of Sherlock Holmes from the dead (he had "died" in 1891 in "The Final Problem"). This, it became clear, was not the case. Holmes was still dead and this chronicle was merely one of Watson's reminiscences. Despite intense public pressure, Sir Arthur Conan Doyle remained adamant that the detective was to remain at the bottom of the Reichenbach Falls (he would stay there until 1903). Nevertheless, the public lined up outside the offices of the *Strand* to buy copies. Cleverly, the installments always kept the reader breathlessly waiting for the next month. For example, the first part ended with the now famous exchange between Holmes and Dr. Mortimer:

" 'Footprints?'
'Footprints.'
'A man's or a woman's?'
Dr. Mortimer looked strangely at us for an instant, and his voice sank almost to a whisper as he answered:
'Mr. Holmes, they were the footprints of a gigantic hound.' "

During the run in the *Strand*, the *Hound* increased the magazine's circulation by some 30,000 copies, a testament to the public's love of Holmes and Watson and a demonstration that readers were going to continue to insist that the detective return from his watery grave.

HOUND OF THE BASKERVILLES, THE. England 1931 or 1932. Dir: V. Gareth Gundrey. Cast: Robert Rendel (Holmes), Fred Lloyd (Watson), John Stuart (Henry Baskerville), Wilfrid Shine (Dr. Mortimer). The fourth film version of the novel (See Appendix for complete list of films), and one of the least effective, despite the attention to detail and the generally competent performance by Rendel. Harshly viewed by critics who disliked its plotting and lack of suspense, the film did poorly, insuring that Rendel would have only one appearance as the detective. Film historians point to Lloyd's work as Watson as particularly noteworthy, applauding his competence and absence of the dull-wittedness so much a characteristic of other Watsons.

HOUND OF THE BASKERVILLES, THE. U.S. 1939. Dir: Sidney Lanfield. Cast: Basil Rathbone (Holmes), Nigel Bruce (Watson), Richard Greene (Sir Henry Baskerville), Lionel Atwill (Dr. Mortimer), John Carradine (Barryman), Wendy Barrie (Beryl Stapleton). The beloved first film featuring Rathbone and Bruce as the dynamic duo inaugurated the long-running cycle of movies that made them the most popular Holmes and Watson of all time. *The Hound of the Baskervilles* remains the most respected version of the novel, despite the multitude of remakes and new adaptations. With its moody atmosphere, fog-filled sets of the Grimpen Mire, and excellent performances throughout, this inaugural production was a major hit both with critics and at the box office. It is generally faithful to the original material, although some changes were made: Holmes descends into the hound's pit and is there trapped by Stapleton, escaping in time to rescue Sir Henry from a glass of poison; and there is a seance, without Holmes, that actually serves to enhance the supernatural elements of the tale. Throughout, Rathbone gave wonderful life to the detective, while Bruce was at

A poster from *The Hound of the Baskervilles* (1939) with Basil Rathbone and Nigel Bruce, the first of their beloved long-running cycle of films. Note that Richard Greene received top billing.

his best as Watson. Ironically, the studio, 20th Century-Fox, was uncertain about the picture, especially the box office potential of Sherlock Holmes. In their advertising, Holmes was not the prime lure—that would be the Hound itself. Even in the credits, Richard Greene was given top billing. The studio need not have worried. The dog, by the way, was a 140-pound great dane named Chief, from the San Fernando Valley.

HOUND OF THE BASKERVILLES, THE.

England 1959. Dir: Terence Fisher. Cast: Peter Cushing (Holmes), Andre Morrell (Watson), Christopher Lee (Sir Henry Baskerville), Ewen Solon (Stapleton), and Francis de Wolff (Dr. Mortimer). The first Holmes film ever released in color, produced by Hammer Films, the English studio best known for its lurid, gory, and colorful horror movies such as *Frankenstein* (1957) and *Horror of Dracula* (1958). For audiences familiar with Hammer Films, this version did not come as a surprise, but for the uninitiated it may have been bewildering, for Hammer had the habit of taking original plots and changing them around until only the spirit of the source material remained. This was true with their Dracula films and was especially the case with the Hound. The changes (including the use of a mine shaft and having Beryl Stapleton a fey woman of the moor) certainly spiced things up, but faithful Sherlockians were probably horrified at seeing Sir Henry Baskerville threatened with a tarantula! Hammer made much of its use of color, advertising "It's ten times the terror in Technicolor! The most horror-dripping tale ever written!" The studio was never accused of understatement.

Holmes (Stewart Granger) confers with the dutiful Watson (Bernard Fox) in *The Hound of the Baskervilles* (1972). Note the rather spacious Baker Street.

Dennis Hoey (l. with the rope), a memorable performer as Inspector Lestrade, in *The House of Fear* (1943), with Basil Rathbone (r. as Holmes) and Nigel Bruce (far r. as Watson).

"HOUND OF THE BASKERVILLES, THE."

U.S. 1972. Dir: Barry Crane. Cast: Stewart Granger (Holmes), Bernard Fox (Watson), Anthony Berke (Mortimer), William Shatner (Stapleton), and Jane Merrow (Beryl Stapleton). A made-for-television film, broadcast in the United States on ABC that brought screen legend Granger, perhaps belatedly, to the role of the Great Detective. He is, unfortunately, very old in the film, and a little too heavy, while Fox as Watson does nothing to assist him in energizing their moments together. This version of *The Hound of the Baskervilles* is also hampered by a claustrophobic set, a frantically paced script, and the debilitating sense that the viewer has seen all this before. Two excellent performances were given by Shatner and Merrow.

"HOUND OF THE BASKERVILLES, THE."

England 1983. Dir: Douglas Hickox. Cast: Ian Richardson (Holmes), Donald Churchill (Wat-son), Nicholas Clay (Stapleton), Ronald Lacey (Lestrade), Denholm Elliot (Dr. Mortimer). A made-for-television film featuring Ian Richardson as the Great Detective for the second time—he played Holmes in "The Sign of Four" the same year. The production was first rate although Richardson's Holmes was a bit too amiable. The villain, as if anyone familiar with the story did not know, is revealed in the opening moments through a flashback to the early Baskerville falling prey to the hound's curse. Ronald Lacey, excellent as Lestrade, would later appear in the Jeremy Brett (Holmes) version of *The Sign of Four* in the dual role of the Sholto Brothers.

"HOUND OF THE BASKERVILLES, THE"

England 1987. Dir: Brian Mills. Cast: Jeremy Brett (Holmes), Edward Hardwicke (Watson), James Faulkner (Stapleton). Granada Television's virtually mandatory filming of the most famous of all of Holmes's cases, giving the viewers the pleasure of seeing Jeremy Brett's Holmes investigate the dread Hound of the Baskervilles. The photography and performances are first rate, with only a few changes made from the original. Brett, in an interview, was of the opinion that this one should have been done differently—he would like to do it over again.

HOUSE OF FEAR, THE.   U.S. 1945. Dir: Roy William Neill. Cast: Basil Rathbone (Holmes), Nigel Bruce (Watson), Dennis Hoey (Lestrade), Aubrey Mather (Alastair), and Paul Cavanagh (Simon Merivale). The tenth outing of Rathbone and Bruce, this time in a film supposedly based upon "The Five Orange Pips," although the plot seems to be more of a reworking of Agatha Christie's "And Then There Were None." At the request of an insurance agent, Holmes and Watson journey to West Scotland to investigate the strange goings-on at Drearcliff, a seaside manorhouse that is owned and inhabited by the members of "The Good Comrades," an association of seven middle-aged men who moved to Drearcliff six months earlier and who all have insurance policies, with each other as the beneficiaries. Naturally they start dropping like flies. Two are horribly murdered after receiving an envelope containing the infamous orange pips (or seeds), and the others soon follow in unique fashions—one is blown to bits and another crushed beneath a rock. The set used for *The House of Fear* was the same as the one found in *Sherlock Holmes Faces Death*.

HOWELLS, RACHEL.   The second housemaid at Hurlstone, in Sussex, in "The Musgrave Ritual" who was of "an excitable Welsh temperament." Howells loved and was engaged to the butler Richard Brunton, but was cast aside by him for another, an act that had the most terrible consequences for the treasure-hunting manservant.

"HOW WATSON LEARNED THE TRICK."
A delightful parody of Holmes and Watson, written by Sir Arthur Conan Doyle, published in 1924 in *The Book of the Queen's Doll's House Library* in a limited edition of 1500 copies. Conan Doyle was one of a number of noted writers asked to contribute short stories or passages to the "library" being assembled for the so-called Queen's Doll's House. This was a magnificent miniature house, designed by the architect Sir Edward Lutyens, complete with electric lights, running water, and working

appliances that was presented to Her Majesty Queen Anne, wife of King George V, as "a token or symbol of goodwill." The "books" for the miniature library were from such luminaries as G. K. Chesterton, Rudyard Kipling, Thomas Hardy, Joseph Conrad, J. M. Barrie (a friend of Conan Doyle's), and Conan Doyle himself. Doyle authored "How Watson Learned the Trick" for the special occasion—a humorous exchange between Holmes and Watson in which the good doctor mistakenly believes he has mastered the art of deduction.

HUDSON.   The sole survivor of the crew of the barque *Gloria Scott* which was destroyed in an explosion following its takeover by the convicts being transported to Australia. Hudson was pulled out of the water by the convicts who had taken a new boat. He turned up many years later in England, precipitating the events described in "The 'Gloria Scott'." He worked as a gardener to Trevor Senior and then as butler. Trevor Junior noted: "The maids complained of his drunken habits and his vile language. The dad raised their wages all round to compensate them for the annoyances."

Another figure named Hudson, probably a member of the Ku Klux Klan, was mentioned in "The Five Orange Pips." The name appears in the notebook of Elias Openshaw, in the entry dated March, 1869: "4th. Hudson came. Same old platform."

HUDSON, MRS.   The long-suffering landlady of 221B Baker Street who, surprisingly, was never directly involved in any of the published cases of the Canon, although she aided Holmes in "The Empty House," summoned Dr. Watson into the affair of "The Dying Detective," and was always there to give Holmes (and Watson when he resided at Baker Street) all of his needed comforts, particularly his meals, especially breakfast. Holmes was apt to complain of her presence in his rooms while he was on a case, but he also rewarded her with money and, on a few occasions, with his praise; he once declared, for example, in "The Naval Treaty," that "her cuisine is a little limited, but she has as good an idea of breakfast as a Scotchwoman." Watson's assessment of her was much more effusive in his account of "The Dying Detective." "Mrs. Hudson, the landlady of Sherlock Holmes, was a long-suffering woman. Not only was her first-floor flat invaded at all hours by throngs of singular and often undesirable characters but her remarkable lodger showed an eccentricity and irregularity in

his life which must have sorely tried her patience . . . The landlady stood in the deepest awe of him [Holmes] and never dared to interfere with him, however outrageous his proceedings might seem. She was fond of him, too, for he had a remarkable gentleness and courtesy in his dealings with women."

Her deep regard for Holmes was such that she responded with great emotion upon his return to Baker Street in 1894 in "The Empty House" after the Great Hiatus. In that case, Mrs. Hudson had her moment of glory, moving the wax bust of Holmes that was serving as a decoy for the gunman planning to shoot the detective so that it appeared that Sherlock was home. An early demonstration of her concern was given in *The Sign of Four* when Watson tried to put her fears at ease about the restlessness of Sherlock Holmes. Despite her exasperations and exclamations of displeasure, Mrs. Hudson was astonishingly patient with the peculiar parade of clients and assorted associates of Holmes's who went through Baker Street, though she was not particularly fond of the Baker Street Irregulars.

She frequently brought Holmes cards of visitors or telegrams from the police or other clients. She awoke early to let in the terrified Helen Stoner in "The Speckled Band," retorting upon Holmes about it. Among the persons shown in to Holmes's rooms by Mrs. Hudson were Inspectors Baynes and Gregson in "Wisteria Lodge"; the sailors looking for Captain Basil in "Black Peter"; Cecil Barker in *The Valley of Fear*; and the future Mrs. Watson, Mary Morstan, in *The Sign of Four*. It is possible that she may have had a hand in the employment of the page, often called Billy, as Holmes's practice had grown over the years and as she was getting on in age. Holmes noted that she had a "stately tread" in *A Study in Scarlet* and acknowledged that the bell that rang at Baker Street at the start of "The Five Orange Pips" was probably "some crony of the landlady's," although John Openshaw was actually the caller.

Mrs. Hudson has become a mainstay of Holmes films, the cinematic precedent established by such actresses as Minnie Rayner (in the series with Arthur Wontner) and Mary Gordon (in the Rathbone-Bruce series). (See also BAKER STREET.)

HUDSON, MORSE.   The owner of a shop on Kensington Road that sold pictures and statues, including the busts of the emperor in "The Six Napoleons." Hudson at one time possessed three of the six Napoleons, two of which were sold to Dr. Barnicot and a third that was destroyed in broad daylight on his own counter. "Disgraceful sir! A Nihilst plot—that is what I make of it. No one but an anarchist would go around breaking statues. Red republicans that's what I call 'em." Watson described Hudson as "a small stout man with a red face and a peppery manner."

HUDSON STREET.   A quiet street in Aldershot where Henry Wood had lodgings in "The Crooked Man." Mrs. Barclay and Miss Morrison met the Crooked Man on Hudson Street.

HUGUENOTS.   The French Protestants who were persecuted in the sixteenth and seventeenth centuries. After wrapping up his explanations of the details surrounding *The Hound of the Baskervilles*, Holmes invited Watson to a performance of the De Reszkes in *Les Huguenots* for which the detective had a box, after dinner at Marcini's. Charles Gorot in "The Naval Treaty" was of Huguenot extraction.

HUND VON BASKERVILLE, DER (1). Germany. 1914–1920. Dirs: Rudolf Meinert, Richard Oswald, and Willy Zehn. Cast: Alwin Neuss, Erich Kaiser-Titz, Eugen Burg, and probably others as Holmes. Actually a series of films released by the German company Vitascope from June 1914 to 1920, based initially on *The Hound of the Baskervilles*. The first entry, *Der Hund von Baskerville* (1914), starred Alwin Neuss and was so successful that the company made sequels, essentially picking up where the last one left off. Neuss appeared subsequently in *Das Einsame Haus* (*The Isolated House*, 1914), *Das Unheimliche Zimmer* (*The Uncanny Room*, 1915), and *Wie Entstand der Hund von Baskervilles* (*How the Hound of the Baskervilles Arose*, 1915). At the same time as *The Uncanny Room* was released, a rival version, *Das Dunkle Schloss* (*The Dark Castle*) was released, starring Eugen Burg and directed by Willy Zehn. The next two installments of the regular series were *Dr. Macdonald's Sanatorium* (1920), and *Das Haus Ohne Fenster* (*The House Without Windows*, 1920). It is uncertain who the stars of these last two were, possibly Erich Kaiser-Titz in the former film.

HUND VON BASKERVILLE, DER (2). Germany. 1929. Dir: Richard Oswald. Cast: Carlyle Blackwell (Holmes), Georges Seroff (Watson). A

Memorable Mrs. Hudsons

MRS. HUDSON IN FILM AND TELEVISION

ACTRESS	FILM OR PROGRAM	ACTRESS	FILM OR PROGRAM
Mme. D'Esterre	The Adventures of Sherlock Holmes (film series—1921)		The Pearl of Death (1944) The Woman in Green (1945) Dressed to Kill (1946)
	Further Adventures of Sherlock Holmes (film series—1922)	Barbara Leake Irene Handl	A Study in Terror (1965) The Private Life of Sherlock Holmes (1970)
	The Last Adventures of Sherlock Holmes (film series—1923)	Alison Leggatt	The Seven-Per-Cent Solution (1976)
		Pat Keen	Without a Clue (1990)
Tempe Pigott	A Study in Scarlet (1933)	Enid Lindsey	"Sherlock Holmes" (TV—1965)
Marie Ault	The Speckled Band (1931)		
Minnie Rayner	The Sleeping Cardinal (1931) The Missing Rembrandt (1932)	Grace Arnold	"Sherlock Holmes" (TV—1968)
Clare Greet	The Sign of Four (1932)	Marguerite Young	"Dr. Watson and the Darkwater Hall Mystery" (TV—1974)
Minnie Rayner	The Triumph of Sherlock Holmes (1935) Silver Blaze (1937)	Marjorie Bennett	"Sherlock Holmes in New York" (TV—1976)
Gertrude Walle	Der Hund von Baskerville (1929)	Betty Woolfe	Murder By Decree (1979)
		Rosalie Williams	"The Adventures of Sherlock Holmes" (TV series, on-going in "The Return of Sherlock Holmes," and "The Casebook of Sherlock Holmes")
Mary Gordon	The Hound of the Baskervilles (1939)		
	The Adventures of Sherlock Holmes (1939)		
	Sherlock Holmes and the Voice of Terror (1942)		
	Sherlock Holmes and the Secret Weapon (1942)	Iris Vandeleur	"Sherlock Holmes" (TV—1951)
	Sherlock Holmes Faces Death (1943)	Mary Holder	"The Speckled Band" (TV—1964)
	The Spider Woman (1944)		

film generally considered the last silent Sherlock Holmes picture, although some purists cede the title to *The Return of Sherlock Holmes* (1929) with Clive Brook. If *Der Hund* is taken as the last silent work featuring Holmes, then American-born Carlyle Blackwell (d. 1955) holds the distinction of being the last silent Sherlock. Directed by Oswald, who had worked on the earlier *Der Hund von Baskerville* (1914–1920), this version reportedly followed the novel very closely but was a box office failure, largely because of the growing market for sound pictures, as proven by *The Return of Sherlock*

Holmes. Nevertheless, this was the third screen version of the novel-length account of *The Hound of the Baskervilles*; many more would follow.

HUNTER, NED.   A stableboy at King's Pyland who had been on guard the night that Silver Blaze was taken from the stables in "Silver Blaze." He had been drugged with opium in his curried mutton and was thus unconscious when Silver Blaze disappeared.

HUNTER, VIOLET.   A young woman who introduces Holmes to the case of the "Copper Beeches" by asking his advice on whether she should accept a situation that had been offered her, a request that caused Holmes to sink into despair about the degeneration of his practice into an agency for recovering lost lead pencils and giving advice to young ladies from boarding schools. Miss Hunter of Montague Place had served as a governess for five years, but the departure of her employer, Colonel Spence Munro, to Halifax, forced her to seek a new position. She was offered an excellent one by Jephro Rucastle in Hampshire, with the condition that she cut her hair. Watson wrote that "she was plainly but neatly dressed, with a bright, quick face, freckled like a plover's egg, and with the brisk manner of a woman who has had her own way to make in the world." The doctor was pleased to report at the end of his account that Miss Hunter had become the head of a private school at Walsall.

HUNTING CROP.   A hunting crop was Holmes's preferred weapon. He used it to smash the last bust of Napoleon in "The Six Napoleons," strike the revolver from the hand of John Clay in "The Red-Headed League," and threaten James Windibank in "A Case of Identity." Grimesby Roylott shook a hunting crop at Holmes in "The Speckled Band." Other persons who used the weapon were Sir Henry Baskerville in *The Hound of the Baskervilles* and Silas Brown in "Silver Blaze."

HURET.   The so-called Boulevard Assassin who, in 1894, was tracked down and arrested by Holmes. The detective was rewarded with the Order of the Legion of Honour and an autographed letter of thanks from the French president ("The Golden Pince-Nez").

HURLSTONE.   The family estate of the Musgraves, in Sussex in "The Musgrave Ritual." Holmes said that it was a famous old building, "built in the shape of an L, the longer arm being the more modern portion, and the shorter the ancient nucleus from which the other was developed. Over the low, heavy lintelled door, in the centre of this old part, is chiselled the date, 1607, but experts are agreed that the beams and stonework are really much older than this. The enormously thick walls and tiny windows of this part had in the last century driven the family into building the new wing, and the old one was used now as a storehouse and a cellar, when it was used at all."

HUXTABLE, THORNEYCROFT.   Ph.D., M.A., etc. The founder of the Priory School, the most select preparatory school in England, near Mackleton, in Hallamshire, and the author of *Huxtable's Sidelights on Horace* in "The Priory School." Watson wrote that he could not "recollect anything more sudden or startling than the first appearance of Dr. Thorneycroft Huxtable," as the school principal staggered into 221B and engaged Holmes to find the missing Lord Saltire, son of the duke of Holdernesse.

HYAMS.   The tailor of Jonas Oldacre in "The Norwood Builder." Among the ashes of the burned woodpile near Oldacre's residence was a trouser button marked with the name "Hyams." This was taken by the police to be evidence that the unfortunate body in the fire had been Oldacre.

HYDE PARK.   The largest park in London. Hatty Doran was last seen walking in Hyde Park in the company of Flora Millar, so the police dragged the Serpentine, the large artificial lake in the park, in the hopes of finding her body in "The Noble Bachelor." Other cases in which the park was mentioned were "The Red-Headed League," "The Empty House," "The Yellow Face," "A Scandal in Bohemia," and *The Hound of the Baskervilles*.

HYNES, HYNES.   A neighbor of Aloysius Garcia who owned the large house Purdey Place, in Surrey in "Wisteria Lodge."

I

**"ILLUSTRIOUS CLIENT, THE ADVEN-
TURE OF THE" (ILLU).** Published: *Col-
lier's*, November 1924, *Strand*, May 1925; collected
in *The Case Book of Sherlock Holmes* (1927). Case
date: September 1902. Major players: Holmes,
Watson, Baron Adalbert Gruner, Violet De Merville, Colonel James Damery, and Kitty Winter.
One of Sir Arthur Conan Doyle's favorite cases, the
"Illustrious Client" presented a believable, reprehensible, and utterly vile villain in the person of
Baron Gruner, an Austrian nobleman who almost
certainly murdered his late wife in the Splugen Pass
and who is now planning to wed Violet De Merville, daughter of old General De Merville, of Khyber fame. The planned union has broken the old
general. At the request of "The Illustrious Client,"
generally believed to be King Edward, Sir James
Damery engages Holmes's services, as he often did
for the nobility, to break off their wedding. The
detective attempts to negotiate with Gruner with
the result being the most shocking headline of the
Canon:

MURDEROUS ATTACK UPON
SHERLOCK HOLMES

IMPERIAL THEATRE. A Westminster theater. Violet Smith's father, the late James Smith, had
been the orchestra conductor at the "old Imperial
Theatre." ("The Solitary Cyclist.")

INCREDIBLE UMBRELLA, THE. A highly
innovative 1979 novel written by Marvin Kaye,
presenting the exploits of one J. Adrian Fillmore,
an English literature professor. Fillmore purchases a
strange looking bumbershoot umbrella, discovering
in it a device that transports him into a series of

imagined worlds. Among them are a Gilbert and
Sullivan country (from the *Mikado* and *The Pirates
of Penzance*), a peculiar Holmesian world (with
Ormond Sacher and Sherringford Holmes); a place
with Dracula; another one with Frankenstein; and
a world of the Canon where Moriarty has his own
umbrella. Along the way, Fillmore saves Holmes
from death and visits Flatland. The joke is that
Fillmore becomes James Phillimore, the man who

The most terrible headline of the Canon in "The Illustrious Client"; by Howard Elcock.

Holmes recovers from the attack of Baron Gruner's agents in "The Illustrious Client"; by John Richard Flanagan.

forgot his umbrella, went back into his house to retrieve it, and was never seen again (A case originally mentioned in "Thor Bridge"). A sequel, *The Amorous Umbrella*, followed, but Holmes did not make an appearance.

INDIA.   The prized possession of the British Empire, India was the background for several cases investigated by Holmes and a number of persons involved in them. Watson had personal experience with India, having been attached to the Northumberland Fusiliers, a regiment stationed in India at the time (*A Study in Scarlet*). He later wrote of his "service in India," noting that it had trained him "to stand heat better than cold" ("The Cardboard Box"). The flavor of India was pervasive throughout *The Sign of Four*, as the events told by Watson had their origin in that distant land—with the treasure of the Agra originally owned by a rajah. Dr. Grimesby Roylott ("The Speckled Band"), Colonel Barclay ("The Crooked Man"), and Colonel

Sebastian Moran ("The Empty House") all had spent time in India. Each left behind deeds of shame, particularly Roylott and Barclay. Moran was held to be the finest heavy game shot that the Eastern Empire ever produced, once crawling into an Indian drain in pursuit of a wounded tiger. Roylott also smoked Indian cigars and had a passion for Indian animals—especially the swamp adder, the so-called deadliest snake in India. Major Sholto, in *The Sign of Four*, decorated Pondicherry Lodge with a wide assortment of Indian curiosities, and stuffed the house with Indian servants. India was also one of the specialisms of Mycroft Holmes ("The Bruce-Partington Plans").

INDIAN ARMY.   The armed forces of British India, a separate institution from the British army, were divided into three armies, the Bengal, Madras, and Bombay. Several individuals served in the Indian army, starting, of course, with "John H. Watson, M.D., Late Indian Army." Others include:

Captain Morstan and Major Sholto (*The Sign of Four*) of the Thirty-fourth Bombay Infantry, Major-General Stoner ("The Speckled Band"), of the Bengal Artillery, and Colonel Sebastian Moran ("The Empty House") of the First Bengalore Pioneers. Other mentioned regiments were the Third Bengal Fusiliers, and the Guides.

INFERNAL DEVICE, THE. A 1979 novel by Michael Kurland that features not only Holmes but Professor Moriarty, Queen Victoria, and Trepoff. The latter was mentioned in "A Scandal in Bohemia" under the name the Trepoff murder, a case investigated by Holmes in 1888 in Odessa. The plot centers around the nefarious plans of the evil Russian Trepoff toward Queen Victoria. His ambitions are foiled by Holmes and his ally Professor Moriarty, a twist on the Canon also seen in Holmes's autobiography, *Sherlock Holmes, My Life and Crimes*, by Michael Hardwick.

INFLUENCE OF A TRADE UPON THE FORM OF THE HAND. In full, *A Study of the Influence of a Trade upon the Form of the Hand with Lithotypes of the Hands of Slaters, Sailors, Corkcutters, Compositors, Weavers, and Diamond-cutters*, a monograph written by Holmes sometime in or before 1887. It was, Holmes told Watson in *The Sign of Four*, "a matter of great practical interest to the scientific detective—especially in cases of unclaimed bodies, or in discovering the antecedents of criminals." At the time of the affair of the Four,

this mongraph, with other works of the detective, was being translated into French by Francois le Villard.

INTERLAKEN. A town in central Switzerland on the Aar River, the main tourist center of the Bernese Alps. In their journey across the Continent in "The Final Problem," Holmes and Watson passed through Interlaken on their way to Meiringen.

IRIS. The horse of the duke of Balmoral that ran in the Wessex Cup in "Silver Blaze." It finished a disappointing third.

"IS DISEASE A REVERSION?" An essay written by Dr. Mortimer that won him the Jackson Prize in Comparative Pathology in *The Hound of the Baskervilles*.

ISONOMY. A highly successful racehorse, foaled in 1875, and owned by Frederick Gretton (1839–1882). "Silver Blaze" was said to be from Isonomy stock and was considered to hold "as brilliant a record as his famous ancestor."

IVY PLANT. A Westminster pub "round the corner" from Godolphin Street in "The Second Stain." When the young woman he had allowed in the house of Eduardo Lucas to see the murder scene fainted, Constable MacPherson repaired to the pub to fetch a brandy.

JACK-IN-OFFICE. A perjorative English term used to describe an arrogant police officer or public official. In "The Speckled Band," Dr. Grimesby Roylott called Holmes a scoundrel, meddler, busybody, and "the Scotland Yard Jack-in-Office!" It was also used in *The Sign of Four*.

JACKSON. A physician who would look after Watson's medical practice when he was away with Holmes. Jackson took over while Watson journeyed with Holmes to Aldershot to look into the death of Colonel Barclay in "The Crooked Man." Watson also wrote of Dr. Anstruther ("The Boscombe Valley Mystery") and an "accomodating neighbor" who would look after the practice ("The Final Problem," "The Stockbroker's Clerk.")

JACK THE RIPPER. One of the most infamous mass murderers in history. The Ripper's reign of terror in London's East End, in the Whitechapel area, lasted from August 7 to November 10, 1888. The bloody case of Jack the Ripper remains unsolved over a century after its abrupt end, although there are many theories and proposed solutions as to his identity. The Ripper affair has also offered writers and filmmakers an intriguing opportunity to match the wits of Holmes with the murderer, a struggle that has extended into the psychological and sexual aspects of both figures. In his brilliant work *Sherlock Holmes of Baker Street* (1962), W. S. Baring-Gould speculated that Inspector Athelney Jones of Scotland Yard was the Ripper, his unmasking accomplished by Watson. Another novel, *The Last Sherlock Holmes Case* by Michael Dibdin, took a shocking view of the detective's relationship with the serial killer, one that is *very* upsetting to first-time readers who might also be devoted Sherlockians. Other novels involving a Holmes-Ripper connection are John Gardner's *The Return of Sherlock Holmes* (1975; in which Professor Moriarty brings the Ripper's terror to an end), and Edward Hanna's *The Whitechapel Horror* (1992). (See also STUDY IN TERROR, A and MURDER BY DECREE.)

JACOBS. The butler to the Trelawney Hopes at Whitehall Terrace in "The Second Stain."

JACOBSON'S YARD. A boat repair yard on the Surrey side of the Thames, opposite the Tower of London. In *The Sign of Four*, Jonathan Small hid the steam launch *Aurora* here, ostensibly to have minor repairs done on the rudder.

JAMES. The name used once by Mrs. Watson when speaking to her husband John in "Wisteria Lodge." The apparent error on her part has been the subject of a tremendous amount of speculation by Sherlockians as to its significance and possible meaning. James is also the name of the son of the postmaster of Grimpen, Devonshire in *The Hound of the Baskervilles*. He delivered a telegram to John Barrymore at Baskerville Hall.

JAMES, JACK. An American citizen in the pay of the German spymaster Von Bork in "His Last Bow," James was arrested and sentenced to Portland Prison just before the start of World War I. Von Bork told the Irish-American Altamont: "It was James's own fault. You know that yourself. He was too self-willed for the job."

JEW'S HARP. A small musical instrument with a metal frame shaped like a lyre that is held between the teeth, with a projecting steel tongue that is struck or plucked to produce a variety of sounds and tones. In "The Empty House," Holmes noted that Parker, a sentinel posted by Colonel Sebastian Moran, was a garrotter who was also said to be a remarkable performer upon the jew's harp. The instrument is also called the jews' harp.

JEZAIL. A type of musket frequently used by the opponents of the British Empire in parts of Asia. Dr. Watson was wounded by the famous "Jezail bullet" at the Battle of Maiwand, writing in *A Study in Scarlet* that he was struck in the shoulder, shattering the bone and grazing the subclavian artery. Later, however, in *The Sign of Four*, he sat nursing his leg, declaring: "I had had a Jezail bullet through it some time before, and though it did not prevent me from walking, it ached wearily at every change of the weather." A third reference to the transient wound was made in the account of "The Noble Bachelor." "I had remained indoors all day, for the weather had taken a sudden turn to rain, with high autumnal winds, and the jezail bullet I brought back in one of my limbs as a relic of my Afghan campaigns, throbbed with dull persistency." (See also WATSON, DR. JOHN.)

JOHANNESBURG. A city in South Africa where, according to Bob Carruthers and Jack Woodley, Violet Smith's father Ralph had died in poverty in "The Solitary Cyclist." Jack Woodley was also known in the area, his name said to be "a holy terror from Kimberley to Johannesburg."

JOHN. Not surprisingly, characters named John appear in a number of Holmes's cases, such as the pompous butler in the service of Dr. Leslie Armstrong in "The Missing Three-Quarter." On the order of his employer, he ushered Holmes and Watson severely to the door. In "A Scandal in Bohemia," Irene Adler's coachman, John, drove her to the Church of St. Monica in the Edgeware Road for her wedding. He later kept watch on the injured Nonconformist clergyman who had been assisted into Adler's sitting-room. And a coachman named John was hired by Holmes during his investigation into the disappearance of Neville St. Clair in "The Man With the Twisted Lip." He picked up Holmes and Watson near the Bar of Gold opium den.

JOHNSON. A member of the Oxford rugby team in "The Missing Three-Quarter." According to Cyril Overton, Johnson was one of the two "Oxford fliers" who could romp around the Cambridge first reserve player Moorhouse, stressing the need for Holmes to find the missing three-quarter Godfrey Staunton.

JOHNSON, SHINWELL. Also Porky Shinwell, a member of Holmes's agency early in this century. "A huge, coarse, red-faced, scorbutic man, with a pair of vivid black eyes which were the only external sign of the cunning mind within," Johnson assisted Holmes in his efforts to end the planned marriage of Violet De Merville and Baron Adalbert Gruner in "The Illustrious Client." Of him, Watson wrote: "Johnson, I grieve to say, made his name first as a very dangerous villain and served two terms at Parkhurst. Finally he repented and allied himself to Holmes, acting as his agent in the huge criminal underground of London and obtaining information which proved to be of vital importance."

JOHNSON, SIDNEY. The senior clerk and draughtsman at the Woolwich arsenal, and one of two men who had a key to the safe from which were stolen the Bruce-Partington Submarine Plans in "The Bruce-Partington Plans." Mycroft Holmes described him as "a man of forty, married, with five children. He is a silent, morose man, but he has, on the whole, an excellent record in the public service. He is unpopular with his colleagues, but a hard worker."

JOHNSON, THEOPHILUS. A coal owner from Newcastle who, with his family, was staying at the Northumberland Hotel in London, at the same time as Sir Henry Baskerville in *The Hound of the Baskervilles*.

JOHNSTON. One of the four principal elders of the Mormons in *A Study in Scarlet*.

JONES, ATHELNEY. An officer from Scotland Yard who was in charge of the investigation into the murder of Bartholomew Sholto in *The Sign of Four*. Jones "was red-faced, burly, and plethoric, with a pair of very small twinkling eyes which looked keenly out from between swollen and puffy pouches." He was once a member of the audience for a lecture by Holmes "on causes and inferences and effects in the Bishopgate jewel case." According to the Holmesian W. S. Baring-Gould, in his biography *Sherlock Holmes of Baker Street*, Jones was also the notorious Jack the Ripper, his true nature revealed by Dr. Watson.

JONES, PETER. A Scotland Yard inspector who was brought into the strange affair of "The Red-Headed League" by Holmes. He represented the law in the long vigil held in the City and Suburban Bank vault waiting for the appearance of thieves Holmes was expecting. The detective said of him: "I thought it well to have Jones with us also, he is not a bad fellow, though an absolute imbecile in his profession. He has one positive virtue. He is brave as a bulldog, and tenacious as a lobster if he gets his claws upon anyone."

JOSE. The personal servant to Don Murillo in "Wisteria Lodge." It was Jose who delivered the fatal note to Aloysius Garcia.

KEMP, WILSON. The accomplice of Harold Latimer in the affair of "The Greek Interpreter." Mr. Melas reported that Kemp "was a small, mean-looking, middle-aged man with round shoulders. As he turned towards us the glint of the light showed me that he was wearing glasses . . . He spoke in a nervous, jerky fashion, and with little giggling laughs in between."

KENNINGTON ROAD. A street in Lambeth where Morse Hudson's shop was situated in "The Six Napoleons." Dr. Barnicot, who purchased two busts of Napoleon from Hudson, kept a residence and principal consulting room just a few yards away. Philip Green also followed Annie Fraser up the Kennington Road in the hopes of learning the whereabouts of the missing Lady Frances Carfax in "The Disappearance of Lady Frances Carfax."

KENSINGTON. A London borough where Watson had a small practice and his residence in "The Empty House" and "The Red-Headed League." At the time that Holmes began his investigation into the affair of the unfortunate John Hector McFarlane in "The Norwood Builder," Watson had sold his practice at the request of the detective and moved back into 221B Baker Street.

"A young doctor, named Verner, had purchased my small Kensington practice, and given with astonishingly little demur the highest price that I ventured to ask—an incident which only explained itself years later, when I found that Verner was a distant relation of Holmes, and it was my friend who had really found the money." Other Kensington residents included Horace Harker ("The Six Napoleons"), Mr. Melville ("Wisteria Lodge"), and Hugo Oberstein ("The Bruce-Partington Plans"). Harold Latimer claimed to live in Kensington ("The Greek Interpreter").

KENT. Holmes conducted several investigations in Kent in southeastern England: "The Golden Pince-Nez," "The Abbey Grange," and "The Lion's Mane." Several others took place near Kent: "The Man With the Twisted Lip" (Holmes declared Lee, home of The Cedars and Neville St Clair, to be in Kent), and *The Valley of Fear* (Birlstone was in Sussex on the border of Kent). Jonathan Small also stated in *The Sign of Four* that before the Mutiny, India was as peaceful as Surrey or Kent. Kent is also a medical practitioner who resided temporarily in a "detached house" at Tuxbury Old Park, where he cared for a patient in "The Blanched Soldier."

KESWICK. A respected paperhanger at 13 Duncan Street, Houndsditch, London in *A Study in Scarlet*. Holmes looked for Mrs. Sawyer at that address but found only the paperhanger and that no one by the name of Sawyer had ever lived there.

KHALIFA. See GREAT HIATUS.

KHAN, ABDULLAH. One of the Four in *The Sign of Four*. He was a tall, fierce-looking Sikh.

KHITMUTGAR. The name used in India for a kind of butler or manservant. The *khitmutgar* was under the authority of the *khansamah*, the house steward. Dr. Grimesby Roylott served a prison term for beating his native butler to death ("The Speckled Band"), while both Thaddeus and Bartholomew Sholto had a *khitmutgar* (*The Sign of Four*).

KIDNAPPING. Criminal abduction of various kinds took place in the Canon. Sophy and Paul Kratides were kidnapped in "The Greek Interpreter," as was Mr. Melas; he was forced to translate for the kidnappers to convince Paul Kratides to surrender to their will. Violet Smith in "The Solitary Cyclist," Miss Burnet in "Wisteria Lodge," and Lady Carfax in "The Disappearance of Lady Frances Carfax" were all abducted. Hatty Doran was thought to have been abducted in "The Noble Bachelor" and Holmes suggested to Lord Mount-James that Godfrey Staunton had been kidnapped for ransom in "The Missing Three-Quarter." One of the most complicated kidnappings with which Holmes was associated was detailed in "The Priory School," featuring the kidnapping of Lord Saltire, son of the duke of Holdernesse.

KING, MRS. The cook at Ridling Thorpe Manor, Norfolk in "The Dancing Men." She was awakened one night by a series of explosions and, with the housemaid Saunders, rushed downstairs to find Mr. Hilton Cubitt dead and his wife Elsie horribly wounded in the head.

KING EDWARD STREET. The address given by Duncan Ross in his alias as the solicitor William Morris in "The Red-Headed League." His offices were supposedly at 17 King Edward Street, north of St. Paul's. When Jabez Wilson went there to learn why the Red-Headed League had been dissolved, he found not the solicitor but a factory producing artificial kneecaps, and no one there had ever heard of Duncan Ross or William Morris.

KING'S COLLEGE HOSPITAL. A London hospital where Dr. Percy Trevelyan occupied a minor position after graduating from London University in "The Resident Patient." While there, he devoted himself to research into nervous diseases.

KING'S CROSS STATION. A London railway station where Holmes and Watson took a train to Cambridge to look into the disappearance of Godfrey Staunton in "The Missing Three-Quarter." The nearby St. Saviour's Church, situated in King's Cross, was to have been the site of the marriage of Mary Sutherland and Hosmer Angel.

KING'S PYLAND. The Dartmoor training stables owned by Colonel Ross in "Silver Blaze." The horse Silver Blaze disappeared from here.

KINGSTON-ON-THAMES. A town in Surrey on the south bank of the Thames in "The Illustrious Client." The odious Baron Adalbert Gruner lived near Kingston, at Vernon Lodge.

KIRWIN, WILLIAM. Coachman and servant to the Cunninghams at their estate of Reigate, in Surrey in "The Reigate Squires." He was murdered during an apparent burglary. His mother, Mrs. Kirwin, went half crazy when informed of her son's death.

KLEIN, ISADORA. A wealthy voluptuary and widow of Klein, the German sugar king in "The Three Gables." Originally from Pernambuco, Klein resided at Grosvenor Square, taking numerous lovers, including the late Douglas Maberley. Having treated Maberley's affections in a cavalier fashion, Klein learned that her onetime lover had written a novel that was a thinly disguised account of the affair, a work that, if published, would ruin her forthcoming marriage to the duke of Lomond. She thus bent her entire will toward acquiring the manuscript, precipitating the events recounted in "The Adventure of the Three Gables." Watson wrote of his and Holmes's encounter with her: "A minute later we were in an Arabian Nights drawing-room, vast and wonderful, in a half gloom, picked out in an occasional pink electrical light. The lady had come, I felt, to that time of life when even the proudest beauty finds the half light more welcome. She rose from a settee as we entered: tall, queenly, a perfect figure, a lovely mask-like face, with two wonderful Spanish eyes which looked murder at us both."

KLOPMAN.   A Nihilist who planned to murder Count Von und Zu Grafenstein, the uncle of the German spymaster Von Bork. Holmes prevented the death as recorded in "His Last Bow."

KNELLER, SIR GODFREY.   A portrait artist (1646–1723) who painted one of the Baskerville family portraits that hung in the gallery. The painting helped Holmes to identify the evil mind behind the affair of *The Hound of the Baskervilles*.

KNIGHTHOOD.   Sherlock Holmes was offered a knighthood in June, 1902 ("The Three Garridebs"), but refused. He also had no interest in seeing his name upon the honor list ("The Bruce-Partington Plans"), accepting instead a remarkably fine emerald tiepin from "a certain gracious lady"

(1895), for his service in recovering the Bruce-Partington Submarine Plans. The novel *Enter the Lion* (1979) by Michael Hodel and Sean M. Wright proposed that both Holmes and Mycroft were offered knighthoods very early in their careers, but declined stating the difficulties of being "sirs" at such young ages.

KRATIDES, PAUL.   Brother of **Sophy Kratides**, who was abducted and brutally tortured by Harold Latimer and Wilson Kemp in "The Greek Interpreter." From a wealthy Greek family in Athens, Paul learned that his sister had fallen under the influence of Harold Latimer, a murderous fortune hunter, in England and so travelled from Greece to rescue her. He placed himself in the power of Latimer and Kemp, however, and was soon imprisoned, starved, and beaten by them in the hopes that he would sign over the Kratides property. By the time that Mr. Melas, the Greek interpreter, met him, Kratides was in terrible condition. "He was deadly pale and terribly emaciated, with the protruding, brilliant eyes of a man whose

Mr. Melas meets the battered Paul Kratides in "The Greek Interpreter"; by Sidney Paget.

spirit was greater than his strength. But what shocked me more than any signs of physical weakness was that his face was grotesquely criss-crossed with sticking-plaster, and that one large pad of it was fastened over his mouth." Kratides utterly refused to give in to his captors, paying the ultimate price. After it became clear that Paul would never sign, and with the law closing in, Latimer and Kemp fled, taking Sophy with them. Her fate remained unknown, although a press clipping reached Holmes and Watson from Budapest that two Englishmen had been found stabbed to death.

It was assumed by the Hungarian police that the two had quarrelled and killed each other. It was also possible that Sophy had finally exacted her revenge.

KU KLUX KLAN.   Holmes became enmeshed in Klan activity as a result of his investigation into the apparently cursed family of the Openshaws in "The Five Orange Pips." He consulted the *American Encyclopedia* for information about the Klan, a racist secret society founded in 1866.

LABURNUM VALE.   Josiah Brown, whose plaster cast of Napoleon was stolen and destroyed, resided at Laburnum Vale, a street in Chiswick, in Laburnum Lodge or Villa in "The Six Napoleons."

LAFTER HALL.   The residence of Old Frankland, on the moor, in Devonshire in *The Hound of the Baskervilles*. He was in the habit of observing the moor from Lafter Hall with his telescope. Watson visited him and learned that Frankland had seen a boy running with a bundle upon the moor day after day. Using Frankland's telescope Watson saw the boy, followed his route, and eventually encountered the Man on the Tor.

LAGONI, OTTO.   Danish actor who followed the successful Viggo LARSEN in the role of Holmes on screen in the Nordisk series of silent films (1908–1911). Lagoni's first known contact with the detective came in 1902 when he played Holmes on the stage in the Danish version of the William Gillette play *Sherlock Holmes*. For Nordisk, he starred as Holmes in *La Femme* (1910); and

Sherlock Holmes I Bondefangerklor (*Sherlock Holmes in the Clutches of the Confidence Men*, 1910). He may have been Holmes in *Den Forklaedte Guvernante* (*The Bogus Governess*, 1911), and at least took part in *Mordet I Bakerstreet* (*Murder in Baker Street*, 1911), with Holger Rasmussen as Holmes. As is the case with the Nordisk films in general, there is question concerning both the exact number of films made and who appeared in what.

LAKE SALOON.   A saloon in Chicago where the criminal Jonas Pinto was supposedly shot by John McMurdo in *The Valley of Fear*.

LAL CHOWDAR.   The faithful manservant of Major Sholto in *The Sign of Four*. Lal admitted Captain Morstan into Pondicherry Lodge to meet Sholto about the disposition of the Agra Treasure. When Morstan died a few minutes later, Lal assumed that Sholto had killed him, assuring his master that his lips were sealed. He assisted Sholto in disposing of Morstan's body. By the time of Sholto's death, Lal Chowdar was dead.

LAL RAO. The Indian butler (*khitmutgar*) of Bartholomew Sholto, at Pondicherry Lodge, Upper Norwood in *The Sign of Four*. Lal was an ally of Jonathan Small.

LAMA. A Buddhist monk in Mongolia or especially Tibet. During the Great Hiatus (1891–1894), Holmes supposedly visited the "head Lama," or Llama as spelled by Watson, (Dalai Lama) in Tibet. This is historically improbable as the Dalai Lama at the time, the thirteenth, was very young and was still undergoing instruction. Similarly, Holmes would have been unable to meet the Panchen Lama, the second head of the Tibetan Buddhist priesthood, the eighth, who was also young and, too, was undergoing his instructional period at Shigatse, Tibet. Precisely who Holmes met is thus unclear; a possible solution was offered by Richard Wincor in his peculiar novel, *Sherlock Holmes in Tibet* (1968), in which Holmes, as Ole Sigerson, attends a lecture by Lama Nordup, Tibet's leading metaphysician. The lecture is followed by a private interview that has a surprising climax.

LAMBERLEY. The town in Sussex, where Robert Ferguson and family resided at Cheeseman's in "The Sussex Vampire," was situated south of Horsham. At the start of his investigation into suspected vampirism in Sussex, Holmes suggested, "I rather fancy we shall know a good deal more about Cheeseman's Lamberley, before we are through." As usual, the detective was correct.

LANCASTER GATE. An exclusive residential area, Lancaster Gate, a street just north of Hyde Park, was the site of a furnished house taken by Aloysius Doran, father of Hatty Doran in "The Noble Bachelor." Following the marriage of Hatty and Lord St. Simon, the wedding party returned there.

LANCASTER, JAMES. A harpooner who came to 221B to be interviewed by Captain Basil for an arctic expedition in "Black Peter." He was informed that the berth was full. As recompense for his troubles, Lancaster was given half a sovereign.

LANCET. A British medical journal founded in 1823. Dr. Mortimer authored an article in the *Lancet*, "Some Freaks of Atavism" in *The Hound of the Baskervilles*. In "The Blanched Soldier," Holmes also asked James Dodd what paper Godfrey Ems-

worth's keeper was reading, in the hopes that Dodd would say the *Lancet*, stating at the end of the case that it would have been helpful to his case had Dodd said the *Lancet* or the *British Medical Journal*.

LANGELLA, FRANK. The American Tony Award–winning actor (b. 1947), best known for his brilliant interpretation of Dracula on the stage and in the 1979 film version, has also played Holmes in several productions, including a 1977 performance at the Williamstown Theatre Festival of the William Gillette play, *Sherlock Holmes*. In 1981, his revival of the play was aired on the American cable channel Home Box Office. Langella was supported by Richard Woods (Watson), Laurie Kennedy (Alice Faulkner), and George Morfogen (Moriarty).

LANGHAM HOTEL. Among the guests at this very exclusive West End hotel were the Honorable Philip Green ("The Disappearance of Lady Frances Carfax"), the king of Bohemia (registered under the name of Count Von Kramme in "A Scandal in Bohemia"), and Captain Morstan (*The*

Frank Langella, Tony Award-winning actor, seen as Holmes, from his appearance in the play *Sherlock Holmes*. (Courtesy Frank Langella.)

Sign of Four). Morstan stayed at the Langham in 1878 when he was planning to visit his daughter Mary. He listed the hotel as his address, and Mary went there to meet him. She was informed that he had gone out the night before and not returned. After Mary had waited all day, the manager of the Langham suggested she contact the police.

LANGMERE.   A hamlet in Norfolk, just south of Donnithorpe, site of Holmes's first known investigation, "The 'Gloria Scott'."

LANGUR.   A species of long-tailed Asian monkey, also known as the "leaf monkey." A black-faced langur was used in the rejuvenescent serum prepared by Lowenstein for Professor Presbury in "The Creeping Man."

LANNER, INSPECTOR.   The Scotland Yard inspector was in charge of the investigation into what he initially believed to be the suicide of Blessington in "The Resident Patient." His assumptions were changed by Holmes, who proved that Blessington had actually been murdered. Lanner was described as "a smart-looking police inspector who was taking notes [about the case] in a pocketbook."

LARBEY.   A man who was beaten nearly to death by the Scowrers, on the orders of Boss McGinty in *The Valley of Fear*. His wife, Mrs. Larbey, was shot while caring for him.

LA ROTHIERE, LOUIS.   An international agent residing at Campden Mansions, Notting Hill. Mycroft Holmes considered him one of the three agents, with Hugo Oberstein and Eduardo Lucas, to be capable of masterminding the theft of the Bruce-Partington Plans. He was also a likely suspect in the disappearance of the sensitive document from the dispatch box of Trelawney Hope in "The Second Stain."

LARSEN, VIGGO.   Danish actor who starred in and directed the Nordisk series of silent Holmes films. An ex-sergeant, he was an accomplished performer and director, completing a vast number of projects for the Danish film company. In his Holmes films, Larsen commonly paired the detective with some kind of rollicking archcriminal such as Raffles or Arsene Lupin. This was the case at Nordisk and later when Larsen associated himself with German filmmakers. His films for Nordisk

were: *Sherlock Holmes I Livsfare* (Sherlock Holmes Risks His Life, 1908), also called *Sherlock Holmes I*; *Sherlock Holmes II* (1908); *Sangerindens Diamanter* (*The Singer's Diamonds*, 1909); *Droske No. 519* (*Cab No. 519*, 1909); *Den Graa Dame* (*The Grey Lady*, 1909). For Vitascope he starred in and directed the series of films under the title of *Arsene Lupin contra Sherlock Holmes* (1910–1911). He also made *Sherlock Holmes contra Professor Moriarty* (1911) for Vitascope, and *Rotterdamamsterdam* (1918) for Mester-Film. See also OTTO LAGONI.

LASCAR.   Generally, a name used for an East Indian sailor, specifically the proprietor of the Bar of Gold opium den in "The Man With the Twisted Lip." Described by Holmes as "rascally," the lascar had sworn to have vengeance upon the detective, as Holmes used it before for his own purposes. The lascar was suspected of complicity in the disappearance and possible death of Neville St. Clair.

LASSUS, ORLANDUS.   The sixteenth century composer, also known as Roland de Lassus, Orlando Lasso, and originally Roland Delattre, who composed mostly sacred music, including masses, madrigals, and hundreds of motets. He was the object of study by Holmes in November 1895 as part of his hobby researching the music of the Middle Ages. In the third week of November, because of the dense yellow fog, Holmes remained indoors, spending Monday cross-indexing his book of references, and the second and third days on musical research. By Thursday, of course, the detective was pacing restlessly, his ennui finally broken by the affair of "The Bruce-Partington Plans." With the solution of the case, Holmes returned to his studies on Lassus, producing a "monograph upon the Polyphonic Motets of Lassus, which has since been published for private circulation, and is said by experts to be the last word upon the subject."

LAST SHERLOCK HOLMES STORY, THE.
A 1978 novel by Michael Dibdin that examines the always interesting case of JACK THE RIPPER. This work, however, is an intense psychological thriller. Crucial to the story is Holmes's belief that the crimes are being committed by none other than Professor James Moriarty. The intrepid Lestrade brings Holmes a letter from the Ripper, a missive that attracts the detective's attention and draws him into the case. The bodies continue to mount,

with murders of the most horrible kind, so awful that even the seasoned medical man Watson is sickened. Holmes jumps into the case and begins tracking the elusive professor. Over time, a pattern to the killings is established as the apparent danger to Holmes increases. The detective sets a trap that prevents the murder one night, only to have two occur on a different night. Finally, with the net seemingly ready to close around Moriarty, Holmes goes to Whitechapel for the climax. Watson follows him, making a discovery of the most shocking kind, setting off a chain of events that culminates at the Reichenbach Falls. Very controversial, shocking to faithful Sherlockians, and highly revisionist.

LATIMER, HAROLD.   The associate of Wilson Kemp who used intimidation, torture, and murder in his efforts to acquire the property of the wealthy Kratides family in "The Greek Interpreter." A "fashionably dressed," "powerful, broad-shouldered young fellow," he met Sophy Kratides while she was visiting England and somehow gained ascendancy over her. When her brother, Paul, arrived to terminate their relationship, Latimer and Kemp imprisoned him, applying torture and starvation in an effort to secure Paul's signature. When they needed a translator, Latimer sought Mr. Melas, bringing him under threat to translate the words of Paul. When it became clear that Kratides would never relent, Latimer, Kemp, and Sophy fled. Latimer, along with Kemp, was found stabbed to death in Budapest some time after.

LATIMER'S.   A boot maker's in Oxford Street from whom Watson purchased his boots in "The Disappearance of Lady Frances Carfax." The shoes, or more properly the laces, were the object of discussion between Holmes and Watson, focusing on the way the laces were tied.

LAURISTON GARDENS.   A group of houses just off the Brixton Road where, at No.3 Lauriston Gardens, was found the body of Enoch J. Drebber in *A Study in Scarlet*. Watson wrote that "Number 3, Lauriston Gardens wore an ill-omened and minatory look. It was one of four which stood back some little way from the street, two being occupied and two empty. The latter looked out with three tiers of vacant melancholy windows, which were blank and dreary, save that here and there a 'To Let' card had developed like a cataract upon the bleared

panes. A small garden sprinkled over with a scattered eruption of sickly plants separated each of these houses from the street, and was traversed by a narrow pathway, yellowish in colour, and consisting of a mixture of clay and of gravel." It was here that Watson first saw Holmes in action as a detective.

LAUSANNE.   Lady Carfax stayed here at the Hotel National in this picturesque town in Switzerland, near Lake Geneva, and was last heard from here in "The Disappearance of Lady Frances Carfax." Watson was sent to Lausanne by Holmes to look into her disappearance.

LEADENHALL STREET.   A street in London where Mary Sutherland addressed her letters to Hosmer Angel, at the post office in "A Case of Identity." Hosmer Angel supposedly worked as a cashier in the Leadenhall Street office, claiming to reside on the premises and thus requiring that Mary reach him through the post office.

LE BRUN.   A French agent who looked into the affairs of Baron Gruner ("The Illustrious Client"). The baron warned Holmes that his fate might be the same as Le Brun—he was attacked by Apaches in the Montmarte district of Paris and was crippled for life.

LECOQ, MONSIEUR.   The detective created by Emile Gaboriau who appeared in a series of novels from 1866 to 1869. Watson and Holmes discussed Lecoq early in their association; Watson asked Holmes: "Have you read Gaboriau's works? Does Lecoq come up to your idea of a detective?" Holmes, sniffing sardonically, replied: "Lecoq was a miserable bungler ... he had only one thing to recommend him, and that was his energy. It might be made a textbook for detectives to teach them what to avoid."

LEE, CHRISTOPHER.   The famous English actor (b. 1922), the son of an Italian countess and a colonel in the King's Royal Rifle Corps, who has had a long career in mainstream horror films. He is particularly known through his work with Hammer Films, the English production company. He appeared as the Mummy, Frankenstein's Monster, and Count Dracula. A natural to play Sherlock Holmes, Lee appeared in a Holmes film for the first time with his friend and frequent screen compan-

Christopher Lee (Holmes) and Watson veteran Thorley Walters (in another outing as the good doctor) at work in *Sherlock Holmes und das Hlasband des Todes* (*Sherlock Holmes and the Necklace of Death,* 1962). Note Lee's artificial nose worn for the film.

ion, Peter Cushing, in Hammer's *The Hound of the Baskervilles* (1959); Lee played Sir Henry Baskerville. In 1962, he assumed the deerstalker and pipe himself, starring in the German film *Sherlock Holmes und das Halsband des Todes* (*Sherlock Holmes and the Necklace of Death*) with Thorley Walters (Watson). In *The Private Life of Sherlock Holmes* (1970), he portrayed Mycroft Holmes, making him the only known actor to portray both siblings on the screen. Currently, he is starring in a series of European television productions with Patrick Macnee (Watson), featuring Holmes in his later years. Thus far he has made "Sherlock Holmes, Incident at Victoria Falls" (1991) and "Sherlock Holmes and the Leading Lady" (1992).

LEFEVRE. A criminal who was able to escape justice at Montpelier because there was, at the time, no reliable test for bloodstains. Holmes, however, discovered such a test in *A Study in Scarlet.*

LEGION OF HONOR, ORDER OF THE. Also Order of the Legion of Honour, a high medal of honor established by Napoleon in 1802 that was given to Holmes by the French government for tracking down and arresting Huret, the Boulevard Assassin ("The Golden Pince-Nez"). This was only

one of many awards given to the detective by various governments and sovereigns.

LEONARDO. A strongman in the Ronder Circus who was the lover of Eugenia Ronder in "The Veiled Lodger." Leonardo directed the plan to kill Eugenia's husband, but lost his nerve at the last second and deserted her when she was attacked by the lion Sahara King. His photograph showed "clearly a professional acrobat, a man of magnificent physique, taken with his huge arms folded across his swollen chest and a smile breaking from under his heavy moustache—the self-satisfied smile of the man of many conquests." Years after the incident, in 1896, Leonardo drowned when bathing near Margate.

LEPROSY. The disease figured in Holmes's theorizing about the possible fate of John Hebron—he thought it possible that Effie Munro's first husband, John, was not dead but had become a leper ("The Yellow Face"). Leprosy was also incorrectly thought to be at work in the case of Godfrey Emsworth ("The Blanched Soldier"). Holmes commented to Watson that Violet De Merville received him and Kitty Winter like "two rather leperous mendicants" ("The Illustrious Client").

LESTRADE, INSPECTOR G. An inspector of Scotland Yard and the most well known policeman of the Canon, Lestrade has also appeared repeatedly as a character in several non-Canonical works, including films, pastiches, and parodies.

Inspector Lestrade appeared frequently in the published cases of Holmes and was definitely involved in a number of unpublished and otherwise unknown investigations. He first appeared in *A Study in Scarlet* looking into the murder of Enoch Drebber at Lauriston Garden, and competing with Inspector Gregson to solve the mysterious killing. Watson wrote that Lestrade was "lean and ferret-like" and Holmes declared that he and Gregson were "the pick of a bad lot. They are quick and energetic, but conventional—shockingly so. They have their knives into one another, too. They are as jealous as a pair of professional beauties." He would later admit that Lestrade possessed "bull dog tenacity," a characteristic that had propelled him to the top of Scotland Yard ("The Cardboard Box"), even though he lacked imagination ("The Norwood Builder") and was customarily out of his depth (*The Sign of Four*).

Lestrade was in charge of numerous cases in which Holmes became involved or was summoned directly by the inspector. Despite his jibes and sneeringly patronizing attitude toward the consulting detective, Lestrade swallowed his pride to engage Holmes's services in an early forgery case (*A Study in Scarlet*), the so-called Cardboard Box affair, the murder of Enoch Drebber (*A Study in Scarlet*), and the strange matter of "The Six Napoleons." He was also heading up the following cases in which Holmes rendered service, invariably solving the case, proving the representative of Scotland Yard wrong, and yet taking no credit for the solution: "The Norwood Builder," "The Bruce-Partington Plans," and "The Noble Bachelor." Lestrade was in command of the investigations into the deaths of Charles Milverton ("Charles Augustus Milverton") and Eduardo Lucas ("The Second Stain"). He was also part of the trap laid by Holmes to capture the murderer of Ronald Adair in "The Empty House" and worked with Holmes on "the bogus laundry affair" ("The Cardboard Box"). The detective also noted that during the Great Hiatus, Lestrade failed to solve three murders in one year, but was successful in the Molesey Mystery, telling the inspector, "you handled it fairly well." Holmes called in Lestrade at the climax of *The Hound of the Baskervilles* and consulted him in the search for Frances Carfax in "The Disappearance of Lady Frances Carfax." Finally, he was engaged by the friends of James McCarthy to clear him of the charge of murdering his father in "The Boscombe Valley Mystery," and he turned the matter over to Holmes. It is unclear how old Lestrade was during the time of Holmes's career, but it was reported that in the 1880s he had put in twenty years with the CID, making him very seasoned by the time that Holmes retired in 1903.

More than any other policeman in the Canon, Lestrade appeared in a wide variety of non-Canonical writings and productions, serving as the often slow, bumbling, but confident foil to the genius of the Great Detective. This has been especially true of Holmes films, reaching absurd heights with the characterization of Lestrade in the Basil Rathbone-Nigel Bruce films from Universal Pictures (1939–1946), in which the inspector was portrayed as a complete idiot by Dennis Hoey. Recent films have attempted to treat Lestrade more fairly, most notably *Murder By Decree* (1979, with Frank Finlay as the policeman) and the Granada Television series starring Jeremy Brett as Holmes (with Colin Jeavons as Lestrade.)

LESURIER, MADAME. A milliner on Bond Street in "Silver Blaze." John Straker had on his body, in a pocket, a milliner's account for thirty-seven pounds fifteen made out by Madame Lesurier, of Bond Street, to William Darbyshire. Holmes subsequently visited Madame Lesurier; the information learned there was used to help solve the case.

LETURIER. The victim of murder in Montpellier, by poison. In discussing his solution of the case recounted in *A Study in Scarlet*, Holmes told Watson: "Having sniffed the dead man's lips, I detected a slightly sour smell, and I came to the conclusion that he had had poison forced upon him from the hatred and fear expressed upon his face. By the method of exclusion, I had arrived at the result, for no other hypothesis would meet the facts. Do not imagine that it was a very unheard-of idea. The forcible administration of poison is by no means a new thing in criminal annals. The cases of Dolsky in Odessa, and of Leturier in Montpellier, will occur at once to any toxicologist."

LEVERSTOKE, LORD. The noble father of one of the students at the "Priory School" run by Thorneycroft Huxtable.

LEVERTON. A detective of the Pinkerton Agency who pursued the killer Giuseppe Gorgiano from New York to London in "The Red Circle." As part of his work in London, he assumed the disguise of a cab driver. Inspector Gregson, who assisted him in the hunt for Gorgiano, introduced Leverton to Holmes, who surprised and flattered the American by saying: "The hero of the Long Island Cave mystery? Sir, I am pleased to meet you." He was "a quiet, businesslike young man, with a clean-shaven, hatchet-face."

LEWISHAM. A southeastern borough of London where Josiah Amberley lived, at the Haven in "The Retired Colourman." The Randalls, described by Inspector Stanley Hopkins as "that Lewisham gang of burglars" in "The Abbey Grange," were suspected of responsibility in the death of Sir Eustace Brackenstall at the Abbey Grange.

Inspector Lestrade on Film and Television

ACTOR	PROGRAM OR FILM	ACTOR	PROGRAM OR FILM
Arthur Bell	*The Adventure of Sherlock Holmes* (series of films—1921)	Bill Owen	"Sherlock Holmes" (TV—1951)
Tom Beaumont	*The Last Adventures of Sherlock Holmes* (series of films—1923)	Archie Duncan	"Sherlock Holmes" (TV—1954)
		Peter Madden	"Sherlock Holmes" (TV—1965)
Alan Mowbray	*A Study in Scarlet* (1933)	William Lucas	"Sherlock Holmes" (TV—1968, "A Study in Scarlet")
Philip Hewland	*The Sleeping Cardinal* (1931)		
	The Missing Rembrandt (1932)	Alan Caillou	"The Hound of the Baskervilles" (TV—1972)
Charles Mortimer	*The Triumph of Sherlock Holmes* (1935)	Hubert Rees	"The Hound of the Baskervilles" (TV—1982)
John Turnbull	*Silver Blaze* (1937)		
Dennis Hoey	*Sherlock Holmes and the Secret Weapon* (1942)	Ronald Lacey	"The Hound of the Baskervilles" (TV—1983)
	Sherlock Holmes Faces Death (1943)	Colin Jeavons	"The Adventures of Sherlock Holmes" (on-going role in series: "The Return of Sherlock Holmes" and "The Casebook of Sherlock Holmes")
	Spider Woman (1944)		
	The Pearl of Death (1944)		
	The House of Fear (1945)		
	Terror By Night (1946)		
Frank Finlay	*A Study in Terror* (1965)	Roger Ashton-Griffiths	*Young Sherlock Holmes* (1985)
	Murder By Death (1979)		
George Benson	*The Private Life of Sherlock Holmes* (1970)	Jeffrey Jones	*Without a Clue* (1990)

LEXINGTON, MRS. The housekeeper of Jonas Oldacre in "The Norwood Builder." She testified to the police after the apparent murder of her employer that she admitted Jonas's killer, John Hector McFarlane, into Oldacre's home and retired for the evening, claiming that she had heard nothing of what may have transpired. She later found what seemed to be absolutely damning evidence against McFarlane. Holmes described her as "a little, dark, silent person, with suspicious and sidelong eyes. She could tell us something if she would—I am convinced of it."

LINDER.   See MAX LINDER & CO.

LION.   The animal was hunted by Dr. Leon Sterndale ("The Devil's Foot") and Count Negretto Sylvius in "The Mazarin Stone." Count Sylvius had shot the animal in Algeria. The lion Sahara King attacked and mutilated Eugenia Ronder in "The Veiled Lodger."

LION'S MANE.   See CYANEA CAPILLATA.

"LION'S MANE, THE ADVENTURE OF THE" (LION).   Published: *Strand*, December 1926, *Liberty* magazine, November 1926; collected in *The Case Book of Sherlock Holmes* (1927). Case

Holmes in repose and retirement in "The Lion's Mane"; by Frederic Dorr Steele.

LIST OF 7, THE. This 1993 novel by Mark Frost (co-creator of the cult television show "Twin Peaks") is not a direct pastiche of Holmes stories but instead offers up a lurid tale involving Arthur Conan Doyle. Dark, grim, at times even grotesque, the novel is nevertheless a compelling and exceedingly well researched story of sorcery and black magic. A young doctor, Conan Doyle receives an urgent plea for help on Christmas Day, 1884, from a mysterious woman. Her request takes him to a seance where his skills in exposing charlatan spiritualists allow him to unmask a group of frauds; but his foray turns out to be an encounter with legitimate sorcerers, the Brotherhood, who are involved in some unholy cabal. Much as Nicholas Meyer sprinkles his Sherlockian novels with historical characters, so too does Frost introduce some intriguing real life figures such as Madame Helena Blavatsky, a founder of the Theosophical Society. Doyle is aided by a mysterious and enigmatic detective named Jack Sparks who possesses many similarities to Doyle's later literary creation, Sherlock Holmes. As the story progresses, in fact, it assumes increasingly the feel of a Holmesian pastiche, with Doyle fulfilling the Watson role to the eccentric and secretly tormented Holmes in Sparks. An impressive work on a seldom examined subject.

LITTLE GEORGE STREET. A street near Euston Station. Halliday's Private Hotel was located on Little George Street. Here was found Joseph Stangerson, stabbed to death in his room in *A Study in Scarlet*.

LITERATURE. In his early appraisal of Holmes's limits, Watson wrote that Holmes's knowledge of literature was "nil," adding, however, that the detective's knowledge of "sensational literature" was "immense. He appears to know every detail of every horror perpetrated in the century" (*A Study in Scarlet*). Watson recalled some years later this assessment with much humor ("The Five Orange Pips").

LITTLE PURLINGTON. A small village in Essex, not far from Trinton in "The Retired Colourman." Described by Watson as "the most primitive village in England," Little Purlington was the home of J. C. Elman, vicar of Mossmoor-cum-Little Purlington, the supposed sender of a telegram to Josiah Amberley concerning Amberley's missing

date: Summer, 1907. Major players: Holmes, Fitzroy McPherson, Ian Murdoch, Harold Stackhurst, Maud Bellamy. One of the few cases written by the Great Detective himself, penned after his 1903 retirement to the Sussex Downs. The account, dated by Holmes to July, 1907, is particularly notable because of the major glimpses it provides into the Master's retirement life. Holmes solves the bizarre and horrible deaths of Fitzroy McPherson and his dog, and the vicious attack upon the leading suspect, Ian Murdoch. The detective writes: "At this period of my life the good Watson had passed almost beyond my ken. An occasional week-end visit was the most that I ever saw of him. Thus I must act as my own chronicler. Ah! had he but been with me, how much he might have made of so wonderful a happening and of my eventual triumph against every difficulty!" He solves the case not through any extensive deductions but thanks to his phenomenal memory, from recollections of a book he had once read.

wife. The message sent Amberley and Watson to Little Purlington, a wasted journey as Elman denied ever sending the telegram.

LITTLE RYDER STREET.   A street in London where Nathan Garrideb lived in "The Three Garridebs." "One of the smaller offshoots from the Edgeware Road, within a stone-cast of old Tyburn Tree of Evil Memory," the house in which Garrideb resided "was a large, old fashioned, Early Georgian edifice, with a flat brick face broken only by two deep bay windows on the ground floor."

LIVERPOOL.   The large seaport from where the much pursued Enoch J. Drebber and Joseph Stangerson planned to sail to New York in *A Study in Scarlet*. Drebber had in his pockets two letters from the Guion Steamship Company, referring to their intended sailing. Count Negretto Sylvius

hoped to divert Holmes to Liverpool ("The Mazarin Stone"), and the Birlstone murder was reported from Liverpool and nineteen other places (*The Valley of Fear*). A clue found in the Priory School sent Holmes to Liverpool, an investigation that led to nought ("The Priory School").

LIVERPOOL, DUBLIN, AND LONDON STEAM PACKET CO.   A sailing company for whom James Browner worked as a steward in "The Cardboard Box," working aboard one of their vessels, the SS *May Day*.

LLOYD'S.   The well-known association of underwriters, founded in London and initially specializing in marine insurance. Holmes consulted the *Lloyd's Register of British Law and Foreign Shipping*, published annually, and spent one whole day poring over Lloyd's registers and files of old paper,

London at the time of Sherlock Holmes and Jack the Ripper in the film *Murder by Decree* (1979), starring Christopher Plummer and James Mason.

in an effort to locate the vessel *Lone Star* in "The Five Orange Pips."

LOMAX.   Sublibrarian at the London Library, at St. James Square and a friend of Watson's in "The Illustrious Client." He assisted the doctor in finding a "goodly volume" on Chinese pottery so that Watson could study the subject, at Holmes's insistence, in preparation for an encounter with the dangerous Baron Gruner.

LOMOND, DUKE OF.   The betrothed of the voluptuary Isadora Klein in "The Three Gables." Holmes said of Klein, "I hear that she is about to marry the young Duke of Lomond, who might almost be her son. His Grace's ma might overlook the age, but a big scandal would be a different matter . . ." She was thus desperately trying to acquire the novel written by her former lover, a work that revealed her true nature and her cruel behavior.

LONDON.   Sherlock Holmes lived and practiced in London from around 1877 or 1878 until his retirement in 1903. It is unclear how well Holmes knew the sprawling metropolis of London before settling at Montague Street in 1878, or, indeed, how many times he had even visited, the assumption being that he was the son of country squires. Nevertheless, once established in the city, he came to know it in ways unmatched by others. His exacting knowledge of London included its geography, history, people, boroughs, culture, and precise order of shops in many districts. Thus, in "The Red-Headed League," he tells Watson "I should like to remember the order of the houses here. It is a hobby of mine to have an exact knowledge of London." The detective was even familiar with the wide variety of soils found throughout the area, a skill in observation that allowed him to deduce many things about a client or suspect, including their possible place of origin or their route of travel, points of interest that might prove extremely useful in solving a case or detecting a falsehood. It is believed that crucial to Holmes's successful use of disguises and hence his ability to learn information from all classes of English life was his clever application of at least five safe houses throughout the city ("Black Peter"). He could leave Baker Street in one disguise, wander about for a time, retire to the safe house and come out as someone entirely different. Thus, in a single afternoon, he might go

to the East End and talk, in person, with the worst elements of society and still meet Watson for "something nutritious" at Simpson's Dining Room in the Strand. No doubt such London safe houses would have been useful while evading the assassins sent out by Professor Moriarty to kill him in "The Final Problem." (For a listing of the excellent studies on Holmes's London, please see the Bibliography in the Appendices.)

LONDON BRIDGE.   The oldest of the bridges over the River Thames in London. The opium den Bar of Gold lay in Upper Swandam Lane, said by Watson in "The Man With the Twisted Lip" to be "a vile alley lurking behind the high wharves which line the north side of the river to the east of London Bridge." The London Bridge (later moved from London to Arizona), was featured in the made-for-television film "The Return of Sherlock Holmes" (1987), with Michael Pennington and Margaret Colin. **London Bridge Station** was located in Bermondsey in London. John Hector McFarlane travelled from Norwood to London Bridge Station ("The Norwood Builder"). He was then followed by the police to Baker Street and was certain that they were only waiting for the warrant to arrest him. Holmes and Watson used London Bridge Station in at least two cases, "The Greek Interpreter" and "The Bruce-Partington Plans," and Watson returned here from Blackheath in "The Retired Colourman."

LONDON UNIVERSITY.   A university situated in Bloomsbury, most known by Sherlockians as being the institution from which Dr. Watson took his degree of doctor of medicine in 1878 (*A Study in Scarlet*). Dr. Percy Trevelyan in "The Resident Patient" was also a recipient of a degree from the university, telling Holmes and Watson, "I am a London University man, you know, and I am sure that you will not think that I am unduly singing my own praises if I say that my student career was considered by my professors to be a very promising one."

LOPEZ.   The secretary of Don Murillo, onetime ruler of San Pedro in "Wisteria Lodge." Lopez escaped with his master from San Pedro during the revolt that overthrew Murillo, the so-called Tiger of San Pedro. He subsequently travelled with Murillo throughout Europe until his narrow escape from England and from assassination with his

master in the Hotel Escurial. Lopez used the aliases Rulli and Lucas.

LOWENSTEIN, H. An obscure but notorious scientist in Prague "who was striving in some unknown way for the secret of rejuvenescence and the elixir of life" in "The Creeping Man." Although his so-called Serum of Anthropoid was tabooed by the medical profession because he refused to divulge its source, Lowenstein was able to find a client for his wonder drug in England.

LOWER BURKE STREET. A street situated between Kensington and Notting Hill. Culverton Smith lived here, at 13 Lower Burke Street in "The Dying Detective."

LOWER GILL MOOR. An expanse of moor that stretched just to the north of the Priory School and Chesterfield High Road in "The Priory School."

LOWER GROVE ROAD. The street in Reading where Mr. Sandeford, an owner of one of the six busts of Napoleon, lived in "The Six Napoleons."

LUCAS, EDUARDO. An international agent who resided at 16 Godolphin Street, in Westminster in "The Second Stain." Lucas was "well known in society circles both on account of his charming personality and because he has a well-deserved reputation of being one of the best amateur tenors in the country. Mr. Lucas is an unmarried man, thirty-four years of age, and his establishment consists of Mrs. Pringle, an elderly housekeeper, and of Mitton, his valet." He was also a spy and blackmailer who was able to apply sufficient pressure upon a victim to steal an important document from the dispatch-box of the Rt. Hon. Trelawney Hope, secretary for European affairs. It was subsequently revealed that Lucas led a double life, posing as Eduardo Lucas in London and Henri Fournaye in Paris, where he was married to a French woman, Madame Fournaye, who was mentally unstable.

LUCCA, EMILIA. Wife of Gennaro Lucca and daughter of Augusto Barelli in "The Red Circle." Emilia was born in Posilippo, near Naples. She fell in love with one of her father's employers, Gennaro, but Augusto forbade their union because Gennaro had neither money nor position. Nev-

Emilia Lucca looks out pensively in "The Red Circle": by H. M. Brock.

ertheless, Emilia fled with him to Bari where they were married and then to Brooklyn, New York. Gennaro's ties to the Red Circle, however, forced them to leave America and sail to England where the events recounted in "The Adventure of the Red Circle" transpired. (See next entry.)

LUCCA, GENNARO. An Italian originally from around Naples who was impressed into the terror organization of the "Red Circle." While in Italy, Gennaro worked as an employee of Augusto Barelli, meeting and falling in love with his daughter Emilia. When Barelli refused to accept their union because Lucca was without money or position, he and Emilia fled to Bari where they were wed and then sailed to New York where they settled in Brooklyn. In New York, however, Gennaro once more met the blood-stained killer Giuseppe

Gorgiano, the Red Circle member who had, in Italy, initiated Gennaro into the terrible organization. Forced to participate in the crimes of the Red Circle, and despite knowing that "once within its rule no escape was possible," Gennaro and Emilia resolved to flee, going to England. Gorgiano pursued them, and the events described in "The Adventure of the Red Circle" followed.

LUMBER ROOM. Holmes declared in "The Five Orange Pips": "A man should keep his little brain attic stored with all the furniture he is likely to use and the rest he can put away in the lumber-room of his library." The detective would later write about his own mind being a crowded box-room ("The Lion's Mane"), but he also once said that only fools took in "all the lumber of every sort" that they might come across (*A Study in Scarlet*). Baker Street had a lumber room itself, used to hold file copies of old daily newspapers ("The Six Napoleons"). Another lumber room was used by Elias Openshaw ("The Five Orange Pips").

LUPIN, ARSENE. The well-known literary creation of playwright and onetime court reporter Maurice Leblanc (1864–1941). Called The Prince of Thieves, Lupin first appeared in 1907. He was a brilliant and very elusive criminal who, tiring of his profession, retired and became a private detective. Because of his daring, use of aliases, and remarkable skill in avoiding the police, Lupin seemed a natural opponent of Sherlock Holmes, and Leblanc tried unsuccessfully to secure permission from Conan Doyle to use the Great Detective in one of his adventures. Refusing to give up, Leblanc wrote his book anyway, merely changing the sleuth's name to Herlock Sholmes. Herlock first appeared in a short story "Herlock Sholmes Comes Too Late," opposite Lupin, in the collection *Arsene Lupin, Gentleman Burglar* (1907). An entire book devoted to the pair, *Arsene Lupin contre Herlock Sholmes* (1908), was published the next year. The German film company Vitascope soon purchased the idea and, ignoring copyright laws (which was common at the time), produced several Lupin movies (1910–1911), using the name Holmes. Starring and directed by Viggo Larsen, the five films came under the overall name *Arsene Lupin contra Sherlock Holmes*. Interestingly, save for the last episode, *Arsene Lupins Ende* (*The End of Arsene Lupin*), the criminal consistently outfoxed Holmes and even had better disguises.

LUXEMBOURG. The capital of the Grand Duchy of Luxembourg through which Holmes and Watson passed on their way to Switzerland in "The Final Problem."

LYCEUM THEATRE. A major theatre in London in the Strand. In *The Sign of Four*, Holmes, Watson, and Mary Morstan went to the Lyceum as per the instructions of the mysterious note delivered to her. "Be at the third pillar from the left outside the Lyceum Theatre tonight at seven o'clock. If you are distrustful bring two friends. You are a wronged woman, and shall have justice. Do not bring the police. If you do, all will be in vain. Your unknown friend."

LYNCH, VICTOR. A forger who was listed under V in Holmes's "good old index" containing his "record of old cases, mixed with the accumulated information of a lifetime" ("The Sussex Vampire").

LYON PLACE. A street in Camberwell. Mary Sutherland, her mother, and stepfather resided here at 31 Lyon Place Camberwell in "A Case of Identity."

LYONS (1). Watson received a telegram from the French city on April 14, 1887, informing him that Holmes was lying ill in Lyons at the Hotel Dulong ("The Reigate Squires"). The physician hurried to his side.

LYONS (2). An artist who lived upon Dartmoor, Devonshire in *The Hound of the Baskervilles*. He married Laura, daughter of Old Franklin despite her father's opposition, and then deserted her. (See next entry.)

LYONS, LAURA. Of Coombe Tracey, the daughter of Old Frankland who had wed, despite her father's opposition, the artist Lyons in *The Hound of the Baskervilles*. Lyons subsequently deserted her, and she was forced to take up typewriting as her father refused to have anything further to do with her. She found a friend in Sir Charles Baskerville and was supposed to meet him the night he died.

M. Holmes told Watson in "The Empty House" that his collection of M's in the index of biographies was "a fine one." The detective observed: "**Moriarty** himself is enough to make any letter illustrious, and here is **Morgan** the poisoner, and **Merridew** of abominable memory, and **Matthews,** who knocked out my left canine in the waiting-room at Charing Cross . . ." Also included in the M's was "**Moran, Sebastian, Colonel.**"

MABERLEY, DOUGLAS. The son of Mary and Mortimer Maberley in "The Three Gables" who became attaché at Rome before his death of pneumonia. Holmes remembered Douglas as a "magnificent creature," but Mary watched him become a "moody, morose, brooding creature," a "gallant boy" turned into "a worn-out cynical man." Holmes deduced that a woman was behind his fall and was proven correct.

MABERLEY, MARY. The mother of Douglas Maberley and widow of Mortimer Maberley, one of Holmes's early clients in "The Three Gables." Mary consulted Holmes over the affair of the Three Gables, namely the very aggressive efforts of someone attempting to buy her house, the Three Gables, with the proviso that she leave behind all of her furniture and, with a few exceptions, her goods and private possessions. The detective undertook to look into the matter and soon connected the strange events with the untimely passing of her son. Watson wrote that she was "a most engaging elderly person, who bore every mark of refinement and culture."

MABERLEY, MORTIMER. The late husband of Mary Maberley and father of Douglas Maberley, who was one of Holmes's early clients in "The Three Gables." The detective assisted Maberley in what Holmes called "some trifling matter." His widow remembered Holmes's work well enough to consult him about her own strange experiences.

MACDONALD, ALEC. A Scotland Yard inspector, originally from Aberdeen, who had been assisted by Holmes twice prior to his working with the detective in the Birlstone affair (*The Valley of Fear*). Watson wrote: "He was a young but trusted member of the detective force who had distinguished himself in several cases which had been entrusted to him. His tall, bony figure gave promise of exceptional physical strength, while his great cranium and deep set, lustrous eyes spoke no less clearly of the keen intelligence which looked out from behind his bushy eyebrows. He was a silent, precise man, with a dour nature and hard Aberdonian accent."

MACKINNON. "A smart young police inspector" from Scotland Yard who was in charge of the investigation into the disappearance of Josiah Amberley's wife, her lover, and Amberley's fortune ("The Retired Colourman"). He was grateful at the case's resolution that Holmes was not going to take credit, declaring, "That is very handsome of you, Mr. Holmes. Praise or blame can matter little to you, but it is very different to us when the newspapers begin to ask questions." The *North Surrey Observer* would report under the "flaming headlines" THE HAVEN HORROR and BRILLIANT POLICE INVESTIGATION of MacKinnon's success.

MACKLETON. A town in northern England in Hallamshire near Dr. Thorneycroft Huxtable's Priory School in "The Priory School." Huxtable took the train to London from Mackleton Station.

MacNamara.   A widow who owned a boardinghouse in Vermissa Valley in *The Valley of Fear*. She gave lodgings to Mike Scanlan and Jack McMurdo after McMurdo was kicked out of Jacob Shafter's boardinghouse for his dealings with the Scowrers.

Macnee, Patrick.   English actor and onetime schoolmate of Christopher Lee who is now quite active in the role of Dr. Watson. The veteran of "The Avengers" (with Honor Blackman, Diana Rigg, and Linda Thorson), Macnee first donned the mantle and took up the pen of Dr. Watson in the 1976 television movie "Sherlock Holmes in New York," with Roger Moore as Holmes, John Huston as Moriarty, and Charlotte Rampling as Irene Adler. His performance has been criticized by Sherlockians as leaning too far toward Nigel Bruce's own style of buffoonery, but he took to the part with considerable enthusiasm. Recently, Macnee returned to the part, this time with Christopher Lee, in the European television production of "Sherlock Holmes and the Incident at Victoria Falls" (1991) and "Sherlock Holmes and the Leading Lady" (1992). As with Lee, Macnee's age may be hindering the believability of his character. Macnee also did a delightful turn on the "Magnum p.i." television series as a lunatic Englishman convinced that he is Holmes. John Hillerman, a regular on the show, naturally was his Watson.

Macphail.   The coachman of Professor Presbury in "The Creeping Man."

MacPherson.   A constable who was on duty at 16 Godolphin Street, in Westminster, the murder site of the international agent Eduardo Lucas in "The Second Stain." While standing guard, he met a young woman who wanted to see where the crime had taken place. "She was a very respectable, well-spoken young woman, sir, and I saw no problem in letting her have a peep. When she saw that mark on the carpet, down she dropped on the floor, and lay as if she were dead. I ran to the back and got some water, but I could not bring her to. Then I went round the corner to the Ivy Plant for some brandy, and by the time I had brought it back the young woman had recovered and was off—ashamed of herself, I dare say, and dared not face me." Having explained the disturbed crime scene, Holmes amazed the "very hot and penitent" policeman by showing him a picture of the beautiful visitor. Lestrade warned him, "it's lucky for you, my

man, that nothing is missing, or you would find yourself in Queer Street."

Madrid.   The capital of Spain where Don Murillo, "the Tiger of San Pedro," was finally murdered with his secretary at the Hotel Escurial in "The Wisteria Lodge." One of the letters in the dispatch box of Trelawney Hope came from Madrid in "The Second Stain."

Mafia.   The dangerous secret criminal organization said by Inspector Lestrade to enforce "its decrees by murder" in "The Six Napoleons." The Inspector believed the Mafia to be at work in the murder of Pietro Venucci, who was connected to the society. (See also the RED CIRCLE.)

Magnifying Lens.   Or simply lens, is now closely identified with Holmes, seen regularly in the public imagination with his pipe, deerstalker, and cape. The Canon is replete with instances of the detective employing his magnifying lens according to Mycroft Holmes, "to run here and run there, to cross-question railway guards, and lie on my face with a lens to my eye—it is not my metier" ("The Bruce-Partington Plans"). The importance of the instrument to Holmes was also noted by Watson. "Grit in a sensitive instrument, or a crack in one of his own high-power lenses, would not be more disturbing than a strong emotion in a nature such as his" ("A Scandal in Bohemia"). The magnifying lens was used, among many other cases, to perform the brilliant analysis of Henry Baker's hat ("The Blue Carbuncle"), to examine the room where Enoch Drebber's body was discovered (*A Study in Scarlet*), to study Dr. Mortimer's walking stick (*The Hound of the Baskervilles*), to look over the watch that had been belonged to Dr. Watson's brother (*The Sign of Four*), and to study the area around Boscombe Pool where Charles McCarthy was found murdered ("The Boscombe Valley Mystery"). In film, the lens has become a fixed part of any would-be Holmes's kit, so much so that it has been very successfully caricatured in such productions as *The Great Mouse Detective* (1986), *The Adventure of Sherlock Holmes' Smarter Brother* (1974), and especially *Without a Clue* (1990). Probably the best practitioner of using the lens productively and interestingly in film was Basil Rathbone.

Mahomet Singh.   One of the Four in *The Sign of Four*.

Holmes (Basil Rathbone) using his beloved magnifying lens in *The Hound of the Baskervilles* (1939).

MAIWAND, BATTLE OF.   A bloody engagement fought in Afghanistan on July 27, 1880 between the Afghans and a British force sent from Candahar. The battle was a disaster for the British, who were outflanked and forced to retreat with very heavy losses, particularly among the Berkshires (the Princess Charlotte of Wales's Royal Berkshire Regiment) to which the young Dr. Watson had recently been attached. Watson was wounded at Maiwand by the now famous Jezail bullet, either in the leg or shoulder, and would have been captured by the Afghans had his orderly, Murray, not thrown him across a packhorse and brought him to safety across the British lines (*A Study in Scarlet*).

MALINGERING.   Holmes told Watson at the conclusion of "The Dying Detective," "Malingering is a subject upon which I have sometimes thought of writing a monograph." It is unknown whether Holmes ever did produce such a work, particularly given the difficulties that have been encountered in locating his other more known writings.

MANAOS.   A city in northern Brazil, where the father of Maria Pinto Gibson, wife of J. Neil Gibson, served as a government official in "Thor Bridge."

MANCHESTER STREET.   A street that runs parallel to Baker Street that was mentioned in "The Empty House." While on their way circuitously to Camden House, Holmes and Watson passed through Manchester Street.

MANN, DER SHERLOCK HOLMES WAR, DER.   Germany. 1937. Cast: Hans Albers (Holmes), Heinz Ruhmann (Watson), Paul Bildt (Conan Doyle). In a comedy that proved that Holmes was popular even in Nazi Germany, two detectives attempt to fool passengers on a train by impersonating Holmes and Watson. Their caper is successful long enough for them to become embroiled in a mystery and to recover a stolen Mauritius stamp. Throughout the film, they repeatedly encounter an Englishman who inexplicably goes into hysterics every time he sees them. It turns out, of course, that he is Sir Arthur Conan Doyle, and he manages to have the two cleared of all charges when their identities are revealed.

MANOR HOUSE CASE.   A case that was solved by Holmes shortly before he undertook the Melas affair in "The Greek Interpreter." Mycroft Holmes said that he had expected to see Holmes for a consultation on the Manor House case, adding that he thought his brother might be a little out of his depth. Holmes, of course, had cleared up the matter, but Mycroft declared: " 'It was Adams, of course.' 'Yes, it was Adams.' 'I was sure of it from the first.' "

"MAN WHO WAS WANTED, THE CASE OF."   This pastiche was such an authentic seeming story that it was widely believed to have been written by Arthur Conan Doyle and was even published under his name in *Cosmopolitan* in August 1948 and the *Sunday Dispatch* in January 1949. The real author, however, was Arthur Whitaker. In 1910, Whitaker completed his story and sent it to Conan Doyle. An unemployed architect at the time, Whitaker suggested that he and Conan Doyle might collaborate. Sir Arthur, of course, declined the request, but in a courteous letter suggested that Whitaker develop it on his own with different characters or accept 10 pounds for the plot, although no guarantee could be given that it would ever be used—in fact, it never was. Whitaker accepted the 10 pounds, but kept a carbon of the story and Conan Doyle's letter.

Forgotten among the papers of Doyle after his death in 1930, the adventure was discovered in 1942 by Hesketh Pearson during his research for a biography and subsequently published in part in the biography (1943) and then in full (1948–1949). Whitaker, by then retired, wrote the estate, proving authorship and causing immense embarrassment to the Doyles. Incidentally, Whitaker was paid 150 pounds to keep silent. His story was written in a superbly Watsonian manner, presenting the challenging case of a criminal who robs twelve banks by forging checks, successfully eluding capture until his whereabouts are revealed by Holmes.

"MAN WITH THE TWISTED LIP, THE" (TWIS).   Published: *Strand*, December 1891; collected in *The Adventures of Sherlock Holmes* (1892). Case date: June 1889. Major players: Holmes, Watson, Hugh Boone, Neville St. Clair, Isa Whitney, and Mrs. Neville St. Clair. Watson begins his account by describing the sad story of Isa Whitney, an opium addict. In trying to save the unfortunate Whitney, Watson journeys to the opium den, Bar of Gold. There he finds Whitney, but he also stumbles upon Sherlock Holmes. The detective assures him that he has not taken up opium along with his other vices; he is on a case, searching for the missing Neville St. Clair. St. Clair's wife saw her husband at a window of the Bar of Gold, but was then unable to find him and the police were summoned. In the bar, they discovered traces of blood and St. Clair's coat, washed up on a mud bank and stuffed with 421 pennies and 70 half-pennies, and arrested the one person in the room, the beggar extraordinaire Hugh Boone, a character well known in London. His incarceration unfortunately does nothing to locate the missing man. In desperation, Mrs. St. Clair turns to Holmes, who solves the case after an entire night of pondering with his pipe, one of the most intense smoking sessions in the entire Canon. Of the case, Holmes remarked, "I cannot recall any case within my experience which looked at first glance so simple, and yet which presented such difficulties."

"MAN WITH THE WATCHES, THE." A short story written by Sir Arthur Conan Doyle that first appeared in the *Strand* in July, 1898 and was later published in the collection *Round the Fire Stories* (1908). While not part of the Canon, the case presented in the story is certainly equal to any faced by the detective. An inexplicable murder is committed on a train: a man carrying six watches has been shot through the heart. He was not an original passenger so his arrival on board is a mystery. The puzzle is compounded by the disappearance of three passengers, seemingly into thin air. The police are baffled and various theories are offered by the public, including a letter in the *Daily Gazette* "over the signature of a well-known criminal investigator" in which a long solution is proposed. When the truth is finally revealed, it turns out that the "sleuth" author of the letter is utterly mistaken—a private (and public) joke by Conan Doyle at the expense of the Great Detective, who was at the time supposedly dead. The respected Sherlockian Edgar Smith thought that "The Man With the Watches" and "The Lost Special" were so excellently Holmesian that they should be subsumed into the Canon.

MAP. Holmes consults maps in several cases, including a map of London during "The Bruce-Partington Plans," and an ordnance map in "The Engineer's Thumb," *The Hound of the Baskervilles*, and "The Priory School."

MARCINI'S. A restaurant in London where Holmes and Watson dined in *The Hound of the Baskervilles*. They ate there after the Baskerville affair, prior to going to hear the De Reszkes in *Les Huguenots*.

MARGATE. A case investigated by Holmes and Watson at the Kent seaside resort of Margate that was mentioned in "The Second Stain." Holmes suspected a woman of a crime because she maneuvered to have the light at her back, believing that she desired to make her facial expressions unreadable. The solution, however, was that she wished to conceal the fact that she had no powder on her nose. The detective noted that his experience was similar to that of Lady Trelawney Hope, who also put the light at her back. In "The Veiled Lodger," Leonardo, the onetime strongman of the Ronder Circus, drowned while bathing in Margate.

MARKER, MRS. The sad-faced housekeeper to Professor Coram at Yoxley Old Place in "The Golden Pince-Nez."

MARKET SQUARE. A square in the town of Vermissa in the Vermissa Valley in *The Valley of Fear*. Here could be found John McGinty's saloon, the favorite gathering place of the local Scowrers.

MARSEILLES. The southern French city is mentioned in "A Case of Identity." At the time Holmes was introduced to a case by Mary Sutherland, the disappearance of her fiance Hosmer Angel, the detective was involved in several cases, but none were of interest "save for one rather intricate matter which has been referred to me from Marseilles."

MARTHA. The housekeeper to the German spymaster Von Bork who was actually a counter-espionage agent working for Holmes in "His Last Bow." On the night that Holmes concluded his operations against the German spyring, Martha proved very helpful. There has been speculation that Martha was, in fact, Martha Hudson, Holmes's long-suffering landlady.

MARTIN, INSPECTOR. A member of the Norfolk constabulary who was assigned to investigate the murder of Hilton Cubitt at Ridling Thorpe

Manor in "The Dancing Men." Unlike other officers of the police, Martin was pleased to have Holmes's assistance in the case. Watson wrote that the trim inspector "had the good sense to allow my friend [Holmes] to do things in his own fashion, and contented himself with carefully noting the results." Throughout the investigation, Martin was astounded at Holmes's work, exclaiming "Capital! Capital!" at one point.

MARTIN, LIEUTENANT.   An officer serving on board the *Gloria Scott* in "The 'Gloria Scott'." He remained loyal to the captain when the convict revolt broke out and was killed in the unsuccessful attempt to suppress it.

MARTYRDOM OF MAN.   A work written in 1872 by the English traveller William Winwood Reade. An ethnological and historical attack on Christianity, *The Martyrdom of Man* was considered by Holmes in *The Sign of Four* to be one of the most remarkable books ever penned.

"MARVELOUS MISADVENTURES OF SHERLOCK HOLMES, THE."   In full "The Marvelous Misadventures of Sherlock Holmes: A Musical Mystery for Children," a musical written by Thom Racina that debuted in Chicago at the Goodman Theatre in July 1971. It starred Michael Kerns (Holmes), Donald Livesay (Watson), and Linda Taccki (Countess von Hassenfeffer).

MARX & CO.   A London clothier, of High Holborn. Aloysius Garcia of "Wisteria Lodge" purchased clothes from the company. They could supply no information about the murdered Garcia save that he was a good payer.

MARY.   A servant in the Horsham home of the Openshaws in "The Five Orange Pips." She prepared a fire in the room of Elias Openshaw, at his instruction, in which he burned the contents of his brass box. On the top of the box was printed the treble K (KKK). The maid to Mary Maberley in "The Three Gables" is also named Mary. She heard robbers in the house struggling with Mrs. Maberley and screamed out a window, summoning the police and forcing the intruders to flee.

MARY JANE.   A servant girl in the employ of the Watsons in "A Scandal in Bohemia." She was

described by Dr. Watson as "incorrigible" and his wife was forced to give her notice. Among her failings was the scarring of the doctor's shoes by carelessly scraping around the edges of the sole in order to remove some encrusted mud. Holmes naturally deduced that Watson had "a clumsy and careless servant girl" by observing the inside of Watson's left shoe, where the leather was scored by six almost parallel cuts.

MARYLEBONE LANE.   A street in the West End from which a van rushed into Bentinck Street, nearly running down Holmes and vanishing in an instant in "The Final Problem."

MASK OF MORIARTY, THE.   A 1985 play by Hugh Leonard, directed by Brian de Salvo, and starring Tom Baker (Holmes), Alan Stanford (Watson), and Brian Munn (Moriarty). This production was a lighthearted lampoon of the Canon by Leonard, who had written for earlier series on British television. It was "based" on an unknown and suppressed story by Watson, written apparently while in the throes of some of Holmes's drugs. The play included such bizarre points as a murder on Waterloo Bridge, the appearance of Jack the Ripper, and assorted deeds by the nefarious Professor Moriarty. The play opened in Dublin.

"MASKS OF DEATH, THE."   A 1984 British television film with Peter Cushing (Holmes), John Mills (Watson), Gordon Jackson (Alec MacDonald), and Anne Baxter (Irene Adler), directed by Roy Ward Baker, from a screenplay by John Elder, of Hammer Films fame. "The Masks of Death" marked the return of Peter Cushing to the role of Holmes after some sixteen years (he had starred in the British television series "Sherlock Holmes" in 1968). Here the Great Detective is brought out of retirement in 1913 to investigate three deaths in the East End, his inquiries ultimately involving him with the mysterious disappearance of a German convoy.

MASON.   A platelayer in "The Bruce-Partington Plans" who, one Tuesday morning at six o'clock, discovered the dead body of Arthur Cadogan West "just outside Aldgate Station on the Underground system in London." In *A Study in Scarlet*, Mason, a criminal in Bradford, escaped justice because there was at the time no reliable test for bloodstains (*A Study in Scarlet*). Holmes was thus jubilant that he had discovered one.

MASON, JOHN. The head trainer at Shoscombe stables who engaged Holmes's services because of the very peculiar behavior of his employer, Sir Robert Norberton, in "Shoscombe Old Place." Mason opened his account of events by declaring, "I think that my employer, Sir Robert, has gone mad," adding "when a man does one queer thing, or two queer things, there may be a meaning to it, but when everything he does is queer, then you begin to wonder. I believe Shoscombe Prince and the Derby have turned his brain." Watson described Mason as "a tall, clean-shaven man with the firm, austere expression which is only seen upon those who have to control horses or boys. Mr. John Mason had many of both under his sway, and he looked equal to the task."

MASON, MRS. The nurse to the Ferguson baby in "The Sussex Vampire." She was a tall, gaunt woman but, according to Robert Ferguson, had a heart of gold and was devoted to the children. It was she who first reported to Ferguson that his wife was apparently vampirizing the infant, witnessing with him a short time later Mrs. Ferguson rising from the baby's cot with blood on her lips.

MASTIFF. A type of large hound such as Carlo, the fierce dog owned by Jephro Rucastle in "The Copper Beeches." The most terrible mastiff Holmes would encounter was, of course, the Hound of the Baskervilles, described as a combination of a bloodhound and mastiff. Based on the little marks found on the walking stick of Dr. Mortimer in *The Hound of the Baskervilles*, Holmes was able to deduce that the dog was smaller than a mastiff but larger than a terrier.

MAUDSLEY. A friend of James Ryder's whom he hoped to involve in the affair of "The Blue Carbuncle." Ryder told Holmes and Watson: "I had a friend once called Maudsley, who went to the bad, and has just been serving his time in Pentonville. One day he had met me, and fell into talk about the ways of thieves and how they could get rid of what they stole."

MAUPERTUIS, BARON. The most accomplished swindler in Europe who was able to escape from the police of three countries but who was finally caught by Holmes ("The Reigate Squires"), in 1887. Watson wrote: "The whole question of the Netherland-Sumatra Company and of the colossal schemes of Baron Maupertuis are too recent in the minds of the public, and are too intimately concerned with politics and finance to be fitting subjects for this series of sketches." The affair, however, took a terrible toll on the detective, who finally collapsed from his incessant exertions. The rest he subsequently took in Reigate, Surrey, led to his involvement in the case of the Reigate Squires.

MAURITIUS. An island in the Indian Ocean where Mr. Fowler took a government appointment after his marriage to Alice Rucastle in "The Copper Beeches."

MAWSON & WILLIAMS'. A stockbroking firm in London, located on Lombard Street in "The Stockbroker's Clerk." They gave a position to Hall Pycroft, onetime stockbroking clerk at Coxon & Woodhouse.

MAYNOOTH, EARL OF. A governor of one of the Australian colonies who was serving there in spring 1894 ("The Empty House"). His wife, the **Lady Maynooth,** daughter Hilda Adair, and son Ronald Adair, returned to England at that time because Lady Maynooth required an operation for a cataract. They took up residence at 427 Park Lane. Ronald was later murdered under bizarre circumstances.

"MAZARIN STONE, THE ADVENTURE OF THE" (MAZA). Published: *Strand*, October 1921, *Hearst's International*, November 1921; collected in *The Case Book of Sherlock Holmes* (1927). Case date: 1903. Major players: Holmes, Watson, Billy, Count Negretto Sylvius, Sam Merton. A case, ranked with "The Veiled Lodger" as one of the least effective and most poorly constructed in the entire Canon. It is generally agreed that this account was based upon the one-act play *The Crown Diamond: An Evening with Sherlock Holmes*, by Sir Arthur Conan Doyle, performed in 1921. The origins of the story on the stage are clear right from the start as the opening passage is written in an unusual third person. Watson arrives at 221B Baker Street and is greeted by the page Billy. The doctor's subsequent exchange with Holmes includes the dialogue " 'I am expecting something

The Maxims of Sherlock Holmes

In his capacity as assistant, friend, and chronicler to Sherlock Holmes, Dr. Watson recorded a number of sayings or maxims of the detective that are now world famous. Some of them had a Shakespearian origin ("The Game is afoot!"), some a biblical one ("Sufficient for to-morrow is the evil thereof."). All of them, however, served to illustrate both the method and the genius of the world's first consulting detective. The most famous of his maxims, "Elementary, my dear Watson," was not actually said by the sleuth anywhere in the Canon. The following are among his most notable maxims:

There is nothing new under the sun. It has all been done before. (*A Study in Scarlet*)

It is a capital mistake to theorize before you have all the evidence. It biases the judgment. (*A Study in Scarlet*)

They say that genius is an infinite capacity for taking pains. (*A Study in Scarlet*)

Where there is no imagination, there is no horror. (*A Study in Scarlet*)

To a great mind, nothing is little. (*A Study in Scarlet*)

I am the last and highest court of appeal in detection. (*The Sign of Four*)

Detection is or ought to be, an exact science.... (*The Sign of Four*)

I never guess. It is a shocking habit—destructive to the logical faculty. (*The Sign of Four*)

When you have eliminated the impossible, whatever remains, *however improbable*, must be the truth. (*The Sign of Four*)

Women are never to be entirely trusted—not the best of them. (*The Sign of Four*)

It is a capital mistake to theorize before one has data. ("A Scandal in Bohemia")

Women are naturally secretive, and they like to do their own secreting. ("A Scandal in Bohemia")

As a rule, the more bizarre a thing is the less mysterious it proves to be. ("The Red-Headed League")

It is my business to know things. ("A Case of Identity")

It has long been an axiom of mine that the little things are infinitely the most important. ("A Case of Identity")

Singularity is almost invariably a clue. ("The Boscombe Valley Mystery")

Circumstantial evidence is a very tricky thing. ("The Boscombe Valley Mystery")

You know my method. It is founded upon the observation of trifles. ("The Boscombe Valley Mystery")

It is, of course, a trifle, but there is nothing so important as trifles. ("The Man With the Twisted Lip")

My name is Sherlock Holmes. It is my business to know what other people don't know. ("The Blue Carbuncle")

I am not retained by the police to supply their deficiencies. ("The Blue Carbuncle")

Circumstantial evidence is occasionally very convincing, as when you find a trout in the milk, to quote Thoreau's example. ("The Noble Bachelor")

I make a point of never having any prejudices, and of following docilely wherever fact may lead me. ("The Reigate Squires")

A loaf of bread and a clean collar. What does man want more? (*The Hound of the Baskervilles*)

Sufficient for to-morrow is the evil thereof. (*The Hound of the Baskervilles*)

The Press, Watson, is a most valuable institution, if you only know how to use it. ("The Six Napoleons")

Come, Watson, come! The Game is afoot! ("The Abbey Grange")

'I followed you.'

'I saw no one.'

'That is what you may expect to see when I follow you.' ("The Devil's Foot")

I am a believer in the genius loci. (*The Valley of Fear*)

Woman's heart and mind are insoluble puzzles to the male. ("The Illustrious Client")

When an object is good and the client is sufficiently illustrious, even the rigid British law becomes human and elastic. ("The Illustrious Client")

this evening.' 'Expecting what?' 'To be murdered, Watson.' " There follow events roughly similar to those recounted in "The Empty House." The Mazarin Stone, also called the Crown Diamond, is a great yellow stone that was stolen from Whitehall. Described as a "hundred-thousand-pound burglary," the disappearance of the stone prompted the prime minister and the home secretary to journey to Baker Street to enlist the aid of Holmes.

MCCARTHY, CHARLES.   A onetime wagon driver in the Australian goldfields and an acquaintance of the wealthy John Turner in "The Boscombe Valley Mystery." McCarthy lived on Hatherley, one of Turner's best farms and seemed to have some power over Turner although the latter was more than reluctant to allow his daughter to wed McCarthy's son, James. The elder McCarthy also had poor relations with his son, **James McCarthy,** and was witnessed by a young girl quarreling with him near Boscombe Pool. A short time later, McCarthy was found dead, his son the obvious suspect. The young McCarthy did nothing to improve his position by refusing to divulge the nature of the argument and by declaring that his father, as he died, mumbled some allusion to a rat. James McCarthy said of his father: "He was not a popular man, being somewhat cold and forbidding in his manner. . . ." Holmes believed McCarthy to be innocent and was successful in clearing him.

MCCAULEY.   A man who was sent The Five Orange Pips as a threatening gesture by the Ku Klux Klan and who was mentioned in the notebook of Elias Openshaw for March 1969: "7th. Set the pips on McCauley, Paramore, and Swain of St. Augustine. 8th McCauley cleared."

MCFARLANE, JOHN HECTOR.   "A bachelor, a solicitor, a Freemason, and an asthmatic" who came to Holmes in the desperate hope that the detective might be able to clear him of the murder of Jonas Oldacre in Norwood in "The Norwood Builder." A resident of Torrington Lodge,

McFarlane was hired by Oldacre to prepare his will, gaping in astonishment when he found that Oldacre, with some reservations, had left all of his property to him. McFarlane visited Oldacre that night at his Norwood home to look over a number of documents, spending the night at the Anerley Arms because of the late hour of his departure from Oldacre's company. The case against McFarlane seemed bleak, but Holmes was able to clear him. It was the discovery of the apparently absolutely damning evidence against his client that was the final impetus to Holmes to solve the mystery and the clinching proof in his mind of McFarlane's innocence.

MCFARLANE, MRS.   The mother of the unhappy John Hector McFarlane, who was arrested for the murder of Jonas Oldacre in "The Norwood Builder." Mrs. McFarlane knew Oldacre in the past for he was an old suitor of hers. She was engaged to him at one time but was so shocked at the story of how he had loosed a cat in an aviary that she would have nothing to do with him, marrying a better, if poorer man. She said "he was more like a malignant and cunning ape than a human being." On her wedding morning, Oldacre sent her a photograph of her that was shamefully defaced and mutilated with a knife. Mrs. McFarlane was absolutely convinced of her son's innocence.

MCFARLANE'S.   A carriage building depot situated around the corner from Jabez Wilson's pawnshop in Coburg Square in "The Red-Headed League."

MCGINTY, JOHN.   The so-called bodymaster of Lodge 341 of the Ancient Order of Freemen, the SCOWRERS, in Vermissa Valley in *The Valley of Fear.* The cruel and pitiless leader of the Scowrers, McGinty was also supposedly a respected leader in the valley, owning the Union Hotel and Saloon in Vermissa, and "was a high public official, a municipal councillor, and a commissioner of roads, elected to the office through the votes of the ruffians who in turn expected to receive favours at his hands." McGinty "was a black-maned giant, bearded to the cheek-bones, and with a shock of raven hair which fell to his collar. His complexion was as swarthy as that of an Italian and his eyes were of a strange dead black, which, combined with a slight squint, gave them a paricularly sinister appearance." McGinty accepted John McMurdo into Lodge 341, but came to regret this action. He was also known as "Jack" or "Black Jack."

McGregor, Mrs.   A member of the Ferrier wagon party in *A Study in Scarlet*. She did not survive the journey across the Great Alkali Plain.

McLaren, Miles.   A student at the College of St. Luke's who was also competing for the Fortescue Scholarship in "The Three Students." Hilton Soames, lecturer at the college, considered him to be the prime suspect in cheating on the examination for the scholarship. "He is a brilliant fellow when he chooses to work—one of the brightest intellects of the university; but he is weyward, dissipated, and undisciplined. He was nearly expelled over a card scandal in his first year. He has been idling all this term, and he must look forward with dread to the examination."

McMurdo.   A onetime prizefighter who served as a porter to Batholomew Sholto at Pondicherry Lodge, Upper Norwood in *The Sign of Four*. A "short, deep-chested man," he once boxed three rounds with Holmes at Alison's rooms for a benefit four years before meeting the detective at Pondicherry. At first not recognizing Holmes he roared: "God's truth! How could I have mistook you? If instead o'standing there so quiet you had just stepped and given me that cross-hit of yours under the jaw, I'd ha' known you without a question. Ah, you're one who has worked your gifts, you have! You might have aimed high, if you had joined the fancy."

McPherson, Fitzroy.   The science master at Harold Stackhurst's coaching establishment, The Gables, in "The Lion's Mane." He was apparently brutally murdered, dying in the presence of Holmes and Stackhurst. The detective wrote: "His back was covered with dark red lines as though he had been terribly flogged by a thin wire scourge. The instrument with which this punishment had been inflicted was clearly flexible, for the long, angry weals curved round his shoulders and ribs. There was blood dripping down his chin, for he had bitten through his lower lip in the paroxysm of his agony. His drawn and distorted face told how terrible that agony had been." At the time of his death, he was engaged to Maud Bellamy, who was convinced that "no single person could ever have inflicted such an outrage upon him." The death of his

dog, the body found down on the beach "at the very place where its master met his end," proved immensely helpful to Holmes in solving the case.

McQuire's Camp.   A mining camp or prospecting settlement near the Rockies in "The Noble Bachelor." Francis Hay Moulton and Aloysius Doran both worked claims in the area; Doran succeeded in "making his pile" (becoming wealthy) while Moulton's claim petered out. It was at McQuire's Camp that Moulton met Hatty Doran.

Mecca.   A city in Arabia, the site of the annual pilgrimage, the hajj, made by Muslims from all around the world. During the Great Hiatus, Holmes claimed to have "looked in" at Mecca, an action that, if true, was an extremely risky one as he might have been killed by the faithful there if exposed as an unbeliever ("The Empty House"). Jonathan Small and Tonga were picked up by a vessel carrying pilgrims to Jiddah in *The Sign of Four*.

Medical Directory.   A directory of all recognized medical practitioners enrolled on the government's medical register. Watson looked up the record of Dr. James Mortimer in the *Medical Directory*, confirming the deductions made by Holmes on Mortimer's walking stick in *The Hound of the Baskervilles*.

Meek, Sir Jasper.   A well-known physician, and according to Watson, one of the best medical practitioners in London. In "The Dying Detective," Watson was eager to consult him about Holmes's apparently terrible illness, but the detective would not allow him to do so.

Meiringen.   A city in central Switzerland where Holmes and Watson spent a night at the Englischer Hof during their attempted flight from Moriarty in "The Final Problem."

Melas.   A Greek linguist and interpreter, a neighbor of Mycroft Holmes, and the title figure in the case recounted in "The Greek Interpreter." Mycroft told Holmes and Watson: "Mr. Melas is a Greek by extraction, as I understand, and he is a remarkable linguist. He earns his living partly as interpreter in the law courts and partly by acting as guide to any wealthy Orientals who may visit the Northumberland Avenue hotels." He consulted

Mycroft and then Holmes about his very peculiar and frightening abduction by a gang of criminals who used his linguistic skills to translate the words of their unfortunate kidnap and torture victim Paul Kratides.

MELVILLE.   A retired brewer and resident of Albemarle Mansion, Kensington in "Wisteria Lodge." He introduced John Scott Eccles to Aloysius Garcia, a meeting that led to Garcia inviting Scott Eccles to his home at Wisteria Lodge.

MEMOIRS OF SHERLOCK HOLMES, THE.
The second collection of Sherlock Holmes cases was published in 1894. The stories included in the collection were "Silver Blaze," "The Adventure of the Cardboard Box," "The Yellow Face," "The Stockbroker's Clerk," "The 'Gloria Scott'," "The Musgrave Ritual," "The Reigate Squires," "The Crooked Man," "The Resident Patient," "The Greek Interpreter," "The Naval Treaty," and "The Final Problem." The omission in their titles of the customary words "The Adventure of" is notable; the one exception is "The Adventure of the Cardboard Box." This case, considered by Conan Doyle to be a little too sensational and objected to by some readers because of its treatment of adultery, was subsequently left out of many editions of the *Memoirs*. It was later included in the collection *His Last Bow* (1917).

MENDELSSOHN, FELIX.   Noted German composer (1809–1847), some of whose lieder (*Lieder ohne Worter*, "Songs without Words") were played by Holmes, at Watson's request as they were favorites of the doctor (*A Study in Scarlet*). Watson wrote that he knew Holmes could play difficult pieces because he played some Mendelssohn and other favorites.

MERCER (1).   A member of Holmes's agency who served as a "general utility man who looks up routine business" and who was said in "The Creeping Man" to have entered the detective's employ since Dr. Watson's time. Mercer assisted Holmes in finding details about Dorak, his telegram about the elderly bohemian helping to clear up the case.

MERCER (2).   The second mate of the barque *Gloria Scott* in "The 'Gloria Scott'." He was bribed to join the mutiny of convicts and was thus in league with Jack Prendergast. In the explosion that

destroyed the *Gloria Scott*, Mercer was killed. His name has been spelled Mereer in some editions.

MEREDITH, GEORGE.   English poet (1828–1909). After discussing the pertinent points of "The Boscombe Valley Mystery," Holmes told Watson, "And now let us talk about George Meredith, if you please, and we shall leave all minor matters until to-morrow."

MERIVALE.   A member of Scotland Yard who asked Holmes to look into the St. Pancras case ("Shoscombe Old Place"). Holmes solved the case by using his microscope to connect a suspect with a cap found at the scene of the crime.

MERRILOW, MRS.   The landlady of Eugenia Ronder in "The Veiled Lodger." Of South Brixton, she was "an elderly, motherly woman of the buxom landlady type" who consulted Holmes about her lodger, a mutilated woman whose face she had seen only once in seven years, and she wished to God she had not. Concerned about Ronder's declining health, Mrs. Merrilow had suggested the police or the clergy, but Ronder would not agree. Finally, when Merrilow suggested Holmes, Ronder exclaimed "That's the man."

MERRIPIT HOUSE.   The residence of the Stapletons, on Dartmoor, in Devonshire in *The Hound of the Baskervilles*.

MERRYWEATHER.   Chairman of directors of the City and Suburban Bank who participated with Holmes, Watson, and Inspector Peter Jones, in the vigil in the cellar of the Coburg branch of the bank in "The Red-Headed League." Merryweather was initially contemptuous of Holmes, stating, "I hope a wild goose may not prove to be the end of our chase," but later gushed with gratitude, "I do not know how the bank can thank or repay you. There is no doubt that you have detected and defeated in the most complete manner one of the most determined attempts at bank robbery that have ever come within my experience." It was also Merryweather's custom to play a rubber of whist every Saturday night, a game that he had not missed in twenty-seven years until the night he accompanied Peter Jones to the rendezvous with Holmes.

MERTON COUNTY.   A county in the region of the Gilmerton Mountains in the United States in *The Valley of Fear*. An agricultural area, it was near Vermissa Valley.

MERTON, SAM.   A prizefighter and accomplice to Count Negretto Sylvius in the theft of "The Mazarin Stone." He was "a heavily built young man with a stupid, slab-sided face," whom Holmes described as: "Not a bad fellow. He is a big silly bullheaded gudgeon. But he is flopping about in my net all the same."

MEUNIER, OSCAR.   A French sculptor of Grenoble who created the wax bust of Sherlock Holmes that was used as a decoy on the night of Holmes's capture of the murderer of Ronald Adair in "The Empty House." Meunier spent some days doing the molding, and so excellent was his work that Watson, upon seeing it, threw out his hand to make sure that the man himself was standing beside him. The bust was damaged in the affair by a bullet, fired by an air gun, that passed through the head and flattened itself on the wall. A similar bust was created of Holmes years later by Tavernier for use in the recovery of the Mazarin Stone.

MEYER, ADOLPH.   An international agent who resided at 13 Great George Street, Westminster in "The Bruce-Partington Plans," Mycroft Holmes considered him one of the foreign spies in London capable of masterminding so big an affair as the theft of the Bruce-Partington Submarine Plans, along with Louis La Rothiere and Hugo Oberstein.

MICHAEL.   The stablehand at Cheeseman's, in Sussex, in the employ of Robert Ferguson in "The Sussex Vampire." He slept in the house.

MICROSCOPE.   Holmes used a high-powered magnifying instrument as part of his methods of detection. He told Watson, "Since I ran down that coiner by the zinc and copper filings in the seam of his cuff [Scotland Yard] have begun to realize the importance of the microscope." He did feel, however, that microscopic examinations of stains for identifying blood corpuscles to be clumsy and uncertain—hence his jubilation at having found a test for bloodstains that he considered to be infallible (*A Study in Scarlet*). The microscope was pivotal in the solution of the St. Pancras case ("Shoscombe Old Place"), and at the start of the affair of Shoscombe Old Place, the detective was "bending

for a long time over a low-power microscope." Watson also wrote, "Grit in a sensitive instrument, or a crack in one of his own high-power lenses, would not be more disturbing than a strong emotion in a nature such as his" ("A Scandal in Bohemia"). The microscope (and MAGNIFYING LENS) has appeared in numerous films, one of the best ways to establish the detective as a man of science and logic.

MIDDLESEX.   A county to the west of London. The village of Pinner, home of Effie Hebron's maiden aunt in "The Yellow Face," was in Middlesex. Grant Munro met Effie Hebron in Pinner. The city of Harrow or Harrow-on-the-Hill was also in Middlesex. Honoria Westphail lived near Harrow in "The Speckled Band."

MIDIANITES.   A tribe mentioned in the Old Testament that lived in the land of Moab. In "The Disappearance of Lady Frances Carfax," while supposedly recovering from a disease contracted in South America, Dr. Shlessinger claimed that he "was preparing a map of the Holy Land, with special reference to the Kingdom of the Midianites, upon which he was writing a monograph."

MIDLAND ELECTRIC COMPANY.   A company in Coventry that employed Cyril Morton, fiance to Violet Smith in "The Solitary Cyclist."

MILES, HONORABLE MISS.   A victim of the blackmailer Charles Augustus Milverton who had her planned wedding to Colonel Dorking called off only two days before it was to take place because of the blackmailer's wicked activities in "Charles Augustus Milverton."

MILLAR, FLORA.   Onetime danseuse at the Allegro who was an intimate of Lord St. Simon in "The Noble Bachelor." St. Simon said of her: "Flora was a dear little thing, but exceedingly hot-headed and devotedly attached to me. She wrote me dreadful letters when she heard I was about to be married, and, to tell the truth, the reason why I had the marriage celebrated so quietly was that I feared lest there be a scandal in the church." Millar attempted to disrupt the wedding of St. Simon and Hatty Doran. She "endeavored to force her way into the house after the bridal party, alleging that she had some claim upon Lord St. Simon. It was only after a painful and prolonged scene that she was ejected by the butler and the footman." Because she was seen in the company of Hatty Doran just before the bride's disappearance, Millar was arrested on suspicion of murdering her.

MILLER HILL.   An ill-kept public park in the center of Vermissa in *The Valley of Fear.* Jack McMurdo and Brother Morris met there.

MILNER, GODFREY.   An associate of Ronald Adair who played cards with him, Lord Balmoral, and Colonel Sebastian Moran in "The Empty House" some weeks prior to the terrible murder of Adair. It was reported that Adair, in partnership with Moran, had won as much as 420 pounds in one sitting from Milner and Lord Balmoral.

MILVERTON, CHARLES AUGUSTUS. The so-called King of All Blackmailers whom Holmes considered "the worst man in London" in "Charles Augustus Milverton." The detective was forced to do business with the odious Milverton on behalf of a client, Lady Eva Brackwell, who was being blackmailed, an involvement that led Holmes to extreme measures. Watson wrote that "Milverton was a man of fifty, with a large, intellectual head, a round, plump, hairless face, a perpetual frozen smile, and two keen gray eyes, which gleemed brightly from behind broad, gold-rimmed

Robert Hardy is Charles August Milverton, "The Master Blackmailer," in a recent television production. (Photo courtesy of MYSTERY/WGBH Boston).

glasses. There was something of Mr. Pickwick's benevolence in his appearance, marred only by the insincerity of the fixed smile and by the hard glitter of those restless and penetrating eyes."

MIRACLE PLAYS.   A type of religious drama depicting events from the Bible or the lives of saints, that flourished in the Middle Ages. Holmes was able to speak authoritatively on the subject in *The Sign of Four.*

MISADVENTURES OF SHERLOCK HOLMES, THE.   A famous collection of pastiches and parodies of the Canon, edited by Ellery Queen and published in 1944. The first such collection, *The Misadventures* was remarkable for the authors who were included: Agatha Christie, Mark Twain, James M. Barrie, and Vincent Starrett. Among the stories are "The Unique Hamlet" by Vincent Starrett (1920), "The Case of the Missing Lady" by Agatha Christie (1929), "The Adventure of Shamrock Jolnes" by O. Henry (1914), and "The Adventure of the Murdered Art Editor" by Frederic Dorr Steele (1933). Potentially very popular, it was ultimately suppressed by the Conan Doyle estate.

MISADVENTURES OF SHERLOCK HOLMES, THE.   An excellent collection of patiches and parodies of the Canon published in 1989 and edited by Sebastian Wolfe. As Wolfe declares in the introduction, the distinctions between parodies, pastiches, and burlesques have not always been clear, so he included examples of each in the book, providing a useful demonstration of the flexibility not only of Holmes but the Canon itself. *The Misadventures* includes some truly excellent works: "Martian Crown Jewels" by Poul Anderson, "The Anomaly of the Empty Man" by Anthony Boucher, "The Adventure of the Snitch in Time" by August Derleth and Mack Reynolds, and two pieces by the revered John Dickson Carr, "The Adventure of the Paradol Chamber," and "The Adventure of the Conk-Singleton Papers."

MISSING REMBRANDT, THE.   England 1932. Dir: Leslie Hiscott. Cast: Arthur Wontner (Sherlock Holmes), Ian Fleming (Watson), Minnie Raynor (Mrs. Hudson), Francis L. Sullivan (Baron von Guntermann). The second film featuring Wontner as Holmes, released by Twickemham Studios, and based in part on "The Adventure of

Charles Augustus Milverton," presents the duel between Holmes and the odious art dealer and blackmailer Baron von Guntermann (played by the well-known character actor Francis L. Sullivan). The baron, who portrays a thinly disguised Milverton, works as a society blackmailer when he is not attempting to steal precious art—in this case the title Rembrandt from the Louvre. As in the original story, Holmes becomes involved on behalf of Lady Violet, one of the baron's victims. The detective ultimately exposes Guntermann and recovers the missing painting, but, it may be presumed, the baron receives his just deserts as per the bloody end of Milverton. Critics were pleased with Wontner's performance, prompting a third release, *The Sign of the Four*, produced by Associated Radio Pictures.

"MISSING THREE-QUARTER, THE AD-VENTURE OF THE" (MISS).

Published: *Strand*, August 1904, *Collier's*, November 1904; collected in *The Return of Sherlock Holmes* (1905). Case date: December 1896. Major players: Holmes, Watson, Cyril Overton, Lord Mount-James, Dr. Leslie Armstrong, Godfrey Staunton, and Pompey. Cyril Overton, skipper of the varsity rugby team for Cambridge, consults Holmes on a matter of supreme importance: the star third quarter of the Cambridge team, Godfrey Staunton, has disappeared and without him the team faces certain defeat at the hands of Oxford. Overton is stunned that Holmes has never heard of either the skipper or his star player. Holmes knows Arthur Staunton, a rising young forger, and Henry Staunton, whom Holmes helped to hang, but he knows no Godfrey. Holmes and Watson take the case, ignorance notwithstanding, and journey to Cambridge to search for Staunton in the villages of the area. Their investigation leads them to the impressive Dr. Leslie Armstrong, who proves a more than able opponent to Holmes, impeding the detective's hunt at every turn. Eventually, with the help of Pompey, "pride of the local draghounds," they locate the rugby star; alas, it is too late to save Cambridge from defeat.

MILTON, JOHN.   The valet to Eduardo Lucas at 16 Godolphin Street, Westminster in "The Second Stain." Milton claimed to be out for the evening, visiting a friend at Hammersmith, while his employer was being stabbed to death, but was arrested anyway by the police "as an alternative to absolute inaction." His alibi, however, was complete and he was subsequently released.

MOLESEY MYSTERY.   An investigation successfully undertaken by Inspector Lestrade while Holmes was still presumed dead (during the Great Hiatus) that was mentioned in "The Empty House." Holmes commented on the case by saying, "you handled the Molesey Mystery with less than your usual—that's to say, you handled it fairly well." It is unclear whether Molesey refers to a person or to a location.

MONTAGUE PLACE.   A street in London just off of Montague Street, near the British Museum. In "The Copper Beeches," Violet Hunter apparently lived here as her note to Holmes was addressed from this location.

MONTAGUE STREET.   A street in London, near the British Museum where Holmes kept rooms from around 1878 until 1881, when he began his career as a detective. He told Watson: "When I first came to London I had rooms in Montague Street, just round the corner from the British Museum, and there I waited, filling in my too abundant leisure time by studying all those branches of science which might make me more efficient. Now and again cases came my way, principally through the introduction of old-fellow students, for during my last years at the university there was a good deal of talk there about myself and my methods." The third of these early cases was "The Musgrave Ritual." Much effort has been undertaken to determine where exactly on Montague Street the young detective may have lived, as there has been much effort to find the actual 221B Baker Street. Coincidentally, Arthur Conan Doyle lived at 23 Montague Street when he went to London in 1891. An interesting picture of Holmes's domestic arrangements was presented in the novel *Enter the Lion* by Sean Wright and Michael Hodel (1979).

MONTGOMERY.   An inspector from Scotland Yard who took the statement of Jim Browner at the Shadwell police station in "The Cardboard Box."

MONTPELLIER.   A city in the south of France where Holmes spent at least several months during the Great Hiatus ("The Empty House"). While there, Holmes conducted some research into coal-tar derivatives. At least two crimes of which the detective was familiar were committed at Montpellier; Leturier was the victim of the forcible administration of poison (*A Study in Scarlet*); and

Lefevre escaped justice because there was at the time no reliable test for bloodstains (*A Study in Scarlet*). Watson also located Marie Devine, the maid of Lady Carfax, at Montpellier (although he spelled it "Montpelier") in "The Disappearance of Lady Frances Carfax."

MONTPENSIER, MADAME. A French woman whom Holmes defended "from the charge of murder which hung over her in connection with the death of her stepdaughter, Mlle. Carere, "the young lady who, as it will be remembered, was found six months later alive and married in New York" (*The Hound of the Baskervilles*). The case of Madame Montpensier was presented in detail in "The Adventure of the Black Baronet" by John Dickson Carr and Adrian Conan Doyle in the collection, *The Exploits of Sherlock Holmes* (1954).

MOORHOUSE. A member of the Cambridge rugby team whom Cyril Overton, the team captain, considered the logical player to replace the missing Godfrey Staunton, in "The Missing Three-Quarter," who had vanished just before a match with Oxford. Overton had serious reservations about Moorhouse, saying that "he is trained as a half, and he always edges right in onto the scrum instead of keeping out on the touchline. He's a fine place-kick, it's true, but, then, he has no judgement, and he can't sprint for nuts."

MOORSIDE GARDENS. A street in London. Count Negretto Sylvius lived here, at 136 Moorside Gardens, N.W. in "The Mazarin Stone."

MORAN, COLONEL SEBASTIAN. Former army officer, noted big-game hunter, and chief of staff to Professor Moriarty. According to Holmes's own biographical index, his entry read:

"Moran, Sebastian, Colonel. Unemployed. Formerly 1st Bangalore Pioneers. Born London, 1840. Son of Sir Augustus Moran, C.B., once British Minister to Persia. Educated Eton and Oxford. Served in Jowaki Campaign, Afghan Campaign, Charasiab (despatches), Sherpur, and Cabul. Author of *Heavy Game of the Western Himalayas* (1881); *Three Months in the Jungle* (1884). Address: Conduit Street. Clubs: The Anglo-Indian, the Tankerville, the Bagatelle Card Club.

In the margin, written in Holmes's 'precise hand' was 'The second most dangerous man in London.' "

Holmes's assessment was proven totally correct in 1894 when, upon returning to England from the Great Hiatus, the detective became Moran's target for revenge for the death of the late Professor Moriarty and the destruction of the Napoleon of Crime's vast network of illegal activity. It was Moran, who three years before, had witnessed the demise of Moriarty at the Reichenbach Falls and who had fired upon Holmes, giving the detective an "evil five minutes upon the Reichenbach ledge." A man of nerve and courage, Moran had a record of tiger kills that remained unmatched, and he once crawled down a sewer after a wounded man-eating tiger. Nevertheless, his own dubious habits and morals forced him to leave India and retire, albeit without any open scandal. Holmes added: "It was at this time that he was sought out by Professor Moriarty, to whom for a time he was chief of staff. Moriarty supplied him liberally with money, and used him only in one or two very high-class jobs, which no ordinary criminal could have undertaken." Moran was trapped by Holmes in the affair of "The Empty House," but somehow avoided a death sentence and was still alive, in prison, in 1914 as mentioned in "His Last Bow."

MORAN, PATIENCE. The daughter of Moran, lodgekeeper of the Boscombe Valley Estate in "The Boscombe Valley Mystery." She was a witness to some of the events in the murder of Charles McCarthy. The fourteen year old reported to her mother that while she was picking flowers in one of the woods, she overheard McCarthy and his son engaged in a violent quarrel. "She heard Mr. McCarthy the elder using very strong language to his son, and she saw the latter raise up his hand as if to strike his father." Her testimony only added to what Watson called a "damning case" against young McCarthy.

MORCAR, COUNTESS OF. The owner of the Blue Carbuncle who had the gem stolen from her jewel case at the Hotel Cosmopolitan in "The Blue Carbuncle."

MORECROFT. A name used by Killer Evans in "The Three Garridebs."

MORIARTY, COLONEL JAMES. One of the two brothers of the infamous Professor Moriarty. Little is known about this colonel, save that he forced Watson to write the account of Holmes's last days in 1891—"The Final Problem." Watson wrote: "My hand has been forced . . . by the recent letters in which Colonel James Moriarty defends the memory of his brother, and I have no choice but to lay the facts before the public exactly as they occured." It has been a matter of great curiosity to Sherlockians that this Moriarty should have the same name as his more reprehensible sibling—James, leading some to speculate that the family's name might be the compound James Moriarty. In his play *Sherlock Holmes*, William Gillette obviated the theorizing by naming the professor Robert. A third brother was a station master in the West of England, encountered in *The Valley of Fear*.

MORIARTY, PROFESSOR. According to Holmes, the Napoleon of Crime (d. 1891) was the near equal in intellectual ability to Sherlock himself, and the grand master of a criminal organization that controlled much of Britain's underworld and probably extended its influence to the Continent. Professor James Moriarty technically appeared only briefly in the Canon: he journeyed past

John Huston in a memorable outing as Professor Moriarty in *Sherlock Holmes in New York* (1976), one of the finest of all screen Moriartys.

Holmes and Watson on a train (a special) in "The Final Problem" and was visible to Watson near the Reichenbach Falls, the only times that Watson ever saw him. However, the professor played a major role in the events of "The Final Problem," was present in spirit in *The Valley of Fear*, and his malign influence was at work in "The Empty House." According to Holmes, Moriarty "is the Napoleon of Crime, Watson. He is the organizer of half that is evil and of nearly all that is undetected in this great city. He is a genius, a philosopher, an abstract thinker. He has a brain of the first order. He sits motionless, like a spider in the centre of its web, but that web has a thousand radiations, and he knows every quiver of each of them." Like Mycroft Holmes, Sherlock's elder brother, Moriarty participated in only a small portion of the cases recounted by Watson, but he loomed large indeed among the major figures of the Canon.

Canon. Waging private war upon the criminal classes of England, Holmes inevitably would have

The Napoleon of Crime, Professor Moriarty, from "The Final Problem"; by Sidney Paget.

The coat of arms of Professor Moriarty, according to the scholar William S. Hall, bears the motto *Aspera me juvant* ("Peril delights me").

become aware of a shadowy and elusive figure on the order of Professor Moriarty, and the detective ultimately became the world's leading expert on the criminal genius. The degree to which Holmes had investigated the professor was made clear in *The Valley of Fear* when he told Inspector Mac-Donald that he had paid three visits to Moriarty's memorable offices, "twice waiting for him under different pretexts and leaving before he came. Once—well, I can hardly tell about the once to an official detective. It was on the last occasion that I took the liberty of running over his papers . . ."

In "The Empty House," Holmes told Watson, "His career has been an extraordinary one. He is a man of good birth and excellent education, endowed by Nature with a phenomenal mathematical faculty. At the age of twenty-one he wrote a treatise upon the Binomial Theorem, which had a European vogue. On the strength of it, he won the Mathematical Chair at one of our smaller Universities, and had, to all appearance, a most brilliant career before him. But the man had hereditary tendencies of the most diabolical kind. A criminal strain ran in his blood, which, instead of being modified, was increased and rendered infinitely more dangerous by his extraordinary mental powers. Dark rumours gathered round him in the University town, and eventually he was compelled to resign his Chair and to come down to London . . . For years past I have continually been conscious of some power behind the malefactor,

some deep organizing power which for ever stands in the way of the law, and throws its shield over the wrong-doer. Again and again in cases of the most varying sorts—forgery cases, robberies, murders—I have felt the presence of this force, and I have deduced its action in many of those undiscovered crimes in which I have not been personally consulted. For years I have endeavoured to break through the veil which shrouded it, and at last the time came when I seized my thread and followed it, until it led me, after a thousand cunning windings, to ex-Professor Moriarty of mathematical celebrity."

An estimate of the professor's vast intake of money from his criminal activities was calculated by Holmes based on the salary that was paid to his chief of staff (6,000 pounds per annum), the fact that he had over twenty banking accounts, and his ownership of a painting by Jean Baptiste Greuze, an artist whose work could fetch up to 40,000 pounds at auction.

Holmes acknowledged that Moriarty was a genius and that despite his horror at the man's crimes, he was lost in admiration for his skills. Interestingly, it was the dangerous intellect of the professor's that was probably a major impetus in the detective's determination to unravel and destroy the web of nefarious doings over which the villain presided. Such intrusions could not be permitted by Moriarty, of course, and a titanic struggle was inevitable. The war between them began with Moriarty's visit to 221B Baker Street to warn off Holmes, during which Moriarty assured him: "You hope to beat me. I tell you that you will never beat me. If you are clever enough to bring destruction upon me, rest assured that I shall do as much to you."

Holmes responded: "You have paid me several compliments, Mr. Moriarty . . . Let me pay you one in return when I say that if I were assured of the former eventuality I would, in the interest of the public, cheerfully accept the latter." The duel ended on May 4, 1891 at the Reichenbach Falls in a personal struggle between the two from which only Holmes survived. In later years, however, he expressed a certain regret that so excellent an opponent was gone. In "The Norwood Builder" he laments to Watson: "From the point of view of the criminal expert, London has become a singularly uninteresting city since the death of the late lamented Professor Moriarty" (similar statements were made in "The Illustrious Client," "His Last Bow," and "The Missing Three-Quarter"). Readers of the *Strand* would no doubt have agreed, at least

Veteran actor George Zucco, as Professor Moriarty, in *The Adventures of Sherlock Holmes* (1939).

in so far as their desire to know more about the dread Napoleon of Crime.

Non-Canon.   It was only a matter of time before Professor Moriarty reappeared against Sherlock Holmes in some capacity. Fans, in fact, had to wait only a few years, for WILLIAM GILLETTE chose to use the professor as the villain in his play *Sherlock Holmes*, although the professor's first name was changed from James to Robert. The wicked mathematician did his part to make the play such a huge success. Henceforth, he was *the* villain to challenge the wits of the Great Detective, viler even than the deadly snake wielder Dr. Grimesby Roylott. Throughout this century, Moriarty has appeared in novels, new plays, and films, proving himself one of the most memorable of baddies, not only of the Canon, but in the literature of crime in general.

Much speculation has been devoted to the possible genesis of the Holmes-Moriarty struggle. W. S. Baring-Gould first postulated in his *Sherlock Holmes of Baker Street* that Moriarty had been the mathematics tutor of the young Sherlock Holmes.

Nicholas Meyer, in his renowned novel, and later film, *The Seven-Per-Cent Solution*, theorized that Moriarty was not only a tutor to the child Sherlock but that he had conducted an illicit affair with his student's mother. Still another cause was offered by Sean Wright and Michael Hodel in their novel *Enter the Lion* (1979). They proposed that the young James Moriarty had lost his father to suicide as the result of the efforts of Sherlock and his brother Mycroft in uncovering a treasonous conspiracy in which the elder Moriarty was involved; shamed and ruined, James swore revenge. In film, meanwhile, the 1985 *Young Sherlock Holmes* adopted the tutor hypothesis, adding to it the notion that the future Moriarty was responsible for the death of Holmes's one great love.

MORMONS.   Members of the church that was originally founded in 1830 by Joseph Smith, known in full as The Church of Jesus Christ of Latter-Day Saints. The Mormons were presented in the first case recounted by Dr. Watson, *A Study in Scarlet*, although the details of Mormon life and activities were not particularly accurate.

MORPHINE.   One of the drugs, with cocaine, that Holmes took on occasion. At the start of the case recounted in *The Sign of Four*, Watson could not restrain himself about Holmes's addiction, blurting out, " 'Which is it to-day,' I asked, 'morphine or cocaine?' " After his attack by Baron Gruner's thugs in "The Illustrious Client," Holmes was given morphine. Ironically, Baron Gruner required morphine himself at the end of the case, the result of being splashed with vitriol. Professor Presbury needed morphine in "The Creeping Man," and Ian Murdoch called for some after his encounter with "The Lion's Mane."

MORPHY, ALICE.   The daughter of **Professor Morphy**, of Camford University, holder of the Chair of Comparative Anatomy with Professor Presbury to whom Alice was engaged in "The Creeping Man." Presbury won her hand, overcoming other candidates who were more her age as well as his own eccentricities. His increasingly peculiar behavior, however, endangered their union. According to Presbury's assistant Trevor Bennett, Miss Morphy was "a very perfect girl both in mind and body, so that there was every excuse for the professor's infatuation."

Memorable Moriartys

PROFESSOR MORIARTY ON FILM AND TELEVISION

ACTOR	PROGRAM OR FILM	ACTOR	PROGRAM OR FILM
Booth Conway	*The Valley of Fear* (1916)	Leo McKern	*Adventures of Sherlock*
Ernest Maupain	*Sherlock Holmes* (1916)		*Holmes' Smarter Brother*
Percy Standing	*The Final Problem* (1923)		(1975)
Gustav von Seyffertitz	*Sherlock Holmes* (1922)	John Huston	*Sherlock Holmes in New York*
Harry T. Morey	*The Return of Sherlock Holmes*		(1976)
	(1929)	Laurence Olivier	*The Seven-Per-Cent Solution*
Ernest Torrence	*Sherlock Holmes* (1932)		(1976)
Norman McKinnel	*The Sleeping Cardinal* (1931)	Eric Porter	"The Adventures of
Lyn Harding	*The Triumph of Sherlock*		Sherlock Holmes"
	Holmes (1935)		(TV—1985)
	Silver Blaze (1937)	Anthony Higgins	*Young Sherlock Holmes*
George Zucco	*The Adventures of Sherlock*		(1985)
	Holmes (1939)	Anthony Andrews	"Hands of a Murderer"
Lionel Atwill	*Sherlock Holmes and the Secret*		(TV—1990)
	Weapon (1942)	Paul Freeman	*Without a Clue* (1990)
Henry Daniell	*The Woman in Green* (1945)	Daniel Davis	"STAR TREK: The Next
Hans Söhnker	*Sherlock Holmes und das*		Generation" (TV series)
	Halsband des Todes (1962)		

MORRIS, WILLIAM. One of the names used by Duncan Ross during the affair of "The Red-Headed League."

MORRISON, ANNIE. A woman whose name appeared in the note that had been sent to the murdered William Kirwin and that decoyed him to his death in "The Reigate Squires." It is unclear, however, what Morrison's relationship to Kirwin constituted that he could be so easily drawn into a trap.

MORRISON, MORRISON, AND DODD. A firm of London solicitors who represented Robert Ferguson in "The Sussex Vampire." They were consulted by Ferguson about vampires and wrote to Holmes, "As our firm specializes entirely upon the machinery the matter hardly comes within our purview, and we have therefore recommended Mr. Ferguson to call upon you and lay the matter before you." The solicitors had apparently been previously associated with the detective in the case of the *Matilda Briggs*, a ship connected with the giant rat of Sumatra, a story for which the world was not yet prepared.

MORSTAN, CAPTAIN ARTHUR. Father of Mary Morstan and an officer in the Indian army who had been a friend of Major John Sholto, serving with him at the Blair Island penal colony in the Andaman Islands in *The Sign of Four*. While in the islands, Morstan met Jonathan Small and became involved, with Sholto, in the disappearance of the AGRA TREASURE. Returning to England in 1878, he was supposed to be reunited with his daughter but mysteriously disappeared, leaving her waiting at the Langham Hotel.

MORSTAN, MARY. Later Mary Watson (1868–ca.1891–94), daughter of Captain Arthur Morstan, who brought to Holmes the complex case of *The Sign of Four* and who later married DR. WATSON. She approached Holmes in the hopes that he might be able to solve the mysterious disappearance of her father years before and the strange events that had recently befallen her. As a result of her request, Holmes and Watson became involved in murder, revenge, and one of the detective's bloodiest and darkest investigations. Throughout the case, Watson grew increasingly enamored of her, finally asking her for her hand in marriage. At the end of the affair, Watson told Holmes that she had accepted him as "a husband in prospective." Subsequently, Watson mentioned his marriage ("The Boscombe Valley Mystery," "The Stockbroker's Clerk," and "A Scandal in Bohemia"), noting in "The Stockbroker's Clerk" that shortly after his wedding he purchased a practice in the Paddington district. Mary apparently died some time between 1891 and 1894, during Holmes's Great Hiatus. Her husband wrote that Holmes "had learned of my own sad bereavement, and his sympathy was shown in his manner rather than in his words" ("The Empty House").

MORTIMER. The gardener at Yoxley Old Place in "The Golden Pince-Nez." Among his duties was to push the invalid Professor Coram around the grounds in a bath chair. Mortimer, "an Army pensioner—an old Crimean man of excellent character," lived in a three-roomed cottage at the other end of the garden.

MORTIMER, DR. JAMES. A country physician from Grimpen, on Dartmoor, in Devonshire, who introduced Holmes to the legend and subsequent case of *The Hound of the Baskervilles*. Mortimer lived with his wife in Grimpen and had been a friend of Sir Charles Baskerville, a relationship that added to his sense of responsibility toward young Sir Henry Baskerville, who had the curse of the family looming over his future. His career was listed in Holmes's *Medical Directory*. Watson wrote that

he "was a very tall, thin man, with a long nose like a beak, which jutted out between two keen gray eyes, set closely together and sparkling brightly from behind a pair of gold-rimmed glasses. He was clad in a professional but rather slovenly fashion, for his frock-coat was dingy and his trousers frayed." He said of himself, "a dabbler in science, Mr. Holmes, a picker up of shells on the shores of the great unknown ocean." A forgetful person, Mortimer left his walking stick on his first visit to 221B, an item upon which both Holmes and Watson made deductions.

MORTIMER'S. A firm that backed onto the pawnshop of Jabez Wilson in "The Red-Headed League."

MORTIMER STREET. A street in the West End of London that supposedly ran behind Watson's house, stretching behind Regent Street and Goodge Street. During the case recounted in "The Final Problem," Holmes climbed over the garden wall of Watson's house into Mortimer Street to escape possible surveillance by agents of Moriarty. Watson, however, wrote of practices in Paddington ("The Engineer's Thumb," "The Stockbroker's Clerk") and Kensington ("The Empty House," "The Norwood Builder," "The Red-Headed League"), neither of which were anywhere near Mortimer Street. (See also under WATSON, JOHN H.)

MORTON. A member of the Oxford rugby team who was described by Cyril Overton, captain of the Cambridge team, as one of the two "Oxford fliers" who "could romp round" Moorhouse, the substitute for the missing three-quarter Godfrey Staunton in "The Missing Three-Quarter." Morton was also the name of an inspector from Scotland Yard who was in charge of the investigation into the death of Victor Savage in "The Dying Detective." An old acquaintance of Holmes, he assisted the detective in capturing Savage's murderer.

MORTON, CYRIL. The fiancé of Violet Hunter who was employed by the Midland Electrical Company, at Coventry in "The Solitary Cyclist." He eventually married Hunter and became the senior partner of Morton & Kennedy, the famous Westminster electricians.

MOSER. The well-known manager of the Hotel National in Lausanne in "The Disappearance of

Lady Frances Carfax." Dr. Watson journeyed to Lausanne in search of the missing Lady Carfax and "received every courtesy at the hands of M. Moser," learning from him information that the doctor considered useful: "Lady Carfax, as he informed me, had stayed there for several weeks. She had been much liked by all who met her. Her age was not more than forty. She was still handsome and bore every sign of having in her youth been a very lovely woman. M. Moser knew nothing of any valuable jewellery, but it had been remarked by the staff that the heavy trunk in the lady's bedroom was always scrupulously locked."

MOULTON, FRANCIS HAY.   An American gold prospector who met and married Hatty Doran in "The Noble Bachelor." Moulton first came to know Doran in 1884, in McQuire's Camp, near the Rockies where Aloysius Doran, her father, was working a claim. They were soon engaged, but her father struck a rich pocket while Moulton's claim petered out, and her father came to oppose their union. The couple remained in love, however, and Moulton followed the Dorans to San Francisco. There, they were secretly married and Moulton set out to make his fortune. Doran heard that her husband was in Montana, and then Arizona, and finally New Mexico: "After that came a long newspaper story about how a miner's camp had been attacked by Apache Indians and there was my Frank's name among the killed. I fainted dead away and I was very sick for months after." Her assumption that Moulton was dead allowed her to accept Lord St. Simon's request of marriage.

MOUNT-JAMES, LORD.   The uncle of Godfrey Staunton, The Missing Three-Quarter of the Cambridge rugby team. Mount-James was one of the richest men in England and a miser. He at first would have nothing to do with Holmes, but repented and was more cooperative when the detective posed the theory that Staunton may have been abducted with the aim of acquiring his vast fortune. Mount-James then instructed Holmes: "I beg you to leave no stone unturned to bring him safely back. As to money, well, so far as a fiver or even a tenner goes you can always look to me." Watson described him as "a queer little old man, jerking and twitching in the doorway. He was dressed in rusty black, with a broad-rimmed hat and a loose white necktie—the whole effect being that of a very rustic person or of an undertaker's mule. Yet,

in spite of his shabby and even absurd appearance, his voice had a sharp crackle, and his manners a quick intensity which commanded attention."

MOUNTS BAY.   A bay situated on the southern coast of Cornwall near the cottage taken by Holmes and Watson for their vacation in 1897 in "The Devil's Foot." Watson wrote of the scenery: "From the windows of our little whitewashed house, which stood high upon a grassy headland, we looked down upon the whole sinister semicircle of Mounts Bay, that old death-trap of sailing vessels, with its fringe of black cliffs and surge-swept reefs on which innumerable seamen have met their end. With a northerly breeze it lies placid and sheltered, inviting the storm-tossed craft to tack into it for rest and protection.

"Then come the sudden swirls round of the wind, the blistering gale from the south-west, the dragging anchor, the lee shore, and the last battle in the creaming breakers. The wise mariner stands far out from that evil place."

MULLER.   A criminal who escaped justice because there was, at the time, no reliable test for bloodstains (A Study in Scarlet). Holmes was thus jubilant over his discovery of a test that was infallible.

MUNICH.   The Bavarian city where Holmes said there occured a case in 1871 that paralleled the one brought to him by Lord Robert St. Simon in "The Noble Bachelor."

MUNRO, EFFIE.   Wife of GRANT ("Jack") MUNRO, whose strange behavior prompted her husband to consult Holmes in "The Yellow Face." According to Grant Munro's account, Effie "went out to America when she was young and lived in the town of Atlanta, where she married this Hebron, who was a lawyer with a good practice. They had one child, but the yellow fever broke out badly in the place, and both husband and child died of it. I have seen his death certificate. This sickened her of America, and she came back to live with a maiden aunt at Pinner, in Middlesex. I may mention that her husband had left her comfortably off, and that she had a capital of about four thousand five hundred pounds, which had been so well invested by him that it returned an average of seven percent. She had been six months at Pinner when I met her; we fell in love with each other, and we married a few weeks later."

MUNRO, GRANT.   A hop merchant who resided in an 80-pound-a-year villa in Norbury with his wife, Effie, in "The Yellow Face." He consulted Holmes about the strange behavior of his wife, EFFIE MUNRO, but assured the detective that Effie loved him "with her whole heart and soul, never more than now." Munro "was well but quietly dressed in a dark gray suit and carried a brown wideawake [a type of felt hat] in his hand. I [Watson] should have put him at about thirty, though he was really some years older." He was also called "Jack" Munro.

MURCHER, HENRY.   A police constable with the Holland Grove beat in *A Study in Scarlet*.

On the night of the murder of Enoch J. Drebber, Murcher met Constable John Rance at the corner of Henrietta Street and was later summoned to the scene of the crime at Lauriston Gardens, just off the Brixton Road.

MURDER BY DECREE.   England-Canada 1979. Dir: Bob Clark. Cast: Christopher Plummer (Holmes), James Mason (Watson), Frank Finlay (Lestrade), Betty Woolfe (Mrs. Hudson). One of the finest of all Holmes films, featuring the detective pursuing Jack the Ripper. Based on *The Ripper File* by John Lloyd and Elwyn Jones, with a screenplay by John Hopkins, *Murder By Decree* is a complex thriller that goes beyond the Ripper legend into high political speculation that the gruesome murders in Whitechapel were conducted by a group of Freemasons anxious to end a political

Holmes (Christopher Plummer), Watson (James Mason), and Lestrade (Frank Finlay) look upon the terrible remains of a victim of Jack the Ripper in *Murder by Decree* (1979).

scandal involving the duke of Clarence—historically considered a possible suspect as the Ripper. Holmes, of course, uncovers the entire plot, his solution plunging into the very corrupt heart of the British government. This is all very interesting, but the true delight of the film is the chemistry between Plummer and Mason. Their scenes together in Baker Street capture succinctly the give and take of the original relationship. Mason plays Watson as a competent and complete personality, while Plummer's Holmes is very much the deductive machine of the Canon, with a helpful injection of passion and compassion. The overall production is excellent, with nice photography in the East End scenes—presented in a kind of maze of alleys and seedy streets, the perfect place for the Ripper's predations. A particularly memorable scene involves Holmes ruthlessly squashing a pea to the consternation of the good doctor. (See also *STUDY IN TERROR, A.*)

MURDER WILL OUT. U.S. 1930. Cast: Clive Brook (Holmes), William Powell (Philo Vance), and Warner Oland (Dr. Fu Manchu). Also known under the title *A Travesty of Detective Mysteries*, this was actually a sequence in the revue film *Paramount on Parade*, featuring such stars as Jean Arthur, Gary Cooper, Frederic March, and Fay Wray. The segment featured Holmes and Watson (H. Reeves-Smith), along with Philo Vance in pursuit of FU MANCHU. Interestingly, this is the only film in which the Great Detective dies on screen.

MURDOCH, IAN. A mathematics coach (tutor) at Harold Stackhurst's coaching establishment, The Gables, in "The Lion's Mane." Known for his terrible temper, Murdoch was a suspect in the grisly death of Fitzroy McPherson, his behavior doing nothing to exonerate him. Holmes wrote that he was "a tall, dark man, so taciturn and aloof that none can be said to have been his friend. He seemed to live in some high, abstract region of surds and conic sections, with little to connect him to ordinary life. He was looked upon as an oddity by the students, and would have been their butt, but there was some strange outlandish blood in the man, which showed itself not only in his coal-black eyes but also in occasional outbreaks of temper, which could only be described as ferocious. On one occasion, being plagued by a little dog owned by Mr. McPherson, he had caught the creature and hurled it through a plate-glass window. . . ."

William Powell, star of the 1930s and 1940s, who appeared as detective Philo Vance in *Murder Will Out*, part of *Paramount on Parade*.

MURGER, HENRI. French writer (1822–1861), author of *Vie de Boheme* (1848). While Watson was waiting for Holmes to return to 221B from his search for the mysterious Mrs. Sawyer in *A Study in Scarlet*, he skipped through the pages of Murger's work.

MURILLO, DON JUAN. The so-called Tiger of San Pedro, the cruel and bloodthirsty president of San Pedro who was ultimately overthrown and forced to flee to Europe. Searched for by his enemies, Murillo was cornered in England in the case chronicled under the title "Adventure of Wisteria Lodge," but he escaped once more. He was assassinated in the Hotel Escurial in Madrid.

MURPHY. The supposed acquaintance of John McMurdo in Chicago in *The Valley of Fear*. McMurdo told Jack Shafter that Murphy had given him the address of Jack Shafter's boardinghouse in Vermissa Valley. In *The Hound of the Baskervilles*, Murphy was the gipsy horse dealer on Dartmoor who claimed to be on the moor the night Sir

Charles Baskerville died. Although he had been drinking, Murphy heard the cries of Sir Charles, but was unable to distinguish their direction.

MURPHY, MAJOR.   An officer of the Royal Mallows (Royal Munsters) at Aldershot who served under Colonel James Barclay and who called in Holmes to investigate the mysterious death of the colonel in "The Crooked Man." Murphy was the principal informant of Holmes in the case.

MURRAY.   Dr. Watson's orderly during the Afghan War (*A Study in Scarlet*). When Watson was wounded at the Battle of Maiwand (1880), he would have fallen into the hands of the Afghans had Murray not saved him by throwing him across a packhorse and bringing him to safety behind the British lines. Murray is also the name of a member of the Bagatelle Card Club who played whist with Ronald Adair, Sir John Hardy, and Colonel Sebastian Moran on the afternoon of the day that Adair was brutally and mysteriously murdered in "The Empty House."

MUSGRAVE, SIR RALPH.   A member of the cadet branch of the Musgraves which was established at Hurlstone in western Sussex in "The Musgrave Ritual." Sir Ralph was said to be a prominent cavalier and close companion of Charles II in his wanderings.

MUSGRAVE, REGINALD.   A descendent of Sir Ralph Musgrave and an acquaintance of Holmes from his college days who hired the detective to investigate the disappearance of the butler and the second housemaid at Hurlstone, the Musgrave family estate in "The Musgrave Ritual." Holmes's involvement led not only to the finding of Brunton the butler but the unraveling of the Musgrave Ritual and the discovery of a long lost family heirloom. The detective observed: "In appearance he was a man of an exceedingly aristocratic type, thin, high nosed, and large eyed, with languid and yet courtly manners. He was indeed a scion of one of the very oldest families in the kingdom . . . I never looked at his pale, keen face or the poise of his head without associating him with gray archways and mullioned windows and all the venerable wreckage of a feudal keep."

MUSGRAVE RITUAL.   This peculiar catechism was memorized by each Musgrave as he en-

tered the man's house in "The Musgrave Ritual." It had its origins in the middle of the seventeenth century based on the spelling found in the original document, dating probably to the time of Sir Ralph Musgrave, the cavalier and close companion to Charles II in his wanderings. The meaning of the ritual was lost over time, and Reginald Musgrave described it as "rather an absurd business, this ritual of ours . . . But it has at least the saving grace of antiquity to excuse it." The butler Richard Brunton and Holmes were both able to solve the mystery of the ritual, and its significance. The 1943 film *Sherlock Holmes Faces Death*, starring Basil Rathbone and Nigel Bruce as Holmes and Watson, was loosely based on the Musgrave Ritual, replete with a Musgrave and the scheming butler Richard Brunton (Halliwell Hobbes).

The Musgrave Ritual

Whose Was It?

His who is gone.

Who shall have it?

He who will come.
Where was the sun?
Over the oak.
Where was the shadow?
Under the elm.
How was it stepped?
North by ten and by ten, east by
five and by five, south by two and
by two, west by one and by one, and
    so under.
What shall we give for it?
All that is ours.
Why should we give it?
For the sake of the trust.

—"The Musgrave Ritual."

"MUSGRAVE RITUAL, THE" (MUSG).
Published: *Strand*, May 1893, *Harper's*, May 13, 1893; collected in *The Memoirs of Sherlock Holmes*. Case date: ca. October 1879. Major players: Holmes, Reginald Musgrave, Brunton, Rachel Howells, Janet Tregellis. The third case of Holmes's professional career (or possibly the third case brought to him by a former classmate, depending

upon the interpretation of the statement). The case is recounted by Holmes to Watson after the pair open a large tin box containing records of Holmes's early work; including such unchronicled cases as the Tarleton murders, the case of Vamberry, the wine merchant, and the old Russian woman, among others. "The Musgrave Ritual" refers to an arcane ritual recited by members of the Musgrave family. Reginald Musgrave of Hurlstone Manor involves Holmes in the affair. Brunton, the family butler, has disappeared, vanishing so completely that the police can find no trace of him. The young detective soon learns that Brunton and the Musgrave Ritual are somehow connected. The retained relics of the case are a crumpled piece of paper, an old-fashioned brass key, a peg of wood with a ball of string attached to it, and three rusty old discs of metal. Years later, in "The Yellow Face," Watson

wrote of the affair as one of those cases in which the truth came to light even though Holmes had erred. This statement is not borne out by the details of the investigation. In some editions of "The Yellow Face," this reference is not to the Musgrave Ritual but to the "second stain." The date of the case is somewhat in dispute as it took place during a time period while Holmes resided in Montague Street (1878–1881), about which little is known.

MYRTLES, THE.   A residence in Backenham that was rented by Harold Latimer in "The Greek Interpreter." At the time of the brief abduction and frightening employment of Mr. Melas, Sophy Kratides was staying at the Myrtles. J. Davenport, a friend of hers, supplied her address in response to a newspaper advertisement placed by Mycroft Holmes.

NAPLES.   An Italian seaport from where Pietro Venucci hailed in "The Six Napoleons." Emilio and Gennaro Lucca came from Posilippo, near Naples, in "The Red Circle."

NAPOLEON.   The French general and emperor who was the model for the six plaster casts based on the head of Napoleon by Devine that were being smashed by an unknown assailant and that became the focus of Holmes's investigation in "The Six Napoleons." The genius of the emperor was the inspiration for Holmes's declaration that Moriarty was the Napoleon of Crime ("The Final Problem," *The Valley of Fear*).

NAPOLEON OF CRIME.   The name used by Holmes to describe the talents and ambitions of

PROFESSOR MORIARTY in "The Final Problem" and "The Naval Treaty."

NARBONNE.   A French city from where Watson received a note from Holmes while the detective was engaged in an investigation on behalf of the French government ("The Final Problem").

"NAVAL TREATY, THE" (NAVA).   Published: *Strand*, October and November 1893, *Harper's*, October 14 and 21, 1893; collected in *The Memoirs of Sherlock Holmes* (1894). Major players: Holmes, Watson, Percy Phelps, Annie Harrison, Joseph Harrison, Forbes, Mrs. Tangey. Case date: Baring-Gould 1889. A long chronicle in the Canon, originally published in two editions both in America and England that fully justifies the audience's patience. An old schoolmate of Watson's, Percy Phelps (who, while at school, was the object of cruelties by schoolmates because of his relation to the powerful Lord Holdhurst) asked the doctor to intercede for him with Sherlock Holmes. A member of the Foreign Office, Phelps had stolen from his desk a naval treaty that he was copying. The theft could have the most grievous consequences internationally, but, strangely, after two months it had not surfaced anywhere. Meanwhile, Phelps, always a sensitive person, suffered a complete collapse, recovering through the ministrations of his impressive fiancée Annie Harrison. Taking the case, Holmes later declared that it was "certainly one of the darkest which I have ever investigated." He managed to return the document, however, with considerable panache. Of the thief, Holmes declared that he "is a gentleman to whose mercy I should be extremely unwilling to trust." Watson mentioned "The Naval Treaty" in "The Final Problem," writing that his work "had the unquestionable effect of preventing a serious international complication." "The Naval Treaty" was also intended originally to be the last of Watson's accounts of the detective before the events forced him to write "The Final Problem."

NEALE.   In full, Neale, Outfitter, Vermissa, U.S.A., a clothing outfitter in Vermissa (*The Valley of Fear*). An overcoat fished out of the moat surrounding the manor house of Birlstone had the name Neale on the tailor's tab on the neck.

NED, UNCLE.   The uncle of Mary Sutherland in "A Case of Identity." He left her 2,500 pounds in New Zealand stock, paying 4½ percent.

NEGRO, THE.   A racehorse owned by Mr. Heath Newton that ran in the Wessex Cup but lost to Silver Blaze in "Silver Blaze."

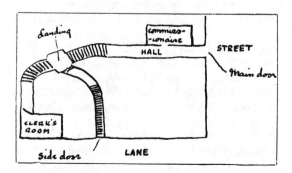

NELIGAN.   A banker of the firm of Dawson & Neligan in Cornwall who disappeared following the failure of the bank. His son, John Hopley Neligan, labored to clear his father's name, and Holmes's investigation into the murder of Captain Peter Carey uncovered what had become of the missing Neligan in "Black Peter." Young Neligan used some securities that his father had supposedly stolen to track down Captain Peter Carey. The captain, called Black Peter, was soon murdered, and Neligan was arrested for the crime by Inspector Stanley Hopkins.

NETHERLANDS, THE.   The European country whose ruling family Holmes aided by accomplishing a mission of such delicacy that he was unable to discuss the details with anyone, including Watson ("A Case of Identity"). Other Canonical references to the Netherlands include the *Friesland*, a Dutch vessel ("The Norwood Builder"); the lepers whom Godfrey Emsworth encountered in South Africa and who spoke Dutch in "The Blanched Soldier"; Altamont, the agent of Von Bork, who declared that he was intending to escape from England to the Netherlands in "His Last Bow"; and Count Sylvius and Sam Merton, who planned to flee to the Netherlands, following Syvlius's courier, Van Sedddar ("The Mazarin Stone").

NETHERLANDS-SUMATRA   COMPANY.
A firm apparently involved in the schemes of Baron Maupertuis ("The Reigate Squires"). The details of the case were not recorded by Watson because "the whole question of the Netherlands-Sumatra Company and the colossal schemes of Baron Maupertuis is too recent in the minds of the public, and too intimately concerned with politics and finances, to be a fitting subject for this series of sketches."

NETLEY HOSPITAL.   A hospital in the Hampshire village of Netley that was the primary medical institution serving the military in Great Britain. In *A Study in Scarlet*, following his receiving a degree as doctor of medicine from the University of London in 1878, Watson "proceeded to Netley to go through the course prescribed for surgeons in the Army."

NEUSS, ALWIN.   The actor was an early success as Holmes in both the Danish Nordisk series (1908–1911) and the German Vitascope series based on *The Hound of the Baskervilles* (1914–1920). As with the Nordisk series in general, there is some uncertaintly related to Neuss's work in Denmark. He probably played Watson in the early productions with Viggo Larsen, Holger Rasmussen, and Otto Lagoni, but this is not absolutely confirmed. It is also unclear in which films he portrayed the Great Detective, for the director/actor Forrest Holger-Madsen also played Holmes and was the director in Neuss's apparent Holmesian outings. If he did play Watson, Neuss was the doctor in *Sherlock Holmes I* (1908); *Sherlock II* (1908); *Sherlock Holmes I Gaskjeldfren* (*Sherlock Holmes in the Gas Cellar*, 1908); *Sangerindens Diamanter* (*The Singer's Diamond*, 1909); *Droske No. 519* (*Cab No. 519*, 1909); *Den Graa Dame* (*The Grey Lady*, 1909); *La Femme* (*The Woman*, 1910); *Sherlock Holmes I Bondefangerklor* (*Sherlock Holmes in the Claws of the Confidence Men*, 1910); *Den Forklaedte Guvernante* (*The Bogus Government*, 1911); *Mordet I Bakerstreet* (*Murder in Baker Street*, 1911); and, possibly, *The Adventures of Sherlock Holmes* (1908). For Nordisk he was probably Holmes in *Millionobligationen* (*The One Million Bond*, 1911) and possibly *Hotelmysterierne* (*The Hotel Mystery*, 1911). For Vitascope, Neuss played Holmes in *Der Hund von Baskerville*, a series of films; he was the detective in the first four installments: *Der Hund von Baskerville* (1914), *Das Einsame Haus* (*The Isolated House*, 1914), *Das Unheimliche Zimmer* (*The Uncanny Room*, 1915), and *Wie Enstand der Hund von Baskerville* (*How the Hound of the Baskervilles Arose*, 1915). Neuss left the Baskerville series to star in and direct the Holmes film *Ein Schrei in der Nacht* (*A Scream in the Night*, 1915).

"NEW ADVENTURES OF SHERLOCK HOLMES, THE."
U.S. 1954–1955. Dir: Sheldon Reynolds. Cast: Ronald Howard (Holmes), H. Marion Crawford (Watson), and Archie Duncan (Lestrade). An American television series filmed in France, created by Sheldon Reynolds who would produce the 1982 Holmes series with Godfrey Whitehead and Donald Pickering. Produced by Guild Films, the series was, with one exception, comprised of thirty-nine original stories; the one segment drawn from the Canon was based on "The Red-Headed League." Ronald Howard was considered too young to be a memorable Holmes, and the son of the star Leslie Howard was frequently overshadowed by his Watson. The first episode was "The Case of the Cunningham Heritage," which

offered a version of how the dynamic duo first met. Crawford's Watson was written and performed with the specific intention of reversing the buffoonery long on display with Nigel Bruce's many Watsonian incarnations.

NEW ADVENTURES OF SHERLOCK HOLMES, THE.
A 1987 collection of new Holmes stories, edited by Martin Harry Greenberg and Carol-Lynn Rossel Waugh, and featuring the fresh efforts of such Eminent Mystery Writers as John Gardner, Stephen King, Loren D. Estelman, and Michael Harrison. The stories include "The Infernal Machine" by John Lutz; "The Return of the Speckled Band" by Edward D. Hoch; "Sherlock Holmes and 'The Woman'" by Michael Harrison; "Dr. and Mrs. Watson at Home" by Loren D. Estelman; "The Adventure of the Persistent Marksman" by Lillian de la Torre; and "The Doctor's Case" by Stephen King.

NEW BRIGHTON.
A town in Cheshire to which James Browner followed his wife, Mary, and her lover in "The Cardbord Box."

NEW FOREST.
A once forested region in Hampshire that Watson wished to visit. He wrote at the start of "The Cardboard Box": "I yearned for the glades of the New Forest or the shingle of Southsea. A depleted bank account had caused me to postpone my holiday, and as to my companion, neither the country nor the sea presented the slightest attraction to him." This wish was included in some editions of "The Resident Patient."

NEWHAVEN.
A port in Sussex from where Holmes and Watson left England, rather than at Dover, to go across the Channel to Dieppe in "The Final Problem." They travelled overland after leaving the Continental Express at Canterbury.

NEWSPAPERS.
Holmes routinely read newspapers for information on the criminal goings-on in London and consulted them for their agony columns of which the detective had the opinion: "What a chorus of groans, cries, and bleatings! What a ragbag of singular happenings! But surely the most valuable hunting-ground that ever was given to a student of the unusual." A number of newspapers were mentioned in the Canon. Watson read the *Daily Chronicle,* a London morning paper, for an account of the delivery of the horrific

cardboard box to Susan Cushing in "The Cardboard Box." It also covered the disappearance of the horse Silver Blaze in "Silver Blaze." Mary Sutherland placed an advertisement in the paper in the hopes of finding her fiancé Hosmer Angel in "A Case of Identity." The **Daily Gazette,** a London paper, was read by Holmes for its agony column; he used it to solve the mystery of Mrs. Warren's strange lodger in "The Red Circle." The **Daily Herald** was the newspaper edited by James Stanger in Vermissa Valley that opposed the Scowrers in *The Valley of Fear.* The **Daily News** was a London morning newspaper in which Mycroft Holmes advertised for Paul and Sophy Kratides in "The Greek Interpreter." In *A Study in Scarlet,* an editorial in the publication called the murder of Enoch Drebber a political crime. The **Daily Telegraph** of London was one of Holmes's major sources for details on crime and strange events in the city and country. The paper carried an editorial on the murder of Enoch Drebber, declaring that all the evidence pointed to the work of political refugees and revolutionists and that in the history of crime there had seldom been a tragedy which presented stranger features. Holmes read the *Telegraph* for details about the "murder" of Jonas Oldacre in "The Norwood Builder" and the murder of Eduardo Lucas, in a story filed in Paris, in "The Second Stain." The foreign agent Hugo Oberstein communicated with the thief of "The Bruce-Partington Plans" through the *Telegraph's* agony column. Holmes advertised in the two London papers **Evening Standard** and **Evening News** in the hopes of locating Henry Baker, owner of a hat and a remarkable goose in "The Blue Carbuncle." He also advertised in the **Pall Mall Gazette,** the **St. James Gazette,** and the **Globe.** Watson read the *Evening Standard* about the London robbery of Mawson & Williams in "The Stockbroker's Clerk." The *Globe* reported the rumor that Lord Saltire, the son of the duke of Holdernesse, had been abducted in "The Priory School," despite the best efforts of Thorneycroft Huxtable (head of the Priory School where the young lord was a student) to keep the news away from the press. As noted, Holmes advertised in the paper for Henry Baker. The **Journal de Geneve,** a leading newspaper in Geneva, Switzerland, published in French an account of the death of Professor Moriarty in "The Final Problem." The London daily, **Morning Chronicle,** carried an advertisement for a vacancy in "The Red-Headed League" on April 27, 1890. Curiously, the paper

had gone bankrupt in 1862, another problem with Watson's apparently error-filled account of the case. The oldest London paper, the **Morning Post,** announced the impending marriage of Lord Robert St. Simon and Hatty Doran in "The Noble Bachelor," and the cancellations of the marriages between Baron Gruner and Violet de Merville in "The Illustrious Client," and between Colonel Dorking and the Honorable Miss Miles in "Charles Agustus Milverton." The major London daily paper, **The Times,** was read by Holmes for information in "The Engineer's Thumb," "The Blue Carbuncle," *The Sign of Four*, and "The Missing Three-Quarter." The paper was used to advertise for Mary Morstan by the Sholtos in *The Sign of Four,* and Violet Smith by Jack Woodley and Bob Carruthers in "The Solitary Cyclist." The note of warning sent to Henry Baskerville at the Northumberland Hotel was put together with clippings from the newspaper in *The Hound of the Baskervilles.* The **Pink 'Un** was the name popularly used for the **Sporting Times,** a weekly paper for racing. In "The Blue Carbuncle," Holmes was able to learn everything he wanted to know from John Breckinridge by making his inquiries appear to be part of a bet. He told Watson afterward, "When you see a man with whiskers of that cut and the Pink 'Un protruding from out of his pocket, you can always draw him with a bet . . . I daresay that if I had put a £100 in front of him, that man would not have given me such complete information as was drawn from him by the idea that he was doing me in a bet."

NEW STREET. A street in Wallington where Sarah Cushing resided in "The Cardboard Box."

NEW YORK. Holmes had possibly visited New York prior to his embarking on his illustrious career, and accounts of his visit have been published in *The Adventure of the Stalwart Companions; Sherlock Holmes, My Life and Crimes;* and the biography of Holmes by W. S. Baring-Gould, *Sherlock Holmes of Baker Street.* The city also plays a role in numerous adventures. Holmes knew Wilson Hargreave of the New York Police Bureau and used some information sent by him to clear up the details of the Dancing Men affair. Enoch Drebber and Joseph Stangerson planned to sail to New York, but they were killed before leaving London in *A Study in Scarlet.* The Randalls, suspected of killing Sir Eustace Brackenstall, had an airtight alibi—they were arrested in New York on the day after the murder in "The Abbey Grange." It was thought that Mlle. Carere, believed dead, was actually alive and married in New York (*The Hound of the Baskervilles*). Archie Swindon fled to New York from the terror of the Scowrers in *The Valley of Fear*. The Luccas settled in Brooklyn, but were forced to flee America because of The Red Circle. Holmes was seen in the city in the Roger Moore (as Holmes) film project *Sherlock Holmes in New York*.

NEW ZEALAND. The island in the South Pacific where Mary Sutherland's Uncle Ned lived; he appeared in "A Case of Identity," living in the city of Auckland. Holmes stunned Trevor Senior by deducing that he had once been in New Zealand in "The 'Gloria Scott'."

NIGHT GLASS. A type of telescope that had been adapted for use at night. Holmes used a night glass to help in the tracking and capturing of the *Aurora* and Jonathan Small in *The Sign of Four*.

NIHILISM. A type of revolutionary philosophy that became popular with the intelligentsia of Russia in the 1860s. In "The Golden Pince-Nez," Professor Coram, known at the time as Sergius, was involved with his wife in the Nihilist Movement in Russia. The revolutionaries were said by Morse Hudson in "The Six Napoleons" to be responsible for the smashing of his Napoleonic busts, declaring it to be "A Nihilist plot—that's what I make it. No one but an anarchist would go about breaking statues. Red republicans—that's what I call 'em." The murders of Don Murillo and his secretary in Madrid in "Wisteria Lodge" were ascribed to Nihilists.

NIMOY, LEONARD. The American actor known around the world as Mr. Spock from the classic "Star Trek" television series and films has also played Sherlock Holmes several times on stage and television. His first outing came in the early 1970s, when he appeared in the short film "The Hidden Motive," for Kentucky Educational Television, in which he attempts to deduce the contents of a globe without opening it. He later devoted an episode of the speculative series "In Search of . . ." to seeking out Sherlock. He clearly found him in 1975–1976 when he donned the cap and deerstalker for the William Gillette play *Sherlock Holmes* with performances in Detroit, Los Angeles, and Chicago. His work as Holmes was perfectly

logical given his years as the emotionless Vulcan, Spock; and certain Holmesian references appeared in the *Star Trek* films such as in *Star Trek VI* (1991) when Spock declares Holmes to be an ancestor.

"NOBLE BACHELOR, THE ADVENTURE OF THE" (NOBL). Published: *Strand*, April 1892; collected in *The Adventures of Sherlock Holmes* (1892). Case date: October 1886 to 1888. Major players: Holmes, Watson, Lord Robert St. Simon, Hatty Doran, Flora Millar, and Francis Hay Moulton. One of the many cases investigated by Holmes (both chronicled and unchronicled) in which his assistance is enlisted by a member of the nobility. Lord Robert St. Simon comes to the detective to ask his help in finding his wife, the onetime Hatty Doran, who had disappeared shortly after their wedding. Doran was subsequently seen in Hyde Park with Flora Millar, a former dancer who had once been involved with St. Simon. Inspector Lestrade of course arrests Millar on suspicion of murder, but the arrest does nothing to

The wedding of Hatty Doran and Lord St. Simon in "The Noble Bachelor"; by Sidney Paget.

locate the missing woman. Watson's account includes a mention of his infamous wound from the Jezail bullet "which I had brought back in one of my limbs as a relic of my Afghan campaign . . ."

NONCONFORMIST.   A term used to refer to someone who is not a member of the Church of England. One of Holmes's disguises, that of a Nonconformist clergyman, was used to fool Irene Adler and gain entry into Briony Lodge in "A Scandal in Bohemia."

NONPAREIL CLUB.   A club that became involved in a card scandal. Holmes's investigation into the affair led to his exposing of "the atrocious conduct of Colonel Upwood." A full explanation of *The Hound of the Baskervilles* had to wait until Holmes completed two cases of "the utmost importance." One of them was the Nonpareil Club. The details of the case were presented in "The Adventure of the Abbas Ruby" by Adrian Conan Doyle and John Dickson Carr in the collection *The Exploits of Sherlock Holmes* (1954).

NORBERTON, SIR ROBERT.   A famous but penniless nobleman who resided at Shoscombe Old Place with his sister Lady Beatrice Falder on whom he relied for money in "Shoscombe Old Place." Considered an eccentric, he raced horses and once nearly horsewhipped to death Sam Brewery, a Curzon Street moneylender, on Newmarket Street. Watson, always a betting man, was well informed about Sir Robert: "Well, he has the name of being a dangerous man. He is about the most daredevil rider in England—second in the Grand National a few years back. He is one of those men who have overshot their true generation. He should have been in the days of the Regency—a boxer, an athlete, a plunger on the turf, a lover of fair ladies, and, by all accounts, so far down Queer Street that he may never find his way back again." Norberton's increasingly odd behavior prompted his trainer, John Mason, to consult Holmes. Norberton "was a terrible figure, huge in stature and fierce in manner. A large stable-lantern which he held in front of him shown upward upon a strong, heavily moustached face and angry eyes" [that glared round him into every recess of the vault].

NORBURY.   A suburb of London where Holmes investigated the case of "The Yellow Face." Grant Munro, the detective's client, owned an

eighty-pound-a-year villa there. As Holmes considered the investigation a complete failure, he told Watson "if it should strike you that I am getting a little over-confident in my powers, or giving less pains to a case than it deserves, kindly whisper 'Norbury' in my ear, and I shall be infinitely obliged to you."

NORFOLK.   A county in eastern England where Trevor Senior in "The 'Gloria Scott' " and Hilton Cubitt in "The Dancing Men" were squires.

NORLETT, CARRIE.   In "Shoscombe Old Place," she worked as a maid to Lady Beatrice Falder under the name Carrie Evans. Her husband, Norlett, was an actor. He was hired by Norberton to give a secret and peculiar performance. Norlett was described as "a small rat-faced man with a disagreeably furtive manner."

NORMAN-NERUDA, WILHELMINE.   A well-known violinist from Austria (1834–1911), born Wilhelmine Neruda. She wed the Swedish musician Ludwig Norman in 1864. Holmes speeded up his investigation into the death of Enoch Drebber in *A Study in Scarlet* in order to hear Norman-Neruda at Halles in the afternoon. He said: "Her attack and her bowing are splendid. What's that little thing of Chopin's she plays so magnificently: Tra-la-la-lira-lira-lay."

NORTHUMBERLAND AVENUE.   A Westminster avenue where Holmes and Watson enjoyed a Turkish bath at the start of "The Illustrious Client." Francis Hay Moulton lived for a time on Northumberland Avenue in "The Illustrious Client," while Mr. Melas worked as an interpreter for wealthy London visitors staying in hotels on the street in "The Greek Interpreter."

NORTON, GODFREY.   A London lawyer, a resident of the Inner Temple, and a close friend of Irene Adler in "A Scandal in Bohemia." "A remarkably handsome man, dark, aqualine, and moustached," Norton eventually married Adler at the Church of St. Monica in the Edgeware Road. Holmes, disguised as an unemployed groom, acted as witness at the wedding.

NORWAY.   The Scandinavian country figures in "Black Peter," as the banker Neligan, of the failed West Counties bank Dawson & Neligan, set off in a private yacht for Norway, taking a number of securities with him in the hopes of investing them. He was subsequently lost at sea, although the true facts were uncovered during Holmes's investigation into the murder of Captain Peter Carey. Holmes and Watson journeyed to Norway to follow up the case. During the Great Hiatus (1891–1894), when it was widely believed that Holmes had been killed at the Reichenbach Falls, the detective was actually travelling around Tibet under the name Sigerson. Watson had heard of the "Norwegian explorer" but had no way of knowing that it was really his old friend until told so by Holmes in "The Empty House."

NORWOOD. A district stretching from Surrey to Lambeth and divided into three areas of South, Lower, and Upper Norwood. Holmes investigated the apparent murder of Jonas Oldacre in "The Norwood Builder" in Lower Norwood. The detective's involvement in the Sholto affair, chronicled in *The Sign of Four*, took him to Pondicherry Lodge, home of the Sholtos in Upper Norwood. Interestingly, Athelney Jones was at the Norwood police station at the time of the first alarm concerning the tragic events at Pondicherry Lodge.

"NORWOOD BUILDER, THE ADVEN-TURE OF THE" (NORW). Published: *Collier's*, October 1903, *Strand*, November 1903; collected in *The Return of Sherlock Holmes* (1905). Major players: Holmes, Watson, John Hector McFarlane, Inspector Lestrade, Jonas Oldacre, and Mrs. Lexington. Case date: 1894, possibly 1895, a short time after the return of Holmes from the Great Hiatus. A case brought to Holmes by the leading suspect, "the unhappy John Hector McFarlane," in the apparent murder of Jonas Oldacre of Norwood. While telling his story to Holmes and Watson, Inspector Lestrade arrives to arrest McFarlane. The evidence against him is considerable. Oldacre had come to the young solicitor to have his will written up, a testament leaving everything to McFarlane. Following this, McFarlane supposedly murdered Oldacre and burned his body in a fire of timber. Evidence found at the scene included a set of trouser buttons belonging to Oldacre, some organic remains, and a bloodstained stick of McFarlane's. Holmes's subsequent investigation is further complicated by the later discovery of McFarlane's bloody thumb print upon a wall. Fortunately for McFarlane,

however, Holmes does not give up so easily. The case is solved with the help of wet straw, a bucket of water, and several constables with good loud voices.

NORWOOD DISAPPEARANCE CASE. The name used by Holmes for the case that he investigated in "The Norwood Builder." His precise choice of words was proven correct at the conclusion of the affair.

NORWOOD, EILLE. English actor (1861–1948), unfortunately little known today, who was, nevertheless, one of the foremost of all Holmeses, appearing forty-seven times in three film series for Stoll Pictures (1921–1923). Norwood did not begin playing Holmes until he was sixty years old, but his remarkable performances soon won him a wide public following, including the admiration of none other than Sir Arthur Conan Doyle, who once said that Norwood "has that rare quality that can only be described as glamour, which compels you to watch an actor even when he is doing nothing. His wonderful impersonation of Holmes has amazed me." Aside from his careful study of Holmes as he was originally written, Norwood also perfected the use of the detective's diguises, astounding audiences with a dizzying array of faces and body shapes, from an old woman to a Chinese lascar, complete with moustache and slick black hair. Regrettably, very few of the Stoll pictures of Holmes have survived so the skill of Norwood's interpretation can be assessed from the few productions that are extant and the stills of others. Effort has been made over the last years by the Baker Street Cinematograph, of the *Baker Street Irregulars*, to save surviving Norwood reels in the possession of the British Film Institute. In 1923, Norwood starred on stage in *The Return of Sherlock Holmes*, written by his nephew, and produced by Norwood himself with Conan Doyle's approval. His principal screen Watson was the character actor Hubert Willis who joined him in forty-six of the films. The one exception was *The Sign of the Four* (1923), when he was replaced by Arthur Cullin.

NOTEBOOK. Holmes (and Watson) were in the habit of jotting down many details about the cases in which they were involved in a series of notebooks. The detective had complete information on the nefarious activities of Count Sylvius in

"The Mazarin Stone," maintained in a fat note-book. He also used his notebook to hold a record of the Emsworth affair in "The Blanched Soldier"; some notes from the Priory School kidnapping in "The Priory School"; a quotation from Ecker-mann's *Voodooism and the Negroid Religions* in "Wisteria Lodge"; and the bill from Dr. Leslie Arm-strong in "The Missing Three-Quarter." Dr. Wat-son certainly carried his own notebook as Holmes remarked to him at the end of the affair of The Dancing Men, "I think that I have fufilled my promise of giving you something unusual for your notebook." The good doctor also referred to his "notebook for the year 1895" at the start of his account of "The Solitary Cyclist," implying that Watson's notebook may actually have been a for-mal diary. (See also CASEBOOK and COMMON-PLACE BOOK.)

NOTTING HILL.   A district in Kensington where the international agent Louis La Rothiere lived, at Campden Mansions; he was considered one of only three foreign agents capable of carrying out so big an operation as the theft of the Bruce-Partington Plans. Selden, the killer who would eventually be killed by the Hound of the Basker-villes, was known as "the Notting Hill murderer," his crimes presumably carried out in the area.

OAKSHOTT, MAGGIE.   The sister of James Ryder in "The Blue Carbuncle." She resided at 17 Brixton Road and raised eggs and poultry for dealers. She sold the geese to Mrs. Breckenridge of the Covent Garden that eventually ended up dis-tributed to the members of the goose club of the Alpha Inn, including one bird that carried in its crop an extraordinary surprise.

OAKSHOTT, SIR LESLIE.   A famous surgeon who attended Holmes following the brutal attack upon the detective outside the Cafe Royal by the agents of Baron Gruner in "The Illustrious Client."

OBERSTEIN, HUGO.   An international agent, residing at 13 Caulfield Gardens, Ken-sington, who was considered one of the foreign operatives capable of stealing the Bruce-Partington Submarine Plans in "The Bruce-Partington Plans." Holmes considered the other two agents, Louis La Rothiere and Adolph Meyer, to be obvious sus-pects, but found the location of Oberstein's resi-dence to be of tremendous significance to the case. In the previous case of high political intrigue re-corded in "The Second Stain," Holmes considered Oberstein, La Rothiere, and Eduardo Lucas to be possible suspects in the theft of the secret letter from the dispatch box of Trelawney Hope.

ODESSA.   A Russian port on the Black Sea where Holmes was summoned to investigate the Trepoff murder. Writing in "A Scandal in Bo-hemia" that he had "seen little of Holmes lately," Watson noted that "from time to time I heard some vague account of his doings," including the Trepoff case. Odessa was also the site of a poisoning that Holmes, in *A Study in Scarlet*, said was similar to that of Enoch Drebber: "The forcible adminstra-tion of poison is by no means a new thing in the criminal annals. The cases of Dolsky in Odessa, and of Leturier in Montpellier, will occur at once to any toxicologist."

OLDACRE, JONAS. A well-known and successful builder, of Lower Norwood, who was apparently murdered and burned in "The Norwood Builder." The *Daily Telegraph* reported: "Mr. Oldacre is a bachelor, fifty-two years of age, and lives in Deep Dene House, at the Sydenham end of the road of that name. He has had the reputation of being a man of eccentric habits, secretive and retiring. For some years he has practically withdrawn from the business, in which he is said to have amassed considerable wealth." Just prior to his death, Oldacre had instructed the solicitor John Hector McFarlane to draw up a will that, with some reservations, left all his property to McFarlane, supposedly because Oldacre had once been engaged to McFarlane's mother. It was assumed by the police under Inspector Lestrade that McFarlane had murdered Oldacre for his money, finding what appeared to be damning evidence against him. McFarlane's mother told Holmes of Oldacre: "Thank heaven that I had the sense to turn away from him and to marry a better, if poorer man. I was engaged to him, Mr. Holmes, when I heard a shocking story of how he had turned a cat loose in an aviary, and I was so horrified at his brutal cruelty that I would have nothing more to do with him."

OLD RUSSIAN WOMAN. In full, The Adventure of the Old Russian Woman, one of the early cases undertaken by Holmes, dating to the time before the detective's association with Dr. Watson. The case was mentioned in "The Musgrave Ritual."

OLDMORE, MRS. The wife, or widow, of Oldmore—a former mayor of Gloucester—who, by custom, stayed at the Northumberland Hotel while in London. She was a guest at the hotel at the time that Henry Baskerville was staying there in *The Hound of the Baskervilles*.

OPENSHAW, COLONEL ELIAS. The uncle of JOHN OPENSHAW and an emigré to England from America was found dead in a shallow pool of water shortly after receiving a mysterious letter from the KKK and the infamous Five Orange Pips. After serving in the Confederate army during the American Civil War, Openshaw settled in a small estate in Sussex, near Horsham. John Openshaw said of him: "He was a singular man, quick-tempered, and very foulmouthed when he was angry, and of a most retiring disposition. During all the years he lived at

Horsham, I doubt if he ever set foot in the town. He had a garden and two or three fields round his house, and there he would take his exercise, though very often for weeks on end he would never leave his room. He drank a great deal of brandy and smoked heavily, but he would see no society and did not want any friends, not even his own brother." The reason for his anti-social behavior plays a major part in the case.

OPENSHAW, JOHN. The son of JOSEPH OPENSHAW and the nephew of COLONEL ELIAS OPENSHAW and the man who brought to Holmes the terrible affair chronicled in "The Five Orange Pips." Openshaw first watches his uncle and then his father die after receiving from an unseen force Five Orange Pips. Young Openshaw thus inherited his uncle's estate through his father, receiving as well, however, their terrible legacy of the pips.

The body of John Openshaw is fished out of the Thames in "The Five Orange Pips"; by an unknown French artist, around 1920.

Unable to comprehend the matter, he consulted Holmes, who made the mistake of allowing him to set off alone for his home in Sussex, at Horsham, and he never arrived. Holmes would seek revenge upon his murderers.

OPENSHAW, JOSEPH.   The father of JOHN OPENSHAW and brother of COLONEL ELIAS OPENSHAW who, like his brother, received the dreaded Five Orange Pips. According to John Openshaw, he "had a small factory in Coventry, which he enlarged at the time of invention of bicycling. He was the patentee of the Openshaw unbreakable tire, and his business met with such success that he was able to sell it, and to retire upon a handsome competence." After his brother's untimely demise in a shallow pool, Joseph inherited his estate, but soon after was the recipient of Five Orange Pips. A short time later, he was found dead in a chalk pit.

OPIUM.   A narcotic prepared from the juice of the poppy. According to Watson's depiction of Holmes's areas of knowledge in *A Study in Scarlet*—"Sherlock Holmes—his limits," the detective was "well up in belladonna, opium, and poisons generally." The doctor later helped Kate Whitney by finding her husband Ira in an opium den, the Bar of Gold, in "The Man With the Twisted Lip." Watson wrote that Whitney had "a yellow, pasty face, drooping lids, and pin-point pupils, all huddled in a chair, the wreck and ruin of a noble man," the results of his terrible addiction to the drug. Miss Burnet in "Wisteria Lodge" and the stablehand Ned Hunter in "Silver Blaze" were both drugged with opium. Ian Murdoch, suffering from the attack of the Lion's Mane, shouted for opium for the pain in "The Lion's Mane."

ORIGIN OF TREE WORSHIP, THE.   One of the books that Holmes carried while in the disguise of a deformed, elderly bibliophile. Watson ran into the disguised detective, of course not recognizing his friend Holmes whom he thought dead. Writing in "The Empty House": "I struck against an elderly, deformed man, who had been behind me, and I knocked down several books he was carrying. I remember that as I picked them up, I observed the title of one of them, *The Origin of Tree Worship*, and it struck me that the fellow must be some poor bibliophile, who, either in trade or as a hobby, was a collector of obscure volumes."

OSTLER.   A type of stablehand. In "A Scandal in Bohemia," Holmes impersonated an ostler and thus learned a great deal from the other ostlers of Serpentine Mews concerning Irene Adler.

OVERTON, CYRIL.   Captain of the Cambridge rugby team who engaged the services of Holmes to find Godfrey Staunton, the title character in "The Missing Three-Quarter." Overton was "an enormous man, sixteen stone of solid bone and muscle, who spanned the doorway with his broad shoulders. . . ." By his own account, he "was first reserve for England against Wales, and [he] skippered the Varsity all this year." He cried out, however, that such achievements were nothing compared to Godfrey Staunton, the crack three-quarter of Cambridge, Blackheath, and five internationals. Desperate when Staunton became missing, Overton first went to Scotland Yard, but Inspector Stanley Hopkins advised him to consult Holmes. The detective was able to find Staunton, but not in time to prevent Overton's crushing defeat by Oxford. Overton expressed total surprise that Holmes had never heard of him or Staunton, asking the detective "Good Lord! Mr. Holmes where have you lived?"

OWEN, REGINALD.   British actor (1887–1972) who appeared both as Watson and Holmes. Owen starred as Watson opposite Clive Brook in *Sherlock Holmes* (1932), with Ernest Torrence (Professor Moriarty), and Miriam Jordan (Alice Faulkner). In the role, he was provided only two brief moments on screen, and his Watson is even more pompous and obnoxious than Nigel Bruce's (the Watson opposite Basil Rathbone). The following year, Owen played Holmes, in *A Study in Scarlet* (1933). He had hoped that this would be the first in a series of American-made Holmes films, but the generally poor reception of the film ended any such aspirations. His Watson here was Warburton Gamble, with Holmes alumnus Alan Mowbray as Inspector Lestrade.

OXFORD STREET.   A main street in LONDON that was frequently used by Holmes and Watson as a route to and from 221B Baker Street. Sir Henry Baskerville and Dr. Mortimer in *The Hound of the Baskervilles* and Stanley Hopkins in "The Golden Pince-Nez" travelled on this road. Located here were Bradley's tobacco shop in "The Disappearance of Lady Frances Carfax," Holmes's branch of the

Reginald Owen as a rather chunky Sherlock Holmes, from *A Study in Scarlet* (1931).

Capital and Counties Bank in "The Priory School," and Latimer's boot shop in "Lady Carfax." The residence of the Adairs was located at the Oxford Street terminus of Park Lane in "The Empty House." The street will be remembered most, however, as the route to which Holmes was headed to conduct business when he was attacked by the agents of Professor Moriarty in "The Final Problem."

OXFORD UNIVERSITY.   This great English university is considered by scholars as a possible alma mater of Sherlock Holmes. As with the other potential university, Cambridge, no specific mention was ever made in the Canon about Holmes's education, even in the two cases that covered those early years, "The 'Gloria Scott'" and "The Musgrave Ritual," where Watson remains deliberately ambiguous. He does refer to a Camford University in "The Creeping Man," a clever name that could be a reference to either Cambridge or Oxford. Holmes may have visited Oxford in his pursuit of research into early English charters in "The Three Students." The Oxford rugby team defeated that of Cambridge in "The Missing Three-Quarter," mainly because the Cambridge star Godfrey Staunton was missing; Holmes found him, but not in time to save Cambridge from ignomy. Colonel Sebastian Moran in "The Empty House" and John Clay in "The Red-Headed League" were both educated at Oxford. These were two onetime students of whom the university could hardly be proud.

OXSHOTT COMMON.   A common that was situated about a mile from the Wisteria Lodge where the body of Aloysius Garcia was found in "Wisteria Lodge." Oxshott Towers, in the Surrey district of Oxshott, was owned by George Folliot.

OYSTERS.   Holmes apparently enjoyed oysters, as he served them during the dinner he gave for Watson and Inspector Athelney Jones in *The Sign of Four*. During the case recorded in "The Dying Detective," Holmes, supposedly afflicted with a terrible Far Eastern malady, raved about oysters: "Indeed, I cannot think why the whole bed of the ocean is not one mass of oysters, so prolific the creatures seem. No doubt there are natural enemies which limit the increase of the creatures. You and I, Watson, we have done our part. Shall the world, then, be overrun by oysters? No, no; horrible."

PADDINGTON. An area in LONDON where Watson purchased a general practice from old Mr. Farquhar in "The Stockbroker's Clerk." Paddington Station, in Paddington, was near Watson's practice, and Watson acquired a few patients from among the rail staff there. One of his patients who was brought to him from Paddington Station was Victor Hatherley, a man who had lost his thumb in a strange fashion in "The Engineer's Thumb." Holmes waited for Watson at Paddington so that they could travel together to Herefordshire in "The Boscombe Valley Mystery." Watson wrote: "Sherlock Holmes was pacing up and down the platform, his tall, gaunt figure made even gaunter and taller by his long gray travelling-cloak and close-fitting cloth cap." Holmes and Watson journeyed to Exeter from here in "Silver Blaze," and Henry Baskerville left from here to Dartmoor in *The Hound of the Baskervilles.*

PAGANINI, NICCOLO. Great Italian violinist (1782–1840) about whom Holmes revealed he knew a great deal in "The Cardboard Box." He discussed Paganini with Dr. Watson, sitting with him for an hour over a bottle of claret while he told him "anecdote after anecdote of that extraordinary man."

PAGE. Customarily a young boy who has the duty to escort guests from the door to the master of the house or office. Throughout the years covered in the Canon, there were apparently several pages, two of whom were named Billy ("The Mazarin Stone," "Thor Bridge," *The Valley of Fear*). In "A Case of Identity," the page was described as "the boy in buttons," reappearing in "The Naval Treaty," "The Noble Bachelor," "Wisteria Lodge," and "The Yellow Face."

PAGET, SIDNEY. English artist who became famous for his long-running illustrations for the stories of the Canon for the *Strand*. Those many casual readers of the Holmes stories in the magazine who appreciate Paget's talents may be surprised to learn that he was not the *Strand*'s first choice. When searching for a suitable artist, the editors chose Sidney's brother **Walter.** A mix up occurred, however, and the request for services went instead to Sidney. The magazine never regretted its mistake. With the exception of Frederic Dorr Steele, Sidney became the most famous of all illustrators of the Canon, his art doing much to establish the public image of Holmes. Ironically, Sidney used Walter as his model for the Great Detective. After Sidney's death, Walter illustrated one story for the *Strand*, "The Dying Detective." (See also Appendix for Artists of the Canon.)

PAINFUL PREDICAMENT OF SHERLOCK HOLMES, THE. In full *The Painful Predicament of Sherlock Holmes, A Fantasy in about One-Tenth of an Act*, a short comedy play written by William Gillette and first performed on March 24, 1905. It was created by Gillette hurriedly as part of a benefit for an unfortunate actor named Joseph Jefferson Holland. Originally planning to perform at the benefit with Ethel Barrymore in the *The Silent System*, Gillette was forced to improvise a substitute play when, for some reason, the drama originally planned proved unworkable. Gillette took the opportunity to poke fun at the character of Holmes, at his own critics (who always criticized his interpretation of the Great Detective), and at the play *Sherlock Holmes* that had been such a hit over the previous few years. As Jack Tracy, in his *Sherlock Holmes: The Published Apocrypha* (1980), wrote:
"He had the laugh on them all by a very simple

device. In all the pandemonious action of The Painful Predicament, he uttered not one sound. Miss Barrymore has virtually every line (bracketed by Billy's at the beginning and end), and Gillette spent the whole time going through the pantomimic business to which his audiences had become accustomed—only this time it was his Holmes could get no word in as his client kept up an uninterrupted dialogue."

Critics adored the short play, and Gillette repeated his nonverbal performance on several occasions using it to try and save a dying London play, *Clarice*, in September, 1905. The characters of the sketch were Sherlock Holmes, Gwendolyn Cobb (the extremely loquacious female lead), and the page Billy. The setting was "Sherlock Holmes's Baker Street apartments somewhere about the date of day before yesterday. The time of day is not stated."

PALIMPSET. A vellum or parchment manuscript that has been written upon several times, often preserving fragments of earlier work beneath the washings. At the time of his involvement in the affair of Professor Coram in "The Golden Pince-Nez," Holmes was working upon deciphering a palimpset. He found, however, that the original inscription was nothing more exciting than an abbey's accounts from the second half of the fifteenth century.

PALL MALL. A street in Westminster known for its many and famous clubs such as the Baldwin Club, the Carlton Club, and the Diogenes Club. Mycroft Holmes, a founding member of the Diogenes Club, resided opposite the club in Pall Mall. "At the end of Pall Mall" could be found the offices of the Adelaide-Southampton steamship line in "The Abbey Grange."

PALMER (1). In full, William Palmer, a notorious doctor who was hanged for poisoning his wife. In "The Speckled Band," Holmes used Palmer, and Pritchard, as examples of physicians who were at the head of their profession but who became murderers. "When a doctor does go wrong he is the first of criminals. He has nerve and he has knowledge."

PALMER (2). An English company that manufactured bicycle tyres (tires). Palmer tyres were crucial to the solution of the disappearance of Lord Saltire, son of the duke of Holernesse in "The Priory School."

PARADOL CHAMBER. One of Holmes's unchronicled cases, occuring in 1887 and recorded by Watson as the adventure of the Paradol Chamber in "The Five Orange Pips." John Dickson Carr, in his 1949 **The Adventure of the Paradol Chamber,"** offered a possible, albeit whimsical version of the case. It was performed at the Mystery Writers of America Annual Dinner Show, The March of Crime, and published in the *Unicorn Mystery Book Club News*. The short story presents Holmes and Watson at Baker Street solving the case of why Lord Matchlock, the foreign minister, was seen leaving Buckingham Palace and walking up Constitution Hill without his pants. The cast of characters includes Lady Imogene Ferrers, M. de Marquis de Paradol, and, of course, Colonel Sebastian Moran.

PARAMORE. A man who, in 1869, was threatened by the Ku Klux Klan in "The Five Orange Pips." In his notebook, Elias Openshaw, recorded for the seventh of March, 1869 that the pips had been set on McCauley, Paramore, and Swain. On the twelfth he wrote, "Visited Paramore. All well."

PARIS. Jefferson Hope pursued Enoch Drebber and Joseph Stangerson to the capital of France in *A Study in Scarlet*. The international agent Eduardo Lucas led a double life in England and France, maintaining a wife and villa in Paris. He was known there by the name Fournaye. Following his murder in "The Second Stain," the Paris police were able to uncover useful facts that were related to Holmes's investigation in London. They were ignorant of the true facts until given a demonstration by the Great Detective in "The Naval Treaty." In Paris, an attempt was made on the life of Don Murillo in "Wisteria Lodge," and Hugo Oberstein could be reached there at the Hotel du Louvre in "The Bruce-Partington Plans." Paris also figured in John Gardner's pastiche novel *The Return of Moriarty*, as the professor attempted to establish a European criminal network.

PARKER (1). The vicar of Hilton Cubitt's parish in Norfolk. He stayed at a boardinghouse in London, in Russell Square, meeting Cubitt, who stayed at the same boarding establishment, during the Jubilee of Queen Victoria in "The Dancing

Men." While there, Cubitt met Elsie Patrick, his future wife.

PARKER (2).   A member of the Moriarty Gang who was posted as a sentinel over 221B by the professor's onetime lieutenant who was eager to avenge his master's death upon Holmes in "The Empty House." Returning to Baker Street, Holmes saw Parker, telling Watson later: "He is a harmless enough fellow, Parker by name, a garroter by trade, and a remarkable performer upon the jew's harp. I cared nothing for him. But I cared a great deal for the much more formidable person behind him, the bosom friend of Moriarty . . ."

PARK LANE MYSTERY.   The name popularly used to describe the bizarre and puzzling murder of the Hon. Ronald Adair in "The Empty House." The name was derived from Adair's address—427 Park Lane—where the murder occurred.

PARR, LUCY.   The second waiting maid at Fairbank, the home of Alexander Holder in "The Beryl Coronet." Because she had been in service for only a few months, she was under suspicion in the theft of the Beryl Coronet.

PATRICK.   Father of Elsie Patrick and a joint, or gang, leader in Chicago in "The Dancing Men." He was the inventor of the Dancing Men cipher, a secret code that appeared as a kind of child's writing.

PATTERSON.   An inspector from Scotland Yard who was in charge of the effort to round up the gang of Professor Moriarty in "The Final Problem." In his note to Watson left at the Reichenbach Falls, Holmes told him: "Tell Inspector Patterson that the papers which he needs to convict the gang are in pigeonhole M., done up in a blue envelope and inscribed 'Moriarty'."

PATTINS, HUGH.   A harpooner who desired employment in the arctic expedition planned by Captain Basil (Holmes) in "Black Peter." He applied at 221B Baker Street but was informed that the berth was full, the same thing told to James Lancaster. Pattins was described as "a long, dried-up creature, with lank hair and sallow cheeks."

PEACE, CHARLES.   A well-known real-life murderer (1832–1879) who was hanged. While discussing the accomplishments of Baron Gruner in "The Illustrious Client," Holmes commented that he had a "complex mind," adding "all great criminals have that. My old friend Charlie Peace was a violin virtuoso." It was thus assumed that he was referring to the murderer Charles Peace, and it can be surmised that either he knew the man or, less likely, had a hand in his apprehension.

PEARL OF BORGIA, THE BLACK.   A precious pearl that was associated with the famous Borgias in "The Six Napoleons." Said by Holmes to be "the most famous pearl now existing in the world," it was stolen from the prince of Colonna's bedroom at the Dacre Hotel. Holmes was called in on the case after the London police failed to recover it, but he, too, "was unable to shed any light upon it." Given a second opportunity, the Great Detective did not fail.

PEARL OF DEATH, THE.   U.S. 1944. Dir: Roy William Neill. Cast: Basil Rathbone (Holmes), Nigel Bruce (Watson), Evelyn Ankers (Naomi Drake), Miles Mander (Giles Conover), Dennis Hoey (Lestrade). The ninth film with Rathbone and Bruce as Holmes and Watson, based in part on "The Adventure of the Six Napoleons." The film features a trio of villains, the elegant thief Naomi Drake, the vicious criminal Giles Conover, and his grotesque henchman, the Creeper (played by Rondo Hatton, a real-life victim of acromegaly) who snaps men's spines, always at the third vertebra, and who would appear again in such films as *House of Horror* and *The Brute Man*. As in the original story, the focus of the criminals seems to be in finding and destroying six busts of Napoleon, but their aim is actually to acquire the precious Borgia Pearl. Holmes displays brilliant moments as well as clumsy ones, such as turning off the alarm in a museum which allows the pearl to be stolen. He naturally recovers and thwarts the machinations of Conover of whom he makes the Moriarty-like statement, "If I could free society of this sinister creature, I should feel that my own career had reached its summit." Not surprisingly, the Creeper turns on his master and Holmes is forced to kill the monster, the first time in the Universal series that Holmes slays a major criminal with his own hands. Watson and Lestrade are their usual bumbling selves, although Watson displays the degree of his loyalty to Holmes by attacking the newspaper reporters who poked fun at the detective after he allowed the pearl to be stolen.

PEERLESS PEER, THE ADVENTURE OF THE.

A 1974 pastiche novel by Philip Jose Farmer, written under the name of Dr. John H. Watson M.D., with the addition of "Edited by Philip Jose Farmer, American Agent for the Estates of Dr. Watson, Lord Greystoke, David Copperfield, Martin Eden, and Don Quixote." This is a unique work in that it presents Holmes and Watson meeting Tarzan of the apes. Their encounter takes place while the detective and the doctor are on a secret mission to Africa in 1916 in pursuit of the German master spy. The book was, unfortunately, suppressed by the estate of Edgar Rice Burroughs which held copyright on the Tarzan character, unbeknownst to Farmer, and thus the novel is now a very much sought after item in peripheral Sherlockiana.

PENANG LAWYER.

A type of walking stick with a head made of wood from the Malaysian island of Penang. Both Dr. Mortiner in *The Hound of the Baskervilles* and Fitzroy Simpson in "The Lion's Mane" carried one.

PENNSYLVANIA.

Ezekiah Hopkins, founder of "The Red-Headed League," supposedly hailed from this state. He was said to be from Lebanon, Pennsylvania.

PENNSYLVANIA SMALL ARMS COMPANY.

An American manufacturer of weapons in *The Valley of Fear*, that was said to be well known. The sawed-off shotgun used to kill John Douglas at Birlstone Manor, Sussex, was made by the firm. Its initials "PEN" could be seen on the fluting between the barrels.

PERFUME.

A fragrance whose prompt recognition Holmes felt could be crucial to solving a case in *The Hound of the Baskervilles*. He stated that a criminal expert should be able to distinguish one essence from another.

PERKINS.

The groom for Baskerville Hall, on Dartmoor, in Devonshire in *The Hound of the Baskervilles*. He was sent for by Dr. Mortimer when the body of Sir Charles Baskerville was discovered. Perkins was also a young man who was apparently killed outside the Holborn Bar by the prizefighter Steve Dixie in "The Three Gables." Holmes confronted the fighter about the death.

PERSANO, ISADORA.

One of the unchronicled cases found in the travel-worn and battered tin dispatch box with "John H. Watson, M.D., late Indian Army," painted upon the lid. The case of Isadora Persano was included in Watson's list of unfinished investigations such as those of James Phillimore and the cutter *Alicia* in "Thor Bridge." Watson wrote: "The third case worthy of note is that of Isadora Persano, a well-known journalist and duellist, who was found stark staring mad with a match box in front of him which contained a remarkable worm said to be unknown to science." Persano appeared in the bizarre short story "The Problem of the Sore Bridge—Among Others" by Philip Jose Farmer, a tale that connected Persano, the *Alicia*, and James Phillimore.

PERSIA.

During the Great Hiatus (1891–1894), Holmes "passed through Persia," the region of western Asia known today by the name Iran ("The Empty House"), and in "A Case of Identity" quoted the Persian writer Hafiz. Colonel Sebastian Moran's father had once been the British minister to Persia ("The Empty House").

PESHAWAR.

Also Peshawur, a town in India where Watson was moved to the base hospital after receiving his wound at the Battle of Maiwand in *A Study in Scarlet*.

PETER.

A groom at Chiltern Grange in the employ of Bob Carruthers in "The Solitary Cyclist." He was given the task of driving Violet Smith in a dogcart to Farnham Station, but they were attacked on the way. Peter was pulled off the cart and clubbed and Violet Smith was carried off.

PETERS, "HOLY."

Or Henry Peters, an unscrupulous Australian rascal who posed as a Dr. Shlessinger to win the trust of Lady Frances Carfax in "The Disappearance of Lady Frances Carfax." Holmes, who was familiar with him, declared: "His particular specialty is the beguiling of lonely ladies by playing upon their religious feelings, and his so-called wife, an English woman named Fraser, is a worthy helpmate." His left ear was badly torn, the result of a saloon fight at Adelaide in 1889 in which it was badly bitten. As Dr. Shlessinger, he pretended to be a missionary to South America who was recovering at the Englischer Hof in Baden from a disease he contracted while performing his many duties. "He was preparing a map of the Holy Land, with special reference to the Kingdom of the Midianites, upon which he was writing a monograph." He resided at No. 36 Poultney Square, in Brixton.

PETERSON.   A commissionaire who brought to Holmes the hat and Christmas goose belonging to Henry Baker in "The Blue Carbuncle." Holmes kept the hat and gave Peterson the goose. A short time later, the commissionaire burst into 221B as his wife had made an astonishing discovery in the bird's crop.

PETRARCH.   Holmes read the works of this Italian poet (1304–1374), published in a pocket edition, while on the train to Boscombe Valley to investigate the murder of Charles McCarthy in "The Boscombe Valley Mystery."

PHEASANT.   This game bird figured in the lethal coded message sent to Trevor Senior by Beddoes in "The 'Gloria Scott' ": "The supply of game for London is going steadily up. Head-keeper Hudson, we believe, has been now told to receive all orders for fly-paper and for preservation of your hen-pheasant's life." At the cold supper for Mr. and Mrs. Francis Hay Moulton in "The Noble Bachelor," Holmes had pheasant served, an entree that has convinced many scholars that the detective was actually an accomplished gourmet.

PHELPS, PERCY.   Nicknamed "Tadpole," an old schoolmate of Dr. Watson whose potentially excellent career in the Foreign Office was severely threatened by the mysterious theft of a secret Naval Treaty that had been entrusted into his care. Watson wrote: "He was, I remember, extremely well connected, and even when we were all little boys together we knew that his mother's brother was Lord Holdhurst, the great conservative politician. This gaudy relationship did him little good at school. On the contrary, it seemed rather a piquant thing to us to chevy him about the playground and hit him over the shins with a wicket." Phelps appealed to Watson to procure the help of Holmes in recovering the document. Ironically, it would prove that the brain fever and near total mental collapse that Phelps underwent after the theft were crucial to the successful return of the document and the rescue of his political future.

PHILADELPHIA.   Jephro Rucastle claimed that his daughter, Alice, was on a trip from England to Philadelphia in "The Copper Beeches." The companies that were buying their way into Vermissa Valley in *The Valley of Fear* had no fear of the Scowrers because they were headquartered in New York and Philadelphia.

PHILLIMORE, JAMES.   An unfinished investigation by Holmes, the details of which, Watson wrote, were included in a battered tin dispatch box in the vaults of the bank of Cox and Co. mentioned in "Thor Bridge." "Among these unfinished tales is that of Mr. James Phillimore, who, stepping back into his house to get an umbrella, was never more seen in this world." Phillimore has been the subject of considerable speculation by writers who have offered possible explanations for his disappearance. Among the most interesting are: "The Adventure of the Highgate Miracle" by Adrian Conan Doyle and John Dickson Carr in the collection *The Exploits of Sherlock Holmes*; "The Problem of Sore Bridge—Among Others," by Philip Jose Farmer; and the *Incredible Umbrella* by Marvin Kaye.

PHILOSOPHER'S RING, THE CASE OF THE.   A 1978 novel by Randall Collins, written supposedly by John Watson. Similar to the novel *The Case of the Revolutionist's Daughter*, this is a detailed glimpse into the intellectual and philosophical world of England early in this century, presented as a Sherlock Holmes case, although the presence of the detective is somewhat superfluous as much of the work is devoted to philosophical disquisition. Holmes is engaged by Bertrand Russell to find the missing Ludwig Wittgenstein, his investigation bringing him in contact with the leading philosophical lights of the time. He also encounters such spiritualists as Annie Besant and Leila Waddell, the so-called Scarlet Woman, finally meeting the Beast himself, Aleister Crowley. Readers generally unfamiliar with the issues of the era will probably have a hard time keeping up with the case.

PHOTOGRAPHY.   Holmes claimed that photography was one of his methods of criminal detection in "The Lion's Mane." As part of his efforts to deceive his employer, Jabez Wilson, and to ensure undisturbed periods of time beneath Wilson's pawnshop, Vincent Spaulding supposedly took up photography as a hobby in "The Red-Headed League." Jephro Rucastle also worked on photography in "The Copper Beeches."

PICKLOCK HOLES.   The earliest known parody of Sherlock Holmes, created by R. C. Lehmann and first appearing in *Punch* in 1893. The humorous adventures of the detective were recorded by Cunnin Toil. Picklock Holes was unique among detectives as he hired criminals to keep himself busy and generally created the evidence he would need to solve a case. Among his "investigations" were "The Bishop's Crime" (1893), "Lady Hilda's Mystery" (1893), and "Picklock's Disappearance" (1894).

PICKPOCKET.   A criminal activity said by Holmes in *The Valley of Fear* to be part of Professor Moriarty's vast criminal network. "I happen to know who is the first link in his chain—a chain with this Napoleon-gone-wrong on one end, and a hundred fighting men, pickpockets, blackmailers, and card sharpers at the other, with every sort of crime in between."

"PIERROT."   The code name used by the international agent seeking The Bruce-Partington Plans in the advertisements placed in the "agony column" of the *Daily Telegraph* to communicate with his partner. After his discovery of the name, Holmes used it to trap the agent in the Charing Cross Hotel.

PIKE, LANGDALE.   Holmes referred to Pike as a "human book of reference upon all matters of scandal" in "The Three Gables." Watson wrote: "This strange languid creature spent his waking hours in the bow-window of a St. James Street club and was the receiving station as well as the transmitter for all gossip in the metropolis. He made, it was said, a four-figure income by the paragraphs he contributed every week to the garbage papers which cater to the inquisitive public. If ever, far down in the turbid depths of London life, there was some strange swirl or eddy, it was marked with automatic exactness by this human dial upon the surface. Holmes discreetly helped Langdale to knowledge, and on occasion was helped in turn." Clearly a pseudonym, Langdale Pike was possibly a member of high society.

PINCE-NEZ.   A type of eyeglass fastened to the nose with a clip or spring. Holmes performed one of his foremost acts of deduction on a gold pince-nez that belonged to Anna Coram, a vital piece of evidence in the murder of Willoughby-Smith in "The Golden Pince-Nez." Based on his observations, he wrote: "Wanted a lady of good address, attired like a lady. She has a remarkably thick nose, with eyes which are set close on either side of it. She has a puckered forehead, a peering expression, and probably rounded shoulders. There are indications she has had recourse to an optician at least twice during the last few months. As her glasses are of remarkable strength, and as opticians are not very numerous, there should be no difficulty in tracing her." He explained each of these points to an astonished Stanley Hopkins. Meanwhile, in "A Case of Identity," the two dents on either side of Mary Sutherland's nose told Holmes that she wore pince-nez. In "The Five Orange Pips," John Openshaw also wore them.

PINKERTON, ALLAN.   Founder (1819–1884) of the famous Pinkerton Detective Agency that won considerable notoriety for its activities during the Civil War in the United States (1861–1865). According to the autobiography *Sherlock Holmes, My Life and Crimes*, by Michael Hardwick, the detective, while touring America as a younger man, became associated with Allan Pinkerton, serving for a time as a member of the agency and learning some lessons in criminal detection that would be useful in his later career. Two Pinkerton detectives appeared in the Canon: Birdy Edwards who labored to destroy the Scowrers of Vermissa Valley in *The Valley of Fear*; and Leverton, the hero of the Long Island Cave Mystery, who was "on the trail" of his life in pursuit of the dangerous Gorgiano of "The Red Circle."

PINNER.   A small town in Middlesex in "The Yellow Face." Following the death of her husband in Atlanta, Effie Hebron returned to England and stayed with her aunt in Pinner. While living there, she met Grant Munro. (Also see BEDDINGTON.)

PINTO, JAMES.   A criminal who was shot to death in the Lake Saloon, Market Street, in the New Year week of 1874 in *The Valley of Fear*. His killer was, by his own admission, John McMurdo. McMurdo claimed that he had been producing counterfeit money and that Pinto had helped to "shove the queer" or pass the money into circulation. Pinto then threatened to "split" or inform, so McMurdo killed him and "lighted out for the coal country."

PIPE. With the deerstalker, the pipe was Sherlock Holmes's most recognized possession, described by Dr. Watson in his chronicles, sketched in the illustrations accompanying them, and appearing in film and onstage. It is now generally accepted that Holmes smokes almost exclusively a meerschaum pipe—a pipe with a bowl made out of meerschaum (a type of mineral) and distinguished by its curving design. This, of course, is incorrect as Holmes possessed a wide variety of pipes, many with a specific purpose and place in his meditations. The detective had a litter of pipes scattered over the mantelpiece in his bedroom ("The Dying Detective"), while others were stored in the coal-scuttle where he also kept his cigars ("The Mazarin Stone"). His tobacco, particularly his thick coarse shag, was kept in the toe end of a Persian slipper ("The Empty House," "The Illustrious Client," "The Musgrave Ritual," "The Naval Treaty"), in the aforementioned coal-scuttle ("The Mazarin Stone"), or in the various tobacco pouches also found on the mantelpiece. Each morning, he would make his before-breakfast pipe, composed of "all the plugs and dottles left from his smokes of the day before, all carefully dried and collected on the corner of the mantelpiece" ("The Engineer's Thumb"). Following his morning meal, the detective smoked an after-breakfast pipe, although its composition was never revealed ("Thor Bridge"). It may be guessed that he began here to work toward his next before breakfast smoke. Arguably, Holmes's most important pipe was his "old black pipe" ("The Creeping Man"), said by Watson to be an institution in the detective's life. This "old and oily" pipe ("A Case of Identity") was kept with other pipes in a rack and served him as a "counsellor." It was described also as a black clay pipe ("The Blue Carbuncle," "The Copper Beeches," "The Red-Headed League," and *The Hound of the Baskervilles*), his meditative pipe ("The Solitary Cyclist"), and "the unsavoury pipe which was the companion of his deepest meditations" (*The Valley of Fear*). It was this black clay pipe that Holmes smoked for several hours straight while pondering on the Baskerville case, the smoke from it turning the rooms at Baker Street positively poisonous.

Holmes also smoked a cherrywood, a briar, and a pipe with an amber stem. The cherrywood replaced the clay pipe when the sleuth's mood was disputatious rather than meditative ("The Copper Beeches"). The briar, seen also in *The Sign of Four*, was used in "The Man With the Twisted Lip" to meditate upon the disappearance of Neville St. Clair; Holmes smoked it all night, consuming an ounce of shag. These were all, however, essentially straight pipes, the shapes confirmed by the early illustrations in the *Strand* by Sidney Paget. A radical change of pipes began in 1899 in William Gillette's play *Sherlock Holmes*. The renowned actor, who did much to establish the public image of the detective, portrayed Holmes smoking a large, curved pipe. Gillette found that he had an easier time with a curved meerschaum as he could clamp it between his teeth and still deliver his lines. This image soon stuck and before long it seemed that virtually every Holmes, on stage or in film, was smoking a curved pipe or the even more pronounced meerschaum. Subsequent illustrators of the Canon, also influenced by Gillette, began drawing Holmes with a curved pipe, although some, such as Frank Wiles, remained purists. Over time, the smoking device became so synonymous with the Great Detective that it was subject to being caricatured; this was done to notable effect in such films as *The Private Life of Sherlock Holmes* (1970), *They Might Be Giants* (1971), and *Young Sherlock Holmes* (1985).

"PLOT FOR A SHERLOCK HOLMES STORY." A "scenario for an uncompleted tale" possibly written by Arthur Conan Doyle that was discovered by the writer Hesketh Pearson during the preparation for his 1943 biography *Conan Doyle*. Of uncertain date and possibly not even by Conan Doyle, the plot presents a young woman approaching Holmes for help after her uncle was found murdered in his bedroom, seemingly shot through an open window. The young girl's lover has been arrested as the evidence points clearly to him, particularly a revolver found with his initials carved on the butt and because he is the only person in the village with a light ladder. Holmes and Watson journey to the village where after making some preliminary investigations, Holmes has the well searched. A pair of stilts is found, but the rest of the evidence against the young man remains. Holmes, however, traps the real killer by hiring a man to walk up to the guilty man's window on stilts, impersonating the dead victim. Already wracked with guilt, the killer reveals all. If Conan Doyle had plans for the story, he never used them.

PLUMBER. One of the many disguises used by Holmes during his investigations. As a means of penetrating the household of Charles Augustus Milverton in "Charles Augustsus Milverton," he posed as Escott, a plumber with a rising business, wooing Milverton's housemaid Agatha. Actual plumbers mentioned in the Canon were John Horner in "The Blue Carbuncle" and the late father of Mary Sutherland in "A Case of Identity."

PLUMMER, CHRISTOPHER.   The distinguished Canadian stage, television, and film actor had two outings as the Great Detective: the 1977 British television film "Silver Blaze," with Thorley Walters (Watson); and the riveting 1979 film *Murder By Decree*, with James Mason (Watson) and Frank Finlay (Lestrade), in which he investigates the Ripper murders of Whitechapel, with shocking results.

PLYMOUTH.   A seaport in Devonshire where Holmes claimed to have met Mrs. Straker in "Silver Blaze." It was here also that Leon Sterndale heard of the death of Brenda Tregennis in "The Devil's Foot." The decorators and furnishers hired for the remodelling of Baskerville Hall in *The Hound of the Baskervilles* were from Plymouth.

POE, EDGAR ALLAN.   The highly influential American writer (1809–1849) of mystery, horror, and detective fiction is considered to be a founder of the detective story through his creation of C. Auguste Dupin, who appeared in such well-known works as *The Murders in the Rue Morgue* (1841) and *The Purloined Letter* (1845). In *A Study in Scarlet*, Holmes naturally knew of Dupin and took umbrage that Watson should compare him with that "fictional" sleuth. "No doubt you think that you are complimenting me in comparing me to Dupin . . . Now, in my opinion, Dupin was a very inferior fellow. That trick of his of breaking in on his friend's thoughts with an apropos remark after a quarter of an hour's silence is really very showy and superficial. He had some analytical genius, no doubt; but he was by no means such a phenomenon as Poe appeared to imagine." Holmes mentioned the trick again in "The Cardboard Box," giving a demonstration of it himself.

POLDHU BAY.   Also Poldhu Cove, a bay in Cornwall where Holmes, on doctor's orders, took a vacation in the spring of 1897 recorded in "The Devil's Foot." He and Watson stayed at Poldhu Cottage "near Poldhu Bay, at the further extremity

of the Cornish peninsula." They were soon embroiled in what Holmes called the "Cornish horror—strangest case I have handled."

"POLICE NEWS OF THE PAST."   The title suggested by young Stamford in *A Study in Scarlet* for a paper Holmes could start owing to the fact that he was "a walking calendar of crime." Holmes said it might be made to be "very interesting reading."

"POLITICIAN, THE LIGHTHOUSE, AND THE TRAINED CORMORANT, THE." One of Holmes's unchronicled cases that was, apparently, the potential source for a major scandal ("The Veiled Lodger"). Because of the explosive nature of Holmes's memoirs, Watson was compelled to assure his readers and those persons involved that "the discretion and high sense of honour which have always distinguished my friend are still at work in the choice of these memoirs, and no confidence will be abused." He was forced to add, however, that attempts had been made to destroy the papers. "The source of these outrages is known, and if they are repeated I have Mr. Holmes's authority for saying that the whole story concerning the politician, the lighthouse, and the trained cormorant will be given to the public."

POLLOCK, CONSTABLE.   A policeman who, with Sargeant Tuson, was successful in arresting Beddington, the well-known forger after the attempted robbery of the London stockbroking firm of Mawson & Williams in "The Stockbroker's Clerk."

POLYPHONIC MOTETS.   A type of vocal composition based on some sacred or religious text and sung without musical accompaniment. At the start of "The Bruce-Partington Plans," Holmes was conducting research into the music of the Middle Ages, study that led to a monograph "Upon the Polyphonic Motets of Lassus." It was printed for private circulation and "was said by the experts to be the last word on the subject."

POMPEY.   A local draghound (a dog trained to follow an artificial scent) used by Holmes in his efforts to find the missing Godfrey Staunton in "The Missing Three-Quarter." Pompey was "a squat, lop-eared, white-and-tan dog, something between a beagle and a foxhound." Holmes told Watson, "Pompey is the pride of the local draghounds—no very great flier, as his build will show, but a staunch hound on the scent."

PONDICHERRY. A town on the eastern coast of India from which Elias Openshaw received a letter containing the dreaded Five Orange Pips that signalled his impending death in "The Five Orange Pips." Of note, the barque *Lone Star*, out of Savannah, Georgia, had stopped at Pondicherry in January and February 1883.

PONDICHERRY LODGE. The large home in Norwood that belonged to Major Sholto and later his son Bartholomew in *The Sign of Four*. Watson wrote: "The square, massive house, with its black, empty windows and high, bare walls, towered up, sad and forlorn, behind us. Our course led right across the grounds, in and out among the trenches and pits with which they were scarred and intersected. The whole place, with its scattered dirtheaps and ill-grown shrubs, had a blighted, ill-omened look which harmonized with the black tragedy which hung over it."

POPE'S COURT. A lane just off of Fleet Street where the offices of The Red-Headed League were situated. Jabez Wilson told Holmes that the day he went to apply for a position, "Fleet Street was choked with red-headed folk, and Pope's Court looked like a coster's orange barrow. I should not have thought there were so many in the whole country as were brought together by that single advertisement."

PORLOCK, FRED. The *nom de plume* of Holmes's informant in the criminal organization of Professor Moriarty in *The Valley of Fear*. According to the detective, the name Porlock was a "mere identification mark; but behind it lies a shifty and evasive personality . . . Led on by some rudimentary aspirations toward right, and encouraged by an occasional ten-pound note sent to him by devious methods, he has once or twice given me advance information which has been of value—that highest value which anticipates and prevents rather than avenges crime." Through his ciphered letter, Porlock introduced Holmes to the tragedy that was to occur at Birlstone Manor, a murder that became an all too dreadful reality.

PORTER, MRS. The elderly Cornish cook and housekeeper who, aided by a young girl, took care of the Tregennis family in "The Devil's Foot." Mrs. Porter discovered the Tregennises one morning in terrible condition: Brenda Tregennis was dead and her two brothers George and Owen were "gibbering like two great apes." She had fainted at the horror but, upon recovering, opened the window to let in the morning air. Unable to remain in the house another night she left to rejoin her family at St. Ives.

PORTSDOWN HILL. A hill in Hampshire that was dominated by several forts overlooking the Solent, the strait in the English Channel between Hampshire and the Isle of Wight. One of the forts was commanded by Major Freebody, a friend of Joseph Openshaw's in "The Five Orange Pips."

PORTSMOUTH. The major seaport in Hampshire, southern England. Watson arrived home from Afghanistan at Portsmouth aboard the *Orontes* (*A Study in Scarlet*). Von Bork, the German master spy in "His Last Bow," had papers in his safe on the Portsmouth forts, but Steiner, one of his agents was arrested there. More than coincidentally, Altamont telegrammed Von Bork from Portsmouth.

PRAGUE. The king of Bohemia journeyed to England from Prague, capital of the former nation of Czechoslovakia and chief city of Bohemia, in the hopes of engaging the services of Holmes in recovering a compromising photograph in "A Scandal in Bohemia." Professor Presbury of Camford University travelled secretly to Prague to meet with the infamous H. Lowenstein in "The Creeping Man." Baron Adalbert Gruner, suspect in the death of his wife in the Splugen Pass in "The Illustrious Client," managed to escape justice, but Holmes had definite news: "Who could possibly have read what happened at Prague and have any doubts as to the man's guilt! It was a purely technical legal point and the suspicious death of a witness that saved him!"

PRENDERGAST, JACK. A criminal "of incurably vicious habits, who had by an ingenious system of fraud obtained huge sums of money from the leading London merchants" in "The 'Gloria Scott'." Arrested in 1855, this "man of great family and of great ability" was sentenced to deportation

Jack Prendergast.

that Prendergast had said too much and that he had been beaten four times—three times by men, and once by a woman.

PRESBURY, PROFESSOR. A famous professor of physiology at Camford University whose peculiar behavior prompted his personal assistant, Trevor Bennett, and his only daughter, **Edith Presbury**, to consult Holmes in "The Creeping Man." A sixty-one year old widower, Presbury was a man of European reputation about whom there had never been a breath of scandal. He became engaged, however, to Alice Morphy, daughter of his colleague in the chair of comparative anatomy. As Presbury was wealthy, Professor Morphy had no objection to their union, although the difference in ages was considerable. In his pursuit of the girl, the professor exhibited "the passionate frenzy of youth" and Edith felt that his infatuation was "excessive and a little violent and unnatural." His behavior became increasingly curious and "those around him had always the feeling that he was not the man they had known, but that he was under some shadow which had darkened his brighter qualities." Of later significance were his trip to Prague under secret circumstances and his communications with an unknown agent who wrote directly to him, the letter identified by a cross under the stamp. Watson described Edith Presbury as "a bright, handsome girl of a conventional English type."

PRESCOTT, RODGER.   A onetime forger and counterfeiter in Chicago who moved to London to continue his criminal career in "The Three Garridebs." It was said by Killer Evans that "no living man could tell a Prescott [forgery] from a Bank of England." He was shot by Evans in the Waterloo Road in January, 1895, but his printing plates were never found. Their recovery by Holmes in the case "caused several worthy C.I.D. men to sleep the sounder, for the counterfeiter stands in a class by himself as a public danger." He also used the alias Waldron.

PRICE.   In his interview with Harry Pinner in "The Stockbroker's Clerk," Watson impersonated Mr. Price, a clerk from Birmingham.

PRIME MINISTER.   Known also in the Canon as the premier, the head of the majority party in Parliament and leader of the cabinet. As he was

to the Australian colonies aboard the barque *Gloria Scott*. During the voyage, he organized a convict revolt with the help of the prisoners Evans and Armitage. In the explosion that subsequently destroyed the *Gloria Scott*, Prendergast was killed.

PRENDERGAST, MAJOR.   An officer whom Holmes cleared of wrongful accusations that he cheated at cards in the Tankerville Club scandal ("The Five Orange Pips"). Prendergast recommended Holmes to John Openshaw, telling him that the detective could solve anything and had never been beaten. Holmes responded by saying consulted by foreign rulers throughout the Continent, so too was Holmes engaged by several prime ministers in matters of great national importance. Lord Bellinger, two-time premier, went to Baker Street to enlist the aid of Holmes in recovering of the missing letter from a foreign potentate in "The Second Stain." In the case of "The Mazarin Stone," the prime minister himself arrived at 221B. Mycroft Holmes reported that he had never seen the prime minister so upset as he was over the missing Bruce-Partington Plans. Finally, Holmes performed one last mission for the government when the prime minister visited Holmes at the retirement villa in the Sussex Downs and secured his willingness to undertake a complicated penetration of the German spy ring before the start of World War I that culminated in "His Last Bow."

PRINGLE, MRS. The elderly housekeeper at 16 Godolphin Street, the Westminster residence of the international agent Eduardo Lucas in "The Second Stain." On the night of his brutal murder, Mrs. Pringle had apparently heard nothing.

"PRIORY SCHOOL, THE ADVENTURE OF THE" (PRIO).

Published: *Collier's*, January 1904, *Strand*, February 1904; collected in *The Return of Sherlock Holmes* (1905). Major players: Holmes, Watson, Dr. Thorneycroft Huxtable, Lord Saltire, Heidegger, Reuben Hays, James Wilder. Case date: Various, possibly 1901. A popular and controversial investigation, much discussed by Holmes scholars, largely because of the interesting figures involved and a clue that largely led to its

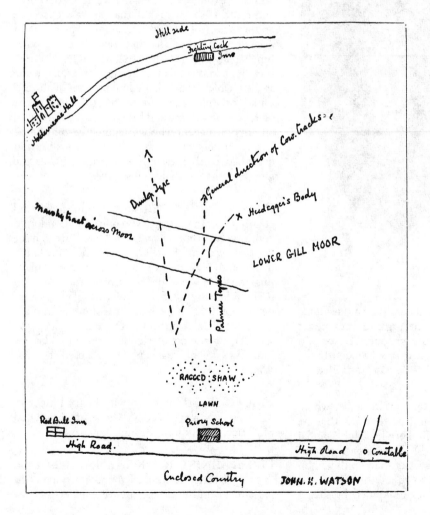

Sketch of Priory School.

Robert Stephens (Holmes) and Colin Blakely (Watson) from *The Private Life of Sherlock Holmes* (1970); they were one of the most real of all the screen duos.

solution. Holmes is engaged by Dr. Thorneycroft Huxtable (none other than the author of *Huxtable's Sidelights on Horace*! and founder of the most exclusive preparatory school in England) to locate Lord Saltire, the son of the duke of Holdernesse who disappeared from Huxtable's own Priory School, near Mackleton. His disappearance prompts Dr. Huxtable to journey to London in the desperate hope of enlisting the services of Sherlock Holmes. Holmes journeys to the prep school and nearby Holdernesse Hall, meeting the duke, "one of the greatest subjects of the Crown!" The famous clue in question is a set of bicycle tracks found in the dirt; viewing the tracks Holmes is able to determine the direction of the vehicle. At the time of the story's publication, many readers argued that such a deduction would be impossible. Two points, however, proved Holmes to be correct: first, the wheels made a deeper impression when going uphill and a more shallow one when going downhill; secondly, when travelling along a muddy road, the direction could be detected by the way in which the mud has splattered. "The Priory School" is also notable as one of the few instances in Holmes's career that the detective accepted a large financial reward, an event noted by Watson in "Black Peter." Holmes himself mentioned the affair in his own work "The Blanched Soldier," writing about "the case which my friend Watson has described as that of the Abbey School, in which the Duke of Greyminster was so deeply involved."

PRISONER OF THE DEVIL. A 1979 pastiche written by the renowned Holmesian Michael Hardwick. Written in the style and flavor of Dr. Watson's narratives, the story focuses on Holmes's involvement in the infamous Dreyfuss Case that occured in France in 1894–1898. *Prisoner of the Devil* was mentioned in Hardwick's 1987 novel *The Revenge of the Hound*.

PRITCHARD, EDWARD WILLIAM. An English surgeon who was hanged in 1865 in Glasgow for poisoning his wife and mother-in-law. In discussing criminal physicians in "The Speckled Band," Holmes said: "When a doctor does go wrong he is the first of criminals . . . Palmer and Pritchard were among the heads of their profession."

PRIVATE LIFE OF SHERLOCK HOLMES, THE. U.S. 1970. Dir: Billy Wilder. Cast: Robert Stephens (Holmes), Colin Blakely (Dr. Watson), Irene Handl (Mrs. Hudson), Genevieve Page (Madame Valladon), Christopher Lee (Mycroft Holmes). Billy Wilder's affectionate homage to the Great Detective was a major failure at the box office, in part because of its often heretical treatment of Holmes and the rather downbeat ending in which Holmes fails as a detective and loses his love interest. Despite these drawbacks, *The Private Life* is generally considered a good film, offering not only a sumptuous glimpse into the era and world of Holmes but a delightful picture of his unique relationship with Watson. The plot centers of Holmes's efforts to assist the forlorn Mme. Valladon (Page) in finding her husband. His investigation takes him to Scotland, where, despite the warnings of his brother Mycroft (played menacingly by CHRISTOPHER LEE), he becomes involved in espionage and a secret government program very reminiscent of the Bruce-Partington Submarine. It is soon clear that his mighty powers have been used against him, largely because he ignored his long-standing suspicion of women and allowed himself to be manipulated. As Holmes, Stephens captured the genius of the sleuth while making him remarkably human; Holmes has been deeply affected by his past and has been left hurt and vulnerable. Colin Blakely, as Watson, is the woman chaser and drinker so long suspected by Sherlockians, but he is also goodnatured, bright, and stalwart. He, too, possesses foibles and eccentricities, serving as a genuine associate of the detective, instead of his unimaginative chronicler and straightman. The version of the film released to the theaters was heavily edited, cut by the nervous studio United Artists. Also originally included was an epilogue in which Holmes, still shaken by recent events, turns down Scotland Yard's plea for help in the case of Jack the Ripper, thereby explaining Holmes's absence from this sensational historical episode.

"PROBLEM OF THOR BRIDGE, THE" (THOR).

Published: *Strand*, February and March 1922; collected in *The Case Book of Sherlock Holmes* (1927). Major players: Holmes, Watson, J. Neil Gibson, Grace Dunbar, Marlow Bates, Maria Pinto Gibson. Case date: October 1900 or 1901. A case that has come from Dr. Watson's "travel-worn and battered tin dispatch–box" stored in the vaults of Cox & Co. bank, Charing Cross branch, the narrative begins on "a wild morning in October" as Holmes is consulted by the American senator and "Gold King" J. Neil Gibson. His governess, Grace Dunbar (of whom Gibson writes to Holmes, "I can't see the best woman God ever made go to her death without doing all that is possible to save her") has been arrested for the murder of Gibson's wife, Maria, who had been found on Thor Bridge on Gibson's estate. Dunbar, of course, is eventually cleared by Holmes in one of the cleverest of his solutions.

PROSPER, FRANCIS.

A greengrocer with a wooden leg who supplied the household of Alexander Holder in "The Beryl Coronet." He was the sweetheart of Lucy Parr, the second waiting-maid to the Holders.

PUGILIST.

The horse of Colonel Whitelaw that ran and lost in the Wessex Cup in "Silver Blaze."

PURSUIT TO ALGIERS.

U.S. 1945. Dir: Roy William Neill. Cast: Basil Rathbone (Holmes), Nigel Bruce (Watson), Marjorie Riordan (Sheila), Rosalind Ivan (Agatha Dunham), and Morton Lowry (Sanford). The twelfth in the long-running Rathbone-Bruce cycle, ranked by critics as the worst outing by the duo, and an episode that pointed conclusively to the decline of the series on the whole. Holmes is given the task of protecting the life of the heir to the throne of the mythical kingdom of Rovenia, accompanying him on a sea voyage aboard the SS *Friesland* (a subtle reference to the vessel on which Holmes and Watson nearly lost their lives). While Rathbone was often criticized for seeming disinterested, his Holmes here is as competent as ever, if a bit melancholy, referring at one point to the late Professor Moriarty. Watson begins to tell some fellow passengers about the "giant rat of Sumatra," but, maddeningly, the camera pans away and the audience is deprived of what surely would have been the most interesting moment of the entire film.

PYCROFT, HALL.

A stockbroker's clerk, residing at 17 Potter's Terrace "out Hampstead way," who introduced Holmes to the case chronicled in "The Stockbroker's Clerk." A onetime clerk at Coxon & Woodhouse, he was turned loose when the firm suffered from a bad decision on a Venezuelan loan. He was offered a position with the company Mawson & Williams' but accepted a berth with the Franco-Midland Hardware Company instead. The subsequently strange experiences of his employment, however, compelled him to consult Holmes. Pycroft "was a well-built, fresh-complexioned young fellow, with a frank, honest face, and a slight, crisp, yellow moustache. He wore a very shiny top-hat and a neat suit of sober black, which made him look like what he was—a smart young City man, of the class who have been labelled cockneys, but who have given us our crack volunteer regiments, and who turn out more fine athletes and sportsmen than any body of men in these islands."

QUALLSFORD INHERITANCE, THE. In full, *The Quallsford Inheritance, A Memoir of Sherlock Holmes from the Papers of Edward Porter Jones, His Late Assistant*, by Lloyd Biggle, Jr. A 1986 novel that is quite different from the usual pastiches—this is written from the perspective of Edward Porter Jones (Porter) a member of the Baker Street Irregulars (BSI). Dr. Watson is mentioned but does not figure prominently; his role in the tale as chronicler and joint investigator for Holmes is assumed by Porter. The basic premise is that Porter grew up as a BSI and, at the age of sixteen, asked Holmes if he would accept an apprentice. Porter learns his craft well and is more of a help to the investigation than Watson would have been. The case begins with the BSI bringing Holmes the strange word "Pitahaygas," a word uttered by an old woman wandering through the Spitafields Market in London carrying an empty basket. Holmes is unable to decide on the significance of the word and so places an advertisement in the agony column concerning it. Perhaps in response, he is visited by Miss Emmeline Quallsford, who begs him to find her brother's murderer. Edmund, her brother, was killed, even though the evidence points to suicide. The significance of the word? None, save that Edmund said "Pitahaya" quite often.

QUEEN ANNE STREET. A street in London's West End where, in 1902, Watson had rooms at the time of the affair of the Illustrious Client.

RACHE. The German word for revenge that was scrawled in blood upon the wall in the room at Lauriston Gardens where the body of Enoch Drebber was found in *A Study in Scarlet*. Inspector Lestrade was of the view after its discovery that the writer was going to put down the name Rachel but was disturbed before he or she had time to finish. The *Daily Telegraph*, however, theorized that the "sinister inscription" pointed to "political refugees and revolutionists." Holmes, of course, had his own views.

Radio

Throughout the so-called Golden Age of Radio, Sherlock Holmes and Dr. Watson were a beloved mainstay of broadcasting in the United States and Great Britain. The first of the well-known radio series featuring the detective was the program "The Adventures of Sherlock Holmes," originally starring Richard Gordon (Holmes) and Leigh Lovell (Watson) from 1930 to 1933. The first episode, "The Adventure of the Speckled Band," starred WILLIAM GILLETTE as Holmes, one of the last performances in a long and distinguished career. It aired on October 20, 1930.

The most famous radio duo was also film history's greatest Holmes-Watson combination: BASIL RATH-BONE and NIGEL BRUCE. Together, they appeared in six separate series of adventures, many original creations, from 1939 to 1946. After performing in over 200 programs, Rathbone terminated his ties to the Master and set out to try and rebuild his career without Holmes. Bruce would carry on as Watson with Tom Conway from 1946 to 1947. Special mention must be made of Edith Meiser, who wrote every Holmes radio story that was aired in the United States from 1930 to 1943, playing a vital role in developing the long-lasting popularity of the radio sleuth.

The following is a chronological list of the many Holmes-Watson series that were aired in England and the United States from 1930 to 1978. (Holmes is always listed first, followed by Watson.)

ENGLAND

DATE	PROGRAM OR SERIES	ACTORS	DATE	PROGRAM OR SERIES	ACTORS
1938	"Sherlock Holmes and the Adventure of Silver Blaze"	F. Wyndham Goldie, Hugh Harber Bramber Wills	1949	"A Book at Bedtime" (stories including "The Bruce-Partington Plans" and "The Norwood Builder")	Laidman Browne (reader)
1943	"The Boscombe Valley Mystery"	Arthur Wontner and Carleton Hobbs			
1945	"The Adventure of the Speckled Band"	Sir Cedric Hardwicke and Finlay Currie	1952	"Sherlock Holmes" BBC "Children's Hour"	Carleton Hobbs and Norman Shelley
	"Silver Blaze"	Laidman Browne and Norman Shelley	1953	"Sherlock Holmes" (Gillette play)	Carleton Hobbs and Norman Shelley
1948	"The Adventure of the Speckled Band"	H. Marion Crawford and Finlay Currie	1954	"The Adventures of Sherlock Holmes"	John Gielgud and Ralph Richardson

ENGLAND

Date	Program or Series	Actors	Date	Program or Series	Actors
1957	"The Hound of the Baskervilles"	Noel Johnson (reader)	1963	"The Sign of Four"	" "
1958	"The Hound of the Baskervilles"	Carleton Hobbs and Norman Shelley	1964–1965	"Sherlock Holmes Returns"	" "
1959	"The Sign of Four"	Richard Hurndall and Bryan Coleman	1966–1967	"Sherlock Holmes Again"	" "
	"Sherlock Holmes" BBC "Thirty Minute Theatre"	Carleton Hobbs and Norman Shelley	1969	"Sherlock Holmes"	" "
				"The Hound of the Baskervilles"	Nigel Stock (reader)
1960	"The Valley of Fear"	" "	1974	"A Study in Scarlet"	Robert Powell and Dinsdale Landen
	"Sherlock Holmes"	" "	1976	"The Baker Street Regulars"	Stephen Thorne and Wilfrid Carter
1961–1962	"Sherlock Holmes" BBC "Light Programme"	" "	1976–1977	"The Adventures of Sherlock Holmes"	Nigel Stock (reader)
1962	"A Study in Scarlet"	" "	1978	"Sherlock Holmes Stories" on the BBC	Barry Foster and David Buck

UNITED STATES

Date	Program or Series	Actors	Date	Program or Series	Actors
1930	"The Adventure of the Speckled Band"	William Gillette and Leigh Lovell	1939–1940	"The Adventures of Sherlock Holmes"	Basil Rathbone and Nigel Bruce
1930–1933	"The Adventures of Sherlock Holmes" (Three series of broadcasts)	Richard Gordon and Leigh Lovell	1940–1943	"Sherlock Holmes"	" "
			1943–1946	"Sherlock Holmes"	" "
			1946–1947	"The New Adventures of Sherlock Holmes"	" "
1934–1935	"The Adventures of Sherlock Holmes" (Fourth broadcast)	Louis Hector and Leigh Lovell	1947–1948	"Sherlock Holmes"	John Stanley and Alfred Shirley
			1948–1949	"Sherlock Holmes"	John Stanley and Ian Martin
1935	"Sherlock Holmes"	William Gillette and Reginald Mason	1949–1950	"The Adventures of Sherlock Holmes"	Ben Wright and Eric Snowden
1938	"Sherlock Holmes"	Orson Welles and Ray Collins, The Mercury Theatre	1968	"The Adventures of Sherlock Holmes"	Carl Pilo and Lou Tripani

Lestrade points the mysterious word RACHE to Holmes and Watson, in *A Study in Scarlet*; by D.H. Friston.

Over the last few years, fans of the original broadcasts have had the opportunity to hear them again, via cassette recordings. Particularly excellent is the recent series of cassettes featuring Rathbone and Bruce. Included on each tape are introductions and epilogues presenting anecdotes and information on the Canon or the productions; the recordings also retain the original commercials.

RADIX PEDIS DIABOLI.   Known commonly as the Devil's Foot root, an obscure ordeal poison found in West Africa that played an important role in the events of "The Devil's Foot." The name was derived from the peculiar shape of the root; said by a botanical missionary to be like a foot, half-human, half-goat. Kept a secret, its brownish powder was used by the medicine men in certain areas

of West Africa, its fumes producing a horrible death or insanity. At Holmes's time, there were only two samples available in Europe—one in Buda and the other in the possession of the African explorer Leon Sterndale. He had acquired his root "under very extraordinary circumstances in the Ubangi country." The root appeared most prominently in the case referred to by Holmes as the Cornish horror and was used in one of the wildest and most dangerous experiments ever attempted by Holmes. The Devil's Foot root made an appearance in the 1991 production *Sherlock Holmes, Incident at Victoria Falls*, although its use was not consistent with the prescribed application in the Canon.

RAFFLES, A. J.   The popular literary creation of E. W. Hornung, the friend and brother-in-law of Arthur Conan Doyle, who dedicated the first Raffles book, *The Amateur Cracksman* (1899) "To A.C.D. This form of flattery." A. J. Raffles, of course, was the brilliant, urbane, and talented criminal, a cracksman whose exploits were recorded by his faithful companion Bunny Manders. Conan Doyle thought highly of Hornung's work, but he felt that Raffles, like Holmes, did terrible harm to his creator's literary reputation. Nevertheless, because of the friendship and the ties of the two men, it was inevitable that someone would suggest a meeting of Holmes and Raffles. This was opposed for years by Conan Doyle, although a tentative agreement was made in 1913 in which a third party would write a story, with the permission of Hornung and Conan Doyle. The project, however, was cut short by World War I and the death of Hornung. A Raffles-Holmes confrontation was filmed as early as 1908, by the Nordisk Film Co., in *Sherlock Holmes II* (or *Raffles Escapes from Prison* in England). Both Raffles and Holmes went on to have illustrious film careers, independent of each other. (See also RIVALS OF SHERLOCK HOLMES and "SORE-BRIDGE, THE ADVENTURE OF.")

RAILWAY.   Trains were used by Holmes as his principal means of travel while conducting his investigations throughout England and on the Continent. So frequent and extensive was his railway usage that J. Alan Rannie, in his 1935 article "The Railway Journeys of Mr. Sherlock Holmes" in the *Railway Magazine* wrote that Holmes was "more than a casual traveller; he had the makings of a railwayist, and though his technical knowledge was usually employed in connection with his professional problems, this was not always the case. On one occasion, whilst on his way to investigate the mystery of Silver Blaze, he is known to have timed a train, and though his method might be considered inadequate by competent modern observers, he arrived at a very reasonable result." In "The Bruce-Partington Plans," the detective also solved the puzzling murder of Arthur Cadogan West using his knowledge of the rails not only to determine the circumstances of Cadogan West's death but also who killed him and where. A rail journey also figures in the interesting non-Canonical tale "The Man with the Watches" and *The Seven-Per-Cent Solution*.

RALPH.   The butler to the Emsworth family at Tuxbury Old Hall in "The Blanched Soldier." James Dodd told Holmes that Ralph "seemed about the same age as the house, and there was his wife, who might have been older." Ralph's wife had been Godfrey Emsworth's nurse. He considered her to be "second to his mother in his affections."

RANCE, JOHN.   A London constable who discovered the body of Enoch J. Drebber at No. 3 Lauriston Gardens, just off the Brixton Road in *A Study in Scarlet*. Holmes interviewed him at his home at 46 Audley Court, Kensington Park Gate, ending the discussion by telling the constable: "I am afraid, Rance, that you will never rise in the force. That head of yours should be for use as well as

Holmes and Watson converse on a train during their trip to investigate murder and theft in "Silver Blaze"; by Sidney Paget.

ornament." The detective was disappointed in Rance because he allowed a drunk at the scene of the murder to go on his way unmolested. "You might have gained your sergeant's stripes last night. The man you held in your hands is the man who holds the clue of this mystery, and whom we are seeking."

RANDALL.   The name of a gang of burglars in "The Abbey Grange" in Lewisham, headed by the elder Randall and his two sons. A fortnight before the murder of Sir Eustace Brackenstall at the Abbey Grange, the Randalls committed a burglary at Sydenham and were thus suspected in Sir Eustace's death. The evidence in the case seemed to point circumstantially to their involvement, but they had an air-tight alibi—they were arrested in New York the morning after the murder.

RAS, DAULAT.   An Indian student at the College of St. Luke's who was also a contestant for the Fortescue Scholarship in "The Three Students," Ras lived on the same floor as the tutor Hilton Soames and was one of the suspects in the cheating scandal investigated by Holmes at the college. According to Soames, Ras was "a quiet, inscrutable fellow, as most of those Indians are. He is well up on his work, though Greek is his weak subject. He is steady and methodical."

RASPER.   The horse of Lord Singleford that ran in the Wessex Cup in "Silver Blaze." It lost to Silver Blaze.

RAT.   A rodent figures twice in the Canon. John McCarthy thought that his father was making some dying allusion to a rat in "The Boscombe Valley Mystery." One of Holmes's unchronicled cases mentioned in "The Sussex Vampire," the *Matilda Briggs*, was associated with the GIANT RAT OF SUMATRA, a story for which the world is not yet prepared.

RATCLIFF HIGHWAY.   A thoroughfare in Stepney on which was situated the Sumner Shipping Agency in "Black Peter." Captain Basil (impersonated by Holmes) solicited three harpooners for his arctic expedition from the agency. The **Ratcliff Highway Murders** were a series of brutal murders committed by John Williams in 1812 that took place on the Ratcliff Highway and its environs. In an editorial on the Drebber murder in *A Study in*

Basil Rathbone, considered the ultimate Sherlock Holmes by many, violin in hand, in *The Hound of the Baskervilles* (1939).

Scarlet, the *Daily Telegraph* made mention of the Ratcliff crimes.

RATHBONE, BASIL. This English actor (1892–1967) became the most beloved and recognized portrayor of Sherlock Holmes through his numerous film and stage appearances and his long-running radio program. Throughout his Holmesian career, Rathbone was ably accompanied by Nigel Bruce as Dr. Watson. With the possible exception of WILLIAM GILLETTE before him, no actor has been more identified with the Great Detective than Rathbone. While this association earned him a huge following, it was also a terrible burden and a deep frustration for the gifted and Shakespearian-trained actor. Try as he might, Rathbone was never able to free himself from the demanding and all-consuming role as sleuth of Baker Street.

Rathbone was born Philip St. John Basil Rathbone in Johannesburg, South Africa. The son of a mining engineer, he and his family journeyed to England in 1896. Attending Repton School, the future Sherlock discovered a taste for acting, deciding that he wanted to pursue a theatrical career. He made his stage debut in 1911 in *The Taming of the Shrew* and first performed in London in 1914 at the Savoy Theatre in the play *The Sin of David*. Serving in World War I, he was awarded the Military Cross, while his brother John was killed.

Returning to the stage after the war, Rathbone enjoyed a highly successful career, playing in London, New York, and elsewhere in the United States and England. In 1911, he appeared in his first film, *The Fruitful Vine*, produced by the Stoll Company that was famous for its Eille Norwood Holmes films. The next years brought more stage work and increasing movie roles, culminating in his memorable performances in a host of films: *Captain Blood* (1935), *Romeo and Juliet* (1936; Oscar nomination as Tybalt); *The Adventure of Marco Polo* (1938), and *The Adventures of Robin Hood* (1938).

How Rathbone came to the role of Sherlock Holmes is a matter of some debate. One story tells of a chance meeting between the actor and Darryl F. Zanuck (head of 20th Century-Fox) at a cocktail party in 1939. The movie studio chief supposedly remarked to the actor that he would make a perfect Holmes. Another version, also at a party, gives the writer Gene Markey credit for suggesting to another guest, Zanuck, that Rathbone would be ideal as Holmes should the studio follow up Zanuck's idea of filming a Holmes story. (Markey also recommended

Nigel Bruce as Watson.) Regardless of how Holmes found Rathbone, Zanuck settled on the tall, distinguished actor, pairing him with Bruce in *The Hound of the Baskervilles* (1939), although Fox hedged its bets and gave top billing to the better-known Richard Greene in the role of Sir Henry Baskerville.

The monumental success of the *Hound* made a sequel inevitable: *The Adventures of Sherlock Holmes* (1939) with Ida Lupino and George Zucco as Professor Moriarty. This was another hit that did much to cement Rathbone and Bruce as the definitive Holmes-Watson duo. Surprisingly, however, Fox chose not to pursue any additional Holmesian ventures, largely because of the increasingly bleak national and international mood in the wake of Hitler's march across Europe. It was decided that the last thing the audience wanted to see was a movie full of dark, fog-enshrouded alleys and bloodthirsty murderers. Not everyone shared that sentiment and in October 1939, Rathbone and Bruce began a series of radio adaptations, written by Edith Meiser. The two would continue their radio broadcasts until 1946.

Starting in 1942, Rathbone, with the ever present Bruce, was back in film as the sleuth in *Sherlock Holmes and the Voice of Terror*, the first of twelve outings produced by Universal Pictures. The other films were *Sherlock Holmes and the Secret Weapon* (1942), *Sherlock Holmes in Washington* (1943), *Sherlock Holmes Faces Death* (1943), *The Scarlet Claw* (1944), *Sherlock Holmes and the Spider Woman* (1944), *The Pearl of Death* (1944), *The House of Fear* (1945), *The Woman in Green* (1945), *Pursuit to Algiers* (1945), *Terror By Night* (1946), and *Dressed to Kill* (1946).

By 1946, Rathbone had grown bored with being Holmes and increasingly in despair of ever freeing himself from the part. Rathbone would endure the humiliation of people asking not for his autograph but for that of Sherlock Holmes. In retrospect, particularly in view of Rathbone's memoirs, it should have been no surprise that when the opportunity presented itself to cut himself loose from Holmes in 1946, he took it. By a useful coincidence, Rathbone's contracts for both radio and film were up and, contrary to the advice of his friends, he chose not to renew. The news came as a major shock to fans, the radio producers, and Nigel Bruce. Tom Conway would replace him in the episodes with Nigel Bruce.

Rathbone moved to New York with his beloved wife Ouida where he hoped to return to the stage. Some success did follow, but Holmes would not go

The famed duo of Basil Rathbone and Nigel Bruce, from *The Woman in Green* (1945).

into the grave. Rathbone discovered that the image was truly a part of him now and from time to time on television he would appear as the detective on "The Milton Berle Show," "The Bob Hope Show," and in an adaptation of "The Adventure of the Black Baronet." In 1950, he also starred in the play *Sherlock Holmes*, written by his wife. Rathbone died on July 21, 1967 of a heart attack.

READING. A town in Berkshire, the home of Mr. Sandeford, owner of the last of the six busts of Napoleon by Devine to be destroyed in "The Six Naploeons," residing on Lower Grove Road. Mr. Armitage lived at Crane Water near Reading in "The Speckled Band."

RED BULL. An inn on the High Road, near Mackleton, situated upon the road to the "Priory School." As the landlady was sick on the night of Lord Saltire's disappearance from the school, the guests were all awake waiting for the doctor and could verify that no one passed the inn—especially Lord Saltire and the suspected German master Heidegger.

RED CIRCLE. The secret Italian political terror organization, based in Naples and allied to the old Carbonari, was featured in "The Red Circle." According to Emilia Lucca, "the oaths and secrets of the brotherhood were frightful, but once within its rule no escape was possible." Many years before, her husband, Gennaro, had become a member in Naples, initiated by the terrible killer Gorgiano. Emilia and Gennaro had fled Italy, hoping that he had escaped its clutches. In New York, however, they met Gorgiano again, and Gennaro was once more forced into its ranks, the society expecting him to take part in its many criminal activities.

"RED CIRCLE, THE ADVENTURE OF THE" (REDC). Published: *Strand*, March and April 1911, *Strand* (U.S.), April and May 1911; collected in *His Last Bow* (1917). Major players: Holmes, Watson, Mrs. Warren, Emilia Lucca, Gennaro Lucca, Inspector Gregson, Leverton, Giuseppe Gorgiano. Case date: September 1902, according to W. S. Baring-Gould, although opinion among scholars varies. Holmes wrote of this affair: "This is an instructive case. There is neither money or credit in it, and yet one would wish to tidy it up." It begins with a visit by a Mrs. Warren, a landlady of "a high, thin, yellow-brick edifice in Great Orme Street, a narrow thoroughfare at the northeast side of the British Museum." She uses flattery to convince Holmes to look into the mystery surrounding her lodger, a puzzle that has become even darker given the abduction of her husband and subsequent release when his captors realized they had made a mistake and grabbed the wrong man—obviously they were after the lodger. Holmes meets a member of the Pinkerton Detective Agency, Leverton, best known to Holmes through the Long Island Cave Mystery.

"RED-HEADED LEAGUE, THE" (REDH). Published: *Strand*, August 1891; collected in *The Adventures of Sherlock Holmes* (1892). Case date: see below. Major players: Holmes, Watson, Jabez Wilson, John Clay (Vincent Spaulding), Duncan Ross, Peter Jones, Mr. Merryweather. An immensely popular entry in the Canon, ranked by both Conan Doyle and the readers of the *Baker Street Journal* (in 1959) second on their lists of favorite cases. Its success owes much to an intricately intriguing plot, a colorful client, and fine interplay between Holmes and Watson. Mr. Jabez Wilson, owner of a pawnbroker's shop in Coburg Square, comes to Holmes with a strange tale. His assistant, Vincent Spaulding (who came at half wages), pointed out that there was an opening in the Red-Headed League, an organization dedicated to "the propogation and spread of the red-heads as well as for their maintenance." Spaulding told Wilson that the group "was founded by an American millionaire, Ezekiah Hopkins, who was very peculiar in his ways. He was himself red-headed, and had a great sympathy for all red-headed men; so when he died it was found that he had left his enormous fortune in the hands of trustees, with instructions to apply the interest to the providing of easy berths to men whose hair was of that colour. From all I hear it is splendid pay and very little to do." Spaulding (also known as John Clay) thus encouraged Wilson to apply, as the latter had a tremendous head of red hair. Meeting with Duncan Ross, one of the league's founders, at 7 Pope's Court, Fleet Street, Wilson was immediately given a post. For the salary of 4 pounds a week, he was given the task of copying the *Encyclopedia Britannica* in the league's offices, with the added proviso that he must never leave the office of the league during set hours each day. After eight weeks of writing "Abbots and Archery and Armour and Architecture and Attica," Wilson went to work and read pinned to the door the stunning notice:

THE RED-HAIRED LEAGUE
IS
DISSOLVED
OCTOBER 9, 1890

The mystery only deepened when Wilson attempted to locate Ross. Going to Ross's supposed new offices at 17 King Edward Street, he learned that "it was a place for manufacturing artificial knee-caps." Utterly perplexed, Wilson approached Holmes, to investigate.

"The Red-Headed League" represents one of the most glaring examples of an error in dating by Dr. Watson, for Wilson first read of the organization in April 1890, and learned of its demise some eight weeks later.

REGENT CIRCUS.   It was at Westminster circus, or circle, that Holmes and Watson walked toward on their way to the Diogenes Club to meet Mycroft Holmes in "The Greek Interpreter." Following the death of the blackmailer Charles

Augustus Milverton, Holmes and Watson went down Oxford Street toward Regent Circus—there they saw a photograph of his murderer.

REGENT STREET.   The London street that will be remembered with infamy as the site of the vicious, murderous attack upon Holmes by the agents of Baron Gruner in "The Illustrious Client." It was also on Regent Street that Holmes noticed a man with a bushy black beard following Sir Henry Baskerville and Dr. Mortimer in *The Hound of the Baskervilles*. Gross and Hankey's, the jewelry establishment, was situated on the street in "A Scandal in Bohemia." John Turner and Charlie McCarthy met here in "The Boscombe Valley Mystery."

REGISTRATION AGENT.   Holmes impersonated a registration agent, who compiles lists of eligible voters, when he interviewed Henry Wood's landlady in "The Crooked Man."

REICHENBACH FALLS.   Second to 221B Baker Street, this is the most famous site in all of the Canon for it was here that Holmes apparently met his demise on May 4, 1891 at the hands of Professor Moriarty in "The Final Problem." The Reichenbach Falls are situated along the Reichenbach River in central Switzerland, near the village of Meiringen. Holmes, based on Watson's deductions, had entered into his struggles with the evil professor on the ledge overlooking the Falls. Watson wrote: "An examination by experts leaves little doubt that a personal conflict between the two men ended, as it could hardly fail to end in such a situation, in their reeling over locked in each other's arms. Any attempts at recovering the bodies was absolutely hopeless, and there, deep down in that dreadful cauldron of swirling water and seething foam, will lie for all time the most dangerous criminal and the foremost champion of law of their generation." In 1968, the Sherlock Holmes Society of London conducted a tour of Switzerland tracing the path of Holmes. On May 1, the members reenacted the climactic fight at the Falls, with Sir Paul Gore-Booth (later Lord Gore-Booth) as Holmes, and Charles Scholefield as Moriarty, although Scholefield was mercifully spared the professor's watery fate. The tour attracted considerable worldwide attention.

"REIGATE SQUIRES, THE" (REIG).
Published: *Strand*, June 1893, *Harper's*, June 17,

The personal struggle of Holmes and Moriarty comes to an end in "The Final Problem"; by Sidney Paget.

Holmes "accidentally" knocks over a table in "The Reigate Squires"; by Sidney Paget.

1893; collected in *The Memoirs of Sherlock Holmes* (1894). Major players: Holmes, Watson, Colonel Hayter, William Kirwin, Cunningham, Alec Cunningham. Case date: April 1887. In this tale Holmes's health is once again damaged by the relentless demands of a case (see also "DEVIL'S FOOT, THE ADVENTURE OF THE"). The investigation in question took place in spring 1887 and was concerned with the colossal schemes of Baron Maupertuis and the Netherland-Sumatra Company. "Even [Holmes's] iron constitution, however, had broken down under the strain of an investigation which had extended over two months, during which period he had never worked less than fifteen hours a day and had more than once, as he assured me, kept to his task for five days at a stretch." To ensure a proper rest, Watson takes him to stay with Colonel Hayter, whom Watson had known in Afghanistan, in Reigate, Surrey, whose "establishment was a bachelor one." His recuperation is soon marred, however, by a series of robberies. Holmes solves the murder and uses his investigation as a kind of therapy. When first published, the story was called "The Reigate Squire," the plural being added when it was collected into *The Memoirs of Sherlock*

Holmes (1894); American versions of the title have used the word "Puzzle" instead of "Squires."

"REMINISCENCES."   Dr. Watson's narratives of Holmes's adventures, on which the cases of the Canon are based, were originally gathered as his Reminiscences. At the start of *A Study in Scarlet* was written: **"Being a reprint from the Reminiscences of John H. Watson, M.D., Late of the Army Medical Department."** This has led Sherlockians to deduce that the vast career of Holmes and the memoirs of Dr. Watson were already published at the time that the good doctor's cases were reprinted in the *Strand* and elsewhere. There is some question as to whether the reminiscences had been published, but the use of the term "reprint" would indicate an earlier publication. If so, such a work would be the most important in all of Sherlockiana. Unfortunately, despite the efforts of scholars and aficionados, no copy has ever been found, a lack of discovery that would seem to give credence to those who say that the "Reminiscences" remained unpublished.

"RESIDENT PATIENT, THE" (RESI). Published: *Strand*, August 1893, *Harper's*, August 12, 1893; collected in *The Memoirs of Sherlock Holmes* (1894). Major players: Holmes, Watson, Percy Trevelyan, Mr. Blessington, Worthingdon Bank Gang. Case date: See below. An investigation brought to Holmes and Watson by Dr. Percy Trevelyan, a specialist in nervous diseases. Young Trevelyan had accepted the offer of the enigmatic Blessington to set him up in practice in a Brook Street address in return for a percentage of all profits and free medical care. The arrangement worked for some years. Suddenly, however, Blessington became increasingly agitated and nervous. Holmes's demands that Blessington tell all are refused and the next morning Trevelyan's patron is found hanged in his room. Holmes's examination of the room is brilliant, allowing him to formulate a remarkably clear picture of the men who had brought about Blessington's death. The dating of the case is difficult because of Watson's admitted ambiguity. He writes that it took place in October, while providing no year, owing to the loss of memoranda on the matter. This passage was included in the first editions of the case and in the edition collected in book form but was omitted from the American and subsequent editions. The noted Holmesian W. S. Baring-Gould dates it to October

Holmes and Watson converse in "The Retired Colourman"; by Frank Wiles.

1886. (See also "CARDBOARD BOX, THE ADVENTURE OF THE.")

"RETIRED COLOURMAN, THE ADVENTURE OF THE" (RETI).

Published: *Liberty*, December 18, 1926, *Strand*, January 1927; collected in *The Case Book of Sherlock Holmes* (1927). Major players: Holmes, Watson, Josiah Amberley, Barker. Case date: 1898. One of the last cases recorded in the Canon, published originally before "The Veiled Lodger" and "Shoscombe Old Place," although it has been collected in some editions as the last of all stories. Dealing with adultery and murder, the story has been subject to much debate as to why Watson seems to have tried intentionally to ensure that it not be published last. It has thus been speculated that Holmes was still traumatized by the death of his mother under mysterious or even terrible circumstances, perhaps murdered by his father for committing adultery. As this tragic episode had perhaps left him scarred for life, the events of the case cause him to lament to Watson about his client Josiah Amberley: "Pathetic and futile. But is not life pathetic and futile? Is not his story a microcosm of the whole? We reach. We grasp. And what is left in our hands at the end? A shadow. Or worse than a shadow—misery." The cause of Holmes's gloom is the affair brought to him by Amberley. The man's wife has apparently left him with her lover, taking with her Amberley's box of deeds. The grim case is distinguished by the presence of the detective Barker, said by Holmes to be his "hated rival upon the Surrey shore." Holmes also demonstrates his skills as a burglar.

THE RETURN OF MORIARTY.

A major pastiche (with *The Revenge of Moriarty*) published in 1974 by John Gardner, the author best known for his James Bond novels. In the *Return*, Holmes in fact figures almost not at all, the focus being on Professor Moriarty and to a lesser extent, Inspector Angus McCready Crow, a brilliant Scotland Yard policeman. As the "editor" of the novel, Gardner cites two main sources for his account: Crow's journals, notebooks, and correspondence, and, most importantly, the privately ciphered (coded) journals of Professor James Moriarty. The story is richly populated by a major cast of characters, including the dangerous associates of Moriarty, especially his so-called Praetorian Guard—Pip Paget, Spear, and the dangerous Lee Chow—and their "ladies." The plot begins with the return of the professor to London in April 1894, at the same time as Sherlock Holmes. How he survived the Reichenbach Falls is revealed in the reminiscences of the professor, as is his role in resolving the Ripper case in 1888. His arrival coincides with Holmes's adventure of "The Empty House," and thus he suffers the loss of Colonel Sebastian Moran because of the colonel's insistence on seeking revenge against Holmes for the "death" of the professor. The colonel's actions reveal the instability of his empire and much of the book is spent detailing his struggle to regain preeminence over England's criminal element. He faces considerable threats from such rivals as Michael the Peg and Peter the Butler. While his true aim is to unite all of the criminal masterminds of Europe and America, his ambitious plan to win their confidence nearly costs him his liberty. The attention to Victorian detail is impressive, and Gardner aids the reader with a glossary of slang and common terms from the era, a glossary useful to readers of the Canon itself. The Moriarty that emerges from the tale is fully three-dimensional and highly plausible. This Napoleon of Crime, however, is quite different from that depicted in the Canon, his appearance in the stories the result of a clever disguise—his true origins revealed only slowly.

RETURN OF SHERLOCK HOLMES, THE.

The third collection of Sherlock Holmes's cases, published in 1908, featured those adventures that were released following the detective's triumphant return to practice in 1894 after the GREAT HIATUS. The stories of the collection were "The Adventure of the Empty House," "The Adventure of the Norwood Builder," "The Adventure of the Dancing

Men," "The Adventure of the Solitary Cyclist," "The Adventure of the Priory School," "The Adventure of Black Peter," "The Adventure of Charles Augustus Milverton," "The Adventure of the Six Napoleons," "The Adventure of the Three Students," "The Adventure of the Golden Pince-Nez," "The Adventure of the Missing Three-Quarter," "The Adventure of the Abbey Grange," and "The Adventure of the Second Stain."

RETURN OF SHERLOCK HOLMES, THE.

U.S. 1929. Dir: Basil Dean, and Clive Brook. Cast: Clive Brook (Holmes), H. Reeves-Smith (Watson), Harry J. Morey (Professor Moriarty), Donald Crisp (Colonel Sebastian Moran), and Betty Moran (Mary Watson). This was the first sound film featuring Sherlock Holmes, although a silent version was released to accommodate those theaters that were not yet able to present sound pictures, so one might say that this was the last silent Holmes picture. (A foreign language version was also released without H. Reeves-Smith, but with Brook.) Released by Paramount and produced by David O. Selznick, *Return* introduced Clive Brook as the detective, placing him in an all-original story, with plot elements from "The Dying Detective" and "His Last Bow" included, along with, of course, Professor Moriarty and Colonel Moran. The plot involves the kidnapping of Watson's son-in-law, Roger Longmore (Hubert Druce), and the pursuit of the culprits by Holmes, Watson, and the good doctor's daughter Mary onto an ocean liner. (Several shots were actually filmed on board a ship, very rare for the era.) Holmes poses as a violinist and a ship's steward, using phosphorescent paint to trace a suspect. Professor Moriarty, of course, is at the bottom of everything, attempting to murder the detective with a poison thorn hidden in a cigarette case. Critics liked Brook, but disliked the movie, to the effect that the film is largely unknown today.

"RETURN OF SHERLOCK HOLMES, THE."

The third season (1986) of episodes in the outstanding series of adaptations by Granada Television, starring Jeremy Brett (Holmes), Edward Hardwicke (Watson), and Rosalie Williams (Mrs. Hudson). This season marked the departure of David Burke and the arrival of Edward Hardwicke as Watson. This Watson is more serious, more competent, although he literally passes out when

Holmes turns up from the "dead" in "The Empty House"—the detective was thought dead in the last episode ("The Final Problem") the previous season. The quality of the episodes remained high, and Brett's Holmes continued to be one of the finest of all time. Among the stories covered were "The Abbey Grange," "The Second Stain," and "The Musgrave Ritual." One point of note: not all the stories are from the collection of *The Return of Sherlock Holmes* (e.g. "The Musgrave Ritual"), a frustrating detail to Sherlockian purists.

"RETURN OF SHERLOCK HOLMES, THE."

U.S. 1987. Dir: Kevin Connor. Cast: Margaret Colin (Watson), Michael Pennington (Holmes). An inventive made-for-television movie that suggests that Holmes was able somehow to cheat death. Set in the present, the story proposes that a descendent of Watson, a Boston detective (Colin), journeys to England to inherit an English manor. She finds a body frozen in suspended animation and revives it, discovering that it is Sherlock Holmes. Much of the film is devoted to the Great Detective attempting to familiarize himself with the modern world, aided by Watson's descendent. A female Watson works very nicely, and was used previously in both the stage and film versions of *They Might Be Giants* and in the 1976 comedy *The Return of the World's Greatest Detective* with Larry Hagman and Jenny O'Hara.

REVENGE OF MORIARTY, THE.

A 1975 pastiche and sequel by John Gardner to his immensely successful *The Return of Moriarty*, The *Revenge* picks up where the first story left off, with the professor leaving England in 1894, his plot to assemble a continental (if not world-wide) criminal organization having been thwarted by Inspector Crow and Sherlock Holmes. The main storyline centers around Moriarty's plan to inflict vengeance upon all those who worked against him in the past, especially Crow and Holmes. Moriarty fled England for America where, assuming aliases such as Jacques Meunier, a French businessman, he amasses a tremendous fortune and returns to England in secret to put his vengeance into action. Once again, Gardner's attention to historical and social detail is very impressive. He centers his plot on Moriarty, but, more than in the *Return*, Holmes is given a greater role. The climax is somewhat rushed and abrupt, no doubt with the aim of another sequel.

REVENGE OF THE HOUND, THE.   A 1987 pastiche novel by the well-respected Holmesian Michael Hardwick. While the title would suggest a sequel to the Canonical novel *The Hound of the Baskervilles* and is a nicely sensational "grabber," the work does not deal with the dread Baskerville curse. Instead, Holmes and Watson are engaged on a complex series of investigations into murder, body-snatching, and the apparent return of the Hound, sighted on Hampstead Heath. Throughout, the spirit and style of Watson's writing is maintained (as with the other Hardwick pastiche, *Prisoner of the Devil*).

REYNOLDS, SIR JOSHUA.   The famed English portrait painter (1723–1792) who is said to have painted a member of the Baskerville family (*The Hound of the Baskervilles*). The work hung in Baskerville Hall and was noticed by Holmes, who immediately recognized its similarity to a living person involved in the case.

RICHARDS, DR.   The physician who was called to Tredannick Wartha, the home of the Tregennis family, following the discovery by Mrs. Porter, the housekeeper, that Brenda Tregennis was dead and her brothers George and Owen were "gibbering like two great apes" in "The Devil's Foot." The scene was so horrible that Dr. Richards turned "as white as a sheet" and "fell into a chair in a sort of faint."

RICOLETTI.   One of Holmes's early but unchronicled cases, dating from a time before the association of Holmes and Watson ("The Musgrave Ritual"). Watson wrote that Holmes had "a full account of Ricoletti of the club-foot, and his abominable wife."

RIDLING THORPE MANOR.   The home in Norfolk of Hilton and Elsie Cubitt in "The Dancing Men." Also known in some editions as Ridling Manor or Ridling Thorp Manor, it was the site of the appearance of the so-called Dancing Men and the tragedy that overtook the Cubitts.

RIGA.   A Russian port city situated on the Baltic Sea. It was the site of an 1857 case that Holmes said was one of the two parallel cases to the one

referred to him by Francois le Villard (*The Sign of Four*).

RIPLEY.   A village in Surrey, near Woking, that Holmes visited during his labors in recovering the missing Naval Treaty in "The Naval Treaty." He told Watson and Percy Phelps: "After leaving you at the station I went for a charming walk through some admirable Surrey scenery to the pretty little village called Ripley, where I had my tea at an inn and took the precaution of filling my flask and of putting a paper of sandwiches in my pocket. There I remained until evening, when I set off for Woking again and found myself in the highroad outside Briarbrae just after sunset."

RIVAL SHERLOCK HOLMES.   Italian 1907 or 1908. Prod: Arturo Ambrosio. An important early Holmes film, silent and running six minutes and fifty seconds, known originally in Italy as *Le Rival de Sherlock Holmes* (or *Sherlock Holmes' Enemy*). It is unclear whether Holmes actually appeared in the film as a character, but its success in Italy and the United States demonstrated the drawing power of the detective. The *Moving Picture World* (May, 1908) declared: "A pictorial detective story of merit, with many lightning changes of disguise by the detective in his pursuit of the lawbreakers. Exciting scenes and physical encounters are numerous."

RIVALS OF SHERLOCK HOLMES.   The name given to a large number of fictional detectives who appeared in print around the same time as Sherlock Holmes, many springing up during the period when the reading public believed the Great Detective was dead at the bottom of the Reichenbach Falls (1893–1903). Many of these rivals were far from memorable, but some were both impressive and genuinely interesting. Unfortunately for them, they have been long in the shadow of their giant contemporary and remain, even today, virtually unknown by the reading public. Among the better known or remarkable detectives are Father Brown, by G. K. Chesterson, who appeared in a number of books starting in 1911; Nick Carter, the most enduring of the rivals, who premiered in 1886 and was the creation of the American Ormond G. Smith; Martin Hewitt, by Arthur Morrison, who appeared in 1894 in the *Strand*, with illustrations by Sidney Paget; Dr. John Thorndyke, by R. Austin Freeman, debuting in 1907 and described as "the greatest medico-legal detective of all time"; Professor A. S. F. X. Van Dusen, by Jacques Futrelle, who appeared first in 1906 and who was known as "The Thinking Machine," using pure logic to solve his cases and sending out his assistants to gather evidence and clues, à la Nero Wolfe. Effort has been made to rescue the Rivals from oblivion—Sir Hugh Greene, the expert historian on the detective story, compiled many stories into several collections: *The Rivals of Sherlock Holmes* (1970), *More Rivals of Sherlock Holmes* (1971), *Cosmopolitan Crimes: Foreign Rivals of Sherlock Holmes* (1971), and *The American Rivals of Sherlock Holmes* (1976) among others. Alan Russell assembled another forty stories into his work, *Rivals of Sherlock Holmes* (1978). Thames Television also aired a television series called "The Rivals of Sherlock Holmes" based on Hugh Greene's works (1975–1976). Splendidly produced and directed, the series offered seasoned Holmesians such as John Neville (who played Dr. Thorndyke), Robert Stephens (Max Carrados, the blind detective), Douglas Wilmer (Professor Van Dusen), and Charles Gray (Monsieur Valmont, a French detective). (See also LUPIN, ARSENE and RAFFLES, A. J.)

RIVER POLICE.   The Thames Division of the Metropolitan Police that helped to bring several Holmes cases to a climax. The river police played a critical role in the pursuit and capture of Jonathan Small on the Thames in *The Sign of Four* and were used in the recovery of John Openshaw's body in "The Five Orange Pips" and the arrest of James Brown in "The Cardboard Box."

RIVIERA.   The coastal region of southeastern France along the Mediterranean. Holmes had, in a squat notebook, the facts concerning "the robbery in the train de-luxe to the Riviera on February 13, 1892," in which Count Sylvius was involved in "The Mazarin Stone."

ROBINSON, JOHN.   The name used by James Ryder when he first met Holmes and Watson in "The Blue Carbuncle."

ROME.   The Italian city where Douglas Maberley served as attache and where he died of pneumonia in "The Three Gables." Don Murillo stayed in Rome for a short time as noted in "Wisteria Lodge." (See also VATICAN).

RONDER.   Owner of the Ronder Circus in "The Veiled Lodger" and "one of the greatest showmen of his day." Ronder was also a "devil" who tormented his wife **Eugenia**. She told Holmes and Watson: "I was raised a poor circus girl brought up on the sawdust, and doing springs through the hoop before I was ten. When I became a woman this man loved me, if such lust as his can be called love, and in an evil moment I became his wife. From that day I was in hell, and he the devil who tormented me." "He deserted me for others," she claimed. "He tied me down and lashed me with his riding-whip when I complained." His picture displayed "a dreadful face—a human pig, or rather a human wild boar, for it was formidable in its bestiality . . . Ruffian, bully, beast—it was all written on that heavy-jowled face." She was later involved in her husband's death and was mauled by the lion King Sahara, an attack that destroyed her beauty and left her emotionally and spiritually crippled. Desirous of telling her grisly story, she allowed Holmes to be her confessor before her death. Her plans for a premature demise were prevented by Holmes with the words: "Your life is not your own . . . Keep your hands off it."

ROSA, SALVATOR.   An Italian artist (1615–1673) known for his landscapes. Thaddeus Sholto owned a Rosa that a connoisseur might have had some doubts about. (*The Sign of Four*).

ROSE.   The Great Detective lyrically commented of the flower in "The Naval Treaty": "Our highest assurance of the goodness of Providence seems to me to rest in the flowers. All other things, our powers, our desires, our food, are all really necessary for our existence in the first instance. But this rose is extra. Its smell and its colour are an embellishment of life, not a condition of it. It is only goodness which gives extras, and so I say again that we have much to hope from the flowers."

ROSENLAUI.   Properly Rosenlaui Bad, a hamlet in central Switzerland near Meiringen. In "The Final Problem" on May 4, 1891, Holmes and Watson set out from Meiringen with the plan of spending the night at Rosenlaui. While walking, however, they decided to stop at the Reichenbach Falls—with all the consequences.

ROSS, COLONEL.   The owner of King's Pyland stables on Dartmoor and the horse Silver

Blaze, the favorite for the Wessex Cup in "Silver Blaze." When his racehorse was apparently stolen and his trainer John Straker murdered, Colonel Ross asked Holmes to look into the matter, in cooperation with Inspector Gregory. He was skeptical of Holmes's skill, at one point saying, "I must say that I am rather disappointed in our London consultant." The detective, however, proved Ross's doubts groundless, managing to play a trick on the colonel upon returning Silver Blaze to its owner.

ROSS, DUNCAN.   The name used by the manager of the offices of The Red-Headed League in Pope's Court, London. Ross accepted Jabez Wilson into the league and gave him the task of copying the *Encyclopedia Britannica*. He was also the accomplice of the clever and dangerous John Clay and was apparently actually named Archie. Another alias that he used was William Morris.

ROSS AND MANGLES.   Animal dealers on the Fullman Road in *The Hound of the Baskervilles* who sold to a neighbor of Baskerville Hall the dog that "was the strongest and most savage in their possession."

ROSYTH.   A naval base in Scotland about which the master spy Von Bork attempted to acquire information in "His Last Bow." One of the pigeon-holes in his safe was marked Rosyth.

ROTHERHITHE.   An area in Bermondsey, a borough of London, where Holmes had been working on a case involving Chinese sailors down on the docks when he contracted the disease that was to play so prominent a role in the case known as "The Dying Detective."

ROTTERDAM.   The seaport in the Netherlands from where the master spy Von Bork said his agent Altamont could catch a boat to New York in "His Last Bow." The cigar found at the scene of the murder of Charles McCarthy in "The Boscombe Valley Mystery" was, Holmes said, of an Indian variety, of a type rolled in Rotterdam.

ROUNDHAY, MR.   The vicar of the parish around the hamlet of Tredannick Wollas in "The Devil's Foot." According to Watson, Roundhay "was something of an archaeologist, and as such Holmes had made his acquaintance. He was a middle-aged man, portly, and affable, with a con-

siderable fund of local lore." The vicar introduced Holmes and Watson to the case that the detective called "the Cornish horror," at one point exclaiming "We are devil-ridden, Mr. Holmes! My poor parish is devil-ridden! Satan himself is loose in it! We are given over into his hands!"

ROY.   The wolfhound of Professor Presbury in "The Creeping Man." Always a loyal and faithful hound, Roy suddenly and inexplicably turned on his master, attempting twice to bite him. Roy's behavior was of interest to Holmes.

ROYAL MALLOWS.   A regiment in the British army stationed at Aldershot and under the command of Colonel James Barclay in "The Crooked Man." The name Royal Munsters was used in some editions.

ROYAL MARINE LIGHT INFANTRY.   The commissionaire who delivered the summons to Holmes from Inspector Gregson in *A Study in Scarlet* was retired from this regiment of marines. Holmes deduced this from the man's appearance and manner and told a disbelieving Watson. The doctor was later astonished when the commissionaire identified himself as a former sergeant of the Royal Marine Light Infantry.

ROYLOTT, GRIMESBY.   One of the most terrible villains from the Canon who appeared in "The Speckled Band" and its stage version by Arthur Conan Doyle. A member of the once rich and influential family of the Roylotts of Stoke Moran, Roylott inherited an estate that had been reduced to near poverty by profligate heirs in the eighteenth century and a particularly wasteful gambler during the Regency. His father finished off any hopes of salvaging the family's fortune. Grimesby was thus forced to seek his own living, serving as a doctor in Calcutta. Marrying Helen Stoner in India, he returned to England and Stoke Moran after her death in 1875. He raised his two step-daughters, Julia and Helen, but their life was not happy, culminating with Julia's death a short time before her planned marriage. At the request of Helen, Holmes investigated the matter, revealing just how wicked Roylott truly was. Examples of Roylott's vicious nature included beating his native butler to death on suspicion of robbery in India, and hurling the blacksmith near Stoke Moran over a parapet into a stream. Watson wrote of him: "A large face, seared with a thousand wrinkles, burned yellow with the sun, and marked with every evil passion, was turned from one to the other of us, while his deep-set, bile-shot eyes, and his high, thin, fleshless nose, gave him somewhat the resemblance to a fierce old bird of prey." Resurrected in the 1910 stage play *The Speckled Band*, Roylott (here spelled Rylott) was played with consummate skill by Lyn Harding. He would return to the role in the 1931 film version *The Speckled Band* with Raymond Massey (Holmes) and Athole Stewart (Watson).

RUCASTLE, ALICE. Daughter of Jephro Rucastle by his first wife in "The Copper Beeches." She was away in Philadelphia at the time that Violet Hunter was hired by Mr. Rucastle as governess. Alice's fiancé, Mr. Fowler, however, had great doubts that she was in fact out of England, and was quite persistent in discovering what her family had done with her. Alice eventually wed Fowler by special license in Southampton.

RUCASTLE, EDWARD. Son of Jephro Rucastle and his first wife for whom Jephro Rucastle hired Violet Hunter as governess in "The Copper Beeches." She described him to Holmes and Watson: "He is small for his age, with a head disproportionately large. His whole life appears to be spent in an alternation between savage fits of passion and gloomy intervals of sulking. Giving pain to any creature weaker than himself seems to be his one idea of amusement, and he shows quite remarkable talent in planning the capture of mice, little birds, and insects." Holmes found the child's behavior most enlightening about the parents.

RUCASTLE, JEPHRO. Owner of The Copper Beeches, in Hampshire, near Winchester, who resided with his second wife, his son Edward, and his daughter Alice. He searched for a governess for his son, finding Violet Hunter through an employment agency, and insisted that she sit in a particular chair and cut her hair very short. Miss Hunter described him as "a prodigiously stout man with a very smiling face and great hairy chin which rolled down in fold upon fold over his throat . . . a pair of glasses on his nose . . ." **Mrs. Rucastle,** second wife of Jephro Rucastle, was younger than her husband and was utterly devoted to Jephro and their son Andrew. Violet Hunter thought her "colorless in mind as well as in feature. She impressed me neither favorably nor the reverse. She was a nonentity. It was easy

to see that she was devoted both to her husband and her little son. Her light gray eyes wandered from one to the other, noting every little want and forestalling it if possible. He was kind to her also in his bluff, boisterous fashion, and on the whole they seemed to be a happy couple. And yet she had some secret sorrow, this woman. She would often be lost in thought, with the saddest look upon her face."

RUGBY. Watson played rugby, a type of football in which the participants can kick, carry, or dribble the ball, presumably wearing the number 31 which he described as his "old school number" ("The Retired Colourman"). He played at one time for Blackheath, competing against Richmond and Bob Ferguson, the man involved in the affair of "The Sussex Vampire." Cambridge and Oxford played matches at the Queen's Club in Kensington and the sudden disappearance of the crack three-quarter Godfrey Staunton in "The Missing Three-Quarter," of Cambridge, prompted the captain of the team, Cyril Overton, to consult Holmes. The detective found Staunton, but too late to save Cambridge from defeat.

RUSSELL, WILLIAM CLARK. American writer, best known for his tales of the sea. He was read by Dr. Watson who "was deep in one of Clark Russell's fine sea-stories" when John Openshaw arrived at Baker Street in "The Five Orange Pips."

RUSSIA. During Holmes's career, Russia remained a major European empire. Prior to the meeting of Watson and Holmes, the young detective solved the adventure of the old Russsian woman ("The Musgrave Ritual"), and just before the case recounted in "A Scandal in Bohemia," Watson heard from time to time "some vague account of his [Holmes's] doings" such as his summons to Odessa in the case of the Trepoff murder. In England, Holmes became embroiled in Russian affairs during "The Golden Pince-Nez" with Professor Coram and his wife, Anna, former member of the Russian Nihilists. In the same chronicle, Holmes and Watson delivered papers to the Russian embassy in order to secure the freedom of Alexis, the love of Anna. Dr. Percy Trevelyan had a Russian count and his son come to his office, a mysterious visit that was connected to the terrible murder of the Resident Patient. The Russian embassy was also said to be willing to pay handsomely for the Naval Treaty.

RYDER, JAMES. Nicknamed Jem, the upper attendant at the Hotel Cosmopolitan, in London, from where the Blue Carbuncle, owned by the Countess Morcar, was stolen in "The Blue Carbuncle." He tried desperately to recover a goose that had been promised to him but that had been accidentally sold. His search for the goose led him to an encounter with Sherlock Holmes. Watson described him as "a little rat-faced fellow."

SACKER, ORMOND. Sir Arthur Conan Doyle considered this as an early name for Dr. John Watson. The name was used in the film *The Adventures of Sherlock Holmes' Smarter Brother* (1975) for Sigerson Holmes's assistant played by Marty Feldman. Another, more remarkable Sacker appeared in Mark Frost's 1993 novel *The List of 7*.

SAHARA KING. The North African lion was one of the exhibits of the Ronder wild beast show in "The Veiled Lodger." Sahara King was responsible for mutilating Eugenia Ronder. The inquest declared that there had been some signs that the lion was dangerous, but familiarity begat contempt and no notice of its true nature was taken.

ST. BARTHOLOMEW'S HOSPITAL. Known popularly as Bart's or Barts, a London hospital associated with the University of London, serving as one of the university's medical schools. Dr. Watson worked as a staff surgeon at St. Bartholomew's in *A Study in Scarlet*. Young Stamford, who will always be remembered for introducing Watson to Holmes, served as Watson's dresser at the hospital. The institution is itself remarkable to all students of the Canon because the famous first meeting between the duo took place in St. Bart's chemical laboratory and is commemorated with a plaque.

ST. CLAIR, NEVILLE. A man of apparently comfortable finances who resided in Lee at a villa called the Cedars with his family in "The Man With the Twisted Lip," St. Claire disappeared one day in the room of the beggar Hugh Boone in the opium den Bar of Gold. Holmes said of him: "He had no occupation, but was interested in several companies and went to town as a rule in the morning, and returning by the 5:14 from Cannon Street every night. Mr. St. Clair is now thirty-seven years of age, is a man of temperate habits, a good husband, a very affectionate father and a man who is popular with all who know him. I may add that his whole debts at the present moment, as far as we have been able to ascertain, amount to £88 10s., while he has £220 to his credit at the Capital and Counties Bank. There is no reason, therefore, to think that money troubles have been weighing upon his mind." **Mrs. Neville St. Clair** engaged Holmes to find her husband. Evidence found at the scene of his disappearance included his clothes, a box of children's bricks, and traces of blood on the windowsill and floor. On a nearby mudbank, the police found his coat stuffed with 421 pennies and 270 half-pennies. On her way to the Aberdeen Shipping Company to pick up a package one day, Mrs. St. Clair saw her husband in the second-floor window of the Bar of Gold opium den, watching in horror as he was apparently dragged away. Bursting into the room, she could not find anyone save a wretched beggar, Hugh Boone, who was arrested.

ST. GEORGES.   A London church, situated in Hanover Square, where Lord Robert St. Simon and Hatty Doran were married in "The Noble Bachelor."

ST. JAMES'S HALL.   A Westminster concert hall. In "The Red-Headed League," Holmes invited Watson to attend a performance of Sarasate at the Hall, interrupting their investigations of the Red-Headed League. Watson wrote: "All the afternoon he sat in the stalls wrapped in the most perfect happiness, gently waving his long, thin fingers in time to the music, while his gently smiling face, and languid, dreamy eyes were unlike those of Holmes, the sleuthhound, Holmes, the relentless keen-witted, ready-handed criminal agent, as it was possible to conceive . . . When I saw him that afternoon enwrapped in the music at St. James's Hall I felt that an evil time might be coming upon those whom he had set himself to hunting down."

ST. JAMES'S STREET.   A street in Westminster noted for its many clubs. Longdale Pike, "the receiving station, as well as the transmitter, for all the gossip of the Metropolis," spent his waking hours in a bow window of a St. James's street club in "The Three Gables."

ST. LOUIS.   A city in the state of Missouri, mentioned in A Study in Scarlet. Jefferson Hope was from St. Louis, and Hope's father, Jefferson Senior, had been a good friend of John Ferrier. Holmes also noted an 1871 case in St. Louis that was parallel to one referred to him by Francois Le Villard (The Sign of Four).

ST. LUKE'S.   A university college, in one of England's great university towns, where Holmes investigated the case recorded in "The Three Students." Hilton Soames, who brought the case to Holmes's attention, was a lecturer at the College of St. Luke's. It remains unclear as to what university St. Luke's belonged, particularly as Watson was careful to avoid giving any details that might assist the reader in identifying the school.

ST. MONICA.   A church on Edgeware Road where Godfrey Norton and Irene Adler were married in "A Scandal in Bohemia."

ST. OLIVER'S.   A Yorkshire private school that was run by Mr. and Mrs. Vandeleur, actually Jack and Beryl Stapleton (The Hound of the Baskervilles). Mr. Vandeleur established the school with the assistance of a consumptive tutor named Fraser who made the school a success. Fraser soon died, and the school "sank from disrepute into infamy."

ST. PANCRAS.   A case investigated by Holmes that was brought to him by Merivale of Scotland Yard. The detective solved the matter by using his microscope to link the suspect, a picture-frame maker who habitually handled glue, to a cap found beside the body of a policeman ("Shoscombe Old Place").

ST. SAVIOUR'S.   A church near King's Cross where Mary Sutherland and Hosmer Angel were to be married, followed by a wedding breakfast at the St. Pancras Hotel in central London ("A Case of Identity"). The wedding never took place.

ST. SIMON, LORD ROBERT.   In full, Lord Robert Walsingham de Vere St. Simon, second son of the duke of Balmoral, and onetime undersecretary for the colonies in a late administration in "The Noble Bachelor." Lord St. Simon engaged Holmes's services to find his bride, Hatty Doran, who disappeared mysteriously and abruptly after the wedding. Watson described him: "A gentleman entered [Holmes's rooms], with a pleasant, cultured face, high-nosed and pale, with something like petulence about the mouth, and with the steady, well-opened eye of a man whose pleasant lot it had ever been to command and to be obeyed. His manner was brisk, and yet his general appearance gave an undue impression of age, for he had a slight forward stoop and a little bend of the knees as he walked. His hair, too, as he swept off his very curly brimmed hat, was grizzled round the edges and thin upon the top. As to his dress, it was careful to the verge of foppishness, with high collar, black frock-coat, white waistcoat, yellow gloves, patent-leather shoes, and light-coloured gaiters."

SALTIRE, LORD.   The title held by the son and heir of the duke of Holdernesse in "The Priory School," actually an inferior title to that of the

Lord Robert St. Simon, from "The Noble Bachelor"; by Sidney Paget.

duke himself. Holmes was engaged by Dr. Thorneycroft Huxtable to find Lord Saltire as he had disappeared from the Priory School run by Huxtable.

SAMSON.   A criminal in New Orleans who escaped from justice because there was, at the time, no reliable test for bloodstains (*A Study in Scarlet*). Holmes was thus jubilant that he had found a test that was infallible.

SANDERS, IKEY.   A gem cutter who refused to cut the stolen Crown Diamond for Count Negretto Sylvius in "The Mazarin Stone." Holmes told the count that he had "peached" (informed).

SAN FRANCISCO.   Aloysius Doran took his daughter Hatty to the California city so that she would not marry Francis Hay Moulton in "The Noble Bachelor." Hatty married Moulton there anyway, but later learned that he had been killed. Lord Robert St. Simon, whom she would eventually wed, first met her in San Francisco. It has been theorized that Dr. Watson once visited San Francisco, possibly meeting and falling in love with one

of his wives, an idea suggested in David Dvorkin's *Time for Sherlock Holmes*, W. S. Baring-Gould's *Sherlock Holmes of Baker Street*, and probably part of the unpublished *Angels of Darkness* by Conan Doyle.

SANGER, JOHN.   Known as "Lord John" Sanger, an English circus owner (1816–1889) who was considered one of the greatest showmen of the day, he was a rival of the circus owners Ronder and Wombwell in "The Veiled Lodger."

SAN PAULO.   Properly Saõ Paulo, the city in Brazil was a heading in the notebook, containing stock exchange securities, found in the cabin where Captain Peter Carey was murdered in "Black Peter."

SAN PEDRO.   A supposed Central American country that was ruled for ten or twelve years by the cruel dictator Don Murillo, known as the Tiger of San Pedro in "Wisteria Lodge." He was eventually overthrown by revolution, but he escaped and fled to Europe. San Pedro's colors were green and white.

SARASATE.   In full Pablo Martin Meliton Sarasate y Navascues, a Spanish composer and violinist (1844–1908) whom Holmes and Watson heard perform at St. James's Hall, interrupting their investigation into "The Red-Headed League."

SAUNDERS.   Housemaid to Mr. and Mrs. Hilton Cubitt at Ridling Thorpe Manor, Norfolk in "The Dancing Men." She and Mrs. King, the housekeeper, were awakened by an explosion, followed a minute later by another one. Going downstairs, they discovered Mr. Cubitt quite dead and Mrs. Cubitt horribly wounded in the head.

SAUNDERS, MRS.   The caretaker of the house on Little Ryder Street where Nathan Garrideb had his rooms in "The Three Garridebs." It was practice for her to leave the building each day at four o'clock.

SAUNDERS, SIR JAMES.   A respected specialist in dermatology for whom Holmes did a professional service. He aided the detective in the case recounted by Holmes in "The Adventure of the Blanched Soldier."

SAVAGE, VICTOR.   The nephew of Culverton Smith, the well-known resident of Sumatra and expert on Eastern diseases in "The Dying Detective." Savage mysteriously "contracted an out-of-the-way Asiatic disease in the heart of London" and was dead within four days, suffering horribly throughout. Holmes investigated the strange death and apparently contracted a tropical illness himself while working among Chinese sailors down in the docks.

SAWYER, MRS. "A very old and wrinkled woman" who claimed a wedding ring which Holmes had advertised as being found in the roadway between the White Hart Tavern and Holland Grove in *A Study in Scarlet*. Mrs. Sawyer was actually an accomplice of the killer of Enoch Drebber disguised to appear as an old woman. Holmes attempted to follow "her" but lost the trail, discovering that the address provided by Mrs. Sawyer, 13 Duncan Street, Houndsditch, was occupied by a respectable paperhanger named Keswick and that no one by the name of Sawyer had ever lived there. (See also DENNIS.)

SAXE-COBURG SQUARE. A London square near the Strand where the pawnshop of Jabez Wilson was located in "The Red-Headed League." "It was a poky, little, shabby-genteel place, where four lines of dingy two-storied brick houses looked out onto a small railed-in enclosure, where a lawn of weedy grass and a few clumps of faded laurel bushes made a hard fight against the smoke-laden and uncongenial atmosphere."

"SCANDAL IN BOHEMIA, A (SCAN)." Published: *Strand*, July 1891; collected in *The Adventures of Sherlock Holmes* (1892). Major players: Holmes, Watson, the king of Bohemia, Irene Adler. Case date: March 1888. The first short account by Dr. Watson, published after *A Study in Scarlet* and *The Sign of Four*, that begins with the tantalizing statement: "To Sherlock Holmes she is always the woman. I have seldom heard him mention her under any other name. In his eyes she eclipses and predominates her sex. It was not that he felt any emotion akin to love for Irene Adler. All emotions, and that one particularly, were abhorrent to his cold, precise but admirably balanced mind." From this grand opening the narrative assures the reader that the impending union of Watson and Mary Morstan mentioned in *The Sign of Four* has taken place, that Holmes continues to use cocaine, and that the

detective's career is flourishing (including a summons to Odessa in the case of the Trepoff murder). As was to occur throughout his active years, Holmes is engaged by a member of the European aristocracy, in this case none other than Wilhelm Gottsreich Sigismund von Ormstein, grandduke of Cassel-Felstein, and hereditary king of Bohemia. The monarch enlists his services to recover a compromising photograph of the king with the American born opera singer Adler. She has threatened to use the photograph to wreck his planned marriage to a Scandinavian princess, and all efforts to recover it, legally and illegally, have failed. Holmes uses several clever disguises throughout the case, but even he is ultimately unsuccessful, his plans for a dramatic recovery of the picture wrecked by Adler herself. All turns out well, however, and Watson writes that "he used to make merry over the cleverness of women, but I have not heard him do it of late. And when he speaks of Irene Adler, or when he refers to her photograph, it is always under the honourable title of the woman." A photograph of Adler, left by her for the king, becomes one of Holmes's most prized possessions. He later also accepted a gold snuffbox from the king. Watson made note ("The Blue Carbuncle," "The Copper Beeches"), that the case was free from legal crime.

SCANDINAVIA, KING OF. Probably King Oscar II (r. 1872–1905), monarch of the united Norway and Sweden, although after 1905 Oscar was ruler of Sweden only. Holmes assisted the royal family of Scandinavia just before taking on the affair brought to him by Lord Robert St. Simon in "The Noble Bachelor," enabling the detective to inform the nobleman that he was descending, not ascending, in the social class of his client. The resolution of the case for the royal family probably earned Holmes a high medal (perhaps the medal of St. Olaf) and certainly gained him a large financial reward. This last award, in conjunction with the assistance he gave to the French Republic, had left him in such a position financially that by the time of "The Final Problem," Holmes could, if he so wished, continue to live in a quiet fashion and to focus on his chemical researches. The detective was also connected to the royal house through his work for the king of Bohemia. In "A Scandal in Bohemia," that ruler was planning to wed Clotilde Lothman von Saxe-Meningen, second daughter of the king of Scandinavia, a union threatened by

Irene Adler, who owned a compromising photo of the king of Bohemia.

SCARLET CLAW, THE.

U.S. 1944. Dir: Roy William Neill. Cast: Basil Rathbone (Holmes), Nigel Bruce (Watson), Gerald Hamer (Potts), Paul Cavanagh (Lord Penrose). The eighth entry in the long running Rathbone-Bruce cycle of films. This time around, the dynamic duo journeys to Canada, becoming embroiled in a dark, murder-filled mystery in a gloomy village in the Canadian backwoods. One of the least known of the many Holmes films by Universal, *The Scarlet Claw* is actually one of the finest of the entire cycle, mixing murder, revenge, and dark mayhem with what appears to be a supernatural apparition as the name of the village is La Morte Rouge (The Red Death). Investigating the death of Lady Penrose, Holmes uncovers a tale of vengeance and nearly becomes a victim of the Scarlet Claw while out on the marsh that bears a striking resemblance to the moor in *The Hound of the Baskervilles* (it was the same set). As seemed frequently the case in Rathbone movies, the detective has a hard time keeping the intended victims of the killer from meeting their gruesome ends, and this time he is able to save only one of them. At the end Holmes quotes Churchill about Canada, the Commonwealth, and the United States.

"SCHLOCK HOLMES."

A very popular and imaginative parody of the detective by Robert L. Fish, appearing in *Ellery Queen's Mystery Magazine* on a regular basis from 1960 to 1970. The stories featured Schlock Holmes and Dr. Watnet, who had quarters at 221-B Bagel Street and were visited by Inspector Balustrade from Scotland Yard. The housekeeper was Mrs. Essex. The Holmes cases included "The Adventure of the Double-Bogey Man" (1962), "The Adventure of the Perforated Ulster" (1967), and "The Adventure of the Dog in the Knight" (1970). A collection of the stories, *The Incredible Schlock Holmes* (1966), was edited by Anthony Boucher.

SCIENCE-FICTIONAL SHERLOCK HOLMES, THE.

A 1960 collection of parodies and pastiches of the Canon, edited by Robert C. Peterson, with contributions from such well-known writers as Poul Anderson, Anthony Boucher, August Derleth and Mack Reynolds, and Gordon R. Dickson. Among the stories are "Sherlock Holmes and Science Fiction" by Anthony Boucher; "The Martian Crown Jewels" by Poul Anderson and Gordon R. Dickson; "The Adventure of the Snitch in Time" by Mack Reynolds and August Derleth; and "The Anomaly of the Empty Man" by Anthony Boucher. A number of the works in the collection have been reprinted subsequently in such anthologies as *Sherlock Holmes Through Time and Space* (1984) and *The Misadventures of Sherlock Holmes* (1989).

SCOTLAND.

The home of several figures in the Canon, the most important being the long-suffering housekeeper, Mrs. Hudson. Other Scots included: Inspector MacDonald (*The Valley of Fear*), Menzies, the engineer of the Crow Hill Mine murdered by the Scowrers (*The Valley of Fear*), and the nurse of Lucy Hebron ("The Yellow Face"). Holmes and Watson journeyed to Scotland in the 1971 film *The Private Life of Sherlock Holmes*, meeting Queen Victoria and encountering a seagoing vessel strikingly similar to the Loch Ness Monster.

SCOTLAND YARD.

The name given to the London Metropolitan Police, in particular the Criminal Investigation Department (CID); Scotland Yard also refers to the headquarters of the London Metropolitan Police located in Holmes's time on the Thames embankment (from 1890), the so-called New Scotland Yard, built after the original Scotland Yard (or Great Scotland Yard) was almost completely destroyed in a bombing in May 1884. Throughout his long career, Holmes had extensive and repeated dealings with the officers and men of Scotland Yard. The Great Detective never had patience for lesser minds and was particularly short of compassion when working with the members of the Yard, justifying Watson's observation in "The Bruce-Partington Plans" that "it was one of my friend's most obvious weaknesses that he was impatient with less alert intelligences than his own." As T. S. Blakeney wrote in his book *Sherlock Holmes*, in the chapter "Holmes and Scotland Yard":

"Sherlock Holmes is nothing if not a contrast to Scotland Yard. His reputation, indeed, has largely been built up by the regularity of his successes over the official forces, successes due to his entirely different attitude towards the cases he investigated, and to the original methods adopted in their solution. The Yard attitude was that of the promoted policemen they were . . . 'Facts alone are wanted in life. Plant nothing else, and root up everything else . . .'

Sherlock Holmes
and Science Fiction

Sherlock Holmes and science fiction have blended surprisingly well together over the years. The detective has chased Professor Moriarty through time, repulsed an invasion of the earth by Martians, and appeared in a remakable number of incarnations, including a dog, an old man, and a weird alien, a crime-solving creature in "The Martian Crown Jewels" by Poul Anderson. The most notable appearance of the detective and the professor on television has been on "STAR TREK: The Next Generation." In two episodes of the series, the android character Data (Brent Spiner) has pretended to be the Great Detective, opposite Moriarty (well played by Daniel Davis) who has been recreated on what is called a "holodeck," a device for creating artificial environments and entertainments. Assorted other Holmesian references have been used from time to time, especially by the Vulcan character Spock, who in "Star Trek VI" claims Holmes as an ancestor.

The following are major works featuring Holmes in a sci-fi setting:

TITLE (DATE)	AUTHOR	TITLE (DATE)	AUTHOR
The Demon Device (1979)	Robert Saffron	*The Probability Pad* (1970)	T. A. Waters
Doctor Jekyl and Mr. Holmes (1981)	Michael Hardwick	*The Science-Fictional Sherlock Holmes* (1960, Collection)	Robert Peterson, Ed.
The Earthquake Machine (1976)	Austin Mitchelson and Nicholas Utechin	*The Second War of the Worlds* (1976)	George Smith
Exit, Sherlock Holmes (1977)	Robert Hall	*Sherlock Holmes Through Time and Space* (1984, Collection)	Martin Greenberg, Ed.
The Incredible Umbrella (1979)	Marvin Kaye		
The Infernal Device (1979)	Michael Kurland	*Sherlock Holmes' War of the Worlds* (1975)	Manly Wade Wellman
The Other Log of Phileas Fogg (1973)	Philip Jose Farmer	*Time for Sherlock Holmes* (1979)	Michael Dibdin
The Adventure of the Peerless Peer (1974)	Philip Jose Farmer		

But the imagination necessary for the proper handling of the facts they accumulated was lacking in the Scotland Yarders, and the want of it frequently led to their overlooking the really important data for their case."

In case after case in which Holmes was involved, he proved the investigating officer of the Yard to be wrong either in specific examinations of the clues and evidence or in the entire approach and theorizing. His string of successes naturally produced some antagonisms, as was evidenced by the jealous comments of the Yard officer Forbes, who was looking into the missing Naval Treaty in "The Naval Treaty": "You are ready enough to use all the information that the police can lay at your disposal, and then you try to finish the case yourself and bring discredit on them." Holmes responds: "On the contrary, out of my last fifty-three cases my name has only appeared in four, and the police have had all the credit in forty-nine. I don't blame you for not knowing this, for you are young and inexperienced, but if you wish to get on in your new duties you will work with me and not against me."

Certainly some, if not many, detectives of the Yard put aside their pride and envy and went hat in hand to 221B or wired the detective for help when faced with a truly baffling case. His most regular associates on the Yard were Gregson, Hopkins, Bradstreet, and especially Lestrade. Gregson, in *A Study in Scarlet*, was mentioned by Holmes as "the smartest of the Scotland Yarders"; with Lestrade he was "the pick of a bad lot," but in all of the cases in which he served as the representative of law he seemed a complete incompetent. Stanley Hopkins appeared at first to be a protege of sorts to Holmes, and some Sherlockians have even speculated that he might have been Holmes's son. Holmes, however, was quite severe in his criticism and obvious in his disappointment in the way the policeman handled the Black Peter affair.

Lestrade, of them all, seems to have been the most perpetually in need of Holmes's assistance, even if he remained sneeringly condescending of the detective's methods and astonishingly immune to learning anything of value from the detective who so routinely proved him to be in error. Still, Lestrade did manage to establish reasonably cordial relations with the Master. In "The Six Napoleons" we find him visiting 221B and Watson writes: "It was no very unusual thing for Mr. Lestrade of Scotland Yard, to look in upon us of an evening, and his visits were welcome to Sherlock Holmes, for they enabled him to keep in touch with all that was going on at the police headquarters. In return for the news which Lestrade would bring, Holmes was always ready to listen with attention to the details of any case upon which the detective was engaged, and was able occasionally, without any active interference, to give some hint or suggestion." It was in this affair of the Six Napoleons that Lestrade paid Holmes the highest compliment possible: "I've seen you handle a good many cases, Mr. Holmes, but I don't know that I ever knew a more workmanlike one than that. We're not jealous of you at Scotland Yard. No, sir, we are very proud of you, and if you come down to-morrow, there's not a man, from the oldest inspector to the youngest constable, who wouldn't be glad to shake your hand."

SCOTT ECCLES, JOHN. The man who introduced Holmes to the case of Wisteria Lodge with the telegram: "Have just had most incredible and grotesque experience. May I consult you? Scott Eccles, Post Office, Charing Cross." A resident of Popham House in Lee, he was invited to Wisteria Lodge by Aloysius Garcia, suffering the experience of which he wrote and subsequently being suspected in the murder that took place. He was "a stout, tall, gray-whiskered and solemnly respectable person . . . His life history was written in his heavy features and pompous manner. From his spats to his gold-rimmed spectacles he was a Conservative, a churchman, a good citizen, orthodox and conventional to the last degree. But some amazing experience had disturbed his native composure and left its traces in his bristling hair, his flushed, angry cheeks, and his flurried, excited manner."

SCOWRERS, THE. The name used in Vermissa Valley for the members of Lodge 341 of the Ancient Order of Freemen (*The Valley of Fear*). While elsewhere the Freemen were thought to be a benevolent fraternal organization, in Vermissa the members used their secret society to practice murder and intimidation against what they held to be the oppression of railway and mining companies. In organizing the workers, the Scowrers would not tolerate any opposition or dissent, threatening and punishing anyone who stood in their way or spoke out in favor of moderation. The head of the lodge (known as the bodymaster) was Jack McGinty, the "black-maned giant" with "strange dead black" eyes. Through the efforts of Birdy Edwards and the Pinkertons, the Scowrers were suppressed in 1875.

Aside from Bodymaster McGinty, the Scowrers were headed by several equally unsavory individuals. The county delegate for the Ancient Order of Freedmen was **Evans Pott;** he had authority over all of the Scowrers in Vermissa Valley, including the ruthless McGinty. He lived at Hobson's Patch. The treasurer was **Carter,** considered a gifted organizer, "and the actual details of nearly every outrage had sprung from his plotting brain." The secretary was **Harraway,** "a man of incorruptible fidelity where the finances of the Order were concerned, and with no notion of justice or honesty to anyone beyond." The members of the Scowrers mentioned in *The Valley of Fear* were the following: **Ted Baldwin; Jack McMurdo; Jim Carnaway,** who was killed in the attempt on Chester Wilcox; **Tiger**

Cormac, a thick set, dark faced, and brutal looking murderer; **Egan,** who, with the Scowrer **Lander,** claimed head money for the shooting of old man Crable at Stylestown; **Gower,** a participant in the attack upon James Stanger, editor of the *Daily Herald* in Vermissa; **Lawler,** who lodged with Jack McMurdo and who was dispatched by the county delegate Evans Pott to murder the manager of the Crow Hill Mine; **Manders,** a young member of the Freemen and partner of McMurdo in the unsuccessful murder attempt on Chester Wilcox; **Mansel,** a participant in the attack on Stanger; **Morris,** "an elderly, clean-shaven man, with a kindly face and a good brow" who had a son named Fred and who spoke to the Scowrers in favor of moderation (dangerous sympathies for a member of that society); **Reilly,** a companion of McMurdo's in the murder attempt on Wilcox; **Mike Scanlan,** a friend of McMurdo's who shared a room with him; **Arthur Willaby,** who stood guard outside the editorial office of the Vermissa *Daily Herald* with McMurdo while several other Scowrers assaulted the editor (he vowed revenge upon Birdy Edwards after his release from prison with his brothers of the lodge); and **Wilson,** who, despite his youth, volunteered to murder Andrew Rae. Members of the Ancient Order outside of Vermissa included: **Bartholomew Wilson,** the district leader of Lodge 29, at Chicago; **James H. Scott,** Bodymaster of Lodge 29, Chicago; **J.W. Windle,** the division master of Lodge 249 in Merton County, who petitioned the Scowrers of Vermissa Valley to murder Andrew Rae; and **Higgins** the treasurer of the Merton County Lodge. A lawyer named **Reilly** was retained by the Scowrers. He helped free from jail the men arrested for the brutal attack on Stanger.

The Scowrers were able to intimidate and terrorize many individuals and even entire companies in the Vermissa Valley. **Atwood, Van Deker,** and **Manson,** owners of ironworks, sold out their businesses to the **West Wilmerton General Mining Co.** out of fear for their lives. **Lee,** a mine owner, sold his firm to the **State and Merton Railroad Company. Archie Swindon** also sold his business rather than pay protection money; he apparently fled to New York. **Max Linder & Co.** paid five hundred dollars to the Scowrers to be left alone. The coal-mining firm of **Walker Brothers** tried the same tactic, sending the Scowrers one-hundred dollars to be left unharassed, but the Scowrers demanded five hundred.

Many individuals could not pay to escape the wrath of the lodge, however, and the number of innocent persons killed, beaten, or mutilated by the Scowrers in *The Valley of Fear* was large. Among the (apparently) murdered were **Simon Bird, Josiah H. Dunn** (manager of the **Crow Hill Mine**), **William Hales** (a mine owner in Gilmerton), the two **Jenkins** brothers, **Menzies** (the engineer of the Crow Hill mine), the **Nicholson** family, **Andrew Rae** (co-owner of the coal firm **Rae and Sturmash** in Merton County), members of the **Stendal** family and **Van Shorst. Old Man Crable,** of Stylestown, was murdered by two Scowrers, Lander and Egan; they subsequently claimed head money for the shooting. **Hyam, Milman, Billy James,** and **Charles Williams** were also victims. The **Staphouse** family was wiped out in an explosion. **Larbey** was almost beaten to death on the orders of Boss McGinty; his wife, **Mrs. Larbey,** was shot while caring for him. **Murdoch** was mutilated. **Chester Wilcox,** of Marley Creek and a mine foreman of the **Iron Dyke Company,** was a target of an assassination plot by the lodge. In the attempt on his life, the Scowrer Jim Carnaway was killed and Jack McMurdo led another unsuccessful try. Finally, **James Stanger,** editor of the Vermissa *Daily Herald*, was beaten by a group of Scowrers because of his outspoken editorials against them.

Not everyone was terrified or intimidated by the brutal members of Lodge 241. **Jacob Shafter** was an opponent of their activities, not even allowing the Scowrer Jack McMurdo to stay in his boardinghouse. Two other enemies of the Scowrers were **Herman Strauss** and **Jack Knox.** The Scowrers were ultimately destroyed by the Pinkerton agent Birdy Edwards, who was a part of the aggressive campaign launched against them by five firms with interests in the valley, probably including the **West Wilmerton General Mining Co.** West Wilmerton purchased several ironworks in Vermissa Valley from local owners who were anxious to escape the predations of the Scowrers.

SCRAPBOOK. A collection of clippings, materials, and assorted extracts was apparently kept by Holmes to record details about his cases. Several references were made to Holmes's scrapbooks ("The Empty House," "The Red Circle," and "The Three Students"), but it seems that these collections were synonymous with his massive commonplace books, a collection so vast that he probably had an index to it. Watson also kept a scrapbook, only this one was on Holmes's career. For example, he collected clippings from the murder case of Enoch Drebber in *A Study in Scarlet.*

"SECOND STAIN, THE ADVENTURE OF THE" (SECO).

Published: *Strand*, December 1904, *Collier's* January 28, 1905; collected in *The Return of Sherlock Holmes* (1905). Major players: Holmes, Watson, Lord Bellinger, Rt. Hon. Trelawney Hope, Eduardo Lucas, Lady Hilda Trelawney Hope. Case date: See below. An investigation brought to Holmes by none other than the two-time Prime Minister Lord Bellinger and the secretary for European affairs, the Rt. Hon. Trelawney Hope. As in the "The Naval Treaty," Holmes is engaged to find a missing document of national importance, one that if not found could have the most dire international consequences, including "the expenditure of a thousand millions and the lives of a hundred thousand men." The document in question was stolen from Trelawney Hope's dispatch box, in his bedroom, an event utterly inexplicable to both him and his wife. It is acknowledged that three secret agents in London could have pulled off such a theft: Oberstein, Louis La Rothiere, and Eduardo Lucas. Matters are soon complicated, however, by the appearance of Lady Hilda Trelawney Hope asking questions about the affair, the murder of Lucas in his fashionable residence at 16 Godolphin Street, Westminster, and the presence of an out of place bloodstain, a "second stain," on a carpet at the murder scene in Westminster. The detective succeeds brilliantly, and Lord Bellinger is forced to remark, "There is more in this than meets the eye."

The dating of the case presents a number of difficulties as Watson deliberately refrained from providing any useful information because of the extreme sensitivity of the affair, writing that it occurred "in a year, and even in a decade, that shall be nameless." He does admit that the matter was first brought to them in autumn, on a Tuesday morning. The proposed date by scholars has varied from 1886 to 1894; W. S. Baring-Gould placed it in October 1886. In "The Naval Treaty," Watson writes that "no case, however, in which Holmes was engaged has ever illustrated the value of his analytical methods so clearly or has impressed those who were associated with him so deeply. I still retain an almost *verbatim* report of the interview in which he demonstrated the true facts of the case to Monsieur Dubuque of the Paris police, and Fritz

von Waldbaum, the well-known specialist of Dantzig . . ."

SECOND WAR OF THE WORLDS, THE.

A 1976 pastiche science-fiction novel by George H. Smith that transfers Holmes into the literary environment of H. G. Wells's *War of the Worlds*, although only the title bears any similarity to the original Wells work. Here Holmes and Watson are transported to the world of Annwn, a twin of earth. There they team up with two Annwnians, Dylan MacBride and Clarinda, to stop another Martian invasion. A similar theme was developed in Manly Wade Wellman's *Sherlock Holmes' War of the Worlds* (1975).

SECRET WRITINGS.

In full, *Secret Writings: Analyses of 160 Separate Ciphers*, a monograph written by Holmes sometime before 1898 and his involvement in the affair of the Dancing Men. As the detective commented while working on the Dancing Men cipher, "I am familiar with all forms of secret writings, and am myself the author of a trifling monograph upon the subject." *Secret Writings* is the last of Holmes's technical monographs mentioned in the Canon. (See CRYPTOGRAPHY.)

SELDEN.

The so-called Notting Hill murderer who was sentenced to Princetown Prison, from which he later escaped (*The Hound of the Baskervilles*). Selden hid on the moor near Baskerville Hall but was later killed on it by the Hound. His reasons for remaining close to the Hall were exposed by Sir Henry Baskerville and Dr. Watson, the former ironically contributing to Selden's death by giving him some of his clothes. Watson wrote of him: "I remembered the case well, for it was one in which Holmes had taken an interest on account of the peculiar ferocity of the crime and the wanton brutality which had marked all the actions of the assassin. The commutation of his death sentence had been due to some doubts as to his complete sanity, so atrocious was his conduct."

SENEGAMBIA.

Holmes felt that there were cases in India and Senegambia, a onetime French possession in western Africa, that were parallel to the murder of Bartholomew Sholto that he investigated in *The Sign of Four.*

SEPOY REBELLION.

An uprising that occurred in India from 1857 to 1858. The Sepoy

Rebellion was taking place at the time of the theft of the Agra Treasure (*The Sign of Four*). It involved the mutiny of the native Indian soldiers of the Indian army (Sepoys).

SEVEN-PER-CENT SOLUTION, THE.

The bestselling 1974 pastiche novel by Nicholas Meyer, known in full as *The Seven-Per-Cent Solution, Being a Reprint from the Reminiscences of John H. Watson, M.D., as edited by Nicholas Meyer*. The most successful pastiche of the Canonical Writings of Dr. Watson, this work involves itself with the dark corners of the Great Detective's mind, boldly examining his addiction to cocaine and the underlying psychological causes of his dependancy. It gives the heretofore unpublished events of what happened in 1891, in the case originally recounted as "The Final Problem." Fast approaching near total ruin from cocaine, Holmes is lured out of London by a clever conspiracy organized by his brother Mycroft, with the help of Dr. Watson (as always the narrator), and the reluctant assistance of Professor Moriarty, whom Holmes is persecuting remorselessly. Taking the bait that Moriarty has fled from London, Holmes gathers Watson and pursues the professor to Vienna. There he makes his fateful encounter, not with the Napoleon of Crime, but with the one man in Europe capable of saving him from his terrible addiction, Sigmund Freud. Much of Watson's account focuses on Holmes's courageous effort to free himself from the grip of the insidious drug. An interesting side plot involves Holmes's defeat of the ambitions of the wicked Baron Von Leinsdorf, thereby delaying, albeit for a few years, a European war. While not a flawless rendering of Dr. Watson's style, the novel captures the spirit and atmosphere of the Canon, while offering a splendid glimpse at decadent Vienna near the turn of the century. (See also COCAINE, WEST END HORROR, THE and CANARY TRAINER, THE.)

SEVEN-PER-CENT SOLUTION, THE.

U.S. 1976. Dir: Herbert Ross. Cast: Nicol Williamson (Holmes), Robert Duvall (Watson), Alan Arkin (Sigmund Freud), Laurence Olivier (Moriarty). This immensely stylish film version of the Nicholas Meyer novel of the same name, with its screenplay adapted by Meyer with some major changes made in the plot. At its heart, the film is faithful to the novel, presenting the meeting of Holmes with Dr. Sigmund Freud in Vienna and their painful efforts

Sherlock Holmes (Nicol Williamson) confers with Dr. Sigmund Freud (Alan Arkin) in a moment of crisis in *The Seven-Per-Cent Solution* (1976), based on Nicholas Meyer's novel.

to rid the detective of his addiction to cocaine. The principal alteration in the story is the emphasis placed on the role of Baron Von Leinsdorf (played with devilish enthusiasm by Jeremy Kemp), allowing the introduction of the singer Lola Deveraux (Vanessa Redgrave). Still included is the exciting train chase, only here the detective, Watson, and Freud race to prevent Von Leinsdorf and an Ottoman *pasha* from making off with the lovely Miss Deveraux. Holmes embarks on his Hiatus, as per the novel, but he discovers Deveraux will be travelling with him, a touch of romance bringing to mind Holmes's association with Irene Adler.

SHAFTER, ETTIE.

Daughter of Jacob Shafter in *The Valley of Fear*. She helped her father run a boardinghouse on Sheridan Street in Vermissa where Jack McMurdo stayed for a brief time. Ettie later married Birdy Edwards in Chicago (1875), but died of typhoid in California. **Jacob Shafter** would not allow McMurdo to remain in the boardinghouse because of his associations with the Scowrers in the valley.

SHAG.

A type of coarse tobacco that was much favored by Holmes. Watson wrote about himself in "The Creeping Man": "As an institution I was like the violin, the shag tobacco, the old black pipe, the index books, and others perhaps less excusable."

The detective was known to have smoked an entire ounce of shag during the night spent at the Cedars while pondering the strange case of "The Man With the Twisted Lip" and to have charged and recharged his pipe "with the strongest black tobacco" while awaiting fresh news about the missing horse Silver Blaze in "Silver Blaze." Holmes also ordered a pound of shag from the tobacconist Bradley when starting his initial inquiries into the strange death of Sir Charles Baskerville in *The Hound of the Baskervilles*. Finally, as a reward for helping them in their labors, the disguised Holmes was given two fills of shag by the ostlers of the Serpentine Mews in "A Scandal in Bohemia."

SHAKESPEARE, WILLIAM. Holmes had considerable familiarity with the writings of the bard (1564–1616) despite Dr. Watson's assessment that the detective's knowledge of literature was "nil" (*A Study in Scarlet*). Holmes quoted *King Henry VI*, part II, act 3, scene 2 in "The Disappearance of Lady Frances Carfax": "Thrice is he armed that hath his quarrel just," but misquotes *Twelfth Night*, act 2, scene 3: "Journeys end in lovers' meetings" (properly "Jorneys end in lovers meeting"; "The Empty House" and "The Red Circle"), saying that it came from "the old play."

SHEERLUCK OHMS. A parody of the Great Detective written by Dr. Watts Ion whose stories appeared from 1947 to 1951 in the *Anaconda Wire* under the title "The Adventures of Sheerluck Ohms." Among the "investigations" in which he was involved were "The Case of the Chain Reaction," "The Case of the Fish That Wouldn't Keep," "The Case of the Persian Parsnip," and "The Case of the Tootsbury Typist." The name of the detective was similar to the general parody "Sheerluck Holmes" that began appearing soon after Holmes became popular with the public.

SHERLAW KOMBS. The first parody ever written on the Great Detective, created by Robert Barr under the pseudonym Luke Sharp in 1892. Sherlaw Kombs appeared in the May 1892 edition of the *Idler Magazine* in "Detective Stories Gone Wrong: The Adventures of Sherlaw Kombs." Immediately entertaining the public, the detective was given the honor of being included in the well-known collection by Ellery Queen, *The Misadventures of Sherlock Holmes* (1944). He was aided by the faithful Whatson.

SHERLOCK BROWN. U.S. 1921. Dir: Bayard Veiller. Cast: Bert Lytell, Ora Carew, DeWitt Jennings. A silent comedy released by the Metro Picture Corp., produced, written, and directed by Bayard Veiller; he was later to assist in the screenplay for *Sherlock Holmes* (1930) with Clive Brook. *Sherlock Brown* merely uses the pale shadow of Holmes, presenting a young detective, William Brown, in a frantic chase to recover a secret formula that had been stolen from the government. Three years later, the Metro Picture Corp. would release *Sherlock, Jr.*, starring Buster Keaton.

SHERLOCK HOLMES. This drama in four acts, written by Sir Arthur Conan Doyle and WILLIAM GILLETTE that premiered in Buffalo on October 23, 1899, and then in New York on November 6, 1899, made Gillette one of the most famous Holmeses on both sides of the Atlantic. Sir Arthur had been desirous of writing for the theater, but the already successful novelist found breaking into the different medium less than a blazing success. Apparently, in the early 1890s Conan Doyle had been approached by the Broadway producer and impressario Charles Frohman about securing the rights to Sherlock Holmes for dramatic use. Nothing immediately came of their association. Around 1897 or early 1898, however, Conan Doyle had decided that he might have greater theatrical opportunities if he wrote a piece about the Great Detective. He sat down and wrote a five-act play featuring Holmes and Professor Moriarty based on the period of the detective's early career. The work found its way to Frohman, who decided that it was unfit for production. Frohman nevertheless recognized its possibilities and journeyed to England to meet with Conan Doyle. He told Sir Arthur that a rewrite should be undertaken, suggesting that the person to do it (and to play Holmes) was the respected actor William Gillette.

With Conan Doyle's authorization, and giving credit to Conan Doyle, Gillette went to work revising the Holmes play. The change was staggering with wholesale adjustments in plot and character. At one point, Gillette telegraphed Sir Arthur with the astonishing question: "MAY I MARRY HOLMES?" Conan Doyle, accepting reality and acknowledging both his faith in Gillette and his own fading interest in the subject, wired back: "YOU MAY MARRY HIM, OR MURDER HIM, OR DO WHAT YOU LIKE WITH HIM."

William Gillette, one of the famous portrayors of Holmes, seated on his beloved cushions, from *Sherlock Holmes,* the play he wrote.

In May 1899, Gillette travelled himself to England to meet Sir Arthur, securing his blessing for the play, including Conan Doyle's grudging acceptance of a romantic aspect to the plot. Returning to the United States, Gillette took the play into production. After opening in Buffalo, it moved to New York, where it was a smash hit. The play moved to London in September 1901, opening at the Lyceum Theatre, an excellent place for it given the Lyceum's appearance in *The Sign of Four*. As big a success in England as in the United States, the play even drew a visit from the king and queen, on the evening of February 1, 1902. In the touring company of the play, the part of Billy was played by a twelve-year-old actor named Charles Chaplin. Chaplin would reprise his role in September 1905 in the comedy *The Painful Predicament of Sherlock Holmes*, again opposite Gillette as the Great Detective.

Sherlock Holmes was based upon several stories of the Canon, intertwined around a great deal of innovative creating by Gillette. Parts of the plots from "A Scandal in Bohemia" and "The Final Problem" gave Holmes the tasks of recovering a memento from a onetime love affair and confronting the wicked Professor Moriarty, respectively. The famous confrontation between the detective and professor is retained while Irene Adler is replaced by the young, beautiful Alice Faulkner as a woman planning to avenge her dead sister. Holmes convinces her to fall in love with him but is himself the sudden victim of Cupid's arrow, telling his beloved Alice: "Your powers of observation are somewhat remarkable, Miss Faulkner . . . and your deduction is quite correct! I suppose . . . indeed I know . . . that I love you." Despite the heretical nature of the line, the audience adored the play, enjoying as well the complex lighting effects and the moment in the story when Holmes is trapped dramatically in a sealed room by Moriarty with the aim of gassing the detective to death. Most of all, the audiences flocked to see the detective brought to life by Gillette. With his curved pipe, cap, cloak, magnifying lens, violin, and cocaine syringe, Gillette emerged as the ultimate embodiment of Holmes, remaining so for decades.

Through *Sherlock Holmes* the image of Holmes was forever set, thereafter concretized by the illustrators of Holmes stories as they used Gillette as their model instead of the original description given by Watson. The stage play made Holmes a household name, all the while associating him forever with a meerschaum pipe, a magnifying lens

stuck to his eye, and the line "Elementary, my dear Watson," immortalized by Basil Rathbone, which had its start in the play with the line "Oh, this is elementary, my dear Watson." Equally, the play took Holmes out of the Canon and made him a legitimate hero, a man of action in a sharp contrast to the living machine of thought that was the Sherlock Holmes of Watson's writings. *Sherlock Holmes* was very similar to the Hamilton Deane play *Dracula* in the way that it took a literary figure, presented it for stage, and then altered the public view for all time. Like the play *Dracula*, *Sherlock Holmes* has been revived countless times. Notable revivals have starred John Wood, John Neville, Robert Stephens, and Frank Langella.

SHERLOCK HOLMES. U.S. 1916. Dir: Arthur Berthelet. Cast: William Gillette, Edward Fielding, Ernest Maupain (Moriarty), and Marjorie Kay (Alice Faulkner)—an unfortunately lost silent film, the cinematic version of Gillette's monumentally successful stage play. Also known as *Adventures of Sherlock Holmes*, and produced by Essanay Films, this was not, as some have thought, merely a filming of Gillette's performance, but was a complete work in its own right, the plot generally following that of the stage piece, with Holmes meeting and falling in love with the beautiful Alice Faulkner (Kay). Offensive to many devout Sherlockians, the romance of Holmes and Faulkner was, apparently, given added emphasis in the film as Gillette desired it to have appeal with audiences everywhere. The result was a major hit, described in one review as "the Greatest Super feature of the Year." Filmed in Chicago, it lasted a lengthy two hours, in seven reels, and was for many years the most important film featuring Holmes as it recorded the performance of Gillette, considered in his time to be *the* Great Detective. In England, however, H. A. Saintbury was better known and appeared in 1916 in the film *The Valley of Fear*.

SHERLOCK HOLMES. U.S. 1922. Dir: Albert Parker. Cast: John Barrymore (Holmes), Roland Young (Watson), Gustav von Seyffertitz (Moriarty), Carol Dempster (Alice Faulkner). Known in England as *Moriarty*, this was Barrymore's sole Holmesian outing, based on the William Gillette play *Sherlock Holmes* (and especially Gillette's 1916 film version), with a screenplay by Marion Fairfax and Earle Brown. Released by the Samuel Goldwyn Co., *Sherlock Holmes* was a major film, featuring as it

JOHN BARRYMORE
in
SHERLOCK HOLMES

Directed by **ALBERT PARKER**

Adapted from **WILLIAM GILLETTE'S** stage play founded on Sir **CONAN DOYLE'S** stories

A Goldwyn Picture

A poster from the John Barrymore film *Sherlock Holmes* (1922).

Clive Brook as the Great Detective in *Sherlock Holmes* (1932). Holmes film veteran Alan Mowbray stands behind him.

did the great Barrymore. It certainly had the potential of one of the all-time Holmes pictures. The writers very cleverly inserted a prologue to the Gillette material, featuring Holmes and Watson as students at Cambridge. While there, the young sleuth defeats a plot by the already active Moriarty and first meets his love, Alice Faulkner. Holmes's relationship with both characters, the professor and Alice, is explained and is thus more interesting later in the film.

SHERLOCK HOLMES. U.S. 1932. Dir: William K. Howard. Cast: Clive Brook (Holmes), Reginald Owen (Watson), Miriam Jordan (Alice Faulkner), Ernest Torrence (Moriarty), Alan Mowbray. The third outing by Brook as the Great Detective, but the most memorable performance

in the film was by Ernest Torrence as the evil Moriarty, ranked as one of the finest of all time, particularly when compared to the distinctly non-Holmesian Brook. Holmes never once wears the customary deerstalker and is engaged to be married to Alice Faulkner (Jordan). The plot centers on the efforts of Moriarty to seek revenge upon the three men who were responsible for his arrest and conviction, one of whom is Holmes. Reginald Owen would go on to appear as Holmes in *A Study in Scarlet* (1933). This film was also known as *Conan Doyle's Master Detective Sherlock Holmes* (1932).

"SHERLOCK HOLMES." U.S. 1936. Writer: Edith Meiser. An American radio program starring Richard Gordon (Holmes) and Harry West (Watson) that ran from October through December

1936. The series consisted of forty-eight stories adapted or created by Edith Meiser, who also did the adaptation for "Sherlock Holmes" on radio in 1935 for William Gillette. Some of the original cases were "The Hindoo in the Wicker Basket," "The Armchair Solution," and "The Giant Rat of Sumatra." This was the last major American radio program featuring Holmes before the 1939 debut of Basil Rathbone and Nigel Bruce on the airwaves. In 1938, however, there was an adaptation of the Gillette play, *Sherlock Holmes*, by Orson Welles and the Mercury Theatre.

"SHERLOCK HOLMES." England 1951. Cast: Alan Wheatley (Holmes), Raymond Francis (Watson), and Iris Vandeleur (Mrs. Hudson). The first Holmes television series in England, featuring adaptations of six cases from the Canon by C. A. Lejeune, with Ian Atkins as producer. The episodes

were transmitted live on BBC television starting in October 1951. The stories were "The Empty House," "A Scandal in Bohemia," "The Dying Detective," "The Reigate Puzzle," "The Red-Headed League," and "The Second Stain."

SHERLOCK HOLMES.   U.S. 1953. Cast: Basil Rathbone (Holmes), Jack Raine (Watson), Thomas Gomez (Moriarty), and Elwyn Harvey (Mrs. Hudson). A play written by Ouida Rathbone for her husband that opened at the New Century Theatre in New York in October 1953, that, unfortunately, lasted only three performances. *Sherlock Holmes* came about as a result of Basil Rathbone's desire to appear in a stage play about the detective, but he did not wish to star in a revival of Gillette's famous play as he considered it badly dated. His wife Ouida thus undertook the job of creating a new work. She chose as her basic source "The

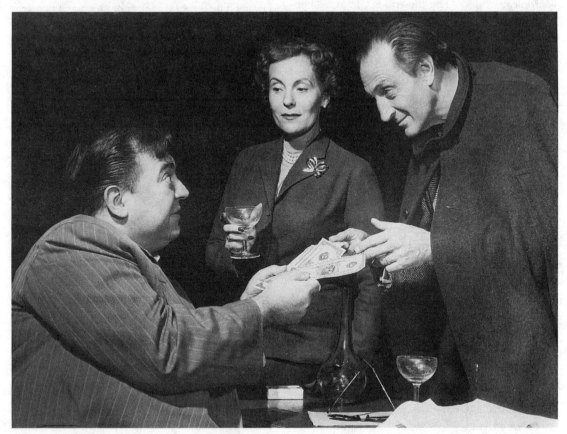

An aging Basil Rathbone is seen here accepting money from Professor Moriarty (Thomas Gomez) in the play *Sherlock Holmes* (1953) written by his wife Ouida Rathbone.

Adventure of the Bruce-Partington Plans," including elements of "A Scandal in Bohemia," "The Final Problem," and "The Second Stain." Despite lavish sets and a large ensemble cast, the play was astonishingly unsuccessful, in large measure because of the weak performance of Rathbone. Nigel Bruce, who had died three weeks before the opening of a heart attack, was sorely missed. In his autobiography, Rathbone wrote: "For myself be it said that, like Conan Doyle at the end of the first *Adventure*, try as I would my heart was not in it."

"SHERLOCK HOLMES." England 1964–1965. Dir: Various, including Peter Sasdy, Max Vernel, and Peter Duguid. Cast: Douglas Wilmer (Holmes), Nigel Stock (Watson), Peter Madden (Lestrade), Mary Holder (Mrs. Hudson). A BBC television series that began as a 1964 television movie version of "The Speckled Band." There followed in 1965 twelve one-hour-long adaptations of Canonical stories: "The Illustrious Client," "The Devil's Foot," "The Copper Beeches," "The Red-Headed League," "the Abbey Grange," "The Six Napoleons," "The Man With the Twisted Lip," "The Beryl Coronet," "The Bruce-Partington Plans," "Charles Augustus Milverton," "The Retired Colourman," and "The Disappearance of Lady Frances Carfax." Both Wilmer and Stock were highly successful in their roles and both would play their respective characters in later productions. This is remembered as one of the best television series on the detective.

"SHERLOCK HOLMES AND DOCTOR WATSON." U.S. 1982. Dir: Sheldon Reynolds and Val Guest. Cast: Geoffrey Whitehead (Holmes) and Donald Pickering (Watson). An American made, but largely unknown, television series, produced and also written by Sheldon Reynolds, creator of the 1954 Ronald Howard series on the Great Detective. Filmed in Poland, the episodes relied only partly on the Canon, using original stories to spice things up. The series made the European television rounds, on West German television, before arriving in the United States. Whitehead took to the role with enthusiasm.

SHERLOCK HOLMES AND THE CASE OF SABINA HALL. The second in a series of pastiche novels by L. B. Greenwood, published in 1987. In this adventure, Holmes and Watson travel to Sabina Hall on the English Channel after the detective receives a letter from an old classmate asking if he knew of anyone in the medical field willing to take up a position as physician to one Silas Andrew, a crusty but terminally ill old gentleman. Holmes decides to accompany Watson to the hall, ostensibly to study examples of fossilized rock along the stretch of the Channel; actually, he suspects that some mischief is about to take place. His private expectations are fulfilled upon their arrival, for Silas Andrew is dead. (See also SHERLOCK HOLMES AND THE RALEIGH LEGACY, and SHERLOCK HOLMES AND THE THISTLE OF SCOTLAND.

SHERLOCK HOLMES AND THE RALEIGH LEGACY. The first in a series of pastiche novels by L. B. Greenwood, published in 1986. Well written in the style of Dr. Watson's accounts, this work presents Holmes and Watson in an investigation into the title inheritance, the so-called Raleigh Legacy. The legacy is a letter or message supposedly *not* written by Sir Walter Raleigh during the reign of Queen Elizabeth I. The writing in the document is apparently total gibberish, and the inheritance seems utterly worthless. Holmes, of course, recognizes that the paper is worth more than one would think and the plot thickens as members of the family begin displaying fascination with the document, an obsession that leads to murder. (See also SHERLOCK HOLMES AND THE CASE OF SABINA HALL, and SHERLOCK HOLMES AND THE THISTLE OF SCOTLAND.

SHERLOCK HOLMES AND THE SECRET WEAPON. U.S. 1942. Dir: Roy William Neill. Cast: Basil Rathbone (Holmes), Nigel Bruce (Watson), Lionel Atwill (Moriarty), Dennis Hoey (Lestrade), Mary Gordon (Mrs. Hudson). The fourth Rathbone-Bruce adventure of the dynamic duo, and the second featuring them in a war-torn London fighting the Nazis in World War II. Under new director Neill, the series underwent a considerable improvement, not the least of which was the introduction of two actors—Lionel Atwill as Professor Moriarty and Hoey as Lestrade. Initially called *Sherlock Holmes Fights Back*, *Secret Weapon* was concerned with Holmes's efforts to protect a new bombsight and the young scientist who invented it. His foe, of course, is the wicked Moriarty who exclaims at one point "Just like old times—a battle of wits!", and who keeps score in his games of skill with the detective on an abacus with miniature skulls on the rods.

SHERLOCK HOLMES AND THE SPIDER WOMAN.

U.S. 1944. Dir: Roy William Neill. Cast: Basil Rathbone (Holmes), Nigel Bruce (Watson), Gale Sondergaard (Adrea Spedding). The seventh entry in the long running series of Universal Studios films. This time the studio set out to find an enemy equal to the Great Detective, but they wanted someone other than Professor Moriarty. They decided to use Gail Sondergaard as the lethal Adrea Spedding, an excellent foil for Holmes who provided a nice battle of the sexes. The story focuses on Holmes's efforts to solve a number of baffling suicides. He faces several attempts on his life from a deadly spider to the fumes of the Devil's Foot root which Watson associates with his recounting of the Cornish Horror. Sondergaard returned three years later as the Spider Woman in *The Spider Woman Strikes Back*. She did not play Adrea Spedding, however, nor did she face Sherlock Holmes.

SHERLOCK HOLMES AND THE THISTLE OF SCOTLAND.

A 1989 pastiche novel by L. B. Greenwood, the third in a series of novels written in a style similar to that of Dr. Watson in the Canon. Not as lively as the other two entries in the series, *The Thistle of Scotland* features Holmes and Watson called in to investigate the apparent theft of the Thistle, a beautiful betrothal gift belonging to Lady Caroline Mowbray that had once been worn by Mary, Queen of Scots.

SHERLOCK HOLMES AND THE VOICE OF TERROR.

U.S. 1942. Dir: John Rawlins. Cast: Basil Rathbone (Holmes), Nigel Bruce (Watson), Evelyn Ankers (Kitty), Henry Daniell (Sir Alfred Lloyd), and Thomas Gomez (Meade). The third Holmes and Watson film starring Rathbone and Bruce, the first for Universal Studios, and the first presenting the detective matching wits with Nazi Germany. Made at a time when audiences needed a boost in morale against the advancing Axis hordes, this was a perfect vehicle for Holmes. He is engaged by the so-called Intelligence Inner Council to find and stop the "Voice of Terror," a broadcast from the Germans that predicts with horrifying accuracy sabotage and destruction in England. Critics were less than impressed with the plot and did not think

much of Holmes pursuing Germans in the modern era—preferring him to remain in his fog-filled, gaslit, Victorian environment. The box office, however, pleased Universal. *The Voice of Terror* was known originally as *Sherlock Holmes Saves London* and was based loosely on "His Last Bow"; the only similarities were the use of the name Von Bork, the famous "east wind coming" speech, and Holmes patriotically working to aid his country. The film is also remembered for Rathbone's peculiar coiffure. His hair was combed forward in a sort of Roman style that was decidedly different from the depictions of Holmes in the *Strand*.

SHERLOCK HOLMES BAFFLED.

U.S. 1903 (filmed perhaps as early as 1900). Photography: Arthur Marvin. Cast: Unknown. The first known film featuring Sherlock Holmes, lasting all of thirty seconds, and produced by the American Mutoscope and Biograph Co., owned by Thomas Edison. Technically, this seminal Holmes work was not made as an actual film but had its start as an entry for the so-called Mutoscope machines that were popular at the time in front of stores or amusement centers. A primitive production, shot with an actor who was clearly not a professional, *Baffled* featured a burglar ransacking a room, presumably the first of all film 221B Baker Streets. He is suddenly disturbed by the detective, who taps him on the shoulder. In a flash, the burglar vanishes in a trick shot worthy of the great filmmaker Melies. The amazed detective sits down and lights a cigar, not a pipe, to ponder the problem. The cigar then explodes in his face. To complicate matters, the burglar reappears on a table, beginning a dizzying episode of vanishing and returning that ends with him outside the house, booty in hand, and Holmes suitably baffled.

SHERLOCK HOLMES FACES DEATH.

U.S. 1943. Dir: Roy William Neill. Cast: Basil Rathbone (Holmes), Nigel Bruce (Watson), Dennis Hoey (Lestrade), Arthur Maretson (Dr. Sexton), Hillary Brooke (Sally Musgrave), and Halliwell Hobbes (Brunton). The sixth Rathbone-Bruce film and the fourth Holmes release by Universal Studios, this outing marked the return of the detective to a more traditional setting (he had been fighting Nazis in the last three films), and to a more conventional hairstyle (see SHERLOCK HOLMES AND THE VOICE OF TERROR). *Faces Death* was based largely upon "The Musgrave Ritual," although, as usual, wholesale changes were made in the original story. The film finds Dr. Watson working in the home of the Musgraves, who have opened their estate in Northumberland to officers suffering from nervous disorders. The manor is splendidly moody, the perfect setting for a series of murders. At one point, the detective declares to Watson: "Houses, like people, have definite personalities, and this place is positively ghoulish!"

"Sherlock Holmes in New York."

U.S. 1976. Dir: Boris Sagal. Cast: Roger Moore (Holmes), Patrick Macnee (Watson), John Huston (Moriarty), Charlotte Rampling (Irene Adler), Marjorie Bennett (Mrs. Hudson). A star-studded made-for-television movie that brings the detective to America, although he is still plagued by the evil machinations of Professor Moriarty, played marvellously by John Huston. The plot revolves around the efforts of the professor to discredit Holmes, as in *Sherlock Holmes* (1932) and *The Adventures of Sherlock Holmes* (1939). Moriarty concocts a devilishly clever bank robbery, and complicates the detective's work by kidnapping Holmes's son. The film presents Holmes with a son, the result of the romance of the detective with *the* Woman, Irene Adler, ten years before. Dominating the production is Huston, perfectly cast and immensely believable as Moriarty. In a delightful

New York at the time of Sherlock Holmes, from *Sherlock Holmes in New York*, with Roger Moore (r.) and Patrick Macnee (l.)

scene, the professor has on his desk the Maltese Falcon, an unspoken homage to Huston's classic 1941 film.

Sherlock Holmes in Washington.

U.S. 1943. Dir: Roy William Neill. Cast: Basil Rathbone (Holmes), Nigel Bruce (Watson), George Zucco (Heinrich Hinkle), Marjorie Lord (Nancy Partridge), and Henry Daniell (William Easter). The fifth Rathbone-Bruce film and the third and last outing for the duo against the Germans. *Washington* took an abrupt change of course from the previous Universal Studios entries in the increasingly popular series. The detective leaves behind the familiar and comfortable surroundings of pseudo-Victorian England for America. This time around, Holmes and his bumbling companion try to recover a missing set of microfilmed plans that the Germans want very badly. Holmes's investigation takes him to Washington where, thanks to some nice deductions back in England, he knows that the missing documents are hidden on a microfilm in a matchbook. The next entry was *Sherlock Holmes Faces Death* (1943).

Sherlock Holmes in the Great Murder Mystery.

U.S. 1908. This early silent Holmes film released by the Crescent Film Manufacturing Co. was based on Edgar Allan Poe's *Murders in the Rue Morgue*, with the Great Detective taking the part originally played by the fictional sleuth C. Auguste Dupin. Thus, Holmes pursues a dangerous gorilla and works to free a young man falsely accused of murder. The one-reel film was significant for its use of an anonymously billed Watson and for its portrayal of the detective's acts of deductive reasoning. This is shown by Holmes plucking away on his violin while pondering the mystery, his thought process examining the clues and evidence. The story also presents Holmes and Watson as old schoolmates, an idea used again in *Sherlock Holmes* (1922) and *Young Sherlock Holmes* (1985).

Sherlock Holmes in Tibet.

A strange and intriguing 1968 pastiche by Richard Wincor that is of interest to Sherlockians in providing some details about Holmes's movements during the Great Hiatus (1891–1894). As Ole Sigerson, Holmes supposedly attends a lecture by Lama Nordup, Tibet's leading metaphysician, the discourse of the learned monk comprising the bulk of the text. Holmes joins the vice-chancellor of Lhassa University; a Professor Horst Hummel, acting chairman of the Department of Metaphysics, the University of Berlin; Colonel H. Bagby Holland-Bennett, an explorer; Mr. Cornelius Dimitriev, a spy; and an American millionaire, Rick Weaver. Holmes is impressed by Nordup, noting that his normal powers of observation and deduction seem useless when trying to analyze him. He does note, however, that Nordup wears boots by Capucinni of Nottingham, suppliers to the pope. A private meeting with the lama leads to a surprise ending.

"SHERLOCK HOLMES RETURNS." A
1993 made-for-television film. Cast: Anthony Higgins (Holmes), Deborah Farentino (Amy Winslow), Ken Pogue (James Moriarty Booth). Dir: Kenneth Johnson. A surprisingly enjoyable film that has Holmes returning to life after many decades in a state of mechanically induced sleep. Similar in structure to "The Return of Sherlock Holmes" (1987), this one has the detective awakening in modern San Francisco and, like "The Return," his Watson is a woman. Higgins is excellent as Holmes and is distinguished for having played both Holmes and his archnemesis Professor Moriarty (in *Young Sherlock Holmes*). The plot here centers on his efforts to bring to justice the equally wicked grandson of Moriarty, solving a nicely convoluted series of gruesome murders.

SHERLOCK HOLMES SOLVES THE SIGN OF THE FOUR. U.S. 1913. Cast: Harry Benham (Holmes). A two-reel silent film, known in Great Britain as *The Sign of Four*, this was the first film version of the novel, reportedly stressing the oriental mystery of the tale and the Agra Treasure. Harry Benham was a somewhat heavier Holmes than routinely seen.

SHERLOCK HOLMES THROUGH TIME AND SPACE. An excellent 1984 collection of science-fictional tales featuring Holmes, edited by Isaac Asimov, Martin Harry Greenberg, and Charles G. Waugh. This offering of the fertile imaginations of such writers as Philip Jose Farmer, Poul Anderson, Gordon R. Dickson, and, of course, Isaac Asimov is further evidence of how well Holmes and his world move into the realm of the fantastic. Among the stories are: "The Problem of Sore Bridge—Among Others" (Farmer); "The Adventure of the Global Traveller" (Anne Lear); "The Adventure of the Misplaced Hound" (Anderson and Dickson); "A Father's Tale" (Sterling Lanier); "The Adventure of the Extraterrestrial" (Mack Reynolds); "God of the Naked Unicorn" (Richard Lupoff); and "The Ultimate Crime" (Asimov).

SHERLOCK HOLMES UND DAS HALSBAND DES TODES. Germany 1962. Dir: Terence Fisher, with Frank Winterstein. Cast: Christopher Lee (Holmes), Thorley Walters (Watson), Hans Sohnker (Professor Moriarty), Edith Schultze-Westrum (Mrs. Hudson), Senta Berger (Ellen Blackburn). Known in English as *Sherlock Holmes and the Necklace of Death*, this was a German film production with English principals—the noted director Terence Fisher from Hammer Films horror fame, Hammer veteran Thorley Walters, and the renowned terror star and Dracula extraordinaire, CHRISTOPHER LEE. The result of their efforts was arguably one of the most peculiar Holmes film ever made. From the detective's seemingly exaggerated checkered suits to the overly Germanic London and Baker Street, the entire movie's feel is decidedly non-Canonical, made all the more so by the plot (derived loosely from *The Valley of Fear*) featuring a rare Egyptian necklace sought after by Moriarty. The climax is hampered severely by the script, which obviously left it clear that a sequel was anticipated.

SHERLOCK HOLMES' WAR OF THE WORLDS. A 1975 collection of stories by Manly Wade Wellman, compiling several short works originally published in the *Magazine of Fantasy and Science Fiction* with some original pieces. The previously published entries were the chapters on "Sherlock Holmes Versus Mars," "The Adventure of the Martian Client," "Venus, Mars, and Baker Street," and the Appendix, a letter from Watson to H. G. Wells. The other chapters are "The Adventure of the Crystal Egg" and "George E. Challenger Versus Mars." The overall plot centers on Holmes's involvement with the famed Martian invasion of the Earth presented in H. G. Wells's novel, *The War of the Worlds*. The detective is joined by Professor George Challenger, with some narration provided by Watson. Wellman also

wrote "The Man Who Was Not Dead" (1941), about how a certain retired detective does his part to repel the German invasion of England.

SHERLOCK, JR.
U.S. 1924. Dirs: Buster Keaton and Clyde Bruckman. Cast: Buster Keaton (The Boy), Kathryn McGuire (The Girl). One of the classics of the silent cinema starring the comic genius Buster Keaton, although the parody of Holmes is a slight one, the film focuses on Keaton's brilliant sight gags and technically superb stunts. Keaton plays a cinema projectionist who falls asleep and has a dream that he actually walks on to the screen, eventually becoming the detective who solves a mystery that occurs while he is awake. The Holmesian references include the use of a magnifying lens and the wearing of a top hat, an image tied probably to John Barrymore's performance in 1922 as the Great Detective.

SHERMAN.
An old bird stuffer who lived at No. 3 Pinchin Lane in the lower quarter of Lambeth in *The Sign of Four*. Sherman owned an extensive menagerie of animals, including the sleuthhound Toby whom Watson was sent to retrieve by Holmes for use at Pondicherry Lodge. Watson described Sherman as "a lanky, lean old man, with stooping shoulders, a stringy neck, and blue-tinted glasses." He is notable for being, with Mycroft Holmes, one of only two figures in the Canon to refer to the Great Detective by the name Sherlock.

SHIPS.
Sailing vessels were mentioned frequently in the Canon, and several were part of the unchronicled cases. Owing to the absence of any details, these ships sound quite fascinating. The vessels in the unchronicled cases include the **Friesland, Sophy Anderson**, and **Matilda Briggs**. The *Friesland* is a case dating to the months just after the return of Holmes to practice in 1894. The detective considered the period uneventful, but Watson disagreed, citing, among other cases, "the shocking affair of the Dutch steamship *Friesland*, which so nearly cost us both our lives" ("The Norwood Builder"). The *Friesland* figured in the bizarre short story "A Father's Tale" by Sterling E. Lanier and the Basil Rathbone–Nigel Bruce film *Pursuit to Algiers* (1945). The *Sophy Anderson* was a British barque that was somehow lost ("The Five Orange Pips"). Holmes investigated the facts of the matter in 1897, one of "a long series of cases of greater or less interest" of which Watson retained the records.

The *Matilda Briggs*, the most intriguing of all of the vessels of the Canon, was first discussed in "The Sussex Vampire." Holmes was reminded of the ship in a letter from the law firm Morrison, Morrison, and Dodd which introduced the detective to the affair of the Sussex Vampire, writing that "we have not forgotten your successful action in the case of Matilda Briggs." Holmes told Watson, "It was the ship which is associated with the giant rat of Sumatra, a story for which the world is not yet prepared."

Some of the vessels mentioned in assorted chronicled cases were destroyed or wrecked under differing circumstances, and others were simply means of transportation that proved to be of mild or considerable interest to Holmes in the resolution of cases he was investigating. The **Esmerelda** was a ship on which Jonathan Small hoped to escape with Tonga and the Great Agra Treasure to Brazil in *The Sign of Four*. It was located at Gravesend, and Small was journeying there aboard the **Aurora** the night he was captured by Holmes, Watson, and Athelney Jones. The *Aurora*, owned by Mordecai Smith, was a steam launch that sailed out of Smith's Wharf at the foot of Broad Street, Lambeth. The **Gloria Scott** was so notable that Watson named one of his stories after it. According to Trevor Senior, "the *Gloria Scott*, an English barque, had been in the Chinese sea-trade, but she was an old-fashioned, heavy-bowed, broad-beamed craft, and the new clippers had cut her out." In 1855, during the Crimean War, it had been pressed into service as a convict ship, transporting prisoners to Australia. Setting sail from Falmouth, it had a crew of twenty-six, with eighteen soldiers, a captain, three mates, a chaplain, a doctor, four warders, and thirty-eight convicts. It never reached Australia and was reported by the Admiralty lost at sea. The **Lone Star** was an American barque, out of Savannah, Georgia, under the command of James Calhoun in "The Five Orange Pips." It was presumed destroyed in the Atlantic gale in 1887, as "a shattered sternpost of a boat was seen swinging in the trough of a wave, with the letters 'L. S.' carved upon it." Holmes spent a whole day poring over the registries of Lloyd's and files of old papers to learn information about the *Lone Star* because of the vessel's possible connection with the murders of the Openshaws. The **Norah Creina,** a steamer, was also apparently lost at sea with all hands off the Portuguese coast, to the north of Oporto. It was believed that the surviving members of the Worthingdon Bank Gang were on board. Their presumed deaths were reported at the end of "The Resident Patient." John and Ivy Douglas in *The Valley of Fear* set sail on the **Palmyra** for South Africa. Tragedy struck one of the passengers during the cruise. Baron Adalbert Gruner planned to leave England on board the **Ruritania,** thereby, he hoped, removing himself from any possible interference with his plans in "The Illustrious Client." A steam sealer, the **Sea Unicorn,** was commanded by Captain Peter Carey from 1883 to 1884 ("Black Peter"). Peter Cairns served aboard the *Sea Unicorn* as a spare harpooner. The vessel also picked up a man in a yacht in the North Sea in 1883, an act that was to come to light during Holmes's investigation into the murder of Carey in July, 1895. Mary Fraser sailed from Adelaide to England on the **Rock of Gibraltar** in "The Abbey Grange." Captain Jack Croker served as first officer. The *Rock of Gibraltar* was described as the "largest and best boat" of the Adelaide-Southampton line. Croker later became captain of the steamer **Bass Rock.** The Liverpool, Dublin and London Steam Packet Company owned the **May Day,** on which James Browner was employed as a steward in "The Cardboard Box." Finally, Watson wrote in *A Study in Scarlet* of his return to England aboard the British troopship **Orontes** following his terrible experiences in Afghanistan. The *Orontes* landed at Portsmouth.

SHOLTO, BARTHOLOMEW. Son of Major John Sholto and brother of **Thaddeus Sholto** in *The Sign of Four*. He and Thaddeus, his twin, searched for six years to find the Agra Treasure that they knew to be hidden somewhere at the home of their late father, Pondicherry Lodge. During that time, Thaddeus was also the anonymous benefactor of Mary Morstan, sending her a pearl each year in secret memory of her father, Captain Arthur Morstan. Bartholomew was opposed to this act of charity, and their difference of opinion was such that Thaddeus eventually moved out of the lodge. His house became "an oasis of art in the howling desert of south London." Upon discovery of the treasure in 1888, Thaddeus summoned Mary Morstan to his house and so involved Holmes in the affair. He was "a small man with a very high head, a bristle of red hair all around the fringe of it, and a bald, shining scalp which shot out from among it like a mountain-peak from fir trees." The finding of the Treasure led to Bartholomew's death in a bizarre fashion. "By the table in a wooden armchair the

master of the house was seated all in a heap, with his head sunk upon his left shoulder and that ghastly inscrutable smile upon his face. He was stiff and cold and had clearly been dead many hours. It seemed to me that not only his features but all his limbs were twisted and turned in the most fantastic fashion."

SHOLTO, MAJOR JOHN.   A onetime officer of the Thirty-fourth Bombay Infantry who became involved with the stolen Agra Treasure in *The Sign of Four*. Sholto served at the Blair Island penal colony in the Andaman Islands with Captain Arthur Morstan. While there, both met the convict John Small, a member of the Four and a participant in the theft of the great Agra Treasure. Joining the conspiracy to retrieve the hidden treasure, Sholto betrayed both Small and Morstan, retiring to England a fabulously wealthy man. He resided at Pondicherry Lodge, Upper Norwood, eventually dying in 1882. On his deathbed, he told his sons, Bartholomew and Thaddeus, of his actions, and of the immense treasure hidden somewhere on the estate. The twins would spend the next six years searching for it. Major Sholto died a terrified man and had spent years in a state of horror toward men with wooden legs, once firing a revolver at a wooden-legged man who turned out to be a harmless trradesman. The morning after his death, the brothers found the window to their father's room forced open, his cupboards and boxes rifled, and a torn piece of paper with the words "The sign of four" fixed upon the major's chest.

"SHOSCOMBE OLD PLACE, THE ADVENTURE OF" (SHOS).   Published: *Liberty*, March 1927; *Strand*, April 1927; collected in *The Case Book of Sherlock Holmes* (1927). Major players: Holmes, Watson, Sir Robert Norberton, John Mason. Case date: Various, late. The final entry in the Canon to be published, although "The Adventure of the Retired Colourman" is often printed in some editions after "Shoscombe Old Place." In a change from usual custom, Watson is able to inform Holmes about a subject, not surprisingly racing, specifically the well-known daredevil, lover of fair ladies, and plunger on the turf, Sir Robert Norberton. His estate and equestrian establishment Shoscombe Old Place, also known as Shoscombe Hall, was situated in the middle of Shoscombe Park. Upon the death of Lady Beatrice Falder, who held it as a "life interest," Shoscombe

Old Place reverted to her late husband's brother, a fact of some importance in the case. Holmes's curiosity in Sir Robert is understandable given the opinion of his head trainer John Mason that Sir Robert has gone mad. Mason's employer has seemingly been pushed over the edge from pressures to win the Derby with his horse Shoscombe Prince. If he fails, the Curzon Street moneylender Sam Brewer and other creditors will ruin him. He has, it seems, also had a falling out with his sister Lady Beatrice Falder, who keeps him alive with money and a place on the estate. Another mystery has come to surround Lady Beatrice herself—she has not been seen by anyone save for her maid for some time and Sir Robert has given away her favorite spaniel. That beloved dog helps solve all of the puzzles. The case reveals much about Watson's proclivities toward gambling. He is most enlightened on the subject of racing and tells Holmes that he ought to know something about racing, "I pay for it with half my wound pension."

SHOSCOMBE PRINCE. The thoroughbred racehorse of Sir Robert Norberton and a favorite of Sir Robert's sister Lady Beatrice Falder in "Shoscombe Old Place." Shoscombe Prince ran in the Derby, winning 80,000 pounds for the race. Sir Robert had fooled the betting touts by using Prince's slower half-brother in practices thereby driving up the odds.

SHOSCOMBE SPANIELS. A very exclusive breed of spaniel deriving its name from Shoscombe Old Place. They were heard of at every dog show and were the special pride of Lady Beatrice Falder. A Shoscombe spaniel helped Holmes solve the mystery of "Shoscombe Old Place."

SIGERSON. Probably the best known of all the aliases used by the detective. He adopted it during his two years of travels in Tibet while on the Great Hiatus (1891–1894). Word of the remarkable explorations of the Norwegian Sigerson reached England, but Watson had no way of knowing that the explorer was actually the Great Detective. The name Sigerson has been used in numerous pastiches.

THE SIGN OF FOUR (SIGN). Also *The Sign of the Four*. Published: *Lippincott's*, February 1890; published in book form by Spencer Blackett, 1890. Major players: Holmes, Watson, Mary Morstan, Thaddeus Sholto, Bartholomew Sholto, Jonathan Small, Inspector Athelney Jones, Tonga, Toby. The second published chronicle by Dr. Watson, originally appearing in *Lippincott's Magazine* with the subtitle "The Problem of the Sholtos," but later organized into chapters for novelization. One of the most famous cases investigated by Holmes, *The Sign of Four* is actually comprised of two tales. The first is Holmes's complex investigation into the death of Bartholomew Sholto and the subsequent theft of the Agra Treasure; the second is the romance between Watson and Holmes's client, Mary Morstan. The investigation by Holmes is one of the finest of his illustrious career as he pursues the murderers from the terrible crime scene at Pondicherry Lodge to the Thames. The climax involves a danger-filled chase down the Thames, during which Holmes kills a human being for the first and only time in the Canon. Meanwhile, Watson wooes Mary with the same ardor Holmes uses to track down the killers. By the end of the affair, she has consented to become his wife. Interestingly, the narrative opens and closes with a straightforward reference to Holmes's cocaine habit, of which Watson clearly disapproves. At the end, Watson tells Holmes: " 'The division seems rather unfair. You have done all the work in this business. I get a wife out of it, Jones gets the credit, pray what remains for you?' 'For me', said Sherlock Holmes, 'there still remains the cocaine-bottle.' And he stretched his long white hand up for it."

The case has been dated to 1888, seven years after the affair recounted in *A Study in Scarlet*. Aside from his indulgence in a three-times-a-day cocaine habit (his seven-per-cent solution), the case provides several opportunities to view Holmes's attitude toward women. He tells Watson: "It is of importance . . . not to allow your judgment to be biased by personal qualities. A client is to me a mere unit, a factor in a problem. The emotional qualities are antagonistic to clear reasoning. I assure you that the most winning woman I ever knew was hanged for poisoning three little children for their insurance-money . . ." and "Women are not to be entirely trusted—not the best of them." *The Sign of Four* has been the basis of several films and was the inspiration for the Paul Giovanni play *Crucifer of Blood*.

SIGN OF FOUR, THE. England 1932. Dir: Graham Cutts. Cast: Arthur Wontner (Holmes), Ian Hunter (Watson), Isla Bevan (Mary Morstan).

The third film featuring the excellent Wontner as Holmes, joined this time by Hunter, who replaced Ian Fleming (Watson in the other Wontner pictures). Hunter was used here to make his wooing of Mary more believable and appealing, much as was done in the 1923 silent version of *The Sign of Four*, in which Hubert Willis was replaced by the younger Arthur Cullin. Despite the use of flashbacks to India in the beginning of the film, this version is generally faithful to the original material. There are, however, several notable deviations: Holmes deduces that a letter's handwriting is that of a one-legged man (the detective noting that an amputated leg causes an increase in the pressure of the downstroke of a pen); he wears the same modern hat as in the last film, *The Missing Rembrandt*; and he is unusually physical. Baker Street is excellent.

"SIGN OF FOUR, THE." England 1983. Dir: Desmond Davis. Cast: Ian Richardson (Holmes), David Healy (Watson), Joe Melia (Jonathan Small), Thorley Walters (Major Sholto), and Cherie Lunghi (Mary Morstan). A made-for-television production that was later broadcast on American television, marking the screen debut of Ian Richardson as the Great Detective. *The Sign of Four* may not be the finest film adaptation ever made of the original case, but it is certainly spirited and is energized by the enthusiastic performance of Richardson. Walters, a longtime Watson, does a fine turn as Sholto, as does Lunghi as Mary.

"SIGN OF FOUR, THE." England 1987. Dir: Peter Hammond. Cast: Jeremy Brett (Holmes), Edward Hardwicke (Watson), and Jenny Seagrove (Mary Morstan). The Granada Television adaptation of the story by the producers of the excellent "Sherlock Holmes" series starring Brett and Hardwicke. "The Sign of Four" was generally faithful to the original source material save that Watson does not woo Mary Morstan, although his reaction to her leaves open the possibility of a postfilm romance. Holmes and Watson are introduced to the case by Mary, their investigation leading them to the Sholtos (played splendidly by Ronald Lacey) and Jonathan Small (John Thaw).

"SILVER BLAZE" (SILV). Published: *Strand*, December 1892, *Harper's*, February 25, 1893; collected in *The Memoirs of Sherlock Holmes* (1894). Major players: Holmes, Watson, Colonel Ross, Inspector Gregory, John Straker, Silver Blaze. Case date: 1881–1891. One of the most popular cases of the Canon with the readers of the *Baker Street Journal* in 1959 (ranked fourth on their list), "Silver Blaze" was, nevertheless, attacked in Conan Doyle's time because of its many errors concerning the rules of racing and training racehorses. Despite the writer's ignorance that, according to Conan Doyle, "cries to heaven," Holmes is definitely "at the top of his form" and the case is one of his most intriguing. Of Isomony stock, Silver Blaze, famed racehorse of Colonel Ross and a heavy favorite in the Wessex Cup, has disappeared from the King's Pyland Stable in Devonshire prior to the race. The trainer, John Straker, has also been found dead, killed from a wicked blow to the head. The obvious suspect, the racing tout Fitzroy Simpson, has been arrested by Inspector Gregory and the Devonshire police. With great vigor, Holmes and Watson journey to Devonshire and launch into an ultimately successful investigation. Having suffered the barbs of Colonel Ross, who doubts his skills, Holmes has some fun at his expense at the end, delaying both the return of Silver Blaze and the unmasking of the killer for as long as possible. Returned to Colonel Ross in time for the Cup, Silver Blaze won the race, defeating Lord Backwater's Desborough, the duke of Balmoral's Iris, and the other entrants Pugilist, The Negro, and Rasper. The case includes the famous exchange between Holmes and Gregory: " 'Is there any point to which you wish to draw my attention?' 'To the curious incident of the dog in the night-time.' 'The dog did nothing in the night-time.' 'That was the curious incident.' "

SILVER BLAZE.   England 1937. Dir: Thomas Bentley. Cast: Arthur Wontner (Holmes), Ian Fleming (Watson), Lyn Harding (Moriarty). Known in the United States as *Murder at the Baskervilles*, this was the last film appearance of Wontner as Holmes. A melange of "Silver Blaze," *The Hound of the Baskervilles*, and "The Empty House," the story has the duo visiting their young friend Henry Baskerville, becoming embroiled in murders in Dartmoor—a stableboy and the trainer of the horse Silver Blaze. The horse, as in the original, is missing. Needless to say, Professor Moriarty is involved (played by the delightful Lyn Harding). He is aided by the nefarious Colonel Moran (Arthur Goullet) with his air gun.

"SILVER BLAZE."   England 1977. Dir: John Davies. Cast: Christopher Plummer (Holmes), Thorley Walters (Watson), Basil Henson (Colonel Ross), and Gary Watson (Inspector Gregory). A British made-for-television movie based on "Silver Blaze" marking the first screen outing for Plummer as the detective; he would later appear as Holmes in *Murder By Decree* (1979). Here he is seconded by Watson veteran Walters, one of the most durable of all screen Watsons.

SILVESTER'S.   A London bank where Lady Frances Carfax maintained an account in "The Disappearance of Lady Frances Carfax." In the search for the missing Lady Frances, Holmes consulted her account at Silvester's, declaring, "Single ladies must live, and their pass-books are compressed diaries."

SIMPSON (1).   A member of the Baker Street Irregulars, described as "a small street Arab," who maintained surveillance on the lodgings of Henry Wood for Holmes in "The Crooked Man."

SIMPSON (2).   Called Baldy Simpson, a member of the same squadron as Godfrey Emsworth and James Dodd during the Boer War in "The Blanched Soldier." During a morning fight at Buffelsspruit, outside Pretoria, Emsworth, Simpson, and another soldier named Anderson were separated from their companions. Simpson and Anderson were later killed at Diamond Hill.

SIMPSON, FITZROY.   A London bookmaker who was the prime suspect in the murder of John Straker, trainer of the horse Silver Blaze at King's Pyland, Dartmoor in "Silver Blaze." Fitzroy Simpson "was a man of excellent birth and education, who had squandered a fortune upon the turf, and who lived now by doing a little quiet and genteel book-making in the sporting clubs of London."

SIMPSON'S.   In full, Simpson's Dining Rooms, a restaurant in the Strand that was frequented three times by Holmes and Watson, once after the capture of the murderer of Victor Savage in "The Dying Detective," when the detective understandably wanted something nutritious to eat, and twice during the affair involving the fiendish Baron Gruner in "The Illustrious Client." Simpson's is thus unique among eateries for it is the only place known with certainty to have been patronized by Holmes more than once.

SINCLAIR, ADMIRAL.   A naval officer, resident of Barclay Square, with whom Sir James Walter dined and spent the entire evening on the night that the Bruce-Partington Submarine Plans were stolen in "The Bruce-Partington Plans," thus providing Sir James with an airtight alibi.

SINGLEFORD, LORD.   The owner of the horse Rasper, which lost to Silver Blaze in the Wessex Cup in "Silver Blaze."

SINGLESTICK.   A type of wooden club or cudgel, often used to train for wielding a sabre, but useful as a weapon itself. Holmes was particularly proficient with the singlestick (*A Study in Scarlet*), which he used when attacked in Regent Street by the ruffian agents of Baron Gruner ("The Illustrious Client").

"SIX NAPOLEONS, THE ADVENTURE OF THE" (SIXN).   Published: *Collier's*, April 1904, *Strand*, May 1904; collected in *The Return of Sherlock Holmes* (1905). Major players: Holmes, Watson, Inspector Lestrade, Beppo, Horace Harker. Case date: 1900. A very popular chronicle, this adventure finds Holmes in pursuit of an apparent madman with a major grudge against Napoleon Bonaparte: busts of the emperor are being smashed throughout South London. Watson declares confidently that the culprit is someone with an *idée fixe* "and under its influence [would] be capable of any fantastic outrage." Holmes dismisses his theory with the simple statement, "That won't do, my dear

Watson." The bizarre affair becomes serious when one of the victims of a bust smashing, Horace Harker, discovers the body of the Mafia thug Pietro Venucci on his doorstep. Holmes naturally deduces the real reason behind the reckless campaign against Napoleon's likeness and reveals the truth of the matter with stunning legerdemain and panache. As Watson writes of the revelation: "Lestrade and I sat silent for a moment, and then, with a spontaneous impulse, we both broke out clapping, as at the well-wrought crisis of a play. A flush of color sprang to Holmes's pale cheeks, and he bowed to us like the master dramatist who receives the homage of his audience. It was at such moments that for an instant he ceased to be a reasoning machine, and betrayed his human love for admiration and applause."

SKIBBAREEN. A coastal town in Ireland where Holmes, posing as Altamont, gave serious trouble to the constabulary in "His Last Bow."

SLANEY, ABE. According to Wilson Hargreave of the New York Police Bureau, "The most dangerous crook in Chicago" ("The Dancing Men"). Slaney had known and loved Elsie Patrick in Chicago, but she could not stand his criminal business so she fled to London. Unable to give her up, he pursued her to England and the tragedy of Ridling Thorpe Manor followed.

SLATER, OSCAR. The cause of this real criminal suspect (d. 1949) was taken up by Arthur Conan Doyle in 1912. Slater had been arrested and convicted in 1908 of murdering an elderly spinster in Glasgow. Conan Doyle, however, felt that evidence in the case was flimsy. Despite caring little for Slater, he continued to work for his release over many years. Finally, in 1927, with public interest renewed in his case and with Conan Doyle paying his legal fees, Slater secured a pardon and was released from Peterhead Prison.

SLEEPING CARDINAL, THE. England 1931. Dir: Leslie Hiscott. Cast: Arthur Wontner (Holmes), Ian Fleming (Watson), Minnie Rayner (Mrs. Hudson), Norman McKinnell (Colonel Henslow), and Leslie Perrins (Ronald Adair). The first Holmes film featuring Wontner and known in the United States as *Sherlock Holmes' Fatal Hour*, originally released by Twickenham Studios. *The Sleeping Cardinal* was based on "The Final Problem" and "The Adventure of the Empty House," thus

The capture of Abe Slaney in "The Dancing Men"; by Sidney Paget.

featuring as villains Professor Moriarty and Colonel Sebastian Moran, although the wicked professor does most of the evil work, Moran reduced to being a mere henchman. The film begins with a bank robbery, shot entirely in silhouette and sound effects. A cut is then made to the flat of Ronald Adair, who, it turns out, is a card cheat. He is taken by force to meet Professor Moriarty. He speaks to Adair from behind a painting of a sleeping Cardinal Richelieu (hence the film title) and tries to blackmail him into aiding his criminal activities. Holmes is first encountered in an excellent version of Baker Street, chatting comfortably with Watson and Mrs. Hudson. The phrase "Elementary, my dear Watson!" is used, as is the name Robert for Moriarty taken from the Gillette play, *Sherlock Holmes. The Sleeping Cardinal* prompted the second Holmes feature, *The Missing Rembrandt*.

SLIPPERS. Holmes kept his tobacco in the toe of a Persian slipper at 221B, considered by Watson to be one of the detective's more bohemian attributes. "The rough and tumble work in Afghanistan, coming on the top of a natural Bohemianism of disposition, has made me more lax than befits a medical man. But with me there is a limit, and when I find a man who keeps cigars in the coal-scuttle, his tobacco in the toe end of a Persian slipper, and his unanswered correspondence transfixed by a jack-knife into the the very centre of his wooden mantelpiece, then I begin to give myself virtuous airs." ("The Musgrave Ritual," also "The Empty House," "The Illustrious Client," and "The Naval Treaty"). Dr. Grimesby Roylott wore Turkish slippers in "The Speckled Band" while Watson wore patent leather slippers in "The Stockbroker's Clerk."

SMALL, JONATHAN.   One of the members of the Four who took part in the theft and murder for the great Agra Treasure in *The Sign of Four*, Small was a onetime soldier in India, in the Third Buffs, before losing his leg to a crocodile while swimming in the Ganges. Discharged, he was given a job on the plantation by Abel White thanks to a good word by the regiment's colonel. Small worked on horseback as an overseer. Soon, however, the Sepoy Rebellion erupted and White was murdered. Small fled to Agra and there took part in the defense of the city. He was soon compelled on threat of death to join in the stealing of the Agra Treasure. The Four were caught, however, and sentenced to penal servitude in the Andaman Islands. Small eventually escaped, with the help of the Andaman Islander named Tonga, to search for the treasure. His quest would take him to England and would lead to murder and one of the most aggressive pursuits of a criminal by Holmes in the Canon.

SMITH, CULVERTON.   A planter and well-known resident of Sumatra who resided at 13 Lower Burke Street while in London in "The Dying Detective." Smith was also unmatched in his knowledge of the disease contracted by Holmes while working among Chinese sailors at the docks. The detective thus asked Watson to consult him. Victor Savage, Smith's nephew, had also contracted a rare disease in London, dying horribly. Watson wrote: "I saw a great yellow face, coarse-grained and greasy, with heavy, double-chin, and two sullen, menacing gray eyes which glared at me from under tufted and sandy brows. A high bald head had a small velvet smoking-cap poised coquettishly upon one side of its pink curve."

SMITH, MORDECAI.   Owner of the steam launch *Aurora*, of Smith's Wharf in *The Sign of Four*. His vessel was chartered by Jonathan Small and became the object of an intense search by Holmes and his Baker Street Irregulars. The detective spoke to **Mrs. Smith,** who expressed concern about the length of time that he had been gone. He worked out of Smith's Wharf at the foot of Broad Street, Lambeth. His two sons were **Jim** and **Jack.** Jack received two shillings from Holmes and Jim accompanied his father on the *Aurora* when it was chartered by Jonathan Small.

SMITH, VIOLET.   Possibly the eponymous cyclist in "The Solitary Cyclist." The daughter of **James Smith**, the onetime conductor at the Imperial Theatre, Violet was a music teacher (as deduced by Holmes from her spatulate fingers) who had been left apparently indigent by the death of her uncle **Ralph Smith**, who had gone to Africa around 1870. Friends of his, Bob Carruthers and Jack Woodley, came to her and declared that they had known Ralph in South Africa and had promised him "to hunt up his relations, and see that they were in no want." Carruthers subsequently offered her the position of music instructor to his only daughter. Her experiences in the Carruthers household were increasingly strange, culminating in the persistent appearances of "a middle-aged man, with a short, dark beard" who would follow her on a bicycle. Watson wrote that she was "the young and beautiful woman, tall, graceful, and queenly, who presented herself at Baker Street late in the evening, and implored [Holmes's] assistance and advice."

SMITH, WILLOUGHBY.   The third secretary in the service of Professor Coram in "The Golden Pince-Nez." As Stanley Hopkins told Holmes: "This Willoughby Smith has nothing against him, either as a boy at Uppingham or as a young man at Cambridge. I have seen his testimonials, and from the first he was a decent, quiet, hardworking fellow, with no weak spot in him at all. And yet this is the lad who has met his death this morning in the professor's study under circumstances which can only point to murder." He was fatally stabbed in the neck with a small sealing wax knife.

SMITH-MORTIMER SUCCESSION CASE.
One of Holmes's many but unchronicled cases during the busy year of 1894.

SNUFF.
A preparation of finely pounded tobacco most often taken by inhalation. Holmes possessed a gold snuffbox with a great amethyst in the center of the lid that had been given to him by the king of Bohemia in "A Scandal in Bohemia." Mycroft Holmes and Jabez Wilson both took snuff in "The Red-Headed League" and "The Greek Interpreter" respectively.

SOAMES, SIR CATHCART.
The father of a student at the Priory School in "The Priory School."

SOAMES, HILTON.
A tutor and lecturer in Greek at the College of St. Luke's in one of the great (but undisclosed) university towns in "The Three Students." Soames engaged Holmes's services when a scandal threatened the examination for the prestigious Fortescue Scholarship—the exam papers had been apparently tampered with and one of the students was attempting to cheat. He "was a tall, spare man, of a nervous and excitable temperament."

SOLAR PONS.
Arguably the greatest of the literary homages to Sherlock Holmes, Solar Pons first came to life in February, 1929, in the short story "The Adventure of the Black Narcissus," published in the *Dragnet Magazine*. The master sleuth of 7B Praed Street, London, was created by August Derleth and assisted in his investigations by his loyal chronicler Dr. Lyndon Parker. Derleth, a great admirer of Conan Doyle, had written him after the publication of the collection *The Case Book of Sherlock Holmes* in 1927 to ask if any more stories would be appearing. When Conan Doyle wrote back in the negative, Derleth began writing his own. Soon, however, he changed the main character from Holmes to Pons, and Watson to Parker. The result was the luminescent detective of Praed Street who was nevertheless so wonderfully Holmesian that many Sherlockians consider Pons to be the son of the Master. So numerous were Pons's adventures that his exploits have been gathered into a number of collections: *"In Re: Sherlock Holmes"—The Adventures of Solar Pons* (1945), *The Memoirs of Solar Pons* (1951), *The Return of Solar Pons* (1958), *The Reminiscences of Solar Pons* (1961), *The Casebook of Solar Pons* (1965), *Solar Pons: Mr. Fairlie's Final Journey* (1968), and *The Chronicles of Solar Pons* (1973). A fan club, "The Praed Street Irregulars," was founded in 1956.

"SOLITARY CYCLIST, THE ADVENTURE OF THE" (SOLI).
Published: *Collier's*, December 1903, *Strand*, January 1904; collected in *The Return of Sherlock Holmes* (1905). Major players: Holmes, Watson, Violet Smith, Robert Carruthers, Jack Woodley. Case date: April 1895. A case brought to Holmes on April 23, 1895, while he was in the midst of investigating the "very abstruse and complicated problem concerning the peculiar persecution to which John Vincent Harden, the well-known tobacco millionaire, had been subjected." While her intrusion was not welcome, "it was impossible to refuse to listen to the story of the young and beautiful woman, tall, graceful, and queenly, who presented herself at Baker Street late in the evening, and implored his assistance and advice." A teacher of music who, because of circumstances, had been left penniless, Smith was offered a position as music instructor to the child of Robert (Bob) Carruthers, a man who, along with Jack Woodley, had known her uncle Ralph in South Africa. Smith's experiences in Carruthers's home grew more bizarre, until finally, she began to be followed by a man on a bicycle, his identity hidden by a short dark beard. As Holmes is temporarily otherwise engaged, he sends Watson to Charlington to investigate in proxy. Holmes's response to his report is one of his most severe of criticisms "as he commented upon the things that I had done and the things that I had not." Once the Great Detective is involved, events move rapidly, but even the Master is unable to prevent a near tragedy.

"SOME FREAKS OF ATAVISM."
An article written by Dr. Mortimer for the *Lancet* (*The Hound of the Baskervilles*).

SOMERTON, DR.
Surgeon at the Blair Island penal colony in the Andaman Islands in *The Sign of Four*. "A fast, sporting young chap," Somerton hosted card parties at which Captain Morstan and Major Sholto played, frequently losing and amassing huge debts.

"SORE BRIDGE—AMONG OTHERS, THE PROBLEM OF."

A wacky 1975 short story by Philip Jose Farmer, published first in the *Magazine of Fantasy and Science Fiction*. This inventive work features Raffles (with his friend Manders) as the main character—the Great Detective makes only a brief appearance. "The Sore Bridge" is concerned with the three unchronicled cases mentioned in "The Problem of Thor Bridge": the disappearance of James Phillimore, the strange affair of Isadora Persano, and the loss of the cutter *Alicia*. The three cases are cleverly tied together with a bizarre science fiction theme.

SOUTH AFRICA.

The name for a region in Africa that was, in Holmes's era, used for both the Boer republics and the imperial British colonies. South Africa was also the site of the Boer War (1899–1902) between the British Empire and the Boers, a struggle that served as part of the backdrop for the case of "The Blanched Soldier," as Godfrey Emsworth and James Dodd served there. Charles Baskerville in *The Hound of the Baskervilles*, the Honorable Philip Green in "The Disappearance of Lady Frances Carfax," and Ralph Smith in "The Solitary Cyclist" all made their fortunes in South Africa. Bob Carruthers and Jack Woodley came from there in "The Solitary Cyclist," and Carruthers was deeply interested in South African gold securities. Watson decided against investing in similar securities in "The Dancing Men." Young Gilchrist in "The Three Students" departed school for Rhodesia to accept a commission in the Rhodesian police.

SOUTHERTON, LORD.

The owner of the wooded preserve that surrounded the Copper Beeches on three sides, home of Jephro Rucastle in "The Copper Beeches."

SPANIEL.

A breed of dog that figured in several cases. The most unique of the Canon's spaniels were those bred by Lady Beatrice Falder, the so-called Shoscombe spaniels in "Shoscombe Old Place." Carlo, the unfortunate dog of the Fergusons in "The Sussex Vampire," was a spaniel, as was Dr. Mortimer's curly-haired companion, the dog later killed by the terrible hound on the moor in *The Hound of the Baskervilles*. The sleuth-hound Toby, owned by Old Sherman and used by Holmes in *The Sign of Four*, was a half-spaniel and half-lurcher.

"SPECKLED BAND, THE ADVENTURE OF THE" (SPEC).

Published: *Strand*, February 1892; collected in *The Adventures of Sherlock Holmes* (1892). Case date: April 1893. Major players: Holmes, Watson, Dr. Grimesby Roylott, Helen Stoner, Julia Stoner. The most popular of all entries in the Canon, ranked first on Conan Doyle's list of favorite stories and first on the poll of favorites by the readers of the *Baker Street Journal* in 1959. "The Speckled Band" certainly contains all of the ingredients for success: a deliciously wicked villain in Dr. Grimesby Roylott, a damsel in distress to please Dr. Watson, and a dark, clever murder mystery to entice Holmes. Watson comments that of the many varied cases of the previous eight years, he "cannot recall any which presented more singular features than that which was associated with the well-known Surrey family of the Roylotts of Stoke Moran." Helen Stoner, stepdaughter of Dr. Roylott, comes to Holmes in absolute terror for her life. She has announced her engagement and fears that she will suffer the same fate as her sister Julia, who died in her arms two years before on the eve of her wedding. Julia's dying words were "Oh, my God! Helen! It was the band! The speckled band!" Holmes naturally takes the case, spurred on by the threats of Roylott, including his bending an iron poker "into a curve with his huge brown hands." Journeying to Stoke Moran, Holmes and Watson set up a vigil in Helen's room, and late in the night uncover the cause of Julia's demise, fulfilling Watson's observation, "Holmes, I seem to see dimly what you are hinting at. We are only just in time to prevent some subtle and horrible crime." The public's interest in the case was confirmed by the success enjoyed by Conan Doyle when he transferred "The Speckled Band" to the stage in 1910.

SPECKLED BAND, THE.

A play written in 1910 by Sir Arthur Conan Doyle, based upon "The Adventure of the Speckled Band" (1892), the work was a monumental success and has been considered by critics to be markedly superior to the other hit play of the time *SHERLOCK HOLMES* by William Gillette. *The Speckled Band* came about as the result of the utter failure of another Conan Doyle play, *The House of Temperley*. An adaptation of Conan Doyle's novel *Rodney Stone* about prizefighting, *Temperley* never drew audiences to the Adelphi Theatre where it was produced, largely because of public displeasure over the sport. Recognizing the need to replace his bomb with a quick money-maker, Conan Doyle decided to write a new Holmes play. He wrote in his autobiography, "When I saw the course that things were taking I shut myself up and devoted my whole mind to making a sensational Sherlock Holmes drama." The result was *The Speckled Band*, supposedly penned in a single week.

Starring as Holmes was H. A. Saintbury, a stage veteran who had already played the detective over a thousand times while on tour with *Sherlock Holmes*. Saintbury would perform as Holmes in the 1916 film adaptation of *The Valley of Fear*. Opposite him was the Shakespearian actor Lyn Harding as the vile Grimesby Rylott (Roylott in the original story); the actor also served as producer. From the start, Harding had disagreements with Conan Doyle over the development of Rylott as the villain. He wanted Rylott to be more central to the drama while Conan Doyle saw him as the classic villain of melodrama. In the end, Harding had his way and took more than a dozen curtain calls from the audience when the play premiered on June 4, 1910, at the Adelphi. Conan Doyle suddenly had a huge success on his hands, a particularly profitable one that paid for the losses of *Temperley* and gave him a property of considerable value.

The Speckled Band was presented in three acts: act 1 The Hall of Stoke Place, Stoke Moran; act 2 (two years later) scene 1, Dr. Roylott's Study, Stoke Place, scene 2, Mr. Sherlock Holmes's Rooms, Upper Baker Street, London; act 3 scene 1, The Hall of Stoke Place, scene 2, Enid's Bedroom, Stoke Place. Among the characters in the play were Sherlock Holmes, Dr. Watson, Grimesby Rylott, Enid Stonor, and Billy (the page of Baker Street, actually created by Gillette in *Sherlock Holmes*.) An early version of the production was *The Stonor Case*.

SPECKLED BAND, THE. England. 1931. Dir: Jack Raymond. Cast: Raymond Massey (Holmes), Athole Stewart (Watson), Lyn Harding (Dr. Grimesby Rylott), and Marie Ault (Mrs. Hudson). The film version of Conan Doyle's stage play of the same name, with Massey making his screen debut and with Harding reprising his brilliant role as the villain Rylott. The plot is roughly that of the play and the original story "The Adventure of the Speckled Band," although the production took a number of liberties with the Holmes of the Canon. For example, 221B is, strangely, 107 Baker Street,

and Watson (capably played by Stewart) enters not to the familiar surroundings of Holmes's rooms but to a machine-filled office, replete with secretaries and stenographers.

SPENCER JOHN GANG. A criminal gang that specialized in murder, theft, assault, and intimidation in "The Three Gables." Members included Steve Dixie, Barney Stockdale, and Susan Stockdale, while one of its clients was the voluptuary Isadora Klein.

SPENDER, ROSE. An old woman who was removed from the Brixton Workhouse Infirmary by Holy Peters and Annie Fraser and taken to their home to die in "The Disappearance of Lady Frances Carfax." They claimed that Spender had once been nurse to Annie Fraser. She died three days later of senile decay, her death certificate signed by Dr. Horsom, of 13 Firbank. The special coffin that was ordered from Stimson & Co. for her funeral helped Holmes to solve the case.

SPLUGEN PASS. A mountain pass through the Alps between Switzerland and Italy where Baron Gruner's wife was killed in an "accident" in "The Illustrious Client." Holmes and many other people were convinced that Gruner was responsible for her death.

STACKHURST, HAROLD. The owner and head of the well-known coaching establishment, The Gables, in Sussex in "The Lion's Mane," Stackhurst was also the best friend of Holmes during the detective's retirement to the South Downs. The Gables was located half a mile from Holmes's villa. Holmes wrote that "Stackhurst himself was a well-known rowing Blue in his day, and an excellent all-round scholar. He and I were always friendly from the day I came to the coast, and he was the one man who was on such terms with me that we could drop in on each other in the evenings without an invitation."

STALWART COMPANIONS, THE ADVENTURE OF THE. An ingenious 1978 pastiche novel by H. Paul Jeffers that presents the enjoyable pairing of Sherlock Holmes with Theodore Roosevelt. The meeting and subsequent adventures occur in 1880, before Holmes met Watson and prior to Roosevelt's entry into politics. Holmes had supposedly been communicating with Roosevelt by

Stage

The first known play to feature Sherlock Holmes was UNDER THE CLOCK, starring and written by Charles Brookfield and Seymour Hicks. The first blockbuster, however, was SHERLOCK HOLMES by William Gillette, a work that proved to be the sire of a host of revivals. It is interesting to note that despite the virtual industry of Holmes films and television productions that the Great Detective remains an immensely popular subject for theatrical treatment.

MAJOR PLAYS FEATURING SHERLOCK HOLMES

DATE	PLAY AND AUTHOR	REMARKS	DATE	PLAY AND AUTHOR	REMARKS
1893	*Under the Clock* (Charles Brookfield and Seymour Hicks)	Earliest known play on the detective.	1929	*Sherlock Holmes: Farewell Appearances of William Gillette*	
1899	*Sherlock Holmes* (William Gillette)	Best known and most successful of all plays.	1933	*The Holmeses of Baker Street* (Basil Mitchell)	Starred Felix Aylmer and Nigel Playfair.
1900	*The Bank of England: An Adventure in the Life of Sherlock Holmes* (Max Goldberg)	Early Holmes play; starred Max Goldberg.	1948	*The Adventure of the Conk-Singleton Papers* (John Dickson Carr)	
1904	*The Sign of the Four* (Charles Rice)		1949	*The Adventures of the Paradol Chamber* (J. Dickson Carr)	
1905	*The Painful Predicament of Sherlock Holmes* (W. Gillette)		1953	*Sherlock Holmes* (Ouida Rathbone)	Starred Basil Rathbone.
			1961	*They Might Be Giants* (James Goldman)	Psychological study; later a film.
1910	*The Speckled Band: An Adventure of Sherlock Holmes* (A. Conan Doyle)	Very successful. Starred stage veteran H. A. Saintbury.	1965	*Baker Street* (James Coopersmith)	Musical
1921	*The Crown Diamond: An Evening with Sherlock Holmes* (A. Conan Doyle)	Forgotten for decades.	1971	*The Hound of the Baskervilles* (Joan Knight)	
			1974	*Sherlock Holmes* (Gillette revival)	Starred John Wood and Tim Pigott-Smith.
1923	*The Return of Sherlock Holmes* (J. E. Harold and Arthur Rose)	Starred Eille Norwood.		*Sherlock's Last Case* (Matthew Lang)	Starred Julian Glover and Peter Bayliss.

MAJOR PLAYS FEATURING SHERLOCK HOLMES

DATE	PLAY AND AUTHOR	REMARKS	DATE	PLAY AND AUTHOR	REMARKS
1975	*Sherlock Holmes and the Curse of the Sign of the Four* (Dennis Rosa)	Also titled "The Mark of Timber Toe."	1977	*The Marvelous Misadventures of Sherlock Holmes: A Musical Mystery for Children* (T. Racina)	Musical.
1976	*Enter Sherlock Holmes* (Mark Woolgar)		1978	*The Incredible Murder of Cardinal Tosca* (Alden Nowlan and Walter Learning)	Starred Jack Medley and Dan MacDonald.
	Sherlock Holmes (Gillette revival)	Starred Leonard Nimoy.		*Crucifer of Blood* (Paul Giovanni)	Very successful play; starred Paxton Whitehead and Timothy Landfield.
	Sherlock Holmes (Gillette revival)	Starred Robert Stephens.			
	Sherlock Holmes (Gillette revival)	Starred Frank Langella and Richard Woods; later shown on American cable television.	1980	*Crucifer of Blood* (Giovanni)	Starred Charlton Heston; later produced for television.
1977	*The Marvelous Musical Adventures of Sherlock Holmes* (William Shrewsbury)	Musical.	1985	*The Mask of Moriarty* (Hugh Leonard)	Starred Tom Baker and Alan Stanford.

letter for some time, finally meeting him in New York while touring as an actor named Escott. He is not only introduced to Roosevelt but to a young policeman named Wilson Hargeave, an officer of the New York police who would later assist Holmes whenever needed, most notably in "The Dancing Men." Hargreave, who had accompanied Roosevelt to the theater, is impressed by Holmes's observations, accepting his help while investigating a murder in Gramercy Park, ironically on the doorstep of Samuel J. Tilden, the loser in America's recent presidential elections. Holmes's investigation leads to the discovery of a mammoth conspiracy that threatens American security. The friendship between Holmes and Roosevelt is an interesting explanation for the fascination of Franklin Roosevelt with the Great Detective.

STAMFORD. An acquaintance of both Holmes and Watson who appeared only once in the Canon—in *A Study in Scarlet*—but who played the most pivotal role in all of the Sacred Writings by introducing the detective and the doctor at St. Barts. Stamford had been Watson's dresser at St. Bartholomew's, meeting the physician some years later in the Criterion Bar in London. Watson, recently invalided home from Afghanistan, was delighted to see Stamford again, particularly as he considered him a crony of his. Looking for cheaper lodgings than his hotel room in the Strand, Watson mentioned this to Stamford, who suggested Sherlock Holmes. The rest is history.

STAMFORD, ARCHIE. A forger who was arrested in Farnham, in Surrey by Holmes and Watson ("The Solitary Cyclist").

STANGER, JAMES. The editor of the Vermissa *Daily Herald* in *The Valley of Fear*, he was attacked and beaten by the Scowrers because of his outspoken editorials against them.

STANGERSON, JOSEPH.   The son of one of the four principal elders of the Mormon Church in *A Study in Scarlet*, Joseph Stangerson, when a young man with "a long, pale face," was a competitor for the affections of Lucy Ferrier, vying with Enoch Drebber. As members of the Avenging Angels, he and Drebber pursued the Ferriers when they attempted to flee, and Stangerson shot Lucy's father, John. Lucy was soon forced to wed Drebber, dying a short time later. Fearing the vengeance of Jefferson Hope, Drebber and Stangerson departed Utah, the latter serving as Drebber's secretary. Their flight took them to Europe, but Lucy's vengeful lover finally caught up with them in London.

STAPLES.   The solemn butler of Culverton Smith in "The Dying Detective."

STAPLETON, BERYL.   The former Beryl Garcia who was the supposed sister of Jack Stapleton of Merripit House, in Devonshire in *The Hound of the Baskervilles*. She attempted to warn Sir Henry Baskerville to keep away from the moor, once mistaking Dr. Watson for the Baskerville heir. Young Sir Henry soon fell in love with her, only to learn the truth about her dark past and the evil future planned by her husband.

STAPLETON, JACK.   An apparently accomplished English entomologist who resided at Merripit House in Devonshire in *The Hound of the Baskervilles* with Beryl Stapleton, supposedly his sister. Despite his charm and air of cordiality, Stapleton had very sinister intentions. Holmes was able to piece together details of his unsavory life, saving Sir Henry Baskerville just in the nick of time from Stapleton's cruel ambitions. (See also FRASER and ST. OLIVER'S.)

STARK, LYSANDER.   A man "with something of a German accent," from Eyford, Berkshire, who hired the young Victor Hatherley to perform a very peculiar job in "The Engineer's Thumb." The engineer described "Colonel" Stark: "I do not think that I have ever seen so thin a man. His whole face sharpened away into nose and chin, and the skin of his cheeks was drawn quite tense over his outstanding bones. Yet this emaciation seemed to be his natural habit, and due to no disease, for his eye was bright, his step brisk, and his bearing assured. He was plainly but neatly dressed, and his age, I should judge, would be nearer forty than thirty." Stark's real name was apparently Fritz.

STARR, LYSANDER.   A fictional correspondent of Holmes's in Topeka in "The Three Garridebs." The detective invented the name in the hopes of trapping a visitor to 221B in a lie. He added that Starr was mayor of Topeka in 1890. The visitor, who claimed to have been a lawyer in Topeka, took the bait, exclaiming, "Good old Starr! . . . His name is still honoured."

STATE AND MERTON COUNTY RAILROAD COMPANY.   A company that ran the railroad running through Vermissa Valley and that owned several mines in the area in *The Valley of Fear*. The firm was active in buying up property in the valley, bringing to bear considerable resources against the Scowrers, who opposed it.

STAUNTON, ARTHUR H.   A rising young forger whose name was entered in one of the volumes of Holmes's commonplace books under the letter S, a volume that was said to be a "mine of varied information" in "The Missing Three-Quarter."

STAUNTON, GODFREY.   A student at Cambridge University and the crack three-quarter of the school's rugby team who mysteriously disappeared just before the planned and important match with Oxford in "The Missing Three-Quarter." According to the team captain, Cyril Overton: "He's simply the hinge that the whole team turns on . . . Whether it's passing, or tackling, or dribbling, there's no one to touch him, and then, he's got the head, and can hold us all together." Staunton was an orphan whose nearest relative was Lord Mount-James, his uncle, one of the richest men in England, a relation that raised the possibility of his having been kidnapped for ransom. Holmes undertook the case and found Staunton, but not in time for the team to be saved from defeat by Oxford.

STAUNTON, HENRY.   Apparently a criminal whom Holmes "helped to hang" ("The Missing Three-Quarter"). Staunton was listed in the volume S of Holmes's commonplace books, a volume that was a "mine of varied information."

STEILER, PETER.   The manager of the Englischer Hof, in Meiringen, Switzerland in "The Final Problem." Watson wrote: "It was on the third of May [1891] that we reached the little village of Meiringen, where we put up at the Englischer Hof, then kept by Peter Steiler the elder. Our landlord was an intelligent man and spoke excellent English, having served for three years as waiter at the Grosvenor Hotel in London. At his advice, on the afternoon of the fourth we set off together, with the intention of crossing the hills and spending the night at the hamlet of Rosenlaui. We had strict injunctions, however, on no account to pass the falls of Reichenbach, which are about halfway up the hills, without making a small detour to see them." It is unclear why Watson referred to him as Steiler the Elder as Steiler the Younger was of no importance.

STEINER.   A member of the German spy ring headed by Von Bork just before the start of World War I in "His Last Bow." Steiner was arrested in Portsmouth just before Von Bork was himself captured by Altamont.

STEPNEY.   An area of London, part of the terrible East End mentioned in "The Six Napoleons." The sculptor works of Gelder and Co. were situated in Stepney. The firm supplied plaster casts of Napoleon by Devine to both Morse Hudson and the Harding Brothers. Holmes and Watson visited Gelder and Co., the doctor describing Stepney as "a riverside city of a hundred thousand souls, where the tenement houses welter and reek with the outcasts of Europe."

STERNDALE, DR. LEON.   The famous lion hunter and African explorer in "The Devil's Foot," who, by his own description, had been outside the law for so many years that he had become ultimately a law unto himself. On the side of his Cornish mother, Sterndale was a cousin to the Tregennis family, and he took particular interest in Brenda Tregennis, who was, with two of her brothers, the victim of a bizarre and horrifying murder. Sterndale was to exact revenge on her killer, using the most fiendish means at his disposal. The explorer had the only supply in England of the so-called Devil's Foot root (*Radix pedis diaboli*), an obscure ordeal poison. Watson wrote: "The huge body, the craggy and deeply seamed face with the fierce eyes and hawk-like nose, the grizzled hair . . .

the beard—golden at the fringes and white near the lips, save for the nicotine stain from his perpetual cigar—all these were as well known in London as in Africa."

STEVENS, BERT.   A "mild-mannered, Sunday-school young man" who had wanted Holmes and Watson to get him off on a charge of murder in 1887. The detective found him to be, however, a "terrible murderer." Holmes used Bert Stevens's case to remind Watson during the affair recounted in "The Adventure of the Norwood Builder" that looks could be deceiving.

STEVENSON.   A member of the Cambridge rugby team who was considered by Cyril Overton to be a possible replacement for the missing Godfrey Staunton in the upcoming game with Oxford in "The Missing Three-Quarter."

STEWART, JANE.   A housemaid to Colonel and Mrs. James Barclay in their villa, Lachine, in Aldershott in "The Crooked Man." She heard the argument between Mrs. Barclay and her husband just prior to the discovery of his dead body and his comatose wife.

STEWART, MRS.   A woman who lived in the central Scottish town of Lauder and who was killed in 1887 ("The Empty House"). While nothing could be proved, Holmes was convinced Colonel Sebastian Moran was at the bottom of it.

STIMSON & CO.   An undertaker in London, on the Kensington Road in "The Disappearance of Lady Frances Carfax." They were hired by Annie Fraser to organize the funeral of Rose Spender. In discussing the special arrangements with Fraser, Mrs. Stimson provided the clue that led to the solution of the mystery and the recovery of the missing Lady Frances Carfax.

STOCK, NIGEL.   An English actor who distinguished himself as Watson in a number of productions, Stock played the good doctor first opposite Douglas Wilmer as Holmes in the 1964 British television adaptation of "The Speckled Band." This was so successful that the pair went on to star in a British television series in 1965. After Wilmer's departure, Stock was paired with Peter Cushing in 1968 in a well-known series of adaptations. He later performed in the one-man play

221B as Watson, describing his life with Holmes. He also did a series of recordings with Robert Hardy as Holmes, written by the well-known Holmesian experts Michael and Mollie Hardwick.

"STOCKBROKER'S CLERK, THE" (STOC).

Published: *Strand*, March 1893, *Harper's*, March 11, 1893; collected in *The Memoirs of Sherlock Holmes* (1894). Major players: Holmes, Watson, Hall Pycroft, Arthur Pinner, Harry Pinner. Case date: 1888 or 1889, after Watson's marriage to Mary Morstan. A case very similar in plot to "The Red-Headed League," but without its colorful characters. Hall Pycroft, a young unemployed stockbroker's clerk, receives an interview appointment with the great London firm Mawson & Williams, but decides instead to accept a post as business manager of the impressive sounding Franco-Midland Hardware Company, Ltd., offered to him by Arthur Pinner, financial agent for the firm. Journeying to the seedy Franco-Midland offices at 126B Corporation Street in Birmingham, Pycroft meets Arthur's brother Harry. It is very obvious to him that the two brothers are one in the same, causing him to consult Holmes. The chronicle mentions Watson's domestic arrangements following his marriage: he purchases a practice in the Paddington district from old Mr. Farquhar, although he does not see much of it as he is off with Holmes to Birmingham.

STOCKDALE, BARNEY.

A member of the Spencer John Gang in "The Three Gables." He was the boss of Steve Dixie and was hired by Isadora Klein, the voluptuary, to intimidate Holmes. His wife was **Susan Stockdale,** a maid at the Three

Holmes visits Watson in "The Stockbroker's Clerk"; by Sidney Paget.

Gables to Mrs. Maberley. She was also a member of the Spencer John Gang, spying in the house on behalf of Isadora Klein until she was caught by Holmes.

STOKE MORAN.

A village in west Surrey that was also the ancestral seat of the Roylotts, at the Stoker Moran Manor in "The Speckled Band." By the time of the affair of the Speckled Band, Stoker Moran had declined considerably under Dr. Grimesby Roylott. "The building was of gray, lichen-blotched stone, with a high central portion and two curving wings, like the claws of a crab, thrown out on each side. In one of these wings the windows were broken and blocked with the wooden boards, the roof was partly caved in, a picture of ruin."

STONE, REV. JOSHUA.

A neighbor of Aloysius Garcia and Wisteria Lodge, in Surrey in "Wisteria Lodge." Stone lived in a large house, Nether Walsling.

STONER, HELEN.

The daughter of **Major General** and **Mrs. Stoner,** and stepdaughter of Dr. Grimesby Roylott, who brought Holmes into the case recorded in "The Speckled Band." Major General Stoner died in 1850 or 1853 and had been an officer of the Bengal Artillery. His widow, **Mrs. Stoner** (née Westphail) married Dr. Grimesby Roylott while still in India. Her twin daughters were only five at the time. After Mrs. Stoner's death in 1875 in a railway accident near Crewe, Helen and her twin sister **Julia Stoner** were raised by Roylott at the Roylott family estate of Stoke Moran. Julia became engaged to a half-pay major in the marines during Christmas, a union to which Dr. Roylott did not object. Within a fortnight of the day that had been set for the marriage, Julia was dead. One night she screamed, collapsed into her sister's arms and, and before dying, exclaimed: "Oh, my God! Helen! It was the band! It was the Speckled Band!" Helen, two years later, feared that she might meet the same end and so consulted Holmes. "She raised her veil as she spoke, and we could see that she was indeed in a pitiable state of agitation, her face was all drawn and gray, with restless, if frightened, eyes, like those of a hunted animal. Her features and figure were those of a woman of thirty, but her hair was shot with premature gray, and her expression was weary and haggard." Helen became engaged to and finally married Percy Armitage, while the detective revealed Julia's murderer.

STOPER, MISS. The manager of Westaway's agency for governesses in the West End in "The Copper Beeches." She was considerably annoyed at Violet Hunter's refusal to cut her hair, the one major stipulation by Jephro Rucastle to which she would not agree and the one obstacle that threatened to ruin Hunter's chances of employment by Rucastle, and Stoper's receiving of a handsome commission. She asked Miss Hunter if she desired to keep her name on the books, declaring: "Well, really, it seems rather useless, since you refuse the most excellent offers in this fashion . . . You can hardly expect us to exert ourselves to find another such opening for you. Good-day to you, Miss Hunter."

STRADIVARIUS. A type of violin made by the Italian violin maker Antonio Stradivarius (1649–1737). Holmes owned a Stradivarius, said by the detective to be worth at least five hundred guineas, purchased on Tottenham Court Road for some fifty-five shillings ("The Cardboard Box"). (See also Music under HOLMES, SHERLOCK.)

STRAKER, JOHN. The trainer of the racehorse Silver Blaze at King's Pyland in "Silver Blaze." He was found murdered upon the moor, about a quarter of a mile from the stables, his head "shattered by a savage blow from some heavy weapon, and he was wounded on the thigh, where there was a long, clean cut, inflicted evidently by some very sharp instrument." Straker was a "retired jockey who rode in Colonel Ross's colours before he became too heavy for the weighing-chair. He has served the colonel for five years as jockey and for seven years as trainer, and has always shown himself to be a zealous and honest servant." His wife, **Mrs. Straker**, had asked her husband not to go out on the night of the murder as she heard the rain pattering against the window. Holmes inquired whether they had ever met in Plymouth at a garden party sometime ago, where she had worn "a costume of dove-coloured silk with ostrich-feather trimming." She was certain that she had never met Holmes and she never owned such a dress, a denial that aided the detective in his investigation. (See also WILLIAM DARBYSHIRE.)

STRAND. A major London thoroughfare where Watson stayed at a private hotel after his being invalided home during the Second Afghan War, "leading a comfortless, meaningless existence, and spending such money as I had, considerably more freely than I ought" (*A Study in Scarlet*). He was thus happy to meet someone looking for a person to share a suite of rooms at Baker Street—Sherlock Holmes. Situated on the Strand were Simpson's in "The Illustrious Client" and "The Dying Detective"; The Lowther Arcade in "The Final Problem"; the shop that sold Henry Baskerville his new boots in *The Hound of the Baskervilles*; and the American Exchange in *A Study in Scarlet*. Holmes and Watson also took a walk one night through London, watching the kaleidoscope of life as it ebbed and flowed through Fleet Street and the Strand in "The Resident Patient."

STRAND MAGAZINE. A long-running popular English magazine founded by George Newnes in

The *Strand* magazine published the first of the Holmes stories, "A Scandal in Bohemia," in July 1881.

1891. The home of a huge number of detective stories, its authors of note over the decades included Agatha Christie, Somerset Maugham, G. K. Chesterton, and Aldous Huxley. But above all, the publication owed its success to the accounts in its pages written by Sir Arthur Conan Doyle, featuring Sherlock Holmes.

Strand Magazine was launched in January, 1891, with what was, at the time, tremendous fanfare and a first print run of some 300,000 copies. This initial success was largely due to the aggressive pre-release publicity orchestrated by Newnes. He used extensive advertising in his other extremely popular publication, *Tit-Bits*, begun in October 1881, and large amounts of publicity to entice readers. His efforts paid off and public interest continued to grow, thanks to the steady and very capable work of H. Greenhough Smith, who held the title literary editor, but who actually ran the paper, with Newnes reaping the rewards while attending Parliament as a Liberal MP for Newmarket.

The magazine probably would have been merely one of several successful publications in England during the period, but in the Spring of 1891 there arrived two short stories from a doctor who had already had one story published by the *Strand*, "The Voice of Science." The new works, "A Scandal in Bohemia" and "The Red-Headed League," featured the still little known literary detective Sherlock Holmes and his faithful chronicler Dr. John Watson. So began the relationship of the *Strand* with Arthur Conan Doyle, an association that helped the publication to reach a circulation of nearly half a million per issue. The last Holmes story it would publish was "Shoscombe Old Place" in 1927. Sadly, the *Strand* could not long survive the turbulent 1940s, and in 1950 it ceased publication. Its place in the history of detective literature, however, was assured.

STRAUBENZEE. A weapons maker who owned a workshop in the Minories and created an air gun for Count Negretto Sylvius in "The Mazarin Stone."

STUDY IN SCARLET, A (STUD). Published: *Beeton's Christmas Annual*, 1887; published as a novel in 1888. Major players: Part One: Holmes, Watson, Inspector Lestrade, Inspector Gregson, Enoch Drebber; Part Two: Jefferson Hope, Joseph Ferrier, Lucy Ferrier. Case date: See below. The first Sherlock Holmes story to be pub-

An early draft of *A Study in Scarlet*. Note the experimentation with possible names for the characters.

lished (if not the REMINISCENCES), *A Study in Scarlet* was particularly notable for detailing the first meeting between Holmes and Watson and for establishing the foundation of their long business and personal relationship, beginning with the now fabled comment by Holmes to Watson at St. Bartholomew's: "How are you? You have been in Afghanistan, I perceive." The account was in two parts. Part One: "Being a Reprint from the Reminiscences of John H. Watson, M.D., Late of the Army Medical Department," and Part Two: "The Country of the Saints." Part One, one of the most important and interesting series of passages in the entire Canon, is written by Dr. Watson and is concerned with his account of his medical career in the army and his meeting Sherlock Holmes before being plunged into Holmes's investigation into the murders first of Enoch Drebber and then Joseph Stangerson. Drebber's murder is both mysterious and gruesome, providing Holmes with ample opportunity to demonstrate his powers as a detective. The sleuth's solution of the crimes leads to Part Two. This is a third person chronicle of the adventures and tragedy endured by John Ferrier, his adopted daughter Lucy, and their dear friend Jefferson Hope; the Mormon community of Utah serves as a backdrop to the narrative. The final two chapters allow Holmes to explain the solution and to wrap up the last details of the case, naming the investigation "our Study in Scarlet," so-called because of "the scarlet thread of murder running through the colorless skein of life." In *The Sign of Four*, Holmes chided Watson for his work in bringing the case to literary life. "Honestly, I cannot congratulate you upon it. Detection is, or ought to be, an exact science and should be treated in the same cold and unemotional manner. You have attempted to tinge it with romanticism, which produces much the same effect as if you worked a love-story or an elopement into the fifth proposition of Euclid." The date of the case is placed at 1881, while the events described in Part Two took place from 1847 to 1860.

The capture of the murderer in A *Study in Scarlet*; by George Hutchinson.

STUDY IN SCARLET, A.   England 1914. Dir: George Pearson. Cast: James Bragington (Holmes), Fred Paul (Jefferson Hope), Agnes Glynne (Lucy Ferrier). The first film version of the first story of the Canon, this adaptation was generally faithful, but, curiously, it omitted Watson entirely, depriving the viewer of the fun of seeing the doctor and the detective meeting for the first time. Holmes was played by Bragington, a nonprofessional actor who was chosen by director Pearson because of his remarkable Holmesian appearance: tall, gaunt, piercing eyes, and excellent in deerstalker and with pipe. He appears only late in the story, the focus of the plot being the events recounted as flashbacks in America.

STUDY IN SCARLET, A.   U.S. 1914. Dir: Francis Ford. Cast: Francis Ford (Holmes), Jack Francis (Watson). A short silent film released by the Gold Seal/Universal Film Co., one day after the release of the other A *Study in Scarlet*, starring James Bragington. This one featured Holmes in a kind of oversized hat, seen previously in the films of Otto Lagoni. Interestingly, Sir Arthur Conan Doyle was not aware of the film as he had sold the rights to someone else. Nevertheless, the advertising for it declared: "This is first of a series of fascinating, mysterious detective stories by the noted author, Sir Arthur Conan Doyle . . ." As was typical for the era, copyright laws meant little to producers.

STUDY IN SCARLET, A.   U.S. 1933. Dir: Edwin L. Marin. Cast: Reginald Owen (Holmes), Warburton Gamble (Watson), Tempe Pigott (Mrs. Hudson), and Alan Mowbray (Lestrade). A production that, according to the credits, was based on the novel A *Study in Scarlet* and "The Adventure of the Red-Headed League," although the film actually had almost nothing to do with either work. REGINALD OWEN, Watson to Clive Brook's Holmes in *Sherlock Holmes* (1932), here graduated to the role of the great detective, with Warburton Gamble as a rather lifeless Watson. Owen was not popular as Holmes, his heaviness and general appearance working against him. He did, however, improve his performance by writing extra dialogue and working on continuity in the screenplay by Robert Florey.

STUDY IN TERROR, A.   England 1965. Dir: James Hill. Cast: John Neville (Holmes), Donald Huston (Watson), Robert Morely (Mycroft), Frank

Holmes (John Neville), Watson (Donald Huston), and Lestrade (Frank Finlay) discuss Jack the Ripper whom they are pursuing in *A Study in Terror* (1965).

Finlay (Lestrade), Barbara Leake (Mrs. Hudson), John Fraser (Lord Carfax), Anthony Quayle (Dr. Murray). This major Holmes production brought to the screen for the first time the intriguing duel of the detective and the infamous Jack the Ripper. The story, production, and subject matter were a radical departure from previous productions, as *A Study in Terror* offered an unvarnished picture of the East End, surpassed only by MURDER BY DE-CREE (1979) in dreariness and squalor, quite a change from the somewhat sanitized London of the Universal Studios Rathbone-Bruce pictures. At the behest of Mycroft, Holmes launches himself into the Ripper case, his investigation taking him into the Whitechapel area where the Ripper has been striking and where the plot slowly works its way to the rather logical climax. John Neville is sound as Holmes, outdone in some scenes by his very able Watson, but the story is undermined by inaccuracy—the details of the crimes are not in keeping with the historical record of the Ripper case. When

first released, the film earned the then undesirable "adults only" X certificate from the British film board.

SUDBURY. A student at Harold Stackhurst's coaching establishment, the Gables in "The Lion's Mane." He was one of several people to discover the carcass of Fitzroy McPherson's Airedale terrier at the spot where its master was found dead.

SUICIDE. Suicide appears several times in the Canon. Elsie Cubitt in "The Dancing Men," Harry Pinner in "The Stockbroker's Clerk," and Josiah Amberley in "The Retired Colourman" all tried to kill themselves, while Anna Coram in "The Golden Pince-Nez" and Maria Gibson in "The Problem of Thor Bridge" were more successful. Jefferson Hope in *A Study in Scarlet* attempted to leap out the window at 221B, but was restrained and gave his assurances that he would not kill himself. Holmes also persuaded Eugenia Ronder to stay her own hand, saying: "Your life is not your own. . . . Keep your hands off it." He also believed that Sir James Walter's sudden death after the theft of the Bruce-Partington Plans was actually suicide in "The Bruce-Partington Plans." In the case of Elias Openshaw in "The Five Orange Pips" and Blessington in "The Resident Patient," murder was disguised as suicide.

SUMATRA. An island in Indonesia, at one time part of the Dutch East Indies. Holmes claimed that he had contracted a coolie disease from Sumatra, an illness that was well known to Culverton Smith, a planter from Sumatra in "The Dying Detective." The detective also investigated the case of the Netherlands-Sumatra Company in "The Reigate Squires." The most famous reference in the Canon (made in "The Sussex Vampire") to Sumatra was the GIANT RAT OF SUMATRA.

SUMMER. A shipping agent in the Ratcliff Highway who assisted Captain Basil (Holmes in disguise) to find three harpooners for an arctic expedition in "Black Peter."

SURREY. A county south of London, Surrey was the site of several investigations by Holmes: "The Naval Treaty," "The Reigate Squires," "The Speckled Band," "Wisteria Lodge," and "The Solitary Cyclist." Holmes declared that he was ravenous upon his return to 221B after his efforts to recover the missing Naval Treaty as he had just "breathed thirty miles of Surrey air."

SUSSEX. A county in southern England where Holmes retired in 1903. "I had given myself up entirely to that soothing life of Nature for which I had so often yearned during the long years spent amid the gloom of London . . . My villa is situated upon the southern slope of the downs, commanding a great view of the Channel" ("The Lion's Mane"). The detective had also investigated several cases in Sussex: "The Sussex Vampire," "Black Peter," *The Valley of Fear*, and "The Musgrave Ritual."

"SUSSEX VAMPIRE, THE ADVENTURE OF THE" (SUSS). Published: *Strand*, January 1924, *Hearst's International*, January 1924; collected in *The Case Book of Sherlock Holmes* (1927). Major

players: Holmes, Watson, Bob Ferguson, Mrs. Ferguson, Mrs. Mason, Dolores, Jack Ferguson. Case date: November 1896 or 1897. Holmes's only Canonical foray into the world of the bloodsucker, a theme subsequently developed by modern writers (see under VAMPIRES and DRACULA). The detective is introduced to a case of apparent vampirism by the firm Morrison, Morrison, and Dodd, a company previously associated with Holmes through his investigation into the ship *Matilda Briggs*, connected with the giant rat of Sumatra, "a story for which the world is not yet prepared." "Big" Bob Ferguson, of the tea brokers Ferguson & Muirhead, is greatly troubled by the inexplicable behavior of his wife, for she has apparently been caught drinking the blood of her infant son. Crucial to the solution of the matter is the condition of the small family dog, Carlo, who has suffered in a way similar to the sheep in "Silver Blaze." Of his conclusions, Holmes tells Watson: "It has been a case for intellectual deduction, but when this original intellectual deduction is confirmed point by point by quite a number of independent incidents, then the subjective becomes objective and we can say confidently that we have reached our goal. I had, in fact, reached it before we left Baker Street, and the rest has merely been observation and information."

SUTHERLAND, MARY. The daughter of a deceased Tottenham Court Road plumber, and stepdaughter of James Windibank, who consulted Holmes and introduced him to the affair recounted in "A Case of Identity." Sutherland hoped that the detective would be able to find her fiance, Hosmer Angel, who disappeared on their wedding day.

SUTRO The lawyer of Mrs. Maberley in "The Three Gables."

SWAIN, JOHN. A man who was threatened by the Ku Klux Klan in 1869 in "The Five Orange Pips." The March 1869 entry in the notebooks of Elias Openshaw was: "7th. Set the pips on McCauley, Paramore, and Swain of St. Augustine." On the tenth, Swain fled the country.

SWAMP ADDER. A very lethal serpent that was said by Holmes in "The Speckled Band" to be "the deadliest snake in India." Its appearance, described as being like a "peculiar yellow band, with brownish speckles," prompted one of its victims to cry out, "It was the band! The speckled band!" There is no snake called the swamp adder anywhere in the world so it is uncertain to which species Watson may have been referring.

SWITZERLAND. The beautiful European country served as the backdrop for the climactic encounter between Holmes and Professor Moriarty in "The Final Problem." After departing England and making their way across Europe, Holmes and Watson entered Switzerland via Luxembourg and Basel. They eventually arrived at Meiringen and then went to Rosenlaui. On May 4, 1891, at the REICHENBACH FALLS, Holmes had his deadly meeting with the professor. (See also: GEMMI PASS, GENEVA, INTERLAKEN, LAUSANNE, MEIRINGEN, ROSENLAUI, and SPLUGEN PASS.)

SYDENHAM. A residential district in south London where the Randalls, a gang of Lewisham robbers, did a job a fortnight before the murder of Sir Eustace Brackenstall in "The Abbey Grange." Captain Jack Croker also lived in Syd-

enham in "The Abbey Grange" and Jonas Oldacre had his residence near there in "The Norwood Builder."

SYLVIUS, COUNT NEGRETTO. A well-known sportsman and big game hunter who resided at 136 Moorside Gardens, N.W. in "The Mazarin Stone," the count was also the thief of the Mazarin Stone (the Crown Diamond). His efforts to dissuade Holmes not to pursue his investigation any further only spurred on the detective. Holmes amassed a considerable record of Count Sylvius's criminal wrongdoings: the gambling away of the Blymer estate, his assumed action against the unfortunate Miss Minnie Warrender, the robbery in the train de-luxe to the Riviera on February 13, 1892, and the forged check in the same year on the Credit Lyonnais. The detective told Watson: "A man of nerve. Possibly you have heard of his reputation as a shooter of big game. It would indeed be a triumphant ending to his excellent sporting record if he added me to his bag."

TANGEY. The commissionaire at the Foreign Office who was on duty the night that the secret Naval Treaty was stolen from the office of Percy Phelps in "The Naval Treaty." An old soldier of the Coldstream Guards, Tangey fell asleep and allowed a kettle for coffee to boil over. Phelps, who had ordered the coffee, was forced to come down to inquire where it was, setting off a series of events that led to the disappearance of the document and Phelps's complete breakdown. His wife, **Mrs. Tangey**, was an early suspect in the crime. She worked as a charwoman in the Foreign Office and had

taken Phelps's order for the coffee, immediately leaving the building to go home. Phelps described her as "a large, coarse-faced, elderly woman, in an apron." They lived at 16 Ivy Lane, Brixton.

TANKERVILLE CLUB. A London club to which Colonel Sebastian Moran belonged, as was revealed in "The Empty House." The club was also involved in a scandal investigated by Holmes ("The Five Orange Pips"). The detective cleared Major Prendergast, who was accused of cheating at cards. The major later told Openshaw of Holmes's success and the young man then consulted Holmes on a case of his own. Prendergast declared that Holmes could solve anything and had never been beaten. The detective replied that Prendergast had said too much and that he had been beaten four times—thrice by men, and once by a woman.

TAPANULI FEVER. A disease, presumably from the Tapanuli region of Sumatra about which Holmes asked Watson if he knew anything in "The Dying Detective." The doctor admitted ignorance, confessing as well to knowing nothing about "Black Formosa corruption."

TARLETON MURDERS. One of Holmes's early cases, dated to the period before his labors with Dr. Watson and mentioned in "The Musgrave Ritual."

TATTOO. Holmes devoted a monograph to the subject, *On Tattoo Marks*, written and possibly published in 1890, around the time of his involvement in the case of "The Red-Headed League." The work may very well be dated to a time earlier than 1890, such as was done by Walter Klinefelter in his excellent 1946 article "The Writings of Mr. Sherlock Holmes." In the case of "The Red-Headed League," Holmes deduced that his client Jabez Wilson had been in China because of the fish tattooed above his right wrist. The pink color was "quite peculiar to China." Holmes nearly caused Trevor Senior to suffer apoplexy by noticing the initials "J.A." tattooed on the bend of his elbow, that he had tried unsuccessfully to have removed in "The 'Gloria Scott'." Holmes also noticed the large blue anchor tattooed on the back of the hand of a retired sergeant of the marines in *A Study in Scarlet*.

TAVERNIER. A French modeler who created the wax bust of Holmes used by the detective to fool Count Negretto Sylvius in "The Mazarin Stone."

TEDDY. The pet mongoose of Henry Wood in "The Crooked Man," Teddy had been taught to catch a defanged cobra as part of Wood's small entertainment show for soldiers. Holmes was able to follow Teddy's activities while in the Aldershot home of Colonel and Mrs. Barclay the night that the colonel died mysteriously. The mongoose was naturally drawn to a canary's cage that was hanging in the window of the room where the colonel's body was found, evidence of Teddy's visit was noted by Holmes and traced on a large sheet of tissue paper.

TELEGRAMS. One of the principal means by which Holmes conducted his extensive communications with friends, associates, and the various professional or legal authorities throughout England or beyond. Watson, too, received telegrams, from the detective, commenting in "The Devil's Foot" that "he has never been known to write where a telegram would serve." Terse and always to the point, Holmes communicated to Watson such intriguing imperatives as: "Why not tell them of the Cornish horror—strangest case I have ever handled" ("The Devil's Foot"); or "Come at once if convenient, if inconvenient come all the same. S.H." ("The Creeping Man"). There was also the episode: "To Holmes I wrote showing how rapidly and surely I had got down to the roots of the matter. In reply I had a telegram asking for a description of Dr. Shlessinger's left ear" ("The Disappearance of Lady Frances Carfax"). As Holmes rarely revealed his entire mind or his full plans, such telegrams often left the recipient confused and confounded. Additionally, at the height of his career, the detective certainly had commissionaires and messengers coming and going through Baker Street. Among the most memorable telegrams of the Canon were from Mycroft to Holmes announcing his unprecedented intention to come to Baker Street in "The Bruce-Partington Plans"; the telegram from Wilson Hargreave that helped clear up the affair of "The Dancing Men"; and the missif from John Scott Eccles to Holmes in "Wisteria Lodge": "Have just had most incredible and grotesque experience. May I consult you?"

TELEPHONE. The modern instrument was apparently installed at Baker Street sometime before 1898 and the case of "The Retired Colourman." Holmes used the telephone during the case, doing so again in his investigation into the affairs of Baron Gruner in "The Illustrious Client" and the Garridebs in "The Three Garridebs." Baker Street also had a telephone directory as Watson looked up the name of Nathan Garrideb in one.

TERRIERS. This breed of small dogs figures in a number of cases. A terrier served as the means of introducing Holmes and Trevor Junior during the future detective's days in university. In "The

Technology comes to Baker Street—Holmes uses a telephone in "The Three Garridebs"; by Howard Elcock.

port: this time a train while *Pursuit* took place on an ocean liner. The choice of locations was a good one as the train took on a claustrophobic and menacing atmosphere. Holmes is engaged by young Ronald Carstairs (Geoffrey Steele) to accompany him and his mother (Mary Forbes) on their trip to Edinburgh while they carry with them the priceless Star of Rhodesia. The detective is joined by Watson and Inspector Lestrade, the inspector returning after a two-film absence.

THAMES.   The famous river in London was either mentioned in or served as the backdrop for several cases: *The Sign of Four*, "The Man With the Twisted Lip," and "The Five Orange Pips." Other references to the Thames were made in "The Golden Pince-Nez," "The Six Napoleons," and "The Dying Detective."

THEY MIGHT BE GIANTS.   U.S. 1971. Dir: Anthony Harvey. Cast: George C. Scott (Holmes), Joanne Woodward (Dr. Mildred Watson). The film version of the 1961 play *They Might Be Giants* by James Goldman, that had been performed in London but never moved to Broadway. This is techni-

'Gloria Scott'," he told Watson that Trevor owned a bull terrier that froze on to Holmes's ankle one morning as he went down to chapel. As Holmes was "laid by the heels" for ten days, Victor Trevor visited and the two became good friends. Holmes later accepted the unpleasant task of euthanizing a terrier belonging to Mrs. Hudson by administering poison (*A Study in Scarlet*). Fitzroy McPherson's dog in "The Lion's Mane" was an Airedale, a type of terrier. Finally, in examining the walking stick left behind by Dr. Mortimer at Baker Street in *The Hound of the Baskervilles*, Holmes deduced that his dog was larger than a terrier.

TERROR BY NIGHT.   U.S. 1946. Dir: Roy William Neill. Cast: Basil Rathbone (Holmes), Nigel Bruce (Watson), Dennis Hoey (Lestrade), and Alan Mowbray (Major Duncan-Bleek). The thirteenth outing of Rathbone and Bruce as Holmes and Watson, and a marked improvement over the previous entry, *Pursuit to Algiers* (1945). The two films were similar in that they presented their story on board some isolated form of trans-

George C. Scott as Justin Playfair, a retired judge who believes he is Sherlock Holmes, in *They Might Be Giants*.

Television

The earliest television program featuring Sherlock Holmes was "The Three Garridebs," starring Louis Hector and William Podmore. It aired on November 27, 1937, and was broadcast from Radio City, New York. Since that night, the detective and his faithful Dr. Watson have appeared in the television series, specials, and movies, remaining a fixture on the air into the 1990s. Beyond these programs, there are also to be found on television repeat showings of classic Holmes films, especially the numerous outings of Basil Rathbone and Nigel Bruce.

DATE	PROGRAM	PERFORMERS	DATE	PROGRAM	PERFORMERS
1937	"The Three Garridebs"	Louis Hector and William Podmore	1974	"Dr. Watson and the Darkwater Hall Mystery" (U.K.)	Edward Fox (Watson)
1949	"The Adventure of the Speckled Band" (U.K.)	Alan Napier and Melville Cooper	1975	"The Interior Motive"	Leonard Nimoy and Burt Blackwell
1951	"Sherlock Holmes" (U.K.)	Alan Wheatley and Raymond Francis	1976	"The Return of the World's Greatest Detective"	Larry Hagman and Jenny O'Hara
	"The Man with the Twisted Lip"	John Longden and Campbell Singer		"Sherlock Holmes in New York"	Roger Moore and Patrick Macnee
1953	"The Adventure of the Black Baronet"	Basil Rathbone and Martyn Green	1977	"My Dear Uncle Sherlock"	Royal Dano and Robbie Rist
1954–1955	"The New Adventures of Sherlock Holmes"	Ronald Howard and H. Marion Crawford		"The Strange Case of the End of Civilization as We Know It" (U.K.)	John Cleese and Arthur Lowe
1964–1965	"Sherlock Holmes" (U.K.)	Douglas Wilmer and Nigel Stock		"Silver Blaze" (U.K.)	Christopher Plummer and Thorley Walters
1968	"Sherlock Holmes" (U.K.)	Peter Cushing and Nigel Stock		"In Search of . . . Sherlock Holmes"	Leonard Nimoy (Host of T.V. series "In Search of . . .")
1969	"High Jinks" (U.K.)	Ray Alan and Derek Dene			
1972	"The Hound of the Baskervilles"	Stewart Granger and Bernard Fox	1981	"Sherlock Holmes" (televised stage play)	Frank Langella and Richard Woods
	"Conan Doyle"	Nigel Davenport (Conan Doyle)		"Sherlock Holmes and the Baskerville Case" (Australia)	Animated (voice of Peter O'Toole)
1973	"Elementary, My Dear Watson" (U.K.)	John Cleese and William Rushton			
1974	"It's a Mystery Charlie Brown"	Animated	1982	"Sherlock Holmes and Dr. Watson"	Geoffrey Whitehead and Donald Pickering

DATE	PROGRAM	PERFORMERS	DATE	PROGRAM	PERFORMERS
	"The Hound of the Baskervilles" (U.K.)	Tom Baker and Terence Rigby	1987	"The Sign of Four" (U.K.)	Jeremy Brett and Edward Hardwicke
	"Young Sherlock" (U.K.)	Guy Henry (Holmes)		"The Return of Sherlock Holmes"	Michael Pennington and Margaret Colin
1983	"The Sign of Four" (U.K.)	Ian Richardson and David Healy	1990	"Hands of a Murderer"	Edward Woodward and John Hillerman
	"The Hound of the Baskervilles" (U.K.)	Ian Richardson and Donald Churchill	1991	"Crucifer of Blood"	Charlton Heston and Richard Johnson
1984	"The Adventures of Sherlock Holmes" (U.K.)	Jeremy Brett and David Burke		"The Casebook of Sherlock Holmes"	Jeremy Brett and Edward Hardwicke
	"The Masks of Death"	Peter Cushing and John Mills		"Sherlock Holmes, Incident at Victoria Falls" (European)	Christopher Lee and Patrick Macnee
1986–1988	"The Return of Sherlock Holmes" (U.K.)	Jeremy Brett and Edward Hardwicke	1992	"Sherlock Holmes and the Leading Lady"	Christopher Lee and Patrick Macnee
1987	"The Hound of the Baskervilles" (U.K.)	Jeremy Brett and Edward Hardwicke			

cally not a Sherlock Holmes film; rather it is a complex psychological comedy featuring Scott as Justin Playfair, a retired judge who has assumed utterly the persona of Sherlock Holmes. His brother, indebted to the mob, is anxious to have him committed so that he can get hold of Justin's wealth. The brother thus summons a psychologist, Dr. Watson (played superbly by Joanne Woodward), to examine him. She is at first fascinated, but soon becomes enamored of "Holmes" and is drawn into his world as his faithful assistant. Scott is immensely powerful as the detective, making the audience wish he had enjoyed the opportunity to portray Holmes in a more straightforward production. Scott's similarity to some of the illustrations drawn by Harry C. Edwards for *McClure's Magazine* is striking.

THOR PLACE.   The estate in Hampshire of J. Neil Gibson, the American senator and Gold King in "Thor Bridge." On the estate spanning Thor Mere, was Thor Bridge where Mrs. Maria Gibson, J. Neil's wife, was found murdered. The bridge proved crucial to the solution of the case by Holmes and the freeing of Grace Dunbar from the charge of murder. Holmes spoke to Watson about

the bridge: "This bridge—a single broad span of stone with balustrated sides—carries the drive on the narrowest part of a long, deep, reed-girt sheet of water. Thor Mere it is called. In the mouth of the bridge lay the dead woman."

"THREE GABLES, THE ADVENTURE OF THE" (3GAB).   Published: *Liberty*, September 1926, *Strand*, October 1926; collected in *The Case Book of Sherlock Holmes* (1927). Major players: Holmes, Watson, Mary Maberley, Isadora Klein, Douglas Maberley, Steve Dixie. Case date: Various. A case generally ranked as one of the poorest of the entire Canon, largely because of the peculiar behavior of the detective throughout. Confronted, for example, at the start of the chronicle by the bruiser Steve Dixie, Holmes cows him with threats and racial epithets quite out of character for the enlightened Holmes. The literary presentation of the black Dixie is weak and strangely jingoistic. The affair itself involves the bizarre experience of a widow, Mrs. Maberley, the owner of the house the Three Gables, situated in Harrow Weald. Watson wrote that the Three Gables was "a brick and timber villa, standing in its own acre of undeveloped grassland. Three small projections

Jeremy Brett, Holmes in the current television series on MYSTERY! (Photo courtesy MYSTERY/WGBH Boston.)

above the upper window made a feeble attempt to justify its name. Behind was a grove of melancholy, half-grown pines, and the whole aspect of the place was poor and depressing." Mrs. Maberley is offered a large sum of money for her house, but with the proviso that she leave *everything* in the house to the new owner; the only exception would be a few personal belongings but even these would have to be examined. Holmes's involvement leads him into conflict with the Spencer John Gang and ultimately causes a climactic meeting with the adventuress and voluptuary Isadora Klein.

"THREE GARRIDEBS, THE ADVENTURE OF THE" (3GAR). Published: *Collier's*, October 1924, *Strand*, January 1925; collected in *The Case Book of Sherlock Holmes* (1927). Major players: Holmes, Watson, Nathan Garrideb, John Garrideb. Case date: June 1902. A case well

remembered by Watson because it occurred in the same month that Holmes refused a knighthood. Watson begins his narrative with the comment: "It may have been a comedy, or it may have been a tragedy. It cost one man his reason, it cost me a bloodletting, and it cost yet another man the penalties of the law. Yet there was certainly an element of comedy." Holmes is engaged by Nathan Garrideb to aid in the search for a third Garrideb. This strange hunt had been launched by the arrival of John Garrideb, counsellor at law in Moorville, Kansas (U.S.A.), who told Nathan that should one more Garrideb be found the vast fortune of the American Alexander Hamilton Garrideb would be divided between them.

"THREE STUDENTS, THE ADVENTURE OF THE" (3STU). Published: *Strand*, June 1904, *Collier's*, September 24, 1904; collected in *The Return of Sherlock Holmes* (1905). Major players: Holmes, Watson, Hilton Soames, Gilchrist, Daulat Ras, Miles McLaren, Bannister. Case

Holmes stares down a criminal in "The Three Garridebs"; by Howard Elcock.

date: 1895. An investigation that takes place "in one of our great university towns" where Holmes and Watson are staying while the detective pursues "some laborious researches in Early English charters." They are consulted by Hilton Soames, tutor and lecturer at the College of St. Luke's. A potential major scandal has befallen the college on the eve of the examination for the Fortescue Scholarship. One of the three students competing for the scholarship has attempted to cheat by looking over the test that had been on Soames's supposedly secure desk. The three suspects are Gilchrist, the Indian Daulat Ras, and the talented but unmotivated Miles McLaren. Vital clues include three lumps of black, doughy clay, shavings, and gloves.

TIBET.   Holmes visited the mountainous land in the high plateau of the Himalayas during the GREAT HIATUS (1891–1894) as reported in "The Empty House." According to Holmes, "I traveled for two years in Tibet, and amused myself by visiting Lhassa, and spending some days with the head lama. You may have read of the remarkable explorations of a Norwegian named Sigerson, but I am sure that it never occurred to you that you were receiving news of your friend." Holmes's trip to Tibet, as with most of his activities during the Great Hiatus, has long been debated by Sherlockians who question its genuineness and theorize that it might have been a shield for activities elsewhere. One book that does seem to demonstrate that Holmes's journey really did take place was *Sherlock Holmes in Tibet* by Richard Wincor.

TIGER.   This big game animal was often pursued by hunters, particularly Colonel Sebastian Moran who, as reported in "The Empty House" owned the unrivalled record for the most bagged tigers in India. He also once reportedly crawled down an Indian sewer to finish off a wounded man-eater. In a less life-threatening episode, Watson supposedly had an adventure with a tiger cub while stationed in Afghanistan as recorded in *The Sign of Four*. Holmes once quoted the Persian writer Hafiz, "There is danger for him who taketh the tiger cub, and danger also for who so snatches a delusion from a woman." ("A Case of Identity.") There were also tiger skin rugs in "The Abbey Grange" and the apartment of Thaddeus Sholto in *The Sign of Four*.

"TIRED CAPTAIN, THE ADVENTURE OF THE."   One of the unfortunately untold cases of Holmes's long career for which Watson wrote that he had notes in "The Naval Treaty." The case was also apparently undertaken by Holmes at the end of the television film "The Crucifer of Blood" with Charlton Heston (Holmes) and Richard Johnson (Watson). Here a sea captain *is* tired, exhausted by his horrible experience with the giant rat of Sumatra, an interesting use of crossover cases.

TIRES.   Also Tyres, provided Holmes with vital evidence in the solution of the Lord Saltire affair chronicled in "The Priory School." Holmes was able to follow the progress of a bicycle, especially its direction, on the basis of the tire tracks. This particular detail struck many readers as peculiar, and it was protested that it was quite impossible to observe direction purely by reading the tracks. The criticism eventually reached Sir Arthur Conan Doyle, and he conducted several experiments, declaring that it was possible. Years later, however, he admitted that he had erred. The only way that tires would indicate direction would be from splash marks of water or mud.

TOBACCO.   Holmes displayed a vast knowledge of the uses and properties of tobacco in solving or clarifying cases; his experience with both tobacco and tobacco ash was certainly broadened by his being such a heavy smoker. Holmes was clearly a habitual, even avid, chain smoker, enjoying the pipe, cigar, and cigarette, prompting Watson to note bitterly that he was a "self-poisoner by cocaine and tobacco." Throughout the Canon, reference is made to Holmes sitting for hours enshrouded in pipe smoke (see also PIPE), such as in *The Hound of the Baskervilles* when Watson returned to Baker Street. "As I entered, however, my fears [of a fire] were set at rest, for it was the acrid fumes of strong coarse tobacco which took me by the throat and set me coughing. Through the haze I had a vague vision of Holmes in his dressing-gown coiled up in an armchair with his black clay pipe between his lips."

Holmes kept his shag (a strong coarse tobacco) in the toe end of a Persian slipper and in assorted tobacco-pouches littered across the mantelpiece of his bedroom ("The Dying Detective"). Cigars were stashed in a coal-scuttle ("The Musgrave Ritual"); so too were pipes and tobacco ("The Mazarin

Stone"). It was his custom to have a before-breakfast pipe that was, according to Watson, "composed of all the plugs and dottles left from his smokes of the day before, all carefully dried and collected on the corner of the mantelpiece ("The Engineer's Thumb"). The tobacconist Bradley's supplied both Holmes and Watson. The good doctor originally seemed to prefer the so-called Ship's Tobacco (*A Study in Scarlet*), a type of tobacco blended and produced in the Netherlands and enjoyed by sailors, but he later smoked an Arcadia Mixture ("The Crooked Man").

Holmes made a particular study of tobacco or its ash, telling Watson that he had also written a monograph upon the subject. Referred to obliquely in *A Study in Scarlet*, Holmes actually mentioned the title in 1889 during his investigation into the murder of Charles McCarthy in "The Boscombe Valley Mystery." He found a cigar which he considered a vital piece of evidence, informing Watson: "I found the ash of a cigar, which my special knowledge of tobacco ashes enables me to pronounce as an Indian cigar. I have, as you know, devoted some attention to this, and written a little monograph on the ashes of 140 different varieties of pipe, cigar, and cigarette tobacco. Having found the ash, I then looked round and discovered the stump among the moss where he had tossed it. It was an Indian cigar, of the variety which are rolled in Rotterdam." He was able to identify a cigar found in *The Sign of Four* as a Trichinopoly, saying that "there is as much difference between the black ash of a Trichinopoly and the white fluff of bird's eye as there is between a cabbage and a potato." The detective also cleverly used some cigarettes made by Ionides of Alexandria to solve the mystery in "The Golden Pince-Nez."

Holmes's abilities with regard to ash and tobacco were no doubt largely ignored or ridiculed by the officers of Scotland Yard, many of whom probably never understood the points he was trying to make. His monograph was thus, in all likelihood, relegated to obscurity, although Holmes seemed extremely pleased with the work. As it was written at least before Holmes met Watson, it may be assumed that the monograph was translated into French around 1887 by Francois le Villard and was probably updated from time to time as the detective encountered new or exotic brands of tobacco.

TOBY.   A very gifted sleuth-hound belonging to Old Sherman of Lambeth who aided Holmes and Watson in tracking Jonathan Small and his small companion in *The Sign of Four*. Watson was sent from Pondicherry Lodge by Holmes to fetch Toby, finding him to be "an ugly, long-haired, lop-eared creature, half spaniel and half lurcher, brown and white in colour, with a very clumsy, waddling gait." The dog reappeared in Nicholas Meyer's novel *The Seven-Per-Cent Solution*, tracking Professor Moriarty, via a trail of vanilla, all the way to Vienna, Austria.

TOLLER.   A groom in the employ of Jephro Rucastle at the Copper Beeches in "The Copper Beeches." Toller was the only member of the estate who could keep control of Carlo, the vicious mastiff. He also was a heavy drinker, a habit used to advantage by Holmes and Violet Hunter. His wife, **Mrs. Toller,** served as housekeeper at the Copper Beeches.

TONGA.   An Andaman Islander who befriended Jonathan Small and who helped him escape from the island in *The Sign of Four*. Tonga then journeyed with Small to England in search of the Agra Treasure. He was present to deadly effect at Pondicherry Lodge, his activities pieced together by Holmes, who was able to pursue Tonga, and hence Small, because the diminutive warrior stepped in creosote. Tonga has the distinction of being the only human being ever shot by Holmes. Watson forever after associated the Thames with Tonga because of the events surrounding him during the pursuit of the ship *Aurora*.

TORQUAY TERRACE.   An area in Camberwell where Madame Charpentier owned a boardinghouse in *A Study in Scarlet*. Enoch Drebber was one of her boarders.

TOSCA, CARDINAL.   An unchronicled investigation carried out by Holmes in 1895. The case centered around "the sudden death of Cardinal Tosca—an inquiry which was carried out by him at the express desire of His Holiness the Pope" ("Black Peter"). This was one of several apparent investigations by Holmes for the VATICAN. Tosca's death was the subject of the play *The Incredible Murder of Cardinal Tosca* (1978), by Alden Nowlan.

TOTTENHAM COURT ROAD.   Holmes purchased his Stradivarius violin, said by him to be worth at least five hundred guineas, from a broker's in London's Tottenham Court Road in "The Cardboard Box." The father of Mary Sutherland had owned a plumbing institution on the road in "A Case of Identity," on the same thoroughfare as Morton and Waylight's, a firm for whom Mr. Warren worked as a timekeeper in "The Red Circle." The road was also the site of the attack by street thugs on Henry Baker in "The Blue Carbuncle."

TOWER OF LONDON. The famed fortress housing the crown jewels, the Tower served as a landmark during the pursuit of Jonathan Small and the *Aurora* by the river police and Holmes and Watson in *The Sign of Four*. The Tower had a more prominent role in the film *The Adventures of Sherlock Holmes*, starring Basil Rathbone and Nigel Bruce. Professor Moriarty attempts to steal the Crown Jewels, the film climaxing with a struggle within and on top of the Tower.

TRACING OF FOOTSTEPS, THE. In full *The Tracing of Footsteps, with Some Remarks upon the Uses of Plaster of Paris as a Preserver of Impresses*, a monograph that had clearly been published before September 1887 or 1888 because the detective showed it to Dr. Watson in *The Sign of Four*. The work was translated into the French by Francois le Villard. (See also FOOTSTEP.)

TREDANNICK WARTHA. The home of the Tregennis Family, near the Cornish hamlet of Tredannick Wollas in "The Devil's Foot," Tredannick Wortha was the site of many of the events described by Holmes as the "Cornish horror." Holmes and Watson visited Tredannick Wollas in the spring of 1897 for an enforced vacation. Instead of rest and relaxation, Holmes became involved in one of the most bizarre murders of his career.

TREGELLIS. The head gamekeeper to the Musgraves at Hurlstone in western Sussex in "The Musgrave Ritual." His daughter, **Janet,** became the lover of the butler Richard Brunton. He left his fiancée, Rachel Howells, for Janet.

TREGENNIS FAMILY. A family in Cornwall that was the victim of the terrible curse described by Holmes as the "Cornish horror" and recorded in "The Devil's Foot." Originally Cornish mine owners, the Tregennises sold out to a larger company in the 1890s, the division of the money proving a source of contention within the family. One

morning, Mrs. Porter—the housekeeper at Tredannick Wartha, the Tregennis home—discovered **Brenda, George,** and **Owen** Tregennis in an unspeakable condition. Brenda was dead, but upon her face lingered "something of that convulsion of horror which had been her last emotion." Her brothers, George and Owen, were still alive, only they "were singing snatches of songs and gibbering like two great apes." Owen and George were taken away to the Helston asylum. A short time later, the other brother, **Mortimer,** was also found dead at the local vicarage where he was staying. Tregennis was "leaning back in his chair, his thin beard projecting, his spectacles up on to his forehead, and his lean dark face turned towards the window and twisted into the same distortion of terror which had marked the features of his dead sister. His limbs were convulsed and his fingers contorted as though he had died in a very paroxysm of fear."

TRELAWNEY HOPE. In full the Right Honourable Trelawney Hope, the secretary for European affairs in the government of Lord Bellinger who had a secret and potentially explosive letter stolen from his dispatch box in the case recounted in "The Second Stain." "The most rising statesman in the country," Trelawney Hope was described as "dark, clear-cut, and elegant, hardly yet of middle age, and endowed with every beauty of body and mind." The fear of the consequences of the theft were such that his "face was distorted with a spasm of despair, and his hands tore at his hair. For a moment we caught a glimpse of the natural man, impulsive, ardent, keenly sensitive." His wife was **Lady Hilda Trelawney Hope,** youngest daughter of the duke of Belminster in "The Second Stain." She went to Holmes to press him for details of the case in which he had been engaged by Lord Bellinger, the prime minister, and her husband. Holmes refused, and she left abruptly, causing the detective to ask Watson: "Now, Watson, the fair sex is your department . . . What was the fair lady's game? What did she really want?" Watson, with his usual eye for the ladies, wrote: "I had often heard of the beauty of the youngest daughter of Belminster, but no description of it, and no contemplation of colourless photographs, had prepared me for the subtle, delicate charm and the beautiful colouring of that exquisite head."

TREPOFF MURDER. A case investigated by Holmes in 1888. In "A Scandal in Bohemia," Watson wrote that from time to time he heard vague accounts of Holmes's activities, such as "his summons to Odessa in the case of the Trepoff murder." Unfortunately, no other details were forthcoming. A version of the affair was presented in the collection *The Exploits of Sherlock Holmes* (1954) in the short story "The Adventure of the Seven Clocks," by Adrian Conan Doyle and John Dickson Carr.

TREVELYAN, DR. PERCY. The London physician introduced Holmes to the case recounted in "The Resident Patient." A medical practitioner of 403 Brook Street, Trevelyan was a graduate of London University. He told Holmes, "After I had graduated, I continued to devote myself to research, occupying a minor position in King's College Hospital, and I was fortunate enough to excite considerable interest by my research into the pathology of catalepsy, and finally to win the Bruce-Pinkerton prize and medal by the monograph on nervous lesions." The monograph was the source of "a most discouraging account of its sales" from his publisher. Unable to afford the kind of lodgings needed to establish himself in practice, Trevelyan suddenly met new prospects when the wealthy Blessington offered to set him up in a Brook Street practice in return for rooms on the premises, medical attention, and three-quarters of all earnings.

TREVILLE, GEORGE. The French actor starred as Holmes in eight films of the Eclair series in 1912–1913. While the productions were shot in England with a British cast, the accent of the French Treville was unimportant because the films were silent. His Watson throughout was a Mr. Moyse, although there is some question as to whether he appeared in the first entry, *The Speckled Band* (1912).

TREVOR, VICTOR. Young Trevor, the son of Victor Senior who brought Holmes into the affair of "The 'Gloria Scott'," the first case of the detective's long career. Trevor was the only friend Sherlock Holmes made during his two years at a university. They had met one morning when Trevor's bull-terrier froze on to Holmes's leg. During the days that he was laid up, Trevor visited and they became good friends. Trevor eventually invited Holmes to visit his father's home in Donnithrope, in Norfolk. There Holmes met Trevor Senior, a widower with one son (his daughter had died of diphtheria years before while on a visit to

Holmes visits with the Trevors at Donnithorpe in "The 'Gloria Scott'" and meets the old sailor Hudson; by Sidney Paget.

Birmingham). "He was a man of little culture, but with a considerable amount of rude strength, both physically and mentally. He knew hardly any books, but he had travelled far, had seen much of the world, and had remembered all that he had learned. In person he was a thick-set, burly man with a shock of grizzled hair, a brown, weather-beaten face, and blue eyes which were keen to the verge of fierceness. Yet he had a reputation for kindness and charity . . ." Trevor Senior was so impressed with young Holmes's deductive abilities that he encouraged him to pursue the career of the detective: "That's your line of life, sir, and you may take the word of a man who has seen something of the world."

Young Trevor later engaged Holmes's help in unravelling the strange events that seemed to be killing his father, but the facts surrounding his father's past that came out were so disturbing to Trevor Junior that he departed England and went out to the Terai tea planting (an area north of the Ganges in India) and, according to Holmes, was doing quite well. Trevor appeared in the pastiche novel *Enter the Lion* by Michael P. Hodel and Sean M. Wright.

TRICHINOPOLY. A type of cigar made from the tobacco grown near the city of Trichinopoly in India. In *A Study in Scarlet*, Holmes was certain that the murderer of Enoch Drebber smoked such a cigar because of the evidence he had found at the murder scene. "I gathered up some scattered ash from the floor. It was dark in colour and flakey— such an ash as is only made by a Trichinopoly." He later asserted, in *The Sign of Four*, that "there is as much difference between the black ash of a Trichinopoly and the white fluff of bird's-eye as there is between a cabbage and a potato." (See also To-BACCO.)

TRINITY COLLEGE.　One of the colleges of Cambridge University, established in 1546 by King Henry VIII. Two of its alumni were involved in a case recorded in the Canon. Cyril Overton, captain of the Cambridge rugby team in "The Missing Three-Quarter" was one; and Jeremy Dixon, owner of the canine sleuth Pompey in the same case, was another.

TRIUMPH OF SHERLOCK HOLMES. England 1935. Dir: Leslie Hiscott. Cast: Arthur Wontner (Holmes), Ian Fleming (Watson), Lyn Harding (Professor Moriarty), Minnie Rayner (Mrs. Hudson), and Leslie Perrins (John Douglas). Wontner's fourth outing as Holmes, reuniting him with director Hiscott and his usual supporting cast (Ian Fleming and Minnie Rayner) after their absence from *The Sign of Four* (1932), which had been made by Wontner with a different studio. Considered by critics to be the best entry in the Wontner series, *Triumph* was a faithful adaptation of the novel *The Valley of Fear*, although two changes were the increased presence of Moriarty and the age of Holmes. The professor was played by Lyn Harding, the memorable Dr. Grimesby Roylott in the stage and film versions of Conan Doyle's play *The Speckled Band*. As Moriarty, he was a fun villain, vying with Wontner not only in the story but for screen time. Wontner, meanwhile, was increasingly old for the role, so the writers Cyril Twyford and H. Fowler Mear decided to have the detective on the verge of retirement to the South Downs when the case is brought to his attention.

TRUMPINGTON.　A village to the south of Cambridge where Holmes finally located the missing Godfrey Staunton in "The Missing Three-Quarter." Unfortunately, his discovery was not in time to prevent the defeat of Camridge in an important rugby match against Oxford as Staunton's absence was keenly felt.

TURKEY.　Also the Ottoman Empire, nick-named by Holmes's time "the Sick Man of Europe," the extensive but weakening empire for whose sultan Holmes performed an important commission in January 1903. While not disclosing the exact nature of his work, Holmes wrote in "The Blanched Soldier" that it "called for immediate action, as political consequences of the gravest kind might arise from its neglect." Holmes also had an encounter with the Turks in the film version of *The Seven-Per-Cent Solution* by Nicholas Meyer. According to Vincent Starrett in his book *221B: Studies in Sherlock Holmes*, the retired but still hale detective was in Constantinople in 1920 as the Turks reported to the *London Times* that he was active in the city "behind the scenes."

TURKISH BATHS.　Both Watson and Holmes had a fondness for the relaxing bath. Watson told Holmes that he preferred the Turkish bath to "the invigorating home-made article" because he had "for the last few days been feeling rheumatic and old. A Turkish bath is what we call an alternative in medicine—a fresh starting-point, a cleanser of the system" ("The Disappearance of Lady Frances Carfax"). The doctor was also to write at the start of "The Illustrious Client": "Both Holmes and I had a weakness for the Turkish bath. It was over a smoke in the pleasant lassitude of the drying-room that I have found him less reticent and more human than anywhere else." They apparently frequented the baths on Northumberland Avenue.

TURNER, JOHN.　The squire in the Boscombe Valley, in Herefordshire had supposedly made his fortune in Australia before returning to England in "The Boscombe Valley Mystery." After meeting an old acquaintance from the colonies, Charles McCarthy, Turner allowed him to rent the choicest farm on his vast estate, and it always seemed that McCarthy had some power over him. Turner, however, was adamant that his daughter **Alice Turner,** should not marry young James McCarthy, son of Charles, whom she loved. When Charles McCarthy is found murdered, Alice enlists the help of Inspector Lestrade to prove James's innocence. Lestrade, puzzled by the case, referred the matter to Holmes. For some inexplicable reason, young McCarthy had refused to propose to Alice, but she never wavered in her love for him, protesting vigorously his innocence. Watson found her "one of the most lovely young women that I have ever seen in my life." Not a well man, the elder Turner was apparently devastated by the news of McCarthy's murder.

TURNER, MRS.   A woman who appeared as housekeeper at 221B Baker Street only once in the Canon, during Holmes's investigation into the Irene Adler matter in "A Scandal in Bohemia." Upon returning to Baker Street from the wedding of Adler and Godfrey Norton, Holmes was quite famished, ringing the bell for the landlady. A Mrs. Turner brought in a tray of food, the only mention of her in the case. She has remained a mystery ever since.

TUSON, SERGEANT.   A member of the city police of London who foiled an attempt to rob the financial house of Mawson & Williams in "The Stockbroker's Clerk." Tuson, aided by Constable Pollock, managed to arrest the thief who turned out to be the notorious forger and cracksman Beddington. The news was so distressing to Beddington's brother that he tried to hang himself.

TUXBURY OLD PARK.   The estate owned by Colonel Emsworth and family near Bedford in "The Blanched Soldier." It was the site of Tuxbury Old Hall, described by James Dodd as a "great wandering house, standing in a considerable park. I should judge it was all sorts of ages and styles, starting on a half-timbered Elizabethan foundation and ending in a Victorian portico. Inside it was all panelling and tapestry and half-effaced old pictures, a house of shadows and mystery."

"TWO COLLABORATORS, THE ADVENTURE OF THE."   A parody of Sherlock Holmes written by J. M. Barrie, author of *Peter Pan* and friend of Sir Arthur Conan Doyle, first published in Conan Doyle's autobiography as he considered it the best parody he had ever read. Barrie first wrote "The Two Collaborators" on the fly-leaves of one of his books, *A Window in Thrums*, and sent it to his friend as a token of his "debonnaire courage," a recognition of their work together in the disastrously unsuccessful play *Jane Annie; Or the Good Conduct Prize* (1893). In the parody, Holmes is visited at Baker Street by his ungrateful creator. The detective's last words, as he is ruthlessly reduced to nothing: "Fool, fool! I have kept you in luxury for years. By my help you have ridden extensively in cabs where no author was ever seen before. *Henceforth you will ride in buses!*" Barrie also wrote "The Late Sherlock Holmes," a clever obituary of the Great Detective that first appeared in the *St. James Gazette* on December 29, 1893, later published in *Collier's* in America. The mood of the obituary is set by the subtitle "Sensational Arrest—Watson Accused of the Crime."

TYPEWRITER.   Holmes considered writing a monograph on the relation of the typewriter to crime, as mentioned in "A Case of Identity." While he apparently never actually completed the little work, he did say: "A typewriter has really quite as much individuality as a man's handwriting. Unless they are quite new, no two of them write exactly alike. Some letters get more worn than others, and some wear only on one side." His knowledge about typewriters helped him solve the matter of "A Case of Identity." Holmes thought momentarily that Violet Smith's spatulate finger-ends were the result of typing rather than her actual piano playing in "The Solitary Cyclist." Both Mary Sutherland ("A Case of Identity") and Laura Lyons (*The Hound of the Baskervilles*) made their living as typists.

"ULTIMATE CRIME, THE." An intriguing short work by Isaac Asimov, published originally in 1976 in the collection *More Tales of the Black Widowers*. Asimov, an enthusiastic and brilliant Sherlockian, used the essay to examine the two most famous writings of Professor Moriarty, *The Dynamics of the Asteroid* and *The Binomial Theorem*, one of the few works to cover the writings of the infamous professor. Another study of the BINOMIAL THEOREM was offered by Poul Anderson in his "A Treatise on the Binomial Theorem" (1955) for *The Baker Street Journal*.

UNDERGROUND RAILWAY. Also called simply the underground, the subway in London was the first such railway under the ground. The underground was featured in "The Bruce-Partington Plans" as the body of Arthur Cadogan West, suspected thief of the Bruce-Partington Submarine Plans, was found just outside Aldgate Station on the line. Holmes's investigation into how the dead man reached the spot allowed the detective to trace the murderer and ultimately recover the plans. In *A Study in Scarlet*, Watson said that he would like to see the author of "The Book of Life" forced to go through third-class carriage in the

underground and give the occupations of the passengers. Holmes, of course, was the author, and he was perfectly capable of doing just that.

UNDER THE CLOCK. A one-act play that opened on November 25, 1893, at the Royal Court Theatre, London. It is noteworthy for being the first stage portrayal of Holmes and Watson. The play was written by the humorists Charles Brookfield (Holmes) and Seymour Hicks (Watson) as a spoof on the detective. Their performances were said at the time to be quite energetic, particularly Hicks's lampooning of the unshakable devotion of Watson for Holmes.

UNDERWOOD, JOHN, AND SONS. A hatter found on 129 Camberwell Road, London in *A Study in Scarlet*. The hat found next to the body of Encoh Drebber was made by John Underwood and Sons, and through them Drebber was traced.

UPWOOD, COLONEL. A participant in the card scandal that occurred in the Nonpareil Club mentioned in *The Hound of the Baskervilles*, the colonel was exposed by Holmes and his conduct was deemed "atrocious."

V.R. The initials of Queen Victoria that became the symbol of one of Holmes's most peculiar eccentricities. In writing of Holmes and his differing strains of bohemianism, Watson noted: "I have always held . . . that pistol practice should be distinctly an open-air pastime; and when Holmes, in one of his queer humours, would sit in an armchair with his hair-trigger and a hundred Boxer cartridges and proceed to adorn the opposite wall with a patriotic V.R. done in bullet-pocks, I felt strongly that neither the atmosphere nor the appearance of our rooms was improved by it."

VALLEY OF FEAR, THE (VALL). Published: *Strand*, September 1914 to May 1915 in serial parts; also published as a novel in 1915. Major players: Part One: Holmes, Watson, Inspector

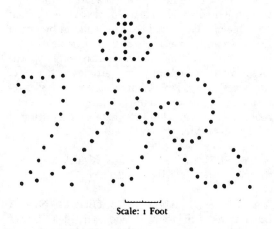

Scale: 1 Foot

With remarkable accuracy, Holmes inscribed the initials of the Queen in bullet-holes on his sitting room wall. (Drawing by Robert Keither Leaveitt, from *Profile by Gaslight*, edited by Edgar W. Smith.

MacDonald, John Douglas, Ivy Douglas, Cecil Barker; Part Two: John McMurdo, Ettie Shafter, Jacob Shafter, Jack McGinty, Ted Baldwin. This novel-length account, written by Dr. Watson, is presented in two very distinct parts. Part One, "The Tragedy of Birlstone," relates a brilliant investigation by Holmes into the apparent murder of John Douglas of Birlstone Manor. Part Two, "The Scowrers," is recounted in the third person, presumably by Birdy Edwards. It tells of the evil predations of the Scowrers of Vermissa Valley in the Gilmerton Mountains, U.S.A., officially the members of Lodge 341 of the Ancient Order of Freemen, and their destruction and arrest by the Pinkertons thanks to the danger-filled work of the agent Birdy Edwards. In general structure, *The Valley of Fear* is similar to *A Study in Scarlet* in that it is divided between Holmes's detecting and the story, told as a retrospection, of the events leading up to the crime presented in the first part. Both sections are then united by an epilogue, in this case an unhappy one. The date of the destruction of the Scowrers is given as 1875, while the Birlstone Manor affair was perhaps in 1888; it probably occurred before 1891 as Holmes makes reference to Professor Moriarty and Colonel Sebastian Moran. Curiously, despite the rather extensive discussion of the professor and his dangerous chief of staff in *The Valley of Fear*, Watson does not remember either of them in "The Final Problem" and "The Empty House." One of the best entries in the entire Canon, *The Valley of Fear* is also one of the least known, certainly overshadowed by the other novel-length chronicles, *A Study in Scarlet*, *The Sign of Four*, and especially *The Hound of the Baskervilles*. In *The Complete Guide to Sherlock Holmes*, Michael Hardwick writes: "The Holmes-Watson relationship, so important to the spirit of the stories, and so missed when it is disregarded or fumbled, shows at its best in this one. More clearly than perhaps anywhere else, they revel in the extent and harmony of their friendship and rapport."

VALLEY OF FEAR, THE.   U.S. 1916. Dir: Alexander Butler. Cast: H. A. Saintbury (Holmes), Daisy Burrell (Ettie Douglas), Arthur Cullin (Watson), Booth Conway (Professor Moriarty). This silent film adaptation of the novel, released by the Samuelson Film Manufacturing Co., starred an actor who had already played Holmes over 1,000 times on stage in England, in the Gillette play *Sherlock Holmes* and in Conan Doyle's *Speckled Band*. In England, in fact, Saintbury was better known than WILLIAM GILLETTE. The story was filled with extensive flashbacks to America. As was to be the case in future productions, such as Arthur Wontner's version of the novel, *The Triumph of*

The branding of Jack McMurdo in *The Valley of Fear* by Frank Wiles.

Sherlock Holmes, Professor Moriarty is much more actively involved in the storyline. Arthur Cullin would reprise his role as Watson in the 1923 *The Sign of Four*.

VAMBERRY.   One of Holmes's early but unchronicled cases, dating to the period before the association of the detective with Dr. Watson that was mentioned in "The Musgrave Ritual." Holmes possessed records of numerous early cases such as that of Vamberry, the wine merchant.

VAMPIRES.   Of the undead, fiendish blood-drinkers Holmes once remarked to Watson in "The Sussex Vampire": "Rubbish, Watson, rubbish! What have we to do with walking corpses who can only be held in their grave by stakes driven through their hearts? It's lunacy . . . Are we to give serious consideration to such things? This agency stands flatfooted upon the ground and there it must remain. The world is big enough for us. No ghosts need apply." Nevertheless, Holmes had accumulated research into vampires, consulting his "good old index" for information on "Vampirism in Hungary" and "Vampires in Transylvania," as well as investigating an apparent outbreak of vampirism in Sussex. This was his only encounter with vampires in the Canon, an investigation that proved very unsupernatural indeed.

A number of writers, however, have theorized that the Great Detective may have met the real undead, perhaps even the Vampire King himself—Count Dracula. The Holmes-Dracula relationship was presented in *The Holmes-Dracula File* by Fred Saberhagen, *Sherlock Holmes vs. Dracula* by Loren D. Estleman, and *A Night in the Lonesome October* (1993) by Roger Zelazny. Other intriguing hypotheses have been made in various articles such as "Re: Vampires" (1957) by William Leonard that covered, among other items, Holmes vs. Dracula, Holmes as Dr. Van Helsing, and most interesting of all, Professor Moriarty as Dracula.

VANDELEUR.   An alias used by Jack Stapleton in *The Hound of the Baskervilles*.

VANDERBILT AND THE YEGGMAN.   A case entered into Holmes's "good old index," one of considerable interest in "The Sussex Vampire." "Vanderbilt and the Yeggman" has been viewed as an affair that might have involved the famous and powerful Vanderbilt family of America.

VAN JANSEN. A murder victim killed in 1834 in Utrecht. No wound appeared on the body, but great gouts and splashes of blood lay all around. These details, Holmes pointed out in *A Study in Scarlet*, were very similar to those attendant in the murder of Enoch Drebber, found dead at the Lauriston Gardens in Brixton.

VAN SEDDAR. An agent of Count Negretto Sylvius, found at Lime Street, who was given the task of transporting the stolen Mazarin Stone to Amsterdam in "The Mazarin Stone." Count Sylvius believed that Holmes knew nothing of Van Seddar.

VATICAN. Holmes was engaged in several cases on behalf of the Catholic Church. According to the scholar Michael Harrison in his study *The World of Sherlock Holmes*, the detective handled five cases for the papacy: the affair of the Vatican Cameos (*The Hound of the Baskervilles*), the Bishopgate Jewel case (*The Sign of Four*), the sudden death of Cardinal Tosca ("Black Peter"), the case of the Two Coptic Patriarchs ("The Retired Colourman"), and the Black Pearl of the Borgias ("The Six Napoleons"). No mention is made directly in the Canon of Holmes's Vatican associations beyond the Vatican cameos and the death of Cardinal Tosca, but it is easy to speculate that the Vatican would have made use of his services, much as the other governments and rulers of Europe did, knowing of both his gifts and discretion. The Pope throughout most of Holmes's career was Leo XIII (r. 1878–1903), followed by Pope St. Pius X (r. 1903–1914).

VATICAN CAMEOS. An affair on which Holmes was working around the time of Sir Charles Baskerville's mysterious death in *The Hound of the Baskervilles*. As he was preoccupied with the matter, he had not pursued Sir Charles's passing with great interest.

VEGETARIAN RESTAURANT. An eatery that backed on to the pawnshop of Jabez Wilson in "The Red-Headed League."

"VEILED LODGER, THE ADVENTURE OF THE" (VEIL). Published: *Liberty*, January 1927, *Strand*, February 1927; collected in *The Case Book of Sherlock Holmes* (1927). Major players: Holmes, Watson, Eugenia Ronder, Mrs. Merrilow.

Holmes admonishes Eugenia Ronder in "The Veiled Lodger"; by Frank Wiles.

Case date: 1896. One of the last cases in the Canon is also one of the least interesting, owing to the fact that Holmes has so little to do. A landlady, Mrs. Merrilow, comes to Holmes out of concern for a longtime lodger, Eugenia Ronder, a woman who, in seven years, has never lifted the veil from her face. Once, Mrs. Merrilow saw her without it by accident and once the milkman saw her face. It was enough to make him drop his milk pail. Recently, however, Ronder has begun to deteriorate and cry out "Murder!" She will not agree to meet with the police or the clergy, but she will talk with Sherlock Holmes. Holmes and Watson journey to Brixton and hear her tragic confession. Watson makes mention of another case that would have been far more interesting, "the politician, the lighthouse, and the trained cormorant."

VENNER & MATHESON. A well-known Greenwich-based engineering firm in "The Engineer's Thumb." Victor Hatherley had worked as an apprentice here for seven years before setting out on his own.

VENUCCI, PIETRO.   An Italian from Naples who was connected to the Mafia and was "one of the greatest cut-throats in London" in "The Six Napoleons." He was found murdered on the doorstep of Horace Harker at No. 131 Pitt Street, Kensington. In his pocket was a photograph of a man, later identified as Beppo. His sister, **Lucretia Venucci,** maid to the princess of Colonna, was a suspect when the Black Pearl of the Borgias was stolen from the prince's bedroom at the Dacre Hotel in London.

VERE STREET.   A street in the West End where Holmes suffered the second attempt on his life by the agents of Professor Moriarty in "The Final Problem." Holmes told Watson: ". . . as I walked down Vere Street a brick came down from the roof of one of the houses and was shattered to fragments at my feet. I called the police and had the place examined. There were slates and bricks piled up on the roof preparatory to some repairs, and they would have me believe that the wind had toppled over one of these. Of course I knew better, but I could prove nothing."

VERMISSA VALLEY.   A valley in the Gilmerton Mountains of the United States known for its coal mines and ironworks in *The Valley of Fear.* The valley was also the site of the pernicious and murderous activities of the SCOWRERS, Lodge 341 of the Ancient Order of Freemen. The second part of *The Valley of Fear* was devoted to chronicling the crimes of the Scowrers in the valley and the ultimate clearing of their evil presence from Vermissa. The town of Vermissa was situated at the head of the valley.

VERNER.   A young London physician who purchased Watson's practice in "The Norwood Builder." Watson wrote at the start of the affair of "the unhappy John Hector McFarlane": "At the time of which I speak, Holmes had been back for some months [from the Great Hiatus], and I at his request had sold my practice and returned to share the old quarters in Baker Street. A young doctor named Verner, had purchased my small Kensington practice, and given with astonishingly little demur

the highest price that I ventured to ask—an incident which only explained itself some years later, when I found that Verner was a distant relation of Holmes, and that it was my friend who had really found the money."

VERNET, EMILE JEAN HORACE.   A noted French painter (1789–1863) and ancestor of Holmes—the detective's grandmother was Vernet's sister ("The Greek Interpreter"). Holmes once remarked that "art in the blood is liable to take the strangest forms," feeling that his and his brother Mycroft's "faculty of observation and . . . peculiar facility for deduction" was hereditary.

VICTORIA, QUEEN.   Ruler of the British Empire (the United Kingdom of Great Britain and Ireland, and empress of India) reigning from 1837 to 1901. The long career of Sherlock Holmes took place almost entirely during her reign, ending only two years after her death. Watson was thus able to write in "The Veiled Lodger" that the row of yearbooks which filled a shelf and dispatch-cases full of documents related to Holmes's investigations were "a perfect quarry for the student not only of crime but of the social and official scandals of the late Victorian era." The detective no doubt earned the regal attention of Queen Victoria through a number of his services for the British government and the crowned heads of Europe, most of whom were relatives of the British queen. In the case of "The Bruce-Partington Plans," Mycroft wrote Holmes: "The Cabinet awaits your final report with the upmost anxiety. Urgent representations have arrived from the very highest quarter. The whole of the State is at your back if you should need it to recover the documents." For his achievement in solving the entire affair, Holmes spent a day at Windsor, returning with a fine emerald pin. Watson wrote: "When I asked him if he had bought it, he answered that it was a present from a certain gracious lady in whose interests he had once been fortunate enough to carry out a small commission." Holmes honored the queen by decorating a wall at Baker Street with a patriotic V.R. (*Victoria Regina*) made of bullet-pocks. Unfortunately, no personal meeting Holmes and Victoria was ever presented in the Canon. In the film *The Private Life of Sherlock Holmes*, the detective met the queen, in the presence of his incensed brother Mycroft.

VICTORIA STREET. A Westminster street where Victor Hatherley had his office at 16A Victoria Street in "The Engineer's Thumb."

VIGOR. The so-called Hammersmith Wonder who was an entry in the especially interesting volume V of Holmes's "good old index," that contained "the record of old cases, mixed with the accumulated information of a lifetime."

VILLARD, FRANCOIS LE. A French detective who consulted Holmes on a case and became an ardent admirer (*The Sign of Four*). Holmes told Watson: "He has all the Celtic power of quick intuition, but he is deficient in the wide range of exact knowledge which is essential to the higher developments of his art . . . He possesses two out of the three qualities necessary for the ideal detective. He has the power of observation and that of deduction. He is only wanting in knowledge, and that may come in time." Le Villard also translated some of Holmes's monographs into French.

VIPER. A type of venomous snake. "Vipers" was an entry in Holmes's "good old index," under the volume V in "The Sussex Vampire." In *The Sign of Four*, old Sherman, not knowing that Dr. Watson had been sent to him by Holmes, threatened the doctor with a "wiper." The "small black and white ivory box with a sliding lid" that caught Watson's eye during the affair of "The Dying Detective" had a "sharp spring like a viper's tooth."

VITRIOL. A name used for sulphuric acid. Vitriol was thrown in two cases: "The Blue Carbuncle" and the "The Illustrious Client."

VITTORIA. A "circus belle" who was an entry in Holmes's "good old index" in the volume V in "The Sussex Vampire."

VIXEN TOR. A tor on Dartmoor where Watson searched for the mysterious Man on the Tor in *The Hound of the Baskervilles*.

VON BISHCOFF. A criminal in Frankfurt who was apparently tried and acquitted for murder because there was no reliable test for bloodstains. Holmes was thus jubilant in *A Study in Scarlet* that he had discovered such a test, saying that Von Bishchoff "would certainly have been hung had this test been in existence."

VON BORK. The gifted German spymaster and head of a secret organization of agents that was gathering information about England (1910–1914) before the start of World War I. In "His Last Bow," it was written: "A remarkable man this Von Bork—a man who could hardly be matched among all the devoted agents of the Kaiser. It was his talents which had first recommended him for the English mission, the most important mission of all, but since he had taken it over those talents had become more and more manifest to the half-dozen people in the world who were really in touch with the truth." As Von Herling, chief secretary of the legation, was to declare: "Nobody takes you seriously. You are a 'good old sport', 'quite a decent fellow for a German', a hard-drinking, night-club, knock-about-town, devil-may-care young fellow. And all the time this quiet country house of yours is the centre of half the mischief in England, and the sporting squire the most astute secret-service man in Europe. Genius, my dear Von Bork—genius!" The genius, however, was undone by an industrious British agent—Sherlock Holmes.

VON HERDER. A blind German mechanic who constructed a deadly air gun on the orders of Professor Moriarty. In "The Empty House," it was used to murder the Hon. Ronald Adair and in the attempted murder of Sherlock Holmes. The weapon, firing soft-nosed revolver bullets, ended up in the Scotland Yard museum.

VON HERLING. Chief secretary of the German legation in London in "His Last Bow." He was an admirer of the master spy VON BORK.

VON KRAMM, COUNT. The name used by the king of Bohemia during his trip to London to engage the services of Holmes in "A Scandal in Bohemia."

VON WALDBAUM, FRITZ. A specialist on crime from Danzig who, with Monsieur Dubuque of the Paris police, had an interview with Holmes to discuss the details of the affair of "The Second Stain." Watson wrote that he had a verbatim report of the interview.

WAINWRIGHT. A criminal mentioned by Holmes to Watson in their discussion about Baron Adalbert Gruner in "The Illustrious Client." The detective said: "A complex mind... All great criminals have that. My old friend Charlie Peace was a violin virtuoso. Wainwright was no mean artist. I could quote many more." Holmes was probably referring to the obscure Thomas Wainwright (1794–1847), a gifted artist who was suspected but never tried for the poisoning of three relatives. He was convicted of forgery and in 1837 was transported to Tasmania.

WALES. Wales, the staunchly nationalistic country bordering England, served as the picturesque backdrop for two pastiches—*The Glendower Conspiracy* by Lloyd Biggle, Jr. and *Ten Years Beyond Baker Street* by Cay Van Ash. In the Canon, the duke of Holdernesse held mineral rights in Wales, and sometimes took up residence at Carston Castle at Bangor ("The Priory School"). Rachel Howells, the second housemaid at Hurlstone, home of the Musgraves, was of excitable Welsh blood in "The Musgrave Ritual."

WALKING STICK. A type of stick carried for walks and decoration, although it has potential as a weapon, as demonstrated by Holmes. The detective was known to carry a walking stick or cane (in, for example, "The Speckled Band," "Thor Bridge," "The Red-Headed League"), using it to defend himself from attack (in "The Illustrious Client"), proving highly proficient with the singlestick (*A Study in Scarlet*). Watson also carried one in "Shoscombe Old Place" and "The Disappearance of Lady Frances Carfax." In *The Hound of the Baskervilles*, Holmes performed a very thorough analysis of Dr.

Mortimer's stick, correcting the incomplete analysis of Dr. Watson.

WALTER, SIR JAMES. The head of the Submarine Department of the Admiralty who was the official caretaker of the Bruce-Partington Submarine Plans in "The Bruce-Partington Plans." The theft of the plans was a crushing blow to him, so much so that he was dead a short time later. Holmes theorized that his unexpected demise may have been suicide. Mycroft Holmes said that his "decorations and sub-titles fill two lines of a book of reference. He has grown gray in the service, is a gentleman, a favoured guest in the most exalted houses, and above all, a man whose patriotism is beyond suspicion." **Colonel Valentine Walter,** his younger brother, was "a very tall, handsome, light-bearded man of fifty... His wild eyes, stained cheeks, and unkempt hair all spoke of the sudden blow which had fallen upon the household." It was later learned that the colonel needed money desperately owing to a stock exchange debt.

WALTERS. A member of the Surrey constabulary who was left in charge of Wisteria Lodge. Constable Walters detected and pursued the mulatto who had returned to Wisteria Lodge. The man was later arrested in a trap laid by Inspector Baynes.

WARBURTON, COLONEL. One of Holmes's unchronicled cases that, with the affair of "The Engineer's Thumb," was brought to the detective's attention by Dr. Watson. Watson described the affair as that of Colonel Warburton's madness. The case was presented in *The Exploits of Sherlock Holmes* in "The Adventure of the Sealed Room" by Adrian Conan Doyle and John Dickson Carr.

WARDLAW, COLONEL. The owner of the racehorse Pugilist that ran and lost in the Wessex Cup in "Silver Blaze."

WARNER, JOHN. The former gardener of High Gable provided Holmes with useful information about Warner's former employer, the elusive Mr. Henderson in "Wisteria Lodge." Warner had been "sacked in a moment of temper by his imperious employer. He in turn had friends among the indoor servants who united in their fear and dislike of their master." The gardener told Holmes that Henderson "sold his soul to the devil in exchange for money . . . and expects his creditor to come up and claim his own."

WARREN, MR. A timekeeper for Morton & Waylight's, on the Tottenham Court Road in "The Red Circle." His wife, **Mrs. Warren,** consulted Holmes about the mysterious behavior of one of their lodgers. Holmes's interest in the case increased when Warren was abducted while walking down the road: "Two men came up behind him, threw a coat over his head, and bundled him into a cab that was beside the curb. They drove him an hour, and then opened the door and shot him out. He lay in the roadway so shaken in his wits that he never saw what became of the cab." Mrs. Warren served as landlady to the lodgers who rented rooms in the Warren home in Bloomsbury, on the Tottenham Court Road. The behavior of one of her lodgers was so peculiar, however, that she consulted Holmes. He at first refused the case, but she "had the pertinacity and also the cunning of her sex." She reminded Holmes of the brilliant work that he had done for Mr. Fairdale Hobbs, one of her lodgers, the previous year. Watson wrote: "Holmes was accessible upon the side of flattery, and also, to do him justice, upon the side of kindliness." "With a sigh of resignation," the detective took on the investigation.

WATERBEACH. A village to the north of Cambridge where Holmes searched for the missing Godfrey Staunton in "The Missing Three-Quarter." The detective found Waterbeach "disappointing."

WATERLOO. The famous battle fought in 1815 between Napoleon and the duke of Wellington and the Prussian Marshal Blucher. During the affair of "The Abbey Grange," Holmes told Watson, "We have not yet met our Waterloo, Watson, but this is our Marengo, for it begins in defeat and ends in victory." At Marengo, in 1800, Napoleon triumphed over the Austrians, snatching a triumph when defeat seemed imminent.

WATSON, JOHN H. Through the writings of this longtime friend, associate, assistant, chronicler, and devoted biographer the world came to know the Great Detective, and it is because of his dogged loyalty and fidelity to the sleuth that Holmes is known in such remarkable detail and color. Ironically, while Holmes is fully formed in the public mind with all of his eccentricities, Watson is much less clearly drawn, the result of his own reticence to discuss himself. It is thus unfortunate that the gifted writer, honorable gentleman, and talented physician has largely been defined by film, television, and radio, and especially by such imaginary Watsons as NIGEL BRUCE. Watson is now seen as the rabidly loyal but hopelessly bungling friend of the detective who spends his life in awe of the radiant genius of Holmes, though the efforts of recent productions—the Granada Television series with Edward Hardwicke and David Burke as the good doctor to Jeremy Brett's Holmes, in particular—attempt to correct this regrettable development. The reality is that even the sleuth proudly told his able friend: "I never get your limits, Watson! There are unexplored possibilities about you."

As a result of references made throughout the Canon, a fairly clear picture of the life of Dr. Watson can be pieced together, although as with his friend Holmes, there are many vital elements that are either missing or unclear. Fortunately, the theories and hypotheses of Sherlockian scholars have provided many possible solutions to any lacunas in the life history of the physician.

Early years. John Hamish Watson was born sometime in the early 1850s (according to the Sherlockian W. S. Baring-Gould on August 7, 1852). His father was Henry Watson and his elder brother, who would die of drink or dissipation around 1888, was Henry, Jr. While still young, Watson's mother apparently passed away and the family went to Australia. He was thus familiar with the goldfields of that country as noted in *The Sign of Four.* He eventually returned to England (c. 1865) and attended the same school as Percy Phelps, whom he would later meet again in "The Naval Treaty."

Unlike Holmes, the young Watson seemed to be both sociable and popular—he took part, for example, in the cruel treatment of young Phelps that was considered such a "piquant thing" by the schoolboys.

That Watson attended the same school as Phelps would seem to indicate that his family was doing reasonably well, for Phelps obviously had excellent connections (his uncle was the powerful politician Lord Holdhurst). A few years later, perhaps around 1872, Watson entered the University of London Medical School to pursue a medical degree. As part of his training, he worked at St. Bartholomew's Hospital in London as a staff surgeon. Stamford, who would have such a crucial role years later in his life, was his dresser. Watson probably played rugby around this time for the Blackheath football team.

As he wrote in A *Study in Scarlet*: "In 1878 I took my degree of Doctor of Medicine of the University of London, and proceeded to Netley to go through the course prescribed for surgeons in the Army. Having completed my studies there, I was duly attached to the Fifth Northumberland Fusiliers as assistant surgeon. The regiment was stationed in India at the time, and before I could join it, the second Afghan War had broken out. On landing at Bombay, I learned that my corps had advanced through the passes, and was already deep in the enemy's country . . ."

Removed from his brigade and attached to the

The coat of arms of John H. Watson, according to the scholar William S. Hall, bears the motto Mea gloria fides ("Fidelity is my glory")

Sixty-sixth Foot (Berkshires), Watson took part in the Battle of Maiwand on July 27, 1880. During the bloody fighting, Watson was wounded by a JEZAIL BULLET and would have been taken by the enemy but for the courage of his orderly, Murray. Removed to Peshawar, he rallied from his wound and was slowly on the road to recovery when he was stricken with enteric fever, "that curse of our Indian possessions." He suffered for months and his "life was despaired of." Finally pulling through, he was sent home by the medical board and journeyed to England on board the troopship *Orontes*. He went on:

"I had neither kith nor kin in England, and was therefore as free as air—or as free as an income of eleven shillings and sixpence a day will permit a man to be. Under such circumstances I naturally gravitated to London, that great cesspool into which all the loungers and idlers of the Empire are irresistibly drained. There I stayed for some time at a private hotel in the Strand, leading a comfortless, meaningless existence, and spending such money as I had, considerably more freely than I ought."

By early January 1881, he had decided to find cheaper lodgings, fortuitously meeting Stamford at the Criterion Bar. Their conversation led to Watson's meeting with Sherlock Holmes and the sharing of lodgings by the two men in Baker Street. Watson's direct involvement in Holmes's life and career began in March 1881, with the investigation into the murder of Enoch Drebber, recounted by Watson in A *Study in Scarlet*.

Years with Sherlock Holmes.   The documenting of the Holmes-Watson partnership is complicated by the ambiguities present in the doctor's narratives concerning his marriages. As his various unions had direct bearings on his relationship with the detective, the years of his dealings with Holmes can be organized largely around his marriages. (See also below under Marriages.)

The first period of the association seems to have lasted from 1881 to 1886, ending with Watson's possible marriage in 1886 or 1887, this assumption based on references in "The Five Orange Pips" and "A Scandal in Bohemia." His first wife having died, Watson returned to Baker Street sometime in late 1888, an arrangement that lasted until May 1889, when he married Mary Morstan. Purchasing a practice in the Paddington district, Watson moved out. This period, during which Watson was busy with his practice, also saw him involved in such affairs as

The first meeting of Holmes and Watson in *A Study in Scarlet*; by George Hutchinson.

"The Crooked Man" and the only two cases he personally brought to the attention of the detective, "The Engineer's Thumb," and "Colonel Warburton's Madness."

The apparent tranquility of his life was ended abruptly on an April day when Holmes clambered through a window in Watson's practice and announced that his war with Professor Moriarty had turned decidedly violent. The following days found the doctor travelling across the Continent with Holmes—Professor Moriarty in hot and vengeful pursuit.

The tragedy of the Reichenbach Falls, in which Watson assumed that Holmes had died in the struggle with the professor, left its mark upon him. As he wrote in "The Final Problem," "It is with a heavy heart that I take up my pen to write the last words in which I shall ever record the singular gifts by which my friend Mr. Sherlock Holmes was distin-

guished." The changes only continued in the months that followed Holmes's death for Watson sold his Paddington practice and returned to Kensington. In July 1891, "A Scandal in Bohemia" was published in the *Strand Magazine*, marking the beginning of Watson's literary career. Yet another tragedy struck in the next few years, however, as his beloved Mary died, possibly of heart trouble (inherited from her father, who also had a weak heart).

The dark years finally came to an end on April 5, 1894 when Holmes "returned to life" and gave Watson such a surprise that "I must have fainted for the first and the last time in my life." After helping Holmes in "The Empty House," Watson sold his Kensington practice and once more took up residence at 221B. Here he would remain until fall 1902, when he left Baker Street for the last time and moved to Queen Anne Street ("The Illustrious Client"). Later that year, he married again, eventually returning to practice.

So began the final period of his professional dealings with Holmes. Their relationship had changed somewhat over the years, the closeness of their friendship assuming a much more utilitarian hue. Holmes considered Watson "an institution" while the doctor used Holmes to provide himself with suitable material to write about for his ever eager public. Finally, in October 1903, Holmes retired to the Sussex Downs. The detective would confirm that Watson remained behind in London in "The Lion's Mane" by noting: "At this period of my life the good Watson had passed almost beyond my ken. An occasional week-end visit was the most that I ever saw of him."

Later Years.　As noted, Watson saw little of the detective after Holmes's retirement in 1903. He remained in practice, however, growing also in girth as he was described in "His Last Bow" as "heavily built." In 1914, Holmes reenlisted "good old Watson" to assist him in finishing up the liquidation of the spy ring of Von Bork recounted in "His Last Bow." He served as chauffeur to the disguised Holmes, joining him in the climax of the detective's brilliant operation. Such, unfortunately, was the last dated reference to the physician in the Canon. He entered once again into the army to serve as surgeon in 1914, a period of activity that would have taxed his medical skill and personal strength given the horrors inflicted upon the combatants in World War I. He continued to write, at least until March 1927, when his last account,

"Shoscombe Old Place," was published in *Liberty Magazine*. His death has been placed by W. S. Baring-Gould at July 24, 1929.

Appearance. Watson is consistently described as sturdy or well built, and Holmes in "The Retired Colourman" noted his "natural advantages" where women were concerned. It is obvious from the good doctor's own admission that he was very handsome in the classic English way, drawing the attentions of ladies, both fair and plain. His numerous marriages would attest to his success in the romantic arts.

Having arrived home from the Second Afghan War, Watson was "as thin as a lath," having endured a Jezail bullet in one of his extremities, a severe bout of enteric fever, and months of convalescence. This extreme thinness was not his normal state. In his younger days, he had played rugby for Blackheath ("The Sussex Vampire") and was thus presumably in excellent physical shape. Lestrade unknowingly described him well in "Charles Augustus Milverton:" "He was a middle-sized, strongly built man—square jaw, thick neck, moustache . . ." A man of remarkable constitution and "reckoned fleet of foot" (*The Hound of the Baskervilles*), he lost his athletic frame when he was described in "His Last Bow" as "heavily built." Watson wore conservative clothing—suits and hats. While in practice, he carried his stethoscope in his hats, its presence visible from the bulge in the side ("A Scandal in Bohemia").

Practices. The confidence on the part of Sherlock Holmes in the medical skill of Dr. Watson would seem to be justified in the general success of Watson's practices throughout London. Having returned to England in 1881, Watson did not enter into medical practice immediately, owing doubtlessly to the shortage of funds at his disposal, his limitations with regard to health, and his increasing fascination with his roommate, Sherlock Holmes. By around 1888, his position had improved substantially so that after meeting Mary Morstan and successfully winning her hand, he took the decisive act of setting himself up in practice. This first London practice was situated in the Paddington district and was purchased from Old Farquhar, he of St. Vitus Dance; it eventually had a "fairly long list" of patients.

Around 1890, Watson and his dear Mary moved to Kensington and another practice ("The Empty House," "The Norwood Builder," and "The Red-Headed League"). This practice was reportedly "small" ("The Norwood Builder") and was "never very absorbing" ("The Red-Headed League"). The lack of patients was possibly due to Watson's attentions being elsewhere. In 1891 Holmes was "killed" at the Reichenbach Falls in Switzerland and a short time later (c. 1891–1894) Mary died. The Kensington practice was sold to a young relative of Holmes named Verner in the period 1894–1895.

The years 1895–1902 are unclear as to the medical activities of the physician, including the peculiar year of 1896 when Watson gives no account of his work. Sometime around 1902, having remarried, Watson entered into a new practice, this time located on Queen Anne Street ("The Illustrious Client"). It was probably associated with his marriage in 1903; to provide a means of support for his domestic arrangement. This practice met with success and "was not inconsiderable" ("The Creeping Man").

Some questions remain about his medical career, however. In "The Final Problem," for example, Watson mentions Mortimer Street as one of the streets near his Kensington practice. This, of course, is not possible; Watson may have been disguising the address, or he may have simply written the wrong street, an understandable lapse given the emotionally distressing nature of the account. Other unclear references were made in "The Crooked Man," "A Case of Identity," and "The Man With the Twisted Lip." The doctor rejoined the Medical Corps in "his old service" ("His Last Bow"), at the start of World War I. (See also Anstruther and Jackson.)

Marriages. One of the most discussed subjects pertaining to Dr. Watson is that of his relationship with women and his subsequent (or frequent) marriages. It is clear from the pages of the Canon that Watson considered himself a womanizer. The personal confession is supported by Holmes's statement in "The Second Stain" that "the fair sex is your department," and Watson's own effusive, colorful, and highly romanticized descriptions of many of the female clients or principals in Holmes's cases. With his literary proclivities for female observation, it would have been very surprising had he not been married or at least amorously involved.

Watson's marriages pose certain difficulties for the chronicle because of their number and the varying references made to them. As has been noted, his handsome physical appearance certainly would have caught the eyes of the ladies, but his own sense of honor would have obviated the kind of rakish or roguish life to which he seemed to allude in his pages. Watson was married at least twice and probably more times than that. W. S. Baring-Gould theorized that Watson first married Constance Adams of San Francisco, whom he met in that American city. This idea is supposedly supported by the unpublished play *Angels of Darkness* by Sir Arthur Conan Doyle and a reference made in "The Five Orange Pips" to his being in a wedded state in September 1887. This first wife had to have died as Watson was a bachelor (it is certainly hoped so) when he met Mary Morstan in July 1888.

His union with Mary occurred sometime before March 1888 (as noted in "A Scandal in Bohemia"). Mary's name is subsequently little used and mentions of his domestic situation merely imply Mary through the date of the case (1888–1891). These cases are "The Engineer's Thumb," "The Final Problem," "The Red-Headed League," and "The Man With the Twisted Lip." Other implied cases are "The Boscombe Valley Mystery" and "The Stockbroker's Clerk." In other cases, there are allusions to his marriage, impending marriage, or simply to his no longer living with Holmes, but there is no evidence, internal or otherwise, to prove his reference is to Mary.

Mary died sometime during Holmes's Great Hiatus (1891–1894). Watson moved back to Baker Street after Holmes's return to England in 1894. By 1903, however, Watson was married yet again and no longer living with Holmes. That he should be married again is not surprising, but what is remarkable is the ease by which he found another wife, given the high rate of mortality among his spouses. Reference to this third marriage is found in "The Blanched Soldier." How many other marriages Watson may have had is unknown and open to speculation.

Watson as a Writer. Holmes made many statements throughout the Canon concerning Watson's literary endeavors. This seems only just, for the doctor contributed greatly to the spreading far and wide of the detective's fame. As Mycroft Holmes observed in "The Greek Interpreter," "I hear of Sherlock everywhere since you became his chronicler." While Holmes would tell Watson, "I am lost without my Boswell" ("A Scandal in Bohemia"), he would also consistently attack Watson's writings. "Your fatal habit of looking at everything from the point of view of a story instead of a scientific exercise has ruined what might have been an instructive and even classical series of demonstrations" ("The Abbey Grange"); and "Honestly, I cannot congratulate you upon it. Detection is, or ought to be, an exact science and should be treated in the same cold and unemotional manner. You have attempted to tinge it with romanticism, which produces much the same effect as if you worked a love-story or an elopement into the fifth proposition of Euclid" (*The Sign of Four*).

Holmes also complained that Watson's accounts were "superficial" ("The Blanched Soldier") and that they embellished the detective's achievements and abilities. However, the sleuth called him "a man of letters" ("Wisteria Lodge"), and took, albeit with some mock disapproval, considerable interest in Watson's literary affairs.

Holmes did seem to approve of Watson's choice of chronicled cases, complimenting Watson for his "power of selection, which atones for much which I deplore in your narratives" ("The Abbey Grange"). He would add in "The Copper Beeches" his appreciation of Watson's choosing not important or "sensational" trials and cases, but "those incidents which may have given room for those faculties of deduction and of logical synthesis which I have made my special province."

It should be noted that Holmes prohibited the publication of many of Watson's accounts of his cases for various reasons—promised secrecy, an aversion to public scrutiny about certain affairs, and his own reticence to have too much revealed to the public. Watson always sought his authorization to publish any case ("The Veiled Lodger") and on occasion received, unbidden, Holmes's suggestion to present a case that might be enjoyed, the Cornish Horror, for example.

As for Watson, he wrote that the cases eventually published were chosen to "illustrate the remarkable mental qualities of my friend, Sherlock Holmes," endeavoring "to select those which presented the minimum of sensationalism." This basis of choice unfortunately did not always produce cases that were particularly riveting ("The Veiled Lodger," for example), and left out some that sound especially enthralling such as The Politician, the Lighthouse, and the Trained Cormorant, to name one of many.

As a writer, Watson had genuine talent and was particularly able to impart superbly wrought but succinct passages of description that gave life to his narratives and made riveting reading what were actually often rather uneventful cases. His high moment came with *The Hound of the Baskervilles*, a novel-length account that is both an excellent detective work and a brilliantly conceived Gothic story.

His enthusiasm, of course, was always heightened when given the chance to write about an encounter with a beautiful lady. Especially notable are his initial appraisals of visitors—women most of all—who are then examined by Holmes with his awesome deductive eye. The descriptions do much to add to both the atmosphere and the clarity of the cases recounted. (For some interesting descriptions, see under the following entries: HUNTER, VIOLET; KLEIN, ISADORA; and TRELAWNEY HOPE, LADY HILDA.)

Critics enjoy pointing to what are now classic Watsonian miscues or errors in the accounts. Among these are the wandering Jezail bullet wound, the mixing up of dates (see "Red-Headed League" for the best known), and the very much talked about scenes where his wife calls him "James" instead of John. Suggested reasons for these lapses have included his emotional states when writing, improper editing, or his own too-frequent enjoyment of spirits.

Relationship with Holmes.   As is the case with any personal relationship, the long association of Holmes and Watson underwent inevitable and gradual changes, although the detective's declaration to his friend in *The Hound of the Baskervilles* remained somewhat of a constant. "It may be that you are not yourself luminous, but you are a conductor of light. Some people without possessing genius have a remarkable power of stimulating it."

Watson deemed Holmes a fascinating individual from the earliest days of their friendship, finding him to be enigmatic and the possessor of some unique talents. He had difficulty, and indeed would for many years, accepting the deductive abilities of the detective, expressing surprise and awe at Holmes's powers. In one instance, Watson was pained by the detective's objective, accurate, but cruel analysis of a watch that had belonged to Watson's dissolute brother. The episode, in *The Sign of Four*, pointed to the fundamental differences between the men: Holmes the pure machine of logic and thought and Watson the man of compassion and subjectivity.

It would be a mistake, however, to assume that

Holmes used Watson throughout his career in the way Watson intimates in "The Crooked Man." "I was a whetstone for his mind. I stimulated him. He liked to think aloud in my presence. His remarks could hardly be said to be made to me—many of them would have been appropriately addresses to his bedstead—but none the less, having formed the habit, it had become in some way helpful that I should register and interject. If I irritated him by a certain methodical slowness in my mentality, that irritation served only to make his own flame-like intuitions and impressions flash up the more vividly and swiftly."

The detective relied upon his friend and chronicler as a partner in his writing of "The Blanched Soldier," noting that "Watson has some remarkable characteristics of his own to which in his modesty he has given small attention amid his exaggerated estimates of my own performance." Equally, Holmes held Watson in considerable respect. Often overlooked, as well, was Holmes's genuine concern for his friend, emotion that came to the surface only on rare occasions—in "The Three Garridebs," "The Devil's Foot," "The Empty House," and "The Bruce-Partington Plans."

Their early years together were quite harmonious and Watson noted in "The Five Orange Pips" that he was the only friend of the detective. After Watson's marriage or marriages, his friendship with Holmes was "to some extent modified" ("The Final Problem") and they drifted apart as noted in "A Scandal in Bohemia."

Recovering from the sudden, unexpected return of Holmes after his presumed death at Reichenbach Falls, Watson aided him again in "The Empty House" and later returned to their Baker Street lodgings, once more serving as the associate on whom Holmes could "thoroughly rely" ("The Boscombe Valley Mystery"). Coincidental to their renewed friendship was the publication of Watson's chronicles in the *Strand Magazine* through his "literary agent" Arthur Conan Doyle. It was incumbent upon him to tie himself to Holmes if for no other reason than to secure his permission to publish some of their more interesting cases together. As the years 1894 through 1901 were busy ones, the doctor had no trouble finding suitable material.

In the time prior to Holmes's retirement, Watson married once more and "the relations between us in those latter days were peculiar . . . He was a man of habits, narrow and concentrated habits, and I had become one of them . . ." Soon, Holmes was gone to the Sussex Downs and the two were separated even further. Nevertheless, when it came time to wrap up the sypmaster Von Bork in 1914, it was unthinkable to Holmes not to go into danger without the friend who had shared in his adventures so faithfully and for so long.

WEISS & CO.

A London manufacturer of cutlery that created the delicate cataract knife that was found in the dead hand of John Straker in "Silver Blaze." It was assumed that Straker had tried to defend himself against his assailant for the blade "was clotted with blood up to the handle."

WESSEX CUP.

Also the Wessex Plate, a horse race held at Winchester that was won by the horse Silver Blaze in "Silver Blaze."

THE WESSEX CUP

The competitors in the race were:

HORSE	OWNER	COLORS
The Negro	Mr. Heath Newton	red cap, cinnamon jacket
Pugilist	Colonel Wardlaw	pink cap, blue and black jacket
Desborough	Lord Backwater	yellow cap and sleeves
Silver Blaze	Colonel Ross	black cap, red jacket
Iris	Duke of Balmoral	yellow and black stripes
Rasper	Lord Singleford	purple cap, black sleeves

Race results:

1st Place—Silver Blaze
2nd Place—Desborough
3rd Place—Iris

WESTBURY, VIOLET.

The fiancée of the murdered Arthur Cadogan West in "The Bruce-Partington Plans." On the night of his death, Cadogan West and Miss Westbury were to go to the theater together, but while they were walking close to his office where the plans to the Bruce-Partington Submarine were kept he gave an exclamation and suddenly dashed off into the fog. She waited, but he never returned. Finally, she walked home alone. Throughout Holmes's investigation, she protested his innocence.

WEST END.

The western region of London where a number of Holmes's investigations took place: "The Beryl Coronet," "The Bruce-Partington Plans," "The Copper Beeches," "The Resident Patient," "the Second Stain," and "The Three Gables." The West End was also the site of the excellent pastiche novel *The West End Horror* by Nicholas Meyer.

WEST END HORROR, THE.

A 1976 pastiche novel by Nicholas Meyer, a sequel to his best-selling work *The Seven-Per-Cent Solution*. This time Holmes and Watson are called into a case in March 1895 to investigate the bizarre murder of Jonathan McCarthy, a hated theater critic in London. The events are then compounded by the murder of Jessie Rutland, a young actress. Even stranger is the mysterious disappearance of the bodies from the morgue, the corpses vanishing along with the police surgeon.

The case is made particularly interesting by the panoply of stars and luminaries who populate Dr. Watson's pages: George Bernard Shaw (who brings Holmes into the affair); Oscar Wilde (hastening on his road to destruction); Ellen Terry, the actress; Gilbert of Gilbert and Sullivan; Henry Irving; and the extremely unpleasant box office clerk and writer Bram Stoker. Each is a suspect, but each is removed for various reasons from suspicion. The most serious suspect is Stoker, who seems to be leading a double life, one that could fit perfectly into the events of the murders. Holmes and Watson locate his secret flat and break in, expecting to find evidence of his associations with Jessie Rutland. Instead they find the work in progress called *Dracula*. Watson is aghast at the portion of the manuscript he reads, the attack of the count upon Mina Harker, exclaiming to Holmes "This is depraved . . . Holmes, what sort of mad work is this?" The final resolution of the affair is accomplished with the help of Dr. Moore Agar, the dramatic meeting described by Watson in "The Devil's Foot" occurring here. The atmosphere is excellent, although Watson does seem to violate his own rule concerning the disguising of names to avoid public embarrassment.

WESTHOUSE & MARBANK.

A London firm located on Fenchurch Street that was a major importer of French claret in "A Case of Identity,"

Watson on Film and Television

While the cinematic and television interpretations of Sherlock Holmes have been intriguing over the years, the work of actors in bringing Watson to life has been often overlooked, despite the fact that some of the portrayals of the good doctor have contributed immensely to the success of the productions. Watsons on film have been distinguished by widely varying characterizations; some actors have chosen at times to adhere carefully to Watson's Canonical personality, but others have sought to put their own stamp on the role, at times with disastrous consequences. Highly esteemed portrayals have been turned in by Edward Hardwicke, Andre Morell, Nigel Stock, and H. Marion Crawford, who managed to make Watson a three dimensional character, interesting and valuable to Holmes. Special mention must be made of NIGEL BRUCE, whose Watson remains the most beloved by audiences even though he allowed the doctor to degenerate into a buffoon in many of the long running cycle of films with Basil Rathbone. In several films Watson has been portrayed by women, proving that gender is not all when one must play the foil to Holmes's deductive powers.

PERFORMER	FILM OR PROGRAM	PERFORMER	FILM OR PROGRAM
Alwin Neuss	*Sherlock Holmes I* (1908)		*The Further Adventures of*
	Sherlock Holmes II (1908)		*Sherlock Holmes* (series—
	Sherlock Holmes III (1908)		1923, except for *The Sign of*
	The Adventures of Sherlock		*Four*)
	Holmes (1908)	Roland Young	*Sherlock Holmes* (1922)
	Sangerindens Diamanter (1909)	Georges Seroff	*Der Hund von Baskerville* (1929)
	Droske No. 519 (1909)	H. Reeves-Smith	*The Return of Sherlock Holmes*
	Den Graa Dame (1909)		(1929)
	La Femme (1910)		*Paramount On Parade* (*Murder*
	Sherlock Holmes I		*Will Out*, 1930)
	Bondefangerklor (1910)	Reginald Owen	*Sherlock Holmes* (1932)
	Forklaedte Barnepige (1911)	Warburton Gamble	*A Study in Scarlet* (1933)
	Mordet I Bakerstreet (1911)	Athole Stewart	*The Speckled Band* (1931)
	Hotelmysterierne (1911)	Fred Lloyd	*The Hound of the Baskervilles*
Mr. Moyse	*The Speckled Band* (1912)		(1931)
	Silver Blaze (1912)	Ian Fleming	*The Sleeping Cardinal* (1931)
	The Beryl Coronet (1912)		*The Missing Rembrandt* (1932)
	The Musgrave Ritual (1913)		*The Triumph of Sherlock Holmes*
	The Reygate Squires (1912)		(1935)
	The Stolen Papers (1912)		*Silver Blaze* (1937)
	A Mystery of Boscombe Vale	Ian Hunter	*The Sign of Four* (1932)
	(1912)	Fritz Odemar	*Der Hund von Baskerville* (1936)
	The Copper Beeches (1912)	Nigel Bruce	*The Hound of the Baskervilles*
Arthur M. Cullin	*The Valley of Fear* (1916)		(1939)
	The Sign of Four (1923)		*The Adventures of Sherlock*
Jack Francis	*A Study in Scarlet* (1914)		*Holmes* (1939)
Edward Fielding	*Sherlock Holmes* (1916)		*Sherlock Holmes and the Voice of*
Hubert Willis	*The Adventures of Sherlock*		*Terror* (1942)
	Holmes (series—1921)		

PERFORMER	FILM OR PROGRAM	PERFORMER	FILM OR PROGRAM
	Sherlock Holmes and the Secret Weapon (1942)	Edward Fox	"Dr. Watson and the Darkwater Hall Mystery" (TV—1974)
	Sherlock Holmes in Washington (1943)	Burt Blackwell	"The Interior Motive" (TV—1975)
	Sherlock Holmes Faces Death (1943)	Jenny O'Hara	"The Return of the World's Greatest Detective" (TV—1976)
	The Spider Woman (1944)		
	The Scarlet Claw (1944)	Patrick Macnee	"Sherlock Holmes in New York" (TV—1976)
	The Pearl of Death (1944)		
	The House of Fear (1944)		"Sherlock Holmes, Incident at Victoria Falls" (TV—1991)
	The Woman in Green (1945)		"Sherlock Holmes and the Leading Lady" (TV—1992)
	Pursuit to Algiers (1945)		
	Terror By Night (1945)	Arthur Lowe	"The End of Civilization as We Know It" (TV—1977)
	Dressed to Kill (1946)		
	Crazy House (1943)		
Andre Morell	The Hound of the Baskervilles (1959)	Richard Woods	"Sherlock Holmes" (TV—1980)
Thorley Walters	Sherlock Holmes und das Halsband des Todes (1962)	Donald Pickering	"Sherlock Holmes and Dr. Watson" (TV—1982)
	The Adventures of Sherlock Holmes' Smarter Brother (1975)	Terence Rigby	"The Hound of the Baskervilles" (TV—1982)
	"Silver Blaze" (TV—1977)	David Healy	"The Sign of Four" (TV—1983)
Donald Huston	A Study in Terror (1965)	Donald Churchill	"The Hound of the Baskervilles" (TV—1983)
Colin Blakely	The Private Life of Sherlock Holmes (1970)	David Burke	"The Adventures of Sherlock Holmes" (TV series—1984–1985)
Heinz Ruhmann	Der Mann, Der Sherlock Holmes War (1937)	John Mills	"The Masks of Death" (TV—1984)
Joanne Woodward	They Might Be Giants (1971; as Dr. Mildred Watson)	Edward Hardwicke	"The Return of Sherlock Holmes" (TV series—1986–1988)
Bernard Fox	"The Hound of the Baskervilles" (TV—1972)		"The Hound of the Baskervilles" (TV—1987)
William Podmore	"The Three Garridebs" (TV—1937)		"The Sign of Four" (TV—1987)
Raymond Francis	"Sherlock Holmes" (TV—1951)		"The Casebook of Sherlock Holmes" (TV series—1991–)
Martyn Green	"The Adventures of the Black Baronet" (TV—1953)	Margaret Colin	"The Return of Sherlock Holmes" (TV—1987)
H. Marion Crawford	"The New Adventures of Sherlock Holmes" (TV—1954–1955)	John Hillerman	"Hands of a Murderer" (TV—1990)
Nigel Stock	"Sherlock Holmes" (TV—1964–1965)	Richard Johnson	"Crucifer of Blood" (TV—1991)
	"Sherlock Holmes" (TV—1968)	Robert Duvall	The Seven-Per-Cent Solution (1976)
Derek Dene	"High Jinks" (TV—1969)	James Mason	Murder by Decree (1979)
William Rushton	"Elementary, My Dear Watson" (TV—1973)	Alan Cox	Young Sherlock Holmes (1985)
		Deborah Farentino	"Sherlock Holmes Returns" (1993)

Edward Hardwicke is Dr. John Watson in the recent television series on MYSTERY! (Photo courtesy MYSTERY!/WGBH Boston.)

with offices in Bordeaux. James Windibank was one of their travelling salesmen.

WESTMINSTER.   The central area of London, noted for the presence of Whitehall, the Houses of Parliament, and Westminster Abbey. Eduardo Lucas, the international agent, resided at 16 Godolphin Street in "The Second Stain." Also located in Westminster were the residence of the international agent Adolph Meyer in "The Bruce-Partington Plans" and the firm Morton & Kennedy in "The Solitary Cyclist."

WESTPHAIL, HONORIA.   The maiden sister of Mrs. Stoner and aunt of Julia and Helen Stoner in "The Speckled Band." While visiting Miss Westphail in Harrow, Julia met the half-pay major of the marines to whom she subsequently became engaged.

WHITE, ABEL.   The owner of an Indian indigo plantation who took pity on Jonathan Small in *The Sign of Four*. He offered the one-legged Small the position of overseer on the plantation. At the start of the Sepoy Rebellion (the Indian mutiny), Abel White was murdered.

WHITE EAGLE.   A tavern on Nine Elms Lane situated across from Broderick and Nelson's timber yard to which the sleuth-hound Toby led Holmes and Watson, via a trail of creosote scent in *The Sign of Four*.

WHITEHALL.   A street in Westminster where a number of government offices are located. Mycroft Holmes worked in Whitehall ("The Bruce-Partington Plans" and "The Greek Interpreter"), walking to his office from his rooms in Pall Mall. The Mazarin Stone was stolen from the Whitehall area in "The Mazarin Stone." The Trelawney Hopes resided at Whitehall Terrace, a street near Whitehall in "The Second Stain."

WHITE MASON.   A chief of the Sussex police who was in charge of the investigation into the apparent death of John Douglas at Birlstone Manor in *The Valley of Fear*. Out of his depths, White Mason summoned Inspector MacDonald of the Metropolitan Police. MacDonald, in turn, engaged the services of Holmes. Watson wrote: "White Mason was a quiet, comfortable-looking person in a loose tweed suit, with a clean-shaved, ruddy face, a stoutish body, and powerful bandy legs adorned with gaiters, looking like a small farmer, a retired gamekeeper, or anything upon earth except a very favourable specimen of the provincial criminal officer."

WHITNEY, ISA.   A friend of Dr. Watson's who was addicted to opium in "The Man With the Twisted Lip." At the urgent plea of Whitney's wife, Watson went to the opium den Bar of Gold in Upper Swandam Lane to rescue his old friend. Watson wrote: "The habit grew upon him, as I understand, from some foolish freak when he was at college; for having read De Quincey's description of his dreams and sensations, he had drenched his tobacco with laudanum in an attempt to produce the same effect . . . I can see him now, with yellow, pasty face, drooping lids, and pin-point pupils, all huddled in a chair, the wreck of a noble man." His wife, **Kate Whitney**, was an old friend and companion of Mary Morstan (Mrs. Watson). Unwittingly, Kate sent Watson into the arms of Holmes and the affair of the Twisted Lip. Isa's brother, **Elias Whitney** is Doctor of Divinity of the Theological College of St. George's.

WHITTINGTON, LADY ALICIA.   A friend of the duke of Balmoral who was present at the wedding of Lord Robert St. Simon and Hatty Doran in "The Noble Bachelor."

WHOLE ART OF DETECTION.

Holmes proposed, but never managed to write this volume. During his investigation of "The Abbey Grange" in 1897, the detective told Watson: "At present I am, as you know, fairly busy, but I propose to devote my declining years to the composition of a textbook which shall focus the whole art of detection into one volume." It would appear that he never completed such a work, particularly as he told Watson four years later that "of late I have been tempted to look into the problems furnished by nature rather than those more superficial ones for which our artificial state of society is responsible."

WIGGINS.

The apparent head and spokesman of the BAKER STREET IRREGULARS. Watson described him: "One of their number, taller and older than the others, stood forward with an air of lounging superiority which was very funny in such a disreputable little scarecrow." It is unclear how long Wiggins remained chief of the BSI, but an interesting bit of speculation of Wiggins's later years was presented in the novel *Exit, Sherlock Holmes*.

WIGMORE STREET.

A West End street where Watson went to the post office. Holmes later deduced that Watson had visited the post office to dispatch a telegram (*The Sign of Four*). Holmes and Watson passed through Wigmore Street on their way to the Alpha Inn in "The Blue Carbuncle."

WILD, JONATHAN.

An infamous eighteenth-century criminal in London who came to control much of the city's criminal underground. In *The Valley of Fear*, Holmes compared Professor Moriarty to Jonathan Wild. Unlike Wild, however, Moriarty was never captured, tried, and hanged.

WILDER, JAMES.

The secretary to the duke of Holdernesse in "The Priory School," Wilder was described as "small, nervous, alert, with intelligent light-blue eyes and mobile features." Wilder played a major role in the events described by Watson in the chronicle of the case.

WILLIAMS.

The prizefighter and onetime lightweight champion of England served as porter and bodyguard to Major John Sholto of Pondi-

cherry Lodge in *The Sign of Four*. The major's son, Thaddeus, later hired him as a servant. It was Williams who met Mary Morstan, Holmes, and Watson at the third pillar from the left outside the Lyceum Theatre to take them to his employer.

WILLIAMS, JAMES BAKER.

The owner of Forton Old Hall in Surrey in "Wisteria Lodge," Williams was a neighbor of Aloysius Garcia at Wisteria Lodge.

WILLIAMSON.

A defrocked clergyman who was an associate of Bob Carruthers and Jack Woodley in "The Solitary Cyclist," Williamson was part of the nefarious plans intended for the unfortunate Violet Smith. According to his realty agent, Williamson was a respectable elderly gentleman.

WILLIS, HUBERT.

The English actor portrayed Dr. Watson some forty-six times, throughout the Eille Norwood (or Stoll Picture) series, from 1921 to 1923. A gifted comic character actor, Willis first came into contact with the works of Conan Doyle in 1913, when he had a part in *The House of Temperley*, based on Doyle's play of the same name, recreating the role of Tom Belcher that he had performed on stage. Willis was in each of the films of Norwood's series, released in three groups, *The Adventures of Sherlock Holmes*, *The Further Adventures of Sherlock Holmes*, and *The Last Adventures of Sherlock Holmes*. The only one in which he did not appear was *The Sign of Four* (1923). For this he was replaced by Arthur Cullin as the producers were looking for a younger performer. For some time, Willis epitomized Watson in the public eye and did much to establish the screen persona of the doctor as a good-natured buffoon.

WILLOWS.

The attending physician to John Turner in "The Boscombe Valley Mystery," he was of the belief that the death of Turner's tenant Charles McCarthy had left his nervous system shattered.

WILMER, DOUGLAS.

The well-known English actor (b. 1920) first donned the deerstalker as Holmes in May 1964, for the British television production of "The Speckled Band," opposite Nigel Stock as Watson. His performance, as well as Stock's, were highly praised and made certain that a full television series would soon follow. It premiered in February 1965, running until May, with twelve episodes. As Holmes, Wilmer was extremely comfortable, appearing at times decidedly Rathbonesque, a similarity in appearance remarked upon by critics. Wilmer later played Holmes in the zany 1975 comedy *The Adventures of Sherlock Holmes' Smarter Brother*.

WILSON.   Several notable figures named Wilson appear in the Canon. The most infamous was the notorious canary trainer who was arrested by Holmes in 1895, thereby removing a plague spot from the East End of London ("Black Peter"). This case was presented in *The Exploits of Sherlock Holmes* with the truly gruesome short story "The Adventure of the Deptford Horror" by Adrian Conan Doyle. Other Wilsons were the chaplain aboard the convict ship *Gloria Scott* in 1855, who was actually the partner of Jack Prendergast and was only impersonating a chaplain so that he could organize a convict uprising on board; the manager of the district messenger office and the employer of young Cartwright, whose good name and perhaps life Holmes had once saved; a constable in Kent who was on duty at Yoxley Old Place after the murder of Willoughby Smith, secretary to Professor Coram in "The Golden Pince-Nez"; and a sergeant in the Sussex constabulary in *The Valley of Fear* who was the first officer to receive word of the terrible events at Birlstone Manor. (See also SCOWRERS.)

WILSON, BARTHOLOMEW.   The district leader of Lodge 29, at Chicago, of the Ancient Order of Freemen, in 1875 in *The Valley of Fear*.

WILSON, JABEZ.   The owner of a small pawnbroker's at Coburg Square who introduced Holmes to the strange case of "The Red-Headed League." At the urging of his assistant Vincent Spaulding, Wilson applied for and secured a position in the League of Red-Headed Men. His duties were not complicated: he was to copy the *Encyclopedia Britannica*, spending four hours a day at his work, never leaving the office for any reason. Paid the generous salary of 4 pounds a week, Wilson was understandably stunned and confused when, after a few weeks, the league was suddenly dissolved. He thus went to Holmes to learn the reasons for his odd experience. Holmes could deduce nothing about him "Beyond the obvious facts that he has at some time done manual labor, that he takes snuff,

and that he is a Freemason, that he has been in China, and that he has done a considerable amount of writing lately." He also had what Watson called a "blazing red head."

WILSON, STEVE.   The name of a supposed Pinkerton agent at Hobson's Patch, who had come into Vermissa Valley to operate against the Scowrers in *The Valley of Fear*.

WINDIBANK, JAMES.   The stepfather of Mary Sutherland and a travelling representative of the great claret importers Westhouse & Marbank in "A Case of Identity." He supported the courtship of Mary by Hosmer Angel but never had the chance to meet his prospective son-in-law in person because he was out of the country for long stretches of time. Holmes considered Windibank a "cold-blooded scoundrel," adding "That fellow will rise from crime to crime until he does something very bad, and ends on a gallows." His wife, Mrs. Windibank, mother of Mary, had been married to a Tottenham Court Road plumber. She later wed Windibank, a man of considerably fewer years than she.

WINDIGATE.   The landlord of the Alpha Inn who also organized a Christmas goose club of which Henry Baker was a member in "The Blue Carbuncle." Holmes and Watson interviewed Windigate, a "ruddyfaced, white aproned landlord" about his geese, and drank two glasses of his beer. Windigate told Holmes of the poultry dealer Breckinridge at Covent Garden, a tip that advanced the case considerably.

WINE.   It is widely acknowledged that Watson was fond of wine, although his propensity for consumption extended to other alcoholic beverages as well. In *The Sign of Four* is recorded an episode of how wine loosened his lips and allowed an obviously long-simmering frustration to boil over. Watson writes: ". . . whether it was the Beaune which I had with my lunch or the additional exasperation produced by the extreme deliberation of his manner, I suddenly felt that I could hold out no longer.
    'Which is it today,' I asked, 'Morphine or cocaine?' "
    While Holmes would frequently go for long stretches of time without food, he was a proven gourmet, some would even say a gourmand, with an extensive knowledge of food and wine. In inviting

Inspector Athelney Jones to dinner in *The Sign of Four*, Holmes declared: "I insist upon your dining with us. It will be ready in half an hour. I have oysters and a brace of grouse, with something a little choice in white wines." In "The Noble Bachelor," the detective organizes a sumptuous meal for some guests, including "a group of ancient and cobwebby bottles." Holmes had an apparent fondness for wine, on occasion drinking, among many vintages, claret ("The Cardboard Box"), Montrachet ("The Veiled Lodger"), and some Imperial Tokay that supposedly came from "Franz Josef's special cellar at the Schoenbrunn Palace" ("His Last Bow"). The presence of beeswing in a wineglass proves a vital clue in Holmes's investigation of "The Abbey Grange."

WINTER, KITTY. The onetime lover of Baron Gruner in "The Illustrious Client." She had been ruined by him and was eager to send him down to a lower hell than the one to which she had been consigned. She was thus quite willing to aid Holmes in his efforts to terminate the planned marriage of Baron Gruner with Violet De Merville, ultimately getting her revenge in a shocking and terrible way. According to Watson, she was "a slim, flame-like young woman with a pale, intense face, youthful, and yet so worn with sin and sorrow that one read the terrible years which had left their leprous mark upon her."

"WISTERIA LODGE" (WIST). Published: *Collier's*, August 1908, *Strand*, September and October 1908; collected in *His Last Bow* (1917). Major players: Holmes, Watson, John Scott Eccles, Inspector Baynes, Aloysius Garcia, Don Juan Murillo. Case date: See below. A moody investigation by Holmes, the account is hampered structurally by the passive nature of Watson's writings—events are more often described in the past tense than actually presented. "Wisteria Lodge" was first published in *Collier's* in the United States as "The Singular Experience of Mr. John Scott Eccles," and was published by the *Strand* in England in two parts, "The Singular Experience of Mr. John Scott Eccles" and "The Tiger of San Pedro." It involves the peculiar night suffered by Scott Eccles in Wisteria Lodge near Esher in Surrey as the guest of Aloysius Garcia, a young, new acquaintance who is subsequently found murdered on Oxshott Common. Holmes is soon involved, encountering the most capable and

competent police officer of the entire Canon— Inspector Baynes. The dating of this case poses a number of problems owing to Dr. Watson's placing of the matter at the end of March 1892, a time when Holmes was presumed dead at the bottom of the Reichenbach Falls. In "The Norwood Builder," however, Watson dates the affair of "the papers of ex-President Murillo" to the months immediately following the detective's return in 1894 from the Great Hiatus (1891–1894).

WITHOUT A CLUE. U.S. 1990. Dir: Thom Eberhardt. Cast: Michael Caine (Holmes), Ben Kingsley (Watson), Jeffrey Jones (Lestrade), Pat Keen (Mrs. Hudson). An all-out Sherlockian comedy that is far more effective than many other similar comedic efforts (most notably *The Hound of the Baskervilles* with Dudley Moore and Peter Cook). This heretical story poses the inventive theory that Holmes was actually a mere front or character to allow the real detective genius, Dr. Watson, to conduct investigations and solve crimes, all the while posing as Holmes's sincere but easily overlooked chronicler. Holmes is really an actor, hired and trained by Watson to do the "sleuthing" and to convince the public and Scotland Yard. Silly, slapstick, and thin in plot, *Without a Clue* was nevertheless thought by critics to be highly entertaining thanks to the chemistry of Caine and Kingsley.

WOLFE, NERO. The detective and literary creation of Rex Stout, noted for his impressive girth and his remarkable habits as a gourmet. So profound were his culinary skills that he was the inspiration for the collection *The Nero Wolfe Cookbook*. As a brilliant detective and a rather great eccentric, Nero Wolfe has been the subject of some speculation concerning his ancestry. It has been suggested that he may have been the son of MYCROFT HOLMES, although that line of descent has been attacked through the years by various Sherlockians as preposterous. Nevertheless, Wolfe did bear a definite physical similarity to Mycroft, an obvious capacity to eat well, and an abhorrence of physical exercise. Other Sherlockians, such as John Clark in *The Baker Street Journal* in 1956, proposed that Mycroft was not the father, but rather his parents were Sherlock himself and IRENE ADLER. Interestingly, Rex Stout, "the literary agent of Archie Goodwin," never completely denied the hypothesis.

WOMAN IN GREEN, THE. U.S. 1945. Dir: Roy William Neill. Cast: Basil Rathbone (Holmes), Nigel Bruce (Watson), Hillary Brooke (Lydia Marlowe), Henry Daniell (Moriarty), Matthew Boulton (Inspector Gregson). The eleventh entry in the Rathbone-Bruce cycle attempted to revive the flagging series by reintroducing the popular and infamous Professor Moriarty, even though he had been twice killed off, in *The Adventures of Sherlock Holmes* (1939) and *Sherlock Holmes and the Secret Weapon* (1942). This time around, Universal cast Henry Daniell, a suave performer who had appeared in minor roles elsewhere in the series. To spice things up even further, the script introduced the seductress Lydia Marlowe (Brooke). Like Daniell, Brooke had appeared previously in the series, in *Sherlock Holmes and the Voice of Terror* and *Sherlock Holmes Faces Death*. Holmes's aid is enlisted by Scotland Yard to help solve the grim "Finger Murders," so-called because the victims, invariably young women, have their right thumbs cut off. The detective soon traces the evil genius behind the affair, Professor Moriarty. Hypnosis figures prominently in the plot, used to try to lead Holmes to his death and to hoodwink the easily controlled Watson. Holmes pretends to be in a trance, escaping an imminent demise high atop a building. It is Moriarty, however, who takes the plunge, marking the final fall for the professor at Universal Studios.

WOMBWELL, GEORGE. The owner of several well-known circuses in "The Veiled Lodger" who was a rival of the showmen Sanger and Ronder.

WONTNER, ARTHUR. One of the most popular portrayors of Holmes (1875–1960) who appeared as the detective on screen, television, and radio. Born in London, Wontner's early career was spent as a romantic lead—he played Raffles, swashbucklers, and Captain Hook. Interestingly, in 1926, he took part in the stage play *The Captive*, in New York, with Basil Rathbone. He did not play Holmes until 1931 when he was fifty-six, quite old for the part, older than Basil Rathbone when he started out as the detective. Nevertheless, Wontner succeeded brilliantly, using his very Holmesian appearance to great effect, although he did wear a toupe in the first films that hid his bald spot but not his high forehead. His Holmes films were *The Sleeping Cardinal* (1932), *The Sign of Four* (1932), *The Triumph of Sherlock Holmes* (1935), and *Silver Blaze*

(1937). In 1943, he returned to Holmes for the BBC radio production of "Boscombe Valley Mystery" with Carleton Hobbs, who was to become a well-known radio Holmes. Finally, in 1951, Wontner appeared as the detective on television as part of the Festival of Britain.

WOOD, DR. A general practitioner from Birlstone, Sussex who examined the body thought to be John Douglas at Birlstone Manor in *The Valley of Fear*. He was considered "brisk and capable."

WOOD, HENRY. A onetime soldier of the 117th in India in "The Crooked Man," Wood competed with Sargent James Barclay for the affections of Nancy Devoy, eventually losing, not to Barclay but because he was captured by Sepoy mutineers during the Indian mutiny. Tortured and held prisoner for many years, he spent time in Nepal before finally escaping. Wandering through Afghanistan and the Punjab, he lived among the natives and survived by performing conjuring tricks. After many years, he returned to England and there encountered the woman he had once loved.

Henry Wood makes a dramatic return in "The Crooked Man"; by Sidney Paget.

An interesting close-up of Arthur Wonter as Holmes, from *The Missing Rembrandt* (1932).

WOOD, J. G.   English writer (1827–1889) on natural history, the author of *Out of Doors* (1874), a collection of essays that proved crucial to Holmes's solution of the death of Fitzroy McPherson in "The Lion's Mane."

WOODHOUSE.   The criminal was one of fifty men mentioned in "The Bruce-Partington Plans" who had "good reason" for taking Holmes's life.

WOODLEY, EDITH.   The onetime fiancée of the Hon. Ronald Adair in "The Empty House." A resident of Carstairs, she and Adair broke off their engagement several months prior to Adair's bizarre murder but "there was no sign that it had left any very profound feeling behind it."

WOODLEY, JACK.   Nicknamed "Roaring Jack" Woodley, "the greatest brute and bully in South Africa" who was a friend and co-conspirator with Bob Carruthers in "The Solitary Cyclist." Woodley was described by Violet Smith as hideous and odious. Holmes was quite successful in ruining Woodley's planned activities, from sending him home half conscious in a cart after a fistfight to destroying his wider plans for Violet Smith.

WORTHINGDON BANK GANG.   The five men who, in 1875, robbed the Worthingdon Bank of 7,000 pounds and killed the bank's caretaker, Tobin. The conspirators were Biddle, Moffat, Hayward, Cartwright, and Sutton. Arrested, Sutton turned informer. Cartwright was hanged and the other three received fifteen years each. Eventually released early, the three fulfilled their vows for revenge upon Sutton in the case recounted in "The Resident Patient."

WRIGHT, THERESA.   The intensely loyal maid and onetime nurse of Lady Mary Brackenstall in "The Abbey Grange." She supported Lady Mary's account that three men had broken into the Abbey Grange and killed Sir Eustace Brackenstall. She also did not approve of Sir Eustace's treatment of Mary.

X-Y-Z

XX.31.   The private phone number of Sir James Damery in "The Illustrious Client." He could be reached there in cases of emergency.

YEAR BOOK.   A series of annual collections of notes and reports related to Holmes's cases was kept by Dr. Watson, who wrote that there was a "long row of year-books which fill a shelf, and there are the dispatch-cases filled with documents, a perfect quarry for the student not only of crime but of the social and official scandals of the late Victorian era." Watson made mention of the books specifically for the years 1887 ("The Five Orange Pips"), 1890 ("The Final Problem"), 1894 ("The Golden Pince-Nez"), and 1895 ("The Solitary Cyclist").

"YELLOW FACE, THE" (YELL).   Published: *Strand*, February 1893, *Harper's*, February 11, 1893; collected in *The Memoirs of Sherlock Holmes* (1894). Major players: Holmes, Watson, Grant Munro, Effie Munro. Case date: Various, 1882–1889 (Baring-Gould date: 1888). One of

Holmes's few investigations that ends in complete failure and that warrants an apology from Watson at the beginning: "It is only natural that I should dwell rather upon his successes than upon his failures . . . Now and again, however, it chanced that even when he erred the truth was still discovered. I have of some half-dozen cases of the kind . . ." Holmes is consulted by Grant Munro, a hop merchant from Norbury. His wife, Effie, has been acting very strangely. She has asked for 100 pounds (of her own money) and has been paying visits at odd hours to a neighboring cottage. To make matters even more confounding, Munro has seen a "yellow livid face" peering out of the window of the cottage. Holmes forms an opinion as to the solution and sticks with it, a surmise that does not fit with Munro's account or his preliminary examinations of the case. Even the usually ever-faithful Watson has to warn the detective that it is "all surmise." As a result of the debacle that follows, Holmes tells Watson, "if it should ever strike you that I am getting a little overconfident in my powers, or giving less pains to a case than it deserves, kindly whisper, 'Norbury' in my ear, and I shall be infinitely obliged to you."

"YOU HAVE BEEN IN AFGHANISTAN, I PERCEIVE." A well-known quote from Holmes, remembered as being his first words to Dr. Watson. In *A Study in Scarlet*, the good doctor wrote:

" 'Dr. Watson, Mr. Sherlock Holmes', said Stamford, introducing us.

'How are you?' he said cordially, gripping my hand with a strength for which I should hardly have given him credit. 'You have been in Afghanistan, I perceive.' "

YOUGHAL. A Scotland Yard officer who assisted Holmes in recovering the Mazarin Stone and arresting the thieves in "The Mazarin Stone."

"YOUNG SHERLOCK." England 1982. Dir: Nicholas Ferguson. Cast: Guy Henry (Holmes). The British television series produced and written by Gerald Frow covers an area of Holmes's life virtually untouched by the Canon—his youth. Guy Henry plays the future detective at sixteen; he is already self-assured, logical, and arrogant, replete with deerstalker and cape. As still a young person

he was presumably too young to smoke. The series, lasting only eight episodes, was probably the inspiration for the Steven Spielberg film *Young Sherlock Holmes* (1985).

YOUNG SHERLOCK HOLMES. U.S. 1985. Dir: Barry Levinson. Cast: Nicholas Rowe (Holmes), Alan Cox (Watson), Anthony Higgins (Rathe) and Roger Ashton-Griffiths (Lestrade). A major production from Amblin Entertainment (Steven Spielberg's production company), that may have taken its inspiration from the British television series "Young Sherlock." It examines in lush detail the early years of Holmes, around the time of his education in a boarding school. He soon meets the equally young Watson and the two are thrown into an adventure featuring Egyptian revenge, a terrifying cult in London, and the terrible machinations of the cult's leader. While the film at times seems more like *Sherlock Holmes and the Temple of Doom*, it does manage to cover such Canonical subjects as Holmes's violin playing, fencing, aversion to women, and the genesis of the Holmes-Moriarty conflict. Nicholas Rowe is excellent as the young detective, with exactly the right look and temperament. Viewers should be warned that some of the scenes are *very* intense for younger children; they should also be sure to watch the credits all the way to the end as a surprise is in store for the patient viewer.

YOXLEY OLD PLACE. A country house in Kent situated seven miles from Chatham that is featured in "The Golden Pince-Nez." It was the site of the murder of Willoughby Smith, secretary to Professor Coram. Stanley Hopkins drew a chart of the house as it related to the case:

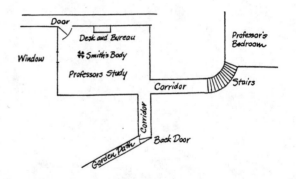

ZAMBA. See CASTALOTTE, TITO.

ZINC. An element that allowed Holmes to track down a counterfeiter in "Shoscombe Old Place." The detective was able to trace the criminal by the zinc and copper filings in the seam of his cuff.

ZUCCO, GEORGE. See ADVENTURES OF SHERLOCK HOLMES, THE (1939); SHERLOCK HOLMES IN WASHINGTON; and MORIARTY, PROFESSOR.

The Writings of Sherlock Holmes

Sherlock Holmes was a surprisingly prolific and gifted writer, authoring a variety of works—from monographs and assorted studies to two chronicles of his cases. Despite the efforts of Sherlockians for decades to find the literary labors of the Great Detective, only two of his writings are extant: "The Adventure of the Blanched Soldier" and "The Adventure of the Lion's Mane." The following is a list of Holmes's writings. (For details of each, please see under individual entries.)

The Book of Life—published anonymously.

Upon the Distinction between the Ashes of the Various Tobaccos: An Enumeration of 140 Forms of Cigar, Cigarette, and Pipe Tobacco, with Coloured Plates Illustrating the Differences in the Ash.

On the Dating of Manuscripts.

The Tracing of Footsteps, with Some Remarks upon the Uses of Plaster of Paris as a Preserver of Impresses.

On Tattoo Marks.

A Study of the Influence of a Trade upon the Form of the Hand, with Lithotypes of the Hands of Slaters, Sailors, Cork-cutters, Compositors, Weavers, and Diamond-cutters.

Explorations in Tibet—published under the name of Sigerson, a Norwegian explorer.

Report of a Visit to the Khalifa at Khartoum—written for the Foreign Office.

A Study of the Chaldean Roots in the Ancient Cornish Language.

On the Polyphonic Motets of Lassus.

Two short monographs on the variations in the shape of the human ear.

Secret Writings: Analyses of 160 Separate Ciphers.

"The Adventure of the Blanched Soldier."

"The Adventure of the Lion's Mane."

Practical Handbook of Bee Culture, with Some Observations Upon the Segregation of the Queen.

The Whole Art of Detection—probably unpublished.

The Typewriter and its Relation to Crime—probably unpublished.

Uses of Dogs in Detection—probably unpublished.

Early English Charters—probably unpublished.

Artists of the Canon

Throughout the long publishing history of the Canon, *Strand, Collier's, Harper's,* and other magazines featured a wide variety of excellent illustrators to add atmosphere and color to the already excellent stories. D. H. Friston was the first illustrator, drawing extensively for *Beeton's Christmas Annual* (1887). When *A Study in Scarlet* was later republished, this time on its own in 1891, the book was illustrated by George Hutchinson. He included the dramatic first meeting of Holmes and Watson. For *The Sign of Four*, published in book form in 1890, there was only one illustration, a frontispiece by Charles Kerr.

The *Strand Magazine* began publishing the stories in July 1891, launching an association with the Great Detective that would last for many years. Their artists included H. M. Brock, H. K. Elcock, Albert Gilbert, and Walter Paget, but the most remembered of all illustrators for the publication was Walter's brother SIDNEY PAGET. Overlooked by many casual readers of Holmes stories is the fact that tales about the detective flourished in the United States as well, especially in *Collier's,* whose greatest artist was Frederic Dorr Steele. The following is a list of artists who contributed illustrations during the initial publishing history of the Canon.

Ball, Alec—*Strand,* "The Disappearance of Lady Frances Carfax."

Benda, W. T.—*Hearst's International,* "The Sussex Vampire."

Brock, H. M.—*Strand,* "The Red Circle," Part One.

Edwards, H. C.—*McClure's* (U.S.), "The Final Problem."

Elcock, H. K.—*Strand,* "The Creeping Man," "The Illustrious Client," "The Lion's Mane," "The Sussex Vampire," "The Three Gables," "The Three Garridebs," "The Blanched Soldier."

Flanagan, J. R.—*Collier's* (U.S.), "The Three Garridebs," "The Illustrious Client."

Gilbert, Albert—*Strand,* "The Mazarin Stone," "His Last Bow," "Thor Bridge."

Haliday, Gilbert—*Strand,* "The Devil's Foot."

Hutchinson, George—*A Study in Scarlet* (second printing).

Hyde, W. H.—*Harper's* (U.S.), "Silver Blaze," "The Yellow Face," "The Stockbroker's Clerk," "The 'Gloria Scott'," "The Musgrave Ritual," "The Reigate Squires," "The Crooked Man," "The Resident Patient," "The Greek Interpreter," "The Naval Treaty."

Keller, A. I.—*Philadelphia Press* (U.S.), *The Valley of Fear.*

Kerr, Charles—*The Sign of Four* (Frontispiece).

Nelson, G. Patrick—*Hearst's International,* "Thor Bridge."

Paget, Sidney—*Strand,* stories appearing in the collections *The Adventures of Sherlock Holmes, The Memoirs of Sherlock Holmes, The Return of Sherlock Holmes,* plus "The Cardboard Box," *A Study in Scarlet,* and *The Hound of the Baskervilles.*

Paget, Walter—*Strand,* "The Dying Detective."

Simpson, Joseph—*Strand,* "The Red Circle," Part Two.

Steele, Frederic Dorr—*Collier's* (U.S.), "The Empty House," "The Norwood Builder," "The Dancing Men," "The Solitary Cyclist," "The Priory School," "Black Peter," "Charles Augustus Milverton," "The Six Napoleons," "The Three Students," "The Golden Pince-Nez," "The Missing Three-Quarter," "The Abbey Grange," "The Second Stain," "Wisteria Lodge," "The Bruce-Partington Plans," "The Disappearance of Lady Frances Carfax," "The Dying Detective," "His Last Bow"; *Hearst's International,* "The Mazarin Stone," "The Creeping Man"; *Liberty,* "The Three Gables," "The Blanched Soldier," "The Lion's Mane," "The Retired Colourman," "The Veiled Lodger," "Shoscombe Old Place."

Wiles, Frank—*Strand, The Valley of Fear,* "The Retired Colourman," "The Veiled Lodger," "Shoscombe Old Place."

Sherlock Holmes in Film

Date	Title	Cast	Date	Title	Cast
1903 or 1905	*Sherlock Holmes Baffled*; American Mutascope and Biograph Co. (U.S.)	Unknown.		*Droske No. 519* (1909; *Cab No. 519*)	Viggo Larsen (Holmes), Alwin Neuss (Watson?), August Blom.
1905	*The Adventures of Sherlock Holmes*; Vitagraph Co. (U.S.)	Maurice Costello (Holmes), Kyrle Bellow.		*Den Graa Dame* (1909; *The Gray Lady*)	Viggo Larsen (Holmes), Alwin Neuss (Watson?).
				La Femme (1910; *The Lady*)	Otto Lagoni (?), Alwin Neuss (?).
1907	*Le Rival de Sherlock Holmes*; Societa Anonima Ambrosio (Italy)	Unknown.		*Sherlock Holmes I Bondefangerklor* (1910, *Sherlock Holmes in the Clutches of the Confidence Men*)	Otto Lagoni (Holmes), Alwin Neuss (Watson).
1908	*Sherlock Holmes in the Great Murder Mystery*; Crescent (U.S.)	Unknown.		*Den Forklaedte Guvernante* (1911; *The Bogus Governess*)	Forrest Holger-Madsen (Holmes), Alwin Neuss (Watson).
	Nordisk Series (1908–1911; Denmark)			*Mordet I Bakerstreet* (1911, *Murder in Baker Street*)	Holger Rasmussen (Holmes), Alwin Neuss (Watson).
	Sherlock Holmes I (1908)	Forrest Holger-Madsen (Raffles), Viggo Larsen (Holmes).		*Millionobligationen* (1911, *The One Million Bond*)	Alwin Neuss (Holmes), Einar Zangenberg.
	Sherlock Holmes II (1908)	Forrest Holger-Madsen (Raffles), Viggo Larsen (Holmes).		*Hotelmysterierne* (1911, *The Hotel Mystery*)	Forrest Holger-Madsen (Holmes), Alwin Neuss (Watson).
	Sherlock Holmes III (1908)	Viggo Larsen (Holmes), Alwin Neuss (Watson?).	1908	*The Adventures of Sherlock Holmes*; Danish	Unknown.
	Sangerindens Diamanter (1909; *The Singer's Diamonds*)	Viggo Larsen (Holmes), Alwin Neuss (Watson?).	1910–1911	*Arsene Lupin contra Sherlock Holmes*; Vitascope (Germany)	Viggo Larsen (Holmes), Paul Otto (Watson).

DATE	TITLE	CAST	DATE	TITLE	CAST
The Franco-British Series (1912–1913):			1914–1920	*Der Hund von Baskerville*; Vitascope GmbH (Germany, film series)	Alwin Neuss, Eugen Burg, Friederick Zellnik, Erich Kaiser-Titz as Holmes.
	The Speckled Band (1912)	Georges Treville (Holmes), Mr. Moyse (Watson).			
	Silver Blaze (1912)	Georges Treville (Holmes), Mr. Moyse (Watson).	1916	*The Valley of Fear*; Samuelson Film (U.K.)	H. A. Saintbury (Holmes), Booth Conway (Professor Moriarty), Daisy Burrell (Ettie Douglas), Arthur Cullin (Watson), Cecil Mannering (McMurdo).
	The Beryl Coronet (1912)	Georges Treville (Holmes), Mr. Moyse (Watson).			
	The Musgrave Ritual (1913)	Georges Treville (Holmes), Mr. Moyse (Watson).		*Sherlock Holmes*; Essanay Film (U.S.)	William Gillette (Holmes), Ernest Maupain (Professor Moriarty), Edward Maupain (Watson), Marjorie Kay (Alice Faulkner).
	The Reigate Squires (1912)	Georges Treville (Holmes), Mr. Moyse (Watson).			
	The Stolen Papers (1912)	Georges Treville (Holmes), Mr. Moyse (Watson).			
	A Mystery of Boscombe Vale (1912)	Georges Treville (Holmes), Mr. Moyse (Watson).	1917	*Der Erdstrommotor* (*The Earthquake Motor*); Kowo Film (Germany)	Hugo Flink (Holmes).
	The Copper Beeches (1912)	Georges Treville (Holmes), Mr. Moyse (Watson).		*Die Kasette* (*The Casket*); Kowo Film (Germany)	Hugo Flink (Holmes).
				Der Schlagenring (*The Snake Ring*); Kowo Film (Germany)	Hugo Flink (Holmes).
1913	*Sherlock Holmes Solves the Sign of Four*; Thanhouser (U.S.)	Harry Benham (Holmes).			
1914	*A Study in Scarlet*; Samuelson Film (U.S.)	James Bragington (Holmes), Fred Paul (Jefferson Hope).	1918	*Die Indische Spinne* (*The Indian Spider*); Kowo Film (Germany)	Hugo Flink (Holmes).
	A Study in Scarlet; Gold Seal-Universal Film (U.S.)	Francis Ford (Holmes), Jack Francis (Watson).		*Was Er Im Spiegel Sah* (*What He Saw in the Mirror*); Kowo Film (Germany)	Ferdinand Bonn (Holmes).

DATE	TITLE	CAST	DATE	TITLE	CAST
	Die Gifteplombe (*The Poisoned Seal*); Kowo Film (Germany)	Ferdinand Bonn (Holmes).		*The Man with the Twisted Lip*	
				The Beryl Coronet	
				The Noble Bachelor	
				Copper Beeches	
	Das Schicksal der Renate Yongk; Kowo Film (Germany)	Ferdinand Bonn (Holmes).		*The Empty House*	
				The Tiger of San Pedro	
				The Priory School	
				The Solitary Cyclist	
	Black Sherlock Holmes; Ebony Pictures (U.S.)	Sam Robinson (Holmes).		*The Hound of the Baskervilles* (1921)	Eille Norwood (Holmes), Hubert Willis (Watson), Rex MacDougal (Sir Henry Baskerville), Lewis Gilbert (John Stapleton), Betty Campbell (Beryl Stapleton), Mme. d'Esterre (Mrs. Hudson).
	Die Dose des Kardinals (*The Cardinal's Snuffbox*); Kowo Film (Germany)	Ferdinand Bonn (Holmes).			
1919	*Der Mord im Splendid Hotel* (*The Murder in the Hotel Splendid*); Kowo Film (Germany)	Kurt Brenkendorff (Holmes).			

Stoll Picture Series (Eille Norwood; 1921–1923)

The Adventures of Sherlock Holmes (1921):

A series of fifteen films starring Eille Norwood (Holmes), Hubert Willis (Watson), and Mme. d'Esterre (Mrs. Hudson). Produced by Stoll Pictures and directed by Maurice Elvey. The fifteen include:

> *The Dying Detective*
> *The Devil's Foot*
> *A Case of Identity*
> *The Yellow Face*
> *The Red-Headed League*
> *The Resident Patient*
> *A Scandal in Bohemia*

The Further Adventures of Sherlock Holmes (1922):

A series of fifteen films starring: Eille Norwood (Holmes), Hubert Willis (Watson), and Mme. d'Esterre (Mrs. Hudson). Produced by Stoll Pictures and directed by George Ridgwell. These fifteen include:

> *Charles Augustus Milverton*
> *The Abbey Grange*
> *The Norwood Builder*
> *The Reigate Squires*
> *The Naval Treaty*
> *The Second Stain*
> *The Red Circle*
> *The Six Napoleons*
> *Black Peter*

DATE	TITLE	CAST	DATE	TITLE	CAST
	The Bruce-Partington Plans *The Stockbroker's Clerk* *The Boscombe Valley Mystery* *The Musgrave Ritual* *The Golden Pince-Nez* *The Greek Interpreter*				Elsom (Mary Morstan), Norman Page (Jonathan Small), Mme. d'Esterre (Mrs. Hudson), Arthur Bell (Inspector Jones).
			1922	*Sherlock Holmes*; Goldwyn Pictures (U.S.)	John Barrymore (Holmes), Roland Young (Watson), Gustav von Seyffertitz (Professor Moriarty), Carol Dempster (Alice Faulkner), John Willard (Inspector Gregson).

The Last Adventures of Sherlock Holmes (1923):

A series of fifteen films starring: Eille Norwood (Holmes), Hubert Willis (Watson), and Mme. d'Esterre (Mrs. Hudson). Produced by Stoll Pictures and directed by George Ridgwell. This group includes:

Silver Blaze
The Speckled Band
The Gloria Scott
The Blue Carbuncle
The Engineer's Thumb
His Last Bow
The Cardboard Box
The Disappearance of Lady Frances Carfax
The Three Students
The Missing Three-Quarter
The Mystery of Thor Bridge
The Mazarin Stone
The Dancing Men
The Crooked Man
The Final Problem

			DATE	TITLE	CAST
			1929	*Der Hund von Baskerville*; Sudfilm (Germany)	Carlyle Blackwell (Holmes), Georges Seroff (Watson), Fritz Rasp (Dr. Stapleton).
				The Return of Sherlock Holmes; Paramount (U.S.)	Clive Brook (Holmes), H. Reeves Smith (Watson), Donald Crisp (Colonel Sebastian Moran).
			1930	*Paramount On Parade—Murder Will Out*; Paramount (U.S.)	Clive Brook (Holmes), William Powell (Philo Vance), Warner Oland (Dr. Fu Manchu), H. H. Reeves-Smith (Watson).

The Sign of Four (1923) — Eille Norwood (Holmes), Arthur Cullin (Watson), Isobel

DATE	TITLE	CAST	DATE	TITLE	CAST
1931	*The Speckled Band;* British and Dominions (U.K.)	Raymond Massey (Holmes), Athole Stewart (Watson), Lyn Harding (Dr. Grimesby Rylott), Marie Ault (Mrs. Hudson).		(1932); Twickenham Studios (U.K.)	Fleming (Watson), Philip Hewland (Inspector Lestrade).
1932	*Sherlock Holmes;* Fox Film Corp. (U.S.)	Clive Brook (Holmes), Reginand Owen (Watson), Miriam Jordan (Alice Faulkner), Ernest Torrence (Professor Moriarty).		*The Sign of Four* (1932); A.R.P. Studios (U.K.)	Arthur Wontner (Holmes), Ian Hunter (Watson), Isla Bevan (Mary Morstan).
	The Hound of the Baskervilles; Gainsborough/ Ideal/Gaumont-British (U.K.)	Robert Rendel (Holmes), Fred Lloyd (Watson), John Stuart (Sir Henry Baskerville).		*The Triumph of Sherlock Holmes* (1935); Real Art Prod. (U.K.)	Arthur Wontner (Holmes); Lyn Harding (Professor Moriarty), Ian Fleming (Watson).
1933	*A Study in Scarlet;* K.B.S. Productions (U.S.)	Reginald Owen (Holmes), Warburton Gamble (Watson), Alan Mowbray (Inspector Lestrade).		*Silver Blaze* (1937, in U.S.: *Murder at the Baskervilles*); Twickenham Film Productions (U.K.)	Arthur Wontner (Holmes), Lyn Harding (Professor Moriarty), Ian Fleming (Watson), Judy Gunn (Diana Baskerville).
	Arthur Wontner (1931–1937) series:		1937	*Der Hund von Baskerville;* Oudra-Lamac-Film (Germany)	Bruno Guttner (Holmes), Fritz Odemar (Watson), Peter Voss (Lord Henry Baskerville).
	The Sleeping Cardinal (1931, in U.S.: *Sherlock Holmes' Fatal Hour*); Twickenham Film Studios (U.K.)	Arthur Wontner (Holmes), Ian Fleming (Watson), Minnie Rayner (Mrs. Hudson), Norman McKinnel (Professor Moriarty).		*Sherlock Holmes, Oder Graue Dame* (*Sherlock Holmes, or the Gray Lady*); Neue Film KG (Germany)	Hermann Speelmans (Holmes), Elizabeth Wendt (Lola), Trude Marlen (Maria Iretzkaja).
				Basil Rathbone and Nigel Bruce Series (1939–1946):	
	The Missing Rembrandt	Arthur Wonter (Holmes), Ian			

DATE	TITLE	CAST	DATE	TITLE	CAST
	The most famous and popular of all the Holmes-Watson duos. They starred in fourteen feature films, the first two for 20th Century-Fox and the rest for Universal Pictures.				Vickery), Dennis Hoey (Inspector Lestrade), Mary Gordon (Mrs. Hudson).
	The Hound of the Baskervilles (1939); 20th Century-Fox (U.S.)	Richard Greene (Sir Henry Baskerville), Wendy Barrie (Beryl Stapleton), Lionel Atwill (Dr. Mortimer), John Carradine (Barryman).		*The Spider Woman* (1944); Universal (U.S.)	Gale Sondergaard (Adrea Spedding), Dennis Hoey (Inspector Lestrade), Mary Gordon (Mrs. Hudson).
	The Adventures of Sherlock Holmes (1939); 20th Century-Fox (U.S.)	Ida Lupino (Ann Brandon), Alan Marshal (Jerrold Hunter), George Zucco (Professor Moriarty).		*The Scarlet Claw* (1944); Universal (U.S.)	Gerald Hamer (Potts), Paul Cavanagh (Lord Penrose), Miles Mander (Judge Brisson), Ian Wolfe (Drake).
	Sherlock Holmes and the Voice of Terror (1942); Universal (U.S.)	Evelyn Ankers (Kitty), Reginald Denny (Sir Evan Barham), Henry Daniell (Sir Alfred Lloyd).		*The Pearl of Death* (1944); Universal (U.S.)	Dennis Hoey (Inspector Lestrade), Evelyn Ankers (Namoi Drake), Ian Wolfe (Amos Hodder), Rondo Hatton (The Creeper).
	Sherlock Holmes and the Secret Weapon (1942); Universal (U.S.)	Karen Verne (Charlotte Eberli), Lionel Atwill (Professor Moriarty), Dennis Hoey (Inspector Lestrade), Mary Gordon (Mrs. Hudson).		*The House of Fear* (1945); Universal (U.S.)	Aubrey Mather (Alastair), Dennis Hoey (Inspector Lestrade), Paul Cavanagh (Simon Merrivale).
	Sherlock Holmes in Washington (1943); (U.S.)	Marjorie Lord (Nancy Partridge), Henry Daniell (William Easter), George Zucco (Stanley).		*The Woman in Green* (1945); Universal (U.S.)	Hillary Brooke (Lydia Marlowe), Henry Daniell (Professor Moriarty), Matthew Boulton (Inspector Gregson), Mary Gordon (Mrs. Hudson).
	Sherlock Holmes Faces Death (1943); Universal (U.S.)	Hillary Brooke (Sally Musgrave), Milburn Stone (Captain			

DATE	TITLE	CAST	DATE	TITLE	CAST
	Pursuit to Algiers (1945); Universal (U.S.)	Marjorie Riordan (Lydia Marlowe), Rosalind Ivan (Agatha Dunham), Leslie Vincent (Nikolas).	1970	*The Private Life of Sherlock Holmes*; Mirisch/United Artists (U.S.)	Robert Stephens (Holmes), Colin Blakeley (Watson), Irene Handl (Mrs. Hudson), Christopher Lee (Mycroft), Genevieve Page (Mme. Valladon).
	Terror By Night (1946); Universal (U.S.)	Alan Mowbray (Major Bleek), Dennis Hoey (Inspector Lestrade), Mary Forbes (Lady Carstairs).			
			1971	*Touha Sherlocka Holmese* (*Sherlock Holmes' Desire*); Czechoslovak Film (Czechoslovakia)	Radovan Lukavsky (Holmes), Vaclav Voska (Watson), Vlasta Fialova (Lady Abraham), Josef Patocka (Sir Arthur Conan Doyle).
	Dressed to Kill (1946, U.K.: *Sherlock Holmes and the Secret Code*); Universal (U.S.)	Patricia Morrison (Hilda Courtney), Edmond Breon (Gilbert Emery), Mary Gordon (Mrs. Hudson).			
			1975	*The Adventures of Sherlock Holmes' Smarter Brother*; 20th Century-Fox (U.S.)	Gene Wilder (Sigerson Holmes), Madeline Kahn (Bessie Bellwood), Marty Feldman (Sergeant Orville Sacker), Leo McKern (Moriarty), Douglas Wilmer (Holmes), Thorley Walters (Watson).
1959	*The Hound of the Baskervilles*; Hammer Films (U.K.)	Peter Cushing (Holmes), Andre Morell (Watson), Christopher Lee (Sir Henry Baskerville), Francis de Wolfe (Dr. Mortimer).			
1962	*Sherlock Holmes und das Halsband des Todes* (*Sherlock Holmes and the Necklace of Death*); CC/ Criterion (German/Italian)	Christopher Lee (Holmes), Thorley Walters (Watson), Senta Berger (Ellen Blackburn), Hans Sohnker (Moriarty).	1976	*The Seven-Per-Cent Solution*; United Artists (U.S.)	Nicol Williamson (Holmes), Robert Duvall (Watson), Alan Arkin (Dr. Sigmund Freud), Laurence Olivier (Moriarty), Vanessa Redgrave (Lola Devereaux).
1965	*A Study in Terror*; Compton-Cameo Films (U.K.)	John Neville (Holmes), Donald Huston (Watson), John Fraser (Lord Carfax), Anthony Quayle (Dr. Murray).			

DATE	TITLE	CAST	DATE	TITLE	CAST
1977	*The Hound of the Baskervilles*; Avco/Embassy (Canada)	Peter Cook (Holmes), Dudley Moore (Watson), Denholm Elliott (Dr. Mortimer), Joan Greenwood (Beryl Stapleton).	1985	*Young Sherlock Holmes*; Paramount (U.S.)	Nicholas Rowe (Holmes), Alan Cox (Watson), Anthony Higgins (Rathe), Roger Ashton-Griffiths (Lestrade)
1979	*Murder By Decree*; Avco/Embassy/Warner (Canada)	Christopher Plummer (Holmes), James Mason (Watson), David Hemmings (Inspector Fox), Betty Woolfe (Mrs. Hudson), Frank Finlay (Inspector Lestrade), Anthony Quayle (Sir Charles Warren).	1990	*Without a Clue*; Orion (U.S.)	Michael Caine (Holmes), Ben Kingsley (Watson), Paul Freeman (Moriarty), Jeffrey Jones (Inspector Lestrade), Pat Keen (Mrs. Hudson)

Appendix

Sir Arthur Conan Doyle (1859–1930)

A Scottish physician, writer, and novelist, the creator of Sherlock Holmes was also an avid sportsman, a war correspondent, and an ardent student of spiritualism.

Arthur Conan Doyle was born on May 22, 1859, in Edinburgh, Scotland, the son of Charles Doyle and Mary Foley. Both parents came from Irish families, but his mother also claimed descent from the Percy family of Northumberland, meaning Arthur could trace himself back to the Plantagenets. His father was a civil servant by profession, but he was also a talented painter. Unfortunately he also suffered from alcoholism and epilepsy, requiring institutionalization for the last years of his life. Doyle's mother instilled in him a romantic streak, regaling him with tales of his Irish ancestors, an upbringing that would influence heavily Doyle's determination to author romantic historical novels on British history.

One of ten children (seven would live to maturity), young Arthur had a difficult childhood. He studied at home and in the local school before entering the Jesuit school of Hodder in Lancashire. After attending the Jesuit secondary school of Stonyhurst, he spent a year in Austria and then spent 1876–1881 at the University of Edinburgh studying medicine. It was while at Edinburgh that Doyle met Dr. Joseph Bell, his tutor. This physician, with his remarkable deductive powers, would serve as a basis for Sherlock Holmes.

After holding several jobs, including a time as a ship's doctor for voyages to the coast of West Africa and the arctic, Doyle accepted an offer in 1882 from Dr. George Budd, a former schoolmate at Edinburgh, to join him in a practice in Plymouth. Their dealings proved less than cordial and Doyle soon moved out, establishing himself instead in a practice as an oculist in Southsea. As the new practice began slowly, Doyle had large amounts of free time to devote to a particular passion of his—writing.

Doyle had sold his first story, "The Mystery of Sassassa Valley," to *Chamber's Journal* while still in school, but his early efforts to publish novels were not particularly successful. For example, one manuscript, *The Narrative of John Smith*, was lost in the mail. He thus gradually came to focus on detective fiction, deciding to attempt to create a literary sleuth. Influenced by the writings of Edgar Allan Poe and Emile Gaboriau, Doyle experimented with several names and attributes for his detective, finally settling on Sherlock Holmes; the tales themselves, he decided, should be narrated by a doctor of Scottish birth, Dr. John H. Watson. The story, *A Study in Scarlet*, was finally purchased by Ward, Lock, and Co. and was published in *Beeton's Christmas Annual* in 1887. Doyle was paid a grand total of 25 pounds for the work, no royalties.

In 1885, Doyle had married Louisa Hawkins, the sister of a patient. She gave birth to two children, a son and a daughter, and encouraged her husband in his literary pursuits. Nicknamed "Touie," she was never in good health. Her eventual bouts with tuberculosis would compel Doyle to take her to winter in Egypt in 1895, a trip that would provide Doyle with the plot for the drama "The Tragedy of the Korosho." Touie died on July 4, 1906.

Meanwhile, *A Study in Scarlet* was moderately successful. Nevertheless, Doyle was encouraged to attempt a longer, more traditional novel, a historical work called *Micah Clarke*, published in 1889. The following year, he was invited to a dinner with J. M. Stoddard, a representative of *Lippincott's Monthly Magazine* of Philadelphia. (Another guest was Oscar Wilde.) As a result of the encounter, Doyle was commissioned to write another Holmes story, what would become *The Sign of Four* (1890). (Wilde was also asked to write a novel, which would become *The Picture of Dorian Gray*, 1891.)

In 1890, Doyle travelled to Vienna to continue medical studies, and returning to London in early 1891, he rented rooms with his wife at Montague

Sir Arthur Conan Doyle's coat of arms as it appears on his bookplate from *The Baker Street Journal*, September 1962).

Place, setting himself up at 2 Devonshire Place. As patients were not visiting in large numbers, Conan Doyle decided to write more Holmes stories, sending "The Science of Vision," "A Scandal in Bohemia" and "The Red-Headed League" to a recently established magazine that had already purchased one of his articles. Their response was enthusiastic and in July 1891 Holmes and Watson first appeared in the pages of *Strand Magazine*.

The reaction was more than Doyle could have hoped for, but within two years he had grown so tired of Holmes that he decided the time had come to kill him off. Already in November of 1891 he had been visited by thoughts of ridding himself of the demanding detective, writing to his mother that Holmes "takes my mind from better things." Those better things to which he referred were the historical novels such as *Micah Clarke* that Doyle felt to be far more important and that he hoped would bring lasting notoriety.

It was probably during a trip to Switzerland in 1893 that Doyle first came up with the actual mechanics of Sherlock's demise. One of the stops on his itinerary was the impressive Reichenbach Falls. Here, looking down at the swirling waters, he perhaps conceived of the epic struggle between Holmes and Moriarty that was to appear in "The Final Problem" in December 1893. (An interesting side note to the Swiss adventure was the oft told legend that Doyle was responsible for introducing skiing to the Alps.)

After their trip to Egypt, during which Doyle had acted as a war correspondent for *The Westminster Gazette* in the bloody conflict with the Dervishes, Doyle moved the family to Surrey. As Holmes was "dead," Doyle concentrated on writing other works, most notably *Rodney Stone*, a novel on the Regency, and the fast moving and highly entertaining character Brigadier Gerard.

In 1900, Doyle became involved in the Boer War in South Africa, volunteering his medical services to his country's armed forces. He sailed for Cape Town in February 1900. Subsequently, he authored two important works on the conflict: *The History of the Great Boer War* (1901) and the pamphlet "The War in South Africa: Its Causes and Conduct" (1902). The latter was written to refute the widespread accusations of British atrocities during the war and to justify the often brutal actions of British troops. It was Doyle's personal opinion that his defense of the war won him a knighthood (Knight of Grace of the Order of St. John of Jerusalem) and appointment as Deputy-Lieutenant of Surrey.

As Louisa had died in 1906, Doyle married Jean Leckie the following year. They had maintained a completely proper friendship during the long period of Touie's illness and their marriage proved a happy one. At their wedding, one of the honored guests was George Edalji, whom Doyle had helped free from prison and wrongful prosecution, only one of the many real-life investigations that people routinely brought to Doyle as the creator of the Great Detective. (Another notable case was that of Oscar Slater.)

The Doyle family moved to Sussex a short time later. More books followed, such as *The Lost World* (1912), marking the arrival of Doyle's third very memorable character (with Holmes and Brigadier Gerard), Professor Challenger. Holmes, however, had also managed to come to back to life, although it had taken many years for Doyle to acquiesce to public demands. The degree to which the public adored Holmes had been made clear to him back in 1893, when angry crowds harangued him for murdering off the detective, or wore black armbands in protest. In August 1901, public jubilation erupted with the publication by the *Strand* of the first installment of *The Hound of the Baskervilles*, but this proved a posthumous account by Dr. Watson. It was not until September 1903 and "The Adventure of the Empty House" that Holmes returned in full glory. Doyle would continue to write new Holmes stories for the next 24 years, culminating with "The Adventure of Shoscombe Old Place," published in March 1927 in the American magazine *Liberty*.

During the interval of those years, Doyle had served in the Crowborough Volunteer Regiment during World War I and had continued to write novels, stories, histories, and even stage plays. His last years, however, particularly from 1916, were devoted almost exclusively to the study of spiritualism. He eventually authored some thirty books on the subject, became a brief friend of Harry Houdini, and travelled extensively to America, Canada, and Australia in the pursuit of legitimate mediums and paranormal experiences.

Sir Arthur died on July 7, 1930, after suffering a severe heart attack. He had promised to send a message from beyond the grave to his loved ones, but no such communication has, apparently, ever arrived.

Doyle, of course, is known the world over for his Sherlock Holmes stories, but he wanted to be remembered for his other writings. These other works were considerable. Aside from his Brigadier Gerard and Professor Challenger books, he wrote such historical novels as *Micah Clarke*, *Uncle Bernac*, and *The White Company* (on the Hundred Years War), and a vast number of short stories on adventure, horror, and the supernatural. Collections of his short stories include: *Dreamland and Ghostland* (1887), *The Captain of the Polestar* (1890), *Round the Fire Stories* (1908), and *The Black Door and Other Tales of Terror and Mystery* (1935, posthumous).

Sherlock Holmes Societies

The following is a list of the more than 300 societies around the world devoted to the study and appreciation of the Great Detective. Readers should be aware, of course, that the addresses are the most current ones available, but organizations often cease functioning and new ones start up with considerable regularity. There almost certainly will be a society located near the reader or one devoted to some area of Sherlockiana that holds special appeal. Anyone interested in joining one of these fine organizations is encouraged to do so. Special thanks must be given to Peter Blau for his kindness in supplying this list.

ACTIVE SHERLOCKIAN SOCIETIES (GEOGRAPHICAL):

The Sydney Passengers
Lionel E. Fredman
History Department
University of Newcastle
New South Wales 2308,
　AUSTRALIA

The Resident Patients of
　Toowoomba
Michael J. Farrell
86 Bridge Street
Toowoomba, Queensland 4350
AUSTRALIA

The Sherlock Holmes Society of
　Australia
Alan C. Olding
P.O. Box 13
Stirling, S.A. 5152
AUSTRALIA

The Elementary Victorians
Steve Duke
P.O. Box 340
Reservoir, Vic. 3073
AUSTRALIA

The Sherlock Holmes Society of
　Western Australia
Douglas Sutherland-Bruce
P.O. Box 74
Sawyers Valley, W.A. 6074
AUSTRALIA

The Singular Society of the Baker
　Street Dozen
Lin Johns
51 Templeridge Place NE
Calgary, AB T1Y 4E4
CANADA

The C.P.R. Stockholder's Society
Peter H. Wood
25 Bellevue Crescent
St. Albert, AB T8N 0A5
CANADA

The Binomial Theorists of
　Nanaimo
W. E. Ricker
3052 Hammond Bay Road
Nanaimo, BC V9T 1E2
CANADA

The Stormy Petrels of British
　Columbia
Fran Martin
10662 129 Street
Surrey, BC V3T 3H4
CANADA

The Great Herd of Bisons of the
　Fertile Plains
Laurie Harper-Winning
6132 Betsworth Avenue
Winnipeg, Man. R3R 0K1
CANADA

The Halifax Spence Munros
Madonna R. Hill
15 Hemming Court
Dartmouth, NS B2W 5E4
CANADA

The Midland Electric Company
Bob Coghill
Woodman's Lee
Griffith, ON X0J 2R0
CANADA

The Whodunit Society
Michael Shumacher
22 Stroud Crescent
London, ON N6E 1Z6
CANADA

Capital Holmes
Sheila Vaudrey
2217 Iris Street
Ottawa, ON K2C 1B7
CANADA

The Bootmakers of Toronto
Maureen Green
47 Manor Road West
Toronto, ON M5P 1E6
CANADA

The Bimetallic Question
Wilfrid de Freitas
Box 883, Stock Exchange Tower
Montréal, PQ H4Z 1K2
CANADA

The Casebook of Saskatoon
William A. S. Sarjeant
Dept. of Geological Sciences
University of Saskatchewan
Saskatoon, Sask. S7N 0W0,
　CANADA

The A. C. Doyle & Sherlock
　Holmes Society of Copenhagen
Lubomir P. Maxa
Abelcathrinesgade 9
DK-1654 Kobenhavn V
DENMARK

Sherlock Holmes Klubben i
   Danmark (The Danish Baker
   Street Irregulars)
Bjarne Nielsen
Nansensgade 70
DK-1366 Kobenhavn K
DENMARK

Les Quincailliers de la Franco-
   Midland
Thierry Saint-Joanis
47 rue de Montmorency
75003 Paris
FRANCE

Le cercle des eleves de Harry
   Dixon
Gerard Dole
10 rue de Buci
Paris 75006
FRANCE

The Sherlock Holmes Society of
   Madras
Dr. G. Krishnamurthi
32 East Mada Street
Mylapore, Madras 600 004
INDIA

The Sherlock Holmes Society of
   India
Ramesh C. Madan
P.O. Box 8854
Vasant Vihar, New Delhi 110057
INDIA

The Sherlock Holmes Society of
   Jerusalem
Moshe Nalick
Kiryat Telshe-Stone 114/3
D.N. Harei Yehuda
ISRAEL

Uno Studio in Holmes
Francesco Leprai
Via Aurelia Antica 268
58046 Marina di Grosseto
ITALY

The Japan Sherlock Holmes Club
   (Marronier Branch)
Kumeo Nakajima
8 Tsukiya-cho
Ashikaga City, Tochigi
JAPAN

The Japan Sherlock Holmes Club
   (Fukuoka Branch)
Shigehide Hayashi
4-38-10 Hibaru, Minami-ku
Fukuoka-shi, Fukuoka 815
JAPAN

The Society of the Three
   Schoolgirls
Miss Kaori Tazuke
Nakachi 1433-9, Itsukaichi-cho
Saeki-ku, Hiroshima-shi 731-51
JAPAN

The Japan Sherlock Holmes Club
   (Kitakyushu Branch)
Masako Tanaka
2-9-17 Tsukida, Yahata-higashi-ku
Kitakyushu-shi, Fukuoka 805
JAPAN

The Japan Sherlock Holmes Club
   (Midland Branch)
Shin-ichi Enomoto
7-105-303 Higashi-umetsubo-cho
Toyota-shi, Aichi 471
JAPAN

The Baskerville Club
Koji Matsuya
241-1 Kawakami-cho
Nara 630
JAPAN

The Red Circle of Niigata
Yukio Yamazaki
2814-2 Utino Katabata
Niigata-shi 950-21
JAPAN

The Adventure of the Empty
   House Club
Mari Hirose
3-14-21 Ihuko-cho
Okayama City, Okayama 700
JAPAN

Butsumetsukai
Ryohei Matsushita
Nakayamadai 1-3-19
Takarazuka, Hiyoga
JAPAN

The Sendai Holmesian Society
Masayuki Kikuchi
1-17-1-115 Tousyougu, Aoba-ku
Sendai-shi, Miyagi 981
JAPAN

The Japan Sherlock Holmes Club
   (Nagano Branch)
Akira Hara
140 Kumashiro Toyooka-Mura
Shimoina-Gun, Nagano-Ken
   399-32
JAPAN

The Japan Sherlock Holmes Club
Tsukasa Kobayashi
Ohizumi-machi 2-55-8
Nerima-ku, Tokyo 178
JAPAN

The Japanese Cabinet
Keith E. Webb
1297-10 Aobadai
Tokorozawa, Saitama 359
JAPAN

The Men with the Twisted Konjo
Yuichi Hirayama
2-10-12 Kamirenjaku, Mitaka-shi
Tokyo 181
JAPAN

The Baritsu Society of Japan
Kiyoshi Tanaka
8-7 Baba cho, Isogo-ku
Yokohama City, Kanagawa 235
JAPAN

The Tokyo Nonpareil Club
Ryoichi Ando
1-14-1-412 Kamoi
Midori-ku, Yokohama 226
JAPAN

The Bird Island Club
Kazumi Hayashi
67-5 Fukuichi
Yonago-shi, Tottori-ken 683
JAPAN

Os Naufragos do Norah Creina
   [The Norah Creina Castaways]
Joel Lima
Largo do Mastro 29-3, Porta D
1100 Lisboa
PORTUGAL

Actas de Baker Street
Joan Proubasta
Camelies 83
08024 Barcelona
SPAIN

The Amateur Mendicant Society
   [Madrid]
Miguel González Pedel
General Margallo 33 (4C)
28020 Madrid
SPAIN

The Baskerville Hall Club of
   Sweden
Anders Wiggström
Byggmästarvägen 29
5-161 45 Bromma
SWEDEN

The Reichenbach Irregulars
Mrs. Bice Musfeld
P.O. Box 678
CH-3860 Meiringen
SWITZERLAND

**The Abbey Grangers of
    Chislehurst**
Colin Prestige
34 Pont Street
London SW1X 0AD
ENGLAND

The Cardboard Boxers of Croydon
Andrew A. P. Butler
64 Frith Road
Croydon, Surrey CR0 1TA
ENGLAND

The Baskerville Hounds
Philip Weller
6 Bramham Moor, Hill Head
Fareham, Hampshire P014 3RU
ENGLAND

The Poor Folk Upon the Moors
Clare Taylor
2 Lynbridge Court, Chapel Street
Tavistock, Devonshire PL19 8DU
ENGLAND

**The Franco-Midland Hardware
    Company**
Philip Weller
6 Bramham Moor, Hill Head
Fareham, Hampshire P014 3RU
ENGLAND

The Priory Scholars of Leicester
Philip Weller
6 Bramham Moor, Hill Head
Fareham, Hampshire P014 3RU
ENGLAND

**The Sherlock Holmes
    International Society**
John Aidiniantz
The Sherlock Holmes Museum
221b Baker Street
London NW1 6XE, ENGLAND

**The Sherlock Holmes Society of
    London**
Cdr. Geoffrey Stavert
3 Outram Road
Southsea, Hants, PO5 1QP
ENGLAND

The Glades of the New Forest
Emma Barrow
87 East Avenue
Bournemouth, Dorset BH3 7BJ
ENGLAND

**The Oxford University Sherlock
    Holmes Society**
Roger Mortimore
University College
Oxford OX1 4BH
ENGLAND

The Fratton Lodgers
Ian Smyth
31 Sandfield Crescent
Cowplain, Hampshire
ENGLAND

The Reichenbach Society
S.T.W. Lew-Gor
1 Townend Street, Crookes
Sheffield, S. Yorks. S10 1NJ
ENGLAND

The Head Llamas
Alan and Catherine Saunders
12 Booth Drive, Laleham
Staines, Middlesex TW18 1PR
ENGLAND

The Northern Musgraves
John Addy
23 East Street, Lightcliffe
Halifax, W. Yorks. HX3 8TU
ENGLAND

The Crew of the S.S. *May Day*
Maurice Milligan
98 Victoria Road
Belfast BT4 1QW, Northern
    Ireland
UNITED KINGDOM

The Bering Straits Irregulars
Candace Olson
6425 Carlos Court
Anchorage, AK 99504

The Genius Loci
Jeremiah E. Abbott
2727 Cherokee Court
Birmingham, AL 35216

**The Wandering Gipsies of
    Grimpen Mire**
Bob Crispen
1308 Runnymead Avenue SW
Decatur, AL 35601

**The Disreputable Little
    Scarecrows of the Shoals**
Frank McClung
612 East Puritan Avenue
Muscle Shoals, AL 35661-1534

**The Arkansas Valley Investors,
    Ltd.**
Jason Rouby
11 McKinley Circle
Little Rock, AR 72207

Moulton's Prospectors
Judith Leary
9459 North 64th Drive
Glendale, AZ 85302

The Family of Col. Moran
Gordon H. Palmer
111 Apache Avenue
Thousand Oaks, CA 91362

The Twisted Lip Society
Molly V. Manaugh
3381 Spear Avenue
Arcata, CA 95521-4831

The Old Soldiers of Quaker Street
John Ruyle
521 Vincente Avenue
Berkeley, CA 94707-1521

**The Diogenes Club of the
    Monterey Peninsula**
Michael H. Kean
3040 Sloat Road
Pebble Beach, CA 93953-2837

**The Goose Club of the Alpha Inn
    [California]**
John P. Sohl
20446 Orey Place
Canoga Park, CA 91306

Bow Street Runners
Fred H. Holt
350 Minnewawa #139
Clovis, CA 93612

The Trained Cormorants
Don Hardenbrook
7208 Premium Street
Long Beach, CA 90808

**The Curious Collectors of Baker
    Street**
Jerry and Chrys Kegley
110 El Nido #41
Pasadena, CA 91107

The Non-Canonical Calabashes
Sean M. Wright
5542 Romaine Street
Los Angeles, CA 90038

The Wisteria-Hysteria
Marilyn Genaro
19944-A Sherman Way
Winnetka, CA 91306-3606

The Pick of a Bad Lot
James H. Stewart
8352 Costello Avenue
Panorama City, CA 91402

The Disjecta Membra of the Greater Bay Area
Brian and Charlotte Erickson
1029 Judson Drive
Mountain View, CA 94040-2310

The Knights of the Gnomon
Robert Bisio
1330 University Drive
Menlo Park, CA 94025

The Napa Valley Napoleons of S.H.
Donald A. Yates
555 Canon Park Drive
St. Helena, CA 94574

The Christopher Morley Whiskey & Sodality Club
Steven E. Whiting
405 West Washington Street #86
San Diego, CA 92103

The Grimpen Admirers of Sherlock Holmes
Steven E. Whiting
405 West Washington Street #86
San Diego, CA 92103

The Old Soldiers of Praed Street
General Hugh Pomfroy
17 Mount Lassen Drive
San Rafael, CA 94903-1127

The Persian Slipper Club of San Francisco
Raymond A. de Groat
S. Holmes Esq.
480 Sutter Street
San Francisco, CA 94108

The Scowrers and Molly Maguires of San Francisco
Charlotte Erickson
Box 341
Mount Eden, CA 94557

The Tide-Waiters of San Francisco Bay
Colonel Ted Schulz
17 Mount Lassen Drive
San Rafael, CA 94903-1127

The Tigers of San Pedro
John Farrell
25314 Woodward Street
Lomita, CA 90717

The Pips of Orange County
Robert A. Dunning
2025 Martha Lane
Santa Ana, CA 92706

The Scion of the Green Dragon
Mary Ellen and Walt Daugherty
1305 Mira Flores Drive
Santa Maria, CA 93455-5609

The Legends of the West Country
Howard Lachtman
926 West Mendocino Avenue
Stockton, CA 95204

The Cardboard Boxers of Susanville
William Ballew
Box 1954
Susanville, CA 96130

The Blustering Gales from the South-West
Paula M. Salo
4421 Pacific Coast Highway #E-112
Torrance, CA 90905

Dr. Watson's Neglected Patients
Steve Robinson
6980 South Bannock Street #3
Littleton, CO 80120

St. Bartholomew's Chemical Laboratory
James K. Butler
8015-D Holland Court
Arvada, CO 80005

The Winter Assizes at Norwich
Charles A. Adams
72 Gifford Lane, R.F.D. 1
Bozrah, CT 06334

The Men on the Tor
Harold E. Niver
Baskerville Hall
29 Woodhaven Road
Rocky Hill, CT 06067-1045

The Yale Sherlock Holmes Society
David F. Musto
Yale Station, Box 4075
New Haven, CT 06520

The Red Circle of Washington, D.C.
Peter E. Blau
3900 Tunlaw Road NW #119
Washington, DC 20007-4830

The Baker Street Irregulars (South Florida Chapter)
Jonathan White
Box 103
Pompano Beach, FL 33061

The Tropical Deerstalkers
Arlyn Katims
6801 S.W. 79th Avenue
Miami, FL 33143

Sherlock Holmes' Dumber Brothers
Richard Bryer
2026 Gray Court
North Fort Myers, FL 33903

The Musgrave Story Society
Ken Nail, Jr.
Box 2361
Merritt Island, FL 32954-2361

The Pleasant Places of Florida
Benton Wood
Box 740
Ellentown, FL 34222-0740

The House of Stuart: The Sherlockian Society of the Treasure Coast
Mr. S. Holmes
Box 221
Palm City, FL 34990

The Confederates of Wisteria Lodge
Mary Leonard
4642 South Hope Springs Road
Stone Mountain, GA 30083

The Tenants of Baker Street
Jennie C. Paton
206 Loblolly Lane
Statesboro, GA 30458

The Andaman Islanders
Marcia Walsh
Box 444
Wahiawa, HI 96786

The Priory School Dropouts
B. Dean Wortman
223 Lynn
Ames, IA 50010

The Younger Stamfords
Richard M. Caplan
708 Greenwood Drive
Iowa City, IA 52246

The Iowa Valley of Fear
Paul A. Tambrino
3702 South Center
Marshalltown, IA 50158

The Camford Scholars
Elizabeth A. Burns
R.R. 3, Box 221
Clinton, IL 61727

The Double-Barrelled Tiger Cubs
284 Illini Union
1401 West Green
Urbana, IL 61801

The Chester Baskerville Society
Michael W. McClure
1415 Swanwick Street
Chester, IL 62233

Altamont's Agents of Chicago
John N. Wilson
11837 West 118th Street
Palos Park, IL 60464

The Criterion Bar Association
Susan Diamond
2851 North Pearl Avenue
Melrose Park, IL 60164-1421

The Dedicated Associates of Lomax
Richard A. Myhre
1319 Poplar Court
Homewood, IL 60430

The Hounds of the Baskerville (sic)
Robert J. Mangler
103 Broadway Avenue
Wilmette, IL 60091

Hugo's Companions
Wayne Siatt
2310 West Burlington Avenue
Downers Grove, IL 60515

The Registrants of the Canonical Convocation and Caper
Jane L. Richardson
3456 East Exchange Road
Crete, IL 60417

The Solar Pons Breakfast Club
Bernadette Donze
7224 South Kidwell Road
Downers Grove, IL 60516

The Sons of Baker Street
Wayne B. Siatt
2310 West Burlington Avenue
Downers Grove, IL 60515

The STUD Sherlockian Society
Donald B. Izban
5334 Wrightwood Avenue
Chicago, IL 60639-1524

The Torists International, S.S.
Claudine Kastner
810 Burning Bush Lane
Mount Prospect, IL 60056

The Scotland Yarders
Susan Richman
472 Burton Avenue
Highland Park, IL 60035

The South Downers
Jane L. Richardson
3456 Exchange Street
Crete, IL 60417

Ferguson's Vampires
Troy Taylor
805 West North #1
Decatur, IL 62522

The Occupants of the Empty House
William R. Cochran
517 North Vine Street
DuQuoin, IL 62832

The Fellowship of the Fallen Elm
Tom Tully
303 East Harrison
Elmhurst, IL 60126

Watson's Bull Pups of Elmhurst
James Cunningham
266 Grace
Elmhurst, IL 60126

The Pinkertons of the Fox River Valley
Barton A. Eberman
405 South First Street
Geneva, IL 60134

The Baker Street Pages
Tim O'Connor
6015 West Route 115
Herscher, IL 60941

The Hansoms of John Clayton
Robert C. Burr
4010 Devon Lane
Peoria, IL 61614-7109

The Alpha Public House Goose Club
John Bowen
109 East Prairie
Roodhouse, IL 62082

Pondicherry Lodge
Glen S. Milner
110 North Marion
Mount Pulaski, IL 62548

The Little Knot of Roughs
Ellen Yocom
420 West Tremont
Waverly, IL 62692

The Friends of Baron Gruner
Brian R. MacDonald
7801 North 700-W
Fairland, IN 46126

The Illustrious Clients of Indianapolis
Mark Gagen
3625-B Glen Arm Road
Indianapolis, IN 46224

The Society of the Solitary Cyclists
Virginia J. K. Young
132 South Scott Street
South Bend, IN 46625

Mapleton Stables at Louisville
Larry DeKay
Box 43546
Louisville, KY 40253

The Silver Blazers
Ralph Hall
2906 Wallingford Court
Louisville, KY 40218-2363

The Speckled Band of Boston
Richard M. Olken
200 Hyslop Road
Brookline, MA 02146

The Friends of Irene Adler
Daniel Posnansky
Box 768
Cambridge, MA 02238

Dr. Watson's Stethoscope
Frank Medlar
Bapst Library
Boston College
Chestnut Hill, MA 02167

A Sherlockian Connection: The Berkshires
Mrs. Henry Arbour
R.D. 2, Notch Road
North Adams, MA 01247

The Truro School Irregulars
Hyman Shrand
Box 336
North Truro, MA 02652-0336

The Carlton Club
James E. Smith II
311 St. Dunstan's Road
Baltimore, MD 21212-3517

The Six Napoleons of Baltimore
Philip Sherman
3011 Fallstaff Road #508
Baltimore, MD 21209-2961

The Sussex Apiarist Society
T. Michael Kaylor
Box 157
Chestertown, MD 21620

The Denizens of the Bar of Gold
Michael F. Whelan
342 Perry Cabin Drive
St. Michaels, MD 21663

Watson's Tin Box
Paul Churchill
2118 Carroll Dale
Eldersburg, MD 21784

The Arcadia Mixture
Frederick C. Page, Jr.
1354 Ardmoor
Ann Arbor, MI 48103

The Amateur Mendicant Society
Peter B. Spivak
3753 Penobscot Building
Detroit, MI 48226

The Greek Interpreters of East Lansing
Gary R. Reed
Box 322
Dewitt, MI 48820

The Ribston-Pippins
Regina S. Stinson
715 Amelia
Royal Oak, MI 48073

The Lady Frances Carfax Society
Linda J. Reed
2809 Fremont Avenue South #211
Minneapolis, MN 55408

Martha Hudson's Cronies
Julia Carraher
4242 Stevens Avenue South #2
Minneapolis, MN 55409

The Norwegian Explorers of Minnesota
E. W. McDiarmid
Wilson Library (Special Coll.)
University of Minnesota
Minneapolis, MN 55455

The Great Alkali Plainsmen of Greater Kansas City
Richard R. Reynolds
Box 9443
Shawnee Mission, KS 66201-2147

The Harpooners of the Sea Unicorn
Michael E. Bragg
Box 799
St. Charles, MO 63302-0799

The Jefferson Hopes of St. Louis
Karen L. Johnson
1419 Shands Court
Kirkwood, MO 63122

The Noble Bachelors of St. Louis
Randall Getz
626 Riverbend Estates Drive
St. Charles, MO 63303-6060

The Parallel Case of St. Louis
Joseph J. Eckrich
914 Oakmoor Drive
Fenton, MO 63026-7008

The Men of the Abbey Grange
Edwin L. Childers, Jr.
506 Hancock Avenue
Warrensburg, MO 64093

The Maiwand Jezails
Richard D. Lesh
1205 Lory Street
Fort Collins, CO 80524-3905

Cox & Co. of New England
James O. Duval
72 Merrimack Street
Penacook, NH 03303

Mrs. Hudson's Cliffdwellers of Cliffside Park, New Jersey
Irving Kamil
32 Overlook Avenue
Cliffside Park, NJ 07010

The Red-Headed League of Jersey
John A. Marchesani
9 Center Street
Westmont, NJ 08108-2609

The Epilogues of Sherlock Holmes
Robert S. Katz
11 Van Beuren Road
Morristown, NJ 07960

The Delaware Valley of Fear
James P. Suszynski
Box 404
Hainesport, NJ 08036

The Goose Club of the Alpha Inn of Princeton University
Thomas Drucker
304 South Hanover Street
Carlisle, PA 17013-3938

The Masters of the Priory School
Fred D. Johnson
4949 San Pedro NE #87
Albuquerque, NM 87109

The Brothers Three of Moriarty
John Bennett Shaw
1917 Fort Union Drive
Santa Fe, NM 87505

The Jarveys of the Metropolis
Steve and Katlin Hecox
1080 Casa Loma Drive
Reno, NV 89503-3128

Dr. Watson's Holmestead
Alfred N. Weiner
4105 Marietta Drive
Vestal, NY 13850

The Montague Street Lodgers of Brooklyn
Thom Utecht
1676 East 55th Street
Brooklyn, NY 11234-3906

An Irish Secret Society at Buffalo
James Powers
443 West Delavan Avenue
Buffalo, NY 14213

Round the Fire
Dolores Rossi Script
887 West Perry Street
Buffalo, NY 14209

The Hudson Valley Sciontists
Nancy Alden
Box 365, High Street
Staatsburg-on-Hudson, NY 12580

The Consulting Detectives
Herbert M. Levy
Box 197
East Meadow, NY 11554

The Three Garridebs
Dante M. Torrese
11 Chestnut Street
Ardsley, NY 10502

The Long Island Cave Sleuths
Beverly Halm
Hillside Junior School 172
81-14 257th Street
Floral Park, NY 11004

The Delaware Deerstalkers
Leonard E. Sienko, Jr.
12 East Main Street
Hancock, NY 13783-1128

The Baker Street Underground
Andrew Jay Peck
185 West End Avenue #11-F
New York, NY 10023

The Isle of Uffa Chowder and Marching Society
Susan Rice
125 Washington Place #2-E
New York, NY 10014

The Priory Scholars
Henry W. Enberg
250 West 27th Street #3-A
New York, NY 10001-5908

The Retired Colourmen of Metroplitan New York
Dave Galerstein
44 Center Drive
New Hyde Park, NY 10040

The Young Sherlockians of New York
Mohamad Bazzi
80-08 35th Avenue #5-F
Jackson Heights, NY 11372

The Federal Street Irregulars of Saratoga Springs
A. T. Retzlaff
1 South Federal Street #510
Saratoga Springs, NY 12866-4255

Altamont's Agents
Thomas A. Dandrew II
R.D. 1, 375 Langley Road
Amsterdam, NY 12010

Watson's Tin Dispatchers
Francine and Dick Kitts
35 Van Cortlandt Avenue
Staten Island, NY 10301

The Long Island Cave Dwellers
Helen E. Heinrich
7 Palfrey Street
Stony Brook, NY 11790-2611

The Mycroft Holmes Society of Syracuse
Carol Cavalluzzi
108 Marvin Road
Syracuse, NY 13207

The Students of Deduction
Stephen Imburgia
1055 Klem Road
Webster, NY 14580

The Inverness Capers
Michael Senuta
881 Columbine Drive
Barberton, OH 44203

The Tankerville Club
Paul D. Herbert
734 Alpine Drive
Milford, OH 45150

The Addleton Barrowists of Circleville, Ohio
P. Thomas Harker
404 South Washington Street
Circleville, OH 43113

Mrs. Hudson's Lodgers
The Stetaks
15529 Diagonal Road
La Grange, OH 44050-9531

Mycroft's Isolated Companions
Dwight J. McDonald
1711 Cypress Avenue
Cleveland, OH 44109

The Seventeen Steps
Patricia Rockwell
4163 Squires Lane
Columbus, OH 43220

The Agra Treasurers
Don Robertson
6055 Brown Deer Place
Dayton, OH 45424

The Darlington Substitutes
Martin Arbagi
History Department
Wright State University
Dayton, OH 45435

The Giant Rats of Massillon
Hugh T. Harrington
1634 Sherwood Avenue NW
Massillon, OH 44646

The Stormy Petrels of Maumee Bay
Ted Cowell
200 Beach Street
Northwood, OH 43619-1708

The Afghanistan Perceivers of Oklahoma
Stafford G. Davis
2144 North Elwood Avenue
Tulsa, OK 74106-3632

The Noble and Most Singular Order of the Blue Carbuncle
Tammy Vale
4505 N.E. 24th
Portland, OR 97211

The Vamberry Wine Merchants
Donald W. Wissusik
32315 N.E. Old Parrett Mt. Road
Newberg, OR 97132

The Lehigh Valley of Fear
Andy Levas
142 Valley Park South
Bethlehem, PA 13018

The Brooks of Carlisle
Thomas Drucker
304 South Hanover Street
Carlisle, PA 17013-3838

The E. Hopkins Trust Company
Jeff Decker
R.D. 3, Box 7631
Racehorse Drive
Jonestown, PA 17038

The Bitches of the Copper Beeches
K. Jeanne O. Jewell
1012 Waltham Road
Berwyn, PA 19312

The Clients of Sherlock Holmes
Sherry Rose-Bond
519 East Allens Lane
Philadelphia, PA 19119-1106

The Sons of the Copper Beeches
Daniel S. Knight
2600 One Commerce Square
Philadelphia, PA 19103-7098

**The Fifth Northumberland
Fusiliers**
Tom Portante
204 Margery Drive
Pittsburgh, PA 15238-3008

The Royal Berkshire Regiment
Karl Suslovic
77 Moon Run Road
McKees Rocks, PA 15136

**The Pennsylvania Small Arm
Company**
Joan G. Ramsey
225 Dan Drive
Mt. Lebanon, PA 15216-1329

Boss McGinty's Bird Watchers
Frederick C. Sauls
Department of Chemistry
King's College
Wilkes-Barre, PA 18711

The Residents of York College
David M. Hershey
1708 West Market Street
York, PA 17404

**The White Rose Irregulars of
York**
Larry D. Williams
718 Harding Street
New Cumberland, PA 17070-1436

The Cornish Horrors
Jan C. Prager
33 Shadow Farm Way
Wakefield, RI 02879

The Hansom Wheels
Myrtle Robinson
6120 Cedar Ridge
Columbia, SC 29206

The Knights of Shag
J. Drew Daubenspeck
403 River Walk Drive
Simpsonville, SC 29681

The Sign of the Four Faces
Cary J. Wencil
2409 South Jefferson
Sioux Falls, SD 57105

The Baker Street Volunteers
Stefanie Kate Hawks
P.O. Box 9486
Knoxville, TN 37940-9486

The Giant Rats of Sumatra
Robert A. Lanier
635 West Drive
Memphis, TN 38112

**The Nashville Scholars of the
Three Pipe Problem**
Gael B. Stahl
1763 Needmore Road
Old Hickory, TN 37138

**The Crew of the Barque "Lone
Star" [Austin]**
Lorre Weidlich
4313 Avenue F
Austin, TX 78751-3722

**The Crew of the Barque "Lone
Star"**
Don Hobbs
Box 36329
Dallas, TX 75235-1329

The Maniac Collectors
Don Hobbs
Box 36329
Dallas, TX 75235-1329

The Mexborough Lodgers
Betty Pierce
300 Shadow Mountain Drive #603
El Paso, TX 79912-4024

The First Bangalore Pioneers
David Dunnett
2508 Sanguinet Street
Forth Worth, TX 76107

The Nonpareil Club
Susan Beasley
3712 Venice
Fort Worth, TX 76180

The Strollers on the Strand
Edgar B. Smith
Dept. of Dermatology
Univ. of Texas Medical Branch
Galveston, TX 77550

The John Openshaw Society
Thomas L. Harman
University of Houston/Clear Lake
2700 Bay Area Blvd. (Box 161)
Houston, TX 77058-1098

The Strange Old Book Collectors
Ben Fairbank
Box 15075
San Antonio, TX 78212-8275

The Country of the Saints
Kevin John
637 North 200 West
Brigham City, UT 84302

The Avenging Angels
Ronald B. De Waal
638 12th Avenue
Salt Lake City, UT 84103-3212

The Game Is Afoot
Gary R. Westmoreland
2002 Jefferson Park Avenue #13
Charlottesville, VA 22903

Doctor Watson's Casual Readers
Ms. Jacque Wood Halpern
The Shady Rest
129 West Rock Street
Harrisonburg, VA 22801

**The Cremona Fiddlers of
Williamsburg**
Ray Betzner
107 Tendril Court
Williamsburg, VA 23188

**The Goose Club of the Alpha Inn
[Vermont]**
William E. Wicker
17 Birchwood Drive
Colchester, VT 05446

The Baker Street Breakfast Club
Sally Sugarman
Box 407
Shaftsbury, VT 05262-0407

The Loungers and Idlers
Janet Bailey
4320 Old Mill Road NE
Bainbridge, WA 98110

**The Persian Slipper Club
Northwest of San Francisco**
Raymond A. de Groat
2147 Lakemoor Drive SW
Olympia, WA 98502-5529

The Sherlock Holmes League
Michael Meaney
4094 West Lake Samm Road SE
Bellevue, WA 98008

The Sound of the Baskervilles
David N. Haugen
346 Del Monte Avenue
Tacoma, WA 98466

The Conductors of Aldersgate Street Station
Fred Zensen
15103 N.E. 27th Avenue
Vancouver, WA 98686

The Thor Bridge Fishers
Alan J. Block
1419 Chapin Street
Beloit, WI 53511

The Canon at Riverside
Elizabeth J. Ash
111 South 9th Street #101
La Crosse, WI 54601

The Notorious Canary-Trainers
Howard Rosenberry
4542 Windsor Road
De Forest, WI 53532

The Bagatelle Card Club
Daniel P. King
5125 North Cumberland Boulevard
Whitefish Bay, WI 53217

Randall's Gang
Paul B. Smedegaard
929 Lathrop Avenue
Racine, WI 53405

The Merripit House Guests
Robert W. Hahn
2707 South 7th Street
Sheboygan, WI 53081

The Scion of the Four
Andrew G. Fusco
2400 Cranberry Square
Morgantown, WV 26505-9209

La Sociedad Sherlockiana de Caracas
Luis Gonzalo Velez Gimon
Av. Los Pinos, Edif. Airosa #5
La Florida, Caracas 1050
VENEZUELA

Active Sherlockian Societies (professional):

The Baker Street Bar Association
lawyers
David R. McCallister
8142 Quail Hollow Boulevard
Wesley Chapel, FL 33544-2021

The Black Pearl of the Borgias
poetry/writing/lecturing
Dolores (Dee) Script
887 West Ferry Street
Buffalo, NY 14209

The Board-School Beacons
educational research and psychometry
Michael H. Kean
3040 Sloat Road
Pebble Beach, CA 93953-2837

The Bruce-Partington Planners Within the Military-Industrial Complex
national security
Jon L. Lellenberg
3133 Connecticut Avenue NW #525
Washington, DC 20008

The Central Press Syndicate
editors of newsletters
Robert W. Hahn
2707 South 7th Street
Sheboygan, WI 53081

Clerks of the Assizes
court clerks felony trial court
James Motylenski
537 Christie Street
South Hempstead, NY 11550

The Colleagues of Lomax, the Sub-Librarian
librarianship
Ronald B. De Waal
638 12th Avenue
Salt Lake City, UT 84103-3212

The Forensic Faces of Sherlock Holmes
forensic science
Marina Stajic
425 East 51st Street #4-A
New York, NY 10022-6465

The Nocturnal Journalists of 131 Pitt Street
journalists, writers, and wordsmiths
Catherine Pfeifer
3939 North Murray Avenue #402
Milwaukee, WI 53211

The Norwood Fire Brigade
fire service
Capt. Randall Getz
Hazelwood Fire Department
6800 Howdershell Road
Hazelwood, MO 63042

The Old Soldiers of Baker Street of the Two Saults (Old SOB's 3)
military Sherlockians
John S. Rabe
2813 Poplar Street
Philadelphia, PA 19130-1222

The Old Soldiers of Baker Street, Detachment 221B (Flying Column)
military and ex-military Sherlockians
Col. Ted Schulz
17 Mount Lassen Drive
San Rafael, CA 94903-1127

The Practical, But Limited, Geologists
geology
Peter E. Blau
3900 Tunlaw Road NW #119
Washington, DC 20007-4830

The Red Lamp League
medicine
Edmond C. Noll
Box 4322
North Hollywood, CA 91602

The Sir James Saunders Society
dermatology
Don E. Hazelrigg
8500 Framewood Drive
Newburgh, IN 47630-2348

Some Freaks of Atavism
historians
Bullitt Lowry
Department of History
Box 13735, North Texas Station
Denton, TX 76203

Stimson & Co.
funeral directors
Michael W. McClure
1415 Swanwick Street
Chester, IL 62233

The Sub-Librarians Scion of The
   Baker Street Irregulars in the
   American Libary Association
librarians
Marsha L. Pollak
1318 Mildred Avenue
San Jose, CA 95125

The Trifling Monographers
practitioners of public relations
Graham Sudbury
1324 East 26th Place
Tulsa, OK 74114-2736

ACTIVE SHERLOCKIAN SOCIETIES (OTHER):

The 140
tobacco-smoking Sherlockians
John F. Farrell
25314 Woodward Avenue
Lomita, CA 90717

221BBS (300/1200/2400 N-8-1
   415-949-1734)
computerized bulletin board
Brian and Charlotte Erickson
1029 Judson Drive
Mountain View, CA 94040-2310

The Abominable Wife of Ross
   County
*a correspondence society
   (unclubbables)*
M. Hellen
694 Jefferson Avenue
Chillicothe, OH 45601

The Adventuresses of Sherlock
   Holmes
women's special-interest group
Evelyn A. Herzog
360 West 21st Street #5-A
New York, NY 10011-3310

alt.fan.holmes (Usenet/Internet)
computerized newsgroup
Chuck Lavazzi
Internet: clavazzi@nyx.cs.du.edu
WWIVnet: 3@3456

The Arthur Conan Doyle Society
study of Conan Doyle's life and works
Christopher Roden
2 Abbottsford Drive, Penyffordd
Chester, Cheshire CH4 0JG
ENGLAND

The Asian Travelers
visitors to the Great Wall of China
Irving Kamil
32 Overlook Avenue
Cliffside Park, NJ 07010

The Baker Street Constables
   (Fans of Jeremy Brett)
a Jeremy Brett fan club
Craig A. Moore
6549 29th Way North
St. Petersburg, FL 33702-6229

The Baker Street Irregulars
American national Sherlockian society
Thomas L. Stix, Jr.
34 Pierson Avenue
Norwood, NJ 07648

The Baker Street Juniors
young Sherlockians
Erika Kobayashi
Ohizumi-machi 2-55-8
Nerima-ku, Tokyo 178
JAPAN

The Baker Street Ladies
*scion of The Japan Sherlock Holmes
   Club*
Yaeko Amano
501, 3-4-27 Sakae-cho
Asaka-shi, Saitama 351
JAPAN

The Baker Street Streakers,
   Irregular!
streaking!!
Henry W. Gould
1239 College Avenue
Morgantown, WV 26605

The Belles of Saint Monica
midwestern Sherlockian women
Ruthann H. Stetak
15529 Diagonal Road
La Grange, OH 44050-9531

The Birdy Edwards Society
19th-century detective literature
J. Randolph Cox
10331 Decker Avenue, Route 5
Northfield, MN 55057

The Blind German Mechanics
a correspondence society
Wally Conger
146-A North Canyon Boulevard
Monrovia, CA 91016

The Boulevard Assassins
social but secretive
Huret, the Boulevard Assassin
11 Greenway North
Albany, NY 12208

C.A.L.A.B.A.S.H. (Convivial
   Attendant Liaisons Among
   B.S.I. and Adventuresses of
   Sherlock Holmes)
*honoring the third buy-law of the
   B.S.I.*
Paul B. Smedegaard
929 Lathrop Avenue
Racine, WI 53405

The Canonical Capricorns
born under the sign of Capricorn
Marlene Aig
123-35 82nd Road #3-B
Kew Gardens, NY 11415

The Canonical Violets
a ladies' group
Nancy B. Hamilton
6224 Forest Acre Circle
Fort Worth, TX 76119

Cartwright's Companions
*sub-scion of Chester Baskerville
   Society*
Michael W. McClure
1415 Swanwick Street
Chester, IL 62233

A Case of Identifiers
preserving photographs of Sherlockians
Bill Vande Water
697 Greenbelt Parkway West
Holbrook, NY 11741

The Clients of Adrian Mulliner
Wodehouseans of BSI—Sherlockians of TWS
Jon L. Lellenberg
3133 Connecticut Avenue NW #525
Washington, DC 20008

The Conan Doyle (Crowborough) Establishment
information on ACD and tours of his home
Malcolm Payne
4 Wealden Close
Crowborough, East Sussex TN6 2ST
ENGLAND

The Constabulary
S'ian students of British police history
John B. Taylor
Box 804
Midlothian, TX 76065

The Dame Adelaide Mathilda Cock-Bullington Memorial Chapter of the Dartmoor Kennel Club
a traveling society
Robert W. Hahn
2707 South 7th Street
Sheboygan, WI 53081

The Dead-Headed League
a geo-academic society
Paul David Rivadue
Garden City High School
Garden City, NY 11530

The Deerstalkers
sub-scion of The Inverness Capers
James Howe
465 Perkins
Akron, OH 44304

The Devils Foot Society
explication of "Adv. of the Devils Foot"
Herbert P. Tinning
93 Sagamore Road
Millburn, NJ 07041

The Diogenes Club of Gothenburg
Sherlock Holmes literature
Lennart Engström
Västes Gata 60
S-421 53 V. Frölunda
Gothenburg, SWEDEN

The Diogenes Club
irregular
George Cleve Haynes
1402 Third Avenue #1318
Seattle, WA 98101

The DioGEnies Club (GEnie WRITERS, INK, page 440, item 1, CATegory 10, TOPic 6)
computerized (GEnie access)
John McGowan

The Dog in the Night-time
individualistic and quietly alert
Wendell Cochran
4351 S.W. Willow Street
Seattle, WA 98136-1769

The Edmonton Deerstalker
members elected by membership committee
Peter H. Wood
25 Bellevue Crescent
St. Albert, Alta. T8N 0A5
CANADA

The Excelsior Guild
honor society of The Baker Street Pages
Tim O'Connor
6015 West Route 115
Herscher, IL 60941

The Five Orange Pips
Sherlockian scholarship
Albert M. Rosenblatt
Box 221-B
Poughkeepsie, NY 12569

The Fragile Philosophical Instruments of Sherlock Holmes
Interntl. Soc. for Philosophical Enquiry
Raymond L. Holly
512 North 11th Street
Herrin, IL 62948

The Franco-Midland Hardware Co. (Colonial Branch Office)
members of Franco-Midland Hardware Co.
Robert W. Wright
R.D. #3, Box 401
Myerstown, PA 17067

The Friends of Mrs. Hudson
Canonical dining and cooking
Francine M. Swift
Sumatra Lodge
4622 Morgan Drive
Chevy Chase, MD 20815-5315

The Great Hiatus
corresponding about foreign translations
John Farrell
25314 Woodward Avenue
Lomita, CA 90717

The H. W.
people whose initials are H. W.
Helen Wesson
826 Golf Drive
Venice, FL 34285

The High Tors
a correspondence society
Larry Waggoner
1649 Yarbro Lane
Paducah, KY 42003

Holmes Fan Club
a correspondence society
Jens Brandebusemeyer
Sperberstrasse 13
D-4506 Hagen a.T.W.
GERMANY

The Holmes Peak Preservation Society
promotion and protection of Holmes Peak
Dick Warner
3168 South Rockford Drive
Tulsa, OK 74105

Holmes' Unofficial Force
a correspondence society
Sandra Buck
R.R. 1, Box 2090
Morrill, ME 04952

Holmesian Studies Special Interest Group
American Mensa special interest group
Michael J. Halm
2062 Yoast Avenue
Cincinnati, OH 45225-1480

The Hounds of the Internet (blocka@beloit.edu)
computerized (Internet access)
Alan J. Block
1419 Chapin Street
Beloit, WI 53511

The Hugh Boone Society
sub-scion of The Red-Headed League
Ann Byerly Marlowe
10324 Castlehedge Terrace
Silver Spring, MD 20902-6807

The Inner Brotherhood of the Holy Four
Holmes & Watson and Gilbert & Sullivan
Colin Prestige
34 Pont Street
London SW1X 0AD
ENGLAND

Irregular Special Railway Company
Holmesians interested in railways
Antony Richards
163 Marine Parade
Leigh-on-Sea, Essex SS9 2RB
ENGLAND

The Last Dog Hung Post-Prandial Club
closing up watering holes after meetings
Paul B. Smedegaard
929 Lathrop Avenue
Racine, WI 53405

The Listeners of the Modern Mazarin Gramophone
Sherlockian radio, stage, and screen
Lawrence P. Nepodahl
1230 Vienna Boulevard
DeKalb, IL 60115

The Maiwand Survivors Society
walking-wounded Sherlockians
Murray, c/o Swift
4622 Morgan Drive
Chevy Chase, MD 20815-5315

The Meiringen Meringues
Sherlockian visitors to Meiringen
Vivian M. Heisler
1025 South Broad Street #2
Trenton, NJ 08611-1459

The Messengers from Porlock
truly ephemeral; studied Porlock 8/7/93
Graham Sudbury
1324 East 26th Place
Tulsa, OK 74114-2736

The Midwest Scion of the Four
a travelling barber-shop quartette
Joseph J. Eckrich
914 Oakmoor Drive
Fenton, MO 63026-7008

The Mini-Tonga Scion Society
collectors of Sherlockian miniatures
Carol Wenk
Box 770554
Lakewood, OH 44107

The Mongooses of Henry Wood
a correspondence society
Mattias Boström
Tordmutevägen 4-B
S-227 35 Lund
SWEDEN

The Montague Street Incorrigibles
a correspondence society
Brad Keefauver
1421 West Shenandoah Drive
Peoria, IL 61614

The Most Prosaic but Effective Order of the Frozen Bull Terrier
scion of Oxf. Univ. Sherlock Holmes Soc.
Roger Mortimore
University College
Oxford OX1 4BH
ENGLAND

The Mrs. Hudson Breakfast
annual breakfast during birthday weekend
The Stetaks
15529 Diagonal Road
La Grange, OH 44050-9531

The Mrs. Turner Thames Club Breakfasters
annual breakfast during birthday weekend
Donald A. Yates
555 Canon Park Drive
St. Helena, CA 94574

The New Black-Headed League
Canonical studies and databases
Masamichi Higurashi
1-28-3 Kichijoji-Honcho #204
Musashino-shi, Tokyo 180
JAPAN

The New Zealand Shareholders
visitors to New Zealand
Irving Kamil
32 Overlook Avenue
Cliffside Park, NJ 07010

Nishichikuma-Shobou Co. Mag.
publishing parodies and pastiches
Kokage Midorikawa
Nishino 6321-648, Kaida
Kiso-gun, Nagano-ken
JAPAN

The Occupants of the Full House
correspondence society (visits welcomed)
Jean Upton
41 Sandford Road
Chelmsford, Essex CM2 6DE
ENGLAND

The One Fixed Point Society for Two-Dimensional Sherlockians
replicas of S'ians who won't leave home
William R. Cochran
517 North Vine Street
DuQuoin, IL 61832

"One of One-Forty"
a correspondence society
Elizabeth J. Ash
111 South 9th Street #101
La Crosse, WI 54601

Over My Dead Body! (300/1200/2400 N-8-1 206-473-4522)
computerized bulletin board (mysteries)
Cherie Jung
6823 South Puget Sound Avenue
Tacoma, WA 98409

The Oxbridge Scholars
Canonical scholarship
Donald G. Jewell
4685 Geeting Road
Westminster, MD 21158

The Page Boys of 221B
young Sherlockians
Robert G. Allison-Gallimore
Route II
18920 Quivira
Spring Hill, KS 66083

Paget's Irregular Horse
equestrian Sherlockians
Norman M. Davis
2215 Davis Street
Blue Island, IL 60406-1668

The Pawky Humorists (Reactivated)
perpetration of Sherlockian puns
Norman M. Davis
2215 Davis Street
Blue Island, IL 60406-1668

The Persian Slipper of the Ribston-Pippins
pipe-smoking subscion of Ribston-Pippins
Sam Stinson
715 Amelia
Royal Oak, MI 48073

The Phoenician Tin Traders Gentlemen's International Corresponding Club
language of the Canon and the S'ian era
John D. Whitehouse
10825 Hitchcock Avenue
El Paso, TX 79935-1419

The Pinchin Lane Irregulars
love and lore of the animal kingdom
Debbie L. Butler
8015-D Holland Court
Arvada, CO 80005

Poor Bibliophiles International
corresponding collectors
John E. Stephenson
7739 South Steele Street
Littleton, CO 80122-3367

The Praed Street Irregulars
American national Pontine society
Theodore G. Schulz
17 Mount Lassen Drive
San Rafael, CA 94903-1127

The Protective Order of the Persian Slipper
pure fun
Steve W. Schaefer
606 North Main Street
Madison, GA 30650

The Quaker Street Irregulars
supporters of Turlock Loams
John Ruyle
521 Vincente Avenue
Berkeley, CA 94707-1521

The Red-Headed League
red-headed Sherlockians
Ann Byerly Marlowe
10324 Castlehedge Terrace
Silver Spring, MD 20902-5807

The Reichenbach Rangers
academic (New Mexico Military Institute)
Darlene Logan
111 West Mathews
Roswell, NM 88201

The Reichenbachian Cliff-Divers
cliff-diving Sherlockians
Kendall J. Pagan
c/o The Lascarian Press
4010 Devon Lane
Peoria, IL 61614-7109

The Sacred Six
Sherlockian inner circle
William P. Schweickert
145 Johnson Road
Scarsdale, NY 10583-6203

The Scrimshanders of the Harpooners of the Sea Unicorn
sub-scion/Harpooners of the Sea Unicorn
John T. Foster
Box 799
St. Charles, MO 63302-0799

Sergeant of Marines
Elementary, my dear Simpson—Gung Ho!!!
Francis J. Carroll, Jr.
712 Prospect Place
Bellmore, NY 11710

The Seven Passengers
study of Solar Pons
Larry DeKay
Box 43546
Louisville, KY 40253

The Shadows of the Elm
a correspondence society (young S'ians)
C. Bryan Gassner
P.O. Drawer G
Corrales, NM 87048

Sherlock Holmes Pipe Club, Ltd., USA
Sherlockian pipe-collectors
Allan H. Rosenfield
Box 221
Westborough, MA 01581

The Sherlock Holmes Research Committee (Japan)
publ. "Studies of the Nippon S.H. Club"
Saburo Hiraga
Tagami-kata 11-15, Houzan-cho
Toyonaka-shi, Osaka 560
JAPAN

The Sherlock Holmes Society of PaNaMa
a correspondence society
Patricia Quardt
Landsegnung 81
D-5470 Andernach 1
GERMANY

The Sherlock Holmes Wireless Society
licensed amateur radio operators
Ken Johnson W6NKE
1813 Moreno Drive
Simi Valley, CA 93063

Sherlock Holmes' Varied Correspondents (sic)
a correspondence society (audiocassette)
Desmond Tyler
162 Leybridge Court, Eltham Road
London SE12 8TL
ENGLAND

Sherlock's Haven BBS (300/1200/2400/9600/19200 N-8-1 516-433-1843)
computerized bulletin board
Steven L. Gardner
Box 489
Jericho, NY 11753

Sherlocktron (300/1200/2400 N-8-1 714-492-0724)
computerized bulletin board
Willis G. Frick
513 Via Presa
San Clemente, CA 92672

The Sign of the Four Noble Student Bachelors
Sherlockian studies
Bob Coghill
Woodman's Lee
Griffith, Ont. X0J 2R0
CANADA

The Slurred Accounts of the Bribed Auditors
insurance/auditors/accountants
Paul H. Brundage
2632 Central Court
Union City, CA 94587-2128

The Society for the Immense Knowledge of Sensational Literature (SIKSL)
a correspondence society
Drew Thomas
150 South Bridge Street #A-17
Somerville, NJ 08876

The Solar Pond Society of London
British scion of Praed Street Irregulars
Roger Johnson
41 Sandford Road
Chelmsford, Essex CM2 6DE
ENGLAND

Solitary Cyclist West
a solitary cycling sawney
DP Griffon
1911 Anderson Place SE
Albuquerque, NM 87108

The Solitary Sherlockian
a correspondence society
Candace Drimmer
1 Quentin Road
Westport, CT 06880

The Strangers' Room
unofficial consulting scion
Andrew Joffe
340 East 63rd Street #4-A
New York, NY 10021

The Street Arabs
a corresponding society (young S'ians)
Zachary Dundas
1735 Gerald Avenue
Missoula, MT 59801

The Trained Cormorants of Gifu
visitors to cormorant fishing at Gifu
Helen Wesson
826 Golf Drive
Venice, FL 34285

The Voices of the Whispering Knights
scion of The Praed Street Irregulars
Frances Van Antwerp
73 East Park Street
Westerville, OH 43081

Von Herder Airguns, Ltd.
a correspondence society
Corinna Koch
Hamburger Allee 66
D-3000 Hannover 1
GERMANY

Watson's Erroneous Deductions
just good Sherlockian friends
Richard J. Kitts
35 Van Cortlandt Avenue
Staten Island, NY 10301

The Watsonians
admirers of Dr. Watson
Robert W. Hahn
2707 South 7th Street
Sheboygan, WI 53081

The Wigmore Street Post Office (Prodigy ID KSNV44A)
users of the Prodigy computer service
Don Meyers
4757 47th Avenue NE
Seattle, WA 98105

The William Gillette Memorial Luncheon
annual luncheon during birthday weekend
Susan Rice
125 Washington Place #2-E
New York, NY 10014

Yottsu-no-shomei-sha [The Sign of Four Co.]
parodies and pastiches
Tatsuo Saneyoshi
3068-5, Naruse Machida
Tokyo 194
JAPAN

Selected Bibliographies

CANONICAL WRITINGS

Baring-Gould, William S. *Sherlock Holmes of Baker Street: A Life of the World's First Consulting Detective*. N.Y.: Clarkson N. Potter, 1962.

Bell, H. E., ed. *Baker Street Studies*. London: Constable & Co., 1934.

———, ed. *Sherlock Holmes and Dr. Watson: The Chronology of Their Adventures*. London: Constable & Co., 1932.

Blackbeard, Bill. *Sherlock Holmes in America*. N.Y.: Harry N. Abrams, 1981.

Blakeney, T. S. *Sherlock Holmes: Fact or Fiction?* London: John Murray, 1932.

Brend, Gavin. *My Dear Holmes: A Study in Sherlock*. London: George Allen and Unwin, 1951.

Christ, Jay Finlay. *An Irregular Chronology of Sherlock Holmes of Baker Street*. Chicago: Fanlight House, 1947.

Dakin, D. Martin. *A Sherlock Holmes Commentary*. N.Y.: Drake Publishers, 1972.

De Waal, Ronald B. *The International Sherlock Holmes*. Hamden, Conn.: Archon Books, 1980.

———. *The World Bibliography of Sherlock Holmes and Dr. Watson*. N.Y.: New York Graphic Society, 1974.

Doyle, Arthur Conan. *The Annotated Sherlock Holmes*. Edited by William S. Baring-Gould. N.Y.: Clarkson N. Potter, 1967.

Eyles, Allen. *Sherlock Holmes, A Centenary Celebration*. London: John Murray, 1966.

Grazebrook, Owen F. *Studies in Sherlock Holmes*. N.Y.: Magico Magazine, 1981.

Green, Richard Lancelyn. *The Uncollected Sherlock Holmes*. Harmondsworth, Middlesex: Penguin Books, 1983.

———, and John Michael Gibson. *A Bibliography of A. Conan Doyle*. Oxford: Clarendon Press, 1983.

Haining, Peter, ed. *The Sherlock Holmes Scrapbook*. London: New English Library, 1974.

Hall, Trevor H. *The Late Sherlock Holmes and Other Literary Studies*. London: George Duckworth, 1971.

———. *Sherlock Holmes: Ten Literary Studies*. N.Y.: St. Martin's Press, 1970.

Hardwick, Michael. *The Complete Guide to Sherlock Holmes*. London: Weidenfeld & Nicholson, 1986.

———, and Mollie Hardwicke. *The Sherlock Holmes Companion*. London: John Murray, 1962.

Harrison, Michael, ed. *Beyond Baker Street: A Sherlockian Anthology*. Indianapolis and N.Y.: Bobbs-Merrill, Co., 1976.

———. *In the Footsteps of Sherlock Holmes*. London: Cassell & Co., 1958.

———. *The World of Sherlock Holmes*. London: Frederick Muller, 1973.

Holroyd, James E., ed. *Seventeen Steps to 221B: A Collection of Sherlockian Pieces by English Writers*. London: George Allen & Unwin, 1967.

———. *Baker Street By-Ways: A Book About Sherlock Holmes*. London: George Allen & Unwin, 1967.

Klinefelter, Walter. *Origins of Sherlock Holmes*. Bloomington, Ind.: Gaslight Publishing, 1983.

———. *Sherlock Holmes in Portrait and Profile*. Syracuse, N.Y.: Syracuse University Press, 1963.

Knox, Ronald A. *Essays in Satire*. London: Sheed & Ward, 1928.

Liebow, Ely M. *Dr. Joe Bell: Model for Sherlock Holmes*. Bowling Green, Ohio: Bowling Green University Popular Press, 1982.

McQueen, Ian. *Sherlock Holmes Detected: The Problem of the Long Stories*. Newton Abbot, U.K.: David & Charles, 1974.

Morgan, Robert S. *Spotlight on a Simple Case, or, Wiggins, Who Was That Horse I Saw You With Last Night?* Wilmington, Del.: 1959.

Pointer, Michael. *The Public Life of Sherlock Holmes*. Newton Abbot, U.K.: David & Charles, 1975.

———. *The Sherlock Holmes File*. N.Y.: Clarkson N. Potter, 1979.

Redmond, Donald A. *Sherlock Holmes: A Study in Sources*. Downsview, Ontario: McGill-McQueen's University Press, 1982.

Roberts, S. C. *Holmes and Watson: A Miscellany*. London: Oxford University Press, 1953.

Rosenberg, Samuel. *Naked Is the Best Disguise: The Death and Resurrection of Sherlock Holmes*. Indianapolis and N.Y.: Bobbs-Merrill, Co., 1974.

Rosenblatt, Julia Carlson, and Frederic H. Sonnenschmidt. *Dining with Sherlock Holmes: A Baker*

Street Cookbook. Indianapolis and N.Y.: Bobbs-Merrill, Co., 1976.

Sayers, Dorothy L. *Unpopular Opinions*. London: Victor Gollanz, 1946.

Shepherd, Michael. *Sherlock Holmes and the Case of Dr. Freud*. London and N.Y.: Tavistock Publications, 1985.

Shreffler, Philip A., ed. *Baker Street Studies—Cornerstone Writings About Sherlock Holmes*. Westport, Conn. and London: Greenwood Press, 1984.

Smith, Edgar W., ed. *A Baker Street Four-Wheeler: Sixteen Pieces of Sherlockiana*. Maplewood, N.J. and N.Y.: The Pamphlet House, 1944.

———. *The Incunabular Sherlock Holmes*. Morristown, N.J.: The Baker Street Irregulars, 1958.

———. *Profile By Gaslight: An Irregular Reader About the Private Life of Sherlock Holmes*. N.Y.: Simon and Schuster, 1944.

Starrett, Vincent. *The Private Life of Sherlock Holmes*. N.Y.: Macmillan, 1933.

———, ed. *221B: Studies in Sherlock Holmes, by Various Hands*. N.Y.: Macmillan, 1940.

Tracy, Jack. *Sherlock Holmes: The Published Apocrypha*. Boston: Houghton-Mifflin, Co. 1980.

Van Liere, Edward J. *A Doctor Enjoys Sherlock Holmes*. N.Y.: Vantage Press, 1959.

Warnack, Guy. *Sherlock Holmes and Music*. London: Faber and Faber, 1957.

Weller, Philip. *The Life and Times of Sherlock Holmes*. London: Crescent, 1993.

Zeisler, Ernest Bloomfield. *Street Chronology—Commentaries on the Sacred Writings of Dr. John H. Watson*. Chicago: Alexander J. Isaacs, 1953.

SIR ARTHUR CONAN DOYLE

Carr, John Dickson. *The Life of Sir Arthur Conan Doyle*. London: John Murray, 1949.

Conan Doyle, Adrian. *The True Conan Doyle*. London: John Murray, 1945.

Conan Doyle, Sir Arthur. *Memories and Adventures*. London: Hodder and Stoughton, 1924.

Costello, Peter. *The Real World of Sherlock Holmes*. N.Y.: Carroll and Graf, 1991.

Edwards, Owen Dudley. *The Quest for Sherlock Holmes*. Edinburgh: Mainstream Publishing, 1983.

Higham, Charles. *The Adventures of Conan Doyle*. London: Hamish & Hamilton, 1976.

Keating, H. R. F. *Sherlock Holmes: The Man and His World*. London: Thames and Hudson, 1979.

Nordon, Pierre. *Sir Arthur Conan Doyle—L'Homme et L'Oeuvre; as Conan Doyle, A Biography*. N.Y.: Holt, Rinehart & Winston, 1964.

Pearsall, Ronald. *Conan Doyle, A Biographical Solution*. London: Weidenfeld & Nicholson, 1977.

Pearson, Hesketh. *Conan Doyle*. N.Y.: Methuen, 1943.

SHERLOCK HOLMES

Baring-Gould, William S. *Sherlock Holmes of Baker Street*. N.Y.: Clarkson N. Potter, 1962.

Hardwick, Michael. *Sherlock Holmes, My Life and Crimes*. London: Harvill Press, 1984.

Harrison, Michael. *I, Sherlock Holmes*. N.Y.: E. P. Dutton, 1977.

WATSON AND MORIARTY

Hardwick, Michael. *The Private Life of Dr. Watson—Being the Personal Reminiscences of John H. Watson, M.D.* N.Y.: E. P. Dutton, 1983.

Roberts, S. C. *Doctor Watson*. London: Faber and Faber, 1931.

Smith, Edgar W. *The Napoleon of Crime*. Summit, N.J.: 1963.

LONDON IN HOLMES'S ERA

Hammer, David. *The Game Is Afoot*. Bloomington, Ind.: Gaslight Publications, 1983.

Harrison, Michael. *The London of Sherlock Holmes*. Newton Abbot, U.K.: David & Charles, 1978.

Kobayashi, Tsukasa. *Sherlock Holmes's London: Following in the Footsteps of London's Master Detective*. San Francisco: Chronicle Books, 1984.

HOLMES ON SCREEN

Druxman, Michael B. *Basil Rathbone, His Life and His Films*. Cranbury, N.J.: A. S. Barnes, 1975.

Haydock, Ron. *Deerstalker! Holmes and Watson on Screen*. Metuchen, N.J.: Scarecrow Press, 1978.

Pohle, Robert W. and Douglas C. Hart. *Sherlock Holmes on the Screen: The Motion Picture Adventures of the World's Most Popular Detective*. South Brunswick, N.J. and N.Y.: A. S. Barnes and Co., 1977.

Rathbone, Basil. *In and Out of Character*. N.Y.: Doubleday, 1962.

Steinbrunner, Chris and Norman Michaels. *The Films of Sherlock Holmes*. Secaucus, N.J.: Citadel Press, 1978.

Tibballs, Geoff. *The Boxtree Encyclopedia of TV Detectives*. London: Boxtree Limited, 1992.